2022 HOROSCOPES

2022
HOROSCOPES

365 daily predictions for every zodiac sign

PATSY BENNETT

ROCKPOOL

Patsy Bennett is a rare combination of astrologer and psychic medium. She contributes horoscopes to magazines both in Australia and internationally and has appeared on several live daytime TV and radio shows. She is a speaker, provides astrology and psychic consultations and holds astrology and psychic development workshops in Byron Bay, Australia, where she lives.

Patsy runs www.astrocast.com.au, www.patsybennett.com, facebook@patsybennettpsychicastrology and instagram @patsybennettastrology

A Rockpool book
PO Box 252
Summer Hill,
NSW 2130
Australia

rockpoolpublishing.co
Follow us! **f** 🄾 rockpoolpublishing
Tag your images with #rockpoolpublishing

Published in 2021 by Rockpool Publishing
Copyright text and astrological charts © Patsy Bennett 2021
Copyright design © Rockpool Publishing 2021

ISBN 9781922579294

Design by Sara Lindberg, Rockpool Publishing
Edited by Lisa Macken
Illustrations by Shutterstock

Printed and bound in China
10 9 8 7 6 5 4 3 2 1

NB: the planetary phenomena and aspects listed on each day are set to Australian Eastern Standard Time (AEST). AEST, also known as Eastern Standard Time (EST), is 10 hours forward of Greenwich Meantime (GMT) and nine hours forward of British Summer Time. To convert times to your locations please see www.timeanddate.com. Astrological interpretations take into account all aspects and the sign the sun and planets are in on each day and are not taken out of context.

CONTENTS

INTRODUCTION

Make 2022 your best year yet! Start the year with clarity: clearly see your amazing year ahead for love, luck, loot and lifestyle. We all consult our horoscopes, but what we really want to know is how best to plan ahead for ourselves personally. Astrology is the study of the movement of celestial objects and their impact on us here on earth, but we need to know what that means on an individual level.

The key throughout the year is to be proactive. This guide doesn't just show you when good things will happen to you. It also shows you how to view positive astrological days as opportunities to initiate new ideas, organise wonderful events and let love into your life, and to see challenging days as days to excel, to draw on your inner reserves and find success by overcoming obstacles. Your greatest achievements will often occur when you conquer hurdles and allow your inner hero to rise to the challenge.

In *2022 Horoscopes* you'll find insight into your own strengths and weaknesses, and into your particular way to move ahead month by month in astrological circumstances. Find out top times for travel, love, communications, domestic circumstances and health and wealth development according to your sun sign. With the benefit of a little foresight, this information will go a long way to making 2022 an extremely rewarding year.

Success is all in the timing and in knowing what to do with your own strengths in mind, and there's no better time than the present to consult your individual guide to success in 2022. This really is the year you can embrace your star power: starting now!

It's likely you are most familiar with the study of your sun sign via your horoscope, and horoscopes are plentiful nowadays for daily guidance. In *2022 Horoscopes* you can find out what's coming up for you personally, which is important because we don't all react the same way to the same phenomena. For example, when the sun is in your own sign it can prove particularly motivational and is a great time to get ahead with projects that resonate with your self-esteem, gut instincts and bigger-picture motivation. In the same way, when planets from Mercury to Pluto pass through your sun sign there will be particular influences that are explained in the diary. It'll be for you to take the initiative and instigate plans and projects that resonate with the prevailing mood.

Astrology isn't a phenomenon that happens to you: you need to take action! When the sun passes through Leo from 23 July to 22 August Leos will tend to feel revitalised, energised and motivated so this is a great time to get things rolling. But for Scorpios this phase may not be the same; there will be more focus on career and direction and hard work as opposed to simply feeling energised. *2022 Horoscopes* will provide invaluable direction to help you find your best-case scenario during various phases of the year and know the pitfalls to avoid.

INTERPLANETARY ASPECTS

Astrologers study the movements of planets in relation to each other; the measurements are in degrees, minutes and seconds. These measurements focus on patterns and particular aspects such as the angles between the planets, the sun and other celestial objects. This book includes mention of the aspects between the sun and the planets; the terminology is explained below.

The angles the planets and the sun make to one another have meaning in astrology. For example, a 'trine' aspect (120 degree angle) can be considered beneficial for the progress of your plans; a 'square' aspect (90 degree angle) can present as a challenge depending on your own attitude to challenges and obstacles. By carefully choosing dates for the fruition of your plans you will be able to move forward with knowledge of the cosmic influences that can help your progress.

Conjunction: when a celestial object is at the same degree as another celestial object and therefore aligned from our point of view here on earth. This can intensify the dynamics between the celestial objects and earth.

Opposition: when a planet is opposite another at a 180 degree angle. This can intensify the interplanetary dynamics.

Quincunx: a 150 degree angle can present a hurdle to be overcome.

Semi-sextile: a 30 degree angle can be a peaceful, harmonious influence or can facilitate the flow of energy between planetary influences.

Sextile: a 60 degree angle can be a peaceful, harmonious influence or can facilitate the flow of energy between planetary influences.

Square: a 90 degree angle can be a challenging aspect; however, as some people get going when the going gets tough it can lead to a breakthrough.

Trine: a 120 degree angle can be a peaceful, harmonious influence or can facilitate the flow of energy between planetary influences.

RETROGRADES

Planets can appear to go backwards from our point of view here on earth; this is known as a retrograde phase. The most well-known retrograde phases are those of Mercury, although several other planets also turn retrograde; these phases are mentioned in the diary. Retrograde phases can be a good time to assimilate, consolidate and integrate recent developments, although traditionally they are associated with delays, a slow down or a difficult process. For example, a Mercury retrograde phase is often aligned with difficult communications or traffic snarls, yet it can be an excellent time to integrate events and to consolidate, review and re-order your ideas. The influences of Mercury and Venus retrograde phases on your sun sign are explained in the diary pages and on page 4.

ECLIPSES, NEW MOONS AND FULL MOONS

Just as retrograde phases can have an impact on your life so, too, can eclipses, new moons and full moons. All of these events are explained and listed in the diary, enabling you to plan ahead with the full knowledge that you're moving in synchronicity with the sun, moon and stars.

ZODIAC SIGNS AND THEIR SYMBOLS/ GLYPHS, RULING PLANET/S AND ELEMENTS

CONSTELLATION	SYMBOL/GLYPH		RULING PLANET/S	ELEMENT
ARIES	Ram	♈	Mars	Fire
TAURUS	Bull	♉	Venus	Earth
GEMINI	Twins	♊	Mercury	Air
CANCER	Crab	♋	Moon	Water
LEO	Lion	♌	Sun	Fire
VIRGO	Virgin	♍	Mercury	Earth
LIBRA	Scales	♎	Venus	Air
SCORPIO	Scorpion	♏	Mars, Pluto	Water
SAGITTARIUS	Archer	♐	Jupiter	Fire
CAPRICORN	Goat	♑	Saturn	Earth
AQUARIUS	Water bearer	♒	Uranus, Saturn	Air
PISCES	Fish	♓	Jupiter, Neptune	Water

MERCURY AND VENUS RETROGRADE PERIODS IN 2022

The dates listed in this section indicate when both Mercury and Venus will be retrograde in 2022. A planet is termed 'retrograde' when it appears to be going backwards around the sun from our point of view here on earth. Of course, no planet actually goes retrograde – it's an optical illusion – but these phases do exhibit certain characteristics.

During the Mercury retrograde phase communications can tend to be a little more difficult than during the 'direct' phase, when the planet has a forwards motion. Travel may also be delayed or cancelled. However, the Mercury retrograde phase can be an excellent time for reviewing your circumstances, for reassessing where you are in life and for re-organising your various duties. Plan to take a slightly slower lane in life, such as a holiday, and don't expect communications to be perfect and for computers to run without a hitch.

During the Venus retrograde phase you might find that relationships are less likely to forge ahead under blue skies, and that sometimes when a Venus retrograde phase coincides with a Mercury retrograde communications may be complex or easily predisposed to arguments. The plus side is that Venus retrograde phases provide an ideal time to take things a little more slowly, to be less demanding on yourself and others within your relationships and practise compassion and kindness. Patience is truly a virtue during the Mercury and Venus retrograde periods.

Mercury retrograde phases in 2022:

14 January to 4 February

10 May to 2 June

10 September to 1 October

29 December to 11 January 2023

Venus retrograde phases in 2022:

1 January to 27 January

THE MOON'S PHASES FOR THE YEAR

The moon's phases, including eclipses, new moons and full moons, can all affect your mood. All of these events are explained and listed in the diary, enabling you to plan ahead with the full knowledge you're moving in synchronicity with the sun and the moon.

On the following four pages are the moon's phases for 2022 for both the southern and northern hemispheres.

2022 SOUTHERN HEMISPHERE MOON PHASES

JANUARY

S	M	T	W	T	F	S
30	31					1
2	3	4	5	6	7	8
9	10	11	12	13	14	15
16	17	18	19	20	21	22
23	24	25	26	27	28	29

FEBRUARY

S	M	T	W	T	F	S
		1	2	3	4	5
6	7	8	9	10	11	12
13	14	15	16	17	18	19
20	21	22	23	24	25	26
27	28					

MARCH

S	M	T	W	T	F	S
		1	2	3	4	5
6	7	8	9	10	11	12
13	14	15	16	17	18	19
20	21	22	23	24	25	26
27	28	29	30	31		

APRIL

S	M	T	W	T	F	S
					1	2
3	4	5	6	7	8	9
10	11	12	13	14	15	16
17	18	19	20	21	22	23
24	25	26	27	28	29	30

MAY

S	M	T	W	T	F	S
1	2	3	4	5	6	7
8	9	10	11	12	13	14
15	16	17	18	19	20	21
22	23	24	25	26	27	28
29	30	31				

JUNE

S	M	T	W	T	F	S
			1	2	3	4
5	6	7	8	9	10	11
12	13	14	15	16	17	18
19	20	21	22	23	24	25
26	27	28	29	30		

2022 SOUTHERN HEMISPHERE MOON PHASES

JULY

S	M	T	W	T	F	S
31					1	2
3	4	5	6	7	8	9
10	11	12	13	14	15	16
17	18	19	20	21	22	23
24	25	26	27	28	29	30

AUGUST

S	M	T	W	T	F	S
	1	2	3	4	5	6
7	8	9	10	11	12	13
14	15	16	17	18	19	20
21	22	23	24	25	26	27
28	29	30	31			

SEPTEMBER

S	M	T	W	T	F	S
				1	2	3
4	5	6	7	8	9	10
11	12	13	14	15	16	17
18	19	20	21	22	23	24
25	26	27	28	29	30	

OCTOBER

S	M	T	W	T	F	S
30	31					1
2	3	4	5	6	7	8
9	10	11	12	13	14	15
16	17	18	19	20	21	22
23	24	25	26	27	28	29

NOVEMBER

S	M	T	W	T	F	S
		1	2	3	4	5
6	7	8	9	10	11	12
13	14	15	16	17	18	19
20	21	22	23	24	25	26
27	28	29	30			

DECEMBER

S	M	T	W	T	F	S
				1	2	3
4	5	6	7	8	9	10
11	12	13	14	15	16	17
18	19	20	21	22	23	24
25	26	27	28	29	30	31

○ New moon ● Full moon

2022 NORTHERN HEMISPHERE MOON PHASES

JANUARY

S	M	T	W	T	F	S
30	31					1
2	3	4	5	6	7	8
9	10	11	12	13	14	15
16	17	18	19	20	21	22
23	24	25	26	27	28	29

FEBRUARY

S	M	T	W	T	F	S
		1	2	3	4	5
6	7	8	9	10	11	12
13	14	15	16	17	18	19
20	21	22	23	24	25	26
27	28					

MARCH

S	M	T	W	T	F	S
		1	2	3	4	5
6	7	8	9	10	11	12
13	14	15	16	17	18	19
20	21	22	23	24	25	26
27	28	29	30	31		

APRIL

S	M	T	W	T	F	S
					1	2
3	4	5	6	7	8	9
10	11	12	13	14	15	16
17	18	19	20	21	22	23
24	25	26	27	28	29	30

MAY

S	M	T	W	T	F	S
1	2	3	4	5	6	7
8	9	10	11	12	13	14
15	16	17	18	19	20	21
22	23	24	25	26	27	28
29	30	31				

JUNE

S	M	T	W	T	F	S
			1	2	3	4
5	6	7	8	9	10	11
12	13	14	15	16	17	18
19	20	21	22	23	24	25
26	27	28	29	30		

2022 NORTHERN HEMISPHERE MOON PHASES

JULY

S	M	T	W	T	F	S
31					1	2
3	4	5	6	7	8	9
10	11	12	13	14	15	16
17	18	19	20	21	22	23
24	25	26	27	28	29	30

AUGUST

S	M	T	W	T	F	S
	1	2	3	4	5	6
7	8	9	10	11	12	13
14	15	16	17	18	19	20
21	22	23	24	25	26	27
28	29	30	31			

SEPTEMBER

S	M	T	W	T	F	S
				1	2	3
4	5	6	7	8	9	10
11	12	13	14	15	16	17
18	19	20	21	22	23	24
25	26	27	28	29	30	

OCTOBER

S	M	T	W	T	F	S
30	31					1
2	3	4	5	6	7	8
9	10	11	12	13	14	15
16	17	18	19	20	21	22
23	24	25	26	27	28	29

NOVEMBER

S	M	T	W	T	F	S
		1	2	3	4	5
6	7	8	9	10	11	12
13	14	15	16	17	18	19
20	21	22	23	24	25	26
27	28	29	30			

DECEMBER

S	M	T	W	T	F	S
				1	2	3
4	5	6	7	8	9	10
11	12	13	14	15	16	17
18	19	20	21	22	23	24
25	26	27	28	29	30	31

○ New moon ● Full moon

THE MOON'S PART IN YOUR LIFE

Your moon sign informs you about your emotional make-up and the way you relate to others, while your sun sign represents your core self. The moon changes signs every two days so, depending on where you were born and at what time, your moon sign will be different. To find out your moon sign it's best to consult an astrologer to guarantee you receive accurate information (see page 873). There are also signs for the placements of all the planets at the time of your birth, and astrologers will consider all of this information when providing a personal consultation for you.

You will find you begin to gain considerable insight into who you are when you combine the information about your moon sign with information about your sun sign and ascendant. It will enable you to choose your best qualities and consciously promote these and minimise your worse qualities, helping you to be the best person you can be.

You will find that when the moon is in your sign, as listed day by day in the calendar, life is either easier or more challenging depending on the planetary aspects to your moon at the time of your birth. Keep a note of the general mood and occurrences when the moon is in your sign as it will enable you to plan ahead more readily with the full knowledge that you can do so according to the sun, moon and stars.

The following pages in this section give a detailed description of your moon sign.

MOON IN ARIES

You tend to be outgoing in your emotional life and will enter relationships on impulse. Your ardour may fire up as rapidly as it wanes, and you can lose interest quickly if you feel your affections are not reciprocated. Always consider carefully who you wish to give your emotional energy and time to, as you may otherwise blow hot and cold. You tend to have a hot temper. Having both the sun and the moon in Aries is a double fire sign, and means you can lose interest quickly in projects. Take the time to formulate plans and stick to them or you will tend to lose enthusiasm and leave many projects unfinished. You have a child-like enthusiasm that is endearing; when you mature your fervour for life could give you an enduringly youthful and fun-loving demeanour.

MOON IN TAURUS

A Taurean moon can provide a sensual, calm emotional state, and when you're involved with a Taurean moon person you're likely to enjoy romantic events such as candlelit dinners, good cooking, good-quality clothes and furnishings and open fireplaces where you warm your toes on a cold winter's night. A Taurean moon person is someone who values friendship and mutual support and has an appreciation for all things luxurious.

Some Taurean moon people can appear self-centred due to super high self-esteem. Another pitfall is a predilection to over-indulgence in all the finer things in life and an unwillingness to see the other side of the coin.

MOON IN GEMINI

Moon in Gemini people tend to be talkative and are likely to reach out to others, although they also like to retain a sense of independence and, when under pressure, will even appear to be detached emotionally. You intellectualise and compartmentalise your emotions, seeming to switch them on and off, which may be infuriating to those who depend on you for support. This may make you appear to be two-faced, yet you are simply embracing the many various qualities you have. You will often find in life you need to agree to disagree with people who cannot see differing points of view.

A Gemini moon person gives emotional support but not in ways you might expect due to your sense of independence and detachment. You get on well with the other air signs, Libra and Aquarius, and with anyone who has the ability to be emotionally independent while still being a loving and supportive character.

MOON IN CANCER

Yours is a fundamentally sensitive emotional make-up. You can be driven by strong emotions, which can take over your thoughts, so it's important to find ways to establish balance in your mind. If you allow emotional expression to overwhelm your intellect and intuition you can feel out of sorts and make mistakes.

You are a hugely intuitive person and may have innate psychic abilities. You need to differentiate between intuition, psychic impressions and emotionally driven impulses so you can be guided by your inner compass rather than being overwhelmed by emotions. Home and family will be important to you, and you are loyal to those you love.

MOON IN LEO

You like to initiate fun projects and are an active, outgoing, emotionally demonstrative and playful character. Being playful may make you seem insincere in your emotional entanglements. You sometimes enter relationships on a whim only to discover you have no interest or affection for the person you have befriended.

You are unlikely to be a wallflower at social events unless you have planets in sensitive signs in your natal chart. Emotionally you are bold and outgoing and like to be the centre of attention. You're a loyal family member who takes your close, personal relationships very seriously. At home you will be the queen or king of the castle.

MOON IN VIRGO

You are considered and careful and unlikely to rush into relationships without forethought (unless you have a strong fire signature in your birth chart). You are unlikely to fall head over heels in love one day and disappear the next, as you like constancy in relationships and exhibit a constancy in your own emotional make-up. You are an earthy person, preferring to take your emotional life step by step. Once you make a commitment it is likely to be long-standing; you do not take responsibilities and duties lightly. In your love life you look for perfection so can tend to be critical, not only of others but also of yourself. You'll take a little time to assimilate that no one is perfect.

You may tend to be choosy about who you bring into your personal inner circle. Professionally you are dependable and hard working.

MOON IN LIBRA

You look for emotional balance and perfection in relationships, both in your love life and at work. Perfect harmony and peace are not always possible, as you learn and hone your interpersonal skills throughout your lifetime. Throughout that process you can tend to seesaw up and down through triumphs and dissatisfactions and success and disappointment. You can be unbalanced emotionally because of your indecision and wish for that elusive perfect X factor. Work actively towards balancing your emotions and you will succeed in gaining what you're looking for. This can be achieved through meditation, yoga and exercise, and your demeanour will attract balanced partners, friends and family.

MOON IN SCORPIO

You are a passionate character who is likely to enter into tempestuous relationships that can extend to the edges of every emotion you've ever felt. While deep, intense, transformative experiences may be exciting and happy, you risk delving into destructive emotional cycles that take your every breath to reconcile. You have an enigmatic and charming emotional presence that is captivating. As you have incredible magnetism it's vital you use this carefully or you risk breaking hearts. You're the one most likely to be wounded by your own intensity, as negative emotions such as jealousy, anger and envy can overwhelm more rational thoughts. Conversely, you are a loyal person who can feel deeply committed to the people around you such as family members.

MOON IN SAGITTARIUS

You are a bright and adventurous character who is unafraid to push yourself forwards into circumstances that others may find daring, such as living in a foreign culture or travelling for extensive periods. You are happy to try all kinds of relationships. However, as you are emotionally self-sufficient you don't actually need them. This independence means it can be difficult to develop a deep relationship with you, but because you are playful, optimistic and fun loving you will often have a large circle of friends and associates. Once you commit to someone you will give them the world.

You are a truly sincere, honest friend, family member and partner, although sometimes your honesty can sting. Moon in Sagittarius is honest to a fault: you see yourself and others through the eyes of blunt honesty rather than flattery.

MOON IN CAPRICORN

You can appear to be emotionally cool and calm unless your astrology chart has a strong fire element. You are practical in your endeavours and will shape your emotions rationally, leading on occasion to the appearance that you are calculating. Once you have a desired outcome in mind you certainly have the capacity to very patiently pursue your goals.

Of all the moon signs you are the one most likely to be a social climber, as you have an emotional need to succeed. You will do what it takes to do so, either by way of hard work, marriage or socialising with people you know can further your agenda.

You express your emotions by action and touch rather than through words, and as such you make an earthy, sensual lover. You have strong parental feelings towards others and will wish to guide and shape, protect and nurture those you love, even if in a seemingly cool or detached way.

MOON IN AQUARIUS

You have an emotional need to be different, which you may express through work, relationships or past-times that challenge the norm. You are quite the enigma, as you can be deeply committed to people or things and then very quickly change your mind and become detached. This may make you seem unreliable, quixotic or downright cruel to those who become emotionally entangled with you. Always be prepared to build bridges.

You wish to experience depth in your feelings, and when this does not seem possible you pursue new adventures in life, testing society's rules and moral codes in the process.

MOON IN PISCES

You are a truly sensitive character and may wonder why you can be moody or why your emotions fluctuate from low to high and back again for no apparent reason. Consider yourself a kind of emotional barometer: you subconsciously pick up on undercurrents that will be felt by you as emotions. For example, you may enter a room where an argument had taken place and become angry for no apparent reason. You will reflect, feel and echo someone's love for you, even if the love does not originate from you. It's vital for you to get a good grip on your own emotions, as you can be easily influenced. Take the time to connect with your intuition, too, to ascertain the true compass in your soul that guides you through life. You have innately strong psychic abilities, which you may wish to develop.

ARIES
20 March – 20 April

THE ESSENCE OF ARIES

Your inner calling is to develop your abilities to such an extent that you are happy to be assertive; that you are brave beyond your own reason; and that your courage shines deep into the crevasses of darkness. Ultimately, you will feel you have conquered the world by acting as a pioneer, being proactive and bringing your inner hero to the surface, taking action and not subscribing to your fears and anxieties.

To do this you'll experience the necessity at various phases in your life to stand apart from others, to feel singularly different and to even feel that you must be a rebel or must be detached from the herd. This can be disheartening to you and you may feel you are acting counter-intuitively as your dearest wish is to be admired, yet how can you be admired if you are set apart from others? Herein lies the paradox: to be truly fulfilled and feel proficient you have to be needed, admired and wanted, yet to do so you may need to remove yourself from the status quo and from what people expect you to do.

Your inner calling is to feel fulfilled by your own independent accomplishments, but in the process you must be inclusive of those who love you and they will respond well to you.

SELF-ESTEEM

To gain self-esteem you must feel you are effective in life, that your presence has some form of positive influence and meaning. You will attempt activities that others may feel less confident of doing, and you may have a tendency to rush into activities or events without a backwards glance let alone forethought.

You are seen as being brave beyond all measure, when in fact it's your need to be looked up to and for excitement and adventure – and also, on occasion, your blind faith (or ignorance) – that lead to impulsiveness. It is not necessarily courage that leads you to take action; it's all of the above! You are seen as courageous to those who do not possess your need for excitement, challenge and spontaneity.

Once you complete difficult tasks your self-esteem blossoms, and you can see yourself as an effective individual who is able to surmount obstacles.

A clear pitfall is that you become impulsive and reckless, that you take calculated risks that can land you in hot water. You also have a tendency to boost your ego through reckless action rather than being brave when you need to be and careful when you must be.

The key to feeling you are answering your inner calling is to accomplish tasks independently, as this will boost your self-esteem. These tasks must resonate with your inner calling and sense of purpose. You must feel that you have entered new territory and have excelled in some way or else your self-esteem will plummet, because deep down you feel that what you do has little meaning.

YOUR INNER LIFE

Your inclination is to be a bright spark, to be the leader and the go-to person. You're going to want to know everyone's secrets: to know all of their dealings and be a part of every decision – and to be the person who has the final say!

Your inner calling is to be loved, which may seem contradictory because a person who always takes the lead may be seen as being bossy and isn't always going to be loved. Thus your dilemma is how to be loved while also being the one setting the pace, taking control and leading others.

The answer lies in compassion. When you approach others with a kind and understanding manner they will always respond well, but when you have an oppositional manner you will only be opposed.

Your motivation and energy levels are infectious, and when these are combined with a focused approach to uplifting activities you will attain the position you seek. However, when your need for excitement and leadership borders on bossiness or control, this is when you will be opposed. To avoid this scenario focus on emotional calm, and the calmness will ripple out from you.

Your home setting risks having a makeshift feel when you are younger, as this is where you recharge from your many activities. Your home may be utilitarian, functioning merely as a place to eat and sleep, as opposed to being a place where you seek comfort and revel in luxury. Yet as you mature you will see there is great merit in your home being not only the place to recharge, but also the place where you find spiritual peace and love in the family that is separate and apart from the chaotic world you engage in away from your home.

Your pitfalls are succumbing to anger, impulsiveness and impetuousness. This we know already: you're an Aries, and are known for your 'leap first, think later' approach!

Perhaps more important is the real risk you run of missing deeper connections with the people you love because you're super busy and super motivated to be a hero, to be larger than life, yet the most important thing for you is to experience a depth of love, friendship and mutual respect. Stop, wait a minute and really look at the value of the relationships you make. If you seek adventure in them rather than in the world at large you will do so at the expense of your relationship.

Take time to filter life events more serenely, to stay in the present and savour life rather than feeling you must conquer another mountain. Rest assured: you are the hero in your own story, and also for many of those whom you meet. Slow down when you can and regain focus when you feel you have strayed from your path.

When you reach peaks of success it's important to rest and savour the sensation for a while before rushing on to the next chapter.

HOW OTHERS SEE YOU

Your need for excitement, adventure and independence can cause you to be seen as being arrogant and aloof or even as a bully. This may be so even if you have not intended to boss others around, and it's not because you feel superior to others or wish to coerce them. People can view your confidence as arrogance, your self-assuredness as bossiness and your impatience with the indecisiveness of others as bullying.

Take a moment to be personable and connect on an equal level with others. Be ready to assert yourself, but be wary of overshadowing people with your bright presence and influence.

Take the time to integrate with others, because a leader must be understood and liked or else they become a tyrant.

HOW TO MAXIMISE YOUR POTENTIAL

Yours is the soul of the true artist, because each action you take is the result of a creative process. The essence of creativity is making something out of nothing, of initiating and forming matter. You express this by initiating and starting great projects that may not appear at first to be creative or even artistic.

Once you are conscious that your actions are a kind of creative process, you will become more invested in setting the intention that your actions align with your heart and resonate with a deeper sense of purpose. In this way you will find fulfilment in your activities, rather than feeling you must constantly conquer new horizons or that the grass is greener elsewhere.

By taking a moment to decipher where your true sense of fulfilment lies and then carefully aligning your actions with this understanding you'll find that doors begin to open in line with the amount of carefully directed focus you exert on your goals.

Your actions will not always necessarily work out in the way you intended, because the artistic and creative process has a dynamic of its own that eventually becomes more enriching than your initial intentions.

It's important to remain open to new ventures and ideas while channelling your considerable energy into your desired outcome.

ARIES AND ITS ASCENDANTS

This chapter is about your sun sign, Aries, and your predictions for the year ahead. The more you know about yourself the better you will be able to take advantage of opportunities, and also to avoid the pitfalls. It's critical to know as much about 'you' as possible.

In astrology your core self is represented by your sun sign, but your personality traits are represented by your ascendant (also known as your rising sign). The ascendant describes your personality, the way other people see you on first meeting you and the way you tend to filter life's events.

When you have intimate knowledge about your sun sign – your engine room or core being – you will be on the way to a happier life. When you add the knowledge about your personality – your ascendant – you will gain even deeper insight into what makes you tick.

Your ascendant sign is determined by the time of your birth on the date and year of your birth. Because the ascendant sign changes approximately every two hours, the best way to determine it is to ask an astrologer to calculate it for you. Certain apps will also calculate your ascendant sign (see page 873).

The following gives you more information about your abilities, characteristics and personality according to your sun sign Aries in combination with your ascendant sign.

ARIES SUN SIGN WITH ARIES ASCENDANT

You're a double Aries and, as such, are doubly dynamic, doubly bossy and doubly a leader! The good news is that people see you for who you are: a fiery, action-oriented, proactive character. They see no alternative agenda in the person you project: you are most definitely an Aries through and through. Your positive traits are energy, entrepreneurship and independent thinking. Your negative traits are super strong (unless you work on self-improvement): impulsiveness, recklessness and bossiness.

You are never duplicitous unless you have a strong element of secrecy in your chart and are always upfront and clear about your motives, and you are a loyal friend.

ARIES SUN SIGN WITH TAURUS ASCENDANT

You will be seen as being a careful, methodical and practical character who is dependable and earthy, someone who enjoys the good things in life and is able to plan ahead. Yet when people get to know you, you may be seen as the fiery, impulsive character you are at your core. You may even confuse yourself with your predisposition to be careful and methodical on some occasions and then fiery and impetuous on others. You may be particularly attracted to people who are intense and sensual, people who like to settle into a routine, while also wishing to retain your individuality. Find ways to combine your independence with your need for comfort and love, and you will establish positive relationships.

ARIES SUN SIGN WITH GEMINI ASCENDANT

You are a mercurial character with many different forms of expression. You may be constantly on the go, fidgety, restless and hard to pin down. You are a dynamo. You can be overtly analytical on occasion and get caught up in your thoughts, so it's important to release tension and the tendency to worry through action-oriented activities that disperse excess energy such as sport and nature rambles.

As a Gemini-rising person you often gesticulate with your arms and hands when you talk. When combined with the Aries energy you are unlikely to carry excess weight, as you are constantly on the go. You need mental stimulation, so follow your heart and study and practise in areas that provide information and learning opportunities

ARIES SUN SIGN WITH CANCER ASCENDANT

You are a force to be reckoned with: two cardinal signs in such prominent positions point to a strong character that, if opposed, will be hard to temper. You can be stubborn, especially if your will is opposed! However, you have a strength of character that lies beneath a sensitive, introspective personality, which can surprise those who get to know you. You do have a kind of extrasensory perception, as the Cancerian personality enables you to pick up information about people and circumstances that other rising signs don't manage.

ARIES SUN SIGN WITH LEO ASCENDANT

You're a double fire sign, so as you can guess you are fiery! You can act up and be a drama magnet, but you can also be extremely productive.

Your personality is very much the Leo type: preferring to be the centre of attention but also being a loving, creative character. The Leo dynamic is able to overcome immense hurdles; when this is combined with kindness the Leo personality is adorable. However, when arrogance and a sense of superiority creep into the mix this Aries–Leo combination can make for a disrespectful character. It is better to harness your strong energy and channel it into productive pursuits that celebrate your humanity.

ARIES SUN SIGN WITH VIRGO ASCENDANT

You are a natural-born healer and want to make the world a better place. Luckily this combination can lead to careful work that executes exactly that outcome, but sometimes the inner tension between the dynamic, outgoing Aries attitude and the careful, methodical, perfectionist Virgo temperament can create indecision or inaction. Professionally, you will be attracted to healing modalities, teaching, being of service to others and activities that improve your own circumstances and those of others. When you combine your dynamic energy levels with careful planning you are a force to be reckoned with.

ARIES SUN SIGN WITH LIBRA ASCENDANT

The initial impression you give is that of a calm, serene and peaceful personality. As your feisty dynamic attributes come to be known you present as a complex character: balanced and reasonable while simultaneously being impatient and fierce. Vacillating between these two approaches can result in indecision, with you not knowing yourself how you are going to react to events. The Libra ascendant tends to temper the ardour of the Aries character so your fiery temperament becomes second nature, but sometimes even you may be surprised by the force of your opinions.

ARIES SUN SIGN WITH SCORPIO ASCENDANT

Passion is your middle name, and you will find your life and relationships take you on many a rollercoaster ride of change and excitement. You are a powerful character who can be intense in your approach to life; you are also serious and do not suffer fools gladly. People may tend to find your charisma attractive, but your drama-magnet personality can be a little overbearing unless you take steps to respect people's opinions and give them space to be who they are. You make a loyal partner, but may be demanding and wish to take control. You are likely to have a strong sex drive, and may also be attracted to alcohol, drugs and other compulsive behaviour.

ARIES SUN SIGN WITH SAGITTARIUS ASCENDANT

You're the zodiac's daredevil adventurer with a larger-than-life personality. Whether you're involved in sport or research, are family oriented or simply a lover of life, you will do what you do energetically and optimistically and with a view to success. You are playful and enjoy life's many upbeat pursuits, with a drive for excitement that is beyond measure; you may be seen as a risk taker for this reason. You aim high in life, and travel, foreign cultures and study will appeal to you. You will prefer fun and excitement over things that are boring and staid, but you may miss out on more established pleasures such as a settled life as a result.

ARIES SUN SIGN WITH CAPRICORN ASCENDANT

While your inner core is a dynamo wishing to unleash its energy and vitality on the world, your calm personality belies this firecracker centre. You may appear staid, traditionalist, measured, self-possessed and even minded, yet beneath this rages the impulsive and reckless mindset of the zodiac's ram. Scratch the surface of the Capricorn ascendant and you will see quite a different character, which can be disconcerting to people first getting to know you. You tend to succeed where others fail through your unique combination of sheer willpower, energy and measured strategy. Career and status are important to you, and when you channel your Aries energy into those you are unlikely to fail. Avoid chopping and changing jobs too often; slow and steady is your recipe for success.

ARIES SUN SIGN WITH AQUARIUS ASCENDANT

You can be quirky, independent and, on occasion, eccentric. Combine a taste for variety and spice in life with the drive to attain your goals quickly and bravely and you have the recipe for an interesting life. You also have a tendency to land yourself in unorthodox and unpredictable circumstances, as you ignore warning signs that the terrain you're about to step into may be out of the ordinary. On the plus side this makes you a great explorer in life: you will go where no one else goes even if this takes you off track. You're bright and willing to learn, and when combined with Aries' drive it makes you a strong character with a fun, quirky twist.

ARIES SUN SIGN WITH PISCES ASCENDANT

Being the dreamer of the zodiac, the Pisces-ascendant personality presents initially as a philosophical, soft and gentle person. When combined with the zest and drive of the Aries you become a determined, diligent and goal-oriented idealist. Your idealism can take you beyond the norm, which for some can result in marvellously talented musical, academic, artistic and creative work. For others this mindset can result in delusional ideals and can lead to disappointment. It's important with this configuration to do your checks and balances and to ensure you always have your feet on the ground, then the Aries drive combined with the Pisces idealism can lead to excellent accomplishments and happiness.

ARIES IN LOVE

You are a particularly independent individual who is likely to be selective about who you spend time with long term. In this section you can check out your compatibility with other sun signs. Remember that we are all complex individuals, so the more you know about someone's astrological birth chart the better you can determine your compatibility. Consider having your astrological birth chart compared with that of a partner, friend or family member, as the compatibility – known as 'synastry' in astrology – goes even deeper than a comparison of sun signs, although this is a good place to begin.

ARIES WITH ARIES

Two powerhouses together can certainly make music when you're both on the same page, but if you disagree with each other there will be fireworks! Where there's a strong initial spark of attraction, dare to go that little bit deeper to find out what your common ground is: are you emotionally on the same track? If not, the spark that got you together could turn into a raging inferno of conflict and bring out adverse qualities such as anger, impatience and bossiness.

If you feel you both have similar values and ethics you could be a real dynamic duo, although there will always be fiery moments. Channel the fire into passion and common aims, or it could turn into temper tantrums and drama.

ARIES WITH TAURUS

You'll appreciate the sensuality and the outward calm of your Taurean but you may be a little frustrated on occasion by their lack of comparative motivation and dynamism unless there is a strong fire element in your Taurean partner's chart. This relationship can be grounding and comforting and can provide the earthiness you sometimes lack in some of your more impulsive moments. One major stumbling block could be that you are both uncompromising in your views once you have decided on something, which can lead to a stalemate. Stubbornness and obstinacy could be real bugbears in this union, but if you can agree to disagree your Taurean partner will find you exciting and you will find your Taurean partner sensual and calming.

ARIES WITH GEMINI

This is a lovely match, even if you both find yourselves so busy in your individual lives that you spend more time missing each other's company than actually being together! When you do make a commitment you should arrange regular together time so you don't miss out on the benefits of this match. You'll appreciate Gemini's intellectual stimulation, freedom of movement and light-hearted attitude, while your partner will feel excited by your independence and ability to take the lead when necessary. Geminis can tend to exist in their heads, so you may find it necessary to avoid getting too involved in debate and indecision. Your proactive stance will feel refreshing to Gemini, who enjoys being spontaneous. Just avoid becoming so impetuous that you become restless.

ARIES WITH CANCER

You are both cardinal signs, which means you are both strong characters, so there has to be give and take or one of you will feel you are playing second fiddle to the other. The Cancerian sensitivity can feel overshadowed by your dominant approach, and you can feel invalidated by Cancer's mood swings, especially when Cancer is usually such a supportive sign. If you can establish a solid platform of mutual respect this match can work. Some might say it is a difficult match, but it largely depends on how willing you are to work on your relationship and whether there is other compatibility in your chart, such as compatible moon signs.

ARIES WITH LEO

You are both fire signs and can be a compatible match, as you are both proactive, upbeat and dynamic. This match can be truly harmonious, as you bring out the best in each other. You will enjoy the same dynamic approach to life and an optimistic attitude to each other along with playful pursuits and adventurous activities, which can create a powerful and energising love life. However, fire breeds fire, and this match spells fireworks if neither of you work on tempering your tendency towards impulsive or explosive behaviour. Some fire–fire sign matches can act as catalysts to ignite a previously serene personality into tempers and outbursts.

ARIES WITH VIRGO

The Virgo personality will feel earthy and appealing to the Aries sun sign, so much so that you may feel truly drawn to this sensual sign. However, the Virgo make-up is essentially careful, prudent

and meticulous in life, which can feel disorienting to your impulsive, spontaneous Aries self. Conversely, the dominance of your entrepreneurial and independent Aries personality can feel a little unsettling to the practical Virgo. If there are other aspects in your synastry that indicate you are a good match there are many ways you can work together harmoniously, as the earthiness of the Virgo acts to ground the fiery Aries rashness and the impulsive and spontaneous Aries feels revitalising and energising to the practical Virgo.

ARIES WITH LIBRA

If you believe that opposites attract then Aries and Libra are made for each other. However, there is a predisposition for disharmony, principally because the drive in Aries (which is symbolised by Mars) is at odds with what the Libra desires (symbolised by Venus). In other words, you will each frequently desire and need very different things in life and from each other. Some matches do thrive on a little tension, so you may find you enjoy the fact that you must constantly keep up with each other's interests and projects. You are coming from different corners of the field, but if you can meet in the middle you may find the rainbow in the midst of a rainy day.

ARIES WITH SCORPIO

Watch out: sparks will fly in this match as both of these sun signs are ruled by Mars, the god of war. In addition, Scorpio is co-ruled by intense Pluto, contributing to a sense of drama and potential explosiveness. This is a high-energy and potentially high-maintenance relationship, as you will both wish to dominate. Also, Scorpio is likely to dampen Aries' fire, which Aries will resent. Passion will abound at first and this will be an engaging relationship full of zest and charm, but all too often it will end as quickly as it began unless care is taken to channel intense energy into positive and constructive pursuits you both enjoy.

ARIES WITH SAGITTARIUS

This is a fire sign match in which both sun signs are comfortable with each other's fundamental approach to life. This can be an adventurous, outgoing and upbeat relationship where both Aries and Sagittarius give space and encouragement to learn about each other and themselves and to learn about life and gain wisdom through the relationship. Unless there are incompatibilities elsewhere in the chart this happy relationship will bring each other's playfulness and action-oriented lust for life into full bloom. There may be some element of competitiveness in the relationship, but it is unlikely to deter the basic underlying harmony.

ARIES WITH CAPRICORN

Aries may be attracted to the Capricorn ability to be calm and measured in their approach to life but may conclude that the Capricorn is staid, overtly traditional or even boring in comparison to the Aries style of dynamic leadership. There is a fundamentally different approach to life here, where the Capricorn seeks carefully attained status and financial gain and the Aries seems foolhardy and impetuous. The Capricorn partner may tend to be older or will wish to guide or protect the Aries sun sign, which the Aries could see as patronising and limiting. That said, this match could provide the chance to experience the other's very different approach to life, but both would need to be super patient.

ARIES WITH AQUARIUS

Both of these signs enjoy excitement and diversity in life, although in disparate ways. Aries is very 'me' oriented, being entrepreneurial, independent, dynamic and outgoing. Aquarius is fundamentally 'us' and 'community' oriented, being socially conscious and humanitarian. Although there is a different focus in both sun signs that may be difficult to reconcile, Aries may appreciate the group consciousness of the Aquarian and Aquarius may appreciate the entrepreneurial and get-up-and-go approach of the Aries. When functioning from the Uranian attributes, Aquarius may also appear too left field to the Aries and Aries too bossy from the Aquarian side. Both have the tendency in each other's eyes to be unpredictable, which can add another gulf to the partnership.

ARIES WITH PISCES

The Pisces soft, dreamy, philosophical approach to life contrasts with the Aries action-oriented approach. And, while Pisces can most surely provide spiritual insight and support to Aries, the Aries' gung-ho approach to life may be anathema to Pisces. There is a tendency here for both signs to miss the point of the other's mindset: the action-driven Aries mindset can seem foolhardy to the more intuitive, instinctive approach of the Pisces, and the philosophical Pisces dreamy and forgetful nature can be annoying to the impulsive, impatient Aries. Romance is possible but may require patience on both sides.

THE YEAR AHEAD FOR ARIES

Affirmation: *'I will embrace change.'*

The immortal words of Franklin D. Roosevelt could be your catchcry in 2022: 'There's nothing as sure as change.' Change is going to affect many aspects of your life from your personal life to work, your interests and what you do in your spare time.

Celestial game-changing Uranus is still in Taurus (and will be until 2025), and by then your life will be completely different to how it is now. So this is the year to customise yourself with change; make it your new best friend because to fight change would be to fight life itself.

Key stress points this year, when you may feel particularly at a crossroads, will be in the second half of the year, although you may also find February taxing as you will be presented with various options. Which one you take will depend on your circumstances. If you wish to broaden your horizons, study, travel and self-development will be paths you may wish to choose this year, even if this arises through trial and error. You will gain the chance to understand what makes you tick so much better. And, if you're ready to retire, the option that offers the most security will appeal.

The entry of Jupiter in your sign on 11 May will augment your influence, so choose your activities wisely as the next 12 months until 2023 could be your luckiest or most abundant.

By the end of the year you'll find, even if through adversity, that you will feel so much more aligned with a sense of purpose than you have for many years, especially if you take up any opportunities that are presented to you.

You may find your work schedules and interests change as the year progresses, and by the end of the year a chance to alter much of what makes you happy may surprise even you as new activities and ideas shape your everyday routine.

HEALTH

Chiron in your sign for the next five years will put the focus firmly on health and well-being, making this period the best for you to focus on your own vitality and health. Uranus in Taurus will continue to bring the unexpected your way and, while you're going to be busy re-inventing at least some aspects of your life, especially your activities, your nerves and general disposition will merit careful focus so you must avoid over-stretching your health.

The aspect of you that understands the benefits of stability and security will wish to keep much the same in your health-care routine, and yet circumstances, in measure with your changing interests and activities, will dictate that you embrace new and interesting modalities that can help support your mental and physical health.

Phases during the year when you may be stretching yourself too far will be during the last six months of the year, and if your health suffers at this time you'll know you must dial down your extra-curricular activities and work commitments as these are the activities that could drain your energy levels in the second half of the year.

A rock-solid activity that engages your mind, body and spirit, such as sports, study and travelling to new and interesting areas of the country, will keep your mind alert and your spirit eager to learn more, but you must avoid over-subscribing to activities that then overwhelm your daily or work routine and subsequently put a strain on your well-being.

FINANCES

You can tend to be impulsive financially, making spontaneous purchases, yet over the past two years you are likely to have earned the benefits of having a slush fund. This year, again, it will be important to build a kitty or you may find that your finances and resources seesaw, especially during stress points in April, May, October and November.

Luckily this year Jupiter, the planet associated with benevolence, good luck and abundance, will be predominantly in your 12th house of work for the first quarter, signalling you will gain the opportunity to broaden your horizons at work and therefore could make money. And, once it enters Aries in May, you will gain every chance to choose your projects and work towards abundance.

However, Jupiter will be retrograde from August until the end of November, suggesting you are best to make hay while the sun shines earlier on in the year. You will still make money during the second half of the year but may not accrue much over and above the rate you already make while Jupiter is retrograde.

The eclipses will be across your money sector, suggesting there could be fluctuating finances especially in May and October-November, so this is why building a kitty for a rainy day will benefit you this year. This may simply be due to additional expenses or overheads and matters beyond your control such as higher prices for some products.

HOME LIFE

Developments in your personal life and at work will determine changes at home. The months of June and July will be the busiest at home, when you will most need to focus on developments there. You may find that a new beginning in some aspect domestically will arise, whether you simply refresh the décor or decide to move.

Developments could be reinvigorating, but if you have not made long-term plans that create stability in your life you may find yourself with a difficult choice. Visitors, a trip or the chance to change your domestic circumstances may appeal, but planning will be the key to success.

Developments around the new moon on 29 June could be positive, as you will gain the opportunity to make the key changes you wish for at home. But once again the key to a successful outcome will reside in good planning, as lack of attention to detail could precipitate loss or a lack of direction.

If you have been planning changes regarding who you share your home with this new moon could be a positive time to welcome new people into your home, as long as you have done relevant checks. The pitter patter of little feet may be signalled by this new moon if you've been trying for a baby.

LOVE

Expect change this year; the eclipses across your partnership and marriage sectors suggest either you or your partner will have significant changes in your lives that impact on each other. Singles could come to the conclusion that freedom is worth more than security and companionship – you are an Aries, after all! Depending on your past circumstances, however, you may discover this year that you wish to find security regardless of what you must sacrifice. If this is the case, ensure you go into your relationships with your eyes wide open.

May and November stand to be months of change in your love life. The eclipses on 16 May and 25 October will both be in Scorpio and suggest a partner will have important news for you, and this could mean considerable changes to come. News may come unexpectedly, or will represent considerable change for you.

Keep an eye out at this time for ways to bring more stability into your life that are not dependent on someone else's circumstances.

CAREER

The full moon in Virgo on 18 March will point to a particular work schedule that will change or simply means less to you than it once did. This will be a time when you may consider your priorities in your working day: what makes you happy, and what is simply a means to a financial end? This year you will wish to embrace more of a sense of fulfilment through your work and career, even if it means retraining or upskilling, finding a fresh avenue or even reinventing things completely.

The new moon in Libra on 25 September suggests changes at work or in your daily routine, which could mean considerable changes to come. Being an Aries you can tend to make rash decisions, but you can also be indecisive due in large to past impulsiveness that has not worked so well for you. Yet this year, the more proactive and progressive you are the better the outcome. Avoid clinging to the past.

Be careful with key choices in May and November, when you may need to decide about a financial or work matter, but if you don't have the full details this is when mistakes can be made; some you may regret.

The 23 December full moon supermoon will point to a fresh career path for you. You may be in the process of changing how you plan your general direction and a change of status may be inevitable.

January

career love home health finance

> Notes: the pie charts such as the one above listed for each month show energy distribution according to the stars for the month ahead. If you wish to make changes in the areas of your finances, health, career, love or home and you see there is a large amount of energy in that sector in the chart your endeavours should succeed as long as you have prepared well in advance. The charts also show which areas will potentially have the most focus in your life during the month.
>
> The moon sign listed for each day's entry in the diary is the position of the moon at the end of the day in Greenwich Mean Time (GMT). To gain the most information about a particular day's circumstances, read the day before and the day after for a complete picture.

1 JANUARY

You'll enjoy an unexpected visit or trip somewhere different. A commitment could be made that brings a refreshing chapter your way. *Moon enters Capricorn late at night.*

2 JANUARY

New moon and supermoon in Capricorn: a good time to turn a corner with a favourite project, endeavour or relationship. Be prepared to commit to an idea that is both practical and exciting.

3 JANUARY

This is a good day to get things done and to turn a new leaf at work if you're back already from the holidays. You'll enjoy socialising in the evening. *Moon enters Aquarius.*

4 JANUARY

You may hear unexpectedly from a friend or associate. If developments are too outside your comfort zone, aim to consider options; avoid impulsive decisions. *Moon in Aquarius.*

5 JANUARY

You'll enjoy a lovely get-together and will appreciate the time to enjoy romance, music, the arts or film. A work matter may be ideal, but ensure you check the details. Be practical. It's a good day for a beauty treatment. *Moon in Aquarius.*

6 JANUARY

You may be feeling a little idealistic so take things one step at a time. Ensure you have the right end of the stick to avoid misunderstandings. *Moon in Pisces.*

7 JANUARY

If you're feeling forgetful blame it on the moon and Neptune! Their conjunction could signal a foggy brain but will also mean you're super inspired if you're an artist or creative person. You may also enjoy meditation and spirituality more than usual. *Moon in Pisces.*

8 JANUARY

This is a good day to enjoy a favourite hobby and activity. Plan to meet favourite people or at least catch up over the phone. *Moon in Aries.*

9 JANUARY

As the sun and Venus align you'll enjoy romance and meeting someone lovely. If you're working you may be busy, and this is certainly a time when you can improve your health and appearance. *Moon in Aries.*

10 JANUARY

You'll appreciate the opportunity to be more practical about your goals and to get things done. Just avoid sensitive topics with people you know can be stubborn for the best measure. *Moon enters Taurus.*

11 JANUARY

You can steam ahead with work and career projects but you must take your time with decisions as you may be forgetful or super idealistic, especially as someone may surprise you. *Moon in Taurus.*

12 JANUARY

The Taurus moon will encourage you to be practical and sensible about your financial decisions and at work. Be aware that not everyone will agree with you now, so be tactful. *Moon in Taurus.*

13 JANUARY

The Gemini moon will bring a more sociable and chatty, light-hearted vibe your way. You'll enjoy get-togethers but must avoid difficult topics unless you really must make a point that could change a relationship or circumstance. *Moon in Gemini.*

14 JANUARY

As Mercury turns retrograde you may receive unexpected news or must attend to something quite out of the ordinary. Analyse circumstances but avoid over-analysing them! Aim to tie up loose ends of paperwork. *Moon in Gemini.*

15 JANUARY

You are likely to feel more intuitive and will enjoy time spent at home – either yours or someone else's. You may enjoy a reunion. *Moon enters Cancer.*

16 JANUARY

You may feel intense emotions surrounding a person, group or situation. Aim to gain perspective if circumstances are difficult. A healing or therapeutic solution is possible. *Moon in Cancer.*

17 JANUARY

The full moon in Cancer this year is an excellent time to consider how to be practical about domestic matters, especially if you feel that your work and home lives are taking different directions. You'll enjoy a meeting or socialising.

18 JANUARY

You'll feel more outgoing and upbeat and more on top of domestic and personal developments. Artistic Aries may also feel more creative. *Moon in Leo.*

19 JANUARY

You'll enjoy doing something fun and different. You may also be more spontaneous and will enjoy an impromptu get-together. *Moon in Leo.*

20 JANUARY

This is a good day to be busy with activities you love. You'll enjoy being spontaneous and will appreciate the chance to alter your usual routine. *Moon in Leo.*

21 JANUARY

You'll feel capable and willing and ready to make changes in your work and daily routines. However, a matter may tend to be exaggerated so maintain perspective, especially at work and regarding health. *Moon in Virgo.*

22 JANUARY

This is a good day for get-togethers, work meetings and socialising. You may hear from an old friend or will receive news you've been waiting for. *Moon in Virgo.*

23 JANUARY

You'll receive news from the past or information you've been looking for. You'll enjoy socialising and doing something different. You may hear from someone unexpectedly. *Moon in Libra.*

24 JANUARY

When the moon is in Libra you tend to be more co-operative and collaborative. You may find you get on with people a little better so it's a good day for talks, but you must be prepared to compromise. *Moon in Libra.*

25 JANUARY

This is a chatty, outgoing day. You'll appreciate the chance to initiate some of the projects or changes you'd like to see take place. *Moon in Scorpio.*

26 JANUARY

You may revisit important matters that are not yet completely decided upon. Aim to be practical with your ideas and avoid obstinacy. *Moon in Scorpio.*

27 JANUARY

You'll appreciate the company of like-minded people but may be bored or frustrated by those who think differently. Choose your company wisely! *Moon in Sagittarius.*

28 JANUARY

This is a good day to overcome differences with those you love and to plan fun events. ***Moon in Sagittarius.***

29 JANUARY

You may need to go over old ground at work or with a project. You'll enjoy getting together with someone you love and admire. Emotions may be intense, so take things one step at a time. ***Moon in Capricorn.***

30 JANUARY

You may hear unexpected news or will need to make sudden changes to plans. Be practical for the best results. ***Moon in Capricorn.***

31 JANUARY

This is an ideal day for enjoying the company of people you love and also indulging in activities you love. You may enjoy improving your health and appearance. If you're working, it could be lucrative. ***Moon in Aquarius.***

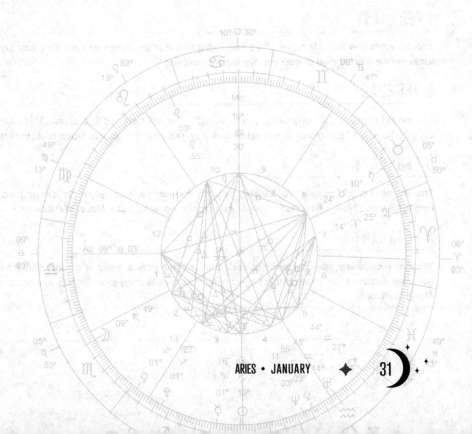

February

career   love   home   health   finance

1 FEBRUARY

The Aquarian new moon is an excellent time to begin something new, and even if projects and ideas involve a great deal of work you are likely to succeed.

2 FEBRUARY

The moon in Aquarius will encourage you to diversify your activities and to socialise. This could perhaps be with a fresh group, or it could be due to an impromptu invitation. *Moon in Aquarius.*

3 FEBRUARY

This is a good day to consider your deeper thoughts and wishes, especially to do with work and health. It's a good day for meditation, yoga and communing with nature. *Moon in Pisces.*

4 FEBRUARY

You may receive key news, for some at work and for some from a friend or organisation. It's a good day to make a commitment to a project or an idea but you must avoid limiting your options. *Moon in Pisces.*

5 FEBRUARY

When the moon is in your own sign you will feel more in touch with your emotions. You may also feel a little impulsive, so be spontaneous but avoid decisions you'll regret. A good day for health and beauty treatments. ***Moon in Aries.***

6 FEBRUARY

You will not always agree with everyone all the time! Take a moment to consider your ideas in relation to someone else's and see if mutual ground can be reached. ***Moon in Aries.***

7 FEBRUARY

As the moon aligns with Uranus you may experience an unexpected development. You may be surprised by your own responses. It's a good day to try something new and to enjoy your fave activities. ***Moon in Taurus.***

8 FEBRUARY

This is another excellent day to be adventurous and to try something new, whether at work or in your own spare time. ***Moon in Taurus.***

9 FEBRUARY

You'll appreciate the chance to reconnect with someone you love or respect. A key meeting at work could be positive, but you must avoid impulsiveness. ***Moon in Gemini.***

10 FEBRUARY

You'll enjoy getting together with someone you love or admire. It's a good day for romance and the arts and for a health or beauty treat. ***Moon in Gemini.***

11 FEBRUARY

Key talks may be intense, so decide early on to maintain perspective. You'll enjoy a reunion, although you may feel super sensitive. ***Moon in Cancer.***

12 FEBRUARY

You'll enjoy cocooning at home. Check to see if your emotions are leading you astray. If not, you'll enjoy a fulfilling time. ***Moon in Cancer.***

13 FEBRUARY

This is another day to ensure your emotions aren't leading you into feeling more sensitive than need be. This aside, you'll appreciate the chance to get together with people you love and enjoy favourite activities. ***Moon in Cancer.***

14 FEBRUARY

Happy St Valentine's Day! This promises to be a busy day and you may experience a surprise as you hear from someone from your past and someone you love. Why not be bold yourself? *Moon in Leo.*

15 FEBRUARY

If a relationship has been a little rocky, take a moment to consider how to smooth things over. There may be an unavoidable meeting. *Moon in Leo.*

16 FEBRUARY

The Leo full moon will spotlight your feelings. You are also due for key news or a meeting that will put things in context. Ensure decisions align with your values.

17 FEBRUARY

An unexpected meeting or out-of-the-ordinary work development could promote your ideas. It's a good day to consider making a commitment to a project or person. *Moon in Virgo.*

18 FEBRUARY

As the sun enters the sign of Pisces you may feel a little more philosophical and introspective. Trust that your previous decisions have merit and be brave. *Moon in Libra.*

19 FEBRUARY

You can achieve a great deal so it's a good time for housekeeping, cleaning and shopping. The moon in Libra can lead you to feel a little indecisive, so take an extra moment before committing to plans. *Moon in Libra.*

20 FEBRUARY

You may be felling more romantic and inclined to indulge in luxuries and laziness. Someone may need your help and, if you need advice, it will be available. *Moon in Libra.*

21 FEBRUARY

You may feel more energised and motivated as the day goes by and can get a great deal done. Any mood swings in the morning may deepen unless you aim to dispel them. *Moon in Scorpio.*

22 FEBRUARY

People in your life may seem a little erratic, so give them a broad berth! You'll gain insight into yourself or someone close. *Moon in Scorpio.*

23 FEBRUARY

Once the moon enters Sagittarius you'll feel more adventurous and outgoing. However, you may feel introspective or even forgetful earlier in the day. The arts, meditation and spiritual endeavours will go well. *Moon in Sagittarius.*

24 FEBRUARY

This is a lovely day to focus on the people, projects and activities you truly love; you'll be glad you did! *Moon in Sagittarius.*

25 FEBRUARY

You may receive an unexpected invitation or will hear out-of-the-ordinary news. A circumstance may change abruptly. Be prepared to be spontaneous, but avoid impulsive behaviour you will come to regret. Communications may be disrupted, so back up your computer. *Moon in Capricorn.*

26 FEBRUARY

Communications should be a lot smoother today than yesterday. This is a better day for talks and meetings. *Moon in Capricorn.*

27 FEBRUARY

You'll enjoy the company of like-minded people. You could make progress with chores, plans and work. *Moon in Aquarius.*

28 FEBRUARY

You'll appreciate the chance to enjoy the company of someone you love, but be prepared for an unexpected change of circumstance or surprise news. *Moon in Aquarius.*

March

career	love	home	health	finance

1 MARCH

You'll feel more relaxed as the day progresses, as less will annoy you and people's opinions and behaviours will not be so frustrating. Plan a romantic and relaxing evening. *Moon in Pisces.*

2 MARCH

The current Pisces new moon phase is ideal for getting in touch with your feelings and taking time to develop your spiritual side. You may wish to begin a new project or health and well-being idea. You'll enjoy meditation, yoga and deepening understanding of those you love.

3 MARCH

Key meetings and developments will ask that you align your ideas with your actions. Today's events may be intense, so take things one step at a time. *Moon in Pisces.*

4 MARCH

There is a close connection with someone from your past or with a matter from the past. This is a good day for a health or beauty treat. *Moon in Aries.*

5 MARCH

You'll enjoy a reunion and a get-together this weekend. If you're working, this is likely to be a busy day. *Moon in Aries.*

6 MARCH

As Venus conjuncts Mars, expect key meetings and developments. You may need to adjust some of your expectations. *Moon in Taurus.*

7 MARCH

You may need to reorganise some of your schedule. Key work news merits focus. Take things one step at a time in practical and realistic ways. *Moon in Taurus.*

8 MARCH

This is a good day for talks, so organise meetings and sensitive communications for today for the best results. *Moon in Gemini.*

9 MARCH

You'll find communications improve now, so take the opportunity to float your ideas and projects with those they concern. Avoid taking the problems of others personally, but help if you can. *Moon in Gemini.*

10 MARCH

Mercury in Pisces for the next two and a half weeks will bring your inner idealist out, so ensure you are being practical with all things. You'll enjoy romance, film, music and dance. Be inspired! *Moon in Gemini.*

11 MARCH

As your attention goes to your home life, family and property, this is a good time to self-nurture and nurture others. *Moon in Cancer.*

12 MARCH

You have natural empathy with others at the moment and will gain insight into them and yourself. It's a good time to support others and to ask for support if you need it. *Moon in Cancer.*

13 MARCH

You'll enjoy relaxing and indulging in your predilection for the luxuries in life. You may return to an old haunt or enjoy a reunion. It's a good day for beauty and health treats. *Moon in Leo.*

14 MARCH

This is a good time for talks and meetings, both socially and at work. You may enjoy an impromptu get-together. *Moon in Leo.*

15 MARCH

When the moon is in Leo you are more expressive and upbeat. Some people may find your behaviour feisty, so if you encounter opposition remember to be tactful, too! *Moon in Leo.*

16 MARCH

You tend to get busy when the moon is in Virgo and, at the least, a little more motivated to get things right in your various activities. Just avoid being self-critical or critical of others. *Moon in Virgo.*

17 MARCH

You may be surprised by news or by an unexpected or impromptu meeting. You may bump into someone you like. *Moon in Virgo.*

18 MARCH

The Virgo full moon will bring into perspective what and who you love to be around in your everyday life. You may begin a fresh health and well-being cycle. It's a good time to focus on spirituality and people who have similar interests to you.

19 MARCH

As the moon enters your seventh house your mind will turn to the people you share your life and love with. You'll appreciate the chance to spend more time with them. *Moon in Libra.*

20 MARCH

The sun in your sign for the next four weeks will add a spring to your step. You'll feel increasingly proactive and may feel drawn to tidy up your home and even let some bad habits go. *Moon in Libra.*

21 MARCH

The Scorpio moon will add passion and deep feelings to your day. You may hear from someone from your past or will return to an old haunt. Health or work news will be relevant. *Moon in Scorpio.*

22 MARCH

A key meeting may bring emotions to the surface. Take things one step at a time at work as you may feel under pressure or must contend with moving goal posts. Expect the unexpected and avoid impulsive decisions. *Moon enters Sagittarius.*

23 MARCH

You'll appreciate the chance to get together with an old friend or partner. Be ready to compromise with someone at work or a friend – within reason. **Moon in Sagittarius.**

24 MARCH

You may feel particularly inspired or drawn to be with someone. You may feel idealistic at work and particularly interested in spiritual quests. A health matter may deserve attention or information. **Moon enters Capricorn.**

25 MARCH

Today's moon will encourage you to be practical about your various options. You may feel impulsive but must be guided by facts and reality. You'll enjoy connecting with an old friend. Work could see an upturn. **Moon in Capricorn.**

26 MARCH

You may hear good news from someone in a position of authority or a particularly charming character. You'll enjoy a get-together or returning to an old haunt. If health has been slow to improve you may see improvements. **Moon in Capricorn.**

27 MARCH

You'll feel sociable now and will enjoy getting together with like-minded people. If you or someone close shows stubbornness, find ways to overcome the impasse. **Moon in Aquarius.**

28 MARCH

This is a good day for work commitments as long as you are happy with the way the big-picture developments fit with your values and principles. You could make great progress at work and could boost health and well-being. **Moon in Aquarius.**

29 MARCH

Your inner dreamer may come out, so ensure you have your feet on the ground. Avoid forgetfulness. You may be drawn to the past. **Moon in Pisces.**

30 MARCH

This is a good day for romance, the arts and creativity. Meetings at work could go well, but you must avoid being super idealistic. **Moon in Pisces.**

31 MARCH

Trust your instincts as they will not be wrong. If you feel vulnerable, ensure you reach out for advice or support. A health or work matter will improve with the correct attention to detail. **Moon in Aries.**

April

career   love   home   health   finance

1 APRIL

The new moon in your sign signals the start of a fresh cycle for you, especially if it's your birthday today. Key health or work news is on the way.

2 APRIL

You'll appreciate the chance to be spontaneous and to do something different. You may hear unexpected news and may enjoy a surprise, for some financially. You'll appreciate a boost to your ego. ***Moon enters Taurus.***

3 APRIL

This is a good day to make changes that may affect your circumstances in the long term. You may enjoy a meeting or talk that could be transformational, for some at work and for others socially. ***Moon in Taurus.***

4 APRIL

Today's developments are positive for travel and, if you've had plans to travel but haven't been able to, your plans may take a step in the right direction, especially regarding a trip to an old haunt. A reunion could be enjoyable. ***Moon in Taurus.***

5 APRIL

You'll experience a change of pace that may have a frustrating aspect to it. A meeting or news could be bittersweet. You'll enjoy soaking up music and the arts and relaxing. *Moon in Gemini.*

6 APRIL

This is a good day for meetings and to talk. If you must negotiate certain arrangements this is a good day for coming to mutually agreeable outcomes. *Moon in Gemini.*

7 APRIL

You'll appreciate the opportunity to talk to key people whose opinions and ideas matter to you. If you have had to undertake difficult talks you could make progress, so take the initiative. *Moon in Cancer.*

8 APRIL

Romance could blossom so make a date if you haven't already! Creative Aries will also find this a productive day. You may feel moved to improve domestic décor or dynamics. *Moon in Cancer.*

9 APRIL

You'll feel motivated to get your plans and projects up and running. If you feel a little lacklustre in the day at first you'll feel increasingly active once you get started, especially with domestic matters. *Moon in Cancer.*

10 APRIL

Keep an eye on communications as you may easily be misunderstood. If you're working, avoid mix-ups and delays by planning ahead. Avoid power struggles; these could escalate quickly. *Moon in Leo.*

11 APRIL

Communications may get stuck and traffic may be slow. Take a moment to ensure you're all on the same page in talks to avoid mix-ups. Be realistic and practical. *Moon in Leo.*

12 APRIL

You'll be drawn to make bold statements and enter fresh territory, either at work or in your personal life. Just ensure your plans sit well with those you work with and care about or today's stars could mean discord. A lovely romantic connection could flourish. *Moon enters Virgo.*

13 APRIL

You can get a great deal done so get busy! If you've been planning to make changes at work or in your personal life, or in your general activities and projects, today's the day. *Moon in Virgo.*

14 APRIL

You'll be drawn to indulge in all the delights in life you enjoy, so if you're working you may need to focus that little bit harder. The arts, music, dance and romance could all flourish now. *Moon enters Libra.*

15 APRIL

Your romantic, idealistic and artistic sides will come out and demand full expression over the coming weeks. Why not consider an arts or dance course? You'll enjoy it. The spiritually minded will enjoy feeling more in tune with yourself, your higher purpose and others. *Moon in Libra.*

16 APRIL

The current full moon in Libra will spotlight a particular business or personal relationship. Consider if you or someone else needs more support.

17 APRIL

You'll feel more passionate about people you love and your ideas and beliefs. Avoid taking impulsive steps to alter agreements at the moment as you may be looking through rose-coloured glasses. *Moon enters Scorpio.*

18 APRIL

You may receive unexpected news and must avoid ego battles. Nevertheless, this is a good day for communications and financial matters as long as you've done adequate research. *Moon in Scorpio.*

19 APRIL

There is a more adventurous, proactive aspect to the day's events so be motivated to initiate fun projects and to be a part of decisions and activities at work. *Moon in Sagittarius.*

20 APRIL

As the sun leaves your sign your attention is likely to turn to practicalities such as financial budgets. You'll enjoy activities that get you in touch with a sense of adventure. You'll also enjoy good food. *Moon in Sagittarius.*

21 APRIL

This is a good day to focus on your health and well-being and that of someone close. Plan a healthy diet and bring fitness into your world.

22 APRIL

You'll feel more inclined to follow your instinct now, especially to do with work and favourite activities. You may even enjoy slowing down a little and taking a break. *Moon in Capricorn.*

23 APRIL

Today's Aquarian moon will bring your inquisitive side out and you'll enjoy exploring new ideas and even social circles. You may hear from an old friend or return to an old haunt. *Moon in Aquarius.*

24 APRIL

This is a good time to take stock, especially financially. Is your budget working for you? Have you overspent, or are you holding the purse strings too tightly? You may feel inspired by art and creativity. Romance could blossom. *Moon in Aquarius.*

25 APRIL

Your insight into the feelings others have for you will be strong over the next two days. Avoid taking their behaviour personally, however. You could deepen your relationship with someone special. *Moon in Pisces.*

26 APRIL

You may receive an ego boost or will feel more confident. Good news about work or from the past will be welcome. *Moon in Pisces.*

27 APRIL

This is a good time to boost your intuitive and spiritual development. However, you may be super sensitive to undercurrents, so ensure you keep your feet on the ground. Good news is on the way. An investment could be ideal but you must be sure of the details. *Moon enters Aries.*

28 APRIL

This is a good time to make long-term changes and to discuss your plans with others, especially regarding work and finances. You may receive good news and will enjoy catching up with someone special. *Moon in Aries.*

29 APRIL

Developments at work may take a turn. Information may come to light that makes things much clearer. An authority figure may have news for you. *Moon in Aries.*

30 APRIL

The partial solar eclipse in Taurus signals a fresh chapter for you in your personal life, and for some Aries at work and financially. Be practical and consider the positives. You may receive ideal news and a reunion could be ideal. *Moon in Taurus.*

May

career   love   home   health   finance

1 MAY

This is a good day to improve your health, well-being and appearance. If you're working, you could also boost your status. It's a good day for socialising and networking. **Moon in Taurus.**

2 MAY

As Venus, the planet of love and money, enters your sign expect more focus on these two aspects over the coming few weeks. It's a good time to discuss your plans with the people they concern in both areas. **Moon in Gemini.**

3 MAY

This is a good day to go with changes occurring in your daily life, such as at work. You may also hear good news that could mean positive changes to come, especially regarding work and health. **Moon in Gemini.**

4 MAY

You may experience a welcome surprise over the coming two days. Be flexible and follow your instincts. This is a chatty day, when you'll enjoy discussing your ideas and plans. **Moon in Gemini.**

5 MAY

Expect a surprise. Being spontaneous and flexible will help you to enjoy your day. *Moon in Cancer.*

6 MAY

This is a good day for get-togethers and socialising. If you need to negotiate financial matters you could be in a good position. *Moon in Cancer.*

7 MAY

This could be a productive weekend, as you'll feel motivated to get things done such as improving home décor. If you're working, it could be a lucrative time. You may feel drawn to update your wardrobe and appearance. It's also a good weekend to boost health and well-being. You'll enjoy a reunion. *Moon in Leo.*

8 MAY

You'll enjoy spending time with those you love. You'll also wish to be busy, so ensure you organise a fun event or outing. *Moon in Leo.*

9 MAY

You may wish to tie up loose ends at work and to nail down a matter that has been up in the air. Be positive and optimistic and you will be successful. *Moon enters Virgo at night.*

10 MAY

As Mercury turns retrograde you may receive important news, financially for some. Aim to get important conversations and ideas floated by the end of the day for the best results. *Moon in Virgo.*

11 MAY

You may sense a change of mood as Jupiter enters your sign. A more adventurous and optimistic time is about to unfold for you. Travel or deepening your spirituality may appeal. *Moon in Virgo.*

12 MAY

The more practical you are with your various ventures the better for you. Be positive but also realistic. *Moon in Libra.*

13 MAY

You'll appreciate the chance to touch base with someone you love or admire. You may make key financial decisions or enquiries now. *Moon in Libra.*

14 MAY

You may feel very strongly about a principle or a financial matter. Take the time to find out the details before you assume the worst. ***Moon in Scorpio.***

15 MAY

This is a good day to focus on your health and well-being. If you have been overworking, find time to unwind. You'll enjoy the company of favourite people. ***Moon in Scorpio.***

16 MAY

The total lunar eclipse in Scorpio is an ideal time to look at how you share space, duties and responsibilities with others. If this is equal you'll enjoy making deeper commitments, but if an aspect of how you share things is uncomfortable it's a good time to talk about it, especially finances. ***Moon enters Sagittarius.***

17 MAY

This is a good day for talks and you'll enjoy your activities, socialising and networking. Be practical and aim for best-case outcomes at work. ***Moon in Sagittarius.***

18 MAY

Be positive about your various plans and projects, as you could make a great deal of progress. If you need the facts this is the day to find out more. Avoid believing the first story you're told. Romance could blossom. ***Moon in Capricorn.***

19 MAY

This is a good day to make tracks with your work projects, and also to make changes financially if you've been planning a new budget. Aim high and be brave. ***Moon in Capricorn.***

20 MAY

This is a good day for talks, especially to do with travel, finances and work, so take the initiative. ***Moon in Aquarius.***

21 MAY

You may receive key news, for some to do with money and for others in your personal life. A trip will take you back to an old haunt or you will enjoy a reunion. ***Moon in Aquarius.***

22 MAY

This is a good day to get things done, so take the initiative. If you're working you will be busy. A sociable day will involve the chance to meet fun people. ***Moon enters Pisces.***

23 MAY

You'll appreciate mixing with upbeat if busy people. If you have been waiting for news it is likely to arrive today. You may be repaid a debt. **Moon in Pisces.**

24 MAY

This is a good day for talks, meetings and negotiations. You may be inclined to make impulse buys or to overspend, so leave the credit card at home if you're already in debt. **Moon enters Aries at night.**

25 MAY

This is a good day to review some of your work projects and long-term plans; you may get deeper insight by doing so. Avoid being impulsive. **Moon in Aries.**

26 MAY

You'll enjoy a little retail therapy. If you have important matters to discuss, this is a good day to do so. **Moon in Aries.**

27 MAY

Be careful with communications, especially at work and with groups, friends and organisations, as you may feel more emotional than usual. If you are instigating change your efforts will be worthwhile, so be brave. **Moon in Taurus.**

28 MAY

You'll appreciate the chance to be a little more self-indulgent over the next two days, and will enjoy good food and company. **Moon in Taurus.**

29 MAY

You may feel super motivated to get things right and to get them done your way. Avoid over-exaggerating your ideas and aim to collaborate for the best results. You'll enjoy the chance to boost your understanding of yourself and someone else. If you're working you're likely to be busy. **Moon enters Gemini at night.**

30 MAY

The Gemini new moon is a good time to launch a financial or written/publishing project. This may also be a good time for launching a financial investment, as long as you have done your research and have not limited your options too much.

31 MAY

This is another good day for get-togethers and planning travel and also for work projects. A health and well-being plan is likely to go well. **Moon in Gemini.**

June

career love home health finance

1 JUNE

Be practical about your plans, especially those to do with friends, groups and organisations. You'll enjoy spending time with someone close or at home. *Moon in Cancer.*

2 JUNE

Chores, work and duties may take up more of your time than you'd prefer, so ensure you make space for fun and relaxing activities too. *Moon in Cancer.*

3 JUNE

You may receive key news to do with work or money and this will help you to better plan ahead. *Moon enters Leo at night.*

4 JUNE

You'll enjoy being active and outgoing; music, dance and creativity will all appeal. You may have chores to complete, and the quicker you do them the more fun you can have! *Moon in Leo.*

5 JUNE

There is a therapeutic aspect to the day. You may wish to relax and spend time with someone whose presence is also relaxing. Romance or family and friends will feel supportive and healing, but if someone lets you down you will find support from someone else. ***Moon in Leo.***

6 JUNE

This is a good time to get your various projects shipshape at work and at home. If making financial transactions, pay attention to the details. ***Moon in Virgo.***

7 JUNE

You may receive a surprise; for some this may be an impromptu get-together or news and for others a boost in finances or well-being or a compliment. ***Moon in Virgo.***

8 JUNE

This is a good day to work towards your health goals. You will find that what may have seemed difficult in the past is easier now. It's a good day for health and beauty appointments. ***Moon enters Libra.***

9 JUNE

You can't agree with everyone all the time, so you may need to compromise and collaborate more than usual. ***Moon in Libra.***

10 JUNE

You may receive good news at work or financially. It's a good day to have talks at work and to improve your well-being, looks and self-esteem. Someone charming could prove to be influential in your life. ***Moon enters Scorpio at night***.

11 JUNE

You may experience a surprise or will receive unexpected praise and be in an unusual circumstance. If, however, you experience a disappointment, look at ways to move forward to create more stability and security, especially financially. ***Moon in Scorpio.***

12 JUNE

Be positive and consider the best outcome in your circumstances. Avoid believing someone who can be negative; make up your own mind. ***Moon enters Sagittarius at night.***

13 JUNE

As Mercury enters Gemini you'll sense a chattier, more light-hearted phase begin. It's a good time to reach out to someone for a talk. *Moon in Sagittarius.*

14 JUNE

The full moon and supermoon in Sagittarius will spotlight a relationship and its true viability. Look for clarity and truth.

15 JUNE

There may be a focus on health and well-being, especially if it's your birthday in early April. Take a moment to ensure you are nurturing yourself and others well. If you need help from an expert, it's available. You may also be asked for help. *Moon in Capricorn.*

16 JUNE

You'll appreciate the opportunity to work methodically towards your goals. Ensure you research facts adequately to avoid mistakes, as you may be forgetful and misunderstandings may arise. *Moon enters Aquarius at night.*

17 JUNE

You'll enjoy a pleasant surprise or impromptu get-together. You may bump into an old friend. *Moon in Aquarius.*

18 JUNE

If you're making considerable commitments, ensure you are on the right track. If you're investing financially, check the details. *Moon in Aquarius.*

19 JUNE

Developments may take more of your time or be more complex than you'd hoped, but they will be worth the effort. Romance could blossom, so make a date. *Moon in Pisces.*

20 JUNE

You'll appreciate the chance to get together with a like-minded friend, group or organisation. Talks will be constructive. *Moon in Pisces.*

21 JUNE

The changes you wish to make in your life are likely to go well now, especially to do with work, finances and your general direction. Be bold and brave. You may also enjoy socialising. *Moon in Aries.*

22 JUNE

When the moon is in Aries you feel more dynamic and proactive but you may also tend to be a little emotional, so take things in your stride if life feels intense. Take a moment to boost health and well-being. ***Moon in Aries.***

23 JUNE

You'll feel more feet on the ground as the day goes by, so take the opportunity to work towards your goals methodically and you'll be pleased with the outcome. ***Moon enters Taurus.***

24 JUNE

Mars in your sign will provide you with extra energy to get things done, so make hay while the sun shines! Avoid clashes with people at home over the next few days; be sensitive to their needs and ask for the same. ***Moon in Taurus.***

25 JUNE

If someone has been behaving irrationally, take some time out to sort out your own feelings and regain a sense of balance and serenity this weekend. ***Moon in Taurus.***

26 JUNE

You'll appreciate the chance to be a little more sociable and outgoing and to touch base with those whose company you love. ***Moon in Gemini.***

27 JUNE

Key talks will be productive, even if they bring out some of your vulnerabilities or sensitivities. You may have a debt repaid or will repay one. This is a good day for medical appointments. ***Moon in Gemini.***

28 JUNE

You may receive unexpected praise or even a financial boost. You'll appreciate the help and attention of someone who has your back. ***Moon enters Cancer.***

29 JUNE

The new moon in Cancer signals that a new chapter is beginning at home, with family or property. If it feels tough or over-exaggerated, take time out to regain perspective. For some this new moon could point to a fresh agreement that may be hard to understand, so take things in your stride.

30 JUNE

You'll gain a better understanding and detente with someone close such as a family member or neighbour. It's a good day to initiate talks, especially at home. ***Moon in Cancer.***

July

career   love   home   health   finance

1 JULY

You'll appreciate the sense that you have more energy and vitality than usual at the end of the week, and even if you're under pressure you will get things done. *Moon in Leo.*

2 JULY

This is a good weekend to sort out your priorities, especially as it's impossible for everything to go your way. Decide early on where you wish to place your attention and map out activities. If you thrive under pressure you'll love this weekend but, if not, take time out when you can. *Moon in Leo.*

3 JULY

Someone you trust who has more experience than you will prove to be a true friend and/or adviser. Avoid misunderstandings and avoid overspending, as you're liable to splurge now. *Moon enters Virgo.*

4 JULY

Some conversations may feel intense so ensure you have your professional hat on at work. For some there will be financial matters to sort out. Stick with the facts to avoid mix-ups and plan ahead as traffic may be delayed. *Moon in Virgo.*

5 JULY

As your sign's ruler, Mars, enters Taurus you will notice a change in mood and you'll feel more practical about certain personal and financial matters in the coming weeks. It's a good day for meetings and negotiations. *Moon enters Libra at night.*

6 JULY

This is a good day for medical and beauty appointments. You may also be drawn to the past. A debt may be repaid, and romance could blossom. Someone may need your help or vice versa. *Moon in Libra.*

7 JULY

When the moon is in Libra you may feel more emotional than usual, so take a moment to regain perspective. Someone may need a shoulder to cry on. If you need support ask for it, as it will be available. *Moon in Libra.*

8 JULY

You may experience a surprise; for some this will involve finances, and for others a person close to you. Someone at home or a domestic matter will need more attention. Avoid feeling vulnerable and make tracks to find out more if you feel compromised. *Moon in Scorpio.*

9 JULY

Communications at home, especially, may be tense so take things in your stride. Avoid miscommunication and mix-ups. Plan ahead, as travel may be delayed. *Moon in Scorpio.*

10 JULY

You'll enjoy a surprise or an unexpected development. You may hear from someone close. This is a good day to get clear if you have had a misunderstanding with someone. *Moon enters Sagittarius.*

11 JULY

Trust your intuition, as it will provide good insight into your circumstances. Someone you love and trust will be a positive influence, so ensure you make time for someone special. *Moon in Sagittarius.*

12 JULY

You may feel super sensitive at the moment so ensure you maintain perspective, especially at home and regarding health and work. Keep communications on an even keel to avoid misunderstandings. *Moon enters Capricorn.*

13 JULY

The full moon and supermoon in Capricorn will shine a light on your status, general direction and career. You may be ready to make positive changes, and these could affect your home as well. You'll enjoy a get-together or visit. It's a good time to make improvements to both home and status. You may enjoy a financial boost.

14 JULY

Your idealism could be a pitfall for you, so ensure you are practical to avoid making mistakes and over-estimating your circumstances. ***Moon enters Aquarius.***

15 JULY

You'll feel motivated to get things done, even if you feel you're up against the odds. If you feel you're fighting against the ideas of others allow things to settle, gain perspective and work towards your goals. ***Moon in Aquarius.***

16 JULY

Take note of key news and developments, for some regarding home, family or your property. A key trip or meeting could be important. You may prefer to get things done quickly but a little more time may be necessary; be patient. ***Moon enters Pisces.***

17 JULY

This is a lovely time for relaxation and to get together with like-minded people. You'll enjoy films, dance, music and romance. Creative Aries will enjoy being productive. ***Moon in Pisces.***

18 JULY

Important meetings and news could lead to key changes but may also be intense, so ensure you stay on top of circumstances. A group, friend or organisation could be influential. A trip could open doors. Trust your intuition. ***Moon enters Aries.***

19 JULY

You may become more active with talks and meetings over the coming weeks, so plan to be busy and sociable. ***Moon in Aries.***

20 JULY

This is a good time to make changes, both at home and at work. If you're doing some DIY or even moving, developments may be intense but will bring the change you want. The consequences of your actions could be long lasting. ***Moon enters Taurus.***

21 JULY

You'll appreciate the opportunity to spend a little time on life's luxuries. Avoid overspending and overindulging; you may regret it! Someone close or perhaps even you may appear unpredictable or stubborn, so take a moment to check you're all on the same page. *Moon in Taurus.*

22 JULY

The sun in Leo for the next four weeks will bring your inner playfulness out. You may feel like spending time on music, dance and people you love, such as more family time. It's also a good phase to focus on being creative. If today's interactions are a little tense, take things slowly. *Moon in Taurus.*

23 JULY

This is an excellent day for getting together with upbeat people who are inspiring. A family get-together or a reunion will be enjoyable. You may enjoy planning travel and/or a spiritual or educational project. *Moon in Gemini.*

24 JULY

The moon in Gemini can tend to bring your inner chatterbox out and you'll enjoy catching up with those you love. If you're working you'll get a great deal done. If you have a lovely Sunday off you'll enjoy reading, writing and generally relaxing. *Moon in Gemini.*

25 JULY

Jupiter in your sign will always make a grand statement, which means you're likely to see things in a slightly larger-than-life way. Today's tough aspects with Venus could point to discord, so ensure you are seeing things clearly and avoid arguments. *Moon enters Cancer.*

26 JULY

While you're not generally known as a stubborn character, you can be as obstinate as anyone. You may simply see life a little on the negative side, seeing only the problems and not the solutions. Aim to find a friendly, conciliatory way out of a tough decision or circumstance. *Moon in Cancer.*

27 JULY

This is a good day for a health check and for improving your circumstances. You may find the advice of a teacher or expert very useful. Someone may ask for your help, and if you need support you will receive it. *Moon in Cancer.*

28 JULY

The current new moon in Leo will kick-start a fresh cycle in your personal life; for some at home and for others in your family or a creative project. However, you may also experience a surprise or an unusual change of plan.

29 JULY

Communications may be tense or very busy, so ensure you pace yourself to avoid mistakes and misunderstandings. A link with someone or a project from your past will be of particular focus, and you'll appreciate the opportunity to catch up with an old connection. *Moon in Leo.*

30 JULY

As such a proactive person you tend to leap before you think about your circumstances, whereas there is merit at the moment in being more thoughtful about how you approach your projects and other people. Avoid being self-critical and too critical of others. *Moon enters Virgo.*

31 JULY

An important decision could be made so you must avoid impulsiveness, as your choice must be well thought out because it represents a commitment. Someone close may surprise you or you will bump into an old friend. An authority figure may have news for you. *Moon in Virgo.*

August

career   love   home   health   finance

1 AUGUST

Talks and developments may be busy or seem at once delayed, blocked and pressured: quite a mix! Someone you feel a fated or destiny link with will be a part of discussions and decisions now. Be clear about your goals. *Moon in Virgo.*

2 AUGUST

You may experience an out-of-the-ordinary change of tempo or a fresh circumstance that comes out of the blue. Be adaptable and try to avoid rushing decisions, even if you must be decisive and/or spontaneous. Look for a balanced outcome. *Moon in Libra.*

3 AUGUST

You'll appreciate surprise help or support from someone. You may experience an unexpected boost in self-esteem via a compliment, visit, domestic development or financial improvement. *Moon in Libra.*

4 AUGUST

It's important at the moment to decide who you must show loyalty to. Family and someone close are important. An authority figure or someone at work may need to be treated carefully. *Moon enters Scorpio.*

5 AUGUST

Hard work, diligence, patience and an open mind will work wonders for you at the moment. Avoid allowing pressure to get the better of you, even if strong emotions enter the mix. Key decisions are best taken with a cool head. ***Moon in Scorpio.***

6 AUGUST

Use your intuition to gain insight into a tricky circumstance or a stalemate. You may find that once the moon is in Sagittarius you gain a more optimistic and outgoing outlook, so avoid allowing intense emotions to run your day. Be inspired by music, art and romance. ***Moon enters Sagittarius.***

7 AUGUST

There is a therapeutic aspect to the weekend as long as you take advantage of the healing potential of this weekend's stars. Avoid being obstinate about matters that must move forward. Avoid reckless spending and focus on finding peace, love and romance at home and in your heart. ***Moon in Sagittarius.***

8 AUGUST

This is a good day for improvements, both of yourself, such as your health, and of your home life and projects such as work commitments. An adviser or expert may be particularly helpful, so seek experienced help if needed. ***Moon enters Capricorn.***

9 AUGUST

Be practical with work and financial matters and you will make progress. Avoid being distracted by matters you can't change for now. You may receive good news to do with work or health. Avoid being misled by strong emotions that get the better of you at work. Romance could flourish, but you must avoid arguments. ***Moon in Capricorn.***

10 AUGUST

This is a fairly changeable time for you, so be prepared to think on your feet. Someone may surprise you or will behave unpredictably. ***Moon enters Aquarius.***

11 AUGUST

You may receive good news from the past. You may be repaid a debt or will repay one yourself. Avoid overspending; you'll regret it. Surprise developments will keep you busy. You'll feel more on top of things as Venus enters Leo for the next few weeks. ***Moon in Aquarius.***

12 AUGUST

The Aquarian full moon will shine a light on your options regarding matters that seem stuck. Consider a fresh perspective, especially if some matters come to a head. *Moon enters Pisces at night.*

13 AUGUST

The Pisces moon will promote a more relaxed outlook on life this weekend, but you must avoid escapism. You may be drawn to overindulge in the good things in life and may regret it tomorrow! A chum or colleague will prove to be a good, loyal friend. *Moon in Pisces.*

14 AUGUST

This is a good day to come to a mutually agreeable arrangement, so sharpen up your negotiation skills. You could make long-term lasting change via a commitment, but you must ensure your plans are practical and realistic. *Moon in Pisces.*

15 AUGUST

You'll hear from a close friend or family member who may have good news. You may meet someone new who seems familiar or who you feel you may have a destiny link with. It's a good day for a reunion. *Moon in Aries.*

16 AUGUST

You'll enjoy doing something different, and someone may be in touch out of the blue. If you need to think outside the box and find new ideas you'll feel inspired. *Moon in Aries.*

17 AUGUST

Keep an eye on the details, especially at work, as there may be some matters that are unclear and need more research. Likewise, if you have a health or beauty decision to make ensure you have all the information. *Moon in Taurus.*

18 AUGUST

A get-together will bring you in touch with like-minded people. You may feel more inclined to spend time doing something fun rather than working, so you'll need to focus a little extra at work. Challenges will be overcome. Romance could blossom, so organise a date! *Moon in Taurus.*

19 AUGUST

You will attain your goals, but you may need to work a little harder at them. A little tension or intensity in the day is best met head on with the intention that you'll succeed: and you will! *Moon in Gemini.*

20 AUGUST

As your sign's ruler, Mars, enters chatty Gemini you are likely to be drawn to be more sociable, to network more and to be inclined to wish to travel. Avoid impulsive decisions and being pressured to make choices unless you're sure. **Moon in Gemini.**

21 AUGUST

There's an escapist element about your weekend. If you've managed to get away for a break you'll enjoy the change of environment, but you must plan ahead to avoid traffic delays. Avoid misunderstandings and forgetfulness, especially if you're working. You may be inclined to overindulge, so pace yourself. It's a good day for a health or beauty treatment but you must be clear about your aims. **Moon in Gemini.**

22 AUGUST

This is a good day for communications and travel, although you must plan ahead and be clear about your intentions. You will enjoy a change of environment via a visit. **Moon in Cancer.**

23 AUGUST

The sun in Virgo for the next four weeks will help you to focus at work and boost your health, so take the initiative. However, you may tend to be self-critical and critical of others, so ensure you maintain perspective. **Moon in Cancer.**

24 AUGUST

There is a therapeutic aspect to the day, making this is a good day for a medical appointment. If you need help or guidance from an expert it's a beneficial time to ask for support. Similarly, you may be asked for help. **Moon enters Leo.**

25 AUGUST

Trust your instincts, especially if developments seem contradictory or pull you in two different directions. Be prepared to make a bold choice. Enlist expert advice if necessary. **Moon in Leo.**

26 AUGUST

In the lead-up to the new moon it is an ideal time to make intentions, especially to do with work and your personal life. Be practical and realistic but also be proactive about what you wish to accomplish in your life. **Moon in Leo.**

27 AUGUST

The Virgo new moon will encourage you to take fresh steps at work and/or regarding health and well-being. If you've been reluctant to make changes, developments now will encourage you to be bold. However, snap decisions will get you into hot water, so be careful.

28 AUGUST

This is a good day for negotiations and financial transactions, as long as you have done your research. You could make a long-term commitment. *Moon in Virgo.*

29 AUGUST

You may find key developments at work will put you in a new position. If you're a creative Aries you could be busy with a key project. A family commitment must be carefully researched and then agreed upon as you could establish common ground. *Moon enters Libra.*

30 AUGUST

You may need to go over old ground with a work or health matter. Be diligent and you will overcome obstacles. Just avoid exaggerating some aspects of circumstances for the best measure. *Moon in Libra.*

31 AUGUST

You'll be drawn to express yourself romantically and creatively, which you'll enjoy if you're in an artistic or romantic environment. If you must get things done at work you may need to focus more on details first and then organise something fun or artistic for later in the day. *Moon in Libra.*

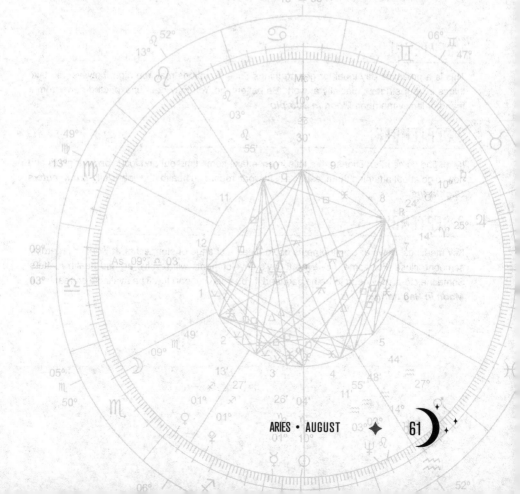

September

career   love   home   health   finance

1 SEPTEMBER

This is a proactive day ideal for getting things done. Emotions may run high, however, so take things in your stride, especially at work. Be patient too. You may hear unexpected news from a friend or family member. *Moon in Scorpio.*

2 SEPTEMBER

If you find some interactions are a little intense take some time out and focus on your goals and how to go about attaining them, especially at work, regarding health and financially. *Moon enters Sagittarius.*

3 SEPTEMBER

Key meetings, news or developments could mean a change of plan, either at work or regarding someone close. For some, however, today's developments will revolve around health matters. Someone close may need to be helped, and if you need support it will be available so reach out. *Moon in Sagittarius.*

4 SEPTEMBER

You'll feel adventurous about your various plans and aims but you must ensure you have a solid basis for believing they'll work, otherwise you may find some activities challenging. Avoid being forgetful and overindulging in the finer things in life; you may regret it! *Moon in Sagittarius.*

5 SEPTEMBER

Developments at work will require delicate handling, so be prepared to be tactful. You may need to attend to a health appointment and gain more information about circumstances. Be practical for the best results. *Moon in Capricorn.*

6 SEPTEMBER

As Venus joins the sun in Virgo you may feel more inclined to be prudent about work and health matters. This is a good time to attend to personal health and well-being. You'll enjoy a reunion but must avoid overspending. *Moon in Capricorn.*

7 SEPTEMBER

You'll enjoy socialising and networking with a diverse group of people, and may also meet an interesting character at work. Humanitarian and spiritual interests could blossom, so take the initiative with your projects. *Moon in Aquarius.*

8 SEPTEMBER

A health, well-being or personal matter will merit careful handling. For some, today's developments will mean you must be more tactful at work and regarding family matters. *Moon in Aquarius.*

9 SEPTEMBER

Take a moment out of your busy schedule, as you could make great progress both with a work and personal matter but may need to take a moment to think things through. Be diligent with your plans and you'll succeed. *Moon in Aquarius.*

10 SEPTEMBER

The Pisces full moon will shine a light on your daily routine, as you are ready for something new. You may receive key news from someone close such as a personal or business partner. Be prepared to think outside the square about your options. It's a good time for spiritual development and meditation. *Moon in Pisces.*

11 SEPTEMBER

Be prepared to think laterally. You'll enjoy an impromptu event and will appreciate the time to get in touch with someone you get on well with, either at work or socially, so make a date! *Moon in Aries.*

12 SEPTEMBER

This is a good day for meetings, both at work and in your personal life. You may enjoy boosting health and vitality through a treatment or visit with a health expert. Avoid feeling you can build Rome in one day; take things one step at a time and you'll accomplish your goals. *Moon in Aries.*

13 SEPTEMBER

You'll get things done more methodically as the day goes by, so avoid feeling rushed. You'll get the chance to focus on finances and practicalities, so don't feel pressured. You'll enjoy relaxing in the evening and may engage in a treat such as a meal out. *Moon enters Taurus.*

14 SEPTEMBER

Your emotions are likely to run deep, especially regarding someone who can be stubborn. You'll feel motivated to get a lot done at work but must avoid feeling you can change something that's ingrained in others overnight. *Moon in Taurus.*

15 SEPTEMBER

You certainly cannot be called inactive or lazy at the moment, as Mars in Gemini is giving you an extra lot of energy, especially with your plans and projects. However, you may tend to be more stubborn than you're usually seen to be, so if some people push against your plans ask if they could be more flexible. *Moon enters Gemini at night.*

16 SEPTEMBER

While you're not generally known as an idealist you may fall into this pitfall at the moment, believing life is rosier than it is and especially concerning work or a health matter. Conversations may be more tense than they need be, so take a moment to unwind if life seems pressured. *Moon in Gemini.*

17 SEPTEMBER

Your chattier, more light-hearted side comes out when the moon is in Gemini, giving you the upper hand in talks, meetings and negotiations. Trust that you can talk the talk! *Moon in Gemini.*

18 SEPTEMBER

Key talks will signal important changes to come, especially if you were born at the end of March. For all Aries this is an important day regarding work, a change of routine or a health matter, so take things in your stride. *Moon enters Cancer.*

19 SEPTEMBER

Important developments at work or within a long-term change of direction will have an impact. This is a good day to initiate a work or personal project *Moon in Cancer.*

20 SEPTEMBER

This is another good day for initiating change, even if you feel there is opposition to your plans. As long as you have laid careful groundwork your plans should succeed. You may experience a surprise. *Moon enters Leo at night.*

21 SEPTEMBER

You'll feel more creative and dynamic about developments even if you know you must be diplomatic and/or take things carefully, especially regarding long-term change. *Moon in Leo.*

22 SEPTEMBER

You'll gain the upper hand with communications as you'll feel more inclined to look for balance and harmony, especially with key people you live and/or work with. The equinox will put your mind to creating more balance and peace in your life, which can sometimes be due to obstacles and challenges. Avoid arguments and look for positive solutions. *Moon in Leo.*

23 SEPTEMBER

Key news will arrive and you may need to review or revise some of your expectations, especially to do with a change of routine either at work or at home. It's a good day for a medical appointment. *Moon in Virgo.*

24 SEPTEMBER

You'll discover if you've been realistic with your expectations or if these need to be tweaked to be more in line with circumstances. Romance could blossom, so organise a treat! It's a good day for a beauty appointment but you must be clear about what you want. *Moon in Virgo.*

25 SEPTEMBER

The Libran new moon will kick-start a fresh chapter in a key business or personal relationship. Long-term change will eventuate from developments, so be careful with your choices.

26 SEPTEMBER

You may hear key news to do with work that may be ideal for you, but if it poses problems this is the time to find out more about your options to ensure you have room to move and to negotiate. *Moon in Libra.*

27 SEPTEMBER

This is a good day to discuss your ideas with the people they concern, especially at work and regarding your general direction and plans for the future, even if you think you're just going over old ground. It's also a good time to boost health and well-being and for meditation and spiritual development. *Moon in Libra.*

28 SEPTEMBER

You are likely to feel motivated and ready for work although you may also feel tempted to overspend, so ensure you are careful with money. It's a good day to make agreements and for negotiations but you may need to give a little. *Moon in Scorpio.*

29 SEPTEMBER

You'll enjoy socialising and networking. The Scorpio moon will add a little charm and charisma to your interactions, making you appear beguiling. Organise romance if you can. *Moon in Scorpio.*

30 SEPTEMBER

You'll appreciate feeling more optimistic and outgoing in your various ventures and this will be noticed by those you interact with. It's a good time to make changes in your usual routine and to try something new. *Moon in Sagittarius.*

career love home health finance

1 OCTOBER

This is a super romantic time, especially for end of March Aries, and you'll enjoy spending time with someone you love. The arts, dance and music will also appeal. You'll appreciate the chance to improve your appearance or wardrobe. *Moon in Sagittarius.*

2 OCTOBER

You may receive key news that will help your plans move forward over the coming weeks, especially to do with work or your health or a change in your daily routine. *Moon in Capricorn.*

3 OCTOBER

You'll enjoy having your feet on the ground this weekend and being more practical about the changes going on in your life. You'll also enjoy treating yourself or someone close to good food and beautiful company, art, music, film and romance. *Moon in Capricorn.*

4 OCTOBER

You'll appreciate spending time with a different circle of people; you may also be invited to a new group or will enjoy a change of scenery. Be adaptable at work and you'll be amazed at what you can do! *Moon enters Aquarius.*

5 OCTOBER

You're not known as being a changeable person but you are open to new ideas, projects and people; you'll enjoy a little diversity and change in your personal and work life. *Moon in Aquarius.*

6 OCTOBER

When the moon is in Pisces you may feel a little more introverted or introspective. It's a good time for reflection, meditation and spiritual development. Trust your instincts. *Moon enters Pisces.*

7 OCTOBER

An unexpected development or unusual news from a business or personal partner may demand you think on your feet. You may experience a change of pace as someone may open your eyes to new information or a fresh perspective. You may find the help of an expert or employer very useful. It's a good day for meetings. *Moon in Pisces.*

8 OCTOBER

Take a moment to allow this week's developments to sink in. You may tend to see life from a very sensitive and vulnerable point of view, yet you have the ability to change your circumstances so they suit you better. *Moon enters Aries.*

9 OCTOBER

The Aries full moon points to a new beginning for you, especially in your personal life and if it's your birthday today (happy birthday!). If you were born later in Aries you may find this a good time to reflect on your health, well-being and work life.

10 OCTOBER

You'll feel more practical and less reflective, just in time for the beginning of the week! It's a good time to rearrange your daily routine so it suits you better and to find ways to boost your appearance, well-being and health. *Moon enters Taurus.*

11 OCTOBER

You'll be looking for more balance and peace in your daily life and at work and it's possible to attain this. You may hear good news to do with someone special or at work. Be adaptable to avoid being thrown off course by an unpredictable character. *Moon in Taurus.*

12 OCTOBER

Someone could make a mountain out of a molehill, perhaps even you, so ensure you have the facts straight before you go in to bat for someone else or for a principle. Misunderstandings could occur. A trip may be ideal but delays are possible, so plan ahead. *Moon in Taurus.*

13 OCTOBER

This is another day to aim to be flexible and adaptable, and the Gemini moon will help you to do so. Schedules, travel and people may be unpredictable, so stay centred. *Moon in Gemini.*

14 OCTOBER

Key talks and developments could lead to positive outcomes, so take the initiative. If it has been difficult to budget this is an excellent time to formulate a new plan. You may even receive good work or financial news. You'll enjoy a meeting. *Moon in Gemini.*

15 OCTOBER

Use your intuition, especially with domestic and personal matters. If you're working this could be a hard work day, and if you're on holiday you'll enjoy being active. *Moon enters Cancer.*

16 OCTOBER

Art, music and creativity and being with like-minded people will appeal to you, although you may need to clear the decks to make space for your favourite activities and romance. *Moon in Cancer.*

17 OCTOBER

This is a good day for work projects as you'll feel motivated and could get a great deal done. However, you may be liable to rush your plans and projects and could make mistakes as a result. Avoid misunderstandings. *Moon in Cancer.*

18 OCTOBER

This is another busy day when you could attain goals, as long as you avoid rushing and pre-empting outcomes. Be positive, but do not cut corners. *Moon in Leo.*

19 OCTOBER

Artistic and creative Aries will find this a productive time, and may even be easily distracted from daily chores. If you can focus on your activities such as work, you will be successful. Avoid butting heads with someone in authority; it could spiral into conflict. *Moon in Leo.*

20 OCTOBER

You may be liable to enter into an ego battle or all-out disagreement, so try to see all sides of the story and remain true to your principles without starting a fight. *Moon enters Virgo at night.*

21 OCTOBER

You'll appreciate the opportunity to pay more attention to the details of your various projects and to the people you love and admire. Avoid being super critical of yourself and others. *Moon in Virgo.*

22 OCTOBER

You can make a great deal of change in your daily life and your status, even if your plans seem difficult. If you have laid solid groundwork your efforts will pay off. You need to be adaptable with a changeable person. *Moon in Virgo.*

23 OCTOBER

This is a good day for negotiations and for establishing common ground with someone important. However, you may feel very passionate about your views, so if you see these threaten other people's peace of mind be tactful. *Moon in Libra.*

24 OCTOBER

The more tactful and diplomatic you can be the better for you, as someone may feel vulnerable or sensitive at the moment. If you feel you need help or support it will be available; just ask. *Moon in Libra.*

25 OCTOBER

Life can get very intense at a solar eclipse. Today's partial eclipse is in Scorpio and points to a new way to share common ground, such as chores, duties and even money, so it's a good time to consider making fresh agreements. Messages could be lost in translation, so be super clear.

26 OCTOBER

You know that you can't agree with everyone all the time, and with so much focus on joint agreements and shared matters at the moment, collaborative efforts must be made. Be patient and look for ways to co-operate. *Moon in Scorpio.*

27 OCTOBER

This is a good day to make agreements and to work on projects. It's also a good day for trips, but you must avoid fast drivers. Avoid also allowing disagreements, especially with people in authority, to become conflict, as it could become long term. *Moon enters Sagittarius.*

28 OCTOBER

You'll appreciate the opportunity to reconsider some of your ideas. You may feel a little more inspired and philosophical, so take particular notice of your ideas. You may be drawn to an old haunt. *Moon in Sagittarius.*

29 OCTOBER

Someone close is likely to have strong ideas and opinions. Take a moment to listen, as they may have important insight that could help you even if it challenges your ideas. A trip may need to be better planned. *Moon enters Capricorn.*

30 OCTOBER

You may feel a little idealistic, so consider your ideas and see that they match up with circumstances then take practical steps to move forward. *Moon in Capricorn.*

31 OCTOBER

Happy Halloween! With the moon in Aquarius tonight, expect the unexpected!

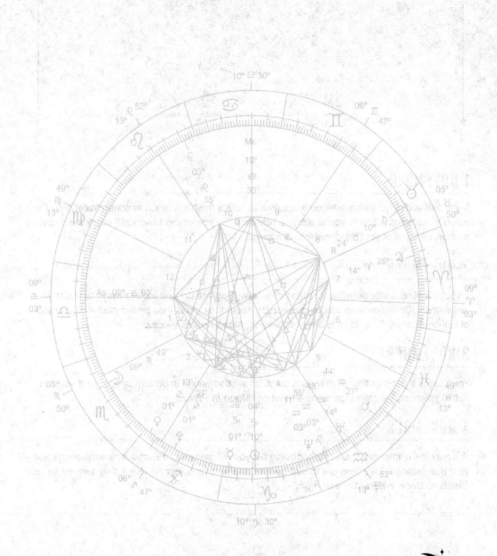

November

career   love   home   health   finance

1 NOVEMBER

If you feel you're not being listened to it's time to take a fresh approach to communications. The moon in Aquarius will help you to adopt a new tack. Try something new; you'll enjoy the chance to improve some of your relationships as a result.

2 NOVEMBER

If you're feeling a little sensitive or vulnerable take short breaks and look for ways to boost your self-esteem. Someone who can be passionate about their ideas may be the cause of your lack of self-confidence. Find ways to boost self-worth. ***Moon enters Pisces.***

3 NOVEMBER

You'll enjoy a get-together or at least a catch-up with someone important to you, so if you have nothing planned yet start organising a meeting. ***Moon in Pisces.***

4 NOVEMBER

You may feel a little sensitive or introspective but you will gain insight into your circumstances and your true feelings. Take time out to self-nurture and to help someone else if they require some attention. ***Moon enters Aries at night.***

5 NOVEMBER

You may be surprised this weekend by developments. Someone close will prove to be helpful and supportive. If you are asked to help someone you will be available for them. Avoid snap decisions but be spontaneous and aim to find practical ways ahead. *Moon in Aries.*

6 NOVEMBER

You have a knack for good communications even if you've been putting your foot in it of late. Take a moment to devise a good plan of action and you'll find you can move ahead despite strong feelings being in your environment. *Moon in Aries.*

7 NOVEMBER

Your diplomatic qualities and tact will be very useful, especially with important negotiations and developments with a friend, group or organisation. Maintain your values and principles, but be prepared to be adaptable to others' needs. *Moon in Taurus.*

8 NOVEMBER

The total lunar eclipse in Taurus will mean a complete change is underway in a personal or financial context. It's important now to see the long-term consequences and outcomes of circumstances. You may receive key news from someone close that may be surprising.

9 NOVEMBER

You'll appreciate the opportunity to put some of your excellent ideas in action to improve your personal life and work. It's a good day to boost looks, health and well-being. A work matter is best decided on in practical terms and on a realistic basis. Avoid arguments; look for solutions instead. Romance could blossom. *Moon enters Gemini.*

10 NOVEMBER

Be careful with communications, as you may be at loggerheads with someone you're better to be agreeing with in the long term. Look for ways to overcome differences but avoid being super idealistic about any agreements you make. *Moon in Gemini.*

11 NOVEMBER

You'll find out if you've been realistic about a partnership, work project, health or beauty matter. If you find your expectations have been too high you'll gain the opportunity to alter your mindset and be more realistic. *Moon in Gemini.*

12 NOVEMBER

This is another day to avoid arguments and to find ways to establish common ground. A work or personal matter will benefit from diplomacy, especially with a figure of authority. You may simply have different plans for the future. *Moon in Cancer.*

13 NOVEMBER

This could be a passionate time when you can overcome differences and establish a fresh path in your relationships. Avoid agreeing to plans on a whim; ensure you have researched your situation adequately before making commitments. Romance could blossom. *Moon in Cancer.*

14 NOVEMBER

This is a good time for being adventurous at work and to make a strong statement. Just avoid appearing rash or brash. *Moon enters Leo.*

15 NOVEMBER

Circumstances are on the up but you must avoid taking anything for granted. Meetings, both social and professional, could go well, so take the initiative but ensure you do your research before committing to long-term plans. *Moon in Leo.*

16 NOVEMBER

You could make a great deal of progress with your various projects. Also, romantically you may find this a super intense but enjoyable time. You'll enjoy socialising with a fresh group or being more outspoken. *Moon in Leo.*

17 NOVEMBER

You may find yourself busier over the coming weeks and today's stars will give you an idea of the kinds of developments that will arise. *Moon in Virgo.*

18 NOVEMBER

This is a good day for making agreements with people in authority such as employers. You may find your career can progress now. If you are looking for a job, send out resumes and organise interviews. *Moon in Virgo.*

19 NOVEMBER

You may be feeling a little head in the clouds and absent-minded, so take a moment to unwind and de-stress. Avoid forgetfulness and find a way to feel more grounded. *Moon enters Libra.*

20 NOVEMBER

You'll enjoy spending time with someone you love or admire. You'll feel more inclined to agree with people and will enjoy collaborations, trips and get-togethers. *Moon in Libra.*

21 NOVEMBER

This is a good day for work projects and collaboration. You may feel particularly motivated and able to get on with colleagues and employers alike. You may hear key financial or personal news. You may enjoy a reunion or a health boost. *Moon enters Scorpio.*

22 NOVEMBER

The sun in Sagittarius for the next four weeks will bring your inner adventurer out. You'll feel drawn to travel and study and generally to broadening your horizons, which you'll enjoy. *Moon in Scorpio.*

23 NOVEMBER

Today's new moon in Sagittarius signals you're ready for something new. Take a moment to formulate exciting plans and choose how you wish to implement them. In the process you may need to re-organise the way you share certain duties or finances or even space at home.

24 NOVEMBER

Developments may have a therapeutic quality about them. If you're involved in legal matters these will move forward fairly rapidly. You'll enjoy exploring new ground. *Moon in Sagittarius.*

25 NOVEMBER

This is a good time to focus on health and well-being, both of your own and that of someone you love. You may be about to alter key elements of your usual routine, and this could be exciting. *Moon enters Capricorn.*

26 NOVEMBER

This is a good day for healing, therapeutic endeavours, meditation and spiritual practices. You may hear from someone who needs your help and you may ask for support yourself, which will be available. Trust your intuition. *Moon in Capricorn.*

27 NOVEMBER

You may be surprised by developments. Be open to being spontaneous, but avoid misunderstandings and mix-ups. *Moon enters Aquarius.*

28 NOVEMBER

This is a good day to feel motivated to get things organised and completed. If you make agreements they are likely to take. You may receive a favourable financial boost or make a career decision that could build stability or wealth. ***Moon in Aquarius.***

29 NOVEMBER

You may be ready to make changes in your environment or financially. If you have been cooped up at home for some time you'll enjoy the chance to spread your wings. Be spontaneous, but avoid impulse buys and gambling. ***Moon in Aquarius.***

30 NOVEMBER

This is a good day for meetings and talks, especially for arranging financial matters, joint duties and responsibilities. A work project could advance. ***Moon in Pisces.***

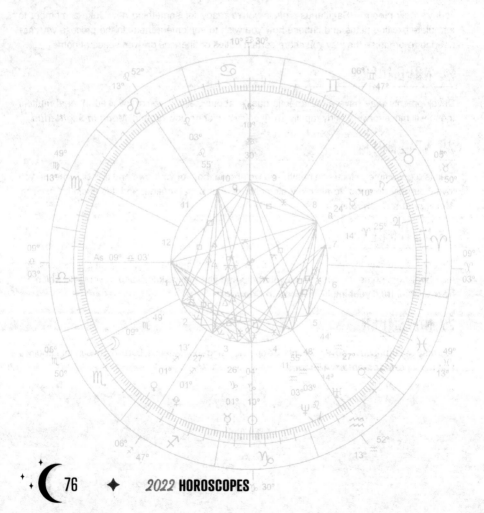

December

career   love   home   health   finance

1 DECEMBER

This is a good day to be active and to meet people. You may get the chance to revisit an old haunt or will need to review some of your plans. **Moon in Pisces.**

2 DECEMBER

Be careful with communications and plans as you may discover a gap in your schedule or a mix-up. This aside, you could make concrete progress with a project, work or health and beauty appointment. **Moon in Aries.**

3 DECEMBER

There is a therapeutic aspect to the day. You'll get the chance to improve your health, appearance or even relationships, so take the initiative and make some improvements. **Moon in Aries.**

4 DECEMBER

You can get ahead with your various projects and will enjoy a get-together and, at the least, a chatty catch-up with someone you love. However, you may tend to be forgetful or may be prone to getting the wrong end of the stick, so be vigilant to avoid mix-ups. **Moon enters Taurus.**

5 DECEMBER

There are certain people and developments that will be hard to avoid, so aim to be positive about the best way forward. If you're at work, be practical and professional for the best measure. *Moon in Taurus.*

6 DECEMBER

Travel and communications may be a little more complex or delayed, so aim to be patient. The more practical and grounded you can be the better for you. *Moon enters Gemini.*

7 DECEMBER

The more adaptable and flexible you can be the better for you, as you may need to change plans at the drop of a hat. *Moon in Gemini.*

8 DECEMBER

The Gemini full moon suggests a fresh chapter regarding a key relationship that involves travel, study, some form of exploration and exciting new plans. You may also need to rearrange finances. Be prepared to change considerably but avoid impulsive decisions. *Moon in Gemini.*

9 DECEMBER

You'll enjoy being spontaneous and may receive an unexpected compliment or invitation. You may also receive an unusual ego or financial boost. *Moon in Cancer.*

10 DECEMBER

It's in your interest to be a little mindful of other people's feelings, as you may tend to be feisty and will step on someone's toes. A change of schedule or a fresh health routine could be difficult to adapt to, but it will be achievable. *Moon in Cancer.*

11 DECEMBER

You'll feel increasingly practical and better organised over the coming weeks and may have already experienced a more grounded approach to and perspective of your status and circumstances. *Moon enters Leo.*

12 DECEMBER

This is a good day to make practical arrangements and for negotiations and agreements, especially with groups, friends and organisations. *Moon in Leo.*

13 DECEMBER

You'll appreciate a feeling of excitement about some of your plans and will enjoy putting some into a more manageable shape. You'll enjoy getting together with like-minded people. It's another good day to make agreements. *Moon in Leo.*

14 DECEMBER

Ensure you are super clear about your intentions as misunderstandings are possible, especially at work and with people you share duties and money with. *Moon enters Virgo.*

15 DECEMBER

This is a better day for financial matters are you're more likely to have an eye for details and be less likely to overspend. *Moon in Virgo.*

16 DECEMBER

Keep an eye on financial transactions as you may be liable to make mistakes or to overspend. If you're making work decisions or negotiating contracts, ask for more time if you're unsure before signing off. *Moon enters Libra.*

17 DECEMBER

This is a better day for financial matters and to make changes in your general circumstances. You may feel like bringing a little more freedom of expression into your life. A pleasant change at work will be enjoyable. *Moon in Libra.*

18 DECEMBER

This is a good day for bringing new ideas, projects and activities into your usual weekend. You'll enjoy getting together with someone charismatic. *Moon in Libra.*

19 DECEMBER

An eye for detail will be needed in your usual interactions and at work. Take time out if you're feeling a little overwhelmed; emotions could be flying high. *Moon in Scorpio.*

20 DECEMBER

You won't get on with everyone all the time, so it's important to choose who you spend quality time with. If possible, avoid those who get your back up at work and, if not, remain professional. *Moon in Scorpio.*

21 DECEMBER

The practicalities of your various projects and ideas may come into question. Take a little time out to work on the details and find new and inspiring ways to plan ahead. A work or personal matter will bring a smile to your face. *Moon in Sagittarius.*

22 DECEMBER

This is a lovely day for get-togthers and to enjoy time with someone you love. You may be pleasantly surprised by news from someone special or at work. You may also receive an unexpected ego or financial boost. *Moon in Sagittarius.*

23 DECEMBER

The new moon and supermoon in Capricorn can anchor your plans and projects. This is a good time to begin something new through practical and well-organised endeavours.

24 DECEMBER

Merry Christmas! This is a lovely day for romance and get-togethers. You'll enjoy a feeling of belonging and being loved. ***Moon in Capricorn.***

25 DECEMBER

There is something new and progressive about this Christmas Day for you; perhaps you have more people around the dinner table or less. Enjoy the difference, as you will appreciate the chance to touch base with those you love. ***Moon in Aquarius.***

26 DECEMBER

There is a healing quality about the next two days. If you overindulged on Christmas Day you'll get the chance to detox. Aim to relax and de-stress as much as possible to enjoy the day. ***Moon in Aquarius.***

27 DECEMBER

You'll appreciate the opportunity to enjoy the company of someone whom you admire or love. A change of company or activity will feel settling and stabilising. You may also enjoy some retail therapy. ***Moon in Pisces.***

28 DECEMBER

This is a good day for a reunion and for enjoying a change of pace. You may enjoy a reunion or a return to an old haunt. ***Moon in Pisces.***

29 DECEMBER

You'll appreciate hearing news you've been waiting for. You may receive a visitor or will take a key trip. Ensure you plan travel ahead as you may be faced with delays. ***Moon in Aries.***

30 DECEMBER

You'll enjoy a little retail therapy but may be inclined to splurge at the sales. Avoid impulsiveness but enjoy being spontaneous. You'll overcome obstacles. ***Moon in Aries.***

31 DECEMBER

Happy New Year! Slowly and surely does it as you face a new year. Emotions may be strong, but you will manage to ride out any disappointments regarding socialising or networking. Someone special will be there and a reunion will arise over the coming days. ***Moon enters Taurus.***

THE ESSENCE OF TAURUS

This is the zodiac's first earth sign. You are practical, have good organisational skills and are inwardly grounded. Your inner calling is to feel you belong, that you have a place in the world and are needed and that you have a sense of purpose. Your true motivation in life is love: you have the highest regard for love and will love those you become close to with all your heart. Your only request is that, in return, you are loved yourself.

Earthly love can be a challenge as humans are not perfect, but your soul will rise to it: to love that is never perfect; love that is nevertheless passionate and without end; love that needs to be fulfilled and in so doing will feel fulfilling. Your inner calling is also to provide for those who respond to the need to be loved and to the need to feel they belong and have an integral purpose in life.

The real challenge for you is to continue to love those who fall short in your eyes, those who perhaps cannot love the way you do and do not have the never-ending resource for love that you do. When this happens your love can turn to stone, and the well from which you derive your values and fulfilment in life will run dry.

Your inner calling is to experience the sensuality of the human experience; to appreciate the divine within the mundane; to experience earthly pleasures while knowing that within these rests the seed of the divine, the eternal and the spiritual.

In a sense you walk between two worlds: the divine and the human. It is easy for you to become lost in either world as this is a fine and delicate line to walk. If you succeed in walking both sides of the line you will find the soul happiness you so crave.

SELF-ESTEEM

To gain self-esteem you need to feel you are flourishing in life and are in charge of your life and your experiences. Above all, you must feel there is value in what you do, in who you are and in your actions. You cannot simply exist and enjoy life; there must be a correlation between what you do, who you are and what you value. You will never stray off the path if you align your experiences with your true loves in life and with the activities that resonate with you on a deep level and lead to a sense of fulfilment.

For example, if you follow your penchant for indulging in the finer things in life such as good food and alcohol or for money for the sake of it you may find that the accomplishments you gain will simply not lead to a sense of fulfilment but rather to a sense of constant craving or a lack in life.

On the other hand, if you rise to your inner calling to establish true values, love and mutual respect and you decide to experience love in all its many guises, both romantic and spiritual, you will find that all else in life falls in place and you gain a true sense of accomplishment.

Your self-esteem will grow largely through your caring and sensuous nature. You will feel rewarded in life through your giving and loving nature, and when you experience the exponential curve of giving and receiving it will make you one very happy bull!

YOUR INNER LIFE

You love to be with people and surround yourself with those who love life and wish to celebrate being alive, just as you do. You are not a fair-weather friend; once you have made your choice of friends you will be loyal and in intimate relationships faithful, as you prefer stability and security to the chase.

As your many friends will confirm you can be stubborn, although you may view this as upholding your beliefs. Being an earth sign means you can be slow to budge once you have formed an opinion, so maintaining a keen eye on the common ground in relationships rather than sticking merely with one established thought will serve you well.

Stubbornness can be a stumbling block for you, especially when you maintain your values to the exclusion of all else. Yet when you embrace an adaptable approach to other people's own destinies, karma, personalities and traits, both positive and negative, you can still uphold your own values, particularly when deep down these revolve around inclusivity, love and mutual respect.

You are a resilient character, and when under pressure have strength beyond your understanding. You appear to be dependable, genuine and loyal, so you do well in industries in which you must project trustworthiness such as financial services, hospitality and all forms of advisory services.

When your ideas and plans are opposed your inner raging bull and obstinacy can be the first traits people notice. Beneath the earthy, placid outer shell of the classic Taurus rests a charging bull; it is no coincidence the bull is your symbolic animal. Anyone who has ever crossed your path and come a cropper will have met the anger and dynamism that can smoulder for years. The more you can train your mind to embrace the inner calm at the seat of your soul the more you will avoid seeing red when life seems to stand in your way, and the more your natural affable self will lead you to success. When you feel respected you are as loyal as the day is long.

The earthy exterior of the Taurean as a placid, practical and methodical person hides the true dynamism of this sign. Scratch the calm surface and you will meet the real bullish breath of the charging fighter beneath.

HOW OTHERS SEE YOU

You are a solid, reliable, practical, friendly and sensual person, and on meeting you people recognise this and respond in kind. They may also experience the charm you automatically radiate, seeing you as being magnetic and personable. You may even wonder why some people are drawn to you when you have done nothing to encourage their attention. It's your animal magnetism, and you're radiating it in bucket loads!

Health, well-being and nutrition will often have strong accents in the Taurean make-up, which may come about by default as your predilection for all things sumptuous and delightful must be tempered and balanced with health and fitness.

There can be a tendency towards addictive or obsessive compulsive behaviour, which may be hidden and only discovered once the behaviour gets out of hand. It's vital that you try to maintain a balanced daily routine.

Taureans may be attracted to work that can be intense, so it's critical to engage checks and balances to ensure a healthy line is drawn between what feeds the soul and what doesn't.

The arts, design, crafts, music and beautiful objects will fuel your spirit. You will enjoy surrounding yourself with beauty, and will no doubt be a creative character yourself. You risk resting on your laurels, and your lust for life can cause you to overindulge in the good things in life.

Your sentimentality can cause you to linger too long in relationships that have outgrown their purpose and in which you continue to remain purely from habit or nostalgia. Your stubbornness and reluctance to move forward into fresh and exciting ventures can predispose you to miss out on new opportunities.

HOW TO MAXIMISE YOUR POTENTIAL

Some may say your pitfall is laziness while others will say it's stubbornness, but it's more a case of being reluctant to move forward without good reason. There is always good reason to go with change, as change is the one certainty in life. That's not to say you should be moving house constantly, ending and beginning relationships or changing jobs every few months or years. What it means is that when you feel deep down that something has to change you must change.

To be aware that something has to change you must be in touch with your instincts, which all too often can be buried behind thoughts and habits. You must rely on your intuition or you really will become stuck.

Your home is your castle, and you appreciate the luxuries of soft furnishings, sensual fabrics and mood lighting. You prefer to stay in one place for many years, as moving too often will be unsettling. You have an emotional connection with your home that is hard to break and you will feel empowered by your home and those within it, so you must avoid ruling the roost with a stick. Allow your softer self and your wish for nurturance of self and others to be expressed at home.

Because your home is where you derive so much pleasure it's important you embellish it with art and music. Just be aware that you do have a tendency to overindulge and keep meals to meal times and sleep to bed time or else your home will become less of a castle and more of a prison.

The best way forward is to be self-assured, as awareness of your abilities and the certainty that your path is the right one are two of your talents. As an earth sign you are one of the most self-confident of the zodiac signs.

TAURUS AND ITS ASCENDANTS

This chapter is about your sun sign, Taurus, and your predictions for the year ahead. The more you know about yourself the better you will be able to take advantage of opportunities, and also to avoid the pitfalls. It's critical to know as much about 'you' as possible.

In astrology your core self is represented by your sun sign, but your personality traits are represented by your ascendant (also known as your rising sign). The ascendant describes your personality, the way other people see you on first meeting you and the way you tend to filter life's events.

When you have intimate knowledge about your sun sign – your engine room or core being – you will be on the way to a happier life. When you add the knowledge about your personality – your ascendant – you will gain even deeper insight into what makes you tick.

Your ascendant sign is determined by the time of your birth on the date and year of your birth. Because the ascendant sign changes approximately every two hours, the best way to determine it is to ask an astrologer to calculate it for you. Certain apps will also calculate your ascendant sign (see page 873).

The following gives you more information about your abilities, characteristics and personality according to your sun sign Taurus in combination with your ascendant sign.

TAURUS SUN SIGN WITH ARIES ASCENDANT

You will be seen at first by those who meet you as being a fiery, impulsive character. As they get to know you better they'll see the careful, methodical and practical character you are at your core, someone who is dependable and earthy who enjoys the good things in life and is able to plan ahead one step at a time. You may even confuse yourself when your predisposition is to be careful and methodical on some occasions yet fiery and impetuous on others. You may be particularly attracted to people who are intense and sensual, people who wish to settle into a routine, yet you may also wish to retain your individuality. Find ways to combine your independence with your need for comfort and love and you will establish positive relationships.

TAURUS SUN SIGN WITH TAURUS ASCENDANT

You are a double Taurean and therefore doubly earthy, doubly practical and potentially also doubly stubborn! But you are also an open book: you are who you seem to be, and your personality and inner self are the same. Consequently, you can be super self-confident and have higher self-esteem while at the same time being principled; it can also be very difficult to change your mind once it's set.

You are a sensual, earthy character and will enjoy the finer things in life. You are a loyal friend and appreciate luxury and comfort. So that you don't get stuck in a particular way of living or get bored it's important to regularly change your usual routine and take steps to learn new aspects of life.

TAURUS SUN SIGN WITH GEMINI ASCENDANT

You are a mercurial character with many different forms of expression. You may be constantly on the go or fidgety, restless and hard to pin down; these are very different to the usual Taurean characteristics. You can be overtly analytical on occasion and can get caught up in your thoughts, so it's important to release tension and the tendency to worry. Consider action-oriented activities that disperse excess energy such as sport and nature rambles.

Gemini rising people often gesticulate with their arms and hands when they talk and can be wiry in appearance. When combined with the Taurus energy there can be inner tension, as your Taurean core self prefers steady progress, not nervous, fidgety expression. Conversely, you are blessed with being an active and analytical communicator while possessing the inner strength and diligence to get things done.

TAURUS SUN SIGN WITH CANCER ASCENDANT

The Cancerian personality gives you a gentle, sensitive, introspective outlook, while underneath your inner resourcefulness and ability to stand your ground may be quite a surprise to people who get to know you. You are a diligent and strong character, and once your mind is made up there is little that will change it. The combination of an earth sign (Taurus) and a water sign (Cancer) provides you with abilities that span the rational and the intuitive, giving you superpowers. You have extrasensory perception, as the Cancerian ascendant enables you to pick up subliminal information about people and circumstances. Combine this with the steadiness of the Taurus underneath and you really are a force to be reckoned with, combining sensitivity and a sixth sense with pragmatism and steadfastness.

TAURUS SUN SIGN WITH LEO ASCENDANT

Your personality is very much the Leo type: preferring to be the centre of attention but also being a loving, creative character. The Taurus–Leo dynamic is able to overcome immense hurdles, is supremely productive and is the king of the jungle. When this is combined with kindness and optimism it makes for an adorable, loyal and productive person. However, when arrogance, laziness and a sense of superiority creep into the mix, this combination can make for a powerful but disrespectful and indolent character. You can act up and be a drama magnet. If you focus on your creativity and productivity instead you will accomplish great feats in life.

TAURUS SUN SIGN WITH VIRGO ASCENDANT

This combination is a double earth mix and points to a trustworthy, loyal and productive character. You will appreciate nature, the earth, being helpful, being of service to others, the simple pleasures in life and generally being a hard worker. You are dependable and will enjoy a responsible role in life. However, the perfectionist nature of Virgo can lead to overtly high expectations, both of self and of others, and to disappointment. If you focus on practicalities, what is possible and achievable, you will move mountains. A pitfall in your character would be overt self-criticism and criticism of others, which will halt your progress. When you focus on your helpful nature and on your values and ability to be kind you will find your life takes you to meaningful places.

TAURUS SUN SIGN WITH LIBRA ASCENDANT

The Libra ascendant gives you the appearance of being balanced, serene and intellectual. You appear to be collected, together and calm. Beneath the surface, however, lies the earthy, slumbering but raging bull. This Taurus-Libra combination, with both signs ruled by love planet Venus, makes for a sexy, seductive and earthy character: you will love good food, wine, company and music. Arts and creativity will appeal to you at various times in your life, and you are likely to have creative or musical abilities yourself. The pitfall with this combination is that you overindulge in the good things in life and live purely to feed your cravings, be these good food, fast cars, status or addiction to drink or drugs. You may also be indecisive, which will create inner tension. When you focus on step-by-step practicalities your inner artist will emerge and you will be able to create the life you want.

TAURUS SUN SIGN WITH SCORPIO ASCENDANT

You are a charismatic, sexy person and will intensely enjoy experiencing all the highs and lows of life. You are an influential character and can be controlling in your approach to life. You are serious and can be obstinate. The combination of earth and water gives you added allure and a strong will, and people may be drawn to your earthy magnetism. You are intuitive and able to work with your sixth sense to your own gain, so you must avoid manipulation and coercion. Deep down you are a trustworthy and loyal character, but your passions may take you into the seesaws of tumultuous relationships. Find the time to express your strong wish for love and compassion, and much of the tumult in your life will disappear.

TAURUS SUN SIGN WITH SAGITTARIUS ASCENDANT

Yours is a larger-than-life personality. Whether you're involved in sport or research, are family oriented or a lover of life you will do what you do energetically and optimistically and with a view to success and winning. You are playful and will enjoy life's many exciting pursuits and are unafraid to try new ventures such as learning through travel, adventure and study. At your core you are focused on creating contentment in life through a sense of stability and security. To avoid inner tension about who you are – the stay-at-home provider of balance and security versus the adventurer – it's important to find expression for both aspects of your nature. You may, for example, express your Sagittarian nature through extreme sport or adventurous holidays or through study. You may express your Taurean nature through art, an enjoyment of nature or the accumulation of wealth and luxury.

TAURUS SUN SIGN WITH CAPRICORN ASCENDANT

You are a double earth character and have a reserved, quiet personality with a predilection for success. Slow and steady is your recipe to the top. You are likely to succeed in your various pursuits even if occasionally your rate of success seems to resemble the tortoise, not the hare. The key to true success lies in determining early in life what your priorities are; you may be attracted to traditional ideas of success such as money and a good job and family life. You may find at different times of your life that alternative priorities arise, such as the need to nurture and be a role model for others and exhibiting compassionate behaviour. You may be seen as a retiring, traditional character but will enjoy expressing your desires for enjoyment and fulfilment in life as much as anyone.

TAURUS SUN SIGN WITH AQUARIUS ASCENDANT

You can appear as a quirky, independent and eccentric person. Combining a taste for variety and spice with your sensuous Taurean nature gives you a lust for life and experience-based wisdom. You are not afraid to taste different foods, to travel to other lands or to investigate new ideas. You do, however, have a tendency to land yourself in unorthodox, unpredictable circumstances. You're bright and willing to learn; when combined with Taurean resilience it makes you a strong character with a fun, quirky twist. The pitfall is that you can be super stubborn. You may also be unwilling to change your life path, especially as you age and despite your willingness to try new experiences. When you rely on that Taurean resilience you know that anything is possible.

TAURUS SUN SIGN WITH PISCES ASCENDANT

Being the dreamer of the zodiac, the Pisces ascendant personality presents initially as a philosophical, soft and gentle person. When combined with the Taurean earthiness it makes for an idealist who is also practical and realistic, a supremely capable person able to work from the ground up to create your ideal life. You may, however, wander between idealism and realism and not be happy with either. To avoid feeling disappointed you should earth yourself through attending to practicalities, so that your ideals manifest in methodical plans.

This Pisces–Taurus combination can point to someone who loves the earth and the ground and wishes to be in nature or working in horticulture, gardening and the environment. You are a sensuous and loving partner and a supportive family member but your idealism can take you beyond the mundane, which can sometimes result in marvellously talented musical, academic, artistic and creative work.

TAURUS IN LOVE

You are such a sensual individual, Taurus, you'll wish to spend considerable time with one partner. In this section you can check out your compatibility with other sun signs. Remember that we are all complex individuals, so the more you know about someone's astrological birth chart the better you can determine your compatibility. Consider having your astrological birth chart compared with that of a partner, friend or family member, as the compatibility – known as 'synastry' in astrology – goes even deeper than a comparison of sun signs, although this is a good place to begin.

TAURUS WITH ARIES

This relationship can be exciting, uplifting and dynamic, even if you find the Aries outlook impulsive. One major stumbling block could be that you can both be uncompromising in your views once you have decided on something, which can lead to a stalemate in which neither of you will budge on important views. Stubbornness and obstinacy could be a real bugbear, but if you can agree to disagree on occasion there is every chance your Aries partner will find you sensual, calming and sexy and that you find your Aries partner exciting, bold and dynamic.

TAURUS WITH TAURUS

Two very sensual and earthy individuals can make merry music together and are a great match, because you both love and appreciate the importance of having strong principles and like to indulge in the good things in life such as fine food and comfort.

You may find this match can predispose you both towards stubbornness, and a deadlock can develop unless you are able to focus on your common ground and on establishing solid foundations in the relationship. Depending on other planetary placements at the time of your birth, this combination can bring out your worst characteristics – or your best. If you are two individuals who are consciously working on being the best version of yourselves this can be a successful combination, but if you are not self-aware then your worst attributes such as laziness, a tendency to get stuck in a rut and overindulgence may come to the fore.

TAURUS WITH GEMINI

This combination with air sign Gemini can be like a breath of fresh air for you or like a hurricane! It will depend on the extent of the Gemini's negative characteristics, such as restlessness, flightiness, inconsistency and unreliability. Your Taurean wish for stability, security, sumptuousness and comfort in life will baulk at the lack of both consistency and level-headedness of the Gemini. However, if your Gemini partner is fun loving, smart, adaptable, exciting and charismatic then you will find these qualities complement yours well. There is likely to be a combination of both good

and bad in your Gemini, as there is in everyone. The restlessness and individuality of the Gemini nature may seem difficult to adapt to when what you are looking for is commitment and calmness in life. A rare Gemini trait is deep-down loyalty; you may need to wait a while to discover this.

TAURUS WITH CANCER

The Taurean approach to life is so much more practical and rational than the Cancerian's intuitive, raw emotional and sensitive approach, so you can feel confused or even overwhelmed by the Cancerian sentiment. There can be compatibility here if both people are willing to work towards a strong relationship and to understand that their approach to life is fundamentally different from each other's. Where yours is earthy and realistic Cancer tends to stride out into new territory, intuitively navigating a way ahead. When you combine both signs' positive attributes and work together with a common aim it can make for a strong union, but if there is no common moral goal in life this combination may simply present as two people missing each other's points.

TAURUS WITH LEO

The Leo nature is very different to the Taurean nature, so much so that you may be at loggerheads. Despite this, Taureans can find the Leo nature exciting, outgoing, fiery and uplifting, especially if your astrology chart has a strong fire signature. A real pitfall in this combination is that the centre-of-attention Leo nature can be at counterpoint with the quiet, calm and earthy Taurean character, which can be grating; Taureans would not be so showy and seemingly selfish as the Leo sun sign. Both sun signs are fundamentally looking for true value and motivation in life, so if you both have the same goals and aims you may find this combination very motivational and ultimately rewarding.

TAURUS WITH VIRGO

These two earth signs can certainly make music together. You have the same fundamental approach to life and this feeds a sense of stability and security in your relationship; it can also point to longevity. You both like to feel settled and that you are working towards a goal, and when your relationship reflects this there can be great reward in the partnership. One pitfall, however, is that you can become too settled at various phases in your lives and are bored or your relationship becomes stagnant. To keep things alive, plan exciting activities or breaks away from everyday routine.

TAURUS WITH LIBRA

Some relationships enjoy a little tension, which can ramp up the passion and romance. Sometimes, however, when tension turns into stress it can be a real passion killer. Both of these signs are ruled by Venus so there is an innate compatibility, but your modus operandi is very different. The Libran analytical and often indecisive frame of mind can be an irritant to the decisive, calm and serious nature of the Taurean, yet the Taurean can provide the calm the Libran is looking for and the Libran can provide the stimulus the Taurean is looking for: the motivation to explore and live life to the fullest. There will be a mutual appreciation of art, music and beauty, which may form the basis of a successful relationship.

TAURUS WITH SCORPIO

This is likely to be a sensuous, passionate relationship; however, as these signs are opposites there is a fundamental difference in your approach to life and in your value systems. The water of the Scorpio sign is likely to dampen the Taurean fervour, and the earthiness of Taurus is likely to feel slow moving or like hard work for the Scorpio. Each sign can benefit the other in a partnership: the Scorpio's intuition may benefit the Taurean's predilection for reason, and the groundedness of the Taurean may be comforting and settling for the intense Scorpio nature. This passionate liaison may be a flash in the pan unless other aspects in the astrological chart such as sun-moon sign compatibility point to more longevity in the relationship.

TAURUS WITH SAGITTARIUS

The outgoing, fiery nature of Sagittarius will be attractive to Taurus but may seem more daring and competitive than Taurus would feel comfortable with in a long-term relationship, because Taurus is looking for stability and security and Sagittarius is looking for adventure and excitement.

Both signs can complement each other. The Taurean caution and reason can be a good leveller for the Sagittarian tendency towards risk taking, while for Taurus the larger-than-life personality and predilection for excitement and risk taking of the Sagittarian may be a breath of fresh air.

TAURUS WITH CAPRICORN

You can certainly make merry music together, as the double earth in this combination makes you compatible. You have the same fundamental approach to life, which feeds a sense of stability, security and longevity in your relationship. You both like to feel settled and that you are working towards a goal, and when your relationship reflects this there can be great reward in the partnership. However, this combination can lead you both towards a materialistic outlook on life. A business partnership is ideal, and a marriage may thrive if it is based on financial goals. You will both enjoy accumulating luxury and experiencing comfort but you may also be drawn to overindulgence and overspending, so take care to achieve balance.

TAURUS WITH AQUARIUS

The steady Taurean approach to life is in stark contrast to the quirky Aquarian approach, which may make for a difficult union unless either sign has other, more compatible traits such as Taurus having your moon in an air sign or Aquarius having their moon in an earth sign. Just based on the sun sign compatibility, Taurus is likely to feel off-kilter in the face of the Aquarian eccentricity, and Aquarius may feel stuck or even bored by the Taurean rationale. There is a real risk that this combination comes head to head in a battle of wills, as neither sign will budge once your minds are made up. Both signs may enjoy the other's attributes at first, and with common goals or values this combination could work but it will involve the necessity for capitulation on both sides.

TAURUS WITH PISCES

The Pisces soft, dreamy, philosophical approach to life contrasts with the Taurean rationale, which is always based on reason, facts and reality and not conjecture. While Pisces can provide

spiritual insight and inspiration to Taurus, the Taurean predilection for reason above all else can be anathema to Pisces. There is a tendency for both signs to miss the point of the other's mindset: the reason-based mindset of Taurus can seem foolhardy to the more intuitive, instinctive approach of Pisces, and the philosophical Pisces dreamy and forgetful nature can be annoying to the practical Taurean. Both signs are sensual signs, and there can be common ground and rewarding enjoyment of art, music and companionship.

THE YEAR AHEAD FOR TAURUS

Affirmation: *'I'm ready for change now.'*

Uranus in your sign for the next three to four years will continue to bring changes in your life. For Taureans born in April this is most likely to be in your personal life, and for May Taureans at work and health-wise.

This year considerable change will also revolve around the areas of your life you share, such as joint duties and finances and even space at home or at work. You want more freedom of movement but also more security; the two may seem mutually exclusive, yet if anyone can make the two run hand in hand it's you this year. This is what the presence of Uranus in your sign is helping you to do: be free while also maintaining a sense of stability.

Certain duties will need to be met, even if you're looking for fresh activities and new frontiers to conquer. And even if some duties may appear to hold you back, they will in fact provide you with the routine or security you need.

You will gain the chance in the second half of the year to indulge more fully in your interests, such as self-development, studies and travel. The first half of the year will revolve more around getting through deep changes occurring in your collaborations, necessitating negotiations and careful analysis of your situation, career and general direction in life.

There's merit in being proactive early in the year to make the changes you have been considering for some time; February in particular will be a good time to float ideas and ventures. The second half of the year will enable you to sit with developments and settle into them.

Finances, especially shared finances such as joint mortgages, tax, investments and super, will benefit from careful thought; you may wish to look for more stable investments or to find ways to invest in more sustainable organisations.

You may alter the groups and organisations you associate with and, ultimately, you may choose new social circles or to socialise differently. Your love life is due to step into fresh territory: singles may look for commitment and couples to renew your vows or to inject your love life with more romance and fun.

HEALTH

You are going to be spending so much time on other people's concerns, issues, health and well-being you must ensure you set aside the time for your own, or you risk fraying your nerves. So much effort going into your career, status and general activities could drain your energy levels unless you prop them up. In the first half of the year you'll progress the most dynamically in your areas of interest, but then in the second half of the year you may need extra breaks and to take time out, especially in June and July and if you were born in mid-May. And, if you find you are overwhelmed with commitments, chores and duties, this is the year to delegate and share these around; you may find that your pleas for help with the housework do not fall so much on deaf ears this year!

The sun, Mercury and Venus in your health sector in October will encourage you to boost your looks and well-being and could help perk up your energy levels. You may be particularly drawn to altering your daily routine then so that it includes more of what you want, such as time spent doing exactly what you love both at home and at work.

FINANCES

In 2022 the major area to keep an eye on is shared finances, as you may find you are more prepared to go it alone with your business ventures even if this flies in the face of reason. You may have more tough calls, especially in relation to negotiations and business agreements. You are in a strong position but may be inclined to undersell yourself and your worth. In this light, negotiations early in the year and from mid-October until December may be particularly significant.

If you find you begin the year on a strong note financially expect to keep accruing wealth and, at the least, to stabilise what you have accomplished. But if you find you are already between a rock and a hard place early on in the year you must be careful to keep a slush fund for a rainy day.

Venus in your finance sector mid-year will encourage you to invest in yourself and your work and status. Be careful not to over- or under-invest and seek financial advice if you're unsure.

Mars will travel through your finance zone from mid-August, which will have a two-pronged effect. If you're generally good with money (many Taureans are) you will find this will be a time – until early September – to make a lot of money. But if you're a Taurean who just loves to spend and to overspend you must be careful at this time to avoid going into debt.

HOME LIFE

This year harmony in your home will come down to sharing and caring and ensuring that equal portions of commitments, duties and chores are shouldered by everyone involved. You may be asked to take the burden of commitments for someone who is unwell or down in the dumps. You may find you are in the position of teacher or guide for your children and must excel at this more than usual.

The eclipses this year are across your personal and partnership sectors, meaning your personal life is due considerable change. This will invariably impact your home life.

The year begins with all hands on deck concerning someone else and their demands and needs; you really may not find too much time for yourself unless you make the time and focus on building true harmony at home.

You may need to review and revise how you share your duties and commitments during the Mercury retrograde phase from mid-January to early February. It's probable that your work and interests will increasingly take you outside your home or that you must make considerable changes at home to accommodate developments regarding work, groups and organisations.

The sun and Venus in your home sector from the end of July and mid-August respectively will encourage you to spend a little more energy on making your home the balanced place you wish it to be.

LOVE

Get set for a fresh approach to someone special, and to yourself! The eclipse seasons in April-May and October-November will prompt you to make long-overdue changes in your personal life. Beforehand, already in January there will be areas concerning joint commitments and duties, activities and interests that you may be drawn to reconsider and see in a new light. Singles may be ready to step into a commitment and couples ready to reconfigure how you share your various chores and duties.

Mars in Sagittarius will add to a sense of urgency that it's now or never: it's time for change at the start of the year. And then the partial solar eclipse on 30 April, together with the total lunar eclipse on 8 November – both in your own sign – point to the fact you will never look back after these turning points in 2022. In other words, your love life is due considerable change now!

A solid commitment is possible, but you will need to remove your rose-coloured glasses first. Couples will be ready to recommit, unless you experience a revelation that changes your circumstances. Singles may meet someone who is truly a match, although it will be important to find out more as a little mystery or enigma may accompany this match. A lovely time for romance will be in November when the sun, Mercury and Venus make a harmonious aspect to Jupiter and Neptune, suggesting, at the very least, a sociable if not a romantic time.

CAREER

Considerable developments at work could change the course of your career; they are likely to stem from your own actions and wish to be more efficient and effective and to be truer to yourself. January, May and November are likely to be turning points when you'll feel motivated to express yourself more actively from your true heart.

Developments may come about through a unique opportunity and, for some, due to a disappointment. And, whether you are promoted or demoted, whether you step up to a new level if you're self-employed or decide to branch out into a new field, you will gain the opportunity to get closer to your true purpose and therefore feel more successful as a result.

Your collaborations and joint duties and commitments will change as a result. At the start of the year you will have an inkling as to how you wish to alter your shared projects and how you wish to move forward more independently – or the opposite. This year, if you've been going it alone at work you will gain the chance to collaborate more, and if you've been working with others and wish to be more independent you'll get the opportunity to do just that.

A work opportunity may arise in October that will seem extraordinarily good luck. As long as you can adapt to the changes it will involve it could be as good as it seems.

January

career love home health finance

Notes: the pie charts such as the one above listed for each month show energy distribution according to the stars for the month ahead. If you wish to make changes in the areas of your finances, health, career, love or home and you see there is a large amount of energy in that sector in the chart, your endeavours should succeed as long as you have prepared well in advance. The charts also show which areas will potentially have the most focus in your life during the month.

The moon sign listed for each day's entry in the diary is the position of the moon at the end of the day in Greenwich Mean Time (GMT). To gain the most information about a particular day's circumstances, read the day before and the day after for a complete picture.

1 JANUARY

Happy New Year! You'll appreciate the chance to do something different. A surprise or a change of routine is likely to lead to a pleasant discovery. *Moon enters Capricorn late at night.*

2 JANUARY

The current new moon and supermoon in Capricorn will help you to feel more grounded and practical. It's a good time to plan in functional terms how you'd like a particular journey, study course or activity to pan out for you this year. It's also a good day for talks at work and for socialising.

3 JANUARY

You'll appreciate the opportunity to think a little outside the box at your various options, both at work and in your big-picture plans. Be inspired! *Moon enters Aquarius.*

4 JANUARY

If you're back at work you'll appreciate the chance to get things shipshape. If you're on holiday you'll enjoy a change of routine and the chance to do something that boosts your health, well-being and looks. *Moon in Aquarius.*

5 JANUARY

As there is a therapeutic quality to the day it is an excellent time to recuperate and plan ahead for the coming year. You may be drawn to working towards better health. If you are asked to help out you will do so willingly. *Moon in Aquarius.*

6 JANUARY

Today's moon in Pisces will bring your inner dreamer out. You'll be drawn to romance and spending time doing something you love. You may also feel particularly inspired and creative. Just avoid forgetfulness. *Moon in Pisces.*

7 JANUARY

There is a therapeutic quality to events. You may be drawn to relax and spend more time on your health and well-being by way of physical activity. It's a good day for deepening your spiritual understanding. Someone may ask for your help, and if you need support it will be available. *Moon in Pisces.*

8 JANUARY

You'll enjoy doing something you love with someone you love! It's a good day for romance and for indulging a little in life's delights. *Moon in Aries.*

9 JANUARY

You'll appreciate the chance to get together with someone important, for some at work and for others in an interest or activity you love. It's also a good day for a beauty or health treat. *Moon in Aries.*

10 JANUARY

When the moon is in your own sign you begin to feel more grounded and less pressured. You'll appreciate the opportunity to take some time out this evening and to get back in touch with someone whose company you love. *Moon enters Taurus.*

11 JANUARY

You'll enjoy a lovely get-together that will be productive as well as enjoyable. However, you may tend to be a little idealistic so if disagreements have been brewing be practical. Avoid absent-mindedness. **Moon in Taurus.**

12 JANUARY

This is a good time to tie up loose ends to do with paperwork and general communications, especially at work, as Mercury will turn retrograde in a couple of days' time and communications may be delayed or complex then. Aim for clear communications now to avoid misunderstandings at a later date. **Moon in Taurus.**

13 JANUARY

You'll appreciate the chance to get in touch with someone whose company you enjoy. Avoid making commitments unless you have all the facts to hand. **Moon in Gemini.**

14 JANUARY

This is a good day for planning and strategy and for getting ahead in a chosen activity or career. You may receive key news that could mean a change of plan at work or even within your general direction. Aim for an innovative approach to your options: think outside the box. **Moon in Gemini.**

15 JANUARY

You are likely to be drawn to adopting a fresh perspective, especially concerning finances and someone special. Aim for an intuitive approach and avoid taking matters personally. **Moon enters Cancer.**

16 JANUARY

Developments may be more intense than they need be at the moment, for some at work and for others concerning someone special or a favourite activity. A relationship may feel more intense than usual, so take things one step at a time. **Moon in Cancer.**

17 JANUARY

The Cancerian full moon shines a light on your general direction in life and, for some, specifically work and your career and how this interrelates with your home life. Avoid getting caught up in the intense emotions of the time and focus instead on practical ways to get ahead.

18 JANUARY

This is a good time for making practical plans, especially in connection with your general purpose and projects moving forward. You could also boost your status and sense of empowerment. Connect with people you know as it can help you to move forward at work. **Moon in Leo.**

19 JANUARY

Today's Mars-Pluto aspect is an excellent time for you to take the initiative, especially at work and to boost your status. It's a good time to collaborate. Romance could sizzle, but you must avoid power struggles as these could escalate quickly. *Moon in Leo.*

20 JANUARY

While you're known as being dependable and practical you can tend to be less willing to adapt to new situations. This is a good time to consider new options and fresh ideas even if they seem out of the ordinary, especially at work and regarding your long-term plans. *Moon enters Virgo.*

21 JANUARY

This is a good day to work in practical and realistic terms to implement new ideas and plans, especially at work and regarding health and well-being. *Moon in Virgo.*

22 JANUARY

You'll enjoy socialising and networking now, so if you have nothing planned yet make a date! A short trip and a plan to take a longer trip could take shape. You may hear good news. *Moon enters Libra.*

23 JANUARY

This is a good day for get-togethers, and you are likely to enjoy a reunion or a visit to an old haunt. You may hear unexpected news from someone. *Moon in Libra.*

24 JANUARY

Key news and developments at work could mean that you must review an idea or a project. You may need to go over old ground, but in the process you will discover something useful. *Moon in Libra.*

25 JANUARY

This is an excellent day to get things done, especially at work. Someone close such as a colleague will help you to complete tasks. If you need co-operation don't hesitate to ask for it; it will be available. *Moon in Scorpio.*

26 JANUARY

If communications have been a little up in the air of late you'll find as the day progresses you gain more certainty about matters you need to be sure about. You'll enjoy a get-together with someone special. *Moon in Scorpio.*

27 JANUARY

You may feel a little more adventurous, especially about how you express yourself with someone close. Be bold and share a secret or encourage them to share their thoughts with you. *Moon in Sagittarius.*

28 JANUARY

You may need to be flexible at the moment, especially with arrangements at work, as plans could be revised without a moment's notice. Be courageous and bold with expressing new ideas. *Moon in Sagittarius.*

29 JANUARY

You may discover something important that could determine a fresh path for you moving forward. Someone close may reveal their true feelings and thoughts or will be keen to get together with you. If you receive intense news take things one step at a time and avoid rushing decisions. *Moon in Capricorn.*

30 JANUARY

Be prepared for an unexpected change of routine or of circumstance. For some this will be to do with work; for others it will be to do with someone close or a health matter. Be practical. *Moon in Capricorn.*

31 JANUARY

This is a good day to focus on good communication skills and put your best foot forward with a work and personal matter. Show your best qualities. *Moon in Aquarius.*

February

career love home health finance

1 FEBRUARY

The Aquarian new moon signals a fresh association and agreement with a group, friend or organisation. Developments may come out of the blue or will require you to think on your feet, so be adaptable and innovative.

2 FEBRUARY

When the moon is in Aquarius it is a good time to think outside the box. You'll enjoy spending time with like-minded people, although a quirky group or organisation may also have a bearing on events. Once the moon is in Pisces later in the day you'll feel more inclined to look at life philosophically. ***Moon in Pisces.***

3 FEBRUARY

Important decisions and matters to do with work are likely to come up for review over the next two days. If you aren't working but are looking for work it is a good time to circulate your resume. A decision that affects your status is best approached carefully. ***Moon in Pisces.***

4 FEBRUARY

A key decision or commitment is likely. You may hear important news from someone close or an organisation that puts a fresh light on your circumstances. ***Moon in Pisces.***

5 FEBRUARY

This is an excellent weekend to spend a little extra time on your health and well-being and on that of someone close. You may be asked for help, and will have support available for you if needed. Just ask. ***Moon in Aries.***

6 FEBRUARY

This is a lovely time to spend with those you love and to indulge in your favourite hobbies and interests. If conflict arises, check if you or someone else has grabbed the wrong end of the stick and correct the situation. ***Moon in Aries.***

7 FEBRUARY

You'll feel more down to earth and practical as the day goes by. This is a good day to take the initiative with new ideas and projects and to think laterally about any problems or issues. ***Moon in Taurus.***

8 FEBRUARY

You may experience a surprise visit or hear unexpected news that could be positive either at work (mostly May Taureans) or in your personal life. Take the initiative with your projects and be positive. ***Moon in Taurus.***

9 FEBRUARY

The Gemini moon is excellent for talks and financial decisions. Just ensure you look at any options from all perspectives to avoid making snap judgements. ***Moon in Gemini.***

10 FEBRUARY

Take a moment to check you're on the same page as someone you must make arrangements or share duties with, as you may have crossed lines. This aside, it is a good time to schedule work and social events. Romance could blossom, so organise an event! ***Moon in Gemini.***

11 FEBRUARY

Key news could be just what you want to hear even if it will mean considerable change moving forward. For some Taureans, though, today's circumstances will include the chance to get together with someone close to you who is influential. Take things slowly if you are feeling super sensitive. ***Moon in Cancer.***

12 FEBRUARY

The Cancer moon will bring strong emotions into the mix. However, if you have good intuition you'll find you are absolutely correct in your analysis of the situation. However, you may feel emotions overwhelm your reason, so be sure to take time out if this is the case. ***Moon in Cancer.***

13 FEBRUARY

This is generally a good time for communications, so where you have important matters to discuss take your cue. *Moon in Cancer.*

14 FEBRUARY

Happy St Valentine's Day! Take a moment to gather your thoughts before you make assumptions, and when you do you'll be glad you allowed your better sense to dominate. There is every chance you'll enjoy a surprise and a fun day; just avoid snap decisions but be bold. *Moon in Leo.*

15 FEBRUARY

Be open to new ideas and to embracing new ways to understand someone close. They may have key news for you. *Moon in Leo.*

16 FEBRUARY

The current Leo full moon shines a light on a key relationship. For some this will be at home; for others at work. You may learn something new that puts a fresh light on things. Ensure you do your research before jumping to conclusions.

17 FEBRUARY

An unexpected development could be just what you want; this may be at work and, for some, socially. Take a moment to decide how you'd prefer things to move forward and take bold steps. *Moon in Virgo.*

18 FEBRUARY

As the sun enters the zodiac sign Pisces your mind will wander to more romantic and creative ideas. You may already be drawn more so than usual to art, movies and dance. Take some time out to enjoy being inspired. *Moon in Libra.*

19 FEBRUARY

You'll enjoy doing something different this weekend and will appreciate the company of like-minded people and family. Collaborations may take you into fresh territory, so be open to new ideas. *Moon in Libra.*

20 FEBRUARY

This is a good day to focus on relaxation and recharging your energy. You may be drawn to help someone who has been down in the dumps. If you need a little help ask for it; it's available. *Moon in Libra.*

21 FEBRUARY

As the moon enters Scorpio later in the day you'll feel more motivated at work and will be productive. If you've been putting chores off this is the day to finally get them done! It's a good day to enquire about new work or health projects. *Moon enters Scorpio.*

22 FEBRUARY

You'll feel inspired by those you work or socialise with and will feel empowered by your connections. However, you won't automatically get on with everyone, so ensure you give those who tend to disagree with you a wide berth. *Moon in Scorpio.*

23 FEBRUARY

You'll enjoy the arts, music and good company, so ensure you make a date with someone you love. Romance could blossom. You may hear from an old friend. A work matter could flourish, but you must pay attention to details. *Moon in Sagittarius.*

24 FEBRUARY

This is another good day for romance, the arts and creativity. However, you may be feeling a little idealistic, so ensure you are looking at life realistically if making key decisions. *Moon in Sagittarius.*

25 FEBRUARY

Be prepared to change your schedule or plans at the last minute; you may find someone's ideas differ from yours. If this is at work, maintain a professional stance for the best measure or you could make mistakes. *Moon enters Capricorn.*

26 FEBRUARY

Communications will improve unless conflict arose yesterday, in which case it will need to be sorted out today. Avoid exacerbating circumstances. *Moon in Capricorn.*

27 FEBRUARY

This is a good day for socialising and improving the feel-good factor in your life. Take a moment to increase the connections and relationships you enjoy and to spend time with those you love. *Moon enters Aquarius.*

28 FEBRUARY

You'll appreciate the opportunity to look at work and your general situation in a new light. You may even uncover new information that provides you with the chance to broaden your horizons. *Moon in Aquarius.*

March

career   love   home   health   finance

1 MARCH

The strong bond you have with someone is hard to ignore. You'll find that a person in a position of power will be helpful to you at the moment. Think laterally if you must overcome a difficult situation. ***Moon enters Pisces.***

2 MARCH

The new moon in Pisces will help you to turn a corner in a work or health situation. Be inspired by reliable information and the facts to do with health and well-being. Someone special has your back. Be prepared to try something different and to meet new people. You'll enjoy a get-together.

3 MARCH

This is likely to be an intense day. Your heart may be on your sleeve or someone in a position of power will have a great deal of influence over your movements and decisions, so ensure you choose your path carefully. Changes at work or in your direction and status will be hard to ignore. A trip could be transformative. ***Moon in Pisces.***

4 MARCH

Today's Aries moon may highlight how you feel about someone close. Avoid feeling dejected or sidelined; find a way to improve your relationship rather than looking for failings in your connection. If you have felt under the weather take short breaks where you can. ***Moon in Aries.***

5 MARCH

Key news or developments are best taken in perspective, as you may have a tendency to see the best or the worst side of things. Be prepared to move into new territory in connection with work or a health matter. Trust your instincts. ***Moon in Aries.***

6 MARCH

A fresh development will ask that you look at your career, status or general direction in a new light. For some this will apply particularly to a friend or an organisation. Be prepared to step into new terrain. ***Moon in Taurus.***

7 MARCH

As the moon in your sign aligns with unpredictable Uranus you may feel a little lopsided. If so, blame it in Mondayitis and look for ways to find more direction and certainty in the areas you feel are unstable. ***Moon in Taurus.***

8 MARCH

Someone close will prove helpful so ensure you reach out to someone you know has your back. Avoid assuming a friend or organisation is an adversary; find time to discuss your plans with them. ***Moon enters Gemini.***

9 MARCH

The Gemini moon will help you to get ahead with your various communications and financial matters. Take the time to ask various questions of those who have the information you need. It's a good day for short trips and to plan longer trips. ***Moon in Gemini.***

10 MARCH

This is a good day to make agreements with people you must get along with, especially at work. It's also a good time to make a commitment to a plan of action. Be inspired, but also be realistic. ***Moon in Gemini.***

11 MARCH

You'll appreciate feeling inspired by someone special in your life. If you have nothing planned yet for an enjoyable event ensure you make a date, as you'll be glad you did. ***Moon in Cancer.***

12 MARCH

Romance, the arts, beauty, music and film will all entice your interests this weekend, so ensure you have something special planned. Enjoy being a little spontaneous and giving your imagination free rein with plans for the future. *Moon in Cancer.*

13 MARCH

This is an ideal day for romance and get-togethers. You'll appreciate spending time with someone special and organising fun events. You'll be inclined to seek out like-minded company. *Moon enters Leo.*

14 MARCH

You can progress well with your various projects and plans so be motivated to get ahead, especially at work. You may find someone influential takes notice of you now. *Moon in Leo.*

15 MARCH

You may feel a little adversarial or will sense that someone in a position of power or someone who has influence over you is adversarial. Be bold, but if you feel conflict is bubbling under the surface take things one step at a time. *Moon in Leo.*

16 MARCH

The more precise and organised you are the better the outcome, as you may otherwise feel a little forgetful or absent-minded. Avoid misplacing valued objects such as keys. *Moon in Virgo.*

17 MARCH

You'll appreciate being spontaneous and may enjoy good news, especially at work or from someone whose company you enjoy. Be flexible, as a sudden change of routine may arise. *Moon in Virgo.*

18 MARCH

The Virgo full moon shines a light on your close relationships, especially those in your family and partnerships. You may discover something new or will have an expectation realised or challenged. If you discover a secret it will be for the best.

19 MARCH

The Libran moon will help you to be practical and at the same time innovative about your various commitments, chores and obligations this weekend. You'll enjoy planning a fun event with an upbeat circle of people. You'll enjoy a reunion and/or the chance to revisit an old haunt. *Moon in Libra.*

20 MARCH

Now that the sun is in Aries for the next four weeks you may find that your work and health lives become real focuses. Find the time to boost your health and vitality as work may become busier over the coming month. *Moon in Scorpio.*

21 MARCH

You'll receive key news; for some this will be at work, and for others it will be to do with health. A reunion and/or the chance to travel could lead to a lovely outcome. Be inspired and discuss new plans, but avoid snap decisions. *Moon in Scorpio.*

22 MARCH

While you'll feel motivated to get ahead with your various projects you must avoid impulsive decisions or feeling that you're under pressure to succeed. Take a moment out of a busy day to gather your thoughts. A key decision to do with finances, work, a friend or health is best decided upon with a calm mind. ***Moon enters Sagittarius.***

23 MARCH

You'll feel thoroughly inspired by someone, by art or even music and your own deeper thoughts, but it's important at the moment to keep your feet on the ground. Someone charming may be super influential, so if you're making key choices do your own research. It's a good day for a beauty or health appointment. ***Moon in Sagittarius.***

24 MARCH

You'll feel more practical and grounded, especially as the day goes by. Rest assured you will adapt to circumstances that may seem out of your control or too good to be true. You'll enjoy a strong connection with someone close. ***Moon enters Capricorn.***

25 MARCH

You are currently learning for the bigger picture to be more adaptable, yet today's Capricorn moon may bring your stubborn side out. Take a moment to decide if you are being obstinate or if someone else is, and make your decisions based on the facts, not expectations. ***Moon in Capricorn.***

26 MARCH

This is a good day for meetings and get-togethers. You'll appreciate the opportunity to be in touch with like-minded but also inspiring people. ***Moon in Capricorn.***

27 MARCH

You'll appreciate a change of pace and will enjoy being with someone whose company you love. A short trip or visit will be enjoyable. Work and your focus on health and well-being are likely to get busier over the coming weeks, so plan ahead. *Moon in Aquarius.*

28 MARCH

This is a good day for making agreements, especially at work and with groups, friends or organisations. Take a moment to work out what your priorities are and then organise your activities accordingly. You'll enjoy a reunion and boosting your appearance. *Moon in Aquarius.*

29 MARCH

The Pisces moon will bring your inner idealist out, so remember to be practical. You may also be inclined to spend time with your favourite people, so ensure you organise a meeting with someone you love. *Moon in Pisces.*

30 MARCH

You'll enjoy being creative but may also tend to be a little head in the clouds. Take a moment to earth your plans and you'll find you could be super productive. Romance could blossom. *Moon in Pisces.*

31 MARCH

The Aries moon spells a busy day, and if you feel restless it's a good time to channel these feelings into activities that bring positive results such as health and fitness, work on projects you love and spending time with someone close. *Moon in Aries.*

April

career   love   home   health   finance

1 APRIL

The Aries new moon will bring fresh ideas your way, especially to do with work and health. You may hear important news in either area. It's a good day for a health or beauty appointment. Your expertise may be in demand.

2 APRIL

You may receive unexpected news or will need to act quickly in response to events. Avoid feeling under pressure, instead finding the most practical way ahead. ***Moon enters Taurus.***

3 APRIL

This is a good day for talks, especially with people you must co-operate with as they are more likely to hear you and may even find your communications uplifting! It's also a good time to make changes that you've been considering for some time. ***Moon in Taurus.***

4 APRIL

If you have important medical matters to attend to you are likely to get ahead with these. Just avoid over-exerting yourself if you have been tired of late. This aside, it is a good day to get things done. ***Moon in Taurus.***

5 APRIL

You'll feel inspired by someone you love or admire, so make time for a get-together or to pick up a book you love or watch a movie you've been meaning to watch. It's also a good day to make a commitment to a new plan of action or to join an inspiring group. *Moon in Gemini.*

6 APRIL

This is an excellent day for talks with people whose co-operation you need. It's also a good day for health and well-being appointments. Good news may be on the way. *Moon in Gemini.*

7 APRIL

You may hear good news from an old friend or at work. A change will be beneficial to you, so ensure you are prepared to make alterations to your usual routine. You could make a commitment that is progressive but also practical. *Moon in Cancer.*

8 APRIL

Romance could blossom. You'll be drawn to being more creative, too, so plan to organise a favourite event that brings your artistic side out. You'll enjoy boosting health and appearance and will enjoy a shopping spree. *Moon in Cancer.*

9 APRIL

You'll appreciate the opportunity to be busy in your usual work circumstance and to get chores done. You'll also appreciate the chance to socialise and network. Just avoid anticipating outcomes and impulsiveness; it might get you into hot water. *Moon in Cancer.*

10 APRIL

You should hear good news from your past or regarding health. A debt may be repaid or you may experience a financial improvement. Someone may surprise you with a compliment or will boost your self-confidence or ego. *Moon in Leo.*

11 APRIL

Chatty and tricky Mercury will be in your sign now for the next few weeks and will improve your communications. You may be drawn to travel and to receiving visitors. Avoid stubbornness over the next two days, and be prepared to collaborate with those in power to avoid conflict. *Moon in Leo.*

12 APRIL

You may experience a lovely event that restores your faith in humankind. If you're interested in spiritual or humanitarian efforts this is a good time to take action with your activities and invest more deeply in areas that interest you. If you experience opposition to your plans, look at it as a way to strengthen your position. *Moon enters Virgo.*

13 APRIL

You will enjoy being in an inspiring environment and letting your imagination run free. You may hear good news to do with work or from someone you love. It's a good day to improve health and your appearance. You can accomplish a great deal at work. **Moon in Virgo.**

14 APRIL

A positive event will stir your senses. You may enjoy socialising and networking. A lovely get-together with like-minded people will boost morale. You'll feel moved by art, romance and creativity. **Moon enters Libra.**

15 APRIL

Your interest in the arts and spirituality or in simply pursuing activities that give you purpose will ramp up over the coming weeks. You may already have a taste of the activities that will catch your attention. Romance could blossom, so organise a get-together. **Moon in Libra.**

16 APRIL

The Libran full moon will shine a light on someone who means a lot to you. You may be particularly drawn to them now and may also enjoy a reunion. For some, the full moon signals a fresh work or health chapter. Aim to find balance if work has taken over your life.

17 APRIL

The Scorpio moon will focus your attention increasingly on chores and daily duties, yet you are more likely to be drawn to enjoying quality time with someone special. Organise your day to get work done in the morning, giving you time for someone special in the afternoon. **Moon in Scorpio.**

18 APRIL

This is going to be an eventful day, so make sure you prepare for considerable developments. You may not agree with everyone and especially not someone who holds a position of power, so aim to be amiable to avoid conflict. You will be surprised by news or a change of routine. **Moon in Scorpio.**

19 APRIL

You'll feel motivated to get things done even if you don't agree with everyone you must collaborate with. There is merit in being industrious, but you must avoid conflict as it could quickly escalate. **Moon in Sagittarius.**

20 APRIL

The sun will enter your sign, which will add to a sense of increasing vitality and optimism over the coming four weeks, so plan to be busy and upbeat. **Moon in Sagittarius.**

21 APRIL

The Capricorn moon will help you be more practical and make grounded decisions, so ensure you take action in small but certain steps. **Moon in Capricorn.**

22 APRIL

The moon at the zenith of your chart may bring your emotions to the surface, especially this morning. Take a moment to ground yourself and adjust your outlook to a more optimistic, self-assured one. You may even surprise yourself with how much you can accomplish. **Moon in Capricorn.**

23 APRIL

You will be in touch with someone important. If you meet someone new there may be a karmic connection between you. **Moon in Aquarius.**

24 APRIL

You will not always agree with everyone, and you'll see this today! However, if you are diligent and careful with your communications you could make great progress, especially at work and with a personal matter. Be practical for the best results. **Moon in Aquarius.**

25 APRIL

The Pisces moon can bring your hopes out to the forefront of your mind. This means you're optimistic but your expectations may also be a little high, so take things one step at a time. **Moon in Pisces.**

26 APRIL

You could make great progress both in your social life and at work but must be prepared to take the initiative. Be inspired by people you admire. **Moon in Pisces.**

27 APRIL

You may receive good news, especially in relation to someone you love or a project that is dear to your heart. You may meet someone who has a fated or predestined link with you. Romance could flourish, so be sure to organise a treat. **Moon enters Aries.**

28 APRIL

This is a good time for talks with your employer, and if you are the employer for talks with your employees! Your points of view will be well received. It's also a good day for initiating change you've been planning for a while. A trip or news may be significant. **Moon in Aries.**

29 APRIL

A key turning point or statement may be made that will involve your status, career or general direction. Be prepared for meetings and get-togethers that could alter the tone of your future. **Moon in Aries.**

30 APRIL

The partial solar eclipse in your own sign spells considerable change for you, especially if it's your birthday. You'll find out exactly who has your back; there is much value in being with those who care for you.

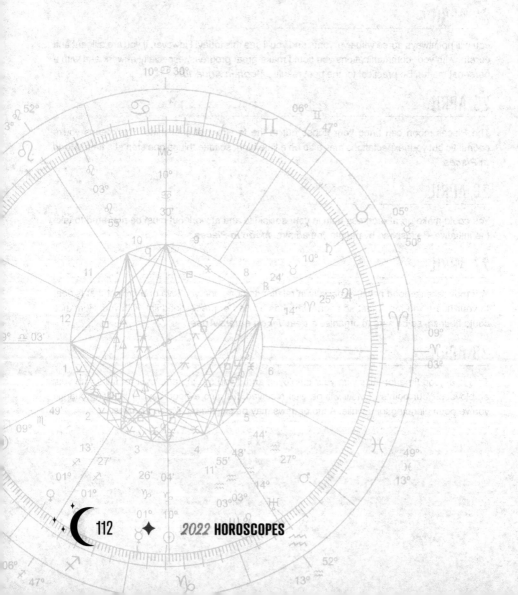

May

career   love   home   health   finance

1 MAY

A lovely day for socialising and networking. If you need to get ahead with certain work projects and ideas, this is an excellent day to make tracks. ***Moon in Taurus.***

2 MAY

As Venus enters Aries you are likely to feel more motivated and outgoing over the next few weeks, especially at work and regarding your health and fitness. It's a good time to consider a fresh look. ***Moon in Gemini.***

3 MAY

This is likely to be a busy day for you at work. If health matters have been on your mind, it's a good day for medical appointments. And, if you'd like to change important aspects of your life, this is a good time to initiate changes. ***Moon in Gemini.***

4 MAY

You'll be drawn to doing something different and opportunities may come from out of the blue. If you've been considering making changes in your daily routine this is a good day to do so, but you must avoid rash decisions as they're likely to backfire. ***Moon in Gemini.***

5 MAY

If you like surprises you'll like today, especially if it's your birthday! But if you prefer life on an even keel it'll be worthwhile taking a deep breath and preparing for something new. You'll enjoy an impromptu meeting or get-together. **Moon in Cancer.**

6 MAY

This is a good day for beauty and health appointments. You'll also feel more confident at work about expressing your ideas and opinions. A financial matter could be sorted out to your satisfaction, so take the initiative. **Moon in Cancer.**

7 MAY

You'll feel motivated to get things done so this is a good time to make tracks down paths that really provide a sense of purpose A group, friend or organisation will prove to be an inspiration. You'll enjoy a reunion. **Moon in Leo.**

8 MAY

You may hear unexpected news unless you already did, and this may be ideal. Romance, art and music will appeal. You may experience a financial boost. **Moon in Leo.**

9 MAY

A project or plan of action may take you into new territory. Be bold and consider how you can courageously go into new terrain. Avoid being inflexible; instead, be adaptable. Try to get key talks and paperwork completed before Mercury turns retrograde tomorrow. **Moon enters Virgo at night.**

10 MAY

You may receive key news that will add perspective to a personal, work or health matter. It's a good day for research. **Moon in Virgo.**

11 MAY

You may notice your routine changes gear today and in the days to come; you may be busier but also more energised as a result. It's a good time to put a new health and fitness schedule in place. **Moon in Virgo.**

12 MAY

You may be called upon to be the voice of reason, so rely on your diplomatic skills and be tactful if you must settle a difference of opinion. Look for balance. **Moon in Libra.**

13 MAY

A special person close to your heart will figure in your life more prominently than usual. Key news is on the way. ***Moon in Libra.***

14 MAY

People around you may appear more emotional or outspoken over the next two days. Give their opinions a wide berth if you disagree. Romance could blossom, so organise a treat! ***Moon in Scorpio.***

15 MAY

It's quite a mixed bag this weekend. It's a good time to attend to health and well-being and to ensure you are on the same page as someone who may need support. It's a good day for rest and recuperation. You or someone close may need to delay a get-together due to health matters. Nevertheless, you will enjoy a reunion. ***Moon in Scorpio.***

16 MAY

The total lunar eclipse in your opposite sign of Scorpio will spotlight a key relationship, especially if it's your birthday. For some, though, the focus will be on work and considerable changes there. It's an intense day, so take things one step at a time. ***Moon enters Sagittarius during the day.***

17 MAY

Aim for the sky but keep your feet on the ground. Be practical to obtain the best-case outcome. A meeting could be successful, so put your best foot forward. ***Moon in Sagittarius.***

18 MAY

You'll discover if you've over- or under-estimated your circumstances. The good news is you'll be able to put things right as a result. ***Moon in Capricorn.***

19 MAY

This is an excellent day to put in motion carefully laid plans as they are likely to come to fruition. You may hear news at work or regarding your status that could effectively transform your life. ***Moon in Capricorn.***

20 MAY

This is a good day for meetings, talks and trips. It's also a good day for health and fitness appointments. You may hear beneficial news from the past or return to an old haunt. A debt may be repaid. ***Moon in Aquarius.***

21 MAY

Key news will arrive, and if you're making an investment this is a good time to double-check facts and figures. You may hear the news you've been waiting for, but if not it's a good time to try again and work towards your goals. *Moon in Aquarius.*

22 MAY

This is a good day to get your various plans and projects shipshape. If you have a favourite activity or hobby you love you'll enjoy devoting time to it. A lovely get-together will be enjoyable. *Moon enters Pisces.*

23 MAY

As Mercury enters your sign expect news to come from your past. You may need to review some of your plans and projects. You'll enjoy a reunion and the chance to discuss travel and work ideas. *Moon in Pisces.*

24 MAY

Currently, the astrological climate favours talks, meetings and negotiations, making this an excellent time to develop relationship and work projects. Take the initiative! *Moon enters Aries.*

25 MAY

A project or interest can go from strength to strength, but if you feel you are losing track or control of circumstances aim to take a step back or slow down the process. *Moon in Aries.*

26 MAY

This is a good day for financial matters, so if you need to repay a debt for example or negotiate your pay with your employer, be positive. You may be repaid a debt. It's also an excellent day for a reunion and for a beauty or health treat. *Moon in Aries.*

27 MAY

The more care and attention you place on communications, especially at work, the better for you. Some of your charm may appear to be dogmatic so take things as they come and avoid conflict with someone in authority or more powerful than you as it could escalate. *Moon in Taurus.*

28 MAY

As Venus enters your sign you'll feel more in your own element over the coming weeks. You may be inclined to overindulge, though, so if you're in debt leave the credit card at home! *Moon in Taurus.*

29 MAY

You'll enjoy a lovely meeting, and socialising is likely to be fun. If you're working it'll be a busy, chatty day. A trip or travel plan may come together now. *Moon enters Gemini.*

30 MAY

The new moon in Gemini signals the chance to turn a corner, for some Taureans in your personal life and for others financially. You may turn a corner at work or will embrace a fresh daily routine that could be beneficial to you health-wise.

31 MAY

You'll be drawn to like-minded people and someone may be super influential. Just ensure you have all the details to hand if you must make a key decision, and avoid making choices you have not researched adequately. *Moon in Gemini.*

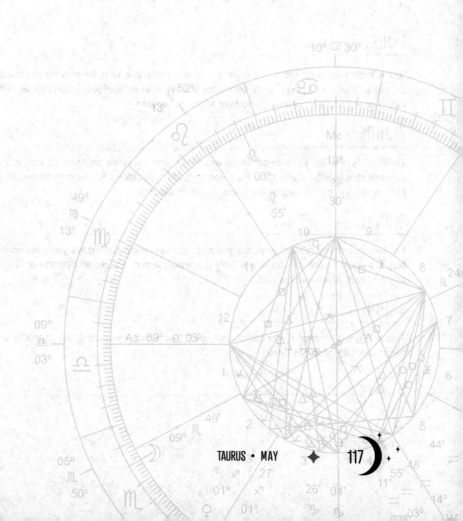

June

career love home health finance

1 JUNE

You're known for your obstinacy when you're uncomfortable with life moving too quickly. The Cancerian moon will bring your emotions out and you may not feel your usual friendly self. Avoid taking other people's opinions personally. *Moon in Cancer.*

2 JUNE

While you prefer life to proceed on an even keel, with everyone together as one, sometimes opinions simply differ. Avoid allowing someone's ideas to sidetrack your own unless, of course, there is merit in their thoughts and plans. *Moon in Cancer.*

3 JUNE

As Mercury ends its retrograde phase you may hear key news, especially if you were born in mid-May. Communications and travel are likely to become less cumbersome over the coming weeks, so take heart. *Moon enters Leo.*

4 JUNE

This is a good time for negotiations and talks. Just avoid pre-empting the outcome and take things carefully. *Moon in Leo.*

5 JUNE

The Leo moon may cause you to question some of your decisions, especially regarding those close to you at home or in your family. This is a good time to look for therapeutic and positive ways ahead rather than looking at the glass as being half full. ***Moon in Leo.***

6 JUNE

When the moon is in Virgo you'll find you are more practical, hands-on and realistic about your various tasks and projects, making this a good time for planning and organisation. ***Moon in Virgo.***

7 JUNE

You may hear unexpected news or will be surprised. A financial matter could be to your benefit, but if not it's your cue to sort things out. You may discover an unexpected solution to any issues that arise. You may bump into an old friend or hear unexpectedly from them. ***Moon in Virgo.***

8 JUNE

Aim for balance in your day or you may be liable to overcommit to various chores and events. Take a moment out of your schedule to work out what and who matter most to you and take it from there. ***Moon enters Libra.***

9 JUNE

This is a good time to be initiating important talks with people who are in a position of influence in your life, such as employers. Find ways to present your ideas in their best light. You could make great progress at work, so take the initiative. A beauty and health matter can also proceed well. ***Moon in Libra.***

10 JUNE

The Libran moon will help you to see both sides to the story and to look for a happy medium. You could make great progress with your various endeavours, especially those that involve the need to communicate well. Trust that you have what it takes to be heard and you will be. ***Moon in Libra.***

11 JUNE

You'll enjoy doing something different this weekend and may also be surprised by developments. A favourite person may be particularly spontaneous, and you'll enjoy being free to make your own decisions. Avoid being impulsive, though, as this could trip you up. ***Moon in Scorpio.***

12 JUNE

You'll enjoy being with someone you love this weekend, so if you have nothing in particular planned yet make a date! Just make sure everyone's on the same page to avoid mix-ups. *Moon enters Sagittarius.*

13 JUNE

Communications, meetings and the necessity to make decisions are likely to become more prevalent over the next fortnight or so, making this a good time to organise your weeks so you make the most of a productive time. You may be drawn to visit somewhere new or to invest in a clever project. *Moon in Sagittarius.*

14 JUNE

The full moon and supermoon in Sagittarius will spotlight your love for someone special. It may also spotlight shared matters such as finances that will benefit from a little more focus. You may discover there has been an error in judgement, which will give you the chance to put things right.

15 JUNE

This is an excellent day to get things shipshape health-wise. If work has been tiring lately it's important to find the time to rest up and recharge your batteries. Avoid minor scrapes and bumps. *Moon in Capricorn.*

16 JUNE

A financial or work matter will be important as you could make great headway. Just avoid making key changes unless you have the full facts. You may be easily misled, so be sure of your information. Romance could blossom, so organise a date. *Moon enters Aquarius.*

17 JUNE

You may hear unexpectedly from someone from your past. If work has been tiring, find a space to take time out. You may be pleased with a surprise change of routine. *Moon in Aquarius.*

18 JUNE

Check your values and principles. Someone you must work or interact with may have different priorities to you. Avoid taking this personally and find common ground if possible. *Moon in Aquarius.*

19 JUNE

You're likely to be feeling generous but may be inclined to overspend or overindulge, so take things one step at a time if you're considering a large investment. Ensure you have checked

the fine print if signing documents. Romance could blossom. Artistic Taureans will enjoy being productive. **Moon in Pisces.**

20 JUNE

The Pisces moon will bring your idealistic, philosophical side out, making this a good day for discussions and meetings as you'll feel inclined to listen to the ideas of others without judgement. Artistic Taureans will be inspired, so take the time to be creative. **Moon in Pisces.**

21 JUNE

This is an excellent time to consider how you could improve your life in the most positive way. It's a good day for a beauty or health boost, and if you're negotiating financial matters be optimistic and believe in yourself! **Moon in Aries.**

22 JUNE

Now that the sun is in Cancer you'll find your more combative, outgoing side will seek expression. Avoid arguments with people who can be adversarial as they have nothing better to do! Use your intuition; it's spot on now. **Moon in Aries.**

23 JUNE

As the moon enters your sign you'll feel more in sync with life and will enjoy treating yourself and others to some of life's delights. A little indulgence never hurt anyone! **Moon enters Taurus.**

24 JUNE

You can tend to be obstinate when the moon is in Taurus, so if you feel this is the case ask yourself if you could cut someone some slack. Avoid being self-critical and critical of others. You'll enjoy socialising but must avoid overindulgence; you'll regret it! **Moon in Taurus.**

25 JUNE

You'll appreciate the opportunity to relax and to get in touch with those you love on a more carefree basis. A commitment could be made but it may mean you must compromise. Choose your path wisely while being adaptable to new options. **Moon in Taurus.**

26 JUNE

You'll enjoy being a little more chatty and relaxed with the people you love. You may enjoy a reunion or will hear good news to do with someone from your past. It's a good day for a health treat. **Moon in Gemini.**

27 JUNE

You may receive positive news at work. If you're not working and health has been a concern you could be in the running for improvements in both areas. Take the initiative. *Moon in Gemini.*

28 JUNE

Think laterally as you'll appreciate the chance to look outside the box at your usual routine and to be a little more spontaneous with upbeat and outgoing people. You may receive a compliment or a financial boost. *Moon enters Cancer.*

29 JUNE

The Cancerian new moon will kick-start a fresh phase in a key relationship. This may be via important news you receive, a trip or simply the chance to alter how you view your relationship. You will benefit from working out your top priorities if a tough call must be made.

30 JUNE

You'll feel more sure of the decisions that must be made now, especially in connection with someone close or work or health matters. Choose a nurturing stance, beginning with your own self-nurture. *Moon in Cancer.*

July

career · love · home · health · finance

1 JULY

You may already intuit tension in the air, so this is an excellent time to find ways to dispel it. You may find exercise useful with this in mind, or meditation or yoga. Aim to find positive ways to avoid conflict as it could escalate quickly. *Moon in Leo.*

2 JULY

If you're working today it's likely to be productive and even lucrative. If you're shopping, avoid random purchases as you're likely to spend big! Misunderstandings are likely, so double-check you're on the same page. *Moon in Leo.*

3 JULY

The tension underlying some communications is likely to continue a little, so let sleeping dogs lie unless you must approach a gnarly topic. Avoid overspending and, if finances are in the red, consider a new budget. *Moon enters Virgo.*

4 JULY

You'll appreciate the sense that you are gradually gaining strength and influence over the coming weeks and months but initially you may feel a little disoriented, especially in a work or health context. Find the time to discuss key matters that are on your mind with those they concern. An expert may be super helpful too. *Moon in Virgo.*

5 JULY

This is another day for believing in your own abilities, as you could make great progress. Just take things one step at a time as you may be inclined to run before you can walk. *Moon enters Libra.*

6 JULY

There is a therapeutic aspect to the day ideal for improving health and well-being. You may also be inclined to boost your spiritual understanding in life. You'll enjoy the chance to improve your appearance. You may receive good news or will appreciate help from an expert. *Moon in Libra.*

7 JULY

You like a balanced and peaceful life, and when the moon is in Libra you will actively pursue qualities that can provide harmony. You may be super drawn to art, music, dance and romance. You may also be inclined to indulge in good food and drinks, so enjoy a treat. *Moon in Libra.*

8 JULY

An obstacle to your plans and ideas may pop up, but it could include a silver lining as a surprise outcome of events could be just what you want. Avoid over-reacting to events if possible. *Moon in Scorpio.*

9 JULY

Financially, this is a good time to look at the fine print in your various agreements, especially if you're considering something new. Choose your words carefully to avoid mix-ups and plan travel ahead of time to avoid delays. If you're shopping, avoid impulse buys as they could get you into hot water. *Moon in Scorpio.*

10 JULY

You'll enjoy an impromptu event, surprise or get-together. A compliment or an ego boost will improve your mood. *Moon enters Sagittarius.*

11 JULY

A partner or colleague may be more outspoken than usual. You may find their joviality endearing, but if they seem tactless avoid taking their mood personally. You'll enjoy being adventurous and meeting new people. *Moon in Sagittarius.*

12 JULY

The Capricorn moon brings out your predilection for good company and good food and entertainment. You'll enjoy being with like-minded people. *Moon enters Capricorn.*

13 JULY

The full moon and supermoon in Capricorn will spotlight an important interest, and you could make great headway with a particular project or plan. A financial matter could be decided upon, and as long as you have done adequate groundwork it looks like a positive agreement. You may receive a financial or ego boost.

14 JULY

You may tend to be a little idealistic or will be lacking key information, so avoid making important decisions unless you've done adequate research, especially financially. *Moon enters Aquarius.*

15 JULY

If you like to feel under pressure and push yourself to meet goals you'll enjoy today's atmosphere. But if you avoid pressure and prefer life at an even pace this could be a tense day, so take things carefully. *Moon in Aquarius.*

16 JULY

A visit or trip will bring your chatty side out. If you're making changes at home these are likely to go well, especially if you gain the help and support of a friend, group or organisation. If obstacles arise you will overcome them. *Moon enters Pisces.*

17 JULY

This is a lovely day to indulge in your senses. You'll enjoy being with someone you love and deepening your connection. The spiritually minded may even experience an epiphany. *Moon in Pisces.*

18 JULY

Developments spell a change of circumstance, for some at home and for others at work. If you're travelling, your environment will bring a sense of transformation your way. Some conversations may be intense, so maintain perspective. *Moon enters Aries.*

19 JULY

This is likely to be a chatty day when information you need will come your way. You may even discover more than you want to! *Moon in Aries.*

20 JULY

The changes in your environment can lead to something better, but you must be realistic and practical and avoid seeing life through rose-coloured glasses – and then dreams could come true! *Moon enters Taurus.*

21 JULY

Some circumstances may be difficult to adjust to at the moment, but you will have the option of seeing things through to a positive outcome. Trust your intuition and be adaptable for the best measure. *Moon in Taurus.*

22 JULY

You may feel sensitive or must communicate difficult news. Avoid assuming other people's problems are yours, but be ready to offer a shoulder for someone to lean on. Don't be afraid to ask for support or advice yourself. *Moon in Taurus.*

23 JULY

You'll enjoy a visitor or a trip that will improve your relationship. If you're willing to do a little DIY or home improvement, this is your weekend! *Moon in Gemini.*

24 JULY

You love to chat, but sometimes you can over share. The next two days are a case in point. Avoid putting your foot in your mouth, especially at work. A financial matter will benefit from focus. *Moon in Gemini.*

25 JULY

If you have recently overspent or have been unable to get on with someone close matters may come to a head, so take the time to step carefully through meetings and talks. Consider expert financial help if necessary. *Moon enters Cancer.*

26 JULY

There's merit in feeling passionate about your projects and ideas, but you risk locking horns with someone you're better to co-operate with. Find a way to overcome differences for the best results. *Moon in Cancer.*

27 JULY

This is a good day for bridging differences between yourself and someone who may be feeling sensitive. If you are feeling vulnerable, find ways to strengthen your stance without appearing stubborn. An expert, adviser or teacher will be super helpful. *Moon in Cancer.*

28 JULY

This new moon in Leo is an excellent time to kick-start a fresh domestic project or improve domestic dynamics. Be positive, and aim to include everyone in your plans. A work matter may be larger than life, so pace yourself. A surprise is on the way. Be flexible if possible and avoid misunderstandings.

29 JULY

The moon in Leo will bring your talkative side out. You may be super effective at work, but those close to you may feel a little at odds with your bright ideas. Take the time to discuss your projects with those they concern to avoid mix-ups.

30 JULY

Some things in life are simply meant to be, such as family ties. The better you can work with someone the better will be your peace of mind. Avoid complex topics and find ways to establish common ground. *Moon enters Virgo.*

31 JULY

You'll enjoy a reunion or a return to an old haunt, even if some conversations are difficult. This is a good time to make a commitment to someone, but you must be on the same page or your agreements could seem restrictive. Finances can be decided upon with attention to detail. *Moon in Virgo.*

August

career love home health finance

1 AUGUST

Key transactions, news or conversations will be more significant than meets the eye. You may bump into someone you feel a strong or predestined link with. Be clear about your goals, especially at work, to avoid disappointment. *Moon in Virgo.*

2 AUGUST

Expect something out of the ordinary; look out for surprises! You'll enjoy a lovely get-together with someone special. Avoid being impulsive; it could backfire. *Moon in Libra.*

3 AUGUST

This is another day on which you may be faced with an unusual circumstance. You'll enjoy being spontaneous and welcoming something or someone new into your environment. *Moon in Libra.*

4 AUGUST

While there is a fair degree of change going on around you, it's in your interest to keep your feet on the ground to avoid mistakes. You may have a difficult task or challenge ahead, but the stars suggest you will overcome any obstacles. A little attention to finances will pay off. *Moon enters Scorpio.*

5 AUGUST

Your hard work and focus on improving your circumstances will not go unnoticed. Just avoid entering into any agreements that could effectively curtail your movements or present strict financial restrictions moving forward. It's a good day to negotiate. ***Moon in Scorpio.***

6 AUGUST

You'll appreciate the chance to experience a little more freedom of movement. Your optimistic outlook is something that brings its rewards. Tread carefully with someone who may not share your optimism to avoid disagreements. ***Moon enters Sagittarius.***

7 AUGUST

You'll enjoy throwing caution to the wind and may also tend to overindulge, so if you're a little short on funds avoid splurging at the shops! It's a good day to rest if you over-extended yourself yesterday. Avoid arguments with someone you know can easily fire up. ***Moon in Sagittarius.***

8 AUGUST

There is a healing or therapeutic aspect to the day, making this a good time to mend bridges with anyone you've quarrelled with. It's also a good day for medical and health appointments and to consult experts. ***Moon enters Capricorn.***

9 AUGUST

Take a moment to decide the best way to approach a thorny topic. Avoid jumping into difficult conversations, as they could escalate quickly. It's a good day for romance, and passion could go off the dial! ***Moon in Capricorn.***

10 AUGUST

Consider looking at important aspects of your life from a fresh perspective. Avoid being stuck in one thought form and play with new ideas. You may discover a fresh viewpoint that has merit. ***Moon enters Aquarius.***

11 AUGUST

This is a good day to go with the flow and avoid impulsiveness. Nevertheless, you may need to make snap decisions, so ensure you look at the positives and the reality of the outcome of your decisions. ***Moon in Aquarius.***

12 AUGUST

The full moon in Aquarius is spotlighting important decisions. For some these will be to do with work and your general direction in life, and for others personal matters that are changing and must be adjusted to. Look at your ideas and those of others from a lateral point of view. You could make progress by being innovative. **Moon enters Pisces** at night.

13 AUGUST

Important decisions merit careful attention to detail, but you must also be happy with the big-picture scenario. If in doubt about how to move forward, trust your instincts. Avoid being easily influenced. **Moon in Pisces.**

14 AUGUST

A commitment may be made that could bring more stability to your life. You must avoid limiting your options too much, though, so be prepared to negotiate. It's a good day for meetings and to make long-overdue changes. **Moon enters Aries.**

15 AUGUST

Someone will prove to be a great help to you, so ensure you reach out for advice from a loyal and knowledgeable source if necessary. It's a good day for meetings and to decide on personal, family and work matters. **Moon in Aries.**

16 AUGUST

You'll appreciate the chance to do something different. You may enjoy an impromptu trip or get-together. You'll also appreciate the chance to boost your friendship circle and to be with those you love. **Moon in Aries.**

17 AUGUST

You may be a little forgetful or simply a little wistful or nostalgic. Avoid making key decisions unless you have all the facts at hand. **Moon in Taurus.**

18 AUGUST

This is a good day for domestic improvements, whether you're considering DIY, some fresh décor or an improvement to interpersonal dynamics. Just avoid imposing your ideas on someone who likes to have their own opinion. A hard-work day will pay off. **Moon in Taurus.**

19 AUGUST

Avoid power struggles as these could leave an unpleasant feeling, especially in the workplace. Aim to work towards your goals both at home and at work and you'll achieve your aims. **Moon in Gemini.**

20 AUGUST

As Mars enters Gemini, prepare to be busy. You may also find that finances deserve a little extra focus. If you're shopping, avoid overspending. That said, you may find the ideal bargain. *Moon in Gemini.*

21 AUGUST

This is an excellent day for romance and to rest up and recuperate, especially if you had a busy day yesterday. You may be inclined to overindulge, so set realistic limits to avoid headaches tomorrow! You or someone close may be absent-minded, so avoid losing important objects such as keys. *Moon in Gemini.*

22 AUGUST

You're communicating well, making this an excellent time to make changes both at work and at home wherever you see them as being necessary. If you're travelling, this will be a transformative trip for you. *Moon in Cancer.*

23 AUGUST

When the sun is in Virgo, as it will be now for four weeks, this is a good time for you to make progress one step at a time with your chosen projects, both at home and at work. It's also a good time to focus on your health and well-being and that of those you love. *Moon in Cancer.*

24 AUGUST

You'll feel drawn to improving your well-being and health. If matters have been strained at work you'll look for ways to improve interpersonal dynamics. It's a good day to seek expert advice and to help someone if they're struggling. *Moon enters Leo.*

25 AUGUST

You are a creative character, and currently your imagination and artistic abilities will begin to peak. Find ways to express this aspect of yourself; you'll find art, music, dance and romance fulfilling. *Moon in Leo.*

26 AUGUST

You'll enjoy exploring romantic places such as beautiful cafés, art galleries and museums. You may be a little idealistic at the moment, so ensure you're seeing life as it really is rather than how you hope it to be. *Moon in Leo.*

27 AUGUST

The Virgo new moon will kick-start a fresh chapter at work. You may be ready to step up into fresh duties or will find time to pay more attention to your own health and well-being. For some

Virgos, this new moon spells a fresh chapter in your personal life. You may be surprised by developments, so take things one step at a time.

28 AUGUST

This is a good time to make a commitment to an idea or plan of action. If you're signing contracts this could be ideal, but you must look at the fine print. If someone's influence over you appears overbearing, find ways to moderate their impact on your life if possible. ***Moon in Virgo.***

29 AUGUST

You'll feel inclined to find ways to establish more balance and harmony in your life. Art, relaxation and music will all provide you with some form of rest in the evening. In the day, choose your words carefully to avoid difficult talks. ***Moon enters Libra.***

30 AUGUST

Your eye for detail will be useful, especially at work. You may not agree with everyone and some talks and travel may be complex or delayed, so aim to be patient for the best results. ***Moon in Libra.***

31 AUGUST

Romance will draw your attention, although you may be seeing life a little through rose-coloured glasses. Yet if you keep your feet on the ground and organise a lovely event, romance could truly flourish. ***Moon enters Scorpio.***

September

career   love   home   health   finance

1 SEPTEMBER

This is an excellent day to get things done. You may find you must attend to financial matters and work could be busy. Take a moment out of your busy schedule to ensure you're on the right track with your various projects to avoid mistakes. A trip or meeting should go well. ***Moon in Scorpio.***

2 SEPTEMBER

While some interactions may be more tense than you'd prefer, you will manage to accomplish your tasks with attention to detail. Just avoid arguments for the best measure. ***Moon enters Sagittarius.***

3 SEPTEMBER

A key meeting will put a work or health matter into perspective. It's a good time for medical and beauty appointments. If you do encounter a hiccup, rest assured you will overcome it with due diligence. ***Moon in Sagittarius.***

4 SEPTEMBER

The Sagittarian moon will bring your curiosity and adventurousness to the surface. You'll enjoy being with upbeat, outgoing people, but if someone in particular proves hard to handle avoid making tension worse; find ways to establish common ground if possible. ***Moon in Sagittarius.***

5 SEPTEMBER

You're likely to feel more comfortable and at ease with yourself and will enjoy finding ways to be more practical and hands-on with your various projects. Avoid seeing only the problems with work or health matters and look for solutions. *Moon in Capricorn.*

6 SEPTEMBER

The moon in Capricorn brings your realistic and practical sides out, especially at work. If you must get things done under pressure, ensure you remain grounded and look at the most feasible ways ahead. *Moon in Capricorn.*

7 SEPTEMBER

You're thinking creatively, which will help you to look outside the box at your various projects and chores. You'll enjoy meeting an upbeat group of people, and if you must research new ideas or overcome hurdles today's the day for lateral thinking. *Moon in Aquarius.*

8 SEPTEMBER

You may benefit from consulting an expert, especially in connection with work and health. A personal matter may benefit from a sensitive approach as someone may be feeling vulnerable or sensitive. Someone may need your help or vice versa. *Moon in Aquarius.*

9 SEPTEMBER

In the lead-up to the full moon emotions can become heated. Find the time to de-escalate tension to avoid unnecessary arguments. If a challenge arises, find ways to overcome it: you can do so. *Moon in Pisces.*

10 SEPTEMBER

The Pisces full moon will spotlight strong feelings, and because Mercury turns retrograde today you may also receive key news. For some this will be to do with work, and for others health. Check you are not approaching a personal matter idealistically to avoid disappointment further down the line. Aim to get important communications such as key paperwork tied up today to avoid delays over the coming days.

11 SEPTEMBER

Emotions are likely to weigh into your life, and your feelings will determine how you react to events. Try to gain perspective. You'll enjoy a spontaneous or uplifting event that alters your usual routine. Someone may be in touch unexpectedly. *Moon in Aries.*

12 SEPTEMBER

Good communication skills are the key to success. You could make some great headway with a project. Romance could blossom, so plan something special. Just avoid taking on too much as this would dull your usual sparkle. *Moon in Aries.*

13 SEPTEMBER

The tension between how you see yourself and how others see you may be an underlying factor in misunderstandings or mix-ups, so consider being super clear and friendly about how you see things as you may find this helps to overcome misconceptions. *Moon enters Taurus.*

14 SEPTEMBER

The Taurean moon helps you to feel comfortable in yourself. You'll appreciate the chance to indulge in some of your favourite interests and to spend time with someone you love, such as a best friend, lover or family member. But be prepared to show how dependable you are at work, even if you feel you must stand up for yourself or your ideas. *Moon in Taurus.*

15 SEPTEMBER

The moon will be in your sign for most of the day, helping you to be practical about your many chores and at work. The more you can demonstrate how dependable and reliable you are the better will be your relationships, especially if they have been a little tense lately. *Moon enters Gemini at night.*

16 SEPTEMBER

Be prepared to consider whether you are being as clear with your various ideas and intentions as you can be. Ask yourself if you or someone close at home or at work has the wrong end of the stick. This could be a good time for romance, but you must ensure you are both on the same page to avoid misunderstandings. *Moon in Gemini.*

17 SEPTEMBER

This is a good day to get ahead with your various tasks, especially at work and financially. However, you may be inclined to make an emotional purchase, so if you're making a large investment ensure you double-check the details. *Moon in Gemini.*

18 SEPTEMBER

You may need to review a situation that came to your attention earlier in the month or at the full moon. Be prepared to look over paperwork or to trace your thoughts back to that time to ensure you're still on the right track. A trip could take you to an old haunt. A reunion may bring up strong emotions, so take things one step at a time. *Moon enters Cancer.*

19 SEPTEMBER

This is an excellent day for work and, if you're looking for work, to circulate your resume and make arrangements for interviews. If you wish to change important aspects of your life this is your day, so plan ahead and get the ball rolling! *Moon in Cancer.*

20 SEPTEMBER

This is another good day to make changes, especially in your personal life and within your daily routine. If you'd like to make changes to your appearance, you may even be drawn to a whole new look. Just ensure if you're making financial decisions that you have double-checked the facts. *Moon enters Leo.*

21 SEPTEMBER

This is another good day to get ahead with your ventures, especially if they involve a degree of transformation such as the chance to change your appearance or a key relationship. Just avoid being too pushy as this would go against you. *Moon in Leo.*

22 SEPTEMBER

You'll appreciate the opportunity to show off a little but you must be careful not to outshine someone in authority such as your employer. Be bold and bright, but avoid allowing pride to rule your day as it comes before a fall. *Moon in Leo.*

23 SEPTEMBER

You may receive key news and a meeting may be more relevant than is at first apparent. The sun in Libra for the next four weeks will provide the opportunity to gain more work/life balance and to find more harmony in your everyday life. Avoid traffic delays by planning ahead. *Moon in Virgo.*

24 SEPTEMBER

This is a great day for romance, the arts and creativity. If you have nothing special planned yet socially organise a date, as you're likely to enjoy it. Artistic Taureans are likely to be inspired. If you're undecided about a key matter, ensure you obtain expert advice. *Moon in Virgo.*

25 SEPTEMBER

The Libran new moon will kick-start a fresh cycle at work and in your personal life for some. Take a moment to decide how you'd ideally like to see your life move forward and make a wish. But be careful what you wish for, as it'll surely come true!

26 SEPTEMBER

This is another excellent day for moving ahead in your various ventures, so take the initiative. Just ensure you're on the same page as someone important such as your partner, friend or employer before taking key action. *Moon in Libra.*

27 SEPTEMBER

This is a good day to discuss your ideas and various plans moving forward, especially to do with work. If a medical or health matter has been on your mind, this is an excellent time to find out more. *Moon in Libra.*

28 SEPTEMBER

Finances are likely to be a focus, as you will gain the chance to invest in something important to you. If you're looking for a loan or must pay one off, this is a good time to obtain information that will help you. You may experience a boost at work or a compliment. *Moon in Scorpio.*

29 SEPTEMBER

The Scorpio moon may bring out your emotions or those of someone close, so if someone is feeling a little out of sorts give them a wide berth. If you are feeling emotional, take a moment to gather your thoughts. Romance could flourish. *Moon in Scorpio.*

30 SEPTEMBER

This is a good day for bonding with colleagues and for getting things done at work. You may not necessarily agree with everyone you must work with, but you could be industrious and will reap the rewards of hard work. You may experience an ego or financial boost. *Moon in Sagittarius.*

October

career   love   home   health   finance

1 OCTOBER

You'll enjoy a get-together, and if you're working you could be busy. A beauty or health treat will appeal. However, some people – perhaps even you – may be feeling tense, so ensure you set aside time to unwind. *Moon in Sagittarius.*

2 OCTOBER

You may receive key news, for some in connection with someone special or at home and for others to do with a key project. Take a moment to work out how you'd like to proceed, as your decision will mean changes moving forward. *Moon in Capricorn.*

3 OCTOBER

You may need to review or oversee a change in the way you do things at work or in your general direction and personal life. Consider how you could communicate with more sensitivity and compassion for the best measure. *Moon in Capricorn.*

4 OCTOBER

You'll feel more adaptable and able to think outside the box, which will improve some of your work connections and discussions there. Just avoid pre-empting outcomes, especially if you are unsure of the details. *Moon enters Aquarius.*

5 OCTOBER

Today's developments will highlight areas in your life in which you could be more flexible and adopt a more open mind. You may feel a little inclined to be stubborn and obstinate, so take a moment to check that you're going with change in the most positive way as opposed to against it. *Moon in Aquarius.*

6 OCTOBER

This could be a very productive two days, especially if you have laid solid groundwork for your various projects and ventures. Just ensure you avoid taking on too much, as you may be inclined to overwork or overexert yourself. A health or beauty check may appeal. *Moon enters Pisces.*

7 OCTOBER

This is a good day for a health or beauty appointment. You may be asked to help someone, and if you need help or advice it will be available. Key meetings should go well, but if you feel under pressure ensure you take extra breaks. *Moon in Pisces.*

8 OCTOBER

You'll appreciate the chance to get on top of chores this weekend, and once you get motivated you could achieve a great deal around the house and/or garden. You'll enjoy a get-together, even if there is some tension involved. This is a good day for a health or beauty appointment. *Moon enters Aries.*

9 OCTOBER

The current Aries full moon will spotlight important health matters, be they yours or those of someone close. You may specifically be drawn to a beauty treat and to improving your appearance, daily routine and domestic circumstances. Avoid taking other people's moods personally. Take a moment to look after your own health. Avoid impulse buys you'll regret.

10 OCTOBER

This is a good day to consider how you could improve your general daily routine so that you feel you are working smarter. Health-wise, this is another good day to focus on your well-being or that of someone close. It's also a good time to boost your appearance through a new look or outfit. *Moon enters Taurus.*

11 OCTOBER

This is a good day for meetings, both socially and at work. Take the time if you're organising events or must collaborate with a group or organisation to reach out, as you're likely to gain results you like even if someone – perhaps even you – feels a little outside their comfort zone. *Moon in Taurus.*

12 OCTOBER

You may uncover a mystery or simply feel absent-minded. A trip to an old haunt may appeal, but you must plan ahead to avoid delays. You may hear from an old work colleague or must go over old ground with a venture or project. Avoid misplacing valuables such as door keys. Be practical for the best measure. *Moon in Taurus.*

13 OCTOBER

The more flexible and accommodating you are the better for you, as there may be unexpected changes to your circumstances. You may find someone at work is unpredictable, and you may be seen as being unreliable unless you make the effort to show just how solid you are. *Moon in Gemini.*

14 OCTOBER

This is a good day for making agreements and for enjoying time with someone you love. You may be ready to make a commitment. You may receive positive work or financial news. If investing, ensure you consult experts to avoid making mistakes. If you're shopping you may be inclined to overspend, so keep an eye on debt! *Moon in Gemini.*

15 OCTOBER

A little retail therapy will appeal to you but if you're already in debt ensure you leave the credit card at home as you may be tempted to make purchases based on emotions alone. You may be easily influenced as well, so unless you get a second opinion about key choices choose carefully. *Moon enters Cancer.*

16 OCTOBER

You'll feel inspired to unwind and will be unlikely to suffer fools gladly. Take some time to enjoy the arts, your favourite music and company. You may be drawn to spend time in nature, too. *Moon in Cancer.*

17 OCTOBER

You may be tempted to act rashly and without forethought, so if you're making important decisions ensure you obtain expert advice. You will enjoy being spontaneous and finding clever ways to express yourself. You may be tempted to overspend or overindulge, so if you're already in the red you may consider putting in place a clever budget. *Moon in Cancer.*

18 OCTOBER

This is a lovely time to focus on your own well-being and a sense of happiness at home. Consider how you could make your home life more comfortable, as it's a good day to make changes there. **Moon in Leo.**

19 OCTOBER

You'll feel bold and outgoing and inclined to make changes at home or within your usual routine. You may even feel a little restless. You may experience an improvement in your work or daily routine, but if you're unsure of any details you must research the facts to avoid mistakes. Avoid conflict; it could escalate quickly. **Moon in Leo.**

20 OCTOBER

Developments could gain momentum very quickly, so ensure you're happy with the way things are and, if not, apply the brakes slightly, especially at work and regarding health matters or a change of routine. Find ways to de-stress. **Moon enters Virgo.**

21 OCTOBER

Your ability to be practical and realistic is a real asset, one you could use for the best results. Avoid being put under pressure unless you really have no alternative. Find ways to unwind when you can. **Moon in Virgo.**

22 OCTOBER

You'll enjoy getting together with like-minded people. Romance could blossom, so ensure you organise a date. If you're single you may meet someone unexpectedly. A sudden or unusual change of schedule can be managed, so put your best foot forward if an unexpected development occurs. Be clear to avoid misunderstandings. **Moon in Virgo.**

23 OCTOBER

As the sun enters your opposite sign of Scorpio you may find that others appear to be more passionate or obstinate than usual. Find a way to navigate around intense circumstances over the coming four weeks. You may feel more passionate about principles yourself. This is a good day for get-togethers and making commitments **Moon in Libra.**

24 OCTOBER

This is a good day for making agreements with work colleagues and those you share duties with. However, someone may bring your vulnerabilities to the surface, so ensure you maintain perspective. **Moon in Libra.**

25 OCTOBER

The partial solar eclipse in Scorpio will be particularly powerful if it's your birthday around 24 April. You are about to begin an entirely new phase in your personal life. All other Taureans are likely to begin a fresh phase at work or within your daily or health routine. Avoid misunderstandings and mix-ups as these are likely. Plan ahead for the best measure. Traffic and travel may be delayed.

26 OCTOBER

There may still be an intense feeling surrounding relationships and, for some, work. Someone close may need special attention or care. If a health matter is on your mind it's a good time to consult an expert. *Moon in Scorpio.*

27 OCTOBER

This is an excellent day for work and improving your general conditions. If you are looking for a job, promotion or pay rise, this is a good day to be more active and to initiate change. Just avoid pushing for results; gently does it. Avoid intense conversations unless you have pre-prepared. If you're shopping, avoid overspending as you're likely to splurge! *Moon enters Sagittarius.*

28 OCTOBER

You may need to review and revise some of your work or health-care programs. You may be feeling particularly idealistic, so ensure you are maintaining perspective. You may enjoy a reunion or a return to a familiar place. *Moon in Sagittarius.*

29 OCTOBER

This weekend you'll enjoy a change of pace and may be more inclined to make changes in your immediate environment and to enjoy a more upbeat and outgoing time. Just ensure the arrangements you make are clear to avoid misunderstandings or delays. *Moon enters Capricorn.*

30 OCTOBER

You can't agree with everyone all the time, so a little compromise may be necessary. You'll appreciate finding the time to enjoy a favourite activity or past-time. You may hear unexpectedly from someone whose company you enjoy. *Moon in Capricorn.*

31 OCTOBER

Happy Halloween! You may enjoy a surprise; for some at work and for others socially. It's certainly always a day when the unexpected can occur, and with the moon in Aquarius later in the day expect a trick or treat! *Moon enters Aquarius.*

November

career   love   home   health   finance

1 NOVEMBER

The Aquarian moon may spotlight your differences of opinion. Avoid feeling antagonistic, as this will simply put your back up and annoy other people into the mix! You'll discover a practical, realistic solution to any conundrums. You'll appreciate relaxing in the evening. *Moon in Aquarius.*

2 NOVEMBER

Conversations may be a little complex, especially at work and/or in connection with health and beauty. Take a few moments before jumping to conclusions to avoid arguments or tension. A light, respectful approach will work wonders. *Moon enters Pisces.*

3 NOVEMBER

A meeting will be more significant than meets the eye. You may meet an old friend or a significant character. If you're single, keep an eye out for meeting someone who seems familiar, especially if you were born in early May. *Moon in Pisces.*

4 NOVEMBER

The bigger picture is this: you have the chance to improve your circumstances, but the more detailed picture involves you taking the time to ensure conversations, talks and communications in general are clear and calm or you risk difficult interactions. Take extra care of work and health matters. *Moon enters Aries at night.*

5 NOVEMBER

You may receive unexpected news, for some from a personal or business partner and for others regarding health and well-being. Take time to find out more about your situation and avoid feeling under pressure. Nevertheless, it's a good time to be spontaneous if need be and to embrace change. You'll enjoy a change of pace. *Moon in Aries.*

6 NOVEMBER

Trust your instincts and avoid feeding bad moods. A reunion or trip to a familiar place may bring emotions to the surface, but if you focus on the positives you'll enjoy a favourite get-together or event. *Moon in Aries.*

7 NOVEMBER

Take time out if need be to reassess your circumstances. A negotiation may have to be undertaken so that everyone involved in the situation is happy with the outcome and can come to terms with the arrangement. You may feel restricted in your movements, so find ways to feel inspired regardless. *Moon in Taurus.*

8 NOVEMBER

The total lunar eclipse in your own sign signals key developments in your life, especially if you were born in mid-May. Taureans born later will begin a fresh chapter at work or in your daily routine. It's a good time to consider how to boost health and well-being in the most practical way. You may receive unexpected news. Avoid snap decisions.

9 NOVEMBER

This is another day of unexpected developments or circumstances that are outside your usual sphere. Take a moment to gather your thoughts. Be flexible and avoid being obstinate, unless you have a key principle you feel you must defend. Place extra focus on good communication skills for the best results. *Moon enters Gemini.*

10 NOVEMBER

You'll be drawn to the arts and romance so make a date if you haven't already! However, there is still a degree of tension in the skies, so ensure you place more attention than usual on good communications or these could be tense or complex. Avoid conflict with someone in authority; find ways to establish mutual ground instead. *Moon in Gemini.*

11 NOVEMBER

Take the time to ensure you are focusing on practical tasks as opposed to chasing rainbows. That said, you can attain any goal with a realistic and positive mindset. *Moon in Gemini.*

12 NOVEMBER

Romance and enjoyable meetings will blossom, making this an excellent day to schedule important talks. You'll be drawn to spending time with like-minded people. However, you will also be easily influenced, so ensure you're maintaining your own goals. *Moon in Cancer.*

13 NOVEMBER

You'll appreciate the opportunity to daydream a little and to let the stresses and strains of last week melt away. Find the time for a beauty or health treat. A lovely change of environment may also appeal. You may be drawn to romance and indulging in luxury. Just avoid overindulgence, as you will pay for it tomorrow! *Moon in Cancer.*

14 NOVEMBER

A more positive and upbeat tone to the start of the week will work wonders for your self-esteem and motivation. This is a good day for meetings and to get down to the bottom line of important matters. A health matter could be looking up. *Moon enters Leo.*

15 NOVEMBER

This is an excellent day for getting your projects and ventures into more positive shape. It's especially positive for artistic and creative ventures. You'll be drawn to romance. It's a good day for meetings of any kind; however, if you're negotiating business deals or a large investment avoid being easily influenced. *Moon in Leo.*

16 NOVEMBER

You may be travelling or organising a trip. It promises to go well as long as you have checked the details and do not rush a project. Talks and meetings should also go well even if you feel under pressure. Bolster self-esteem with a little positive self-talk. Avoid snap decisions. *Moon in Leo.*

17 NOVEMBER

You'll enjoy a lovely social get-together, so organise a treat if you haven't already! Work meetings should go well and will feel more upbeat. You'll feel more outgoing and will be drawn to expand your horizons. *Moon in Virgo.*

18 NOVEMBER

This is an excellent day for enjoying time with someone special. At work, meetings are likely to go well and you may experience a fresh understanding of your role or of your employer's role. Take the time to make changes, as these are likely to take. *Moon in Virgo.*

19 NOVEMBER

You'll enjoy socialising and spending time with your favourite people. But if you're on a spending spree, avoid overspending as you're likely to regret it. You may also be prone to overindulge, so if you're socialising ensure you have a spending limit set to avoid a splurge or leave the credit card at home! Avoid misunderstandings. *Moon enters Libra.*

20 NOVEMBER

You'll enjoy relaxing. If you overdid things yesterday you may feel a little forgetful or absent-minded today, so take things one step at a time. You'll enjoy the arts, music, favourite company and romance. *Moon in Libra.*

21 NOVEMBER

Key news from a personal or business partner will be uplifting, although it may involve a great deal of change. If news today is disappointing, take the time to get together with someone you know has your back as their influence will be uplifting. A journey or meeting may be fortunate. *Moon enters Scorpio.*

22 NOVEMBER

You'll appreciate the feeling that your relationships can obtain a more even keel. You may feel more optimistic, and a partner may as well. Find the time to organise fun, healthy and therapeutic events together. *Moon in Scorpio.*

23 NOVEMBER

The Sagittarian new moon signals a fresh chapter is about to begin in a key personal or business relationship. Be positive about developments moving forward, as they are likely to be therapeutic in many ways.

24 NOVEMBER

Today's moon in Sagittarius will spotlight news from a partner or expert adviser. Take the time to digest the news and conversations, as you'll find there are many positives. It's a good time to be more adventurous in your relationships. *Moon in Sagittarius.*

25 NOVEMBER

This is a good day for health and beauty treats. A medical appointment or health news will be significant. If someone needs your help, be ready to offer support. If you need support it will be available. ***Moon enters Capricorn.***

26 NOVEMBER

This is a good day for healing, therapeutic endeavours, meditation and spiritual practices. You may like to boost your appearance and health. Someone may be particularly influential over you at the moment. If some talks are tense, avoid taking the opinions of others personally unless criticism is merited. ***Moon in Capricorn.***

27 NOVEMBER

An unusual event or unexpected news will arise, so be prepared to think on your feet. You may enjoy hearing from someone from out of the blue. If you have key goals to attain, rest assured you will and that you will overcome any hurdles that arise! ***Moon enters Aquarius.***

28 NOVEMBER

This is an excellent day to get things done, especially at work and financially. If you're making a large investment this could be a positive move, but you must have first done the groundwork. It's a good day to make a commitment. ***Moon in Aquarius.***

29 NOVEMBER

Developments could move forward quickly, so ensure you are on the same page as someone close or you could find you're talking at cross purposes. A financial matter will deserve careful attention. ***Moon in Aquarius.***

30 NOVEMBER

This is another good day for making agreements and for collaborating with others. You may find you can come to mutually agreeable arrangements. It's a good day for meetings, and if you're looking for work it's a good day for interviews. Just ensure you have all the facts at your disposal. ***Moon in Pisces.***

December

career   love   home   health   finance

1 DECEMBER

Someone is likely to voice their opinions, and if you agree with them all will be well. If not, you may need to evaluate your position and avoid a confrontational approach as this will not help you. A financial matter can be decided upon. Avoid purely emotional decisions financially. Romance could flourish, so plan a date! *Moon in Pisces.*

2 DECEMBER

This is a good day for talks and negotiations. It's also a good time to make agreements, both in your personal life and financially or at work. However, you may tend to be a little idealistic about some elements, so if you're making long-term and key decisions ensure you have all the facts at your fingertips. *Moon in Aries.*

3 DECEMBER

There is a therapeutic aspect to the weekend. You'll either enjoy treating yourself to a health or beauty treat or you may simply need to relax. A development could have a therapeutic influence over you. If you need help it will be available. *Moon in Aries.*

4 DECEMBER

You do enjoy a little luxury and comfort, and today you'll enjoy it immensely. Romance could blossom. However, you may have a tendency in conversations to grab the wrong end of the stick, so ensure you have all the facts to hand. Avoid making assumptions. **Moon enters Taurus.**

5 DECEMBER

You may experience some delays, so organise extra time to get things done at work and for travel. Also bear in mind that the next two days could involve misunderstandings, so double-check facts. **Moon in Taurus.**

6 DECEMBER

You may receive news that puts a fresh perspective on some of your agreements or arrangements. Luckily, as Mercury enters Capricorn today you will be able to take practical action if anything needs to be set straight. **Moon enters Gemini.**

7 DECEMBER

An innovative approach to someone who may surprise you will work. Aim to think laterally if you are taken off guard. Your charm is an effective quality, so use it! **Moon in Gemini.**

8 DECEMBER

The Gemini full moon points to a key decision. For many Taureans this will be a financial choice, although for some mid-May–born Taureans it may involve your personal life. You can make a great deal of headway but must avoid making snap decisions, as this full moon will kick-start a new cycle.

9 DECEMBER

A spontaneous approach to life will be enjoyable to you. You may return to an old haunt or will appreciate a reunion. Someone may be in touch from out of the blue. **Moon in Cancer.**

10 DECEMBER

If life has been very up and down of late prepare for another development today. This may be the outcome of some previous developments. If life has been fairly smooth you may still experience something new that asks you to dig deep and express your feelings. Be prepared to listen to someone's feelings in return. **Moon in Cancer.**

11 DECEMBER

Today's developments will bring a more even keel to some of your interactions, but you must avoid being stubborn if change is necessary. Strong emotions may emerge, so find ways to channel these into productive activities. **Moon enters Leo** at night.

12 DECEMBER

This is a good day to be busy, as you are likely to be super productive. It's also a good day to mend bridges and to put plans in place, as they are likely to stick. *Moon in Leo.*

13 DECEMBER

While this is another good day for meetings and to get things done, you may tend to overlook details and be a little idealistic, especially in your personal life. If someone has broken your trust you must ask if you can learn to trust them again, and vice versa. *Moon in Leo.*

14 DECEMBER

Misunderstandings can occur relatively easily, so ensure you are on the same page as those you must collaborate with or mix-ups can occur. You or someone close may be forgetful. Avoid misplacing valuable objects. *Moon enters Virgo.*

15 DECEMBER

Despite some matters being up in the air, today's Virgo moon will enable you to make decisions based on practicalities. You could get a lot done both at work and at home. You'll enjoy a get-together with someone who make you feel at home. *Moon in Virgo.*

16 DECEMBER

There may be a question mark over a trip or project, so avoid pushing for results as decisions will be made in due course. If you must undertake a difficult choice or venture, rest assured you will succeed with due diligence. *Moon enters Libra.*

17 DECEMBER

You'll enjoy a change of pace or even a change of environment. An impromptu get-together will be fun. A trip may take you back to an old haunt. You'll enjoy a reunion. A change at work could be enjoyable. *Moon in Libra.*

18 DECEMBER

A collaboration and romance could be fulfilling, so ensure you organise a lovely get-together. Work matters that need you to co-operate with others or to work as a team could be successful, but you must be super clear about details or misunderstandings can occur. Avoid overwork as you will overtire yourself. Travel may be delayed. Avoid rushing, as minor accidents can occur. *Moon in Libra.*

19 DECEMBER

You can please some people some of the time but not all people all of the time. This adage suits your day, as it's important to realise you can't get on with everyone but you can be pleasant and avoid tense topics. You'll enjoy boosting relationships and romance. *Moon in Scorpio.*

20 DECEMBER

When the moon is in Scorpio people close to you both at work and at home may be more outspoken or passionate. You may feel a little feistier. If problems arise, avoid speaking before you've thought things through. This aside, you'll enjoy a work development or a favourite activity or hobby. *Moon in Scorpio.*

21 DECEMBER

Plans may need to be changed at the last minute. If you've made arrangements with someone special you'll enjoy your get-together, but if the date is delayed it may well be due to matters outside the control of either of you. Be practical and avoid looking for arguments; look for solutions instead. *Moon in Sagittarius.*

22 DECEMBER

A lovely change of environment or of pace will breathe fresh air into your day. If you have nothing special planned yet organise an impromptu treat; you're likely to enjoy it. A business or personal partner may have a surprise in store. *Moon in Sagittarius.*

23 DECEMBER

The new moon and supermoon in Capricorn signals a fresh chapter is about to begin in a shared circumstance, such as shared space at home or at work. For some, a new way to share duties or even finances will begin; you may even enjoy a boost at work. A lovely meeting will add a sense of stability to your life.

24 DECEMBER

There is a lovely, romantic vibe to Christmas, a time to feather your nest and make sure you have your creature comforts all sorted out for yourself and those you love over the next two days. You'll appreciate doing the activities you love, and a trip or visit will be enjoyable. *Moon in Capricorn.*

25 DECEMBER

Merry Christmas! This year's Christmas may be slightly different to that of previous years. If you're missing someone, take a moment to appreciate their existence and focus on your own situation and on enjoying the company you do have. *Moon in Aquarius.*

26 DECEMBER

You'll appreciate the sense that you can approach someone who can sometimes be a little difficult in a new way. You may even feel some of your moods lift as you relax into the holiday season. If you're back at work it could be a busy day with varied influences, so take things one step at a time. *Moon in Aquarius.*

27 DECEMBER

This is a lovely day for get-togethers. You may get on better with someone whose influence you have found overbearing or restrictive in the past. It's a good day to formulate your new year's resolutions as they're likely to stick! *Moon in Pisces.*

28 DECEMBER

This is a lovely day to indulge a little in the arts, music, dance and romance. You'll enjoy a shopping spree at the sales but must avoid overspending, as you are likely to be easily enticed by bargains. You'll enjoy a get-together with a good friend or family member. If you overindulged at Christmas, this is a good time to consider a fresh diet or detox. *Moon in Pisces.*

29 DECEMBER

Key talks or news will present a fresh situation. You may be ready to travel or are looking forward to a fresh venture. Try to get major paperwork and decisions sorted out by today as Mercury turns retrograde and there may be traffic delays or communication glitches to come. *Moon in Aries.*

30 DECEMBER

A certain degree of restlessness needn't get the better of you. Avoid being impulsive, especially with work decisions and financial matters. If obstacles arise, rest assured you will overcome them. *Moon in Aries.*

31 DECEMBER

Happy New Year! You'll feel increasingly in your element as the night goes on, and a comfortable, safe and secure environment will be your happy place as you enter the new year. *Moon enters Taurus.*

THE ESSENCE OF GEMINI

This is the myth: Geminis are insincere and even duplicitous. This is the truth: you are a social butterfly who is upbeat, charming, restless and changeable. Because of this you can be mistaken for being superficial and, even worse, two faced. However, your actions are simply your response to your inner calling, which is to get as much out of life as you can. In the process you'll fly from one event to the next, will appear restless, will be as charming as you are curious about other people and will keep moving in your efforts to gather more information and experience.

Because you are a social butterfly you can be seen as being frivolous, never staying long enough to get to know anyone on any deeper level. It's true that if your curiosity in life goes unchecked you risk being inattentive and self-centred; it is merely a symptom of your wish to get everything possible from life. You tend to flit from one circumstance and activity to another, resting for just a short while before you flit off to the next venture.

To gain a sense of stability it's vital you slow down, rest a little longer between flights here and there and develop your wonderful ability to laugh. You need to see the humour in life and contribute your own typically Zen approach: to take life with a pinch of salt. After all, a little light-heartedness never hurt anyone.

The twin symbol denotes your ability to be flexible, to see life from various angles and to understand how to adapt to new circumstances as if you were two people. The twin icon also demonstrates your ability to multi-skill and multi-task. It's only when you don't provide the people in your life with a sense of substance and sincerity that they question your integrity, so it's important to always show your genuineness or you can be seen as being superficial.

SELF-ESTEEM

You have one of the most resilient of personalities, yet your self-esteem can take a battering as you can be viewed as being distant or frivolous when you allow your mercurial nature to dominate the rest of your personality. When you do become flighty and inconsistent you don't give yourself permission to stay long enough to truly feel the depth of understanding in life and relationships you so crave. This can lead to your being criticised for being insincere or even a phony.

Luckily, your resilient personality, which comes from your ability to see circumstances from many different angles, then takes charge. You are unlikely to take criticism personally or to see someone's criticism of you as being motivated by hatred, and are therefore unlikely to feel vulnerable. You will be aware, though, that you are not appreciated for being the bright person you are. Your ability to see life from many different perspectives can be your downfall, as you tend not to take well-meaning criticism on board. You consequently risk flitting through life without digesting valid information and feedback that could be to your advantage, as it would guide you into a deeper understanding of yourself and the needs of others and lead to a more positive experience in life.

You have an intellect beyond the norm that is informed by instinct and intuition and gives you superpowers! You have an in-built sixth sense that other people envy even if they do not understand it, yet you may not believe in your abilities yourself until you have experience in life and come to realise you do in fact possess deeper insight than many other people.

YOUR INNER LIFE

A pitfall for you can be overindulgence in the finer things in life or a predisposition towards comfort, stability and security at the cost of all else. This can cause inner tension, as your penchant for luxury and easy living may seem counter-intuitive to such a social butterfly and live wire. You do recognise you need your downtime to regenerate your lively mind and body. You may also tend towards secrecy, which again can lead to the impression that you are duplicitous.

Another anomaly in the Gemini make-up is that, despite being a social live wire to the extent you appear aloof, you are in fact a loyal character who would move heaven and earth for those you love. Your unique combination of independence with loyalty and trustworthiness can confuse those who know you, yet once your trust is gained very little can detract from the loyalty you demonstrate.

Your sense of humour may be quirky or dry. You love to laugh, but can therefore be seen as being unable to understand depths of experience. Your penchant for humour and light-heartedness is a manifestation of your ability to see the bigger picture, to see that when laughter stops there can be no progress, no air left to breathe. The worst thing for a Gemini is the feeling that there is no air. You must have your independence, then you are loyal beyond all else.

A real drawback for you can be a tendency towards indecision, which can cause people to see you as being non-committal. Your indecision comes from your ability to see a circumstance from many different vantage points, making your choices all the more difficult. In your case being indecisive can be an asset if your ability to see both sides of the coin is managed well, leading you towards being a skilled mediator, a truly diplomatic and caring character.

Romantic commitment will certainly tend to come later in life; the young twin is likely to enjoy the freedom and independence of being able to flit from one romantic engagement to another. However, if you have points in your astrological chart in earth signs you may be an exception to the rule and wish to settle down earlier in life. Once you find the one it is likely to be a heart connection as strong and as clear as any other sign's romantic relationship. You will demand a similar level of commitment, and if you feel this is lacking you may become elusive and hard to reason with.

HOW OTHERS SEE YOU

If you have met someone who seems constantly on the move it would be someone with strong Gemini in their astrology charts. They may even be physically fidgety and constantly moving their arms as you talk to them.

Always being on the move could lead to a delay in you developing sincerity and creativity until later in life. The stillness necessary to facilitate the creative process may be foreign to your temperament until you mature. When developed your innate creativity and calm will enable you to access so many more experiences, which is what you truly crave. You may also appear to be frustrated, immature or lacking in self-confidence until you allow yourself to experience your own inner calm and creativity.

Your home may have an impermanent, almost traveller feel to it. You may have more than one home or divide your time between two homes. Twins may run in the family, or you may have a blended family or a stepmother or stepfather.

As you are such an adaptable character you should find managing a busy home life easy. However, the sound of your own wheels constantly turning could become too loud even for you to bear. Take the time to rest and breathe or you risk frayed nerves.

HOW TO MAXIMISE YOUR POTENTIAL

You are a social enigma: there is no stopping you once you take to the floor in a meeting room, public space, bar or recreation centre. You are a natural-born mimic and chameleon and can fit in anywhere. To avoid being seen as someone who has no authentic personality of your own it's important you display your solid, dependable attributes as well as your light-hearted ability to blend in wherever you are. The more reliable and punctual you are the better; in this way people will come to know they can rely on you. Otherwise, your chameleon-like behaviour can tend to overshadow your dependability.

You are also a natural-born communicator. You will do well in the media or in any communications industry, as you are a people person who will automatically deliver from the heart what people want from you.

Travel will attract you as a platform for self-development. You should find learning languages easier than most, as you can mimic sounds and hand gestures easily. You do have a tendency for monkey mischief so consider being mischievous in a kind-hearted way, playing pranks that ultimately do no damage and lead only to laughter rather than pranks that cause misunderstandings and conflict.

Take the time to show your serious side. An upbeat, light-hearted approach is appropriate much of the time, but when serious or heart-wrenching events occur in life it's important you show your compassionate and gentle side or you will be seen as being cold, insensitive and unfeeling.

GEMINI AND ITS ASCENDANTS

This chapter is about your sun sign, Gemini, and your predictions for the year ahead. The more you know about yourself the better you will be able to take advantage of opportunities, and also to avoid the pitfalls. It's critical to know as much about 'you' as possible.

In astrology your core self is represented by your sun sign, but your personality traits are represented by your ascendant (also known as your rising sign). The ascendant describes your personality, the way other people see you on first meeting you and the way you tend to filter life's events.

When you have intimate knowledge about your sun sign – your engine room or core being – you will be on the way to a happier life. When you add the knowledge about your personality – your ascendant – you will gain even deeper insight into what makes you tick.

Your ascendant sign is determined by the time of your birth on the date and year of your birth. Because the ascendant sign changes approximately every two hours, the best way to determine it is to ask an astrologer to calculate it for you. Certain apps will also calculate your ascendant sign (see page 873).

The following gives you more information about your abilities, characteristics and personality according to your sun sign Gemini in combination with your ascendant sign.

GEMINI SUN SIGN WITH ARIES ASCENDANT

You are a mercurial character with many different forms of expression. You may be fidgety, restless and hard to pin down; you are a dynamo. Aries rising people are often seen as being truly dynamic to the extent of being bossy. You can be overtly analytical on occasion and get caught

up in your thoughts, so it's important to release tension and the tendency to worry by engaging in action-oriented activities such as sport and nature rambles that disperse excess energy.

You are unlikely to carry excess weight as you are constantly on the go. You need mental stimulation, so follow your heart and study and practise in areas that provide information and learning opportunities.

GEMINI SUN SIGN WITH TAURUS ASCENDANT

You have a sensual, earthy personality and will enjoy the finer things in life. You are a loyal friend and appreciate luxury and comfort. You like to live life at a slower pace and are practical and methodical, which is in contrast with your fast-paced Gemini core. Your outward sense of calm and composed demeanour belie an underlying nervous quality; you may even wonder yourself how you project a rational personality when you have such a busy mind. You can experience inner tension as your Gemini core prefers speed and mental agility while your Taurean personality prefers realistic, steady progress. On the upside, you are blessed with being a good communicator, and with being active and analytical while possessing the inner strength and diligence to get things done.

GEMINI SUN SIGN WITH GEMINI ASCENDANT

You are a double Gemini and are super mercurial, super analytical and super restless. You can also be a great communicator, mediator and conversationalist, a traveller and loyal friend, the latter more so when your friends and family can pin you down on one spot. With both your sun sign and ascendant in Gemini you are likely to be constantly on the move! You have a bright mind but can be so in your head you find it hard to allow your heart to take the lead. At work you are a huge asset to any employer, trade or profession as you have a quick mind, but in your love life your restlessness and independence can make you seem non-committal or preoccupied. Travel, broadening your mind and communications of all forms will entice you as you truly are an active character.

GEMINI SUN SIGN WITH CANCER ASCENDANT

You are seemingly adaptable, but underneath your go with the flow exterior you are a determined individual once you put your mind to certain ideas and projects. You can appear to be sensitive and moody – this is your Cancerian personality – but deep down you are able to detach from emotional circumstances that irk you. It can be confusing for those who see you as being sensitive, intuitive, empathic and sensuous (your Cancerian outer shell), because you can also appear to be cold when your Gemini intellect switches your emotions off without a second thought. Your behaviour may surprise even you. As you mature you will increasingly feel in tune with yourself and able to merge both intellect and emotions into a balanced, well-rounded character.

GEMINI SUN SIGN WITH LEO ASCENDANT

The Leo personality is bright, dynamic and go-getting; you like to be the centre of attention and are driven by success. On first impression you appear strong, dependable and determined, characteristics you can develop. Avoid allowing your Gemini tendency towards indecision to overshadow your Leo self-confidence. Focus on your best qualities from both signs: self-esteem and dynamism from your Leo personality, and intellectual ability and flexibility from your Gemini sun sign. If you allow your

Gemini tendency towards indecision and aloofness to prevail you can seem restless, so it's important to portray dependability and stability, especially when you're trying to make a good impression.

GEMINI SUN SIGN WITH VIRGO ASCENDANT

Both Gemini and Virgo are ruled by Mercury and are different expressions of the same abilities: to serve, to adapt and to think clearly. How you express these qualities may alternate from day to day, which is what makes you such an intriguing, mercurial character. Luckily your earthy Virgo personality will keep your feet on the ground. One pitfall is that you may tend to rely purely on an intellectual understanding of life, so it's important to also feel with your heart and avoid being too introspective.

GEMINI SUN SIGN WITH LIBRA ASCENDANT

As a double air sign you are a great thinker and able to carefully analyse circumstances. You are likely to be intelligent and flexible and have terrific communication skills, and you always look for balance in life. With these two signs comes a tendency to over-analyse to the point of indecision, especially when you're under pressure. Unless there is a prominent earth, fire or water element in your astrology chart you can tend to be a little aloof and indecisive. Be guided by your senses and intuition so you gain the balance you need to be able to empathise, take action and understand the deeper contexts of feelings and interactions.

GEMINI SUN SIGN WITH SCORPIO ASCENDANT

Your passionate, hands-on, outgoing and charismatic personality belies a cool head and detached character that steers your life with a pointedly independent stance. Although you may be seen as being an intense and engaged person, there is much behind this personality that is quite detached. You are an anomaly: hot-headed, passionate and powerful while also being cool and measured. You may experience periods of inner turmoil, and may wonder about the lack of impulse control that can come with the Scorpio ascendant being at odds with the cool Gemini. A great ability you do have is to bounce back from adversity.

GEMINI SUN SIGN WITH SAGITTARIUS ASCENDANT

This is a combination of opposite signs that complement each other: your adventurous, outgoing and upbeat personality meshes well with your Gemini adaptability and desire for freedom and independence. You are a strong character and one of the more loyal in the zodiac, as long as you retain your identity and do not feel caged by work, relationships or family. You enjoy travel and sport and will usually not suffer from weight gain if you remain active. You also have a love of the good things in life, and will not be afraid to pursue your true goals.

GEMINI SUN SIGN WITH CAPRICORN ASCENDANT

Your calm demeanour and measured approach to life is quite the contrast to your changeable, restless core self. Those who meet you will at first see a quiet achiever, the person most likely to succeed, but once they get to know you they will see the light-hearted, fun, mischievous person you are. You can be seen as being quite a complex character, yet you appreciate your ability to be serious when necessary and fun and upbeat with friends and family. You are not afraid to take on responsibility, and can certainly attain the goals you set yourself. You are unlikely to be as

restless as some Geminis, and will appreciate the diligence and staying power your Capricorn ascendant gives you.

GEMINI SUN SIGN WITH AQUARIUS ASCENDANT

These two air signs mix together well: you may be seen as being a quirky and independent individual who is not afraid to try new ideas. You may tend to go off the beaten track, pursuing alternative lifestyles and radical ideas. You are a good thinker but must remember to consult your emotions, especially when you're making decisions, or you may tend to pursue the latest fads without a thought for their emotional impact. You may gain a reputation for being a little left field, so maintain equilibrium to avoid being seen as erratic or unreliable. You can be viewed as being inflexible despite your Gemini adaptability, so allow your inner Gemini room for self-expression.

GEMINI SUN SIGN WITH PISCES ASCENDANT

Pisces being the dreamer of the zodiac, your personality presents initially as philosophical and gentle. Combined with your strong Gemini intellect, you can appear to be a little pensive or reserved, yet you are deeply motivated and enmeshed in life. You have strong feelings, and can be super sensitive and easily swayed by other people's opinions. Those who know you see you for the vulnerable character you are, and know you can override these qualities with your intellect. You may tend to play the martyr, especially when life deals you a lemon. It's important to be more decisive and be aware when you are being influenced, and to identify your true feelings so your actions align with your core self.

GEMINI IN LOVE

You are a particularly independent individual who is likely to be selective about who you spend long-term time with. In this section you can check out your compatibility with other sun signs. Remember that we are all complex individuals, so the more you know about someone's astrological birth chart the better you can determine your compatibility. Consider having your astrological birth chart compared with that of a partner, friend or family member, as the compatibility – known as 'synastry' in astrology – goes even deeper than a comparison of sun signs, although this is a good place to begin.

GEMINI WITH ARIES

This is a lovely match, even if you both find yourselves so busy in your individual lives that you spend more time missing each other's company than actually being together! When you do make a commitment to be together you should arrange regular together time so you don't miss out on the benefits of this match. You'll appreciate the Aries independence and ability to take the lead, and your partner will appreciate your freedom of movement and light-hearted attitude. While you tend to live in your head Aries tends to be action oriented, so you may find it necessary to avoid being too involved in debate and indecision. Even so, your ability to think things through will feel refreshing to Aries, who enjoys being spontaneous but can tend towards being impulsive.

GEMINI WITH TAURUS

This combination of air sign Gemini with Taurus can be like a breath of fresh air for the Taurean – or you can seem like a hurricane! The Taurean is looking for stability and sumptuousness in life, so if you are flighty and unreliable you will be disruptive. Your seeming lack of consistency and level-headedness can be hard for the Taurus to love; Taurus is looking for commitment and calmness in life. If this is what you want this combination can work, especially as your deep-seated loyalty will provide the stability the Taurean is looking for.

GEMINI WITH GEMINI

You are like two peas in a pod, which will make the Gemini twin dynamic super strong. However, this combo can be too much of a good thing. Your ultra light-hearted approach to life can be a source of laughter and fun in your emotional life but you may shy away, somehow missing the earthiness, fire or water of other signs. Depending on your ascendants and moon signs this could be a good match, as you're both independent characters able to get each other and give each other enough freedom to be yourselves. Deep down you have great loyalty; it will simply be a case of making this a priority.

GEMINI WITH CANCER

You are an air sign; Cancer is a water sign. There is some compatibility, but the air in you can feel drowned by the emotions of the Cancerian and the Cancerian can feel you are a little too detached emotionally for this to be love everlasting. If you have a moon in Cancer or a strong water signature in your astrological chart you can feel deeply nurtured and emotionally and intuitively in sync with the Cancerian. If your Cancer partner has a strong air signature in their chart this could be a loving and mutually supportive match. There would need to be allowance given for the fact that individuals in this relationship are coming from different places: one from the head and the other from the heart.

GEMINI WITH LEO

This match makes a fun-loving duo out to enjoy life and live an exciting adventure together. The Leo character will wish to take the lead, which is something you may come to resent in a longer-term relationship as Geminis look for balance and equality in a relationship and especially one based on excitement and adventure. Leo may come to depend on your support, but if you do not have autonomy and the chance to be adaptable and independent this match can end in tears. Leo will look for a settled life, especially in later years, but will wish to be the lion at the centre of the brood. Gemini will not play second fiddle, so give and take is essential in this partnership.

GEMINI WITH VIRGO

While both sun signs are ruled by chatty and mercurial Mercury, these two signs are fundamentally different: they are the two quite opposite expressions of the celestial trickster Mercury. Air sign Gemini looks for flexibility and change in life; earth sign Virgo looks for dependability and routine and can be quite the perfectionist. Gemini will not have the time for this, being always on the go and in pursuit of the next adventure. Moon signs and other placements in the chart aside, this combination can be difficult for both sun signs and is not ideal because of fundamental tension between characteristics.

GEMINI WITH LIBRA

These two air signs will come together in mutual and everlasting understanding and harmony, although sometimes there will not be the spark necessary for romance to ignite as too much air in a relationship can mean too much room to miss each other's relevance. This relationship may become less of a romantic liaison and more of a companionship; extra effort may be needed to romantically nurture it. However, you are fundamentally compatible so this combo will have less drama and stress than some relationships, as both individuals will give each other freedom of movement.

GEMINI WITH SCORPIO

This combination can ignite passion very quickly, although it may be short lived or simply too difficult to sustain long term due to arguments and stress. If both individuals are committed to making the relationship work it can be an exciting and passionate union. It will, however, entail work, as both these sun signs have strong characters. Where the Scorpio will wish to dig down deep and engage in an intense and even possessive relationship, the Gemini will wish to retain some individuality and independence. This can spell fundamental incompatibility.

GEMINI WITH SAGITTARIUS

This is a fun, adventurous and upbeat match and could be perfect for long-term commitment. You both understand how important it is to live life to the fullest, and enjoy travel and broadening your understanding of life. The Sagittarian will appreciate how important independence and mental stimulation is for you and you understand that the Sagittarian cannot be caged or dominated. The mutual understanding and respect for each other's self-expression makes for fundamental compatibility; the lust both signs have for life spells a happy union.

GEMINI WITH CAPRICORN

These two signs are at odds. The earthy Capricorn character can be meticulous and diligent in their progress through life, and is strongly opposed to the impulsiveness, changeability and restlessness of your personality. Both signs would need to work at this relationship to respect their fundamentally different approaches to life. When the effort is made the union could be mutually supportive, as each one's character could complete or complement the other. However, it's likely that without strong connections in other aspects of each person's astrological chart these two sun signs will not engage or understand each other.

GEMINI WITH AQUARIUS

There is fundamental compatibility in this combination, with the Aquarian quirkiness appealing to Gemini's sense of humour. In addition, each sign will give the other the space they need to express themselves. Both signs will understand each other's need for independence as both are free spirits. The Aquarian is most likely to need stability in the relationship, and Gemini's sense of loyalty will respond to this need as long as the Gemini's individuality is respected. This is generally a favourable combo because both signs appreciate uniqueness and independence and have a well-developed sense of humour.

GEMINI WITH PISCES

The Pisces partner may initially find Gemini's chattiness and joie de vivre appealing, yet as time goes by Pisces will wish to see more depth of character than Gemini wishes to display. If Pisces is willing to stay long term in the relationship there will be depth in it, but all too often the Gemini restlessness and changeability can be a turn-off for the sensitive Pisces. Geminis will be attracted to the dreamy, inspired and yet philosophical intelligence of Pisces, but this water sign can unintentionally dampen the Gemini spirit. This union would need effort, or a strong air component in the Pisces' astrological chart and a strong water signature in the Gemini's chart for it to work harmoniously.

THE YEAR AHEAD FOR GEMINI

Affirmation: *'I dare to break into new territory and will avoid risk-taking.'*

Uranus, the celestial game changer, will be bringing great opportunities for change in your everyday life all year, including your work, health and daily routine. It's in your interest to take steps into new territory because this planet will shake up your life whether you want to make changes or not. Therefore, it's best to initiate the change yourself rather than be at the whims of fate.

This year the focus will also be on collaborations, especially in connection with the above. So, for example, developments in your everyday life will revolve around choices between being single or married, rich or poor, kind or cruel and happy or sad. Your career may ask that you are more independent or, on the other hand, if you've been self-employed for some time to consider teamwork and collaborations with other people a little more.

This year is clearly divided into two parts: the first four months and the remaining eight months. You'll find May and June will be excellent times to take stock and to reconfigure elements of your life you'd like to reset or to set on a fresh path. The new moon on 30 May will be an ideal time to reinvent yourself in a way that helps you feel both more empowered and safe and secure within the course you have chosen.

Key turning points will be during January, when your choices about who you spend time with both in your personal life and career will be long-standing. Ensure you are careful about decisions at this time, as you may tend to be seeing life through rose-coloured glasses rather than for what it is.

In May, the eclipses will present broad changes around who you decide to associate with, both in your personal life and at work and especially from the perspective of duties and responsibilities.

From October to November you will wish to create more stability and security both at home and at work. Turning points always offer a choice, so at these crucial times ensure your decisions are based on long-term criteria as the resulting changes will potentially last for decades.

HEALTH

A great deal of your happiness and mental and spiritual health comes from good relationships, and this year it's in your interest to focus on improving relationship skills for peace of mind. You may consider such avenues as assertiveness training or meditation, or activities that help you to calm your mind, as the greatest learning curve for you will revolve around not only your most immediate connections such as partners and family but also those in general, such as relationships with people you meet during business transactions at work or in everyday life.

Travel and study and generally feeling you can develop your own skills, abilities and knowledge will provide a sense of growth, progress and mental well-being. Being in a favourite place will improve your physical well-being, as you do like to be by the sea and/or in a space where you feel vibrant and alive. Consider travel somewhere beautiful if possible, especially in the first half of the year. You may be drawn to return to an old haunt in March-April that will reconnect you with a sense of belonging.

The new moon in your sign on 30 May will be an excellent time to embrace new modalities to boost your health.

Mars will enter your sign at the end of August and could boost your energy levels. Just avoid overwork and fatigue. The sun, Mercury and Venus travelling through your health sector from October onwards will encourage you to focus on improved health and well-being, especially if you must replenish energy levels then.

FINANCES

Financially, it's important to aim for stronger foundations. There will be considerable developments in your financial life this year, for some at home and for others due to changes in your daily routine or work. The more adaptable you are in these areas the better for you, as you will find fresh solid ground to make your investments.

Pluto and, for some mid-June Twins, Saturn in your eighth house will call for important financial decisions this year, when a partnership or collaboration may require review or rearrangement so you are in a strong position moving forward.

Be prepared to look in detail at your options and financial opportunities; it will be in your interest to leave no stone unturned in your effort to gain a clear impression of your best way forward investment-wise at this time.

The eclipses this year will tend to incline you towards gambling and taking financial risks, so this year it's important to be spontaneous but also to research your investments very deeply. Avoid being easily influenced with regard to financial investments or mistakes could be made, especially in the second half of the year.

HOME LIFE

Considerable changes are likely in your home life as people come and go – perhaps even you! Your focus on developing a deeper understanding of yourself and the world at large points to you wishing to travel and to connect with people in new ways.

Key relationships may be impacted upon by developments in the broader world, such as changes in your career or status that affect your domestic relationships and vice versa. As your work changes so will your home life, and your career or that of someone close or at home is due considerable change this year.

Venus in your home sector in September will encourage you to spend a little more energy on making your home the balanced place you wish it to be. And, with Mars in your sign from 20 August, you'll be ready to instigate any changes you'd like to make in this most important part of your life.

However, if some relationships have been strained avoid outbursts and anger at this time; they could trip you up. You may need to compromise or give up one idea or project in favour of your home or family. Be prepared to make the sacrifice, as you will be happy you did.

LOVE

Get set for a fresh chapter in your love life, as you will be prepared to explore new avenues. Singles may be surprised by the unexpected type of characters you are drawn to, and you may even be looking for a commitment where in the past you have considered only how important your freedom is. For some, though, this will be the opposite: you'll be looking for more freedom of movement after a sense of having become entrenched in a rut.

For couples, it's a similar story: you will be looking for a sense of renewal in your relationship, especially in January, May and November. The flavour is very much renewal and breaking out of a rut.

These times may also be tense for you, so even if you feel like breaking out into new territory remain practical and heart-centred, especially in January, May and November. Consider your long-term prospects in your relationships.

The eclipses this year will be across your friendship, love and affairs zones, indicating you will wish to socialise, network and, if you're single, flirt and engage in love affairs.

There's an air of intensity and seduction around Taurus and Scorpio eclipses, which will be in April-May and October-November. Couples may wish to infuse your relationship with more passion through deeper intimacy and connection. However, some Twins may discover secrets at this time, or else your secrets may be revealed.

The Taurus total lunar eclipse on 8 November may be the signal you need to make the changes you've been wishing for. But if you're drawn to maintain the status quo, work out what or who needs to remain in 2022 and who you wish to take forward with you into 2023.

CAREER

Uranus, the celestial game changer, is still in your work sector and this year takes grand steps forward, which means you, too, will proceed into new territory. The key to progress will be ensuring you are not making too much of a risk. On the other hand, it will be important to avoid resisting change and dynamic new options due to fear. Find the balance.

When Jupiter steps into proactive Aries on 10 May you are likely to feel more outgoing and willing to take on big projects. You may also be drawn to new skill sets, to study and broadening your horizons in many ways. You will be stepping from a more ideas-based phase to a more action-oriented, dynamic phase until the end of July and then once again at the end of December.

The year also has Chiron, the 'wounded healer', in your career sector, suggesting you are keen to show just what you know and can teach others. If you feel you are held back, avoid making impulsive decisions. This year is about the long game. Chiron could spell a phase when you feel you are not living up to your full potential. The gift in this feeling is that you get the chance to show just what you're made of.

This year you may be particularly drawn to making changes in your career, and any agreements and collaborations you make must be carefully analysed to ensure you are not making changes that put you at a disadvantage.

A proactive time between May and mid-August could see dynamic developments take place for you, but you must be careful to avoid making changes that could be detrimental to your long-term income or shared interests. At this time, be super careful with the decisions you make.

This applies also to the time around the eclipse on 8 November, which could open doors to a new interest, activity or even relationship. Be open to change then, but as it may also close a door to a long-term alliance you should choose carefully.

January

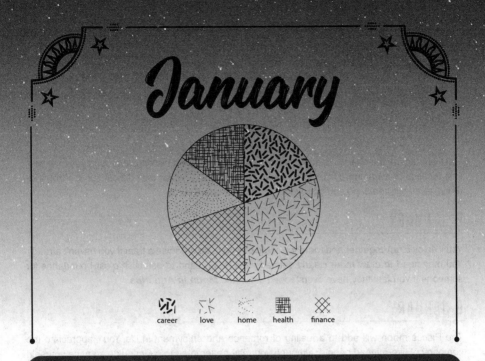

career love home health finance

Notes: the pie charts such as the one above listed for each month show energy distribution according to the stars for the month ahead. If you wish to make changes in the areas of your finances, health, career, love or home and you see there is a large amount of energy in that sector in the chart your endeavours should succeed as long as you have prepared well in advance. The charts also show which areas will potentially have the most focus in your life during the month.

The moon sign listed for each day's entry in the diary is the position of the moon at the end of the day in Greenwich Mean Time (GMT). To gain the most information about a particular day's circumstances, read the day before and the day after for a complete picture.

1 JANUARY

Happy New Year! You'll enjoy a change of pace from your usual New Year's Day, and may receive an unexpected visitor or enjoy a surprise. You'll appreciate the sense that this year will include new horizons. ***Moon enters Capricorn.***

2 JANUARY

The new moon and supermoon in Capricorn will kick-start a fresh phase for you in the areas of you life you share such as duties, responsibilities, finances and space at home. Take a moment to consider your best step forward. You may receive good news to do with work, travel, study or a favourite project.

3 JANUARY

This is a good time to consider how you could make your daily work schedule and your chores a little more streamlined so that you work more efficiently from day to day. A focus on planning ahead this year will be rewarding. ***Moon enters Aquarius.***

4 JANUARY

You'll appreciate the chance to do something different, although the people around you may be a little restless or even unpredictable so aim to be adaptable – which isn't difficult for you! You'll be drawn to music, romance and good food. ***Moon in Aquarius.***

5 JANUARY

You'll enjoy a get-together and romance could blossom, so organise a treat if you haven't already. You may need to draw more clearly defined lines in the sand to establish clear boundaries for someone if you feel they have overstepped the mark. ***Moon in Aquarius.***

6 JANUARY

The Pisces moon will add to a feeling of romance and enjoyment in life. You'll appreciate the company of like-minded people, although you may be tempted to overindulge so pace yourself! ***Moon in Pisces.***

7 JANUARY

Your ability to understand others is strong at the moment so relationships are likely to proceed relatively smoothly, especially those with people you love. But if someone you must share work or duties with surprises you avoid a belligerent approach and aim to progress. ***Moon in Pisces.***

8 JANUARY

You'll get on well with colleagues and those you must share duties and responsibilities with. Take a moment to arrange get-togethers both at work and play as you're likely to enjoy them. ***Moon in Aries.***

9 JANUARY

Romance could go off the dial so ensure you have something special organised with someone you love. Singles: this is a good time to organise a night out or to go to a club you enjoy as you could meet an earthy, dependable character. If you're shopping this weekend avoid overspending. ***Moon in Aries.***

10 JANUARY

You can achieve a great deal, so ensure you put your best foot forward. A meeting and communications are likely to go well, but you must attend to the details or misunderstandings could occur. ***Moon enters Taurus.***

11 JANUARY

You like to achieve goals quickly, so when there are delays you can feel super frustrated. Pace yourself as you could feel impatient as others are going to want to take their time or may miss key details at work. Travel and communications may be complex or even confused. You'll enjoy relaxing and a special meeting is likely to go well. *Moon in Taurus.*

12 JANUARY

Try to get loose ends to do with key communications and negotiations tied up over the next two days before Mercury turns retrograde on Friday, to avoid delays or having to renegotiate at a later time. *Moon in Taurus.*

13 JANUARY

When the moon is in your own sign you'll feel more in your element and be chatty and flexible. However, not everyone will feel the same, so aim to adjust to other people's mindsets and paces if necessary. *Moon in Gemini.*

14 JANUARY

You may receive key news to do with work or a special project or interest. A work matter or health schedule may need to be rethought. You will receive key news while planning a trip or while travelling. If delays occur, be flexible. *Moon in Gemini.*

15 JANUARY

The next two days may be fairly intense for you. For some, this will be in a pleasant way as you boost your status and direction in life and make plans for big change. If you find your situation changes due to matters outside your control, aim to be flexible and work towards the bigger-picture results you want. *Moon enters Cancer.*

16 JANUARY

You may receive key news or will undergo considerable change. For some this will be to do with a project or venture; for others it will be in your work, status and general direction. *Moon in Cancer.*

17 JANUARY

The Cancerian full moon shines a light on your finances and, for some, personal life. Key changes there will mean you must consider the big picture, including health, shared responsibilities and duties. Base decisions on practicalities.

18 JANUARY

This is a good time to make financial and personal decisions that will produce more security and happiness in your life. Look for ways to transform your daily life so it matches your favourite interests and ideas more. **Moon in Leo.**

19 JANUARY

You may receive good news to do with a favourite project or person. Romance could blossom and a trip or venture could open doors, so be proactive. **Moon in Leo.**

20 JANUARY

The sun in Aquarius for the next four weeks will bring your inner adventurer out. You'll feel more inclined to be outgoing and new ventures and social circles will appeal. **Moon in Leo.**

21 JANUARY

These next few days are ideal for socialising and networking. You'll enjoy meeting new people and organising your thoughts and projects too. **Moon in Virgo.**

22 JANUARY

A lovely activity such as a trip or social event will be enjoyable; there may even be a therapeutic quality to events. Teaching, study, research and broadening your horizons will appeal. Avoid being overly sensitive and be practical. **Moon enters Libra.**

23 JANUARY

This is a good day for travel, meetings and furthering your work and personal ventures. You'll enjoy talking with upbeat and innovative people and may even return to an old haunt. **Moon in Libra.**

24 JANUARY

Your charm is shining through at the moment, so be confident and initiate ideas and projects. This is a good time for health and well-being appointments and to boost your energy and appearance. **Moon in Libra.**

25 JANUARY

You're communicating well, so even if you feel under pressure at any point or simply very strongly about an issue, put on your negotiating hat and work your way through talks to gain the best outcome. **Moon in Scorpio.**

26 JANUARY

You may need to go over old ground. You may revisit a topic you believed had already be sewn up, or may enjoy a reunion. *Moon in Scorpio.*

27 JANUARY

When the moon is in Sagittarius you feel more outgoing and adopt a can-do attitude. You'll appreciate putting your back into your work and could create wonderful outcomes now, so be motivated! *Moon in Sagittarius.*

28 JANUARY

The moon in your seventh house spells one thing: romance! And what better time than the end of the week to indulge those you love in some romantic time together. If you're single you'll feel more outgoing and may meet an upbeat, larger-than-life character. *Moon in Sagittarius.*

29 JANUARY

This may feel like an intense time for you as a trip or a get-together will mean you must communicate better. You may hear key financial or personal news. It's a good time to consider a fresh budget if you have overspent. *Moon in Capricorn.*

30 JANUARY

You may hear unexpected news or someone may behave unpredictably. Your usual routine may change. Be prepared to be spontaneous but avoid rash decisions. *Moon in Capricorn.*

31 JANUARY

There is a sense that you will regain a degree of normality and an even keel, especially in your personal life and regarding a project. It's a good day for talks and romance. *Moon in Aquarius.*

February

career   love   home   health   finance

1 FEBRUARY

The new moon in Aquarius will spotlight the chance to begin a fresh project or venture that signifies something new for you. Be bold and adventurous for the best results.

2 FEBRUARY

You'll feel inspired to follow your interests so consider how you could add more of what you love into your life. If you feel there are roadblocks to your plans, find new ways to look at obstacles so you can overcome them. ***Moon enters Pisces.***

3 FEBRUARY

This is a good day to consider your deeper thoughts and wishes, especially to do with work and health. It's a good day for meditation, yoga and communing with nature. ***Moon in Pisces.***

4 FEBRUARY

An important work or personal matter can be decided as you're likely to gain the information you need. You may be drawn to consider a fresh path or project that involves the need to travel or to change some of what you already do. ***Moon in Pisces.***

5 FEBRUARY

When the moon is in Aries you may feel a little impulsive, so be spontaneous but avoid decisions you'll regret. A good day for health and beauty treatments. ***Moon in Aries.***

6 FEBRUARY

Take things one step at a time with a favourite project or interest to avoid rash decisions. Take a moment to consider your ideas in relation to someone else's and see if mutual ground can be reached. *Moon in Aries.*

7 FEBRUARY

As the moon aligns with Uranus you may experience an unexpected development and be surprised by your own responses. It's a good day to try something new and to enjoy your fave activities, but you must remain grounded and practical. *Moon in Taurus.*

8 FEBRUARY

This is a good day to put your back into your work projects, especially those that involve collaborations, as you're likely to achieve a great deal and will appreciate a sense of co-operation. *Moon in Taurus.*

9 FEBRUARY

When the moon is in your own sign you feel chattier and more at ease. You'll appreciate the chance to reconnect with someone you love or admire. A key meeting at work could be positive, but you must avoid impulsiveness. *Moon in Gemini.*

10 FEBRUARY

A work meeting is likely to go well. If you are planning a special event or a social visit this is likely to go well. Just ensure you have planned ahead well to avoid any unnecessary surprises. *Moon in Gemini.*

11 FEBRUARY

You'll appreciate the chance to gain a strong foothold with a project that could mean considerable changes further down the line. You'll also enjoy reconnecting with someone you feel a strong connection with. *Moon in Cancer.*

12 FEBRUARY

Today's Cancerian moon will mean you're more sensitive than usual, so take a moment to unwind and de-stress. Someone may confide their feelings to you, and if you need a little support it will be available so ensure you reach out. Avoid taking the mood swings of others personally. *Moon in Cancer.*

13 FEBRUARY

This is another good day to ensure your emotions aren't leading you into feeling more sensitive than need be. This aside, you'll appreciate the chance to get together with people you love and enjoy favourite activities. A reunion will be enjoyable even if strong emotions arise. *Moon in Cancer.*

14 FEBRUARY

Happy St Valentine's Day! This is always a quirky day when we hear unexpected news or gain the chance to reveal our true feelings. You may be surprised by news you hear. It's a good day to get in touch with someone you love, so be bold! *Moon in Leo.*

15 FEBRUARY

Someone in a position of power may have clear influence over you. You may not immediately agree with them, but you can nevertheless work towards a mutual agreement. *Moon in Leo.*

16 FEBRUARY

The Leo full moon will shine a light on the way you communicate. Aim to be bold, especially at work, and find ways to express yourself confidently and clearly. For some mid-June Geminis this full moon will spotlight the importance of having a solid base at home and making this a priority now even if changes are occurring at work. *Moon enters Virgo late in the day.*

17 FEBRUARY

This is an excellent day for talks at work and concerning your general direction, hopes and aims, especially with a personal or business partner. Romance could flourish. You may receive good news. *Moon in Virgo.*

18 FEBRUARY

As the sun enters the zodiac sign Pisces you are likely to enjoy being more creative and romantic. You may express your imagination more both at work and at home. You may already be drawn to art, movies and dance to a greater degree than usual. Take some time out to enjoy being inspired. *Moon in Libra.*

19 FEBRUARY

This is a good weekend to focus on creating a lovely environment for yourself and those you love. You will be drawn to doing something different and will enjoy a fresh environment or activity. *Moon in Libra.*

20 FEBRUARY

This is a good day to focus on relaxation and recharging your batteries. You may not agree with everyone, so avoid making life difficult by looking for common ground rather than conflict. If you need a little help ask for it; it's available. *Moon in Libra.*

21 FEBRUARY

You'll feel more motivated as the day goes by and will be productive. If you've been putting chores off, this is the day to finally get them done! It's a good day to enquire about new work or health projects and to use your creativity and imagination. *Moon enters Scorpio.*

22 FEBRUARY

You'll feel empowered by your work and social connections. However, you won't automatically get on with everyone so ensure you give those you tend to disagree with a wide berth. *Moon in Scorpio.*

23 FEBRUARY

You'll enjoy being with like-minded people and those who inspire you. Romance could truly blossom so ensure you organise a date or a night in! *Moon in Sagittarius.*

24 FEBRUARY

This is another excellent day for romance. Creative Geminis will feel inspired and the spiritually minded will find this a progressive time. Avoid absent-mindedness and mislaying important valuables. *Moon in Sagittarius.*

25 FEBRUARY

Communications may be a little erratic, so ensure you back up computers and allow extra time for travel as there may be some delays or unexpected changes to your usual routine. Avoid misunderstandings by being super clear and ensuring you are on the same page as those you communicate with. *Moon enters Capricorn.*

26 FEBRUARY

Communications and travel may be better unless obstacles occurred yesterday, in which case this will be a good day to sort them out. This is also a good day for floating ideas at work. You'll appreciate the chance to take part in activities you enjoy. *Moon in Capricorn.*

27 FEBRUARY

You'll appreciate the sense that there is some stability in your relationships. A financial matter may require a little more attention. Someone from your past can help sort out your finances. Take a moment to increase the connections and relationships you enjoy and to spend time with those you love. *Moon enters Aquarius.*

28 FEBRUARY

You'll appreciate the opportunity to look at key relationships and duties in a new light. You may even uncover fresh information that provides you with the chance to broaden your horizons at work or with a project or venture. *Moon in Aquarius.*

March

career	love	home	health	finance

1 MARCH

The strong bond you have with someone is hard to ignore. You'll find that a person you love or who has a strong influence on you will be helpful and supportive. Think laterally but be practical if you must overcome a difficult situation. *Moon enters Pisces.*

2 MARCH

The Pisces new moon signals the chance to turn a corner. For some this will be in your social life and in connection with a group, friend or organisation, and for others at work. Look for inspired ways to move forward.

3 MARCH

Key developments will take your focus. For some these will be at work, and for others via a project, study or travel. Take a moment to ground yourself and then put your best foot forward. Avoid being overcome by emotions and maintain a clear perspective. *Moon in Pisces.*

4 MARCH

Today's Aries moon may highlight someone's feelings or sensitivities; they may feel rejected or sidelined. If it's you who feels like this find a way to improve your situation or relationship rather than looking for failings in your connection. If you have felt under the weather, take short breaks where you can. *Moon in Aries.*

5 MARCH

A key meeting could be fortunate, especially at work. If you're looking for work or a fresh project it's a good time to make calls and circulate your resume. News may be fortunate but may also feel exaggerated in some way, so check the details before making a commitment to a decision. *Moon in Aries.*

6 MARCH

Developments will take you into fresh territory, so be adaptable. For some this will be at work and for others within a change of environment or relationship. Look outside the box at your options. *Moon in Taurus.*

7 MARCH

As the moon in Taurus aligns with unpredictable Uranus events may seem a little out of the ordinary or quirky. A fresh routine or the chance to do something different could be enjoyable. *Moon in Taurus.*

8 MARCH

This is a good day to visit somewhere different and to meet new people. You may be drawn to a fresh environment. Meetings are likely to go well. Reach out to friends and groups as you could make some lovely connections. *Moon enters Gemini.*

9 MARCH

The Gemini moon will help you to get ahead with your various projects. If you have suffered ill health of late this is a good day to consult experts. *Moon in Gemini.*

10 MARCH

As your sign's ruler Mercury enters Pisces you will feel increasingly creative and inspired over the coming weeks. Spiritually minded Geminis will enjoy deepening your interest in the esoteric. This is a good day to make commitments to a project or person. *Moon in Gemini.*

11 MARCH

Your intuition is on top form so trust your gut instincts, especially at work and regarding finances. This is another day when meetings and communications are likely to go well, so take the initiative. *Moon in Cancer.*

12 MARCH

You'll enjoy getting together with like-minded people. A meeting with a friend or family member will be enjoyable. Romance, the arts, beauty, music and film will all entice your interests this weekend, so ensure you have something special planned. *Moon in Cancer.*

13 MARCH

This is an ideal day for romance and get-togethers. You'll appreciate spending time with someone special and organising fun events. You'll also be drawn to movies and art and may feel idealistic and forgetful, so keep your feet on the ground! *Moon enters Leo.*

14 MARCH

You're known as a good communicator and you can certainly show off your abilities. You're particularly good at reading the room, and this quality will come in handy. *Moon in Leo.*

15 MARCH

You're a people person and your charisma is undeniable, but you won't always get on with everyone! You may feel a little adversarial or moody so be bold, but if you feel conflict is bubbling under the surface take things one step at a time. *Moon in Leo.*

16 MARCH

Today's Virgo moon will bring your more practical side out and encourage you to be more accommodating of others. Trust in the advice of someone you know has your back. *Moon in Virgo.*

17 MARCH

You'll enjoy being spontaneous, and an impromptu get-together will be enjoyable. *Moon in Virgo.*

18 MARCH

The Virgo full moon will shine a light on your personal life. You may be ready to embrace a fresh approach to your activities and to welcome new people into your inner circle. On the other hand, if you feel a particular relationship has run its coursethis could be a parting of ways. Avoid being hyper-critical or yourself and others.

19 MARCH

The Libran moon will help you to be inspired and at the same time imaginative about your various commitments, chores and obligations. You can make changes to the way you see your general direction and to your career. Think innovatively. You'll enjoy adding a little luxury to your environment. Dance, music and art will appeal. *Moon in Libra.*

20 MARCH

This is the equinox, when the sun enters Aries. During the next four weeks you may find that your social, work and health lives become a real focus. Find the time to boost your health and vitality as your life may become busier over the coming month. *Moon in Scorpio.*

21 MARCH

A key trip, travel news or developments will be more significant than meets the eye. Arrange for a social event, as you're likely to enjoy it. If you're spiritually minded an event could broaden your horizons. **Moon in Scorpio.**

22 MARCH

You're communicating well at the moment, so trust your skill sets. A change of routine or of schedule may come from out of the blue. If you must begin something new and feel out of your depth, believe in yourself. Avoid snap decisions. **Moon enters Sagittarius.**

23 MARCH

You'll enjoy being with like-minded people. It's a good time for spiritual and artistic endeavours. You may receive key news that is inspiring. **Moon in Sagittarius.**

24 MARCH

You'll feel more practical and grounded, especially if some developments have taken you outside your comfort zone. Rest assured you will adapt to circumstances that may seem out of your control. You'll appreciate encouragement from someone you trust or admire. **Moon enters Capricorn.**

25 MARCH

While certain people and events will be falling into place you may discover someone is a little obstinate. If it's you, find the time to be your usual adaptable self and avoid giving in to someone's demands – unless, on second analysis, they do make sense. **Moon in Capricorn.**

26 MARCH

A change of environment and the chance to meet someone who inspires you will be enjoyable, so be outgoing as a get-together or trip will be fun. **Moon in Capricorn.**

27 MARCH

Be adventurous, as you'll enjoy doing something different. You may meet a new group of people or will enjoy a fun visit. You may make a new friend or deepen an existing friendship. **Moon in Aquarius.**

28 MARCH

This is a good day for making a commitment. For some this will be regarding a work matter, and for others a fun new project. Just ensure you're happy with the bigger-picture principles and ethics involved in what you're planning to do. If not, it's a good day to negotiate. **Moon in Aquarius.**

29 MARCH

The Pisces moon will bring your inner idealist out, so remember to be practical. You may also be inclined to want to spend time with your favourite people, so ensure you organise a meeting with someone you love. *Moon in Pisces.*

30 MARCH

You'll be drawn to romance, the arts, spirituality and music. You may also tend to be seeing the world through rose-coloured glasses, so ensure you have your feet on the ground if you're making key decisions. *Moon in Pisces.*

31 MARCH

The Aries moon spells a busy and sociable day. You may feel restless, so ensure you channel these feelings into activities that bring positive results such as work on projects you love and spending time with like-minded people. *Moon in Aries.*

April

career   love   home   health   finance

1 APRIL

The Aries new moon spells a fresh chapter for you in your personal life, and for some Twins the new beginning will be at work or in relation to a friend, group or organisation. Be bold but avoid making changes in your life purely out of boredom. Move into circles where you already have a natural interest.

2 APRIL

You may receive key news especially if you didn't already yesterday. This may be in connection with a health matter. Someone is likely to ask for your help. If you need support or advice it will be available. You may hear unexpected news or will bump into an old friend. ***Moon enters Taurus.***

3 APRIL

This is a good day for collaborations and co-operation. You may find that by working closely with someone you gain better results. You could make long-term changes financially but must consider your options carefully. ***Moon in Taurus.***

4 APRIL

Take your decisions under advisement so you make the best choices. You'll feel motivated by your goals but may be prone to taking unnecessary risks. A trip or meeting is likely to be a success. *Moon in Taurus.*

5 APRIL

You may be asked to make a choice or a commitment and this will signal a fresh direction or the final stages of much planning and anticipation. If someone is not in agreement with your plans ensure you explain your position carefully. Make sure your plans resonate deeply or you may need to revise them at a later date. *Moon in Gemini.*

6 APRIL

This is a good day to make great strides ahead with a project such as a study course or travel or at work. You may simply feel more fulfilled in your everyday chores and ventures. It's a good day for meetings and for planning, so take the initiative. *Moon in Gemini.*

7 APRIL

This is another good day for meetings and get-togethers, both at work and socially. If you have important matters to discuss you'll make headway so organise talks and meetings. A short trip and plans for a longer one are likely to be met with positive results. However, you may need to persuade someone close of your plans. *Moon in Cancer.*

8 APRIL

This is a lovely day for the arts, romance, dance, music and everything your heart desires! Just ensure you avoid overspending if you're at the shops as you may not be able to stop your impulses! *Moon in Cancer.*

9 APRIL

You'll enjoy socialising as much as you'll enjoy indulging in a favourite activity. If you're studying, this is an excellent time to get ahead with your projects. Someone special may suggest an impromptu get-together, which you'll enjoy. *Moon in Cancer.*

10 APRIL

A tense aspect could bring everyone's anxiety into focus. Take a little extra time for communications as you may misunderstand others and vice versa. Aim to take the tension out of interactions to avoid conflict. *Moon in Leo.*

11 APRIL

If you or someone close tends to be stubborn or uncompromising, take a moment to gather your thoughts or you may reach a stalemate where you cannot even agree to disagree! Communications could settle down later in the day if you approach them sensitively. **Moon in Leo.**

12 APRIL

You may experience an ideal situation, but if you find the opposite occurs check that you haven't been seeing the world through rose-coloured glasses. Someone special will be a true help to you so ensure you reach out for trusted, loyal support. The arts, romance, travel and music will all have a soothing effect. **Moon in Leo.**

13 APRIL

The key to success at the moment for you is co-operation and collaboration. If you work together with others as a team you can only succeed! **Moon in Virgo.**

14 APRIL

A lovely friend, colleague, group or organisation will prove to be a true help and support to you. Artistic and creative Twins will be particularly inspired and/or busy. Romance could blossom now too, so organise a date if you haven't already! **Moon enters Libra.**

15 APRIL

Your focus is likely to change as you embrace an inspired frame of mind or project. Spiritually minded and creative Twins may be particularly busy over the coming few weeks. Make space for your favourite interests. **Moon in Libra.**

16 APRIL

The Libran full moon will spotlight your personal life and the changes going on there. You are completing a long chapter and will be ready to embrace the new. Look for peace, harmony and balance for the best results.

17 APRIL

The Scorpio moon will focus your attention increasingly over the next two days on chores and daily duties, yet you are more likely to be drawn to enjoying quality time with someone special. Organise your day to get work done in the morning, giving you time for someone special in the evening. Avoid tense talks in the morning. **Moon in Scorpio.**

18 APRIL

You can't agree with everyone all the time, but you do have diplomacy on your side and are well equipped to deal with tension in a clever way to dispel conflict. Your charm and tact will be in demand, especially as you may hear unexpected news or will need to alter your usual routine or activities out of the blue. You'll enjoy an impromptu chat or get-together. *Moon in Scorpio.*

19 APRIL

You'll feel motivated to get things done even if you don't agree with everyone you must collaborate with. There is merit in being outgoing and upbeat, but you must avoid conflict as it could quickly escalate. *Moon in Sagittarius.*

20 APRIL

As the sun enters Taurus you'll feel more grounded and able to negotiate unexpected developments. Your decision-making is likely to be increasingly based on practicalities and realities rather than pie-in-the-sky notions. *Moon in Sagittarius.*

21 APRIL

The Capricorn moon will help bring your more practical side out, so rest assured the decisions you make are likely to be reasonable and grounded, enabling you to take action in small but certain steps. *Moon in Capricorn.*

22 APRIL

This is an earthy moon and will bring both your and your partner's more sensuous sides out. It's a good time to plan a lovely night out or in! Avoid accepting criticism or feeling over-sensitive about someone who themselves may simply be overly sensitive. *Moon in Capricorn.*

23 APRIL

You'll enjoy a reunion with someone you love and admire. However, you may also need to make a commitment to a particular path, and if you're unsure you may need to express your uncertainty or do your research so that your path becomes clearer. *Moon in Aquarius.*

24 APRIL

It's possible that you'll get your lines crossed with someone you are generally fairly clear with. If you're working or arranging finances, matters will benefit from additional focus to avoid mistakes being made. You'll enjoy relaxing this evening. *Moon in Aquarius.*

25 APRIL

The Pisces moon can bring your ideals and hopes out to the forefront of your mind. This means you're optimistic but your expectations may also be a little high, so take things one step at a time. **Moon in Pisces.**

26 APRIL

You could make great progress with your various projects and will be galvanised to try something new and may even feel a little head in the clouds, so you must be prepared to be practical. Be inspired by people you admire. **Moon in Pisces.**

27 APRIL

You may receive ideal news and will enjoy a trip or get-together. You may even be in a position where a dream comes true. However, if you undergo a disappointment, consider whether you may have over-estimated your circumstances. If so, you will gain the chance now to put things right. **Moon enters Aries.**

28 APRIL

This is an excellent day for conversations and meetings with those who are influential in your life such as personal and business partners, friends and family. You could also make positive financial changes now with the right advice and guidance. **Moon in Aries.**

29 APRIL

Try to get key paperwork and agreements tied up to avoid having to revise your plans at a later date. Mercury turns retrograde today so find the time to also tie up loose ends of important financial matters. You may receive key news and will enjoy a meeting or news. **Moon in Aries.**

30 APRIL

The partial solar eclipse in Taurus signifies an important turning point for you. For some Geminis this will be due to changes at work; for others due to health; and, for some, simply because you are ready to alter how you go about your life day to day. Be practical and grounded with your decisions for the best results. A social or group involvement may step up to a new level.

May

career love home health finance

1 MAY

Key projects and meetings could make great progress. A lovely social event could bring new people and ideas your way. If you're trying to change major aspects of your life or simply take up new interests, this is it! *Moon in Taurus.*

2 MAY

You'll appreciate the feeling that you are more outgoing and upbeat, especially socially, over the coming weeks. You may attract a fresh social circle or will be drawn to new pursuits and ideas. *Moon in Gemini.*

3 MAY

This is another good day to be adventurous and inquisitive about new projects, ideas and people. You may feel more inclined to broaden your usual social group and to embrace fresh ventures such as travel plans and study. *Moon in Gemini.*

4 MAY

You may hear unexpected news at work or from a friend. You may also realise you can be of great help to someone. If you need advice or support yourself you may find it in unusual places. *Moon in Gemini.*

5 MAY

A change in your usual routine may bring fresh ideas your way. An unexpected development at work will ask that you be more flexible and work spontaneously and under pressure. You may bump into an old friend or hear from someone from out of the blue. If health has been up and down, expect more developments in this area of your life or that of someone close. *Moon in Cancer.*

6 MAY

News is likely to be positive so take the time to look for people who can help you to move forward, especially regarding health and work matters. You may hear from an old friend or will receive the news you're waiting for. *Moon in Cancer.*

7 MAY

Get busy this weekend, as you'll reap the rewards of industriousness. If you'd like to work at tidying up your home or office this is a good time for a working bee. Gardening and work outdoors will also proceed well. Consider enlisting the help of friends and make it a social event! Sports and adventurous activities will prove motivating. *Moon in Leo.*

8 MAY

This is a good day to be adventurous with your collaborations and interests and to indulge in romance, art and music. You may receive an unexpected call or visit unless you already did yesterday. *Moon in Leo.*

9 MAY

You will feel motivated to get things right at work, even if you are suffering from a minor case of Mondayitis. Try to get key talks and paperwork completed before Mercury turns retrograde tomorrow. *Moon enters Virgo.*

10 MAY

You may hear key news at work or regarding health. You'll gain the chance to review some of your decisions over the coming weeks. Your sign's ruler will be retrograde for the next few weeks, so if you find some communications are a little tougher than usual aim to be more patient. Travel may be delayed for some Twins. *Moon in Virgo.*

11 MAY

As Jupiter changes signs from Pisces to Aries you may notice that some people in your midst become a little feistier over these two days. You may also tend to expect more from them. If conflict is brewing, take steps to de-escalate it rather than adding to it for the best results. *Moon in Virgo.*

12 MAY

You may be called upon to be the voice of reason, especially in your personal life, so rely on your diplomatic skills and be tactful if you must settle a difference of opinion. Look for the balance and you'll enjoy seeing concrete results for your hard work. *Moon in Libra.*

13 MAY

You may reconnect with someone from your past or will receive key news from someone you know via work or regarding health. If you meet someone new this person may be more significant than immediately meets the eye. *Moon in Libra.*

14 MAY

People around you may appear more emotional or outspoken over the next two days, especially at work. Give their opinions a wide berth if you disagree. Romance could blossom, so organise a treat! *Moon in Scorpio.*

15 MAY

You won't agree with everyone, so ensure you are tactful if someone in a position of authority challenges your beliefs. A health or work matter will require more attention so that you can make insightful decisions. If you're working this may feel like an inconvenience, so make sure you take things one step at a time. *Moon in Scorpio.*

16 MAY

The total lunar eclipse in Scorpio may feel particularly intense, so aim to maintain a sense of perspective especially regarding work and health. If a change of routine is on the cards, plan ahead to avoid disappointments. Be practical and avoid impulsive decisions. *Moon enters Sagittarius.*

17 MAY

Changes you wish to make may take a turn for the better, especially if you have laid solid groundwork. But if you discover an oversight, take this as your cue to set things right. A commitment could be ideal if you have done adequate research. *Moon in Sagittarius.*

18 MAY

This is a good day for socialising and networking, so aim to make meetings productive and fun. If you have over- or underestimated someone you're likely to find out today, so ensure you take practical steps to remedy any oversights. *Moon in Capricorn.*

19 MAY

This is an excellent day to get ahead with your various projects such as work, travel plans, study and health matters. If you wish to change track this is a productive day to set new plans in motion. *Moon in Capricorn.*

20 MAY

You'll appreciate the chance to talk and truly connect with someone special, so make plans for a get together if you haven't already. You may be drawn to return to an old haunt and a reunion will be pleasant. Travel plans may need to be re-considered or confirmed. *Moon in Aquarius.*

21 MAY

As the sun enters your sign you'll enjoy the sense that communications and relationships are improving, but you must avoid making assumptions. You may receive key news to do with work or health. It's a good day for a catch-up with someone special. *Moon in Aquarius.*

22 MAY

Your projects and ventures will gather their own momentum, so if you're happy with the way things are going you'll be happy with today's outcomes. But if events seem to be going too quickly for you, take steps to slow things down until you're sure. *Moon enters Pisces.*

23 MAY

If you'd like to slow things down such as negotiations or work projects this should be possible, but if you prefer things to speed up you may encounter a delay. Someone may seem a little obstinate or stubborn, so look for ways you could encourage them to be happier. A social or work meeting will be productive. *Moon in Pisces.*

24 MAY

This is an excellent day to get things done, especially at work. If you need the co-operation of a friend, colleague, group or organisation make tracks to set a positive agreement in place as it's likely to take. You'll also enjoy socialising and networking. *Moon in Pisces.*

25 MAY

A change of environment or pace could be ideal for you. A spontaneous meeting will be fruitful, so if you receive an unexpected invitation consider attending. You may bump into an old friend or hear about changes to come at work or in your daily routine. It's a good day to make changes at work or health-wise. *Moon in Aries.*

26 MAY

This is a good day for talks and meetings. If you have a beauty or medical matter to discuss, this is your day! It's a good day for health appointments. *Moon in Aries.*

27 MAY

You may experience difficulty in communications, which is likely to stem from different values and attitudes. Take a moment to de-escalate tension rather than adding to drama or tension. *Moon in Taurus.*

28 MAY

You'll feel more inclined to enjoy life while Venus is in Taurus for the next few weeks. You'll appreciate the time to feather your nest this weekend, with attention to details at home such as adding more of a touch of luxury to your environment. Avoid overindulging and overspending as you'll regret it! *Moon in Taurus.*

29 MAY

This is likely to be a big day, whether you're working or socialising or both! If you're travelling, the trip will take you to a familiar place or one where your nostalgia rises. Take time out if emotions are intense and relax. *Moon enters Gemini.*

30 MAY

The Gemini new moon signals a fresh phase for you, especially if you were born today or earlier in May. If you were born in June you're likely to be turning a corner in a work context, or embracing a new daily routine at the least. It's a good time to get paperwork and health schedules shipshape. *Moon in Gemini.*

31 MAY

Another good day for meetings, both at work and regarding important personal matters such as health and well-being. New plans and ideas will attract you, so be imaginative and adventurous. *Moon in Gemini.*

June

| career | love | home | health | finance |

1 JUNE

The Cancerian moon may bring your emotions out and you may not feel your usual friendly self. Avoid taking other people's opinions personally and take things one step at a time. You will be feeling super intuitive, so trust your instincts. ***Moon in Cancer.***

2 JUNE

You prefer communications to be straightforward, with everyone together as one, but sometimes opinions simply differ. Avoid allowing someone's ideas to sidetrack your own, unless of course there is merit in their thoughts and plans. ***Moon in Cancer.***

3 JUNE

Your sign's ruler, Mercury, ends its retrograde phase today and you may over the coming weeks see that communications and travel become easier to navigate. You may receive key news that will merit close attention, especially to do with work, health and finances and the way these areas relate to a shared circumstance such as taxes or communal space at home. ***Moon enters Leo.***

4 JUNE

Consider your true values and priorities. Ensure you are clear and open to new ideas. You'll enjoy an impromptu get-together, and a health or work development should boost your optimism. **Moon in Leo.**

5 JUNE

The Leo moon may cause you to question some of your decisions, especially regarding those close to you at home or in your family. This is a good time to look for therapeutic and positive ways ahead rather than looking at the glass as being half full. A travel or personal matter will deserve careful attention. Avoid rash decisions. **Moon in Leo.**

6 JUNE

When the moon is in Virgo you'll find you are more practical, hands-on and realistic about your various tasks and projects, especially at home and with family, making this a good time for planning and organisation. **Moon in Virgo.**

7 JUNE

The Virgo moon will provide a little more stability and security to events, enabling you to find a stronger foundation especially in your daily life and work. You may experience a surprise or synchronicitous event. You may bump into an old friend or hear unexpected news. This is a good time for health and beauty appointments. **Moon in Virgo.**

8 JUNE

You can get a great deal done so aim to be hands-on and plan ahead. However, you may be liable to overcommit to various chores and events, so take a moment out of your schedule to work out what and who matter most to you and take it from there. **Moon enters Libra.**

9 JUNE

This is a good time to initiate important talks with people who are in a position of influence in your life such as colleagues, friends, organisations and employers. Find ways to present your ideas in their best light. You could make great progress at work, so take the initiative. A personal matter can proceed well with a balanced outlook. **Moon in Libra.**

10 JUNE

Be practical and take the initiative with your various projects and ventures, as you could make great headway. Your mind is clear and sparking on all cylinders, so trust you have the correct approach and make headway, especially with travel ideas, work, study and health matters. **Moon enters Scorpio.**

11 JUNE

You may be surprised by developments or will enjoy a change of routine. Plan something different. If work presents a challenge, be prepared to discuss your ideas and values to clarify your position. You will overcome any hurdles with clear communications. *Moon in Scorpio.*

12 JUNE

You'll enjoy being with someone you love this weekend, so if you have nothing special planned yet make a date! Just make sure everyone's on the same page to avoid mix-ups and disagreements. *Moon enters Sagittarius.*

13 JUNE

As your sign's ruler Mercury enters your sign you'll find communications will be busy over the coming weeks. You may be particularly sociable and in demand. You may also be asked to help others, and your interest in health and well-being will be the key to success. *Moon in Sagittarius.*

14 JUNE

The full moon and supermoon in Sagittarius is spotlighting how you feel about someone. Some Twins' focus is likely to be on work and health as your feelings become clearer about how you wish to proceed. A friend or organisation is likely to be supportive and will enable you to make well-informed decisions if you're unclear of your path.

15 JUNE

There is great merit in being decisive, but it's important to avoid rash decisions. However, you may be asked to act on impulse or spontaneously to help someone or to ensure you are in a strong position yourself. Be prepared to act swiftly and with full understanding of the repercussions of your actions It's a good day for a health appointment. *Moon in Capricorn.*

16 JUNE

This is an excellent time for progress at work and, for some, financially. You may find that someone at work or from your past will be particularly helpful. A health matter can progress; just ensure that the information you act on is sound to avoid mistakes. *Moon enters Aquarius.*

17 JUNE

This is a good time to make impromptu changes to your usual schedule to give yourself more room to move and to enjoy a little more spontaneity. You may enjoy being more inventive and imaginative at work and in your relationships. Someone may surprise you. *Moon in Aquarius.*

18 JUNE

Take a moment to ensure you're happy with the agreements you make this weekend. If you're simply following the crowd, double-check you wish to be doing what you are doing! A financial or work matter may involve more focus than you prefer, but it will be worthwhile. *Moon in Aquarius.*

19 JUNE

You'll enjoy romance and being with like-minded people. A visit to a venue with music, art and inspiring company may appeal. If a challenge arises, rest assured you can overcome it. *Moon in Pisces.*

20 JUNE

The Pisces moon will bring your wish to be in good compnay to the surface, so you'll seek out like-minded people. Your idealistic, philosophical side may also come out, making this a good day for discussions and meetings as you'll feel inclined to listen to others' ideas without judgement. Artistic Geminis will be inspired, so take the time to be creative. *Moon in Pisces.*

21 JUNE

As the sun enters Cancer, marking the solstice, your attention may turn more towards your values and priorities over the coming weeks. Take a moment to assess what and who makes you happy and ensure you give more time to these areas of your life. A financial or personal matter could blossom. *Moon in Aries.*

22 JUNE

You may find your more combative and outgoing side will seek expression. Avoid arguments with people who can be adversarial as they have nothing better to do! Use your intuition; it's spot on. *Moon in Aries.*

23 JUNE

As the moon enters Taurus you'll focus increasingly on being more practical and realistic about work and your chores. You will also enjoy treating yourself and others to some of life's delights. *Moon enters Taurus.*

24 JUNE

You'll enjoy socialising but must avoid overindulgence as you'll regret it! This is a good time to work on better relationships, and clever planning will work in your favour. *Moon in Taurus.*

25 JUNE

You'll appreciate the opportunity to get in touch with those you love on a more relaxed basis. You'll enjoy doing something different for a change this weekend. A commitment could be made, but it may mean you must compromise. Choose your path wisely while being adaptable to new options. *Moon in Taurus.*

26 JUNE

When the moon is in your own sign you feel more in your element. Words may come more easily and you'll enjoy a sense of spontaneity. A short trip or a visit may appeal. You'll enjoy catching up with favourite people. *Moon in Gemini.*

27 JUNE

This is a good day to get ahead at work, so ensure you get on top of your chores and projects as your efforts won't go unrewarded. It's a good day to mend bridges if you have argued with someone or have found communications difficult lately. *Moon in Gemini.*

28 JUNE

You'll enjoy being spontaneous and an impromptu meeting or event will be a surprise and potentially also enjoyable. You may appreciate a financial improvement and may have a debt repaid or will be able to pay off a debt yourself. You may experience an ego boost or compliment. *Moon enters Cancer.*

29 JUNE

The Cancerian new moon will kick-start a fresh chapter in your personal life and, for some, financially. It's a time to be super careful with your finances and decisions to ensure you have done all the necessary groundwork. Be positive, but avoid grandiose plans that are unproven or untested. *Moon in Cancer.*

30 JUNE

You'll feel surer about which decisions must be made, especially in connection with someone close, work or finances. Choose a nurturing stance, beginning with self-nurture. Trust your instincts. *Moon in Cancer.*

July

career   love   home   health   finance

1 JULY

There is a little tension in the air. If you feel motivated by a little stress you'll enjoy your day, but if stress jangles your nerves you may find exercise, meditation or yoga useful. Aim to find positive ways to avoid conflict as otherwise it could escalate quickly. *Moon in Leo.*

2 JULY

You're communicating well and decisions can be made, especially financially and regarding work. However, if you feel you are under pressure to make decisions you do not fully agree with try to find time to negotiate. Avoid allowing tensions to escalate. Find ways to defuse tense conversations for the best results. *Moon in Leo.*

3 JULY

The tension underlying some communications may continue a little, so let sleeping dogs lie unless you must approach a gnarly topic. Avoid overspending, and if finances are in the red consider a new budget. A little negotiation to do with a work or personal project may be tense, but if you stick with your principles you will succeed. *Moon enters Virgo.*

4 JULY

Be sure to use your considerable communication skills as you may find some interactions are tense. You are intrinsically charming and this is one of your secret super powers, so use it! Avoid stirring up emotions and be practical. *Moon in Virgo.*

5 JULY

This is a much better day for communications than the more recent ones, although if you feel events are running under their own steam and have sped up too quickly it's time to apply the brakes. The more tactful you are during this process the better for you. *Moon enters Libra.*

6 JULY

This is a good day for boosting your mental, spiritual, physical and emotional health. Take a moment to consider how you could be functioning better. Someone may ask for your help. If you need expert advice it will be available. It's also a good day for romance. *Moon in Libra.*

7 JULY

We all like a balanced and peaceful life, and when the moon is in Libra you will actively pursue qualities that can bring harmony into your life. You may be super drawn to art, music, dance and romance. You may also be inclined to indulge in good food and drinks, so enjoy a treat but avoid overindulgence as you'll regret it tomorrow! *Moon in Libra.*

8 JULY

You are one of the most adaptable signs of the zodiac, so when delays or obstacles arise you tend to cope better than most. Your flexible, adaptable approach will go well today with circumstances, putting you on top of any challenges. You may not agree with everyone. Avoid taking other people's personal problems personally. You'll enjoy an unexpected or impromptu development or good news. *Moon in Scorpio.*

9 JULY

This is another day to be careful with communications, as they may not go as well as expected. A delay to do with finances or travel may be a thorn on the rose. Avoid taking other people's grandiose statements to heart, especially if their ideas are clearly exaggerated. If you have overspent in the past, now is the time to consider a fresh budget. *Moon in Scorpio.*

10 JULY

You'll enjoy getting together with like-minded people and may also appreciate an ego boost or compliment. A change in your usual schedule will be enjoyable. Someone you love or admire will add a little extra to your day. If you're single and you meet someone this relationship may be more substantial than meets the eye. *Moon enters Sagittarius.*

11 JULY

Someone at work may be more outspoken than usual. You may find their joviality endearing, but if they seem tactless avoid taking their mood personally. You'll enjoy being adventurous and meeting new people. *Moon in Sagittarius.*

12 JULY

The Capricorn moon brings your predilection for good company out and you'll seek out people who are soothing to your nerves. You'll enjoy being with like-minded people and relaxing in the evening when you can. *Moon enters Capricorn.*

13 JULY

The full moon and supermoon in Capricorn will spotlight an important aspect of your life that is changing. For some this will be a key relationship, and for others it will be a financial situation. It's a good time to make solid plans both at work and financially. An agreement could be advantageous, but you must do adequate research.

14 JULY

Double-check you have the right end of the stick, especially if confusion or delays arise. Misunderstandings and mix-ups may occur, especially at work and with someone close. Trust your instincts and intuition as you may be easily misled. *Moon enters Aquarius.*

15 JULY

Your plans and values may differ from those of someone close, so it's important to make plans you all agree to or arguments could arise. If you need a little tension in romance to feel excited you'll enjoy today's vibe, but if you prefer romance to be on an even keel take things one step at a time. *Moon in Aquarius.*

16 JULY

You are likely to receive news at work or regarding finances. It's a good time to make inroads at work and for making long-term commitments. However, a fresh approach may be needed if you encounter obstacles in your negotiations and talks. Be practical and patient with an authority figure. *Moon enters Pisces.*

17 JULY

This is a good day for talks, especially to do with finances and friends and/or an organisation. Romance could blossom, so make a date if you haven't already! You may be a little absent-minded so focus, especially at work. The arts, spirituality and music will all appeal. *Moon in Pisces.*

18 JULY

Key financial decisions may be made. You may be in a position to make a long-term decision or commitment with someone close that could spell considerable change moving forward. Someone may have strong emotions so ensure you maintain perspective. A trip or conversations could open doors. Key news could change how you see someone. *Moon enters Aries.*

19 JULY

The moon in Aries could bring out your combative side. Avoid power struggles as these could leave an unpleasant feeling, especially with someone close, a family member or a friend. Aim to work towards your goals, both at home and at work, and you'll achieve your aims. *Moon in Aries.*

20 JULY

This is a good time to make changes, especially in your personal life and financially, even if there is an intense mood around developments. Take a moment to focus on good communication skills for the best results. A little negotiation or adjustment may be necessary. *Moon enters Taurus.*

21 JULY

Some circumstances may be difficult to adjust to at the moment, so it's important to avoid impulsiveness and rash decisions. You will gain the option of seeing things through to a positive outcome. Trust your intuition and be adaptable for the best measure. *Moon in Taurus.*

22 JULY

As the sun enters Leo you may begin to feel more positive about developments, especially within your general direction and status. You'll also feel more outgoing and chatty over the coming weeks. *Moon in Taurus.*

23 JULY

This is an excellent day for travel, meetings and financial decisions and transactions, especially if you've done adequate research with key investments. A work meeting or social event is likely to be upbeat and enjoyable. *Moon in Gemini.*

24 JULY

You love to chat, but sometimes you can overshare or simply feel restless when the moon is in your sign. The next two days are a case in point. Avoid overwork and spreading yourself too thin. A financial matter will benefit from focus. *Moon in Gemini.*

25 JULY

Keep an eye on communications, arrangements and interactions as you may not agree with everyone all the time! Finances will also benefit from additional focus. If you're shopping avoid impulse buys, as you may regret overspending and overindulging. *Moon enters Cancer.*

26 JULY

Travel and conversations may be a little delayed or complex, so aim to give yourself extra time with your various projects and ventures to avoid frustration or annoyances and disappointments. You could nevertheless accomplish a great deal with focus. *Moon in Cancer.*

27 JULY

This is an excellent day for health and beauty treats and for medical appointments. If you need to mend bridges with anyone, either at work or at home, this is a good day to build relationships. An expert or adviser will be available if you need support or guidance. *Moon in Cancer.*

28 JULY

The Leo new moon points to a fresh chapter regarding your communications and travel. For some, this new moon points to a fresh financial phase or business agreement. It's a good time to update or check that your communication devices and transportation are all in good working condition. You may receive a surprise or must make impromptu changes to plans. Avoid rash decisions but be spontaneous.

29 JULY

The moon in Leo will bring your talkative side out and you'll enjoy socialising and networking. You may be super effective at work, but those close to you may feel a little at odds with your bright ideas. Take the time to discuss your projects with those they concern to avoid mix-ups. *Moon in Leo.*

30 JULY

You are already an adaptable and flexible person, but sometimes even you can be stubborn. Check if you're being obstinate and consider how you might better adapt to circumstances, enabling you to work more efficiently in all areas of your life. *Moon enters Virgo.*

31 JULY

Your projects and ideas are likely to take a step in the right direction. You can make agreements that could be binding, so ensure you are happy with all the terms and conditions. A meeting or news could be upbeat, and you'll enjoy the sense that you will return to somewhere important to you or will have a reunion. *Moon in Virgo.*

August

career   love   home   health   finance

1 AUGUST

You're known as the zodiac's best communicator, but even you can experience difficulties getting your ideas and thoughts across. Today is one such day, so take this into account and take a little extra time and patience to be heard. ***Moon in Virgo.***

2 AUGUST

You may experience an unexpected change of routine or abrupt developments at work. Communications will be much better and you'll be able to make the most of your good communication skills to work towards beneficial outcomes at work, financially and with someone from your past. You may hear unexpectedly from an old friend. ***Moon in Libra.***

3 AUGUST

You'll appreciate the opportunity to improve your circumstances; for example, you may enjoy a get-together or a health or beauty treat. Someone from your past may repay a debt or pay you a compliment. ***Moon in Libra.***

4 AUGUST

Keep your feet on the ground to avoid mistakes. You may have a difficult task or challenge ahead, but the stars suggest you will overcome any obstacles. A little attention to finances will pay off. ***Moon enters Scorpio.***

5 AUGUST

A work or financial matter is best approached carefully to avoid making waves. You may need to meet a deadline or must simply be more focused than usual, especially in relation to finances and someone special. Rest assured, if an obstacle arises you will overcome it. ***Moon in Scorpio.***

6 AUGUST

You'll appreciate the chance for a change of routine and to be more spontaneous. Your optimistic outlook will bring rewards. Tread carefully with someone who may not share your optimism to avoid disagreements. You'll enjoy being adventurous and the company of like-minded people. Sports and physical activities will appeal. You'll enjoy boosting health. ***Moon enters Sagittarius.***

7 AUGUST

This is a good day for romance and for indulging in activities you love, including socialising and retail therapy! If your views differ from those of someone else it's in your interests to de-stress and unwind from circumstances that have caused frustration. Avoid conflict, as it could escalate. ***Moon in Sagittarius.***

8 AUGUST

This is a good day to build positive relationships where they are needed. For some this will be principally at home or regarding property, while for others it will be at work or with an organisation or friend. If you need expert advice it will be available. If health has been a concern this is a good day to obtain information and book a treatment. ***Moon enters Capricorn.***

9 AUGUST

This may be an intense day as emotions are likely to be at boiling point. If you love a passionate time romance could blossom, but if you prefer life on an even keel you may prefer to pace yourself. Domestic and/or family matters could be sorted out but not without a little soul searching or intense talk. ***Moon in Capricorn.***

10 AUGUST

Consider looking at important aspects of your life from a fresh perspective. Avoid being stuck in one train of thought and play with new ideas. You may discover a fresh viewpoint that has merit. ***Moon enters Aquarius.***

11 AUGUST

You may be surprised by developments, for some at home and for others at work or regarding health. You may remember the idea that never making assumptions has merit. You may discover you have been labouring under a misapprehension, so this will offer the opportunity to be practical about setting things straight so you can move forward. *Moon in Aquarius.*

12 AUGUST

The Aquarius full moon is spotlighting where in your life you could be a little more adventurous and quirky. For many this will be in relation to work, and for others at home. Ask if you can give a little leeway or, contrarily, if you've given too much and must now establish boundaries. *Moon enters Pisces.*

13 AUGUST

Important decisions merit careful attention to the details, but you must be happy with the big-picture scenario. If in doubt about how to move forward trust your instincts, but equally you must avoid being easily influenced. *Moon in Pisces.*

14 AUGUST

This is a good day to make a formal commitment or decision, for some to do with work and your general direction and for others to do with home or a trip. A venture, work or project could gallop ahead, but if you're unhappy with the direction in which things are going it's important to apply the brakes before more momentum is gained. *Moon enters Aries.*

15 AUGUST

You'll appreciate being in touch with an old friend or colleague. If you're making changes at home or with family, some help from someone from your past could be ideal. *Moon in Aries.*

16 AUGUST

This is a good day for visits and for making changes at home. You may be drawn to a new schedule or work practice. Communications with those at home or in your family could improve but you may nevertheless be surprised by someone's news. *Moon in Aries.*

17 AUGUST

Ensure you have all the details at hand to do with a domestic development, family or group venture as mistakes could be made. Ensure arrangements are super clear for all concerned to avoid misunderstandings. *Moon in Taurus.*

18 AUGUST

This is a lovely day to move conversations and important projects forward. You may enjoy a visit or a trip somewhere beautiful. It's also a good day to make home improvements, so if you've been meaning to update your décor today's your day! *Moon in Taurus.*

19 AUGUST

While you're generally an accommodating and amiable person, sometimes people can simply get the wrong end of the stick in conversations and activities. A little more tact and diplomacy, especially at home and with your favourite projects, will work wonders for creating a smoother path forward. *Moon in Gemini.*

20 AUGUST

Mars will now be in your sign until the end of March 2023, providing you with additional energy and motivation as and when you need it. You may feel restless and can get a great deal done, especially with joint projects and in your personal life. Just avoid trying to get everything done at once; pace yourself for the best measure. *Moon in Gemini.*

21 AUGUST

Romance is a big draw card for you, and movies, art, creativity and music will all appeal. Take time out to meet with family and friends as you'll enjoy the event. However, you may be forgetful or someone you generally rely on could let you down. If so, avoid taking matters personally and find other ways to enjoy your Sunday. *Moon in Gemini.*

22 AUGUST

This is an excellent day to make changes that you have been planning for some time. Joint ventures, changes at home with shared areas, for example, and developments at work could go well as you'll be feeling practical. If you are making long-term financial decisions you must do your research and also trust your gut instincts. *Moon in Cancer.*

23 AUGUST

Now that the sun is in Virgo you'll feel so much more practical and grounded about developments at home with family or property. Take the time to formulate realistic plans moving forward, taking all the variables into account. *Moon in Cancer.*

24 AUGUST

Look for positive ways forward, especially at home with family and property. You'll enjoy a little DIY or gardening and freshening up décor. A friend, group or organisation may be particularly helpful with your endeavours. This is also a good day for meetings and gaining expert advice and direction, so take the initiative if you need a little guidance. *Moon enters Leo.*

25 AUGUST

You are a sociable person and your imagination and artistic abilities will begin to peak, especially at home and with family. Find ways to express this aspect of yourself; you'll find art, music, dance and romance fulfilling although perhaps not everyone will agree with all your ideas and choices, so be prepared to put your opinions in the best light. *Moon in Leo.*

26 AUGUST

You'll look for peace and balance at home and in your personal life now that Mercury is in Libra. You may need to act as a mediator or peacemaker for someone in your environment. *Moon in Leo.*

27 AUGUST

The new moon in Virgo is an ideal opportunity to kick-start a fresh chapter at home with family or property. However, you may be tempted to make rash decisions or to rush through projects and ideas, so ensure you seek expert advice and take all the variables into account. You may be surprised by a change of routine or unexpected news. *Moon enters Capricorn.*

28 AUGUST

A commitment may be made at home or regarding a work project. Your domestic life and/or work and career are up for a change, so take the time to consider your projects carefully to avoid making snap decisions. It's a good day to be practical and realistic. Avoid nostalgia as it could lead to an emotion-based decision that is not pragmatic. *Moon in Virgo.*

29 AUGUST

You may feel inclined to establish more peace, balance and harmony in your life. It's a good day to take decisive action regarding your personal life, health and well-being. Art, relaxation and music will all provide you with some form of rest in the evening. In the day, choose your words carefully to avoid difficult talks. *Moon enters Libra.*

30 AUGUST

A group, friend or organisation will have a bearing on some of your domestic decisions. Ensure the advice you follow is expert advice as opposed to someone's assumptions or opinions. You could achieve a great deal but may need to first overcome a hurdle. *Moon in Libra.*

31 AUGUST

You may be a little sensitive to people's opinions, so be clear about where you stand. You may discover that you have over-estimated someone's interest in your circumstances, so ensure you gain perspective and avoid seeing the world through rose-coloured glasses. When you do, you may be pleasantly surprised with the outcome. *Moon enters Scorpio.*

September

career   love   home   health   finance

1 SEPTEMBER

There's little you like more than a good chinwag, yet sometimes people won't feel the same way as you and talks can become stressful. Luckily, today's aspects suggest you'll enjoy both socialising and networking, and your day is likely to be busy so be prepared. *Moon in Scorpio.*

2 SEPTEMBER

If you like a tension in your love life and general interactions you'll enjoy today's conversations, but if you prefer life on an even keel you may need to use your tact and discretion to avoid the odd tense interaction, especially at home. *Moon enters Sagittarius.*

3 SEPTEMBER

A trip or meeting may inspire a deeper sense of direction and your motivation will be to move forward. However, if some of your plans need to be rethought, take a moment to reconfigure how you'd like to see your projects and ventures move forward. *Moon in Sagittarius.*

4 SEPTEMBER

The Sagittarian moon will bring your curiosity and adventurousness to the surface, especially at work and with the people closest to you. You'll enjoy being with upbeat, outgoing people, but if someone proves hard to handle avoid making tension worse; find ways to establish common ground if possible. ***Moon in Sagittarius.***

5 SEPTEMBER

You may feel more comfortable and at ease in yourself and others and will enjoy finding ways to be more practical and hands-on with your various projects. You'll appreciate the chance to relax at home and with loved ones at the end of the day. ***Moon in Capricorn.***

6 SEPTEMBER

The moon in Capricorn can create a sense that the people around you are more realistic and practical. However, some people may also appear more stubborn or even intense so ensure you remain open to co-operating but avoid conflict as it could escalate. If you must get things done under pressure ensure you remain grounded and look at the most feasible ways ahead. ***Moon in Capricorn.***

7 SEPTEMBER

The Aquarian moon will bring your more light-hearted and/or analytical side out, which will enable you to think outside the box with your various projects, plans and ideas. You'll enjoy a reunion and getting domestic or family matters more organised. ***Moon in Aquarius.***

8 SEPTEMBER

A friend, group or organisation will be helpful, even if you feel sometimes that you are more helpful to them than they are to you. You may discover that if you ask for advice or help it will be available. Avoid feeling super sensitive and find clever ways to overcome hurdles. ***Moon in Aquarius.***

9 SEPTEMBER

Someone may be feeling a little worse for wear. If it's you, take time out and avoid adding fuel to the fire if conflict or disagreements are lurking. Find ways to negotiate into a better situation and look for peace at home. ***Moon in Pisces.***

10 SEPTEMBER

The full moon in Pisces is shining a light on your personal life, family and/or a creative project, asking very much how you intend to be practical about moving forward with your treasured plans and projects. Change is in the air, so embrace it!

11 SEPTEMBER

A surprise or change of routine will be enjoyable. If you're working, you may find you enjoy something new in your routine. An impromptu visit or trip will bring you together with a fun group of people. *Moon in Aries.*

12 SEPTEMBER

Many of the changes you're already anticipating may become so much more real, which may be confronting *or* enjoyable and perhaps a mixture of both! Take things one step at a time to ensure you don't over-tire yourself. Avoid overwork, both at home and at work. *Moon in Aries.*

13 SEPTEMBER

The moon in Taurus for the next few days will enable you to be a little more hands-on and practical, especially with plans that have been in the making for a while. For some Twins these will be to do with work, and for others at home or with family. Be adaptable and avoid being stubborn about change. *Moon enters Taurus.*

14 SEPTEMBER

Be prepared to show how dependable you are at work, even if you feel you must stand up for yourself or your ideas. You may experience a change of routine and some developments may come from out of the blue. These will have an impact on your home life or family as the moon spotlights developments that will alter your daily life. *Moon in Taurus.*

15 SEPTEMBER

Mars in your sign will encourage you to be proactive, but it could also produce a fiery, restless quality that could predispose you to rash decisions. Today and tomorrow, keep an eye on the facts and the truth and avoid conflict and being easily led. Arguments could spark up over very little, so keep an eye on maintaining perspective. *Moon enters Gemini.*

16 SEPTEMBER

You'll discover whether some of your plans have been unrealistic and if you must adjust expectations. Take a moment to work on beautifying your home and environment; you'll be glad you did. Avoid arguments at home and at work. Consider if disagreements stem from a basic difference in values and avoid taking them personally. *Moon in Gemini.*

17 SEPTEMBER

This is a good day to get ahead with your various tasks, especially at work and financially. You may be inclined to make emotional judgements that could lead to arguments, so avoid allowing your feelings to run your day. A healing or therapeutic break will appeal. *Moon in Gemini.*

18 SEPTEMBER

This is a good time to look at the information you have and re-evaluate it to ensure it's still relevant, especially to do with your home, personal life, a group, friend or organisation. A decision could be made, but you may need to review the facts first. *Moon enters Cancer.*

19 SEPTEMBER

This is a good day to put changes in motion, especially those that affect or include someone close to you such as someone at home or family member. A collaboration could flourish. Romance could blossom. *Moon in Cancer.*

20 SEPTEMBER

If you need someone's co-operation and collaboration, present your ideas clearly so they can see the merits of your choices, especially at work. A personal or romantic connection can blossom, so ensure you organise a fun night out or in! If obstacles arise rest assured you will overcome them, especially in connection with money. *Moon enters Leo.*

21 SEPTEMBER

This is a good day to get ahead with your ventures. Just avoid appearing too pushy as this will go against you. Someone may not agree with some of your plans, so find the time to enlighten them. *Moon in Leo.*

22 SEPTEMBER

Domestic matters will require a little attention, as there may be a small case of who holds more authority. Be careful not to outshine someone in charge such as your employer. Be bold and bright, but avoid allowing pride to rule your day; pride comes before a fall. *Moon in Leo.*

23 SEPTEMBER

As the sun steps into Libra it marks the equinox, a time where we collectively sense that more balance and harmony can arise. Consider where in your life you could create more peace and work towards it. You may receive key news from someone close that could have an impact on your general direction and decisions moving forward, making it a good time to review your circumstances. *Moon in Virgo.*

24 SEPTEMBER

You'll be drawn to relax through music, the arts and romance. Find an activity or person who provides a sense of beauty and enjoyment in life and spend some time immersing yourself in good vibes. However, you may be a little absent-minded or idealistic, so ensure you avoid forgetfulness and seeing the world through rose-coloured glasses. *Moon in Virgo.*

25 SEPTEMBER

The new moon in Libra points to a fresh circumstance on the way in your personal life. For some this will affect family; for others home and for some a partner. It's a time of great transformation, so ensure you make a wish as it'll surely come true.

26 SEPTEMBER

You'll enjoy spending time with someone you love or will hear from them. A meeting, trip or return to an old haunt will be significant. If you'd like to make long-range changes to your life, this is the time to set the wheels in motion. *Moon in Libra.*

27 SEPTEMBER

This is a good day for conversations and meetings, especially those that can turn your life around. If travel appeals this is a good time for planning, and if you're travelling you're likely to enjoy your new environment. *Moon in Libra.*

28 SEPTEMBER

A commitment could be made that may take you into new territory, especially at work or regarding someone in a position of authority. A commitment made in your personal life is also likely to take. *Moon in Scorpio.*

29 SEPTEMBER

The Scorpio moon may bring out your emotions or those of someone close. If someone is feeling a little out of sorts, give them a wide berth. If you are feeling emotional, take a moment to gather your thoughts. A change of routine may be more emotional than you initially thought, so ensure you pace yourself. *Moon in Scorpio.*

30 SEPTEMBER

This is a good day for bonding with someone special and for getting things done both at work and at home. You may not necessarily agree with everyone you must collaborate or interact with but you could be industrious and will reap the rewards of hard work. You may also receive good news. *Moon in Sagittarius.*

October

career love home health finance

1 OCTOBER

Key news or a get-together this weekend will put a personal relationship or favourite project in perspective. However, some people – perhaps even you – may be feeling tense, so ensure you set aside time to unwind. *Moon in Sagittarius.*

2 OCTOBER

Your sign's ruler, Mercury, ends its recent retrograde phase today, so if communications have been difficult or delayed they will begin to improve over the coming weeks. You may receive key news or will enjoy a get-together. Just stay clear of tense topics if possible to avoid unnecessary arguments. *Moon in Capricorn.*

3 OCTOBER

You may need to review or oversee a change in the way you share some of your duties, either at home or at work. Consider how you could communicate with more sensitivity and compassion for the best measure. *Moon in Capricorn.*

4 OCTOBER

An old argument or point of tension you thought was over with or resolved may re-emerge. Find ways to share positive experiences with those you love and look for ways to move forward in practical, realistic and down-to-earth ways. ***Moon enters Aquarius.***

5 OCTOBER

Developments will highlight areas in your life in which you could be more adventurous and embrace new and exciting projects. Your imagination will be sparking on all cylinders, so this is a good time to innovate and to capture bright ideas and then act on them. ***Moon in Aquarius.***

6 OCTOBER

This could be a very productive two days, especially if you have laid solid groundwork for your various projects and ventures. Ensure you avoid taking on too much as you may be inclined to overwork or over-exert yourself and to expect more than is feasible. Sports and outgoing activities will bring a sense of fulfilment your way. ***Moon enters Pisces.***

7 OCTOBER

You're known more for your ability to communicate well and as a chatty, outgoing character, yet you can be sensitive and take other people's circumstances and opinions to heart. Don't forget: every relationship has its ups and downs. You may feel a little vulnerable or must look after someone's feelings and help them out. If you require expert advice it will be available. ***Moon in Pisces.***

8 OCTOBER

You'll regain some of your usual vitality and lust for life as the day goes by, so be sure to organise a favourite activity for later in the day even if you're not in the mood earlier on! The arts and well-being will draw your attention. It's a good day for a health or beauty appointment. Just be sure to be clear about what you want or need. ***Moon enters Aries.***

9 OCTOBER

The Aries full moon will spotlight how you feel about a particular person, group or organisation. There may be a strong link or focus at the moment concerning study or health in the relationship, and someone may need to express their feelings or need a shoulder to cry on and yours is available!

10 OCTOBER

This is another good day for a health or beauty appointment. You may discover important information about someone close. If you need expert advice or must discuss delicate topics with someone you love, this is your day. ***Moon enters Taurus.***

11 OCTOBER

This is a good day for getting ahead at work and with family and creative projects. You'll be feeling practical and the help of someone in a position of authority will be useful to you, so reach out if you need guidance. You may receive unexpected news. *Moon in Taurus.*

12 OCTOBER

You'll enjoy a trip somewhere beautiful and touching base with a friend or partner. Someone close may need to review some of their ideas. A work project or trip may need to be reviewed. Avoid making big changes in your life unless you have adequately researched the variables. *Moon in Taurus.*

13 OCTOBER

A change of routine or an unexpected development will ask that you're flexible and adaptable and neither of these qualities are difficult for you, so take the initiative and you'll enjoy a varied day. If someone behaves unpredictably, you will overcome any fallout from their decisions. *Moon in Gemini.*

14 OCTOBER

This is a super-productive and potentially enjoyable day, as long as you have made solid arrangements. It's a good day for making commitments, especially at work and regarding your status, general direction in life and personal matters. *Moon in Gemini.*

15 OCTOBER

A lovely event may bring emotions to the surface. A little retail therapy may appeal to you, but if you're already in debt ensure you leave the credit card at home as you may be tempted to make purchases based on emotions alone. You may be easily influenced as well, so unless you get a second opinion about key decisions choose carefully. *Moon enters Cancer.*

16 OCTOBER

Romance and all things beautiful will appeal to you and you'll enjoy immersing yourself in a beautiful environment. However, not everyone will have the same sentiments as you, so avoid taking their opinions or mindset personally. If making key decisions, ensure you have all the facts at your fingertips. *Moon in Cancer.*

17 OCTOBER

This is a proactive day and you'll manage to accomplish a great deal. If you tend to find stress a motivating factor you'll enjoy the day, but if intense behaviour or events tend to leave you cold, take time out and plan for mini breaks during the day. *Moon in Cancer.*

18 OCTOBER

Ensure you have all the details if you're making important statements or have key negotiations to undertake; you may only have part of the picture. This is a good day for art, music, meditation and spiritual activities. A trip may be delayed, so plan well in advance. **Moon in Leo.**

19 OCTOBER

You are likely to be feeling positive about developments and may assume that everyone else is as well. However, someone who has influence over you or who you share space with at home, for example, may not necessarily feel the same way. Take steps to defuse arguments should they arise. **Moon in Leo.**

20 OCTOBER

This is another potentially tense or stressful day, especially in relation to someone close such as a friend or family member. If finances require attention, now is the time to research a fresh budget. **Moon enters Virgo.**

21 OCTOBER

Your ability to be practical and realistic is a real asset, one you could use for the best results especially at home or with work projects. Avoid being put under pressure unless you really have no alternative. Find ways to unwind when you can. **Moon in Virgo.**

22 OCTOBER

You'll enjoy a lovely get-together and being with like-minded people. However, you may not all be on the same page and you may encounter an unexpected development such as an impromptu visitor arriving. Be prepared to be flexible with arrangements as they may change at the drop of a hat. **Moon in Virgo.**

23 OCTOBER

Now that the sun is in Scorpio for the next four weeks there is likely to be more focus on your business and personal partnerships and on the areas of your life you need to reorganise such as your daily schedule and health routine. You may receive good news and will be encouraged to step into new territory either at work or at home. If a hurdle arises or a difficult social situation develops you will overcome it. **Moon in Libra.**

24 OCTOBER

Be prepared to look outside the box at your various personal and business associations, as you could develop good relationships even if some of them bring up your sensitivities or vulnerabilities. **Moon in Libra.**

25 OCTOBER

The partial solar eclipse in Scorpio will spotlight your day-to-day schedule and ways to feel healthier and more efficient. You may appreciate a health or beauty treat. If you find communications a little tense or confusing, take extra time to boost your communication skills, especially listening skills.

26 OCTOBER

You may experience an intense feeling surrounding work and, for some, health. Someone you work with or at home may need special attention. If a health matter is on your mind, it's a good time to consult an expert. **Moon in Scorpio.**

27 OCTOBER

Mars in your sign is encouraging you to be proactive and outgoing, and today's astrological aspects suggest you'll enjoy work and family and friends time equally. That is unless an intense or problematic topic isn't given breathing space in your interactions. Avoid problematic topics and aim to de-escalate tensions should they arise. **Moon enters Sagittarius.**

28 OCTOBER

You may be drawn to an old haunt or wish to reconnect with someone you feel nostalgic about. A previous circumstance may seem rosier in retrospect than it actually was, so gain perspective. A project at work may need to be reviewed. **Moon in Sagittarius.**

29 OCTOBER

Developments may feel a little more intense than usual or, alternatively, events may be delayed or complex. Allow yourself extra time for travel to avoid delays. You may feel a little idealistic, so ensure you remain grounded. **Moon enters Capricorn.**

30 OCTOBER

You'll appreciate finding the time to enjoy someone's company and relaxing and slowing things down. You can't agree with everyone all the time, so a little compromise may be necessary. Someone may surprise you. **Moon in Capricorn.**

31 OCTOBER

Happy Hallowe'en! Expect a quirky day as developments could be a little out of the ordinary – so nothing unusual for the day of the year it is! If you're in doubt about a project or a person, ensure you have enough information to gain certainty. **Moon enters Aquarius.**

November

career   love   home   health   finance

1 NOVEMBER

The Aquarian moon may spotlight your differences of opinion. Avoid feeling antagonistic, as this will add to the frustration and annoy other people into the mix! You'll discover a practical, realistic solution to any conundrums. You'll appreciate relaxing in the evening. *Moon in Aquarius.*

2 NOVEMBER

This is another day when being careful with conversations and interactions will work in your favour, as someone and perhaps even you may be feeling super sensitive and prone to taking casual remarks personally. It's a good day to focus on being supportive of others and to ask for help if you need it. A health or beauty treat could be refreshing. *Moon enters Pisces.*

3 NOVEMBER

You'll enjoy meeting an old friend or colleague. You may need to go over old ground at work or remedy a circumstance that requires attention. You'll enjoy updating your wardrobe or hair style. *Moon in Pisces.*

4 NOVEMBER

The bigger picture is this: you have the chance to improve your circumstances, especially at work and health-wise, but the more detailed picture involves you taking the time to ensure conversations, talks and communications are clear and calm or you risk difficult interactions. *Moon enters Aries.*

5 NOVEMBER

You may be surprised by developments, especially at work and with health matters, so take things one step at a time. Avoid assuming certain outcomes and seek fresh perspective. Be spontaneous and embrace change but avoid making snap decisions. *Moon in Aries.*

6 NOVEMBER

Trust your instincts and avoid fuelling bad moods. A reunion or trip to a familiar place may bring emotions to the surface, but if you focus on the positives you'll enjoy a lovely get-together or event. *Moon in Aries.*

7 NOVEMBER

The key to success lies in good negotiation skills. Take a moment to consider your best responses to situations that demand you accept responsibility for your own actions. A financial matter is best considered from a long-term point of view. You may decide to negotiate a new agreement with someone to ensure a fairer outcome. *Moon in Taurus.*

8 NOVEMBER

The total eclipse of the moon in Taurus will spotlight changes in your working schedule and how you feel about your daily life. Key news is likely either at work or concerning health and it's a good time to consider your circumstances in a realistic light.

9 NOVEMBER

A change of circumstance will take place, if it hasn't already recently, for some Twins regarding a change of routine and for others at work. Some Twins will discover important health-related new. You are the most adaptable of sun signs and, with the moon in your own sign today, you'll manage to adjust to circumstances well. *Moon enters Gemini.*

10 NOVEMBER

It would be an error to assume everyone is on the same page as you are so ensure you listen carefully and double-check you're all coming from the same place, especially if mix-ups occur. Travel or work matters may be delayed, so be patient. You'll enjoy indulging in the arts, music and good company, especially this evening. *Moon in Gemini.*

11 NOVEMBER

Look for the most practical path ahead in your decision-making. Avoid focusing on what isn't working in your personal life and focus on what is working well instead, especially if a personal matter seems stuck. A difficult or stubborn work colleague or personal situation is best approached carefully, and you will find you make great headway. *Moon in Gemini.*

12 NOVEMBER

This will be a romantic time and could also be particularly intense, so organise an event that celebrates your strong connection. You may be feeling more idealistic than usual and could therefore make assumptions about other people's feelings, so ensure you are being realistic. The arts, music, theatre and film will all appeal. *Moon in Cancer.*

13 NOVEMBER

This is a lovely time to spend with people you love. However, you won't automatically agree with everyone and, if there's a work or personal matter that is on your mind, try to dispel anxiety and enjoy good company instead. *Moon in Cancer.*

14 NOVEMBER

A positive and upbeat approach to the start of the week will work wonders for your self-esteem and motivation. This is a good day for meetings and to get down to the bottom of important matters. A health or work matter could be looking up. *Moon enters Leo.*

15 NOVEMBER

This is an excellent day for get-togethers, talks and moving your various plans and projects forward, so take the initiative! If there's someone you need to contact, do so today. However, if some of your ventures have snowballed and you aren't happy with the direction they're moving in they could gain momentum, so ensure you stop them in their tracks if you prefer to slow things down. *Moon in Leo.*

16 NOVEMBER

This is another day when great progress can be made. A travel plan or actual trip should go well, especially if you've laid solid groundwork and prepared ahead. Work and health meetings and discussions could go particularly well. However, it's important you avoid rash decisions. Be practical and realistic. *Moon in Leo.*

17 NOVEMBER

As your sign's ruler Mercury enters the zodiac sign Sagittarius expect more focus to be on travel, broadening your horizons and relationships over the coming weeks. You'll feel more inclined to be upbeat and outgoing in pursuit of adventure and discovery. *Moon in Virgo.*

18 NOVEMBER

This is a good day for making changes to the way you share your various duties and responsibilities, as you're likely to succeed in making solid and agreeable arrangements. ***Moon in Virgo.***

19 NOVEMBER

You'll appreciate the opportunity to be a little more adventurous in your day-to-day activities this weekend and will enjoy activities that boost your status in some way, be this via socialising, networking or even a beauty or health boost. You may be drawn to a mystery, however, one that is alluring but that could lead you astray. If you're tempted to be spontaneous you'll enjoy it, but you may be prone to getting lost or being absent-minded or potentially even led down a garden path. ***Moon enters Libra.***

20 NOVEMBER

You'll enjoy relaxing. If you overdid things yesterday you may feel a little head in the clouds, so take things one step at a time. You'll enjoy the arts, music and favourite company and a special meeting will be enjoyable. A health or beauty treat could appeal but you must be clear about what you want. ***Moon in Libra.***

21 NOVEMBER

This is a good day for meetings, especially with someone special and, for most Twins, at work or regarding health and well-being. You'll enjoy being able to talk freely about your aims and goals. You may even receive good news to do with a group, organisation or friend. ***Moon enters Scorpio.***

22 NOVEMBER

The sun in Sagittarius for the next few weeks will put the focus firmly on someone else such as a business or personal partner. They may be more upbeat and outgoing than usual and their mood will influence you. You may experience a feeling of adventurousness at work and regarding your health regime now too. ***Moon in Scorpio.***

23 NOVEMBER

The Sagittarian new moon will bring a fresh start for you in a work context and, for some, in a close relationship such as a business or personal partnership. This is a good time to begin new projects, health initiatives and, if you are single and meet someone new, in a partnership.

24 NOVEMBER

Today's moon in Sagittarius will spotlight news from a partner or expert adviser. Take the time to digest the news and conversations as you'll find there are many positives. It's a good time to be more adventurous in your relationships. ***Moon in Sagittarius.***

25 NOVEMBER

This is a good day for health and beauty treats and to ensure you are on the right track, both at work and at home. If you feel you need to make adjustments to any aspects of your daily schedule, this is a good day to do so. A friend, partner or even you may need some support or help. If so, this is the day to look for it as you're likely to find it. **Moon enters Capricorn.**

26 NOVEMBER

Another good day to find the support you need and/or to offer it to someone else. If a close relationship has been under pressure this is a good time to boost your relationship, so take the initiative. Romance could blossom. It's an especially good day to boost your appearance with a new outfit or haircut, for example. **Moon in Capricorn.**

27 NOVEMBER

A change of pace or environment may be surprisingly refreshing or different. Developments may be unexpected, especially if you're working. You may decide to alter your appearance to match your feelings and activities. Take the initiative! **Moon enters Aquarius.**

28 NOVEMBER

An excellent day to get things done, especially at work and regarding finances and your personal life. You could make agreements that are binding and that could mean an improvement in your status or direction in life, but you must be certain of the variables. Avoid taking unnecessary risks. **Moon in Aquarius.**

29 NOVEMBER

Key talks and/or a get-together could be more important than meets the eye, so ensure you take your arrangements seriously to avoid committing to something you haven't adequately understood yet. You may receive unexpected news or will need to accommodate a surprise change of routine. **Moon in Aquarius.**

30 NOVEMBER

This is a good day for discussions with someone important such as an employer or a personal partner. If you're looking for work, this is a good day for interviews and to circulate your resume. Take the initiative! You may be ready to make a commitment to someone special or to a particular project. **Moon in Pisces.**

December

career   love   home   health   finance

1 DECEMBER

Mars in your sign will bring your inner rebel out, and if you have full control of this aspect of yourself and are able to channel this upbeat energy into productive outlets you'll enjoy your day. If you tend to rise to conflict easily it's important you avoid intense conversations as they could quickly escalate. A meeting or news will be decisive and romance could blossom. *Moon in Pisces.*

2 DECEMBER

The commitment you're looking for either at work or with people close to you such as a partner is possible. However, you may find that some of your communications are lacking detail and that confusion or even a sense of loss arises. To ensure you remain on top of developments, take the time to research your agreements and ensure you're on the same page. *Moon in Aries.*

3 DECEMBER

A therapeutic aspect this weekend will enable you to truly relax and take time out with people you love. Avoid socialising for the sake of it, as it is unlikely to fulfil you. Choose your company wisely and you'll feel supported as a result. It's a good day for a health treat. *Moon in Aries.*

4 DECEMBER

You'll enjoy the company of someone special or doing a favourite activity, although you may tend to be escapist and could as a result isolate yourself or simply cocoon. To avoid misunderstandings and delays, ensure you double-check arrangements with those they concern. ***Moon enters Taurus.***

5 DECEMBER

You may experience some delays, so organise extra time to get things done at work and for travel. Also bear in mind that the next two days could continue to involve misunderstandings, so double-check facts. ***Moon in Taurus.***

6 DECEMBER

As your sign's ruler, Mercury, steps into the zodiac sign Capricorn, you'll enjoy the sense that communications can begin to even out. To facilitate the process, aim to be practical and take decisions one step at a time. Avoid rush decisions. You may uncover a discrepancy in some communications that enable you to iron out differences. Avoid travel delays by leaving plenty of time for travel. ***Moon enters Gemini.***

7 DECEMBER

You'll gain traction by exhibiting your ability to be flexible and adaptable. An abrupt change of routine or a surprise will mean you need to alter your schedule. This is a day when romance and friendships can flourish. If you've been meaning to ask someone out you may be pleasantly surprised by the result of doing so. ***Moon in Gemini.***

8 DECEMBER

The Gemini full moon shines a light on a fresh chapter in your personal life, especially if you were born in early June. Take a moment to decide how you would like your future to look. Avoid snap decisions, but if a fresh opportunity arises out of nowhere be prepared to grasp it and to research your options.

9 DECEMBER

You'll enjoy an impromptu get-together or will receive encouraging news. If it means you must change some of your routine, rest assured the result will be worth the effort. ***Moon in Cancer.***

10 DECEMBER

This is a good day to make agreements with people with whom you must collaborate. A person in a position of power or who has a powerful influence over you may be particularly supportive, but if not it's important you find ways to co-operate or developments could spell a difficult relationship. Romance can flourish over activities you both enjoy, so take the initiative and plan a treat with someone special. ***Moon in Cancer.***

11 DECEMBER

As Venus joins Mercury in Capricorn you'll appreciate the sense that some of your agreements and relationships can gain a more even keel. But you must avoid obstinacy and, if someone close is behaving stubbornly, encourage them to see this. *Moon enters Leo.*

12 DECEMBER

An excellent day for building bridges with people you may have argued with or with whom you must collaborate. An activity or collaboration such as study that will bring you more kudos could go well. *Moon in Leo.*

13 DECEMBER

While this is another good day for meetings and to get things done, you may tend to overlook details and be a little idealistic, especially in your personal life. If someone has broken your trust, you must ask if you can learn to trust them again and vice versa. *Moon in Leo.*

14 DECEMBER

Communications may be a little complex or even confused, so ensure you take the extra time to be super clear and to navigate carefully through meetings and communications. You may feel a little head in the clouds or someone close may be late or forgetful, so organise extra time for meetings and arrangements if possible. *Moon enters Virgo.*

15 DECEMBER

Even if some matters are up in the air, today's Virgo moon will enable you to make decisions based on practicalities. You could get a lot done in your personal life regarding ensuring certain plans and agreements are in place. You'll enjoy a get-together with someone who makes you feel at home. *Moon in Virgo.*

16 DECEMBER

Certain talks and arrangements may require a little extra research and tact on your part, even if you feel that other people are communicating badly or unpredictably. Be patient and look for harmony and peace in your own heart. *Moon enters Libra.*

17 DECEMBER

You'll enjoy the sense that the big-picture changes in your life are moving forward and that pleasant interactions, developments at work and collaborations and relationships can move ahead in ways that breathe new life into being. *Moon in Libra.*

18 DECEMBER

Certain relationships can deepen, such as those you already have in place including love relationships. Plan for romance as you'll enjoy being with someone you love. However, some relationships could hit a speed bump, especially regarding who has the greater wisdom within the relationship and, for some, regarding health matters. If so, rest assured there will be a good reason for the speed bump that slows down things for now. It's a good time to adjust your expectations of someone else. *Moon in Libra.*

19 DECEMBER

This is another good day for socialising and networking, but if you know there are certain topics that are off limits ensure you avoid them for the best measure! *Moon in Scorpio.*

20 DECEMBER

When the moon is in Scorpio people close to you may be more outspoken or passionate. You may also feel a little feistier and prepared to tackle issues you wouldn't usually presume to do. If problems arise, avoid speaking before you've thought things through. This aside, you'll enjoy a development in your personal life or a favourite activity or hobby. *Moon in Scorpio.*

21 DECEMBER

The solstice is a time of reflection when you can gather your wits as you assimilate your progress so far in the year. News and developments may involve a business or personal partner. Be practical and realistic, and avoid entering into conflict and focus on a constructive plan for moving forward instead. *Moon in Sagittarius.*

22 DECEMBER

The solstice is when the sun enters Capricorn. This can be settling, and you are likely to feel more practical about your various chores and ventures, relationships and ideas. The moon in Sagittarius may produce a restless feel to the day, however, so slow down when possible and avoid arguments. *Moon in Sagittarius.*

23 DECEMBER

The new moon and supermoon in Capricorn signals a fresh start for you in an area you share, such as a communal duty or responsibility, space at home or even a financial matter. For some this new moon signals a fresh chapter in a close relationship. It's a good time to make plans for how you will be meeting and getting together moving forward. You'll enjoy an event or chat that could bring an increased sense of security or stability your way.

24 DECEMBER

This is a lovely time for get-togethers, so enjoy this time of year. A creative, romantic, music-fuelled day will raise spirits. *Moon in Capricorn.*

25 DECEMBER

Merry Christmas! This year's Christmas may be slightly different to that of previous years. If you're missing someone, take a moment to appreciate their existence and focus on your own situation and on enjoying the company you do have. *Moon in Aquarius.*

26 DECEMBER

You'll appreciate being able to approach someone who can sometimes be a little difficult in a new way as you begin to see them in a new light. You may even feel some of your moods lift as you relax into the holiday season. If you're back at work this could be a busy day with varied influences, so take things one step at a time. *Moon in Aquarius.*

27 DECEMBER

You'll enjoy the upbeat and light-hearted atmosphere that the moon in Pisces will bring, and travel may take you somewhere you'll enjoy. If you have entered new territory recently you'll gain an increasing sense of stability. Ensure you establish balance between work and play and find the time to rest. *Moon in Pisces.*

28 DECEMBER

You'll enjoy spending time with those you love. The seasonal sales at the shops may entice you and you'll enjoy your favourite activities and romance in the evening, so plan a treat! *Moon in Pisces.*

29 DECEMBER

You may reconsider your position on various decisions that have been made or fresh news will arise that could alter how you see certain arrangements or agreements. Take a moment to work out shared financial matters before making a financial decision to ensure you're happy with the arrangements. *Moon in Aries.*

30 DECEMBER

You like to get things done swiftly yet currently there is more wisdom in taking things in a measured way unless, of course, you are required to act on impulse. Rest assured your decisions will work out in the long term if you base them on wisdom and experience. *Moon in Aries.*

31 DECEMBER

Happy New Year! You'll feel more grounded, supported and comfortable in a safe and secure environment as you enter the new year, even if developments earlier in the day are busier than you'd prefer. *Moon enters Taurus.*

CANCER

21 June - 22 July

THE ESSENCE OF CANCER

One of the three water signs, you are a caring and intuitive character; you are also one of the strongest members of the zodiac family. A cardinal sign, you have a backbone beyond your own understanding and often only discover your strength when you are challenged and in the midst of difficult circumstances. You're generally known for your sensitive side yet you can be a live wire when you're motivated.

You're better known to circumnavigate trouble and then duck into your shell when under attack, which is why a crab is the symbol for your sign: you tend to walk sideways! Even so, try as you may to circumnavigate trouble you will nevertheless encounter various challenges that will demand you step up and be the strong character you are regardless of the sensitivity that lies beneath the tough shell you hide under. You really are tough through and through, so don't buy into the idea that you're not!

Family, caring for others and being part of a strong social fabric are all very important to you. Nurturance, both in the form of a good diet and emotional support, is also critical, and this is an area in your life you are likely to embrace wholeheartedly. When you think your genuine caring feelings for someone are not being reciprocated you can feel let down, ultimately withdrawing your affections as a result. It is only after a long, hard, extended period of caregiving and nurturance that you give freely.

You may be relatively slower than many other signs to commit to someone, but when you do your feelings run deep and you'll find it hard to extricate yourself from a relationship. Always consult your very accurate instincts when you're choosing friends and a partner.

You are an imaginative and creative character, and fiction, story writing, singing, music and theatre will all appeal to your appreciation of artistic areas. Little Cancerians should be encouraged to express themselves through art at a young age.

Sport will also appeal to the active Cancerian, as it is a great way to teach youngsters how to channel their strong energy into action and activities.

SELF-ESTEEM

One of your true inner resources is that you have high self-esteem and are not afraid to leave your comfort zone to attain your goals. You are adventurous in your interpersonal dealings, especially financially and emotionally. Even if you are shy as a youngster, you know you have inner mettle and determination. You are open to new projects and ideas that other less courageous characters might avoid.

You may wish for a wonderful romantic marriage partner, not only because of your fondness for home life and family but also because you enjoy the stability and security that a partnership can bring. Once committed to a relationship you will not want to relinquish it, but make no mistake: if you feel that your trust is being abused it will take a long time to reinstate it. If respect and equality don't reign in your relationship you have the strength to quickly annul the partnership.

In business you are a solid partner but may be reluctant to move forward with innovations and fresh ideas, so always be ready to look for ways to move ahead in your business and personal collaborations.

YOUR INNER LIFE

Beneath the hard exterior we know there's a soft crab inside, yet what is less known about you is that the sensitivity that characterises you is more to do with your psychic and intuitive abilities and instincts and less to do with your shyness and fear. This isn't to say you're not a shy character – when young you can certainly appear this way – but you're a natural-born sensitive who can feel undercurrents that other zodiac signs may not be aware of. You're able to understand the undercurrents of circumstances and may feel these more readily than other more earthy signs.

Being a sensitive character you can tend to take the problems of others as your own, a true pitfall of the empath. You'll shoulder other people's problems and want to help them and offer support, so much so that sometimes you will mistakenly see their issues as being your issues. The problem is that you are then less able to help because you are ensconced in the problem rather than being an agent for solution. Other people must sort out their own problems irrespective of your help.

Once you mature and are more assertive and can see the fine line between your life and other people's lives you will be a more effective nurturer and carer, and will also have an understanding of your own responsibility to self first and foremost and then to others.

HOW OTHERS SEE YOU

Cancer is ruled by the moon, so you can tend to be seen as being moody. The moon changes signs every two days and you can, as a result, be someone who changes their mind and whose feelings fluctuate fairly frequently. You may be accused of being up and down, and while this may be true you can find out how to work with lunar energy so you are less flighty and more stable.

If you know your moon sign at birth (the sign the moon was in when you were born) you will know that when the moon is in this sign you will be at your most rock steady and potent, barring any afflictions to the moon in your astrological chart. Keep an eye on how you feel during the various phases of the moon; self-knowledge is one of the best tools to contentedness.

HOW TO MAXIMISE YOUR POTENTIAL

Finding your voice is the most important aspect of your self-development, which you can go about in many ways. Public speaking is a good conduit to self-expression and assertiveness. You'll appreciate the opportunity of getting up in front of a crowd of strangers, becoming more open and overcoming feelings of shyness or self-doubt. Finding a toastmaster's club that teaches you how to speak clearly will be a wonderful way to move forward with your self-expression.

Storytelling, writing and talking are all activities that will soothe your soul. You won't necessarily be a best-selling author, a speaker on the international circuit or the person weaving mystery and magic at writer's festivals – although there's nothing to say you can't be – but all these creative pastimes will bring your inner creativity out and help you to connect with friends and family.

To be the best you can be, become conscious that you do, in fact, have strong intuition and even psychic powers. Enrolling in a psychic development class won't necessarily mean you will become a professional psychic, but you will learn the many tips and techniques necessary to use this most important faculty.

Being so naturally inclined to homemaking, family and nesting you'll find that the more stable and secure you feel at home and domestically the more stable and secure you will feel in yourself. In your profession, homemaking, property, maintenance or hospitality will appeal because the place where people rest is the one that attracts you the most.

Because you tend to be easily influenced it's important to establish a strong sense of self and a strong set of ethical codes and values, otherwise you will tend to be drawn this way and that by life's many distractions, activities and personalities. When you realise that you are being led by others or feel you are not expressing your highest sense of purpose, it's important to re-align your activities with your heart-centred code of values and ethics.

CANCER AND ITS ASCENDANTS

This chapter is about your sun sign, Cancer, and your predictions for the year ahead. The more you know about yourself the better you will be able to take advantage of opportunities, and also to avoid the pitfalls. It's critical to know as much about 'you' as possible.

In astrology your core self is represented by your sun sign, but your personality traits are represented by your ascendant (also known as your rising sign). The ascendant describes your personality, the way other people see you on first meeting you and the way you tend to filter life's events.

When you have intimate knowledge about your sun sign – your engine room or core being – you will be on the way to a happier life. When you add the knowledge about your personality – your ascendant – you will gain even deeper insight into what makes you tick.

Your ascendant sign is determined by the time of your birth on the date and year of your birth. Because the ascendant sign changes approximately every two hours, the best way to determine it is to ask an astrologer to calculate it for you. Certain apps will also calculate your ascendant sign (see page 873).

The following gives you more information about your abilities, characteristics and personality according to your sun sign Cancer in combination with your ascendant sign.

CANCER SUN SIGN WITH ARIES ASCENDANT

You are a force to be reckoned with: two cardinal signs in such prominent positions point to a strong character. You can be stubborn, especially if your will is opposed, but you are also a gentle, introspective person underneath, which may be quite surprising to those who get to know you better.

The Aries personality can project a reckless, at times bossy, fiery or even domineering exterior, yet your Cancerian sensitivity lies quietly beneath this strong outer avatar. You have extrasensory perception, as the Cancerian core enables you to intuit information about people and circumstances despite your fiery or brash Aries. Even though you are sensitive you have inner resourcefulness that indicates great strength of character.

CANCER SUN SIGN WITH TAURUS ASCENDANT

The combination of an earth sign and a water sign provides you with abilities that span the divide between the rational and the intuitive, giving you superpowers! The Taurean ascendant enables you to be steadfast, practical and grounded, while the Cancerian core enables you to garner information about people and circumstances that other sun signs don't perceive. Combine the steadiness of the Taurus personality and the instincts of the inner Cancerian, and you really are a force to be reckoned with. The Taurean personality is diligent and strong, and once your mind is made up there is little that can change it; your main pitfall is obstinacy. Aim to be more adaptable, and you'll find your options widen immeasurably.

CANCER SUN SIGN WITH GEMINI ASCENDANT

You are a seemingly happy-go-lucky character, but underneath your bravado lies an inner warmth and gentleness; this is your Cancerian core. On the surface your Gemini personality is able to detach from emotional circumstances that irk you while you appear to remain carefree. Any pain you feel is then on a deeper level and can manifest as moodiness, which can be confusing to those who see you as being light-hearted and fun loving and may even surprise you. As you mature you will feel more in tune with yourself and able to merge both intellect and emotions into a balanced, well-rounded character.

CANCER SUN SIGN WITH CANCER ASCENDANT

You are a double Cancer and, as such, are doubly intuitive and strong and a leader. But you are also doubly moody, introverted and cantankerous when the mood takes you! The key to making this combination work for you is to maximise your best qualities and minimise your worst. Make your intuitive abilities work for you; see them as an inner radar that guides you to making the right decisions, and your life will become so much easier. Don't let sensitivity deter you from your core strength; you are a leader and you feel fulfilled when you take action. Manage moodiness and find ways to avoid sinking into an introverted cycle by joining groups and being outgoing and sociable. You can be easily distracted and may be prone to overindulge in the good things in life, so keep an eye on these tendencies.

CANCER SUN SIGN WITH LEO ASCENDANT

You have a dynamo personality that can appear to be brash at times. Your fiery Leo get up and go personality works well with the iron will of your Cancerian inner self, but when you impulsively charge ahead your sensitive, caring Cancer may take some time to catch up with your own impulsiveness! This can lead to inner tension or disappointment.

Once you learn when to take action and when to allow your intuition to lead a little more the Cancer sun sign with the Leo ascendant makes a strong character able to stand your own ground and lead the pack. Combined with your sixth sense, this is a self-motivated combination and is quite a force to be reckoned with.

CANCER SUN SIGN WITH VIRGO ASCENDANT

This combination can be effective, as your practical personality will enable the sensitive, intuitive Cancerian core to take action in methodical and measured ways. The care and attention you take in life is admirable, but you must make sure your ideals and values are effective as your practical personality will enable the sensitive, intuitive Cancerian core to take action. You are a caring personality who wishes the world to be one big contented, healthy and positive family, so you can become disheartened when faced with the reality that humans are not perfect. You will work towards improving the health and well-being of others in admirable ways. Self-care must always come first or you will burn out due to the near impossible tasks you tend to set yourself.

CANCER SUN SIGN WITH LIBRA ASCENDANT

Having two cardinal signs in such prominent positions indicates a strong personality. Your strength of character may come as a surprise even to you, as you are generally known to have a soft, gentle approach to life. You love music, art, reading, writing and romance but you can be stubborn, especially if your will is opposed. If you feel your will is being challenged it will be hard to change your mind. You do have extrasensory perception, as your Cancerian core can intuit information about people and circumstances that other signs don't perceive. Combine this with your search for peace and harmony in life and you really are a gentle and perceptive yet strong and determined character.

CANCER SUN SIGN WITH SCORPIO ASCENDANT

You are a double water sign and are intuitive, emotional and sometimes super moody. Being moody is no surprise, as you feel your way through life and are a truly empathic character; your moods swing in line with the atmosphere, room or event you are experiencing. As a youngster these qualities may be confusing, as there is little in common between your intuitive approach and the reasoning world. As a youngster you may be easily misled and influenced. You have artistic, even psychic abilities and tend to overindulge in the good things in life, so must avoid co-dependent and addictive behaviour. You will find balance in life by seeing the world through both your practical eyes and your intuitive, artistic senses.

CANCER SUN SIGN WITH SAGITTARIUS ASCENDANT

You are quite the dynamo: upbeat, outgoing, adventurous and a daredevil. The outgoing Sagittarian personality will often mask the gentler yet resolute Cancerian underneath. It will take some time for people to meet the sensitive Cancerian, as the gregarious Sagittarian qualities will take the lead. The care and attention you take in life is admirable, and you are also an upbeat character. There will be an interest in writing, study and storytelling. You may be a chatterbox, especially once you feel comfortable in your surroundings, but you may also be protective of your inner qualities such as your sixth sense. Take the time to cultivate your inner self; your intuition is an additional string to your bow.

CANCER SUN SIGN WITH CAPRICORN ASCENDANT

Two cardinal signs in prominent positions can lead to stubbornness, especially when you are opposed. Yet your Capricorn personality, the person people see on first meeting you, appears to

be down to earth, reasonable and quiet. The Cancerian inner self can also make you appear to be a gentle, introspective person, but when you are challenged your inner resourcefulness and ability to stand your ground will be quite surprising.

You may feel an inner tension between being gentle and perceptive on the one hand and being practical and down to earth on the other. If so, take the time to work on combining your gentleness and earthiness and you will become truly rounded. Combine your Cancerian instincts with the steadfastness of the Capricorn character, and you should find your path an easier one.

CANCER SUN SIGN WITH AQUARIUS ASCENDANT

You are quite the personality: quirky, independent, outgoing, even eccentric and upbeat one day then quiet, traditional and retiring the next. You may be seen as being unusual or as a chameleon. Others with less adaptability will marvel at your ability to mix in with any circumstance, and your adaptability, flexibility and open-mindedness are certainly useful qualities. You are also resolute and determined and can be super stubborn. Depending on the day, you display some or all of these traits! A true pitfall would be to manifest only the negative traits, which include your occasional inability to see the opinions of others and your closed-mindedness and obstinacy. Luckily, your eccentricity means you are rarely stuck in any one particular mindset, which is both a blessing and potentially a difficulty. Mindfulness and meditation work supremely well for you to make you more centred.

CANCER SUN SIGN WITH PISCES ASCENDANT

You are an emotional and intuitive character; two water signs in such prominent positions point to a sensitive character who has deeper perception than many other people. Your Cancerian core self is a gentle, introspective person who is also resourceful and able to stand your ground. This ability may be quite a surprise for those who see only the gentle and dreamy Pisces personality on first meeting. However, the Pisces willpower is also rock solid, with outward gentleness belying inner strength.

You do have a certain extrasensory perception, as both the Cancerian traits and the Piscean psychic abilities make for a supremely intuitive individual. This sensitivity can sometimes lead you to being easily misled and fooled, so base important decisions on facts, not influence.

CANCER IN LOVE

You are a particularly independent individual who is likely to be selective about who you spend long-term time with. In this section you can check out your compatibility with other sun signs. Remember that we are all complex individuals, so the more you know about someone's astrological birth chart the better you can determine your compatibility. Consider having your astrological birth chart compared with that of a partner, friend or family member, as the compatibility – known as 'synastry' in astrology – goes even deeper than a comparison of sun signs, although this is a good place to begin.

CANCER WITH ARIES

You are both cardinal signs, which means you are both strong characters, so there has to be give and take or one of you will feel you are playing second fiddle to the other. Your Cancerian sensitivity can feel overshadowed by the Aries dominant approach and Aries can feel invalidated by Cancerian mood swings, especially when you are usually such a supportive sign. If you can establish a solid platform of mutual respect this match can work. Some might say it is a difficult match, but it largely depends on how willing you are to work on your relationship and whether there is other compatibility in your chart such as compatible moon signs.

CANCER WITH TAURUS

Cancer is a water sign and is inherently intuitive, instinctive, caring and nurturing. Taurus is an earth sign and is practical, methodical and sensual and enjoys the good things in life. Your mutual interest is likely to cross over in areas such as nurturance, caring for each other's well-being and a predisposition for good food and drink. However, your fundamental approach to life is very different and therefore could signal disagreements about essential daily matters.

CANCER WITH GEMINI

The Cancerian personality is gentle, sensitive and introspective, yet underneath your inner resourcefulness and ability to stand your ground may be quite a surprise to Gemini. You are a diligent and strong character, and once your mind is made up there is little that will change it. The combination of an air sign with a water sign could pose difficulties once the initial attraction wears off, as you need different qualities from each other. You need support and stability and Gemini needs freedom of movement and independence despite being a loyal character.

CANCER WITH CANCER

While this may initially present as the ideal twinning, too much of a good thing can be a setback. You are both highly sensitive and intuitive, and unless you have learned to manage your sensitivity and psychic abilities you can easily become confused and misread each other's thoughts and actions. You may tend to see life through each other's eyes, not seeing where you begin and where your partner begins. Blurred lines between you can lead to confusion, but you can make a good pairing if you are conscious about your abilities and tendency to see deeper into each other's actions and talk frequently and constructively about the best way forward in real terms.

CANCER WITH LEO

Leo is ruled by the sun, the centre of the solar system, so Leos like to be the centre of attention; the sun really does shine from them! Cancer would need to initially take the back seat in this relationship or else the Leo will not feel they can shine. The quieter Cancerian personality may play this role in the beginning, but as both these signs are super strong willed this combo can lead to a battle unless both are conscious of each other's boundaries and respectful of each other's power.

CANCER WITH VIRGO

The earthy Virgo will initially appeal as a sensual lover, someone with whom you can feel empathy. You may also enjoy the sense of safety, security and care emanating from Virgo. Virgo will appreciate your apparent emotional intelligence, tenderness and compassion. These signs can certainly gain much from each other and can be mutually supportive, but both can be cantankerous and the Cancerian character will undoubtedly wish to take control over certain issues, which is something Virgo may need to adapt to.

CANCER WITH LIBRA

This is a double cardinal match, so while both these sun signs appear on the surface to be soft, gentle characters both will wish to take the lead. They will do so in different ways: you will want to be heard emotionally and be emotionally fulfilled, while the Libra sun sign will want to be heard and respected and find peace and harmony. As both signs can be indecisive and constantly looking for emotional and mental support from each other, this match can tend to fall flat unless both partners make a conscious effort to constantly support each other. This can be tiring, especially when both are indecisive and looking for personal fulfilment from the other rather than from themselves. If you have strong air in your chart and the Libran strong water, this combination could work.

CANCER WITH SCORPIO

Two water signs make for a passionate, emotional and intense relationship. However, both partners risk feeling overwhelmed by the other, so it's important in this relationship to maintain healthy boundaries and focus on self-care as otherwise it can result in co-dependency. That aside, this is one of the best matches for the Cancerian individual as the two signs are on the same page emotionally: you have similar outlooks in life as you are both intuitive and passionate about your activities. This relationship goes much deeper than many others, so if you are willing to explore the wonders of love it can be fulfilling.

CANCER WITH SAGITTARIUS

It's a case of opposites attracting: you will admire the fire and excitement offered by the Sagittarian, and the Sagittarian will be intrigued and seduced by your tenderness and allure. However, the Cancerian water sign tends to pour cold water on the fire of the Sagittarian, despite initial attraction on both parts. In other words you, driven principally by emotions, can overwhelm the get up and go of the Sagittarian, seemingly clipping their wings albeit unintentionally. Unless that is care is taken to understand the other: the Cancerian is principally a caring, nurturing person, and the Sagittarian principally an outgoing adventurer. Clearly these two people are very different. Embrace your differences and allow them to complement one other and you have a good match.

CANCER WITH CAPRICORN

This is a case of opposites attracting, although you have more common ground than initially meets the eye. You are both cardinal signs, which means you are both strong characters and therefore understand each other's approach life: it's direct and often goal oriented. The earthiness of the Capricorn will represent safety and security to Cancer and your elusiveness and sensitivity can represent a feeling of completion for Capricorn, who is essentially practical, reasonable and intellectual. This is a match for partnership as long as both are willing to give in to the other on occasion and in equal measures.

CANCER WITH AQUARIUS

Cancerians look for safety, security and emotional contentment in a partnership. You are unlikely to find this in the Aquarian, who is essentially quirky, restless and eccentric and can be unreliable, even if unintentionally. While this match may be enticing and even exciting at first, both partners are likely to feel unfulfilled by the other unless there are other indicators in your mutual astrology charts that suggest compatibility such as a sun–moon compatibility. The Cancerian may feel unsupported emotionally by the Aquarian and the Aquarian emotionally beleaguered by the Cancerian. As companions and friends, however, this can be a light-hearted, fun relationship as both approach life with such different attitudes and can teach the other much in life.

CANCER WITH PISCES

This is a recipe for success as you are both water signs and have an innate understanding of each other. You are both intuitive, sensitive and tender partners, although the Pisces tendency for daydreaming may be foreign to the more centred, strong Cancerian. You will wish to take the lead in this relationship, so Pisces must avoid playing the victim-martyr role. Both signs are complex so must give each other space for introspective phases. This, however, is a natural mutually supportive partnership and can be positive for long-term commitment.

THE YEAR AHEAD FOR CANCER

Affirmation for the year: *'I'll embrace the new all the better by being practical.'*

The developments you experienced in 2021 will contribute to your outlook this year, especially with work, your health and daily life, so that any upheaval you experienced in these areas will continue to have a bearing. This doesn't mean drama will follow you into 2022; it means simply that the balls you put in motion in 2021 at work and with your general interests, projects and activities will now develop.

You will gain the chance to evolve the clever ideas that take you into new territory but, as with every new venture, there will be teething problems that will arise principally in the first two months of the year, in May and again towards October/November.

Your level of success in the in-between times will depend on how well you strategise, plan ahead and provide a strong base for yourself, giving you not only room to move but also the solid foundation that enables you to innovate and birth new ventures, skills and ideas. And, while the stress points in your year may require you to dig deep and really rise to any challenges, these will often be the times when you will excel the most.

The month of January and from May to August will be months to remember. It's a time to truly consider your long-term goals as you could complete and attain so much. The real pitfall will be that you make changes on a whim or that changes you considered relatively easy become taxing. The secret to success comes down to good planning earlier in the year and on realising that changes made this year are likely to be long term. Have a five-year plan in the back of your mind, as this will help you to consider the realities and practicalities of your situation and not just your immediate needs.

HEALTH

Your interest in health and well-being is important in 2022 as you will gain the chance to create a more solid base for yourself and those you look after. You are likely not only to be looking after yourself well but also keeping an eye on someone else health-wise.

You will find much mental and spiritual stimulation and support from the people you associate with, so it's important to surround yourself with upbeat, optimistic and confident people this year. You are particularly sensitive to those you mix with, so ensure their moods are positive as these will rub off on you.

January and then again the last quarter of the year are ideal times for making the most effective changes to your daily routine so that you may proceed with the best possible vitality and health.

FINANCES

Going through such changeable times is certainly a test of your financial know-how. The month of January and the phase from May to August will focus particularly on joint and shared duties and finances, and if find yourself in financial strife this year these months are ideal to seek and gain the help of an agency such as an accountant or another expert who can help you get through changes in your finances.

Having Venus in your shared finance zone in April will indicate a good time to focus on taxes and joint assets, giving your finances a decent health check to ensure you are still on track. You may be inclined to overspend or to compensate for a tough daily grind by over-investing, so ensure you are careful with decisions in April and May. You may find that once the sun and Mercury are in Virgo and Libra from the end of August until the end of October you regain a more even keel financially.

As the eclipses will be across your career and home you're most likely to find fluctuations in finances due to changes here, so ensure your investments, both financial and emotional, are for the long term. Avoid speculation, especially in the second half of the year.

HOME LIFE

The stage is set for considerable change in your home life this year. You may feel particularly drawn to making changes domestically. Travel, welcoming visitors or even a move are likely. If you're DIY minded, this is a good year to make changes in your bricks and mortar – however, with the proviso that changes you make at home do not interfere with an already packed and changeable work and health schedule.

It's all in the planning in 2022, which may be a chore for you as you are usually happier being spontaneous and creative. If you see the planning as a foundation stone to creating more joy and happiness at home and a springboard for adventure and travel then you will succeed.

Key turning points at home will be in mid year, then once again towards the end of the year. The eclipses on 16 May and 25 October will be in your home sector and spell major change at home or with family. Someone you live with may be ready to leave home, or you yourself may be inclined to make changes such as a renovation or move.

LOVE

Saturn in your seventh and eighth houses of love and partnerships suggests that there will be change afoot in your closest relationships this year. However, there is also an internal debate that seems to accompany your love life: do you want to commit or do you want freedom? If you're in a committed relationship, freedom of movement in some form will appeal. If you're single you may wish to commit, but in a free kind of a way!

You may even put yourself through the wringer by being unable to decide. Avoid this, as someone close will need your help and attention this year so the more practical and realistic you are the better.

With Jupiter in your eighth house in the first quarter of the year, you will dream big and will be inclined to be positive about your romantic connection. But for couples, much will revolve around the bigger-picture decisions and the direction you both wish to move in. Singles may be seeing prospective partners or those you meet idealistically, so if you experience disappointments in the first quarter aim instead to see people and your relationships in a more realistic light.

Once Jupiter enters Aries on 10 May your love life is likely to get active if it's been lacking in passion. Mars, the sign that brings your dynamic, creative and fun-loving self to the surface, will bring your best aspects out until the end of July, so this is a good time for romance and holidays together. This is the phase for singles to mingle and for couples to reignite passion, as you'll be in your element.

You must make space for romance in the second half of the year, as the eclipses will focus your mind on your activities, career and home. October will be another truly romantic time, so aim for get-togethers then.

CAREER

The eclipses in April-May and October-November will be across your domestic and career sectors, suggesting key changes in both these areas. If you work from home or with property you will find the most change will be in your career, although your home life will be impacted accordingly.

This is an excellent year to focus on good communication skills, as these are the cornerstone of good work relationships. The boundaries in your work relationships will need to be set, otherwise you may find you end up with needless conflict and/or intrigue and obstacles in relationships that should be straightforward.

The new moon on 1 April could kick-start a promising new project. May and then October-November are the key times for change, when you may be drawn to new practices and ideas in your existing career. However, a considerable change at home during these times may put the emphasis on your domestic life, and your work will need to fit around this.

Some lovely collaborations could take place mid year, which will help you to reconsider and reconfigure some of your work practices. You may find an expert, colleague or analyst particularly helpful from June through to August.

January

career   love   home   health   finance

Notes: the pie charts such as the one above listed for each month show energy distribution according to the stars for the month ahead. If you wish to make changes in the areas of your finances, health, career, love or home and you see there is a large amount of energy in that sector in the chart, your endeavours should succeed as long as you have prepared well in advance. The charts also show which areas will potentially have the most focus in your life during the month.

The moon sign listed for each day's entry in the diary is the position of the moon at the end of the day in Greenwich Mean Time (GMT). To gain the most information about a particular day's circumstances, read the day before and the day after for a complete picture.

1 JANUARY

Happy New Year! You may receive an unexpected visitor or enjoy a surprise change in your usual routine for New Year's Day. You'll appreciate the sense that this year will include new horizons. If you're working you may experience something new you'll enjoy. ***Moon enters Capricorn.***

2 JANUARY

The new moon and supermoon in Capricorn will kick-start a fresh phase for you in a personal context, such as a fresh chapter within a key relationship and at work for July Cancerians. For some, though, this year represents the chance to reorganise your health and daily routine so it suits you better. Take a moment to consider your best step forward. You may enjoy a trip or a get-together with someone fun.

3 JANUARY

This is a good time to consider how you could pep up your relationships. A business or personal partner or a friend may suggest something new. A focus on planning ahead this year will be rewarding. *Moon enters Aquarius.*

4 JANUARY

You'll appreciate the chance to do something different, although people around you may be a little restless or even unpredictable so aim to be adaptable as opposed to resisting change. You'll be drawn to enjoying music and indulging in romance and good food. *Moon in Aquarius.*

5 JANUARY

You'll enjoy a get-together and romance could also blossom, so organise a treat if you haven't already. You may reunite with someone you love. A creative project could flourish. *Moon in Aquarius.*

6 JANUARY

The Pisces moon will add to a feeling of romance and mysticism. Spiritually inclined Cancerians will enjoy increasing your understanding of spirituality. You'll appreciate the company of like-minded people although you may be tempted to be a little escapist, so ensure you keep one foot on the ground! *Moon in Pisces.*

7 JANUARY

Your intuition is strong at the moment so relationships are likely to proceed relatively smoothly, especially those with people you love. However, you may see more in a situation than others do, and their lack of insight could be frustrating. Find ways to express your deeper insight if possible to improve mutual understanding. *Moon in Pisces.*

8 JANUARY

This is a good day to get ahead with your various chores, both at home and at work. Romantically inclined Cancerians will enjoy touching base with someone you love over activities you both enjoy, such as creativity and romance and enjoying a good meal. *Moon in Aries.*

9 JANUARY

Romance will appeal especially if you were born in early July. Organise a date with someone special if you haven't already. Singles: this is a good time to organise a night out or to go to a club you enjoy as you could meet an earthy dependable character. Cancerians born later in July may

find this a good time for getting outstanding chores cleared at home or at work. A health or beauty treat will also appeal. **Moon in Aries.**

10 JANUARY

The moon will be in Aries for much of the day, enabling you to complete your various chores and be productive. Once the moon enters Taurus at night you'll enjoy feeling more earthy and will appreciate some down time at the end of the day. **Moon enters Taurus.**

11 JANUARY

As a sensitive character you prefer to get on with everyone all the time. Unfortunately this isn't possible, and you may find that certain people are super helpful and others not so much. Someone may also prove to be forgetful. If it's you, find ways to give yourself reminders and to be more aware, especially at work. **Moon in Taurus.**

12 JANUARY

The moon in Taurus helps you to get things done in the most practical, realistic way. Try to get loose ends to do with key communications and negotiations tied up over the next two days, before Mercury turns retrograde on Friday, to avoid delays or having to renegotiate at a later time. **Moon in Taurus.**

13 JANUARY

When the moon is in Gemini you may notice you and other people feel a little more chatty and flexible, especially at work. Your partner may also feel more inclined to talk freely. However, not everyone will feel the same, so aim to adjust to other people's mindsets and paces if necessary. **Moon in Gemini.**

14 JANUARY

You may receive key news to do with shared matters such as joint finances or a collaboration. You may need to rethink an idea or event. If you're travelling or planning a trip you will receive key news. If delays occur, be flexible. **Moon in Gemini.**

15 JANUARY

The next two days may be fairly intense for you in the run-up to the full moon in your own sign. Developments are likely to revolve around your feelings, especially to do with someone in your personal life, and for some developments will be due to circumstances outside your control so aim to be flexible and work towards the bigger-picture results you want. **Moon enters Cancer.**

16 JANUARY

Someone close has news for you and this may represent considerable change either for you personally, for them or for the relationship. Trust your instincts. Avoid allowing emotions to rule your mind. Find ways to gain perspective. Avoid making snap decisions for the best results. ***Moon in Cancer.***

17 JANUARY

The Cancerian full moon shines a light on your personal life, and for some mid-July Cancerians on a work or health matter. Key changes will mean you must consider the big picture, especially concerning your well-being. Base decisions on practicalities and avoid allowing emotions to overwhelm reason. A commitment can be made.

18 JANUARY

This is a good time to make financial and personal decisions that will produce more security and happiness in your life. Look for ways to express your own values and principles so the activities you do mirror your favourite interests and ideas more. ***Moon in Leo.***

19 JANUARY

You may receive good news to do with work or from someone special. It's a good time to discuss your plans and to make changes in your daily routine so it suits you better. Romance could blossom and a trip or venture could open doors, so be proactive. ***Moon in Leo.***

20 JANUARY

The sun in Aquarius for the next four weeks will encourage you to view the areas of your life you share in a new light. You may feel more outgoing and optimistic about making changes about various commitments, including shared finances such as taxes, shared space at home and joint duties. ***Moon in Leo.***

21 JANUARY

These next few days are ideal for discussing important new ideas with those they concern. You may also be drawn to socialising and networking. You'll enjoy meeting a new circle of people and making plans that are not only practical and viable but also exciting. ***Moon in Virgo.***

22 JANUARY

You'll enjoy a trip or a get-together with someone you admire and understand. A study course, research and broadening your horizons will appeal. Avoid being overly sensitive to other people's bad moods and be practical. ***Moon enters Libra.***

23 JANUARY

This is a good day to sort out finances and also for personal ventures, especially collaborations. You may receive key news from someone you share important matters in your life with. You may enjoy a reunion or will reconsider a recent decision. ***Moon in Libra.***

24 JANUARY

When the moon is in Libra you will be drawn to look for harmony in life. Just ensure it isn't at the cost of anything else such as your principles. Peace of mind at all costs can eventually use up more resources than the actual peace you're looking for. Avoid being stubborn and look for new ways to get on with people if a relationship has hit a speed bump. *Moon in Libra.*

25 JANUARY

Reconsider a work or health matter if necessary. You will receive help from an expert or adviser if need be, so ensure you reach out and make enquiries if you are in need of information as talks could go well. It's a good day for health and well-being appointments. *Moon in Scorpio.*

26 JANUARY

You may need to go over old ground. Someone close such as a partner or work colleague may need to review an agreement. Be flexible and also practical. You may revisit a topic you believed had already been sewn up or may enjoy a reunion. *Moon in Scorpio.*

27 JANUARY

When the moon is in Sagittarius you may be busier at work and will find life a little more exciting or upbeat. You'll appreciate being optimistic and industrious and could create positive outcomes now, so be motivated! *Moon in Sagittarius.*

28 JANUARY

The moon in your sixth house spells a more upbeat day-to-day life. You'll enjoy embracing new activities, and travel and study may appeal to you as ways to express yourself. Plan for a lovely weekend! *Moon in Sagittarius.*

29 JANUARY

Important news is on the way, especially if you were born in mid-July. A personal or business partner or personal acquaintance will have key information for you. It may involve you reconsidering your options or a change in your relationship. *Moon in Capricorn.*

30 JANUARY

You may hear unexpected news or someone may behave unpredictably. Be prepared to adapt to new circumstances but you must avoid rash decisions. *Moon in Capricorn.*

31 JANUARY

You will enjoy a sense that life is regaining a more even keel, especially in your personal life and through work. It's a good day for health and beauty treats and to improve your self-esteem and vitality. *Moon in Aquarius.*

February

career   love   home   health   finance

1 FEBRUARY

The new moon in Aquarius will spotlight new ideas and notions of how you could collaborate and co-operate better with those you work and play with. For some this new moon will bring the chance to begin a fresh project or venture that signifies something new for you. Be bold and adventurous for the best results.

2 FEBRUARY

You'll feel inspired to follow your instincts both at work and at home. Indulging in your personal interests and hobbies will appeal, so consider how you could add more of what you love in your life. If you feel there are roadblocks to your plans find new ways to look at obstacles so you can overcome them. *Moon enters Pisces.*

3 FEBRUARY

This is a good day to consider your deeper thoughts and wishes, especially to do with work and your big-picture aims and goals. Travel, study and generally broadening your horizons will appeal. It's a good day for meditation, yoga and communing with nature, which will feel calming and nurturing. *Moon in Pisces.*

4 FEBRUARY

You are likley to receive key news at work or at home regarding finances or an area you share such as joint duties and responsibilities. If news seems limiting, look for ways to find self-expression even within the restrictions. A partner may have key news for you. *Moon in Pisces.*

5 FEBRUARY

When the moon is in Aries you will feel more motivated to get things shipshape in your life in general, so gardening, planning ahead for the year and arranging plans so they meet your needs will appeal. You'll enjoy being outgoing and upbeat, so organise something exciting! *Moon in Aries.*

6 FEBRUARY

Take things one step at a time with a favourite project or interest to avoid rash decisions. Take a moment to consider your ideas in relation to someone else's and see if mutual ground can be reached. *Moon in Aries.*

7 FEBRUARY

You'll get ahead well now with making changes within your daily routine and setting the ball in motion with your big-picture plans. Be realistic and practical and take things one step at a time, especially with someone who can be sensitive. *Moon in Taurus.*

8 FEBRUARY

This is an excellent day for doing something different and for embracing new groups and organisations, friends and ideas, especially at work. You may be called on to alter your usual routine from out of the blue or hear from someone unexpectedly. *Moon in Taurus.*

9 FEBRUARY

When the moon is in Gemini you may notice that people seem chattier and more likely to get in touch. You'll appreciate hearing from an old friend or acquaintance. A key meeting at work could be positive, but you must avoid impulsiveness. *Moon in Gemini.*

10 FEBRUARY

A work meeting is likely to go well. If you have scheduled a special event or a social visit it is also likely to go well. Just ensure you have planned ahead well to avoid any unnecessary surprises. *Moon in Gemini.*

11 FEBRUARY

Key news and developments suggest longer-term change and developments are to come. Changes are likely to involve someone close such as a partner or colleague, best friend or family member. You'll enjoy a get-together. *Moon in Cancer.*

12 FEBRUARY

Today's Cancerian moon puts you in your element, and you will feel more understanding and in sync with your circumstances. Your intuition is strong so listen to it. If you feel more moody than usual take some time out to regain perspective. Avoid taking the mood swings of others personally. *Moon in Cancer.*

13 FEBRUARY

Ensure other people's and your own emotions aren't making waves. Take a moment to get grounded and practical. You'll appreciate the chance to get together with people you love and enjoy favourite activities. A reunion will be enjoyable even if strong emotions arise. *Moon in Cancer.*

14 FEBRUARY

Happy St Valentine's Day! This is always a quirky day when we hear unexpected news or gain the chance to reveal our true feelings. You may be surprised by news you hear. It's a good day to get in touch with someone you love, so be bold! You may even hear unexpectedly from a lost love or will be feeling nostalgic. *Moon in Leo.*

15 FEBRUARY

You have excellent persuasive powers and this will be a good period to use your influential and charming qualities to create the best outcome, mainly due to the fact that some of your plans may clash with those of someone important to you. Be open to a new path and avoid a battle of egos. *Moon in Leo.*

16 FEBRUARY

The Leo full moon will shine a light on the way you communicate and on key relationships. You'll enjoy a get-together, and for July Cancerians there will be work or health news. Aim to be bold and find ways to express yourself confidently and clearly. For some Cancerians this full moon will spotlight your values and how you spend your time and money, so consider how you can be more balanced so you can do things that are truly meaningful. *Moon enters Virgo late in the day.*

17 FEBRUARY

You may receive unexpected news or hear from someone from out of the blue. It's likely to be good news and it is a good time to make agreements and commitments, as long as you are willing to make the necessary changes. *Moon in Virgo.*

18 FEBRUARY

As the sun enters Pisces you are likely to enjoy indulging more in your favourite interests and hobbies. This could be a particularly spiritual time for you. You may express your imagination more at work and be drawn more than usual to art, movies and dance. *Moon in Libra.*

19 FEBRUARY

This is a good weekend to focus on creative a lovely environment for yourself and those you love. You will be drawn to making changes at home and improving your décor or interpersonal dynamics. Music, dance and romance will appeal. Someone may ask for your help. If you need some advice or support it will be available. *Moon in Libra.*

20 FEBRUARY

This is a good day to focus on relaxation and recharging your batteries and spending time with those you love. You may not agree with everyone, so avoid making life difficult by looking for common ground rather than conflict. If you need a little help ask for it; it's available. *Moon in Libra.*

21 FEBRUARY

You'll feel more motivated as the day goes by and will be productive. If you've been putting chores off, this is the day to finally get them done! You may feel more passionate and be more obstinate, so keep an eye on stubbornness as it could be a pitfall. Spiritually minded Cancerians will be more intuitive while the moon is in Scorpio. *Moon enters Scorpio.*

22 FEBRUARY

You'll feel inspired by other people and by creativity. However, you won't automatically get on with everyone, so ensure you give those you tend to disagree with a wide berth. *Moon in Scorpio.*

23 FEBRUARY

You'll enjoy being with like-minded people and those who inspire you. Work could go particularly well if you have the opportunity to express your more imaginative ideas. Avoid being overly idealistic, forgetful and absent-minded. Romance could truly blossom so ensure you organise a date or a night in! *Moon in Sagittarius.*

24 FEBRUARY

An excellent day for romance. At work you may be particularly charming and influential so if you're in the position to make changes they are likely to take well – that is, as long as your plans are as realistic as they are imaginative. *Moon in Sagittarius.*

25 FEBRUARY

Choose your words carefully as some of what you say may be misunderstood. You may hear unexpected news. Avoid being pressured into making a response and, if you can, ask for time to consider your viewpoints. A group or organisation may alter the terms of their agreement with you. *Moon enters Capricorn.*

26 FEBRUARY

Communications and travel may be better and if obstacles occurred yesterday this will be a good day to sort them out. This is also a good day for floating ideas with someone special such as travel plans. You'll appreciate the chance to take part in activities you enjoy. *Moon in Capricorn.*

27 FEBRUARY

You'll enjoy doing something different. A partner or friend may behave erratically and, if so, try to see their behaviour as being their thing as opposed to a comment on your relationship. A reunion could be enjoyable, so take time to increase the connections and relationships you treasure and be with those you love. *Moon enters Aquarius.*

28 FEBRUARY

You'll appreciate the opportunity to look at key relationships and duties in a new light. A personal matter could benefit from a fresh perspective so that you can see another's point of view more clearly. You may even uncover new information that provides you with the chance to broaden your horizons at work or with a project or venture. *Moon in Aquarius.*

March

career   love   home   health   finance

1 MARCH

The strong bond you have with someone is hard to ignore, but this doesn't mean you'll always agree about everything! Be imaginative about how to boost relationships if they have gone a little flat but be practical if you must overcome a difficult situation. ***Moon enters Pisces.***

2 MARCH

The Pisces new moon signals the chance to turn a corner. For some Cancerians this will involve a favourite activity or interest; for others it will be in connection with study, travel or a creative project. Look for inspired ways to move forward.

3 MARCH

The Venus-Mars-Pluto conjunction will be in your seventh house of partnerships, both business and personal. Someone may have key news for you. This could be a very passionate time, so you must maintain perspective. For some mid-July Crabs there may be key news at work. Take a moment to ground yourself and then put your best foot forward. Avoid being overcome by emotions and maintain a clear perspective. ***Moon in Pisces.***

4 MARCH

Today's Aries moon will create a sense of dynamism and a can-do attitude in you, but you may also tend to fire up fairly quickly so ensure you avoid taking things out of context. Someone at work or who has influence over you may feel super sensitive, rejected or sidelined. If it's you who feels like this find a way to improve your situation or relationship rather than looking for failings in your connection. If you have felt under the weather, take short breaks where you can. *Moon in Aries.*

5 MARCH

An inspiring project or trip is likely to take shape. Reach for the stars and be imaginative about your ventures and be positive about meetings and talks as they could go well. Just ensure you are realistic if your expectations are shown to be overly optimistic. *Moon in Aries.*

6 MARCH

As both Mars and Venus step into Aquarius in your seventh house of partnerships you will experience a change of focus. Someone close to you may have ideas or plans that will take you into new territory. Be innovative but also remember to look at the practicalities. Avoid stubbornness. *Moon in Taurus.*

7 MARCH

The Taurean moon will help you to make decisions based on facts and information as opposed to supposition, but it may also lead you to be a little obstinate where changes must be implemented so ensure you are being open-minded. *Moon in Taurus.*

8 MARCH

This is a good day to build bridges with people you have quarrelled with. Romance could also flourish, so make a date if you haven't already! Meetings are likely to go well. Reach out to friends and groups as you could make some lovely connections. *Moon enters Gemini.*

9 MARCH

The Gemini moon will help you to look at life from many different perspectives, so if you have felt stuck or reluctant to make changes recently this moon will help you to move forward. If you have suffered ill health or fatigue of late this is a good time to consult experts. *Moon in Gemini.*

10 MARCH

As Mercury enters Pisces you will feel increasingly intuitive over the coming weeks, so ensure you trust your sixth sense. Spiritually minded Cancerians will enjoy deepening your interest in the esoteric. This is a good day to make commitments to a project or person. *Moon in Gemini.*

11 MARCH

Your intuition is in top form so trust your gut instincts, especially regarding joint ventures, collaborations and shared duties or finances. This is another day when meetings and communications are likely to go well, so take the initiative. It's a good day to make a commitment. *Moon in Cancer.*

12 MARCH

You'll enjoy the sense that a project such as a study course can move forward well. A meeting in a group or a work situation could be enjoyable. The arts, creativity and your favourite hobbies will all entice you this weekend, so ensure you have something special planned. *Moon in Cancer.*

13 MARCH

This is an excellent day to deepen your understanding of yourself and someone close. Spiritual activities and psychic development could be particularly rewarding. You may feel drawn to a beautiful person or place such as the sea or beach. Someone close may reveal their deeper thoughts and feelings. *Moon enters Leo.*

14 MARCH

Communications are likely to move quickly, so if you like conversations and information to flow you'll enjoy your day. But if you feel sometimes that life is moving too quickly, this is a good time to consider how you could slow it down. Make time for romance; you'll be glad you did! A shared financial matter could move forward. *Moon in Leo.*

15 MARCH

You're a sensitive person, so when you don't get on with everyone you can take this to heart. Some people may seem a little adversarial or moody, so be bold and avoid taking their moods personally. If you feel conflict is bubbling under the surface take things one step at a time, especially financially. *Moon in Leo.*

16 MARCH

Today's Virgo moon will bring your more practical side out and encourage you to be more accommodating of others. Trust in the advice of someone you know has your back, but be careful that you do not give your good hard work away to those who do not appreciate your efforts. *Moon in Virgo.*

17 MARCH

You'll appreciate the opportunity to try something new. A friend, group or organisation may prove particularly helpful or has good news for you, so ensure you reach out if you're waiting for the green light. *Moon in Virgo.*

18 MARCH

The Virgo full moon shines a light on your communications and relationships. You may decide there are better ways you can communicate, such as through a new device or through listening more to others and asking others to listen more to your opinions. This is a good time to consider new travel or study plans. A vehicle may benefit from an overhaul or new tyres, for example. Your spiritual interests could become more of a focus. The full moon will shine a light on which areas of your life need more attention to detail and practicalities.

19 MARCH

The Libran moon will focus your attention on your home life and those you love a little more. You may decide to spend a little more time on your home by giving attention to the décor and the comfort factor. Dance, music and art will appeal. *Moon in Libra.*

20 MARCH

This is the equinox, when the sun enters Aries. During the next four weeks you may find that your work and projects become a real focus. Find the time to boost your sense of accomplishment and fulfilment in life as you could make great progress. *Moon in Scorpio.*

21 MARCH

Key news to do with travel, a project or visitor will arrive. You may feel drawn to spend more time with the people and projects you love and will enjoy the sense that you are communicating well with people you admire. However, you may also be easily influenced at this time. A key financial, study or legal matter will benefit from close attention to ensure you gain ground. *Moon in Scorpio.*

22 MARCH

Your plans can grow, so aim to put your ideas and expertise to good use. If a financial matter needs attention, this is a good time to focus on it. You may be surprised by news you receive from someone you share duties and responsibilities with and may need to adjust your expectations. *Moon enters Sagittarius.*

23 MARCH

You'll enjoy being with like-minded people and being imaginative, artistic and creative. If you love music, you'll enjoy being in a musical environment. This is another day when you may feel easily influenced or even a little absent-minded, so ensure your plans are watertight. You may be drawn to travel to the sea or to a beautiful place. *Moon in Sagittarius.*

24 MARCH

You'll feel more practical and grounded especially at work and regarding health and well-being. If you feel there is opposition to your plans, take a moment to ensure you are on the same page

as misunderstandings could arise. You'll appreciate encouragement from someone you trust or admire. *Moon enters Capricorn.*

25 MARCH

Someone – perhaps even you – will be feeling a little obstinate, so it's worthwhile double-checking you are being your usual friendly self, especially at work. A change of schedule may be a difficult thing to deal with but you will overcome obstacles. *Moon in Capricorn.*

26 MARCH

You'll enjoy the chance to be involved in activities and with people you love spending time with. If you'd like to change some aspects of your agreements with others this is a good day to do so. *Moon in Capricorn.*

27 MARCH

Take the time to organise events both you and those you share time with will enjoy. A collaboration or get-together will be enjoyable. This is a good time for romance, so organise a lovely event with someone special if you haven't already. *Moon in Aquarius.*

28 MARCH

You'll enjoy a lovely get-together with someone special. Communications may be a little up and down, so avoid taking other people's moods or thoughts personally. Communications are likely to get busier over the next few weeks as Mercury enters Aries in your work zone. Take a moment to gather your thoughts and aim to be productive. It's a good day to work out your priorities. *Moon in Aquarius.*

29 MARCH

Be inspired and engage in ventures that you enjoy, but remember to also be practical. You will be drawn to spending time on your favourite projects, so ensure you set time aside for these. *Moon in Pisces.*

30 MARCH

You're commuicating well at the moment, even if you feel a little head in the clouds. Others will see you as inspired or imaginative, so bring your creative side out. You may tend to be seeing the world through rose-coloured glasses, so ensure you have your feet on the ground if you are making key decisions. *Moon in Pisces.*

31 MARCH

The Aries moon spells a busy and sociable day. You may be restless, so ensure you channel this agitation into activities that bring positive results or you may get feisty. Aim to make time to spend with like-minded people. *Moon in Aries.*

1 APRIL

The Aries new moon spells a fresh chapter for you regarding your general direction in life. You may be ready to turn a new leaf, to begin a fresh project or to make changes at home or within your status, for example, from single to married or vice versa. A new liaison with a fresh organisation or group may appeal. This new moon has a healing effect so that, even if you feel vulnerable making changes now, rest assured the long-term outlook is a therapeutic one.

2 APRIL

You may receive key news if you didn't already yesterday; this may be in connection with a health matter. Someone may ask for your help, and if you need support or advice it will be available. You may hear unexpected news from a group or organisation or will bump into an old friend. ***Moon enters Taurus.***

3 APRIL

This is a good day to concentrate on your favourite projects and to find the time to investigate new interests and ideas. A friend, partner or family member may be super helpful with your new ideas or projects. You could make long-term changes financially, but must consider your options carefully. ***Moon in Taurus.***

4 APRIL

You can make a great deal of progress with a venture or project. You'll enjoy meeting a new circle of people or joining in on interesting activities that test your mettle. If conflict is brewing, avoid entering into a Mexican stand-off as it may be one you'll regret. Build bridges instead. *Moon in Taurus.*

5 APRIL

As you enter new territory and, at the least, consider new projects and ideas you'll reach a decision and it could spell considerable change for you, especially work-wise and for some in your personal life, so choose wisely. You may feel a little idealistic, so ensure you keep your feet firmly on the ground. *Moon in Gemini.*

6 APRIL

This is a good day for meetings, both at work and concerning your interests such as a study course, spirituality or travel. You may simply feel more fulfilled in your everyday chores and ventures. It's a good day for planning so take the initiative. *Moon in Gemini.*

7 APRIL

This is another good day for meetings and get-togethers, both at work and socially. If you have important matters to discuss you'll make headway, so organise talks and meetings. A short trip and plans for a longer one are likely to be met with positive results. You may need to persuade someone close of your plans, though. *Moon in Cancer.*

8 APRIL

This is a lovely day for socialising and networking. It's also a good time to indulge in the arts, dance, music and everything your heart desires! You'll also be drawn to romance, so organise a lovely event or a cosy night in! *Moon in Cancer.*

9 APRIL

This is another good day to take the initiative with conversations and your plans, as your efforts are likely to pay off. Be prepared to discuss your ideas with those they concern and with people who can help you, such as teachers, advisers and employers. *Moon in Cancer.*

10 APRIL

Communications may not flow as quickly or as easily as they have more recently, which is a good reason to think your plans through and find a positive way to present and discuss them. Avoid misunderstandings by researching circumstances; avoid relying on someone else to do the hard work for you. A tense situation can be defused with focus and friendliness. *Moon in Leo.*

11 APRIL

As Mercury enters Taurus you may find that some decisions are made and that you must stick with the plans already put in place. The good news is that tense communications are likely to settle down, but you must avoid obstinacy. *Moon in Leo.*

12 APRIL

You'll discover if you've over- or underestimated a circumstance and so will gain the chance to put things right if need be. This aside, a lovely meeting will make your heart soar. And, if you've recently quarrelled with someone, it's a good day to put the past behind you and let sleeping dogs lie. *Moon in Leo.*

13 APRIL

This is a good day to make agreements and commitments, especially at work and regarding a project or interest. Some Cancerians may be in the process of making financial agreements, which are likely to work out well as long as you have researched your circumstances adequately. *Moon in Virgo.*

14 APRIL

If your focus is on your career, status or general direction in life you can be positive that your plans will work out in your favour. A social event is also likely to pan out well for you. You may attain a key goal, so work towards your true aims. *Moon enters Libra.*

15 APRIL

As Mars enters Pisces your focus will be increasingly on areas in your life that make your heart soar. For some this will be spirituality and for others romance and the arts. Take the time over the coming weeks to find the space in your life for activities that feed your soul. *Moon in Libra.*

16 APRIL

The Libran full moon will spotlight your home life and you may find that changes there are due to changes at work or within your status. For some this full moon points to the culmination of a long chapter in your life within your family and the start of a new phase. For others this full moon spotlights a love affair or creative project and is an ideal time to put more energy into these areas.

17 APRIL

The Scorpio moon will focus your attention increasingly over the next two days on your personal life and creative or family projects. Organise your day to get work done in the morning, which will give you time for someone special in the evening. Avoid tense talks in the morning. *Moon in Scorpio.*

18 APRIL

You can't agree with everyone all the time, but you do have diplomacy on your side and are well equipped to deal with tension in a clever way to dispel conflict. Your charm and tact will be in demand, especially as you may hear unexpected news or will need to alter your usual routine or activities from out of the blue. You'll enjoy an impromptu chat or get-together. *Moon in Scorpio.*

19 APRIL

If you appreciate a little pressure in your work life or even at home as it motivates you to get things done you'll enjoy today's astrological influences. But if you prefer life on an even keel be prepared for a surprise and avoid conflict, especially with someone you must collaborate with at work or at home. *Moon in Sagittarius.*

20 APRIL

As the sun enters Taurus you'll feel more grounded and able to manage unexpected developments. Just avoid the tendency when under pressure to be obstinate and find ways to move forward in the most practical and realistic ways. *Moon in Sagittarius.*

21 APRIL

The Capricorn moon will help bring your more practical side out, so rest assured the decisions you make now are likely to be reasonable and grounded, enabling you to take action in small but certain steps. However, it could also bring out your obstinacy, especially regarding how you'd ideally like things to be, yet being adaptable will serve your aims much better. *Moon in Capricorn.*

22 APRIL

This is an earthy moon and will bring both your and your partner's more sensuous sides out. It's a good time to plan a lovely night out or in. You'll manage to get a great deal done at work and around the house, which you'll appreciate. Avoid accepting criticism or feeling overly sensitive about someone who themselves may simply be overly sensitive. *Moon in Capricorn.*

23 APRIL

A meeting with someone special could be truly wonderful. However, if you have recently argued, especially about shared finances or duties, take a moment to work out a mutually agreeable plan otherwise you could escalate your differences. *Moon in Aquarius.*

24 APRIL

Approach financial and personal agreements carefully as it's possible you have different values or goals in the plans you make. You'll enjoy a social get-together or a favourite activity but must avoid overspending and overindulging, which you'll regret. *Moon in Aquarius.*

25 APRIL

The Pisces moon will spotlight how you feel about recent discussions and agreements, especially to do with finances and shared duties. This moon could also bring your ideals and hopes out to the forefront of your mind, making you see the world through rose-coloured glasses, so ensure you maintain perspective. ***Moon in Pisces.***

26 APRIL

You could make great progress with your various projects and will be inspired to indulge in your favourite interests and activities. However, you may feel a little head in the clouds, so you must be prepared to be practical. Be inspired by people you admire. ***Moon in Pisces.***

27 APRIL

A financial agreement could be made now. If you're planning travel or even taking a trip, this is likely to be enjoyable. You may receive ideal news and will enjoy a get-together. You may even be in a position where a dream comes true. However, if you undergo a disappointment, consider if you over-estimated your circumstances. If so you will gain the chance to put things right. ***Moon enters Aries.***

28 APRIL

This is an excellent day for socialising and networking. Meetings with those who are influential in your life such as personal and business partners, friends and family could be transformational, adding a sense that you are progressing with your projects and relationships. You could make positive financial changes now too with the right advice and guidance. ***Moon in Aries.***

29 APRIL

Try to get key paperwork and agreements tied up to avoid having to revise your plans at a later date. Pluto turns retrograde today so find the time to tie up loose ends of important financial matters. You may receive key news and will enjoy a meeting. You may be drawn to step into a new social or networking circle. ***Moon in Aries.***

30 APRIL

The partial solar eclipse in Taurus signifies an important turning point for you. For some Cancerians this will be due to changes at work, for others a change of status and for some a fresh involvement with a group, organisation or friend. Be practical and grounded with decisions for the best results.

May

career   love   home   health   finance

1 MAY

You could make great progress with key projects and meetings so ensure you schedule both important meetings and a lovely social event. If you're trying to change major aspects of your life or simply take up new interests, this is it! Romance could blossom, and you could also overcome disagreements. ***Moon in Taurus.***

2 MAY

As Venus enters Aries you'll enjoy feeling that your career and general activities become a little more dynamic over the coming weeks. You may attract a fresh social circle or will be drawn to new pursuits and ideas. ***Moon in Gemini.***

3 MAY

An excellent day for making changes that involve collaborations, so it's also a good day to work with colleagues and to impress the boss! If you have quarrelled with someone this is a good day to mend bridges. ***Moon in Gemini.***

4 MAY

You'll enjoy being spontaneous and finding the time to alter your usual routine. You may hear unexpectedly from a group or friend and will be drawn to follow your passions in your own spare time. A favourite hobby or a fresh social group may breathe fresh air your way. *Moon in Gemini.*

5 MAY

Expect a surprise that is likely to involve a group, friend or organisation. Take a moment to decide how you'd like to move forward and avoid knee-jerk reactions if the news you receive is not what you want. You'll enjoy being spontaneous and an impromptu get-together could be enjoyable. *Moon in Cancer.*

6 MAY

This is an excellent time for discussions and meetings. You may be drawn to do research on a favourite topic or will meet someone you admire or who inspires you. A medical or beauty matter can be worked on with positive results; just ensure you are clear about what you want. *Moon in Cancer.*

7 MAY

There's little that will hold you back this weekend, so get set for a busy time. This is an excellent day for get-togethers and for indulging in your favourite activities. A trip, sports, study and spiritual endeavours will all appeal depending on your interests, and you'll find the time to muster a group together to enjoy your time together. *Moon in Leo.*

8 MAY

This is a good day to be adventurous with your collaborations and interests and to indulge in activities that test your strength and stamina. Sports, physical exercise and organising your working week in advance will all get you feeling motivated. You may receive an unexpected call or visit unless you already did yesterday. *Moon in Leo.*

9 MAY

If a little tension in the air is motivating for you you'll enjoy today's atmosphere, but if you fall at the first hurdle when you sense arguments or unease you may need to take extra breaks. Some conversations, travel and financial matters will require a little more focus than usual. *Moon enters Virgo.*

10 MAY

As Mercury turns retrograde you're likely to receive key news from someone close, a group or organisation or at work. If health has been a concern you may receive news that merits careful consideration. Try to allow extra time for travel and communications to avoid frustration over the coming weeks. *Moon in Virgo.*

11 MAY

As Jupiter enters Aries you may notice that work speeds up or that issues at work become more prevalent. Avoid allowing emotions to get in the way of your professional attitude. Someone in a position of influence over you may flex their muscles. You may also tend to expect more from your work or employer. If conflict is brewing, take steps to de-escalate it rather than adding to it for the best results. You may be ready to embrace fresh projects or a new direction. *Moon in Virgo.*

12 MAY

You may be called upon to be the voice of reason, especially at home and in your personal life, so rely on your diplomatic skills and be tactful if you must settle a difference of opinion. Look for the balance and you'll enjoy seeing concrete results to your hard work. If work has been tough find the time to relax at home when you can. *Moon in Libra.*

13 MAY

You'll enjoy a reunion, and if you meet someone for the first time there may be more of a connection than immediately meets the eye. Singles may meet someone you have a soul connection with, so if you have nothing planned for an evening or day out now's your chance to arrange something! *Moon in Libra.*

14 MAY

People around you may appear more emotional or outspoken over the next two days, especially at work. Give their opinions a wide berth if you disagree. Romance could blossom, so organise a treat! *Moon in Scorpio.*

15 MAY

Trust your instincts when the moon is in Scorpio, as they're likely to be spot on. You'll get on a little better with someone you share duties or responsibilities with but another relationship may be a little more intense, so ensure you give yourself breaks if you can. *Moon in Scorpio.*

16 MAY

The total lunar eclipse in Scorpio may feel particularly intense so aim to maintain a sense of perspective, especially regarding personal matters. You are likely to have dealings with someone you have an unavoidable connection with and emotions may run high. You could make great headway with treasured projects. *Moon enters Sagittarius.*

17 MAY

You could make ideal changes to some of your agreements and arrangements, so if you need to renegotiate some agreements this is a good time to do so. *Moon in Sagittarius.*

18 MAY

You could make a dream come true, which could catapult a favourite job or project. However, if you've misjudged circumstances you'll find out if you need to adjust arrangements. It's a good day to make commitments. Romance could blossom. ***Moon in Capricorn.***

19 MAY

The changes you wish to see in your life, especially in your personal and social life, are possible now. If you're happy with the way things are going you'll enjoy deepening your ties, both socially and at work. Romance could blossom, so organise a date! ***Moon in Capricorn.***

20 MAY

Another excellent day for meetings, and work projects could also advance. If you're looking for a new job or for a promotion this is a good time to circulate your resume and for interviews. A trip could be enjoyable too. You may enjoy a reunion or a return to an old haunt. ***Moon in Aquarius.***

21 MAY

A get-together or news will be important. You may reconsider your position about a project or a health matter. A trip this weekend could be transformative. ***Moon in Aquarius.***

22 MAY

This is an excellent time to put your energy into your favourite relationships, as you're likely to deepen your ties. But if someone has been feeling a little low or is moody at the moment, avoid raising tense topics. Find the time to relax. ***Moon enters Pisces.***

23 MAY

If you'd like to slow some relationships or activities down this is a good time to do so, as your efforts are likely to take. However, you may find that some projects and interests will get stuck, so if you prefer life to be quick and productive ensure you are patient. A social or work meeting will be rewarding. ***Moon in Pisces.***

24 MAY

This is a good time to make solid progress both at work and in your personal life, as negotiations and agreements can be made relatively constructively. Financial matters could also progress, so aim to put in place a fresh budget if necessary. ***Moon in Pisces.***

25 MAY

You may reconsider certain loyalties or allegiances to people. A close friend or business or personal partner may have key news. You'll enjoy socialising and networking, and this is a good time to meet new people. ***Moon in Aries.***

26 MAY

You may sense that someone close either at work or in your personal life may be feeling a little tense. You'll know to give them a wide berth to avoid arguments. Nevertheless, this is a good day for talks and meetings socially and at work. *Moon in Aries.*

27 MAY

A little tension is brewing, for some Cancerians at work and for others at home. There may be a little tension in the air in general. Take your time to avoid being swept up in other people's dramas. *Moon in Taurus.*

28 MAY

You'll feel inclined to enjoy life while Venus is in Taurus for the next few weeks. You'll feel motivated to find extra value in your work and to bring more luxury and enjoyment into your life. Avoid overindulging and overspending as you'll regret it! *Moon in Taurus.*

29 MAY

Important developments at work or regarding your status will command your attention. Be more attentive to talks and interactions, as they could signal change to come. If you're involved in legal matters these may progress swiftly, so be sure they are leading in the direction you wish to see them go. *Moon enters Gemini.*

30 MAY

The Gemini new moon signals a fresh phase for you, especially regarding your daily routine such as at work or health-wise. For some Cancerians you will be beginning a fresh undertaking with a group or organisation. It's a good time to get paperwork and health schedules shipshape. *Moon in Gemini.*

31 MAY

This is a good day to express your values and principles. If important matters need to be discussed you'll manage to get your valid opinions understood, so take the initiative and let people know where you stand. *Moon in Gemini.*

June

career love home health finance

1 JUNE

The Cancerian moon may bring out your emotions and some of them may surprise you. Avoid taking other people's opinions personally and take things one step at a time. You will be feeling super intuitive, so trust your instincts. *Moon in Cancer.*

2 JUNE

You're generally known as a soft person, one who is sensitive and gentle; however, you know that you are strong and can also be stubborn if the mood takes you! Some opinions will differ today. Avoid being obstinate but, equally, avoid allowing someone's ideas to sidetrack your own – unless, of course, there is merit in their thoughts and plans. *Moon in Cancer.*

3 JUNE

Mercury ends its retrograde phase today and you may over the coming weeks see that communications and travel become easier to navigate. Today, though, you may receive key news that will merit close attention, especially to do with finances and a particular friend or organisation. Take extra time for communications to ensure you avoid misunderstandings and difficult interactions. *Moon enters Leo.*

4 JUNE

Find the time to express your true values and priorities, as those you work and interact with are more likely to understand them now. Ensure you are clear and open to new ideas. You'll enjoy an impromptu get-together, either in a work or social context. *Moon in Leo.*

5 JUNE

The Leo moon may lead you to reconsider some of your decisions, especially to do with finances and commitments. Look for ways to make new arrangements, especially if you feel some commitments could be re-imagined. Avoid rash decisions. *Moon in Leo.*

6 JUNE

When the moon is in Virgo you'll find discussions and travel arrangements will attract your focus. You may need to approach a relationship or interactions in a more serious frame of mind to accomplish your tasks. Avoid over-analysing someone or a project. *Moon in Virgo.*

7 JUNE

You'll enjoy an impromptu meeting or surprise news that will enable you to change your usual routine and enjoy a little more diversity in your day. If developments disrupt your day, however, the Virgo moon will enable you to make practical arrangements to compensate. *Moon in Virgo.*

8 JUNE

You can get a great deal done by being practical and planning ahead. However, you may be liable to overcommit to various chores and events, so take a moment out of your schedule to work out what and who matter most to you and take it from there. *Moon enters Libra.*

9 JUNE

You may need to prioritise who and what is most important as your domestic chores or responsibilities may take more focus than work. If you work from home, aim to set boundaries or simply enjoy relaxing at home rather than working. *Moon in Libra.*

10 JUNE

You can make great progress with your various relationships, both business and personal. Matters you have been reviewing of late will move forward, so be positive. *Moon enters Scorpio.*

11 JUNE

Expect impromptu news or a surprise. You may enjoy getting together with an unpredictable but upbeat character. Someone may behave erratically or will introduce you to a new circle. *Moon in Scorpio.*

12 JUNE

You'll enjoy a reunion this weekend, so if you have nothing special planned yet make a date! Just make sure everyone's on the same page to avoid mix-ups and disagreements. If you're single, you may meet someone you feel is strangely familiar. You may also bump into an ex or an old friend. ***Moon enters Sagittarius.***

13 JUNE

Work is likely to be busy for the next few weeks, and especially communications. Take extra time to learn new communication skills if necessary. A health matter could be improved over coming weeks, so if you've felt fatigued or have a health issue, this is a good time to aim to improve well-being, as your efforts are likely to be successful. ***Moon in Sagittarius.***

14 JUNE

The full moon and supermoon in Sagittarius represents a fresh chapter for you at work and for some Cancerians in your personal life. You are likely to feel adventurous about new ideas and projects, but if not consider a fresh field or interest that does excite you. A new health and beauty regime could appeal.

15 JUNE

You may receive key news at work regarding your status and direction or from a group or friend. If you feel your situation is being compromised or that you must gain expert advice, be assertive. You may be in demand and may be asked for help. ***Moon in Capricorn.***

16 JUNE

This is an excellent time for progress at work and for some financially. Someone at work or from your past will be particularly helpful. A health matter can progress; just ensure that the information you act on is sound to avoid mistakes. Also avoid being easily influenced by someone you do not as yet know too well. ***Moon enters Aquarius.***

17 JUNE

Unexpected developments could be ideal, and being more spontaneous and embracing new ideas and activities will appeal. However, if a stop-start atmosphere in a relationship or at work is beginning to wear you down, it may be time to suggest alternative ways to interact. ***Moon in Aquarius.***

18 JUNE

As a sensitive person you can take other people's mood swings and opinions personally. Today's tough Venus-Saturn aspect could bring differences of opinion to the surface, so try to be philosophical about them. Finances will deserve attention, especially if you're in debt. Avoid lending anyone money. ***Moon in Aquarius.***

19 JUNE

You will enjoy relaxing and focusing on replenishing batteries. However, you may also be drawn to a social group or must complete some chores. Aim to achieve balance in your day or you may resent having no time to unwind. *Moon in Pisces.*

20 JUNE

The Pisces moon will bring your idealistic, philosophical side out, and you may see developments through rose-coloured glasses. If all is going well for you you'll gain a sense of belonging and accomplishment, but if you feel ready to make changes in areas of your life that are lacking in meaning this could be it! *Moon in Pisces.*

21 JUNE

As the sun enters Cancer, marking the solstice, you will feel more energised and ready to take on the world. Today, though, there may be some areas especially at work that irk you. Find a way to constructively channel frustrations into positive outlets such as sports. Romance and creative projects could blossom, so take the initiative. *Moon in Aries.*

22 JUNE

You are certainly no shrinking violet and your combative and assertive sides will seek expression. Avoid arguments with people in authority such as a boss as you may regret outbursts or speaking bluntly. *Moon in Aries.*

23 JUNE

As the moon enters Taurus you'll feel a little more grounded and less likely to fire up over matters you disagree on. That's not to say everyone will feel the same way: someone close may seem a little more intense than usual, so give them a wide berth if conflict seems likely. You will enjoy treating yourself and others to some of life's delights. *Moon enters Taurus.*

24 JUNE

You'll enjoy slowing the pace down at the end of the week. You may be drawn to socialise and yet spending time alone with someone special may prove more alluring. *Moon in Taurus.*

25 JUNE

You'll enjoy feeling more in your element and spending time with those you love. However, you know already that you can't get on with everyone all the time. Avoid allowing a difference of opinion to call the shots this weekend; find a way to get past disagreements. *Moon in Taurus.*

26 JUNE

When the moon is in Gemini you can feel a little restless. Words may come more easily and you'll enjoy a sense of spontaneity, but you may also feel frustrated unless you channel your energy into upbeat pursuits or to serious downtime. Someone may be feeling out of sorts and may require a patient approach. You'll enjoy catching up with favourite people. *Moon in Gemini.*

27 JUNE

This is a good day for health and well-being appointments, and if you've had disagreements with someone in a position of power or influence this is a good day to mend bridges. It's also a good day to gain information you need from an expert or adviser. *Moon in Gemini.*

28 JUNE

You'll relish being spontaneous and may receive unexpected news. You'll enjoy a reunion and the chance to show off a little! *Moon enters Cancer.*

29 JUNE

The Cancerian new moon will kick-start a fresh chapter in your personal life, especially if it's your birthday or if you were born earlier in June. If you were born in July you will kick-start a new phase at work or in your health routine. Be positive, but avoid arguments with people in authority. *Moon in Cancer.*

30 JUNE

You feel more intuitive and in sync when the moon is in your own sign, so trust your instincts. You'll enjoy a reunion or the chance to socialise with someone you find interesting or enigmatic. *Moon in Cancer.*

July

career   love   home   health   financ

1 JULY

You may notice tension in the air. If you feel motivated by a little stress you'll enjoy your day and get things done, but if stress is unsettling you may find exercise, meditation or yoga useful. Aim to find positive ways to avoid conflict as otherwise it could escalate quickly. *Moon in Leo.*

2 JULY

You're communicating well at work and your personal projects and pastimes are likely to get ahead. If you have key financial decisions to make it's a good time for research. However, if you feel you are under pressure to make decisions you do not fully agree with try to find time to negotiate. Avoid snap decisions as you may not know all of the facts. *Moon in Leo.*

3 JULY

The Virgo moon later in the day will help you to look at your situation in more detail without feeling so much under pressure. The tension underlying some communications may continue today, so try to avoid being pressured into choices unless you must deal with a difficult topic. Talks may be tense, but if you stick with your principles you will succeed. *Moon enters Virgo.*

4 JULY

Some interactions may continue to be intense, so be sensitive to other people's opinions but avoid being pressured into decision making if possible. Avoid stirring up both your own and others' emotions and be practical. *Moon in Virgo.*

5 JULY

It will be possible to slow communications and developments down but you must avoid appearing stubborn as this could backfire. If you're happy with the way work and personal matters are going you could make great strides and will enjoy seeing your projects and plans blossom. *Moon enters Libra.*

6 JULY

This is a good day for beauty and health appointments. Someone in a position of power or authority at work could be a great help, so be sure to enlist support if it's needed. You may be asked to help out yourself or to step into a role with more responsibility for the day. *Moon in Libra.*

7 JULY

You appreciate balance at home, and when the moon is in Libra you will pursue qualities that can bring harmony into your domestic realm. You may be super drawn to art, music, dance and romance but you may need to draw a line at work so you don't spend your entire day working rather than enjoying some relaxation time. *Moon in Libra.*

8 JULY

A sudden or unexpected change of circumstance will mean you'll be in need, for some at work and for others concerning a friend or someone close. You may not agree with everyone. Avoid taking other people's personal problems to heart. A health or beauty matter may deserve further attention. Unexpected help or news will arise. *Moon in Scorpio.*

9 JULY

You may wonder if it's you or someone else who is making waves. What is certain is that a travel delay or miscommunication could cause issues unless you're careful with communications and plan ahead. Ensure you back up computers if you work a great deal online. Avoid taking other people's grandiose statements to heart, especially if their ideas are clearly exaggerated. *Moon in Scorpio.*

10 JULY

You'll enjoy an impromptu meeting, for some to do with work and for others purely socially. If you're single and you meet someone this relationship may be more relevant than meets the eye. You may return to an old haunt or hear unexpectedly from someone from your past. *Moon enters Sagittarius.*

11 JULY

You'll feel more outspoken than usual, and work and your general activities can progress well so take the initiative and get things done! If health has been an issue for you, this is a good day to be more outgoing about finding ways to boost well-being. ***Moon in Sagittarius.***

12 JULY

You'll appreciate the opportunity to get your projects and plans up and running. Health and beauty may deserve more attention than usual, and you'll manage to find out more if you are in the dark about some circumstances either at work or health-wise. You'll enjoy being with like-minded people and relaxing in the evening when you can. ***Moon enters Capricorn.***

13 JULY

The full moon and supermoon in Capricorn will spotlight an important personal or business relationship, especially if you were born in June. Strong emotions may arise and news will impact your relationship. July Cancerians are set to turn a page at work or within a daily and health routine. It's a good time to make solid plans both at work and financially. An agreement could be advantageous, but you must do adequate research.

14 JULY

Once again research is necessary, especially if you feel you are in the dark about a personal or work matter. Once you work with experts or advisers to get to the bottom of matters you will gain so much more clarity. ***Moon enters Aquarius.***

15 JULY

You can't always agree with everyone, let alone with someone close, so avoid taking differences of opinion personally. Your plans and values may differ from those of someone close. If you appreciate a little tension romantically you'll enjoy the day, but if you prefer romance to be on an even keel avoid arguments as they could escalate. ***Moon in Aquarius.***

16 JULY

You are likely to receive news, especially if it's your birthday. You'll enjoy an inspired day but some developments may require good planning, so ensure you have laid solid groundwork and particularly with financial agreements. ***Moon enters Pisces.***

17 JULY

This is a good day for talks, meetings, agreements and negotiations. You may be drawn to visiting a beautiful place or indulging in your favourite interests and hobbies that provide you with a sense of fulfilment. Spiritually minded Cancerians will enjoy deepening your appreciation of all things devotional. ***Moon in Pisces.***

18 JULY

Key personal decisions may be made, so if someone wants to talk ensure you are ready and willing! However, some talks may be intense, so ensure you maintain perspective. You may be in a position to make a long-term decision or commitment that could spell considerable change moving forward. A trip or conversations could open doors, for some mid-July Cancerians at work. Key news could change how you see someone. *Moon enters Aries.*

19 JULY

As Mercury enters upbeat Leo you'll feel more outspoken over the coming weeks and may enjoy an ego boost or a sense of entering adventurous new territory. The moon in Aries could bring out your combative side, so avoid power struggles. *Moon in Aries.*

20 JULY

This is another good day to make changes, especially in your personal life even if there is an intense mood around developments. Take a moment to focus on good communication skills for the best results. A little negotiation or adjustment may be necessary. *Moon enters Taurus.*

21 JULY

If you are finding some circumstances difficult to adjust to avoid impulsiveness and rash decisions. But it's also important to avoid being stubborn and averse to change! Trust your intuition and be adaptable for the best measure. *Moon in Taurus.*

22 JULY

As the sun enters Leo you may begin to feel more positive about developments, especially within your personal life and for some financially. You'll feel more outgoing and dynamic over the coming weeks. *Moon in Taurus.*

23 JULY

This is an excellent day for travel, for meetings and also for financial decisions and transactions, especially if you've done adequate research with key investments. A work meeting or financial decision could be a positive move. It's a good time to improve your status. *Moon in Gemini.*

24 JULY

You are sociable and will enjoy getting together with like-minded people. However, you may feel a little choosy over who you will and won't spend time with! A financial matter will benefit from focus. *Moon in Gemini.*

25 JULY

Once again you may tend to look at some people who have a large influence over you in a new light, being more discerning about who you wish to spend time with and/or who you wish to confide in. Avoid conflict by being tactful. Some matters may be delayed, so be patient and diligent. ***Moon enters Cancer.***

26 JULY

You're not known for being impulsive, yet you may be drawn to fire up over delays and misunderstandings. Take extra time for travel and financial transactions to avoid frustration and disappointments. You could nevertheless accomplish a great deal with focus. ***Moon in Cancer.***

27 JULY

This is an excellent day to build bridges with anyone, either at work or at home, and also to build relationships. An expert or adviser will be available if you need support or guidance, so ensure you reach out. Your expertise and wisdom may be in demand. ***Moon in Cancer.***

28 JULY

The Leo new moon points to a fresh chapter regarding finances and, for some, in your personal life. It's a good time to strike new agreements if you already have talked about terms and conditions. Avoid impulsive moves as it's not a good day for signing agreements. If possible, wait until Monday for paperwork to be completed. Avoid rash decisions but be spontaneous.

29 JULY

The moon in Leo will bring your dynamic, upbeat and sociable sides out and you'll enjoy spending time with those you love. If you're working you could get a great deal done but you may feel a little at odds with other people's ideas. Discuss your projects with those they concern to avoid arguments. ***Moon in Leo.***

30 JULY

The Virgo moon will encourage you to be more hands on and practical about matters that may annoy you. Check if you're being obstinate and consider how you might better approach other people to avoid arguments. ***Moon enters Virgo.***

31 JULY

This is a good day to boost your projects and your plans are likely to take a step in the right direction. You can make agreements that could be binding, so ensure you are happy with all the terms and conditions. A surprise or unusual meeting could be upbeat and you'll enjoy meeting people who seem to be forward thinking. ***Moon in Virgo.***

August

career   love   home   health   finance

1 AUGUST

You may meet someone from out of the blue, someone you feel close to even if they're a stranger! If you're making long-term decisions ensure you have all the details at your fingertips, especially financially, to avoid mistakes as misunderstandings could occur. Travel may be delayed so plan ahead to avoid frustration. *Moon in Virgo.*

2 AUGUST

You'll appreciate the chance to be spontaneous and an impromptu meeting, call or get-together could be ideal. Avoid making snap judgements of others. You may be required to act on impulse, so ensure you are prepared for the unexpected. *Moon in Libra.*

3 AUGUST

A friend or organisation may be particularly helpful to you, so ensure you reach out if you need solid advice or guidance. Decide early on in the day what your priorities are and stick with your plan to avoid being distracted from your goals. *Moon in Libra.*

4 AUGUST

You may be feeling a little more emotional or someone at home is demanding your attention, so keep your feet on the ground and attend to chores as they arise. If you have a difficult task or challenge ahead the stars suggest you will overcome any obstacles. A little attention to interpersonal communications will pay off. *Moon enters Scorpio.*

5 AUGUST

A work or financial matter is best approached carefully to avoid making waves. Shared finances and duties will benefit from patience and resilience to overcome bumps in the road. Rest assured, if an obstacle arises you will overcome it. *Moon in Scorpio.*

6 AUGUST

Tread carefully with someone you share finances with and aim to overcome disagreements. Find a practical way forward to organising chores and details at work and at home so that everyone feels they are being treated equally. *Moon enters Sagittarius.*

7 AUGUST

You'll enjoy indulging in life's delights so make time for your favourite interests including spirituality, romance, music and the arts. If tension is still bubbling up in a relationship, find ways to establish a strong framework for co-operation and avoid making rash decisions as you may regret them! *Moon in Sagittarius.*

8 AUGUST

There is a therapeutic and healing aspect to developments. You could potentially overcome a financial or personal disagreement so ensure you make tracks towards collaboration and co-operation. A work matter could also be improved. However, if you encounter an obstacle rest assured there is a silver lining. *Moon enters Capricorn.*

9 AUGUST

Be practical and aim to manifest your inner serenity, as communications and travel may represent some hurdles or will be complex. Delays and frustrations needn't get the better of you if you exercise a balanced outlook. Someone close may have key news for you that brings an intense response. Romance could flourish. If you're single, you may meet an enigmatic character. *Moon in Capricorn.*

10 AUGUST

Be practical, especially if yesterday's events represented obstacles. Consider looking at important aspects of your life from a fresh perspective. Avoid being stuck on one idea and play with new concepts. You may discover a fresh viewpoint. *Moon enters Aquarius.*

11 AUGUST

As Venus leaves your sign you may find that you develop a more objective attitude to recent developments, which will motivate you to take positive action. You may be surprised by developments as you discover more about your circumstances. Avoid making abrupt changes unless you have already researched your position, especially financially. Work on the best-case outcome instead. *Moon in Aquarius.*

12 AUGUST

The Aquarian full moon is spotlighting quirky or unexpected developments. For some these will concern finances, and for others duties and work. Ask if you might be able to give a little leeway or, contrarily, if you've given too much and must now establish boundaries. *Moon enters Pisces.*

13 AUGUST

Important decisions merit careful attention to the details, so ensure you have all the facts at your fingertips. If in doubt about how to move forward trust your instincts, but also avoid being easily influenced by others. *Moon in Pisces.*

14 AUGUST

A commitment or decision can be made, for some financially and for others to a course of action within a key relationship or work project. A social or networking event could go ahead well and bring good results if you have laid careful foundations. Romance could blossom, so organise a treat or a day in! *Moon enters Aries.*

15 AUGUST

You're communicating well and a meeting with someone you find innovative and imaginative will be enjoyable. A trip could bring new and exciting ideas and experiences your way. You'll enjoy a reunion or hearing from an old friend. *Moon in Aries.*

16 AUGUST

This is a good day for visits and for making changes at home. You may be drawn to changing décor, and if you're moving the new situation is likely to be positive even if the logistics are complex. Communications could improve but you may be surprised by someone's news. *Moon in Aries.*

17 AUGUST

Things may not be as they seem or will entail a few conundrums to solve. Ensure arrangements are super clear for all concerned to avoid misunderstandings. You may be absent-minded, so avoid misplacing valuables such as keys. *Moon in Taurus.*

18 AUGUST

This is a lovely day for making progress both at work and in your personal life and for boosting your profile. You may also enjoy a compliment or financial boost. If you're looking for a promotion this could arise, so take the initiative and discuss your position with those in authority. *Moon in Taurus.*

19 AUGUST

While you're an amiable person, sometimes people can get the wrong end of the stick in conversations and circumstances. A little more tact and diplomacy, especially at home and with those closest to you, will work wonders. You'll enjoy socialising and/or a lovely event at home. *Moon in Gemini.*

20 AUGUST

Mars will now be in Gemini until the end of March 2023, encouraging you to communicate more readily. You may feel restless and can get a great deal done, especially with projects at home and in your personal life. You may also be increasingly motivated to spend time on your health and well-being over the coming months. *Moon in Gemini.*

21 AUGUST

A visit at home or a change concerning your home life or status could be ideal, especially if you have planned ahead. If you haven't you may find developments a little disorienting. You may also be forgetful, or someone you generally rely on could let you down. Avoid taking matters personally. A little home improvement may appeal. *Moon in Gemini.*

22 AUGUST

This is an excellent day to make changes that you have been planning for some time. Work collaborations and changes at home could go well as you'll be feeling practical and are communicating effectively. If making long-term financial decisions you must do your research, and also trust your gut instincts. *Moon in Cancer.*

23 AUGUST

Now that the sun is in Virgo you'll feel more practical and grounded about communications, travel plans and, for some, with developments at home, but you may find the pace for the next four weeks a little slow for your liking. Formulate realistic plans, taking all the variables into account. *Moon in Cancer.*

24 AUGUST

As you are sensitive to other people's moods you can tend to be easily influenced by other people's mood swings and find yourself feeling alienated from your own thoughts. Avoid being too distracted by other people's problems. Being compassionate towards them will be a useful trait. A financial or personal matter could flourish, so take the initiative. ***Moon enters Leo.***

25 AUGUST

You will feel motivated to help someone. You are also able to express yourself well, especially at work, so be bold! Not everyone will agree with all your ideas and choices, so be prepared to frame your ideas in the best light. ***Moon in Leo.***

26 AUGUST

You'll look for peace and balance at home and in your personal life now that Mercury is in Libra. You may need to act as a mediator or peacemaker for someone in your environment at work or at home. ***Moon in Leo.***

27 AUGUST

The new moon in Virgo is an ideal opportunity to kick-start a fresh chapter at home, with family or property. For some this new moon points to a new agreement or framework within a key project or relationship. You could make solid agreements but must avoid rash decisions or rushing through projects and ideas. Seek expert advice and take all the variables into account. You may be surprised by a change of routine or unexpected news. ***Moon enters Capricorn.***

28 AUGUST

A commitment may be made but you must be practical. For some key financial decisions will be more important than meets the eye so put your needs first. ***Moon in Virgo.***

29 AUGUST

You may feel inclined to find ways to establish more balance and harmony in your life. It's a good day to take decisive action regarding your personal life, home and family. Art, relaxation and music will all provide you with some form of rest in the evening. In the day, choose your words carefully to avoid misrepresenting your own interests. ***Moon enters Libra.***

30 AUGUST

Key talks may tend to become more intense than they need be, so ensure you maintain perspective and choose your words carefully. A work project or responsibility will benefit from careful appraisal so you must avoid over- or under-estimating circumstances. Travel may be delayed so be patient. ***Moon in Libra.***

31 AUGUST

You may be a little sensitive to people's opinions or will be easily influenced, so be clear about where you stand. You may discover if you have overestimated a financial situation, so ensure you gain perspective. When you do you may be pleasantly surprised by the outcome. ***Moon enters Scorpio.***

September

career   love   home   health   finance

1 SEPTEMBER

You can accomplish a great deal so aim high: you may surprise yourself with how much you can get done. You'll enjoy both socialising and networking and will find this relaxing at the end of the day. Just keep an eye on people who can be fiery; avoid an argument. ***Moon in Scorpio.***

2 SEPTEMBER

If you like tension in your love life and general interactions you'll enjoy today's conversations, but if you prefer life on an even keel you may need to use your tact and discretion to avoid a tense interaction. This may come about due to a basic difference of values or a financial disagreement. Aim to find a solution and you will. ***Moon enters Sagittarius.***

3 SEPTEMBER

A trip, get-together or domestic development will bring people together and may be larger than life in some ways. You'll enjoy getting together with like-minded people. You may need to choose between chores and relaxation but if you are practical you'll manage both. ***Moon in Sagittarius.***

4 SEPTEMBER

The Sagittarian moon will be motivational for you at work and you could truly make great progress with your chores and projects. You'll enjoy being with upbeat, outgoing people, but if someone in particular proves enigmatic or difficult in some way avoid making tension worse; find ways to co-operate if possible. ***Moon in Sagittarius.***

5 SEPTEMBER

As Venus enters Virgo you'll feel more able to plan ahead and pay attention to details, especially financially and at work. You need more time to devote to health and beauty, so be practical about boosting your well-being; you'll be glad you did! ***Moon in Capricorn.***

6 SEPTEMBER

The moon in Capricorn will help you and the people around you be more realistic and practical. However, some may also appear more stubborn or non-committal so remain focused on your plans and you'll make great progress. If you must get things done under pressure ensure you remain grounded and look at the most feasible ways ahead. ***Moon in Capricorn.***

7 SEPTEMBER

The Aquarian moon will bring a change of focus or even a change of mind in someone close who may have news to do with a fresh way of looking at their situation and at the way you collaborate. Relationships may appear a little more light-hearted as the day goes by. You'll enjoy a reunion and finding time for your favourite projects. ***Moon in Aquarius.***

8 SEPTEMBER

A friend, group or organisation will be helpful, even if you feel sometimes that you are more helpful to them than they are to you. You may discover that if you ask for advice or for help it will be available. Avoid feeling super sensitive and find clever ways to overcome hurdles. ***Moon in Aquarius.***

9 SEPTEMBER

This is a good day to spend a little extra time on communications to ensure people you must collaborate with are all on the same page, otherwise you may experience misunderstandings or even disappointments. Plan ahead to avoid travel or logistical delays, especially at work. Try to tie up loose ends with paperwork and agreements before Mercury turns retrograde tomorrow. ***Moon in Pisces.***

10 SEPTEMBER

The full moon in Pisces is shining a light on your projects, career, status and general direction, asking very much how you intend to be practical about moving forward with your treasured plans and projects. Positive change in your personal life is possible, so embrace it!

11 SEPTEMBER

A surprise visit or a trip somewhere different will be enjoyable. You'll enjoy being with a fun group of people and humanitarian interests could draw your focus more than usual. *Moon in Aries.*

12 SEPTEMBER

A lovely get-together with someone you feel comfortable with will be enjoyable. This is a good day to make repairs on your home or vehicle. Some conversations may be a little uncomfortable, however, so if you have sensitive topics to discuss take things one step at a time for the best results. *Moon in Aries.*

13 SEPTEMBER

The moon in Taurus for the next few days will encourage you to be more hands-on and practical, especially with plans that have been in the making for a while. Conversations with a friend, group or organisation could produce concrete results. Be adaptable and avoid being stubborn about change. *Moon enters Taurus.*

14 SEPTEMBER

You'll appreciate the chance to get down to brass tacks with a friend, group or organisation, especially if there are some areas of disagreement. You'll manage to make a new commitment or at least to see the practicalities of certain situations. You may enjoy socialising. *Moon in Taurus.*

15 SEPTEMBER

Mars and Venus will be at a tense square angle for the coming days, which could produce some tension especially with communications in general, so be prepared to make the extra effort to smooth things over to avoid conflict. Arguments could spark up over very little, so maintain perspective. *Moon enters Gemini.*

16 SEPTEMBER

If you're making big changes, either at work or at home, you'll know already that moving and changing jobs can be stressful and know to take things one step at a time and be practical. You'll discover whether some of your plans have been unrealistic and if you must adjust expectations. Avoid arguments, both at home and at work. Consider if disagreements stem from a basic difference in values and avoid taking them personally. *Moon in Gemini.*

17 SEPTEMBER

You may be feeling more emotional about recent developments and conversations, so avoid allowing your feelings to run your day. A healing or therapeutic break will appeal, so take time out. *Moon in Gemini.*

18 SEPTEMBER

A return to an old haunt or to a familiar situation will bring you together with familiar people and places. A trip may be delayed, so ensure you give yourself plenty of space and time to catch up patiently. Changes at home and/or at work will take time to settle down, so ensure you give yourself room to relax. *Moon enters Cancer.*

19 SEPTEMBER

This is a good day to make changes at home and with someone close. A strong business or personal partnership could flourish. A collaboration and romance could blossom. *Moon in Cancer.*

20 SEPTEMBER

Expect the unexpected, especially in connection with your home life, a property or family. You may receive surprise news or an impromptu visitor. If some developments seem limiting, you will find the breathing space you need. *Moon enters Leo.*

21 SEPTEMBER

You may feel a little more emotional, which may be in response to the moods of a partner or their news. Be bold, especially at work, but avoid taking on too much or you risk fatigue. *Moon in Leo.*

22 SEPTEMBER

You'll appreciate the sense you can achieve a great deal at work with good communication skills. Be careful not to outshine someone in charge such as your employer. Be bold and bright, but avoid allowing pride to rule your day as pride comes before a fall. *Moon in Leo.*

23 SEPTEMBER

As the sun steps into Libra this marks the equinox, a time when we collectively sense we can achieve more balance and harmony in our lives. You'll appreciate having the time and motivation over the weekend to spend on developments at home or with someone you love. *Moon in Virgo.*

24 SEPTEMBER

You'll be drawn to spending more time at home and if you're travelling to enjoying a different space. You'll appreciate the time to relax through music, the arts and romance and to immerse yourself in good vibes. You may be a little absent-minded or idealistic, so avoid forgetfulness and seeing the world through rose-coloured glasses. Romance can blossom. *Moon in Virgo.*

25 SEPTEMBER

The new moon in Libra points to a fresh circumstance at home or with family and a property. You may find this impacts on your status. It's a time of great transformation, so ensure you make a wish as it'll surely come true.

26 SEPTEMBER

This is an excellent time to make changes at home or at work. You may find a business or personal partner has good news. What is certain is that change is coming, if it hasn't already taken place! You may return to a familiar place or meet an old friend or colleague. *Moon in Libra.*

27 SEPTEMBER

Be adaptable and ready to listen to other people whose lives touch yours. You are likely to receive news to do with your home, a partner or family. You can make many positive changes now, so be optimistic. *Moon in Libra.*

28 SEPTEMBER

This is a good day to make commitments and be decisive about your projects and collaborations. You can achieve a great deal and negotiations can go well, but you must avoid snap decisions. *Moon in Scorpio.*

29 SEPTEMBER

You'll feel motivated at work and within your relationships to express your more creative and optimistic side. However, the Scorpio moon may bring your emotions or those of someone close out. If you are feeling emotional, take a moment to gather your thoughts. *Moon in Scorpio.*

30 SEPTEMBER

This is a good day for really getting busy at work and with your various chores, as you could attain many goals. You may not necessarily agree with everyone you must collaborate or interact with, so be diplomatic to avoid arguments. You may receive good news. *Moon in Sagittarius.*

October

career   love   home   health   finance

1 OCTOBER

Key news or a get-together this weekend will put a personal relationship or favourite project in perspective, especially at home, to do with family or property. If you're working you may need to prioritise work chores and other duties. Some people and perhaps even you may be feeling tense, so ensure you set aside time to relax. *Moon in Sagittarius.*

2 OCTOBER

You may receive key news, especially in connection with your home life or someone special. It's a good day to plan a trip or to review your travel plans. If communications have been difficult or delayed they will begin to improve over the coming weeks. You may receive key news or will enjoy a get-together. Avoid tense topics if possible to avoid unnecessary arguments. *Moon in Capricorn.*

3 OCTOBER

You may need to review or oversee a change in the way you share some of your duties, either at home or at work. If conflict has been brewing, consider how you could communicate with more sensitivity and compassion for the best measure. *Moon in Capricorn.*

4 OCTOBER

This is a good day to initiate talks with a business or personal partner that could move your joint projects and plans into new territory, so take the initiative. ***Moon enters Aquarius.***

5 OCTOBER

Developments will highlight some differences of opinion, especially with shared duties, finances or collaborations. This is a good time to innovate and express your bright ideas and then to act on them. ***Moon in Aquarius.***

6 OCTOBER

You'll enjoy seeing how some of your collaborations are producing excellent work and results, although you may tend to be increasingly idealistic once the moon is in Pisces as the day goes by so keep things on an even keel. ***Moon enters Pisces.***

7 OCTOBER

Communications are going well with someone you love or admire but some interactions may not go as well. If you feel vulnerable ensure you take breaks. A work matter or change of status could put the spotlight on sensitive topics, so seek expert help if it's needed. ***Moon in Pisces.***

8 OCTOBER

You'll regain some of your usual vitality and lust for life as the day goes by, so be sure to organise a favourite activity for later in the day even if you're not in the mood earlier on! You may need to focus on work at home. It's a good day for a health or beauty appointment. Just be sure to be clear about what you want or need. ***Moon enters Aries.***

9 OCTOBER

The Aries full moon will spotlight how you feel about your work, status and general direction and relates to developments at home. Health and well-being are important to you, so take time out and unwind. You may be asked for help, and if you need it support and advice are available.

10 OCTOBER

This is a good day for remedial work, be this at home or in the office. If you need to repair décor or even a relationship this is the ideal day to do so! It is also a good day for a health or beauty appointment. You may discover important information about someone close. If you need expert advice, this is your day. ***Moon enters Taurus.***

11 OCTOBER

You'll appreciate the opportunity to gain a more even keel and a little peace and balance at home, with family or regarding a property. You will enjoy doing DIY and improving the look of your home; someone will be helpful in this regard. Collaborations could go well. You may receive unexpected news. *Moon in Taurus.*

12 OCTOBER

Important information and key meetings will pave the way for a more enlightened situation either at home or at work. Take the initiative with meetings and travel to move forward with projects and plans. You may need to review past plans. Ensure you have all the facts at your fingertips to avoid mistakes. *Moon in Taurus.*

13 OCTOBER

An unexpected development or impromptu get-together will ask that you're flexible and adaptable. If someone behaves unpredictably you will overcome any fallout from their actions. *Moon in Gemini.*

14 OCTOBER

This is a good day for making commitments, especially at home. Collaborations in general whether at work or at home are likely to go well as long as you have done adequate research. Otherwise, you may discover a spanner in the works unless you already did yesterday. *Moon in Gemini.*

15 OCTOBER

A lovely event such as a reunion or the chance to truly enjoy your home life or a family event may bring emotions to the surface. You may be easily influenced so be careful with decisions. Ask for a second opinion and choose carefully. *Moon enters Cancer.*

16 OCTOBER

Romance and all things beautiful will appeal and you'll enjoy immersing yourself in a beautiful environment. You'll appreciate the chance to enjoy a little luxury and to feather your nest at home, but if some plans don't pan out look for the most practical way forward. A philosophical outlook will help you overcome any disappointments. *Moon in Cancer.*

17 OCTOBER

You can accomplish a great deal, especially if you are working from home or on your home! You or someone at work may be absent-minded so provide extra space to avoid frustrations. *Moon in Cancer.*

18 OCTOBER

The Leo moon tends to bring your inner hero to the surface, and you may even appear more gregarious than usual. But if you're making key decisions ensure you double-check the details and avoid snap decisions. Art, music, meditation and spiritual activities will soothe your nerves. *Moon in Leo.*

19 OCTOBER

Developments regarding your home life, a property or family are likely to gather momentum. Check everyone involved in developments is on the same page, otherwise you may need to contend with an arguments. *Moon in Leo.*

20 OCTOBER

There may be a tendency towards tension at home or concerning someone close, such as someone you must collaborate with. Take a moment to smooth over differences to avoid conflict. *Moon enters Virgo.*

21 OCTOBER

Your ability to be practical and realistic is a real asset, one you could use for the best results, especially with long-term plans. If you feel someone is being critical, avoid behaving the same way in return; find a constructive way forward. Avoid being put under pressure, unless you really have no alternative. Find ways to unwind when you can. *Moon in Virgo.*

22 OCTOBER

You'll enjoy a lovely get-together and being with like-minded people. A domestic development such as a lovely event at your home or with family will be enjoyable. However, you may encounter an unexpected development, such as a visitor or caller, so be prepared to be flexible with arrangements. *Moon in Virgo.*

23 OCTOBER

This is an excellent day for a working bee at home and to collaborate on plans and ventures with helpful people. You may begin to feel more passionate about your plans and ideas and therefore more motived over the coming weeks. If a hurdle arises or a difficult social situation develops, rest assured you will overcome hurdles. *Moon in Libra.*

24 OCTOBER

A meeting or news may bring out your sensitivities or vulnerabilities. Take a moment to gather your thoughts. You could remedy a situation, but must avoid being pressured into a solution that isn't in your interest. *Moon in Libra.*

25 OCTOBER

The partial solar eclipse in Scorpio will spotlight your personal life. For some developments will impact your home life, and for others a creative project or family. Communications could be a little tense or confusing, so take extra time to boost your communication skills for the best results. Trust your intuition.

26 OCTOBER

A changeable or varied situation may bring out your insecurities, but if you trust your gut you will land on the right solution to any problems that occur. You may find intense emotions arise so take things one step at a time, especially if developments take you by surprise. You'll enjoy socialising and meeting a diverse group of people. *Moon in Scorpio.*

27 OCTOBER

Mars in your 12th house can feel frustrating as there is a lot of pent-up energy you'd prefer to express. Find ways to channel restlessness into productive outlets such as fitness training or work. You can achieve a great deal with focus, but you must avoid intense talks and drama and intrigue, especially with someone you share duties or space at home with. *Moon enters Sagittarius.*

28 OCTOBER

You may reconsider some of your recent choices, especially at work. You may be a little tired and idealistic, so avoid making long-term decisions unless you have all the details. A previous circumstance may seem rosier in retrospect than it actually was, so gain perspective. *Moon in Sagittarius.*

29 OCTOBER

Developments may feel a little more intense than usual. Communications may be frustrating and travel delayed. Your intuition is spot on at the moment, so ensure you listen to it. You may feel a little disappointed or idealistic, so ensure you remain grounded. *Moon enters Capricorn.*

30 OCTOBER

You'll appreciate having the time to slow things down. Otherwise, you may feel very intensely about personal matters and could lose perspective. It's impossible to agree with everyone all the time, so a little compromise may be necessary. Someone may pleasantly surprise you. *Moon in Capricorn.*

31 OCTOBER

Happy Hallowe'en! There is more intensity this year than others for you, so aim to find time to unwind where possible. You may meet with an old friend. Expect a quirky day: so nothing unusual for this day of the year! If you're not clear about a project or person, ensure you get enough information to gain certainty. *Moon enters Aquarius.*

November

career   love   home   health   finance

1 NOVEMBER

You can make a great deal of progress at work and with your various collaborations. A reunion could be ideal, however, the Aquarian moon may spotlight a difference of opinion with someone close. Avoid feeling antagonistic, as this will simply add to the frustration and will annoy other people into the mix! A practical, realistic approach will overcome any conundrums. *Moon in Aquarius.*

2 NOVEMBER

Be careful with conversations and interactions as someone, perhaps even you, may be prone to taking casual remarks personally. A reunion or work meeting could be ideal but may require a tactful approach. *Moon enters Pisces.*

3 NOVEMBER

You'll enjoy meeting an old friend or colleague. You may need to go over old ground at work or remedy a circumstance that requires attention. If emotions are super intense, find ways to channel energy into productive duties at work and your favourite activities and interests. *Moon in Pisces.*

4 NOVEMBER

You can improve your circumstances, especially in your personal life, with family, at work and health-wise, but it involves you taking the time to ensure conversations, talks and communications in general are clear and calm or you risk difficult interactions and overwhelming emotions. **Moon enters Aries.**

5 NOVEMBER

Some interactions are going to be a little complex or difficult at the moment. A reunion may bring out your vulnerabilities, so take things one step at a time. Consider how you could strengthen those aspects of yourself you see as being weak. Be prepared to embrace change but avoid snap decisions. **Moon in Aries.**

6 NOVEMBER

You'll feel more proactive and ready to take on your various tasks. A health boost or the chance to catch up with chores will be relaxing. A reunion or a trip to a familiar place may bring emotions to the surface, but if you focus on the positives you'll enjoy a lovely get-together or event. **Moon in Aries.**

7 NOVEMBER

If you are good at negotiating you'll enjoy today's developments, but if you tend to fold at the first hint of disagreement you will need to find another way to proceed such as promising to get back to someone with your response. A financial matter is best considered from a long-term point of view. Avoid feeling under pressure to agree if you disagree. **Moon in Taurus.**

8 NOVEMBER

The total eclipse of the moon in Taurus will spotlight changes in your personal life and how you feel about someone in particular such as a business partner, friend or organisation. If family matters are in the spotlight take a moment to avoid burning bridges and find a positive solution to problems.

9 NOVEMBER

You may enjoy a spontaneous event, but if you prefer life on an even keel you are likely to find some of your circumstances a little chaotic or intense. A friend, group or organisation may have a solution to an issue. If their input muddies the water, look for a fair outcome and propose this. **Moon enters Gemini.**

10 NOVEMBER

A fair outcome can be achieved with careful negotiation. However, you may need to concede a principle or belief. If you feel circumstances are at a stalemate, consider looking for expert advice

or guidance. A work or personal project could flourish, as could romance, so ensure you take the initiative. *Moon in Gemini.*

11 NOVEMBER

Look for the most practical path ahead in your decision-making, as great achievements are rarely won without a challenge. A financial matter is best agreed upon before it spirals. A difficult or stubborn work colleague or personal situation is best approached carefully and you will find you make great headway. *Moon in Gemini.*

12 NOVEMBER

This is a good day for meetings and to persuade important people of your principles and ideas, so take the initiative at work and you'll find positive ways ahead with projects. It's also a good day for romance and family get-togethers, so make a date! If you're still negotiating the terms of an agreement you could reach a good result but must avoid being easily influenced. *Moon in Cancer.*

13 NOVEMBER

Romance could blossom; you'll love music, dance, film, the arts and romantic walks. A creative or family project could progress but you must avoid impulsiveness. If you or someone else is a little tired, take things one step at a time. *Moon in Cancer.*

14 NOVEMBER

A positive and upbeat approach to the start of the week will work wonders for your projects, self-esteem and motivation. This is a good day for meetings and to get to the bottom of important matters. A creative, personal or family matter could be looking up. *Moon enters Leo.*

15 NOVEMBER

This is an excellent day for moving your ideas and plans forward. If there's someone you need to contact, do so today! However, if some of your ventures have snowballed and you aren't happy with the direction they're moving in they could gain momentum, so ensure you stop them in their tracks if you're unhappy with them. *Moon in Leo.*

16 NOVEMBER

You'll feel more outgoing and upbeat about your various projects and plans. A personal matter could move forward into a more proactive and optimistic phase, leaving some of the drama (not all!) behind. Avoid rash decisions. Be inspired but also practical. *Moon in Leo.*

17 NOVEMBER

As Mercury enters the zodiac sign Sagittarius, expect more focus to be on travel, broadening your horizons and on how you can move ahead with your creative ideas and at work over the coming weeks. You'll feel more inclined to be upbeat and outgoing in pursuit of adventure and discovery. *Moon in Virgo.*

18 NOVEMBER

This is a romantic time for you and someone special, so organise a date if you haven't already. If you're single you may meet someone charming and fun, so be sure to go out! You may feel more optimistic about your prospects, which you'll enjoy celebrating. *Moon in Virgo.*

19 NOVEMBER

Duties and responsibilities will need attending to, such as invoices and chores around the home and garden. You may prefer to relax but you will need to stick to various commitments. Find time to relax once all has been attended to. Avoid forgetfulness. *Moon enters Libra.*

20 NOVEMBER

You'll enjoy relaxing at home or at a lovely beauty spot. If you overdid things yesterday you may feel a little absent-minded today, so take things one step at a time. A health or beauty treat could appeal but you must be clear about what you want. *Moon in Libra.*

21 NOVEMBER

This is an excellent day at work and in your career, so ensure you organise interviews if you're looking for work and circulate your resume. You can make great headway with a project. This is also a good day for a medical or beauty appointment. You may even receive good news at work or health-wise. *Moon enters Scorpio.*

22 NOVEMBER

The sun in Sagittarius for the next few weeks will put the focus firmly on your work and health and you can make great progress in both areas, so be optimistic. You may be more upbeat and outgoing than usual and will enjoy increased physical activity. For some Cancerians, the sun in Sagittarius will initially bring a more upbeat social or family life. *Moon in Scorpio.*

23 NOVEMBER

The Sagittarian new moon will bring a fresh start for you in a work context and for some in a close relationship such as that with a family member or a partner. If you are beginning a fresh project this new moon suggests you will find it takes you into exciting new territory.

24 NOVEMBER

Today's moon in Sagittarius will contribute to a feeling of optimism, for some at work and for others in your personal life. It's a good time to boost health and well-being and to improve your image and profile at work. It's a good time to be more adventurous in life. *Moon in Sagittarius.*

25 NOVEMBER

This is a good day for health and beauty treats and to ensure you are on the right track in your general direction. If you feel you need to make adjustments to any aspects of your daily schedule, this is a good day to do so. However, if you experience a disappointment, rest assured developments now have a silver lining. *Moon enters Capricorn.*

26 NOVEMBER

Another good day to find the help and support you need and/or to offer it to someone else. It's an especially good day to boost your appearance with a new outfit or haircut. Just be clear about what you want to avoid disappointment. *Moon in Capricorn.*

27 NOVEMBER

A change of pace at home and at work if you're working today may be surprisingly refreshing or different. Developments may be unexpected. You may decide to alter your appearance to match your feelings and activities but may be surprised by the outcome, so choose your looks carefully. An impromptu get-together may be welcome but could get in the way of existing plans. Choose activities wisely. *Moon enters Aquarius.*

28 NOVEMBER

This is an excellent day to get things done, especially at work and regarding finances and your personal life. You could make agreements that are binding and mean an improvement in your work conditions or pay. Avoid taking unnecessary risks. *Moon in Aquarius.*

29 NOVEMBER

As you are feeling more outgoing and upbeat you are likely to wish to initiate talks and to take the lead at work and within relationships. However, not everyone will agree with your ideas so be prepared to modify or discuss them. Avoid being stubborn. A change of pace may require you to adapt better. *Moon in Aquarius.*

30 NOVEMBER

You're communicating well so organise get-togethers and meetings, especially to do with work and money. You could make a long-term commitment or arrangement. *Moon in Pisces.*

December

career   love   home   health   finance

1 DECEMBER

Aim to channel upbeat energy into productive outlets, especially if you're feeling antagonistic or frustrated, and you'll enjoy your day. Avoid intense conversations as they could quickly escalate, especially at work and regarding health. A meeting or news could be decisive. *Moon in Pisces.*

2 DECEMBER

You can attain your goals, especially with a little sensitivity to the feelings of others. If you have the correct facts at your fingertips you are in a strong position to succeed with your various commitments and chores, but you must focus extra hard. *Moon in Aries.*

3 DECEMBER

This is a great weekend to relax, unwind and build bridges with anyone you have quarrelled with recently. If health has been an issue it's a good day for a treat. An adviser or expert will be useful and you may be asked for support. *Moon in Aries.*

4 DECEMBER

You'll enjoy the company of someone special or doing a favourite activity, although you may tend to be escapist and will enjoy activities that take you somewhere new. Nature walks or being by the sea will appeal. To avoid misunderstandings and delays, ensure you double-check arrangements with those they concern. ***Moon enters Taurus.***

5 DECEMBER

The Taurus moon will encourage you to be practical and realistic, which will be handy as you may experience some delays. Plan ahead to gain extra time to get things done at work and for travel. The next two days could involve misunderstandings, so double-check facts. ***Moon in Taurus.***

6 DECEMBER

Communications may be a little stuck and colleagues or those in charge at work may be a little feisty. Avoid rushing decisions and feeling disoriented by others' issues. You may uncover a discrepancy in some communications, which will enable you to iron out differences. Avoid travel delays by leaving plenty of time. ***Moon enters Gemini.***

7 DECEMBER

An unpredictable or up in the air atmosphere may contribute to a feeling of restlessness, but if you focus on good communication skills you will get through the day well. ***Moon in Gemini.***

8 DECEMBER

The Gemini full moon shines a light on a fresh chapter for you in your personal life, especially if you were born in mid-July. If you were born earlier, a fresh chapter at work or regarding health and a new daily schedule is likely to begin. Take a moment to decide how you would like to see your future. Avoid snap decisions, but be spontaneous if a fresh opportunity arises.

9 DECEMBER

You'll enjoy being spontaneous and may receive unexpected news. You'll enjoy a get-together at work or in your spare time. ***Moon in Cancer.***

10 DECEMBER

You'll notice a change in tempo, not only because it's the weekend but also because some arrangements may change or you may simply feel like slowing things down. Someone close may feel a little stubborn or unwilling to be adventurous. If it's you, rest up as you may need to recharge your batteries. ***Moon in Cancer.***

11 DECEMBER

As Venus joins Mercury in Capricorn you'll get the sense your daily life and schedule can regain a more even keel. But you must avoid obstinacy, and if someone close is behaving stubbornly gently encourage them to see the error of their ways. ***Moon enters Leo.***

12 DECEMBER

This is a good day for making agreements with friends, a partner and family. Set out to make an event of celebrating your commitments to one another if you like! It's also a good day for relaxing and for a health or beauty treat. *Moon in Leo.*

13 DECEMBER

This is another good day for meetings and to get things done. Retail therapy will appeal. You are most likely to be an emotional spender, so ask yourself if you really need what you wish to buy. *Moon in Leo.*

14 DECEMBER

You may be a little idealistic, especially with long-term plans such as travel and family arrangements, so double-check you have the facts straight. Avoid gambling, both financially and emotionally. *Moon enters Virgo.*

15 DECEMBER

This is an excellent day to work on practicalities that need to be completed before you can make big-picture changes at work or in your general direction. Consider the most realistic way forward and then be inspired! *Moon in Virgo.*

16 DECEMBER

You'll enjoy being a little spontaneous, especially at the end of the day when you can relax. Certain talks and arrangements may require a little extra research and tact on your part. You'll enjoy socialising, and the wishes of colleagues and a partner will need to be taken into account. *Moon enters Libra.*

17 DECEMBER

You'll enjoy a change of pace and socialising and networking. A lovely event may take you somewhere different. If you're working or attending a work event, the difference in atmosphere will be enjoyable. *Moon in Libra.*

18 DECEMBER

Frank talks may need to be undertaken to avoid a difficult situation. Be brave and look for ways ahead that improve the circumstances of everyone concerned. A health or well-being situation is best handled sensitively. Avoid minor scrapes and bumps. *Moon in Libra.*

19 DECEMBER

You're getting on well with someone close and this will be inspiring for you, be it at work or in your personal life. Just avoid putting the cart before the horse; take things one step at a time. *Moon in Scorpio.*

20 DECEMBER

When the moon is in Scorpio people in your personal life may be more outspoken or passionate. You may also feel a little more outspoken and demonstrative. If problems arise, avoid a confrontational approach. This aside, you'll enjoy a development in your personal life. *Moon in Scorpio.*

21 DECEMBER

The solstice is a time of reflection when you can gather your wits as you assimilate your progress this year. A difficult situation with an employer or someone close is best handled carefully to avoid arguments. Be practical and realistic, and focus instead on a constructive plan for moving forward. *Moon in Sagittarius.*

22 DECEMBER

You'll enjoy a get-together or social event that puts you in the seasonal spirit. A work development could be encouraging. *Moon in Sagittarius.*

23 DECEMBER

The new moon and supermoon in Capricorn signals a fresh start for you in a close relationship if you were born in June, and a fresh chapter at work or in your daily health routine if you were born in July. You'll enjoy an event or chat that could bring an increased sense of security or stability your way.

24 DECEMBER

You'll enjoy being with someone who inspires you and brings you a feeling of togetherness. A creative, romantic, music-fuelled day will raise your spirits. *Moon in Capricorn.*

25 DECEMBER

Merry Christmas! You'll enjoy doing something different this year or will simply feel a little differently about your circumstances. You'll enjoy a reunion. *Moon in Aquarius.*

26 DECEMBER

A different mood, environment or pace may take a little getting used to. You'll appreciate being able to approach someone in a fresh way who can sometimes be a little difficult as you begin to see them in a new light. You may even feel some of your moods lift as you relax into the holiday season. *Moon in Aquarius.*

27 DECEMBER

You'll enjoy feeling you're getting on better with someone you can tend to disagree with. If you've been working hard this year, find the time to rest and consider a fresh schedule for 2023. *Moon in Pisces.*

28 DECEMBER

If you're shopping avoid overspending as you are likely to buy big. A romantic and for spiritually minded Cancerians mystical time will be inspiring. Try to get important paperwork completed before Mercury turns retrograde tomorrow. *Moon in Pisces.*

29 DECEMBER

Key news or a meeting may lead you to reconsider your position on various decisions. Fresh news will arise that could alter how you see certain arrangements or people. Some Cancerians will be returning to work, and if you had to work over Christmas you may get your time off now. *Moon in Aries.*

30 DECEMBER

A change in routine may involve logistics you'd rather not deal with but rest assured: once you tackle any conundrum that arises you'll be glad you did so. *Moon in Aries.*

31 DECEMBER

Happy New Year! You'll feel more settled as you enter the new year, even if an element of nostalgia or strong feelings arise earlier in the day. Your resolutions for the new year are likely to involve more love and peace. *Moon enters Taurus.*

LEO

22 July - 23 August

THE ESSENCE OF LEO

You are a dynamo, and because the sun rules your sign you are often the centre of attention just as the sun is the star at the centre of the solar system. You are generous to a fault and have a big heart; however, your natural magnetism can tend towards bravado and arrogance if you allow your talents to serve only your ego. Once you mature and realise the energy that emanates from your core is in fact creative and compassionate, you'll find you have a great deal to offer the community and the world at large and that you have enormous positive effects on the people around you. This is not only in relation to your family and friends but also to the bigger-picture social fabric.

Your major pitfall is pride, which can largely stem from knowing on an existential level that you are the centre of the universe rather than from a sense of superiority. If you weren't here would anything else exist? Other people may think you are self-centred and self-indulgent and have an inability to see anyone else's point of view. When you do take care to consciously listen to others rather than simply putting forward your own viewpoint you'll make great progress in understanding how you can collaborate and work with others in ways that lead towards co-operation and happiness.

You have a lion's roar and you do rule supreme, but for your own happiness it's better to rule with a velvet glove than with an iron fist. Those closest to you know you are a kitten at heart. You purr in delight at the attention you receive and react well to comfort and calm.

You do have a tendency towards laziness, which applies more to domestic matters than to work and your accomplishments. You are the ruler of your roost and have an inbuilt expectation that you'll be treated as the royal you are. Spare a thought for those who share space with you: the feeling of being ruled can be tiresome and will not be tolerated for long. To live a peaceful, harmonious life, double-check that the people close to you feel respected and equal and you will continue to purr in comfort.

SELF-ESTEEM

People believe you have high self-esteem because you appear to be dynamic and positive, yet this isn't necessarily always the case. You derive your self-esteem from feeling you have done something well, which may often involve helping others. You are a much more compassionate and helpful person than you are sometimes given credit for and will often go out of your way to be supportive of others, which is what makes you such a lovable Leo.

YOUR INNER LIFE

You have a gentle and caring nature that is often overlooked by people faced with your blustering persona. You truly do care for those you love; family is hugely important to you, and you love to be loyal.

Being such a fiery, proactive character you do require considerable downtime and need to recharge your batteries on a regular basis so you don't burn out. You are as powerful as the star in the

centre of our solar system, but you need to be careful that you replenish your energy levels regularly.

Yours is a sensitive soul. You can take offence at a frown from someone who is not aware they are frowning, or take an ambivalent gesture the wrong way when no insult was intended towards you. When this happens you emanate self-confidence to protect your vulnerability.

HOW OTHERS SEE YOU

You are seen as being a powerful, bright personality who is often the centre of attention, even if you do not consciously or outwardly display a desire for attention. You are someone who sparks on all cylinders and have a natural magnetism that draws people's eye to you, although you can be a drama queen.

Be aware that others can see your self-assuredness and self-centredness as threatening. When you're aware of the perception others have of you you'll learn to reassure people in subtle ways that your behaviour comes from a compassionate, joyful place rather than a place of selfishness. You are one of the least fatalistic signs of the zodiac and your self-confidence comes from your understanding that we are all ultimately responsible for our own actions. Unfortunately, those who are less confident than you can see you as being domineering and proud.

You can be a vain peacock, showing off your physical or inner strength. You do this unconsciously, but by being aware that others see you as a show-off means you can use your sense of humour to transform the negative characteristics into something more playful. And playfulness is, of course, one of your attributes, being a lion with the heart of a kitten.

HOW TO MAXIMISE YOUR POTENTIAL

Yours is one of the most dynamic signs of the zodiac, and you can accomplish great goals. However, you may find that unless you gain clear direction early on in life you become tied up in activities that don't suit your inner purpose and don't provide you with a sense of fulfilment. It's important to direct your considerable energy levels into activities that channel your dynamic energy into outcomes you respect and value.

You are essentially a creative person who enjoys seeing your actions take flight and your ideas and projects becoming something new and beautiful, whether tangible or not. Make sure you value the outcome of your actions. You are likely to be sporty and will enjoy physical activity and work, as these will channel your energy into productive pursuits.

Laziness and arrogance can be major pitfalls, so to maximise your potential you need to work on these negative attributes to minimise their prevalence in your emotional and mental make-up. You may not believe you're arrogant yet find you are often accused of being so. Work on humility and respect for others, and explain your reasons for your opinions and actions so people can understand that your motivation is not to be superior to others. When you're accused of being lazy, lend a helping hand. You are such a caring, heart-centred, compassionate character who is not afraid to muck in when needed. Your help in and around the home will be much appreciated and valued, and you will feel your heart open the more you integrate with the needs of others and work together as a community.

You're a born leader for whom help and compassion have to always be the foundation stones of your actions. This helps you to remain earthed, accepted and respected.

You are deeply loyal and hold respect for others in your heart. When you express your loyalty more on a daily basis you'll find your relationships and communications will thrive.

LEO AND ITS ASCENDANTS

This chapter is about your sun sign, Leo, and your predictions for the year ahead. The more you know about yourself the better you will be able to take advantage of opportunities, and also to avoid the pitfalls. It's critical to know as much about 'you' as possible.

In astrology your core self is represented by your sun sign, but your personality traits are represented by your ascendant (also known as your rising sign). The ascendant describes your personality, the way other people see you on first meeting you and the way you tend to filter life's events.

When you have intimate knowledge about your sun sign – your engine room or core being – you will be on the way to a happier life. When you add the knowledge about your personality – your ascendant – you will gain even deeper insight into what makes you tick.

Your ascendant sign is determined by the time of your birth on the date and year of your birth. Because the ascendant sign changes approximately every two hours, the best way to determine it is to ask an astrologer to calculate it for you. Certain apps will also calculate your ascendant sign (see page 873).

The following gives you more information about your abilities, characteristics and personality according to your sun sign Leo in combination with your ascendant sign.

LEO SUN SIGN WITH ARIES ASCENDANT

You are known as a double fire sign and, as such, are doubly dynamic and doubly a leader! People see you for who you are: a fiery, action-oriented, proactive character who is most definitely a dynamo through and through. Your strong positive traits are that you are energetic, entrepreneurial and independent. Unfortunately, however, your negative traits can be super strong unless you work on self-improvement. You can be lazy, lacking in motivation, pessimistic, arrogant, bossy, domineering and vain. You are never duplicitous, unless you have a strong element of secrecy in your chart. You're always upfront and clear about your motives, and you are a loyal friend. As a double fire character it's important to always maintain perspective to avoid landing yourself in hot water.

LEO SUN SIGN WITH TAURUS ASCENDANT

You will be seen by those who first meet you as being a careful, methodical and practical character who is dependable and earthy, enjoys the good things in life and is able to plan ahead. Yet when people get to know you they see you as being fiery, proactive and also potentially arrogant. You may be confused yourself about your predisposition for being careful on some occasions and reckless on others. You may be particularly attracted to intense and sensual people who wish to settle into a routine, but you may also wish to retain your independence. Find ways to combine your independence with your need for comfort and love and you'll establish positive relationships.

You're happy being comfortable, and once you achieve a level of comfort it will be hard to prise you out of it. Depending on the rest of your astrological chart, you may be supremely motivated by your need for comfort.

LEO SUN SIGN WITH GEMINI ASCENDANT

You are a mercurial character with many different forms of expression. You may be constantly on the go, fidgety, restless and hard to pin down; you are a dynamo. You can get caught up in your thoughts, so it's important to release tension and the tendency to worry through action-oriented activities that disperse excess energy.

As a Gemini-rising person you often gesticulate with your arms and hands when you talk and can be wiry in appearance. When combined with the Leo energy you need mental stimulation, so follow your heart and study and practise in areas that provide information and learning opportunities. One pitfall with this combination is that you can be seen as being aloof to the extent of being uncaring, so it's important to also show your gentler Leo nature: be the kitten that resides inside the lion!

LEO SUN SIGN WITH CANCER ASCENDANT

You have a dynamo character that lies beneath sensitivity, and that can surprise those who see you initially as a giving character. You are strong underneath and have an iron will even if you can appear to be easily influenced, soft or sensitive. You have a gentle, introspective personality, yet your inner resourcefulness and ability to stand your ground may be quite surprising. You do have a kind of extrasensory perception, as the Cancerian personality enables you to pick up information about people and circumstances that other rising signs don't manage.

LEO SUN SIGN WITH LEO ASCENDANT

You're a double Leo sign and are super assertive and adore being the centre of attention. You can act up and be a drama magnet, but you can also be extremely productive. Your personality is very much the Leo type: loving and creative. You have true lust for life; you love fun and will set out to enjoy yourself. It may be hard to explain to a double Leo that fun for you may not be fun for someone else!

You can overcome immense hurdles, and when this is combined with kindness the Leo personality is adorable. But when arrogance creeps into the mix, this double Leo combination can make for a disrespectful character. Learn to harness the double Leo energy and channel it into productive pursuits that celebrate humanity, togetherness and compassion or you may find the fighter in you emerges. You can tend to alienate those you love unless you are extremely careful to be respectful and humble.

LEO SUN SIGN WITH VIRGO ASCENDANT

The Virgo ascendant can often point to a natural-born healer or teacher, someone who wishes to serve and help others and make the world a better place. This combination can lead to careful work that executes exactly that outcome, although sometimes the clash between the dynamic, outgoing Leo attitude and the careful, methodical, earthy and perfectionistic Virgo temperament can point to inner tension. You may tend to hide your light, which will cause frustration. It's important with this configuration to work wholeheartedly at helping others as well as helping yourself shine.

LEO SUN SIGN WITH LIBRA ASCENDANT

Your placid and harmony-loving exterior belies a powerful and strong inner dynamo that may surprise those who meet you and who initially see you as being a gentle, creative, art-and peace-loving individual. You may be indecisive, as on the one hand you will wish to power ahead (Leo) while on the other you wish to make the right decisions. This will slow you down, adding to a sense of frustration. You are likely to be a sociable character, often on the go and being attractive to similarly minded and outgoing people who are artistic, musical or creative.

LEO SUN SIGN WITH SCORPIO ASCENDANT

The Scorpio ascendant is the most charismatic and intense of all ascendants and can be magnetic in personality but also ruthless; think sting in the tail. Ironically, the person you are most likely to sting is yourself, so keep an eye on shooting home goals. You present as a dynamic person who enjoys being the centre of attention, but you must guard against being led by your passions, needs and desires above all else as these impulses could lead you astray. Align yourself with your compassionate, kind heart and allow your Scorpio personality to drive your intentions into positive pursuits. If you allow your Scorpio personality to rule via strong emotions, feelings and impulses you may walk down an exciting but potentially unrewarding path, as your Leo inner self needs optimism and love. Without these you will feel lacklustre, so let your Leo self drive your Scorpio passions.

LEO SUN SIGN WITH SAGITTARIUS ASCENDANT

You are a double fire sign who is active, dynamic and gregarious. You are keen to take the initiative and instigate upbeat, exciting and fun ventures. You may present to others as being overbearing due to your competitiveness which may come as a surprise, especially if you do not see yourself as competitive, yet you cannot fail to wish to win at your various tasks. Even if you are the kitten type of Leo you will still garner attention; you can't help it. You aim to succeed, and succeed you will! Ensure your actions come from a compassionate place or your ego may be torn down a notch or two.

LEO SUN SIGN WITH CAPRICORN ASCENDANT

Your practical, reasonable and sensible personality belies the raging heart of Leo the lion. You can be hugely successful as you are diligent, driven and patient in the execution of your goals. You are unlikely to take 'no' for an answer in your endeavours, and will patiently wait to pounce on projects you have earmarked as yours. You are willing to go the long haul with projects and are hard to dissuade once you have set your mind on an outcome, but you are also fun-loving and loyal beneath your steely determination. Once you look beneath the hard-working and diligent outer shell there is a soft core that enjoys family life and the comforts of home.

LEO SUN SIGN WITH AQUARIUS ASCENDANT

Your personality is very much the Aquarian type: quirky, restless, intelligent and sensitive. You are also a loving and creative character who is able to overcome immense hurdles. When this ability is combined with kindness you are a strong and adorable character, but when arrogance, eccentricity and a sense of superiority creep into your personality a disrespectful streak can emerge. Harness the Aquarian intelligence and channel it into productive humanitarian pursuits. You may experience inner tension between wishing to humanely work with others and wishing to put yourself first. When you work out that it is possible to do both you will overcome this tension.

LEO SUN SIGN WITH PISCES ASCENDANT

Yours is a multi-levelled, complex character. On the one hand you are quite the philosopher, dreamer and savant, being spiritually minded and humanitarian, but on the other hand you are dynamic and active. When you combine your ability to take action in exciting ventures with your spiritually enlightened self you are a force for good. You are likely to be drawn to charity work and are kind at heart, but you may also tend to be easily distracted and see life through rose-coloured glasses; this can result in disappointment and inactivity. It is important to remain heart-centred and steer your interests dynamically towards positive outcomes.

LEO IN LOVE

You are such a dynamic character who is attractive and selective about who you spend your time with in the long term. In this section you can check out your compatibility with other sun signs. Remember that we are all complex individuals, so the more you know about someone's astrological birth chart the better you can determine your compatibility. Consider having your astrological birth chart compared with that of a partner, friend or family member, as the compatibility – known as 'synastry' in astrology – goes even deeper than a comparison of sun signs, although this is a good place to begin.

LEO WITH ARIES

Two powerhouses together can certainly make music when you're both on the same page, but if you ever disagree with each other there will be fireworks! Where there's a strong initial spark of attraction, dare to go that little bit deeper to find out what your common ground is. Are you emotionally on the same track? If not, the spark that initially gets you together could turn into a raging inferno of conflict and, worse, bring out both of your adverse characteristics: anger, impatience and bossiness. If you feel you both have similar values and ethics this really could be a dynamic duo, although there will always be fiery moments. Channel the fire into passion and common aims or it could turn into temper tantrums and drama.

LEO WITH TAURUS

You'll appreciate the sensuality and outward calm of the Taurean, but you may tend to be a little frustrated on occasion by the lack of comparative motivation and dynamism unless there is a strong fire element in your Taurean partner's chart. This relationship can be settling, grounding and comforting and can provide the earthiness you sometimes lack in some of your more impulsive moments. One major stumbling block is that you can both be uncompromising in your views once you have decided on something, and this can lead to a stalemate where neither of you will budge. If you can agree to disagree on occasion there is every chance your Taurean partner will find you exciting if impulsive, and you'll find your Taurean partner sensual, calming and sexy.

LEO WITH GEMINI

This is a lovely match, even if you both find yourselves so busy in your own lives that you spend more time missing each other's company than actually being together. This match makes a fun-loving duo out to enjoy life and live an exciting adventure together. The Leo character will wish to take the lead, which is something the Gemini may come to resent in a longer-term relationship as Geminis look for a balanced relationship based on fun, excitement and adventure. The Leo may come to depend on the support of the Gemini, but if the Gemini does not have autonomy and the chance to be adaptable and independent this match can end in tears. Leo will look for a settled life, especially in later years, but will wish to be the lion at the centre of the brood. Gemini will not play second fiddle, so give and take is essential in this partnership.

LEO WITH CANCER

Leo is ruled by the sun, the centre of the solar system, and likes to be the centre of attention. Cancer would need to take the back seat in this relationship or else you will not feel you can shine. The quieter Cancerian personality may initially play this role, but as both these signs are super strong willed this combo can lead to a battle unless both are conscious of each other's boundaries and mindful of each other's power and self-respect.

LEO WITH LEO

You can be a compatible match as you are both proactive, upbeat and dynamic. This match can be truly harmonious as you work to bring out the best in the other. You will enjoy the same approach to life and have an optimistic attitude to each other, and will enjoy playful pursuits and adventurous activities. In partnerships there can be a powerful and energising love life; however, fire breeds fire and this match spells fireworks if neither of you has worked on tempering your tendency towards impulsive or explosive behaviour. Some fire-fire sign matches can act as catalysts to ignite a previously relatively serene personality into one that exhibits tempers and outbursts.

LEO WITH VIRGO

The Virgo personality is likely to initially attract you as you will be enthralled by their earthy, practical and sensual presence. Your Virgo partner will be excited by your fiery, dynamic self, but you may soon find Virgo lacking in motivation and enthusiasm while Virgo may find you restless, egocentric and impulsive. You both fundamentally come from different sides of the ring, but if you have a strong earth signature in your chart and your Virgo partner has a strong fire element in theirs it could still be a match. Your different attributes can complement each other if you work at this partnership.

LEO WITH LIBRA

There is a fundamental match here: fire needs air to exist and air appreciates the excitement of fire. Leo provides your Libran partner with the motivation they may lack, and your Libran supplies you with the intellect and reason you need. You will appreciate your Libran partner's ability to analyse and plan, and your Libran partner will appreciate your ability to initiate activities and feel excited about life. You complement each other on many levels.

LEO WITH SCORPIO

Scorpio and Leo together make a passionate combination, although with this kind of fire sparks will fly! If you both have good impulse control and have anger under control you'll manage to channel passion into self-fulfilling and mutually enhancing activities, but if you have not come to terms with anger or past issues in your lives this match may be too hot to handle. There may also be ego battles: Leo will wish to be the peacock in the relationship and Scorpio can take this as a personal insult. Both signs wish to control and lead each other, so a pecking order will need to be established.

LEO WITH SAGITTARIUS

There is basic compatibility with this match as you are both fire signs. You will automatically understand where the other is coming from and will enjoy being active, outgoing and upbeat with adventurous pursuits such as travel and sports. You both have strong personalities and are keen to take the lead, but instinctively know one should lead and the other take the back seat. Your lust for life means you can enjoy light-hearted, fun and giggly moments, but you are also able to pull together to mutually support each other in times of need.

LEO WITH CAPRICORN

The resolute, measured, even serious demeanour of the typical Capricorn is quite the opposite to the fundamental Leo, who is outgoing, upbeat and spontaneous. These sun signs are usually at odds, so unless there are other signs of compatibility in the natal astrology chart it can be a difficult match. That is unless you find ways to complete the Capricorn and vice versa. Leo may express the get up and go that the Capricorn is lacking on occasion, and Capricorn may provide you with an improved sense of duty and responsibility. Capricorn will prefer a slow pace of life even while being determined, just like Leo, to succeed and shine. You may feel restricted or limited by this slow pace, and Capricorn can feel unsettled by your fiery spontaneity.

LEO WITH AQUARIUS

Both sun signs in this match complement the other. Aquarius is eccentric and independent and presents Leo with a willing partner for madcap escapades. Leo completes the Aquarian penchant for spontaneity and excitement. This is a good match, as both signs are freedom loving and individualistic. You'll enjoy exciting and quirky activities together, sharing an offbeat sense of humour, yet you can both be serious and wish for a settled family life. This latter desire may kick in a bit later in life than it does for most sun signs.

LEO WITH PISCES

Pisces will be drawn to your Leo generosity and your larger-than-life personality, although they may feel dominated by your strong views and willpower. Avoid overshadowing the delicate Pisces ego. You'll feel attracted to the Pisces personality, as their sensitivity and insight add depth to the relationship and your understanding of the world. This match can feel strained if neither Leo nor Pisces wish to share common ground and stick to it. You are both likely to wander in different worlds and may miss each other along the way unless care is taken to learn more about the other's viewpoints and mindset.

THE YEAR AHEAD FOR LEO

Affirmation for the year: *'I've got this!'*

Changes in the way you live your life, from your everyday routine to your work hours, activities and priorities, will take your focus early on in 2022 as you will gain the opportunity at the very least to see how alternative options could pan out in your life.

You may even experience a sense of wishing to have more freedom of movement in your daily life. A holiday or simply a break from the mundane daily routine may be inconvenient but, on the other hand, it will introduce you to new ideas and plans. And, if you take the bull by the horns and decide to make long-overdue changes, avoid being put off by teething problems as every good plan will have a false start – a situation that will enable you to perfect your plans.

The eclipses in 2022, in April-May and October-November, represent major turning points in your year. For many these will be across your communication and travel zones, suggesting you will be in full flight this year and enjoy being sociable and finding ways to move into new territory in your various interests, even if some of the trips on your bucket list are not feasible this year due to practicalities or other people's circumstances.

The eclipses also point to a fresh phase in a close relationship, as you either get closer or are ready to release someone on their way to the next stage in life.

For others the eclipses will mean major changes at home and/or in your status. Developments in your personal life will represent the major areas of change in 2022, as your family, lover, partner or children become a true focus of change.

Someone or perhaps even you may be ready to fly the coop and, at the least, to consider new ways to share space at home or finances and responsibilities. Negotiations will merit tact and diplomacy to avoid a chaotic or drama-fuelled approach to inevitable change. Consider a new model that will work for all concerned.

HEALTH

Part of your journey in 2022 will revolve around how to make a more enjoyable daily experience sustainable, both financially and in practical, health-related terms. You will find the periods from May through to the end of August and October to December will be particularly conducive to a more relaxed life, and this will benefit your health and well-being.

You may be drawn to improving your appearance during these months as well, and also to changing the look that you have previously been associated with. This will be a full expression of the new way you like to see the world and to be seen.

The Leo new moon on 27 August will be an excellent time to develop a fresh health and fitness routine, as it's more likely to take.

At the start of the year you may be drawn to new and even radical ways to boost your health and appearance. Avoid going too left field: don't undergo surgery unless you feel convinced it's necessary, especially early in the year and in October as this may be something you regret at a later date.

FINANCES

Your finances are due new developments, and specifically in the area of shared finances with family and friends. You may learn new ways to help support each other. This is a year to avoid going into debt, as there is an element of insecurity this will represent for you. But if you have no other choice, opt for lending schemes that are secure and read the fine print, or you may find yourself locked in an agreement that favours only the lender.

The most stressful times this year in terms of debt and finances will be in mid-January, the end of June and in mid-July and mid-October. These times of the year will be useful for you to find clever ways to make your money stretch further, such as working from home, recycling and upcycling.

New investments and ways to save money will also appeal, but the more secure your investment option the better for you in 2022. The eclipse on 8 November could be pivotal, as changes in your status impact on your finances.

People you love will take much of your energy and resources in 2022, so it's essential to ensure your investments and financial strategy are solid as you will free up time to spend with loved ones. Avoid get-rich-quick schemes and legal conundrums by being super clear about the contracts and agreements you forge in 2022.

HOME LIFE

The Capricorn new moon and supermoon on 2 January is an excellent time to set your intentions to maintain your personal identity as an important aspect of your life, or you risk putting too much of your focus on developing your career, work and status. You may tend to be torn in 2022 between duties and commitments at home and work chores, leading to a circumstance where neither your work nor your personal life in the shape of your home are fulfilling.

Family and the development of activities spent with people you love and interests that add meaning to your life will merit much focus. It would be a mistake this year to allow your personal and private life to take a back seat while you pursue your career and work life.

Make the most of Mars in your home sector in January, as you will get the chance to feather your nest for the year to come.

Developments at the end of January will give you a heads-up about how you can best share the various areas of your life so that you can enjoy a balanced existence. Your home life is a vital part of the balance necessary to feel happy and contented now, or you risk overloading with work and chores and leaving little time for those you love, least of all yourself.

LOVE

Relationships in general will undergo considerable change in 2022, so you'll find the year will encompass a lesson in good relationship skills. Be ready to learn and improve your skills and you will sail through any hurdles that are presented to you.

Romance may be particularly powerful in January and in May through to August. If you find your love life is a little chaotic during this time or that communications seem more difficult, take steps to slow your life down and make the time for those you love, especially finding time for romance.

You'll appreciate the opportunity to boost your looks and to spend more time on accumulating your tools and skills for the language of love: good food, comfortable surrounds and peace. October is a particularly positive time to make a commitment to someone.

With Pluto hovering around your descendant for most of the year, especially if you were born around 22 July, and Saturn having a powerful influence in your seventh house all year there is every chance that romance will run amok in your life.

Singles must choose where you place your full romantic attention wisely and avoid being influenced by charm and passion alone, as your love life could alter your existence in the long term in ways that may surprise even you.

CAREER

The moon's north node leaves your career sector and enters your adventure zone, putting the onus on you to feel fulfilled in your career and activities in general. Ask yourself: 'Am I truly happy in my career?' If not this is a good time to make changes, although not without prior research or you may find your duties, commitments and financial obligations get the better of you if you have no secure income.

Proactive Mars in your work sector from the end of January through to early March will present a busy time. You will need to master the art of multi-tasking to stay on top of a hectic schedule, but you could make great progress with your chosen career.

Pluto making a favourable aspect to the sun and Mercury in May also means a busy time. The good news is that you will gain the chance to step into fresh areas and experience new work scenarios, which will increase your marketability and career prospects. However, you will need to be adaptable and willing to take on new roles. You may find that a humanitarian interest will draw you into new avenues.

You'll gain the chance at mid-year to reconsider your options up until the end of the year. This phase is likely to take some of the heat off the busyness of the start of the year, but you will need to instigate a solid health routine to keep your energy levels up.

The total lunar eclipse on 8 November signals fresh interests and ideas will pique your interest this year, and with the eclipses across your travel sector and communications bringing new ideas and environments into your experience you'll enjoy incorporating fresh and exciting projects into your career.

January

career · love · home · health · finance

Notes: the pie charts such as the one above listed for each month show energy distribution according to the stars for the month ahead. If you wish to make changes in the areas of your finances, health, career, love or home and you see there is a large amount of energy in that sector in the chart, your endeavours should succeed as long as you have prepared well in advance. The charts also show which areas will potentially have the most focus in your life during the month.

The moon sign listed for each day's entry in the diary is the position of the moon at the end of the day in Greenwich Mean Time (GMT). To gain the most information about a particular day's circumstances, read the day before and the day after for a complete picture.

1 JANUARY

Happy New Year! You may experience a surprise. You'll enjoy the feeling of a new year beginning and doing something different for a change on the first day of the year. If you're at work you're likely to be busy. *Moon enters Capricorn.*

2 JANUARY

The new moon and supermoon in Capricorn will kick-start a fresh phase such as a new chapter in your personal life and at work, especially for July Leos. For some the new moon is the chance to reorganise your health and daily routine to suit you better. You may enjoy a change in your usual routine or a get-together with someone fun.

3 JANUARY

This is a good time to consider how you could pep up your daily life so it includes more variety and spice. For some the Aquarian moon will promote a sense of fun with someone close, so focus on bringing new ideas and activities into your personal life. ***Moon enters Aquarius.***

4 JANUARY

You won't always agree with everyone, and someone close may have news that merits a patient approach as they may be feeling a little stubborn or simply unwilling to look at their situation laterally. ***Moon in Aquarius.***

5 JANUARY

You'll enjoy indulging in the good things in life so ensure you take time out to source your favourite foods and indulge in the arts, music and romance. ***Moon in Aquarius.***

6 JANUARY

The more understanding of others you can be and the less reactive the better. You may need to review finances or spending habits and work on a new plan of action. You'll enjoy relaxing this evening and allowing your imagination to take flight. ***Moon in Pisces.***

7 JANUARY

You may feel a little escapist and will enjoy daydreaming. If you're on holiday you'll enjoy simply relaxing and exploring new place. However, you could be forgetful, so avoid misplacing valuables such as keys. ***Moon in Pisces.***

8 JANUARY

A little motivation will certainly encourage you to get things done with your various chores, both at home and at work. But if you feel under pressure, avoid allowing this to contribute to mistakes being made. Take things in your stride. ***Moon in Aries.***

9 JANUARY

This a good time for getting outstanding chores cleared at home or at work. A health or beauty treat will also appeal. Working Leos may receive key news to do with work. You may enjoy a change of scenery or of pace. Some Leos will find this a particularly romantic time and may reconnect with an ex. ***Moon in Aries.***

10 JANUARY

The Aries moon will bring your feistiness out. If you channel strong emotions into hard work you will get a lot done, but if you allow frustrations to get the better of you you may find arguments and stress ruin an otherwise productive day. ***Moon enters Taurus.***

11 JANUARY

Romantically, if you find a little stress contributes to the thrill of romance you'll enjoy today's developments, but if you prefer your romantic life to be stress free find the time to take breaks and avoid over-thinking your personal situation. A mystery may be in the making and you could be forgetful, so pace yourself. ***Moon in Taurus.***

12 JANUARY

The moon in Taurus helps you to get things done at work in the most practical, realistic way. Try to get loose ends to do with work tied up over the next two days before Mercury turns retrograde on Friday, to avoid delays or having to renegotiate agreements at a later time. ***Moon in Taurus.***

13 JANUARY

When the moon is in Gemini you may notice you and other people feel a little more chatty and flexible, especially at work. You may also feel more light-hearted about some of your projects and ventures. However, not everyone will feel the same, so aim to embrace other people's mindsets and paces if necessary. ***Moon in Gemini.***

14 JANUARY

You may receive key news to do with work or health. If you were born in July you're likely to hear news from a business or personal partner that requires attention. You may need to reconsider a project. If you're travelling or planning a trip you will receive key news. Delays may occur, so factor in extra time. ***Moon in Gemini.***

15 JANUARY

The next two days may be fairly intense for you in the run-up to the full moon in Cancer. Developments are likely to revolve around your feelings, especially to do with work and health and for some mid-August Leos in your personal life. Aim to be flexible and work towards the bigger-picture results you want. ***Moon enters Cancer.***

16 JANUARY

Key news may represent considerable change either for you personally or within your daily routine. You may alter your usual schedule or must change how you go about your health routine. Avoid snap decisions and allowing emotions to determine your decisions. Instead, find ways to gain perspective. ***Moon in Cancer.***

17 JANUARY

The Cancerian full moon shines a light on a change of routine or circumstance. For many this will be due to developments at work or regarding health matters. A commitment can be made. Key changes will mean you must consider the big picture, especially concerning your general direction in life. Base decisions on practicalities and avoid allowing emotions to overwhelm reason.

18 JANUARY

When the moon is in Leo you feel more in sync with yourself and emotions. However, this doesn't mean you'll naturally agree with everyone. A change in your general routine may bring out your inner warrior, which will be useful for adapting to new circumstances, but you must avoid feistiness. *Moon in Leo.*

19 JANUARY

You may receive good news to do with work or from someone special. It's a good time to discuss your plans and to make changes in your daily routine so it suits you better. Romance could blossom and a trip or venture could open doors, so be proactive. *Moon in Leo.*

20 JANUARY

The sun in Aquarius for the next four weeks will encourage you to be more outgoing and willing to embrace new ideas and projects. You may find that a business or personal partner is also more outgoing. An unpredictable factor may enter your life, and the best way to engage with this could be to focus on improving your communication skills. *Moon in Leo.*

21 JANUARY

These next few days are ideal for discussing important new ideas with those they concern. You may also rework or review some of your work or health schedules. *Moon in Virgo.*

22 JANUARY

You'll enjoy a get-together with someone you admire and understand. Work meetings are likely to go well, as will a trip or reunion. Just factor in extra time for travel and communications to avoid feeling frustrated with delays. You may be drawn to repair a vehicle or digital device. *Moon enters Libra.*

23 JANUARY

This is a good day for meetings and important conversations. If you were born around 26 July you may hear key news from a business or personal partner. Most Leos will receive information to do with work or health. It's a good time to review your work and health practices. *Moon in Libra.*

24 JANUARY

When the moon is in Libra you will be drawn to looking for fairness, and you will uphold your principles and may have more need for value in life. Avoid being stubborn and look for new ways to get on with people if a business or personal relationship has hit a speed bump. ***Moon in Libra.***

25 JANUARY

This is a good time for meetings and talks, both at work and in your personal life. Someone may get in touch from out of the blue and you'll enjoy being spontaneous. ***Moon in Scorpio.***

26 JANUARY

As Mercury retrograde re-enters Capricorn you may find you must go over old ground at work or review health practices. Find ways to align your activities more with interests that provide a sense of purpose. ***Moon in Scorpio.***

27 JANUARY

When the moon is in Sagittarius you may be busier in your personal life and will find value in being with upbeat, optimistic people. You'll be outgoing and industrious and could create positive outcomes, so be motivated! ***Moon in Sagittarius.***

28 JANUARY

The moon will motivate you to get things done at home and with family. You'll feel drawn to meet those who have a positive, healthy effect on your mood. You'll enjoy updating your décor or even moving furniture to provide more space or a sense of the outdoors. ***Moon in Sagittarius.***

29 JANUARY

You'll enjoy a reunion. If you're working you'll be busy. Important news is on the way that may involve reconsidering your options at work or health-wise or a change in your daily routine. ***Moon in Capricorn.***

30 JANUARY

A change of plan may be necessary or will be outside your control. You may hear unexpected news or someone may behave unpredictably. Be prepared to adapt to new circumstances but you must avoid rash decisions. ***Moon in Capricorn.***

31 JANUARY

You will enjoy a health or beauty treat, and work may regain a more even keel or you will receive good news. Some Leos will receive good news from a partner and romance could flourish, so organise a date! ***Moon in Aquarius.***

February

career   love   home   health   finance

1 FEBRUARY

The new moon in Aquarius signifies a fresh start for you. For July and early August Leos this will be in a business or personal relationship, and for those born later in a work and health context.

2 FEBRUARY

Trust your intuition and be sensitive to the mood swings of others without being influenced by them if possible! You'll gain insight into someone's feelings. ***Moon enters Pisces.***

3 FEBRUARY

This is a good day to consider your deeper thoughts and wishes, especially to do with a collaboration or someone close. It's a good day for romance and time with family. ***Moon in Pisces.***

4 FEBRUARY

You will receive key news or make a commitment, especially if you were born in early August. An important work or personal matter can be decided as you're likely to gain the information you need. ***Moon in Pisces.***

5 FEBRUARY

When the moon is in Aries you may feel more outgoing and upbeat, so be spontaneous but avoid decisions you'll regret. This is a good day to improve your health or to help someone with theirs. Avoid arguments as they may be hurtful. *Moon in Aries.*

6 FEBRUARY

You are an independent character and like to do things your way. Today, though, you may need to do things someone else's way! *Moon in Aries.*

7 FEBRUARY

As the moon aligns with Uranus you may experience an unexpected development and will enjoy doing something different. It's a good day to try something new and to enjoy your fave activities, but you must remain grounded and practical. *Moon in Taurus.*

8 FEBRUARY

This is a good day to really focus on the people and projects that mean the most to you. You may be pleasantly surprised as a result, as you can achieve a great deal. You may need to encourage someone to co-operate a little more. *Moon in Taurus.*

9 FEBRUARY

When the moon is at the zenith of your chart as it is today you will feel motivated by your keen interests, and if you love what you do at work you'll enjoy investing time in this. It's a good time to tune in to what and who really motivate you in life and find time for these people and activities. *Moon in Gemini.*

10 FEBRUARY

This is a lovely day to indulge in your favourite treats – just don't go overboard! Romance, music and the arts could all inspire you so organise a special event. If you're shopping just avoid overspending It's a good time to organise a fresh budget if you're in debt. Plan ahead to avoid any unnecessary surprises. *Moon in Gemini.*

11 FEBRUARY

Key meetings and talks will bring clarity to a work or health matter. Avoid feeling under pressure and aim to reveal just how capable and knowledgeable you are. If your health has been under the weather, you could gain direction. *Moon in Cancer.*

12 FEBRUARY

Today's Cancerian moon will mean you're more sensitive than usual but also more intuitive, so take a moment to unwind and de-stress and take note of your instincts. Someone may confide their feelings to you, and if you need a little support it will be available so ensure you reach out. Avoid taking the mood swings of others personally. *Moon in Cancer.*

13 FEBRUARY

Check that your emotions aren't leading you into feeling more sensitive than you should be ,especially concerning work, health or someone close. You'll enjoy a reunion and romance could thrive, so take time out to savour life. *Moon in Cancer.*

14 FEBRUARY

Happy St Valentine's Day! This is always a quirky day with unexpected news or the chance to reveal our true feelings. You may be surprised by news from someone close at home or at work. It's a good day to get in touch with someone you love, so be bold! You'll gain insight into your priorities, especially concerning work and your favourite activities. *Moon in Leo.*

15 FEBRUARY

Today's developments will encourage you to look at fresh ways of interacting with someone close either at home or at work. Take a moment to orient your thoughts, plans and wishes and take direction from them. *Moon in Leo.*

16 FEBRUARY

The Leo full moon will shine a light on your personal life, especially if it's your birthday at the end of July or early in August. You may be ready to turn a corner with someone close, and this decision may come from out of the blue. Some Leos are likely to begin a fresh chapter at work or regarding a health or daily schedule. *Moon enters Virgo late in the day.*

17 FEBRUARY

This is an excellent day for talks at work and concerning a personal or business partner. It is also a good day to make a commitment and to mend bridges if you have argued recently. Romance could flourish and you may receive good news. *Moon in Virgo.*

18 FEBRUARY

As the sun enters the zodiac sign Pisces you are likely to feel more inspired by the people around you. If you aren't already inspired by them you will wish to seek inspiring people! You may tend to idealise someone, so ensure you are realistic or you may feel disappointed. *Moon in Libra.*

19 FEBRUARY

You're likely to be drawn to improving your environment, be this at home or at work or both. You may also be inclined to spend money and to invest in good food and in yourself. If you're already in debt, look for ways to invest in yourself that don't involve money such as fitness training. *Moon in Libra.*

20 FEBRUARY

This is a good day to focus on relaxation and reconnecting with someone you love. You may not agree with everyone so avoid making life difficult by looking for common ground rather than conflict. If you need a little help it's available. ***Moon in Libra.***

21 FEBRUARY

It's a good day to enquire about new work or health options and to use your creativity and imagination. You may feel more intuitive, especially about someone else's feelings, but you must avoid making assumptions. ***Moon enters Scorpio.***

22 FEBRUARY

You'll enjoy being more involved with a family or personal matter. You may be drawn to a little DIY or to improving domestic dynamics. Someone may ask for your help, and if you need support it will be available. ***Moon in Scorpio.***

23 FEBRUARY

A family or personal project could flourish, so be inspired and put your energy into ventures you enjoy. Romance could truly blossom, so ensure you organise a date or a night in! ***Moon in Sagittarius.***

24 FEBRUARY

This is an excellent day for romance. Singles may meet someone new and couples will enjoy rekindling a little mystery and fun in your love life. Creative Leos will feel inspired, and the spiritually minded will also find this an inspiring time. Avoid absent-mindedness and mislaying important valuables. ***Moon in Sagittarius.***

25 FEBRUARY

You may be surprised by news. For some this will involve a change of plan, and for others a change of routine. Communications may be a little erratic, so ensure you back up computers and spare extra time for travel as there may be some delays. Avoid misunderstandings by being super clear and ensuring you are on the same page as those you communicate with. ***Moon enters Capricorn.***

26 FEBRUARY

Communications and travel are likely to be better unless obstacles occurred yesterday and you need to sort them out today. This is a good day for floating ideas at work and with a personal or business partner. This could also be a romantic day, so plan a treat. ***Moon in Capricorn.***

27 FEBRUARY

The earthy moon for most of the day will encourage you to get down to brass tacks with plans and chores. Once the moon is in Aquarius you'll enjoy altering your usual routine and doing something different. ***Moon enters Aquarius.***

28 FEBRUARY

You'll gain the chance to look at key relationships and duties in a new light. Fresh insight will provide the chance to broaden your horizons at work, with a partner or a venture. However, you or someone close may be a little changeable, so aim to be flexible for the best results. *Moon in Aquarius.*

March

| career | love | home | health | finance |

1 MARCH

You're likely to feel on the right track at work and health-wise, so immerse yourself in inspiring projects. Someone close may have an interesting approach to your long-term plans. ***Moon enters Pisces.***

2 MARCH

The Pisces new moon signals the chance to turn a corner, especially in a shared circumstance such as a business or personal partnership. Look for inspired ways to move forward but keep your feet on the ground.

3 MARCH

The Venus-Mars-Pluto conjunction will be in your sixth house of work, daily routine and health. Someone has key news for you. This could be an intense time, so you must maintain perspective. Avoid being overcome by emotions and maintain a clear perspective. ***Moon in Pisces.***

4 MARCH

Today's Aries moon will bring your more proactive, dynamic side into play, enabling you to move forward constructively from any problems or issues. If you have felt under the weather, take short breaks where you can. Someone close may need your help. **Moon in Aries.**

5 MARCH

You may find you need to prioritise between the wishes of someone close and work duties or chores. You may find that the practicalities of a situation are more complex than you'd hoped, so take the time to devise a workable plan everyone is happy with. **Moon in Aries.**

6 MARCH

As both Mars and Venus step into Aquarius you will experience a change of focus and also a new proposition or change of schedule. You'll enjoy stepping into fresh territory. If you're health conscious you may be drawn to looking into ways to be fitter, and complementary therapies may appeal. Avoid stubbornness. **Moon in Taurus.**

7 MARCH

The Taurean moon will help you to be more practical about changes you'd like to make in your activities and ventures and to make decisions based on facts and information. This means this is a good day for planning. **Moon in Taurus.**

8 MARCH

This is a good day to mend bridges with people you have quarrelled with. Romance could flourish, so make a date if you haven't already! Work meetings are likely to go well. It's a good day for health and well-being appointments and to change your looks. **Moon enters Gemini.**

9 MARCH

The Gemini moon at the zenith of your chart helps you to communicate well. It will also help you to be adaptable, especially with changes at work, health-wise or in your status. If you have suffered ill health or fatigue of late this is a good time to consult experts. **Moon in Gemini.**

10 MARCH

This is a good day for making commitments and agreements – that is, as long as you avoid being idealistic. Check facts and ensure those you make arrangements with are definitely on the same page for the best results. **Moon in Gemini.**

11 MARCH

This is a chatty, upbeat day that is ideal for connecting with someone who needs to know your thoughts such as an employer or partner. **Moon in Cancer.**

12 MARCH

When the moon is in Cancer you are more intuitive, so take note of your first impressions if you meet someone new. You'll gain insight into someone close and may make more definite plans for ventures you'll both enjoy. *Moon in Cancer.*

13 MARCH

This is a romantic day, so if you have nothing planned yet arrange a treat. Romance could blossom. If you're meeting friends or family you'll enjoy the get-together but must ensure you all have the same arrangements to avoid mix-ups or missing someone. *Moon enters Leo.*

14 MARCH

This is a good day to get ahead with your various collaborations both at home and at work. It's also a good day for a health, fitness or beauty appointment. *Moon in Leo.*

15 MARCH

You'll enjoy being your dynamic self and will feel in your element as the moon is in your sign. However, some people may see you as a little feisty, so avoid contributing to conflict if possible. *Moon in Leo.*

16 MARCH

Today's Virgo moon will bring your more practical side out and encourage you to focus more on the chores at hand. A financial matter may require further analysis. *Moon in Virgo.*

17 MARCH

You'll appreciate the opportunity to try something new. A venture or interest will take steps forward and you may be pleasantly surprised by news of a positive development from a partner or someone you collaborate with. *Moon in Virgo.*

18 MARCH

The Virgo full moon shines a light on finances for some Leos and on your personal life for others. You may ask yourself how you could share your valuable time and assets better or, on the other hand, if you have been overly generous. The full moon will indicate which areas of your life need more attention to detail and practicalities.

19 MARCH

The Libran moon will bring your analytical and detached qualities out, enabling you to appraise a work, financial or personal situation with objectivity. You'll be looking for fairness and will find a way to establish a more even keel if you feel some aspects of your work, finances or personal life have become unbalanced. *Moon in Libra.*

20 MARCH

When the sun enters Aries this is the vernal equinox. During the next four weeks you may find that your collaborations both in your personal life and at work become a real focus. Find the time to boost your communication skills and relationships as you could make great progress. *Moon in Scorpio.*

21 MARCH

Key news from someone you share important duties, responsibilities or time with will arrive. You may be drawn to travel or to meeting influential people. A key financial or legal matter will benefit from close attention. You may feel idealistic, so keep your feet on the ground. *Moon in Scorpio.*

22 MARCH

This is a good day for making agreements, including financial arrangements, with someone special. You may experience a surprise or a change of routine. If you're disappointed by delays and miscommunications, aim to be patient and focus on good coommunication skills. *Moon enters Sagittarius.*

23 MARCH

You'll be inspired by a beautiful place or person. Romance could flourish, so ensure you arrange a lovely get-together. A trip could be enjoyable. You may be idealistic or forgetful, so if you are making key financial decisions ensure you have all the facts. *Moon in Sagittarius.*

24 MARCH

You'll feel more practical and grounded, especially regarding your home and personal lives. If you feel there is opposition to your plans take a moment to ensure you are on the same page, as misunderstandings could arise. You'll appreciate encouragement from someone you trust or admire. *Moon enters Capricorn.*

25 MARCH

Inconvenient news and delays or frustrating events may be difficult to deal with but you will overcome obstacles. Someone or perhaps even you will be feeling a little obstinate, so it's worthwhile just double-checking you are being your usual friendly self, especially at work. *Moon in Capricorn.*

26 MARCH

This is a positive day for communicating your wishes both at work and at home and for changing some aspects of your agreements with others. *Moon in Capricorn.*

27 MARCH

Take the opportunity to float new ideas and for meetings and get-togethers. A collaboration will be enjoyable. This is a good time for romance, so organise a lovely event with someone special if you haven't already. It's also a good time for getting things shipshape in the office, home or garden. *Moon in Aquarius.*

28 MARCH

A key meeting or news will be decisive. If you agree with the direction those you love and work with are heading you'll be happy. If not, it's important to look at your own options and carve out a path for yourself. You may enjoy a lovely get-together with someone you admire or love. You may also be easily influenced, so keep abreast of the facts. *Moon in Aquarius.*

29 MARCH

The Pisces moon will bring your inner idealist and dreamer out, so remember to also be practical. You may wish to spend time with your favourite people, so ensure you organise a meeting with someone you love. *Moon in Pisces.*

30 MARCH

This is a lovely time for romance, so organise a treat. You'll be drawn to romance, the arts, spirituality and music. You may tend to be seeing the world through rose-coloured glasses, so ensure you have your feet on the ground if you are making key decisions. *Moon in Pisces.*

31 MARCH

The Aries moon will motivate you to be more outspoken, especially about shared matters you may disagree with. You may feel restless, so ensure you channel these feelings into activities that bring positive results such as working on projects you love and spending time with like-minded people. *Moon in Aries.*

April

career love home health finance

1 APRIL

The Aries new moon spells a fresh chapter regarding a favourite project and your general direction in life. You may be ready to turn a new leaf or make changes within your daily activities so they align more with who you are. You may be drawn to study. This new moon has a healing effect so that, even if developments are difficult, the long-term outlook is an uplifting one.

2 APRIL

You may receive key news if you didn't already yesterday. This may be in connection with work or your status in general and may involve a health matter. A trip could be therapeutic. Someone may ask for your help, and if you need support or advice it will be available. You may hear unexpected news from a group or organisation or will bump into an old friend. ***Moon enters Taurus.***

3 APRIL

This is a good day for talks, especially with someone you must share duties, finances or responsibilities with. Aim to establish common ground on shared aims if you wish to move things forward. ***Moon in Taurus.***

4 APRIL

A venture or project can advance, especially to do with travel, legal matters or study. You may be ready to break new ground. Avoid arguments and mend bridges instead. *Moon in Taurus.*

5 APRIL

This is a good day to make a commitment to a plan, schedule or person. Finances may be in the frame, and as you enter new territory consider fresh projects and ideas. You may feel a little idealistic, so ensure you keep your feet firmly on the ground. *Moon in Gemini.*

6 APRIL

You'll appreciate the sense that your plans, such as those for study or travel, are coming together. The people you must collaborate with are likely to be co-operative, so it's a good day for planning and taking the initiative. Financial matters may need to be decided upon. *Moon in Gemini.*

7 APRIL

This is a good day for meetings and get-togethers, both at work and regarding your interests and activities. A travel plan could come together well, and if you are already travelling you'll enjoy discovering new places. It's also a good day to persuade someone close of your plans. *Moon in Cancer.*

8 APRIL

Your interest in the arts, dance, music, spirituality and everything your heart desires will be met by opportunities to indulge in related activities; just clear the space so that you can. A work meeting is likely to be successful. *Moon in Cancer.*

9 APRIL

This is a good day to take the initiative with talks and plans as your efforts are likely to pay off, especially at work and with your collaborations. Be prepared to discuss your ideas with those they concern and with people who can help you such as teachers, advisers and employers. *Moon in Cancer.*

10 APRIL

If you work hard you will gain positive results, but communications may not flow quickly or easily. Take a step back to think your plans through and find a positive way to present them. If you need someone's co-operation ensure you work collaboratively with them. A tense situation can be defused with focus and friendliness. *Moon in Leo.*

11 APRIL

As Mercury enters Taurus you can come to positive agreements, but only if you avoid being stubborn or set in your ways. Look for practical, positive ways to present your ideas to smooth the way forward, especially at work. *Moon in Leo.*

12 APRIL

Romance and your favourite interests could truly take steps forward – that is, unless you've over- or underestimated a circumstance. If so you will gain the chance to put things right if need be. A trip or meeting could be ideal. *Moon in Leo.*

13 APRIL

This is a good day for negotiations and to make agreements and commitments, especially at work and regarding a project or collaboration. If you're ready to make a personal commitment to someone such as through marriage this is a good day to do so. Financial agreements are likely to work out well as long as you have researched your circumstances adequately. *Moon in Virgo.*

14 APRIL

This is a good time to be optimistic and research new ideas, places and plans. A social event or personal interest is likely to pan out well for you. You may attain a key goal in your career, so work towards your true aims. *Moon enters Libra.*

15 APRIL

As Mars enters Pisces you'll be drawn to areas in your life that make your heart soar. Take time over the coming five weeks for activities that feed your soul. However, today's developments may require a little adjustment, especially if someone disagrees with your plans. *Moon in Libra.*

16 APRIL

The Libran full moon will spotlight your home life and you may find that changes there are due to alterations at work or within your status. For some this full moon points to broadening your horizons and the wish for better relationships, which can be achieved by taking the time to better understand someone close and through such options as travel or updating a vehicle or communications device.

17 APRIL

The Scorpio moon will increasingly focus your attention over the next two days on your home and family projects. Organise your day to get chores done in the morning, giving you time for someone special in the evening. Avoid tense talks in the morning. *Moon in Scorpio.*

18 APRIL

This is a good time to discuss areas in your life where you know there are disagreements about changes that are being undertaken. For some this will apply to work, and for others finances or your personal life. Be tactful to dispel conflict. You may hear unexpected news and will enjoy an impromptu chat or get-together. *Moon in Scorpio.*

19 APRIL

The Sagittarian moon will encourage you to get things done at home and to move forward with your plans. Someone you share duties, space at home or finances with may not agree with everything you do, but you'll find a way to move forward. *Moon in Sagittarius.*

20 APRIL

As the sun enters Taurus you'll feel more practical and able to manage unexpected developments or changes at work, in your status or general activities. Just avoid the tendency when under pressure to be obstinate and find ways to move forward in the most realistic ways. *Moon in Sagittarius.*

21 APRIL

While you're known for your dynamic and energetic approach to life, few people acknowledge how practical you can be. Today's moon will help you to keep your feet on the ground with changes. *Moon in Capricorn.*

22 APRIL

This is an earthy moon and you'll manage to get a great deal done at work and around the house, which you'll appreciate. If some things don't go exactly to plan you already know to try and try again. *Moon in Capricorn.*

23 APRIL

A meeting with someone special could be more significant than meets the eye. However, if you have ongoing disagreements, especially about shared finances or duties, you must work out a mutually agreeable plan otherwise you could escalate your differences. If you're workingyou may meet an influential character. *Moon in Aquarius.*

24 APRIL

Ideally you'd like to get on with everyone all the time, but as you know this is impossible. Disagreements needn't escalate if you maintain a flexible and friendly approach. Avoid being super idealistic and be practical instead. You'll enjoy a get-together or a favourite activity but must avoid overspending as you'll regret it! *Moon in Aquarius.*

25 APRIL

The Pisces moon will spotlight how you feel about someone close either at work or in your personal life. Financial and work meetings could see progress, but you may see the world through rose-coloured glasses so ensure you maintain perspective. **Moon in Pisces.**

26 APRIL

Romance, your favourite interests and pastimes will all appeal to you but you may need to knuckle down and do some work first! You'll be inspired by people you admire but may also be easily led, so maintain focus on reality. **Moon in Pisces.**

27 APRIL

This is an excellent day for romance and all things in life you love, so make a date if you haven't already! You may be drawn to improving your home décor or to treating someone special to a lovely event. A financial agreement could be made and you may receive ideal news. If you undergo a disappointment you will get the chance to put things right. **Moon enters Aries.**

28 APRIL

This is an excellent day for work and improving your health and status. If you are looking for work ensure you circulate your resume and arrange interviews. If you are looking for a promotion let your boss know! You could make positive financial changes now with the right advice and guidance. **Moon in Aries.**

29 APRIL

You may hear key work or health news if you didn't already recently. Try to get key paperwork and agreements tied up to avoid having to revise your plans at a later date. You will enjoy a meeting or news. **Moon in Aries.**

30 APRIL

The partial solar eclipse in Taurus will be at the zenith of your chart and signifies an important turning point for you. For some Leos this will be due to changes at work, for others a change of status from single to married for example and for some a fresh project, activity or interest. Be practical and grounded with decisions for the best results.

May

career love home health finance

1 MAY

This is a lovely day to do something you love and to be with someone you love, so make plans if you haven't already to indulge in activities that make your heart sing. Romance could blossom and you could also overcome disagreements. *Moon in Taurus.*

2 MAY

As Venus enters Aries you'll appreciate the sense that your relationships and general interests in life can be more upbeat and that you can be more outgoing. You may be drawn to new pursuits and people over the next few weeks. Be bold! *Moon in Gemini.*

3 MAY

This is an excellent day for work and for collaborations, so it's an optimum time to co-operate and make agreements. Just avoid over-committing to activities you can't possibly complete in a short timeframe. If you have quarrelled with someone this is a good day to mend bridges. *Moon in Gemini.*

4 MAY

You may hear unexpected news that's uplifting. If not, take a moment to re-orient your thoughts and plans and you may surprise yourself with how resourceful you can be. You'll enjoy being spontaneous. *Moon in Gemini.*

5 MAY

Expect a surprise that is likely to involve work, someone influential or a favourite activity. If you're travelling or investigating new projects or options you'll be surprised by the outcome. You'll enjoy being spontaneous and meeting new circles of people. *Moon in Cancer.*

6 MAY

You'll enjoy meetings and talks. Romance could blossom, so be bold if you'd like to ask someone out! You may meet someone you admire or who inspires you. It's a good day to improve your appearance and profile. *Moon in Cancer.*

7 MAY

The more you collaborate and co-operate the more easily you will achieve your goals, so if chores need to be done ensure you enlist help! A trip, sports, study and spiritual endeavours will all appeal depending on your interests, and you'll find the time to muster a group together to enjoy your free time. *Moon in Leo.*

8 MAY

The Leo moon will get you out and about, but you won't necessarily agree with everyone about what you wish to do. You'll appreciate the chance to relax and recharge your energy levels and will enjoy boosting your health and well-being. *Moon in Leo.*

9 MAY

If you find a little tension is motivating for you you'll enjoy today's atmosphere. You may have some hurdles to jump or logistics to take care of. Some talks, travel and work matters will require a little extra focus than usual. Try to tie up loose ends of paperwork before Mercury turns retrograde tomorrow. *Moon enters Virgo.*

10 MAY

As Mercury turns retrograde you're likely to receive key news at work or regarding long-term options in areas such as travel, study or legal matters. If health has been a concern you may receive news that merits careful consideration. Try to allow extra time for travel and communications to avoid frustration over the coming weeks. *Moon in Virgo.*

11 MAY

As Jupiter enters Aries, where it will remain for the upcoming year, you may notice that shared responsibilities such as joint finances, duties and space at home become the focus. You may be drawn to collaborate more or are ready to embrace fresh projects, travel or a new direction. *Moon in Virgo.*

12 MAY

Your feelings are likely to bubble up, especially regarding long-term changes that will involve a great deal of adjustment. Look for balance and you'll enjoy seeing concrete results to your hard work. Find ways to boost communications for the best results. *Moon in Libra.*

13 MAY

You'll enjoy a reunion, and if you meet someone for the first time there may be more significance than immediately meets the eye. Your career or status may be due for change and people you meet could be influential or a catalyst to new circumstances. Singles may meet someone you have a soul connection with. *Moon in Libra.*

14 MAY

The Scorpio moon will motivate you to be more passionate about securing a stable and harmonious home. You'll enjoy putting energy into the relationships of those you love. *Moon in Scorpio.*

15 MAY

You'll find out whether you have over- or under-estimated a circumstance or a person. You may discover positive news to do with an adventurous project, but if the news is disappointing aim to find a clever way forward regardless. Your hard work will be rewarded. *Moon in Scorpio.*

16 MAY

The total lunar eclipse in Scorpio may feel particularly intense, so aim to maintain a sense of perspective especially regarding domestic matters, which are likely to be changing due to bigger-picture circumstances. You could make great headway with treasured projects by being focused. *Moon enters Sagittarius.*

17 MAY

This is a lovely day both for making work agreements and for romance. Thus, depending on where your focus is, find ways to boost either area, as your efforts are likely to pay off! *Moon in Sagittarius.*

18 MAY

This is another day where your efforts should be rewarding – that is, as long as you have not over- or underestimated your circumstances. It's a good day to make commitments. Romance could blossom. ***Moon in Capricorn.***

19 MAY

The changes you wish to see in your life, especially at work and in your status, are now possible. This is a good time to boost your profile and appearance. Romance could blossom, so organise a date! ***Moon in Capricorn.***

20 MAY

This is a good day for meetings, both at work and in your personal life. It's especially ideal for reviewing your plans and for renegotiating agreements if necessary. A trip may be particularly relevant. ***Moon in Aquarius.***

21 MAY

As the sun enters chatty Gemini a get-together or news will be important. This is a good time to discuss your plans with those they concern. You may reconsider your position or will enjoy a reunion. A trip this weekend could be transformative. ***Moon in Aquarius.***

22 MAY

This is an excellent time to deepen ties, especially with the people you must collaborate with on a daily or long-term basis. Not everyone will agree with you even though you're at your charming best! Find the time to relax. ***Moon enters Pisces.***

23 MAY

You will appreciate a chance to shine, for some at work and for others in your personal life. If some talks have stalled avoid being stubborn; if possible, look for fresh ways to get ahead rather than going over old ground. That said, there may be merit in rearranging some agreements. ***Moon in Pisces.***

24 MAY

This is a good time to make solid progress both at work and financially, as negotiations and agreements can be constructive. Your plans could also progress in your personal life. ***Moon in Pisces.***

25 MAY

The green light you have been waiting for is on the way! If you have had to rearrange or renegotiate some work matters these are likely to show progress. A health matter could also be looking up. ***Moon in Aries.***

26 MAY

You may sense that someone close either at work or in your personal life is feeling a little tense. You'll know to give them a wide berth to avoid arguments. Nevertheless, this is a good day for talks and meetings socially and at work. *Moon in Aries.*

27 MAY

You'll appreciate the opportunity to reconnect with someone or to go over old ground that needs a little clarity. Avoid conversations you know could be triggers, as today's stars could contribute to intense talks. *Moon in Taurus.*

28 MAY

Venus in Taurus for the next few weeks will contribute to a tendency to indulge in your favourite activities and interests and is ideal for a holiday. You'll feel motivated to bring more luxury and enjoyment into your life. *Moon in Taurus.*

29 MAY

You'll enjoy being a little more spontaneous than usual and may even surprise yourself. Someone close may have new proposals about how they'd like to enjoy your time together. Romance could blossom, so make a date! *Moon enters Gemini.*

30 MAY

The Gemini new moon signals a fresh phase for you, especially regarding your general direction in life and including such areas as your work, status and interests. You may be inclined to look for more variety and spice in life. *Moon in Gemini.*

31 MAY

Your plans and projects can advance, so make sure you take the initiative. It's a good day for research and talks and to plan a more solid budget, especially if you have recently overspent or have a large outlay to pay off. *Moon in Gemini.*

June

career   love   home   health   finance

1 JUNE

Trust your intuition, which is spot on, and take breaks when you can to unwind. *Moon in Cancer.*

2 JUNE

You're generally known as a dynamic, confident character but few people know just how sensitive you are and your vulnerabilities may surface. You may be asked to help someone. If you need support ask for it as it is available. *Moon in Cancer.*

3 JUNE

Mercury ends its retrograde phase today and you may over the coming weeks see that communications and travel become easier to navigate, especially where they concern work and your big-picture plans. You may receive key news that will merit close attention. *Moon enters Leo.*

4 JUNE

This is a good day to discuss your plans and projects and to put the wheels in motion for fresh ventures such as travel and collaborative projects. *Moon in Leo.*

5 JUNE

The Leo moon helps you to feel more confident and proactive. If you feel at odds with other people's plans find the time to enjoy your day nevertheless. Avoid rash decisions. *Moon in Leo.*

6 JUNE

The Virgo moon is ideal for work and chores as you will feel all the more practical and methodical with your various duties, but you must avoid over-analysing someone or a project. *Moon in Virgo.*

7 JUNE

Unexpected developments may take you by surprise, but if you're waiting for the green light you're likely to hear good news. *Moon in Virgo.*

8 JUNE

This is an excellent day for work and finances and for planning in general. Just avoid taking on too many chores as you have the know-how to get things done but perhaps not enough time. *Moon enters Libra.*

9 JUNE

If indecision is one of your failings be careful to prioritise who and what is more important or you could risk being easily distracted. If you're unsure of a financial or personal matter ensure you gain expert guidance. *Moon in Libra.*

10 JUNE

Get set for changes to take effect. If you have been formulating new ideas and plans these can take great strides forward, but if you are reluctant to embrace fresh ideas and options you may be surprised by developments. *Moon enters Scorpio.*

11 JUNE

Expect unexpected news or a surprise. Avoid rash decisions, as these could be counterproductive. You'll enjoy doing something different and plans for change will get ahead well. If you're reluctant to make changes you may need to be more adaptable. *Moon in Scorpio.*

12 JUNE

A return to a family home or a trip or visit from a family member may be enjoyable. You already know which topics to avoid, so ensure you do that or you could find you get embroiled in complex discussions. *Moon enters Sagittarius.*

13 JUNE

You are likely to be busy for the next few weeks, especially with communications, meetings and, for some, travel. Take extra time to learn new communication skills if necessary. You could boost your kudos, status and profile, so take the initiative. *Moon in Sagittarius.*

14 JUNE

The full moon and supermoon in Sagittarius represents a fresh chapter for you in your personal life and at home. You may feel ready to make key changes such as a little DIY or even to consider a move or a trip away.

15 JUNE

Your vulnerabilities and sensitivities may emerge, so if you feel a little under the weather blame it on the stars! You may be tempted to impulse buy and to overspend. You may be in demand and asked for help. A teacher or adviser may prove particularly helpful. *Moon in Capricorn.*

16 JUNE

You'll appreciate the help of a friend, group or organisation. This is a good time to deepen solid relationships. You may hear unexpectedly from an old friend or employer. If making key decisions ensure you have all the details, especially financially, to avoid mistakes. *Moon enters Aquarius.*

17 JUNE

This is a good day to think laterally, especially if some issues have continued to linger. You'll enjoy being spontaneous. You may receive an unexpected invitation. *Moon in Aquarius.*

18 JUNE

You can't agree with everyone all the time, and today is one such day when your differences may become more obvious. To overcome differences, take discussions more slowly and carefully than usual to ensure a positive outcome. A financial matter may require more focus. *Moon in Aquarius.*

19 JUNE

You will enjoy taking things more slowly and may even prefer quiet times at home with someone you love rather than socialising. Gauge how you feel and take it from there. *Moon in Pisces.*

20 JUNE

The Pisces moon will bring your romantic side out, which you'll enjoy, but you may also see people through rose-coloured glasses. You'll enjoy relaxing and being with like-minded people you don't have to make too much effort with. *Moon in Pisces.*

21 JUNE

As the sun enters Cancer, marking the solstice, you will feel inclined to be a little more philosophical and introspective about life. You may also be more sensitive, so ensure you give yourself extra downtime to process your feelings. This is a go-ahead time for your work and ventures, so be positive! *Moon in Aries.*

22 JUNE

Your assertive side will seek expression and you'll certainly get things done. Avoid arguments with people in authority such as your boss as you may regret outbursts or speaking with insensitivity. *Moon in Aries.*

23 JUNE

As the moon enters Taurus you'll feel more grounded and less likely to fire up over matters about which you disagree. Someone close may need to discuss sensitive matters, and the more understanding you are the better for you. You could reach a new workable agreement with someone. *Moon enters Taurus.*

24 JUNE

You'll enjoy planning a slower pace at the weekend. There are many ways you can plan to relax, beginning right now! There are therapeutic aspects to the weekend, so why not plan a healthy treat. *Moon in Taurus.*

25 JUNE

Activities and people you love will be a true drawcard this weekend, and you'll enjoy a change of routine even if the logistics aren't as straightforward as you'd prefer. *Moon in Taurus.*

26 JUNE

When the moon is in Gemini you'll appreciate the sense that you are somewhat more flexible and free with your spare time. A meeting or get-together such as a sports event or favourite hobby will be enjoyable. *Moon in Gemini.*

27 JUNE

This is a good day for mending bridges with someone if you need to clear the air. It's also a good time for health and well-being appointments. An expert or adviser could prove helpful. *Moon in Gemini.*

28 JUNE

A social or networking event will go well, even if you feel a little nervous about events. An impromptu get-together will be enjoyable and could take you somewhere new. *Moon enters Cancer.*

29 JUNE

The Cancerian new moon will kick-start a fresh chapter, for some at work and for others in a social context. You may be ready to move into a new circle, either at work or socially. *Moon in Cancer.*

30 JUNE

You will feel a little more sensitive when the moon is in Cancer, so if you feel vulnerable now you know why! You may gain insight into a work or personal matter. *Moon in Cancer.*

July

career   love   home   health   finance

1 JULY

You'll enjoy socialising and may even gain the chance to get together with friends at lunchtime. If you feel there is a little tension in a social or work group it would be wise to sidestep it if possible. *Moon in Leo.*

2 JULY

Words will fly so be sure to choose them wisely, as there is a little tension in the air especially with people you care about. Aim to engage in soothing and calming activities to avoid contributing to angst. *Moon in Leo.*

3 JULY

The tension underlying some communications may continue, so look for activities that will dissipate tension rather than magnify it. You have the power to change some aspects of your circumstances, so look for clever ways to be happier in life. *Moon enters Virgo.*

4 JULY

Some interactions may be intense at work and with a particular friend or group. Find ways to avoid being roped into difficult, intense or problematic dramas unless you have no choice but to be involved.Look for logical ways to move forward. *Moon in Virgo.*

5 JULY

This is a much better day for communications, so aim to mend bridges if necessary and plan meetings. *Moon enters Libra.*

6 JULY

This is another good day for mending bridges and for exploring better and new ways to get on with people who you have no alternative but to collaborate with such as work colleagues. *Moon in Libra.*

7 JULY

You may act as a kind of peacemaker and may need to be a mediator for different groups. Find the middle ground if you're unsure of a key decision. Your work and finances could improve, so take the initiative! *Moon in Libra.*

8 JULY

You'll enjoy a change of pace and even a change of scenery. Your help and support may be in demand, and if you need support it will be available from an expert. Avoid taking other people's personal problems personally. *Moon in Scorpio.*

9 JULY

A fairly straightforward matter could be blown out of all proportion so keep an eye on practicalities and maintain perspective.If you're making a large investment ensure you double-check facts. A trip or arrangement may be delayed. *Moon in Scorpio.*

10 JULY

A social or work get-together will be enjoyable, so organise a meeting if you haven't already. Consider a fresh approach to a tired subject if things seem stuck. *Moon enters Sagittarius.*

11 JULY

You may feel more inclined to express your emotions at work, so if you are in a strictly professional environment keep your specialist hat on or risk being seen as incompetent. Someone who seems emotional or uncaring may have their own problems, so try to maintain perspective. *Moon in Sagittarius.*

12 JULY

Be inspired, because many of your plans and relationships can gain ground. Just avoid being too idealistic with some of your plans as you may be a little unrealistic at the moment. *Moon enters Capricorn.*

13 JULY

The full moon and supermoon in Capricorn will spotlight an important personal relationship or creative project. You may be ready to begin a new chapter in your personal life involving family or children. An agreement could be advantageous, but you must do adequate research. You could boost your status, direction and career.

14 JULY

You'll discover whether you've been unrealistic about a plan, person or project. Luckily, this will give you the chance to set your expectations straight and will help with planning moving forward. *Moon enters Aquarius.*

15 JULY

There may be a little tension in the air that could be conducive to romance and mystery, but if stress is a real turn off for you you may wish to take things one step at a time. If an obstacle arises, rest assured you will overcome it. *Moon in Aquarius.*

16 JULY

You'll enjoy a get-together, and if you're working this may get in the way of socialising but will nevertheless serve a purpose. You may need to find ways to get on with a colleague or partner better, so it's a good time to improve your communication skills. *Moon enters Pisces.*

17 JULY

This is a lovely day for romance, spirituality and generally relaxing with people you love. You'll be drawn to art, music and film. *Moon in Pisces.*

18 JULY

Key decisions may be made that could mean long-term change, so ensure you choose wisely especially concerning work and health. News or a meeting could be intense, so find ways to unwind when you can. *Moon enters Aries.*

19 JULY

As Mercury enters upbeat Leo you may discover new information or someone will confide in you. You may also discover your deeper feelings about someone or about work or health matters. *Moon in Aries.*

20 JULY

This is a good day for a health or beauty appointment. If you are looking for work, circulate your resume as it may catch someone's eye. Key meetings could bring about important changes. *Moon enters Taurus.*

21 JULY

The more practical you are about your various activities and projects the better for you. Avoid being rushed and ensure you cover ground thoroughly at work and in your various ventures. *Moon in Taurus.*

22 JULY

As the sun enters your sign you will begin to feel more positive about developments, especially within your personal life and for some at work and with health. You'll feel more outgoing and dynamic over the coming weeks. *Moon in Taurus.*

23 JULY

This is an excellent time for discussions to do with work and for collaborations, both of professional and personal natures. If you have been meaning to make changes to your usual weekend routine this is a good time to do so. For some July Leos a key trip or study course could open doors. Legal matters will move forward. *Moon in Gemini.*

24 JULY

You'll appreciate a sense of freedom and being able to make up your own mind about how you wish your day to be. If you've already committed to some events you may need to honour the commitment to avoid disappointing someone close. *Moon in Gemini.*

25 JULY

People are simply different so you won't automatically get on with everyone! You may have high expectations of someone, so avoid being disappointed if developments do not go to plan. Avoid conflict by being tactful. *Moon enters Cancer.*

26 JULY

Someone may be stubborn and not wish things to move at the same speed as you do. To avoid arguments, find a way to establish common ground. Travel may be delayed, so plan to take extra time. *Moon in Cancer.*

27 JULY

This is an excellent day to mend relationships and to create more harmony for yourself. If you need advice it will be available from an expert. It's an especially good day for beauty and health appointments. *Moon in Cancer.*

28 JULY

The Leo new moon points to a fresh chapter in your personal life, especially if you were born today or in July. August Leos will be starting a fresh daily routine due to new work demands or health circumstances. You may receive unexpected news. Avoid impulsiveness.

29 JULY

The key to moving forward rests in showing you have a compassionate heart and a focus on good communications and health and well-being. *Moon in Leo.*

30 JULY

You're not well known for your obstinacy but you can be immovable if the mood takes you. A key circumstance may make you feel stubborn, but could you actually be happier if you embrace something new? Food for thought. *Moon enters Virgo.*

31 JULY

A trip, meeting or commitment will bring your generosity out. Decisions made now could be advantageous. You may enter a fresh agreement with someone that takes you somewhere new. Be spontaneous, but avoid snap decisions. *Moon in Virgo.*

August

career   love   home   health   finance

1 AUGUST

A change of direction or a new opportunity may represent something completely new. Be bold and trust your instincts. You may enjoy an impromptu reunion or bumping into an old friend. *Moon in Virgo.*

2 AUGUST

There are many coincidences or synchronicities in life, as you'll see today. Be prepared to try something new. *Moon in Libra.*

3 AUGUST

An unexpected surprise or lovely coincidence could raise spirits. You may hear news that is to your advantage. Be enterprising, as you could improve your circumstances. *Moon in Libra.*

4 AUGUST

Emotions may require a little more attention as they catch up with developments. Give yourself time to adjust. A little attention to interpersonal communications will pay off. *Moon enters Scorpio.*

5 AUGUST

Trust your intuition. If you need to reason with someone in a position of authority, make sure you have all the details you need. You will overcome obstacles with persistence. *Moon in Scorpio.*

6 AUGUST

Be adventurous with domestic and personal matters. Find a practical way forward to manage domestic harmony. ***Moon enters Sagittarius.***

7 AUGUST

Work and chores around the house will require more focus than usual and you may not wish to do them, especially as romance and all things self-indulgent and luxurious are likely to catch your attention first! ***Moon in Sagittarius.***

8 AUGUST

There is a therapeutic and healing aspect to today's developments. You could potentially overcome a financial or personal disagreement. If you encounter an obstacle rest assured there is a silver lining. ***Moon enters Capricorn.***

9 AUGUST

Focus a little more on your communication skills and you'll be rewarded with a good outcome, especially financially. If you love intense romance organise a get-together, but if you prefer things on an even keel keep a low profile! ***Moon in Capricorn.***

10 AUGUST

You can accomplish a great deal with attention to details and by being practical and grounded. Avoid being floored by other people's unreliability. ***Moon enters Aquarius.***

11 AUGUST

As Venus enters your sign you'll feel increasingly in your element. However, a change of routine or unexpected development will require you to be all hands on deck. ***Moon in Aquarius.***

12 AUGUST

The Aquarian full moon will spotlight your personal life or that of a business or personal partner, who has news for you. If you were born later in August you may begin a fresh work or health schedule that will require focus and a commitment.

13 AUGUST

The Pisces moon will encourage you to relax and spend time with someone you love. Avoid feeling that you are stuck or that challenges are too big to overcome. You'll feel more capable once you take the time to unwind. ***Moon in Pisces.***

14 AUGUST

A commitment or decision can be made, but if you feel life is moving too quickly take the time to slow down. Someone has key news for you. ***Moon enters Aries.***

15 AUGUST

Talks could be constructive, especially to do with money and your general direction in life. It's a good time to make a commitment to a job or new career path. ***Moon in Aries.***

16 AUGUST

You'll enjoy doing something different and may hear unexpected news to do with work, a project or money. Be bold and ready to initiate new plans. ***Moon in Aries.***

17 AUGUST

Ensure you have all the information you need to get ahead with your various plans. Avoid making mistakes by having the facts. You may be absent-minded, so avoid misplacing valuables such as keys. ***Moon in Taurus.***

18 AUGUST

This is an excellent time to make tracks with a favourite interest, hobby or relationship. You may reunite with someone special or take a trip somewhere beautiful. Check the details if you are making major work or financial moves. ***Moon in Taurus.***

19 AUGUST

Use tact and diplomacy to get along with everyone otherwise you may sense undercurrents that diminish your self-confidence. Be positive and avoid succumbing to dramas, especially if they're not of your own making. ***Moon in Gemini.***

20 AUGUST

Mars will now be in Gemini until the end of March 2023, encouraging you to be more sociable and outgoing. This will keep you busy at work but may also tend to fray nerves, so ensure you organise adequate breaks. You'll enjoy a lovely change of pace and the chance to relax or travel somewhere beautiful. ***Moon in Gemini.***

21 AUGUST

You may discover you made a mistake. If you're shopping be careful with change, and if you're making arrangements ensure everyone is on the same page. Romance could flourish although misunderstandings are possible, so be clear. ***Moon in Gemini.***

22 AUGUST

This is an excellent day for get-togethers, romance and making progress with your various plans. It's a good day for communications and to mend bridges. ***Moon in Cancer.***

23 AUGUST

Now that the sun is in Virgo your attention will go increasingly over the next few weeks to the practicalities of life such as finances. It's a good time to plan something special such as a holiday. *Moon in Cancer.*

24 AUGUST

You'll appreciate the opportunity to boost your well-being, health and appearance. If you need expert advice it will be available, so reach out. You may be asked for help yourself. *Moon enters Leo.*

25 AUGUST

The moon in Leo may bring out a nostalgic part of you that wishes to reconnect with someone special. If you have argued this could be a good time to overcome differences, but you must be prepared to be flexible. *Moon in Leo.*

26 AUGUST

You'll look for peace and balance in your communications and financially, so this is a good time to appraise your finances and personal situation and make adjustments if need be over the next few days and weeks. *Moon in Leo.*

27 AUGUST

The new moon in Virgo may bring a surprise or two your way. For some this will be in your personal life and for others financially or at work. Be prepared to adapt to circumstances. Stubbornness will only lead to a stalemate. *Moon enters Capricorn.*

28 AUGUST

This is a good time to make a commitment to someone or to a project, especially if you were born in mid-August. You may need to make a key decision. Research the facts for the best results. *Moon in Virgo.*

29 AUGUST

You are looking for fair play and the best way ahead in practical terms. The Virgo moon and, later in the day, the Libra moon will help you do so in the most sensible and balanced ways. Look out for how you can stick to your principles while adapting to a changing world. *Moon enters Libra.*

30 AUGUST

The key to a successful day lies in clever and positive communications. Avoid arguments and find ways to establish common ground. *Moon in Libra.*

31 AUGUST

Romance and all things idealistic, creative, luxurious and beautiful will attract you. If you feel disappointed by someone or something, find a more realistic approach to them that will help you feel happier. *Moon enters Scorpio.*

September

career love home health finance

1 SEPTEMBER

Your link with a group, friend or organisation could be truly productive and beneficial. A favourite project, pastime or venture such as study, a trip, a legal matter or sports meet is likely to go well. *Moon in Scorpio.*

2 SEPTEMBER

Some interactions will require more focus than others. You may feel at counterpoint with someone at work or in your personal life, so aim to establish common ground first up to avoid arguments or ill feelings. *Moon enters Sagittarius.*

3 SEPTEMBER

A trip or meeting could be decisive and is more significant than meets the eye. Financial matters will deserve careful appraisal to avoid mistakes. A trip could be delayed or will take you to an old haunt or bring back memories. Singles may meet someone chatty. *Moon in Sagittarius.*

4 SEPTEMBER

The Sagittarian moon will be motivational for you at home and with your personal projects and collaborations, but if someone proves enigmatic or difficult in some way avoid making tension worse. Find ways to co-operate if possible. *Moon in Sagittarius.*

5 SEPTEMBER

As Venus leaves your sign you may reconsider a circumstance or see someone in a new light. Avoid taking anyone's mood swings personally. Someone may need your help, and if you need support it's available. ***Moon in Capricorn.***

6 SEPTEMBER

The moon in Capricorn will help you to get things done, both at home and at work. Make the most of this phase to be productive and decisive. ***Moon in Capricorn.***

7 SEPTEMBER

You like to get things done quickly so the strong, earthy signature in the skies at the moment may be frustrating. The positive side is that it enables you to be more practical and realistic, which is ideal for work and planning. ***Moon in Aquarius.***

8 SEPTEMBER

Pay extra attention to finances and values to ensure you are not tempted to compromise your circumstances. If you feel under pressure from someone or due to a circumstance, find practical ways to work around the situation. ***Moon in Aquarius.***

9 SEPTEMBER

You will not always agree with everyone although today's stars suggest you can, but you may need to compromise or collaborate more. ***Moon in Pisces.***

10 SEPTEMBER

The full moon in Pisces is shining a light on your business and personal relationships, asking that you see them more clearly. You may be seeing some collaborations or relationships in an idealised light. That said, romance could flourish so make a date!

11 SEPTEMBER

A surprise visit or a trip somewhere new will be enjoyable, as you'll enjoy doing something different for a change. If finances have been a focus recently you may receive good yet unexpected news. ***Moon in Aries.***

12 SEPTEMBER

Finances are likely to be looking up, even if work or your daily schedule still require some attention before they are how you'd ideally wish them to be. A debt may be repaid or you may repay one. ***Moon in Aries.***

13 SEPTEMBER

The Aries moon for most of the day will help you maintain a sense of dynamism and get things done. Once the moon is in Taurus for the next few days you'll feel more hands-on and practical, especially with plans that have been in the making for a while. *Moon enters Taurus.*

14 SEPTEMBER

You'll appreciate the chance to get down to brass tacks with someone close. You'll manage to make a new commitment or at least see the practicalities of certain situations. Financially you'll see there is a way forward. *Moon in Taurus.*

15 SEPTEMBER

This is an excellent day to be productive, as your efforts will pay off. Find the time for chores and also your favourite activities. A lovely get-together will feel grounding and leave you with a sense of more stability. *Moon enters Gemini.*

16 SEPTEMBER

You may be tempted by a little retail therapy and may also be tempted to splurge, so if you're already in debt leave the credit card at home! Romance could go off the dial, but you must ensure when making arrangements this weekend that you're on the same page to avoid misunderstandings. *Moon in Gemini.*

17 SEPTEMBER

The moon at the zenith of your chart will bring your mercurial nature out, and you may feel non-committal about which activities to do and who to spend time with. You may simply wish to relax or spend time with a favourite book, person or mini series. *Moon in Gemini.*

18 SEPTEMBER

A trip or meeting will be enjoyable, although there is likely to be some nostalgia involved or a sense you are going over old ground. This is a good time to devise a fresh budget. *Moon enters Cancer.*

19 SEPTEMBER

This is a good day to make changes at work and financially. If you have begun a new job or must budget differently, consider your daily expenses first up and ensure these are covered. A pleasant development will be uplifting. It is a good day for health and well-being appointments or to alter your appearance. *Moon in Cancer.*

20 SEPTEMBER

You will enjoy a change of routine or a surprise development, even if it means there are some logistics you must iron out. *Moon enters Leo.*

21 SEPTEMBER

The moon in your sign will pep you up and contribute to a more positive frame of mind as the day goes by. You'll enjoy organising a fun event or get-together. *Moon in Leo.*

22 SEPTEMBER

You may sense that others are a little stand-offish and may even feel a little combative yourself. Avoid contributing to the mood of the day and find ways to enjoy your time. You'll relish a health or beauty boost. *Moon in Leo.*

23 SEPTEMBER

As the sun steps into Libra this marks the equinox, a time when we collectively sense we can achieve more balance and harmony in our lives. You'll appreciate having the space and motivation over the weekend for getting together with people you love and feeling you are gaining a sense of balance or order, either emotionally or financially. *Moon in Virgo.*

24 SEPTEMBER

This is a truly romantic day, so if you have nothing planned yet organise a treat! You'll appreciate relaxing through music, the arts and romance and spending some time immersing yourself in good vibes. You may, however, be a little absent-minded or idealistic, so ensure you avoid forgetfulness and seeing the world through rose-coloured glasses. *Moon in Virgo.*

25 SEPTEMBER

The new moon in Libra points to a fresh circumstance for you in a key relationship or concerning how you communicate. You'll look for more balance and harmony. You may wish to update a digital device or vehicle.

26 SEPTEMBER

A reunion will be significant and key talks could take you into fresh agreements. If finances have been a concern, this is a good time to devise a fresh budget. You may hear encouraging news at work, with family or financially. *Moon in Libra.*

27 SEPTEMBER

Be positive about making changes at work or in your daily routine. If health has been an issue you can make positive progress. You may receive encouraging financial news and can get ahead. *Moon in Libra.*

28 SEPTEMBER

This is a good day to boost your standing at work and in your personal life. You could improve your status, profile and kudos, so take the initiative. If you are looking for work, circulate your resume as you will get positive feedback. ***Moon in Scorpio.***

29 SEPTEMBER

You'll feel motivated to make changes at home and to spend more time with the people you love. Romance could flourish, so organise a special romantic time if possible. ***Moon in Scorpio.***

30 SEPTEMBER

This is a good time for cocooning with someone you love. If you're working be patient, as you may be tempted to try to speed things along. DIY or improving your home décor will appeal, and you may be drawn to vibrant and beautiful colours and finding some luxurious additions to add comfort to your home. Romance could blossom. ***Moon in Sagittarius.***

October

career   love   home   health   finance

1 OCTOBER

You'll enjoy reconnecting with someone special. You may also be considering a large outlay, so ensure you have the funds in place to avoid unnecessary debt. ***Moon in Sagittarius.***

2 OCTOBER

A get-together or news will add the missing piece to a situation that may have been a little mysterious or unfathomable. You'll gain insight into someone close or into a financial situation, enabling you to know where you stand. ***Moon in Capricorn.***

3 OCTOBER

You may need to review or oversee a change at work. Consider how you could be more practical and find ways to communicate with more sensitivity and compassion for the best measure. ***Moon in Capricorn.***

4 OCTOBER

Your reasonable and practical qualities will be useful especially at work and financially. If you need to negotiate or discuss personal matters be grounded and down to earth for the best outcome. ***Moon enters Aquarius.***

5 OCTOBER

An innovative and imaginative approach to a work issue or to someone close such as a colleague or partner will work wonders. You may be drawn to update your wardrobe or embrace a fresh health routine. *Moon in Aquarius.*

6 OCTOBER

Your intuition, especially in connection with work and someone close, is likely to be spot on. Find the time to combine your insight with a hands-on approach to making your day work for you and it will! *Moon enters Pisces.*

7 OCTOBER

You may be inclined to take on other people's problems and see them as your own even when clearly they are not. An empathic approach is wonderful unless it interferes with your own happiness; look after yourself first. You're communicating well, so take a moment to explain the changes you wish to see at work or at home. *Moon in Pisces.*

8 OCTOBER

You're highly intuitive but also impressionable. Take a moment to work out how to distinguish between your feelings and those of others. Romance could blossom, so organise a treat or simply relax! *Moon enters Aries.*

9 OCTOBER

The Aries full moon will spotlight how you feel about someone close such as someone you love or share space with. If you feel there are fundamental differences it may be time to voice your concerns. For many, though, today's full moon will spotlight lovely plans for a happy future.

10 OCTOBER

Someone may need a little help. If it's you, you'll find support is available. A health or personal matter is best tackled head-on. *Moon enters Taurus.*

11 OCTOBER

This is a go-ahead kind of day when you can achieve a great deal, especially at work and with your chores, so be dynamic! You may need to overcome a logistical matter that comes from out of the blue, which you will do with your usual flair. *Moon in Taurus.*

12 OCTOBER

Matters you have already discussed are likely to come up again and you'll see there has been progress. If not, it's time to rethink the situation. This is likely to involve finances or your personal situation. Ensure you have all the facts. For some, travel will be a hot topic. *Moon in Taurus.*

13 OCTOBER

An unexpected development or impromptu get-together will demand that you're flexible and adaptable. If someone behaves unpredictably you will overcome any fallout from their actions. *Moon in Gemini.*

14 OCTOBER

This is an excellent day for work and projects around the home. You're likely to get on well with anyone you need to rely on and anyone in authority, so it's a good day to discuss ideas and if necessary get permission for your various projects. Just ensure you have done adequate research or your hard work will be in vain. *Moon in Gemini.*

15 OCTOBER

The Gemini moon for much of the day will keep you busy and you'll enjoy a chatty, outgoing and upbeat time. Once the moon is in Cancer you'll enjoy a more relaxed, home-based time with someone truly special to you. *Moon enters Cancer.*

16 OCTOBER

You have high expectations of a relationship or of someone close. Romance and all things beautiful will appeal, but if some plans don't pan out look for the most practical way forward. A philosophical outlook will help you overcome any disappointments. *Moon in Cancer.*

17 OCTOBER

This is an excellent day for getting things done, although you may be more awash with ideas than actual time to implement them so ensure you make notes for future reference! Avoid seeing the world through rose-coloured glasses as this could trip you up. You may be drawn to socialise or to catch up by phone with a friend, group or organisation. *Moon in Cancer.*

18 OCTOBER

The Leo moon helps you to feel more dynamic, although sometimes your larger-than-life personality can seem threatening to others who are less self-confident. Avoid making yourself smaller for anyone else but nevertheless double-check you do not appear overbearing (even if you're not!). *Moon in Leo.*

19 OCTOBER

Conversations may be a little tense. You will achieve a great deal but must be sensitive to the feelings of others to avoid arguments. That said, avoid being coerced or pressured into agreements. *Moon in Leo.*

20 OCTOBER

For some Leos conversations and financial transactions could be tense. In talks, ensure you have all your charming faculties sparking on all cylinders to dispel arguments. Avoid gambling, both financially and emotionally. ***Moon enters Virgo.***

21 OCTOBER

The Virgo moon can bring high expectations into the fold, meaning you could be expecting more than is possible. Avoid feeling disappointed if some matters don't go to plan. A lovely meeting and romance will be enjoyable, but an intense undercurrent will merit careful handling. ***Moon in Virgo.***

22 OCTOBER

This will be a busy day for communications, meetings and, if you're working, at work. You may succeed with your various projects but must be willing to be adaptable. You may hear unexpected news, receive a surprise visitor or take an impromptu trip. ***Moon in Virgo.***

23 OCTOBER

This is an excellent day for discussing important matters with a partner or concerning work. If you're considering a new look or outfit you'll find something perfect for the occasion. Just avoid overspending and overindulging as you'll regret it tomorrow! ***Moon in Libra.***

24 OCTOBER

A meeting or news may bring out your sensitivities or vulnerabilities. Someone close may express their deeper feelings. Take a moment to gather your thoughts. You could remedy a situation, but must avoid being pressured into a solution that isn't in your interest. ***Moon in Libra.***

25 OCTOBER

The partial solar eclipse in Scorpio will spotlight your communications. If you feel there have been deep conversations that give too much information, take time out to reconfigure how deeply you wish to go with your talks with certain people. You may be ready to begin a fresh phase in your relationship. For some, developments will impact your finances as you look for news ways to budget or earn money.

26 OCTOBER

A trip, meeting or communications in general will spotlight for you what must be done. A little research may be necessary so you're clearer about your situation. ***Moon in Scorpio.***

27 OCTOBER

A friend, group or organisation will be helpful as you can gain a great deal of information from them about your personal or financial circumstances. Work may be busy, so ensure you are super focused or you may make mistakes. Avoid arguments, as these will escalate quickly. *Moon enters Sagittarius.*

28 OCTOBER

You may reconsider some of your decisions and may also tend to be nostalgic or sentimental. You may meet an old friend who is a romantic at heart. *Moon in Sagittarius.*

29 OCTOBER

You'll feel more passionate and intense in your opinions and some communications may even be fiery. You may be ready to make changes at home, and a trip or meeting will confirm you are on the right track. *Moon enters Capricorn.*

30 OCTOBER

The Capricorn moon will help you to be practical, so listen to reason even if you are feeling sentimental, nostalgic or unsure of yourself. Find time for yourself and for spending with someone you know has your back. *Moon in Capricorn.*

31 OCTOBER

Happy Hallowe'en! You'll appreciate the opportunity to get down to business at work and be practical about areas in your life you share. Expect a quirky day – so nothing unusual for the day of the year! If you're unsure of a project or a person ensure you research the situation. *Moon enters Aquarius.*

November

career love home health finance

1 NOVEMBER

You're interacting well with people and can rely on your knowledge and experience to make informed choices. You'll get on well with one particularly person you share duties and responsibilities with but may need to choose your words carefully to avoid intense discussions. *Moon in Aquarius.*

2 NOVEMBER

You're a good communicator but may appear to be so much more confident than other people, who may see this as pride or egotism. Be careful with conversations and interactions as someone and perhaps even you may be feeling super sensitive and prone to taking casual remarks personally. A reunion or work meeting could be ideal but may require a tactful approach. *Moon enters Pisces.*

3 NOVEMBER

A get-together or trip will be enjoyable, but once again the more you focus on good communication skills the better. Complex talks such as legal or personal matters are best taken one step at a time for ideal results. *Moon in Pisces.*

4 NOVEMBER

You'll enjoy a meeting of like minds and will feel all the more positive about your prospects moving forward. ***Moon enters Aries.***

5 NOVEMBER

You can improve your circumstances, especially through careful communications in general, or you risk difficult interactions and overwhelming emotions. Someone special has your back, so be sure to discuss ideas with them in a relaxed environment. ***Moon in Aries.***

6 NOVEMBER

You'll feel more proactive and ready to take on your various tasks even if you are feeling vulnerable or must tackle difficult circumstances. A health boost or the chance to catch up with chores will be relaxing. A reunion or trip to a familiar place may bring emotions to the surface, so ensure you focus on the positives. ***Moon in Aries.***

7 NOVEMBER

Put on your negotiating hat, as you'll need it. For some this will be at work, and for others regarding health and well-being. For some Leos it's simply a case of using your charm and empathy so you can understand others better and they understand you. Avoid a Mexican stand-off; it could snowball. ***Moon in Taurus.***

8 NOVEMBER

The total eclipse of the moon in Taurus will spotlight changes in a key project, venture or relationship. You may be surprised by communications and developments. A trip could open a door to a new development. For some Leos this will be in your career and for others due to changes at home. Find ways to constructively organise a stable path forward.

9 NOVEMBER

Expect a surprise, unless you already had one yesterday. Be prepared to be adaptable. You have a tendency to be obstinate when you're under pressure, so look at the positives of current developments. Romance could blossom, so organise a treat with someone special or a quiet night in with a favourite movie or takeaway. ***Moon enters Gemini.***

10 NOVEMBER

You are generally a good communicator but you may currently wonder if this is actually the case. Focus on good interactions and you'll gain ground with your various projects, both at home and at work. This is a good day for romance, but if you're in a difficult situation avoid seeing life through rose-coloured glasses. ***Moon in Gemini.***

11 NOVEMBER

You can achieve a great deal by being practical and grounded. However, you may tend to be stubborn, especially with a work or domestic matter, and this could put you in a rut. Be adaptable without compromising your values. *Moon in Gemini.*

12 NOVEMBER

Pleasant meetings will raise spirits. You will be drawn to art, creativity, romance and lovely people. A spiritual interest could flourish this weekend. *Moon in Cancer.*

13 NOVEMBER

This is a good time for home improvements and to overcome family rows if these have occurred recently. Just avoid complex topics that you know will trigger someone's insecurities for the best measure. *Moon in Cancer.*

14 NOVEMBER

You'll appreciate an increased outgoing and upbeat mood, which will enable you to see circumstances in a more positive light. It's a good time for health and beauty appointments. *Moon enters Leo.*

15 NOVEMBER

This is an excellent day for making progress at home, with someone special and with your work and personal plans. Take the initiative and you'll see your ideas and project take flight. Developments may snowball, so ensure you're happy with your circumstances as they will gain their own momentum. *Moon in Leo.*

16 NOVEMBER

This is a good day for talks, trips and visits and for putting new plans and ideas in gear. If you'd like to do some home renovations or a little DIY or simply improve domestic dynamics, this is it! You'll enjoy planning a holiday unless you're already on one! *Moon in Leo.*

17 NOVEMBER

As Mercury enters the zodiac sign Sagittarius expect more focus to be on travel, broadening your horizons and on how you can move ahead with your creative ideas at home over the coming weeks. You'll feel more inclined to be upbeat and outgoing in pursuit of adventure and discovery. *Moon in Virgo.*

18 NOVEMBER

You'll enjoy feeling more on top of the changes you're instigating and also the change of ambience at home, with family or in your general environment. Be adventurous! *Moon in Virgo.*

19 NOVEMBER

If you are making major financial or personal decisions ensure you have all the facts at your fingertips to avoid mistakes and misunderstandings. You or a friend or partner may be a little absent-minded, so be patient and aim to unwind. ***Moon enters Libra.***

20 NOVEMBER

The moon in Libra engages your analytical, intellectual mind, which will be helpful with planning, financial budgets and generally getting things shipshape. ***Moon in Libra.***

21 NOVEMBER

You can make great strides with a domestic or personal matter. If you're travelling you'll enjoy going into new territory. If you're returning from a trip you'll enjoy the peace of home life. ***Moon enters Scorpio.***

22 NOVEMBER

The sun in Sagittarius for the next few weeks will put the focus firmly on your personal life, creative projects, family, home life, travel and adventure! You'll feel motivated to get things done and to be more outgoing. ***Moon in Scorpio.***

23 NOVEMBER

The Sagittarian new moon signals that you're ready to embrace something new, either at home or in a key relationship such as with someone special or a family member. If you are beginning a fresh project this new moon suggests you will find it takes you into exciting new territory.

24 NOVEMBER

Today's moon in Sagittarius will contribute to a feeling of optimism in your personal life. It's a good time to boost relationships and your home life, such as by improving your comfort at home or even moving. Consider being more adventurous in life. ***Moon in Sagittarius.***

25 NOVEMBER

A therapeutic and healing influence will help you to feel more at home and comfortable with someone special. If talks have been difficult of late you could overcome some of your differences. An expert or adviser can help you to improve domestic décor and dynamics and with plans for travel or other changes at home. ***Moon enters Capricorn.***

26 NOVEMBER

This is a good day to find the help and support you need and/or to offer it to someone else. It's an especially good day to boost your domestic and family dynamics; just be clear about what you want to avoid disappointment. ***Moon in Capricorn.***

27 NOVEMBER

A change of pace at home and at work may be surprisingly refreshing or different. Developments may be unexpected. An impromptu get-together may be welcome but could get in the way of existing plans. Choose activities wisely. ***Moon enters Aquarius.***

28 NOVEMBER

This is an excellent day for meetings and discussions both at work and socially. You'll enjoy making plans that will involve positive outcomes. ***Moon in Aquarius.***

29 NOVEMBER

You are a dynamic and upbeat character and your enthusiasm can be mistaken for bravado. If talks or meetings seem to go askew, check you are being assertive rather than aggressive as people will react much better. ***Moon in Aquarius.***

30 NOVEMBER

You're communicating well so organise get-togethers and meetings, especially to do with work and your home life or business or personal partner. You could make a long-term commitment or arrangement. ***Moon in Pisces.***

December

career love home health finance

1 DECEMBER

Key talks and meetings will enable you to gain more clarity about logistics moving forward. This could be a passionate day for romance. If you like a little tension in your romance you'll enjoy today, but if not you may find some developments stressful so take things one step at a time. *Moon in Pisces.*

2 DECEMBER

You can attain your goals, especially at work and with domestic matters, but you may be prone to misunderstandings and mix-ups so check the details of arrangements carefully. *Moon in Aries.*

3 DECEMBER

There are therapeutic aspects to the weekend. You may find you can get ahead with domestic matters such as home renovations or improving domestic dynamics. A healing or therapeutic activity will be beneficial to you. *Moon in Aries.*

4 DECEMBER

This is a good day for talks, especially about matters that have given you pause for thought recently. If you find someone is evasive there may be good reasons for it. Avoid misunderstandings by being super clear and listening hard to others. *Moon enters Taurus.*

5 DECEMBER

The Taurus moon at the zenith of your chart will help you to be practical at work and with matters that signal long-term change. *Moon in Taurus.*

6 DECEMBER

You or someone close such as a business or personal partner may be prone to misunderstandings, so aim to be super clear. You may be missing someone, in which case it's important to be practical about other areas of your life to avoid mistakes being made due to nostalgia or sentimentality. *Moon enters Gemini.*

7 DECEMBER

You may be surprised by developments, especially in the way they affect your personal life, home or family. It's a good day to get to the bottom of changes you'd like to make and to discuss these with those they affect. *Moon in Gemini.*

8 DECEMBER

The Gemini full moon spotlights a fresh chapter for you at work or regarding something new. You may be ready to make fresh decisions and take steps down a different path that will affect your home or personal lives. Take a moment to decide how you would like to see your future. Avoid snap decisions, but be spontaneous if a fresh opportunity arises.

9 DECEMBER

You'll enjoy being spontaneous and may receive unexpected news. You'll see where some of your options and new opportunities could have positive outcomes. *Moon in Cancer.*

10 DECEMBER

Some of the communication difficulties of last week may arise once again, so if you see the complexities of relationships becoming the issue try to establish common ground and work from there rather than focusing on differences. *Moon in Cancer.*

11 DECEMBER

As Venus joins Mercury in Capricorn you'll gain a sense of greater stability and security but you must avoid obstinacy. If someone close is behaving stubbornly gently encourage them to see the error of their ways. *Moon enters Leo.*

12 DECEMBER

There are many benefits to being practical and reasonable and to making solid arrangements and agreements with someone you see as being a person of authority or knowledge. *Moon in Leo.*

13 DECEMBER

The Leo moon will focus your attention more on who and what really mean the most to you, enabling you to move ahead with your various project with more purpose. Avoid being stubborn. *Moon in Leo.*

14 DECEMBER

You may discover that you or someone close has had overly high expectations and that these need to be adjusted. Take your time to work out the best way forward by researching circumstances carefully, especially financially. *Moon enters Virgo.*

15 DECEMBER

This is an excellent day for sorting out the practicalities of work projects, finances and your personal life. Consider the most realistic way forward and then be inspired! *Moon in Virgo.*

16 DECEMBER

You'll enjoy being spontaneous and getting things done so that you feel you're making progress. If some communications are a little complex, be diligent as you are likely to succeed with your tasks. Just avoid impulsiveness. *Moon enters Libra.*

17 DECEMBER

You'll appreciate a change of pace that may also be a change of company. Family members and those close to you are likely to want your company, and you may need to choose activities wisely. An impromptu get-together will be enjoyable. *Moon in Libra.*

18 DECEMBER

Many of the changes you wish to see in your life are coming together, but some conversations and developments may nevertheless still entail delays and frustrations. Plan extra time for travel and meetings as these may be delayed, and avoid minor scrapes and bumps. Someone may need your help or vice versa. It will be available. *Moon in Libra.*

19 DECEMBER

A change of pace or of place will be enjoyable but may involve a little adaptation. Take things in your stride one step at a time. Avoid rushing. *Moon in Scorpio.*

20 DECEMBER

When the moon is in Scorpio you may feel more intense about your home and personal lives. You'll enjoy cocooning and/or being with like-minded people but may also be more sensitive. This aside, you'll enjoy a development in your personal life. *Moon in Scorpio.*

21 DECEMBER

The solstice is a time of reflection when you can gather your wits as you assimilate your progress this year. You may need to adjust to a new shared situation or take other people's opinions into account even if you disagree with them. Be practical and realistic and focus on a constructive plan for moving forward. *Moon in Sagittarius.*

22 DECEMBER

You'll enjoy an impromptu get-together or social event that puts you in the seasonal spirit. A work development could be encouraging or unexpected. You may be surprised by the attention you receive. *Moon in Sagittarius.*

23 DECEMBER

The new moon and supermoon in Capricorn signals a fresh start for you in your personal life. You may begin a new chapter regarding family or someone close. This is a good time to discuss ways to increase security or stability either at work or in your personal life. It's a good day to make a commitment.

24 DECEMBER

You'll enjoy being with someone who inspires you and provides a sense of togetherness. A creative, romantic, music-fuelled day will raise your spirits. *Moon in Capricorn.*

25 DECEMBER

Merry Christmas! You'll enjoy doing something diverse this year or will simply feel a little differently about your circumstances. You'll enjoy a reunion. *Moon in Aquarius.*

26 DECEMBER

You'll enjoy a different mood, environment or pace so you'll feel inspired to get out of your current situation and visit somewhere new or simply go for long walks. You may even feel some moods lift as you relax into the holiday season. *Moon in Aquarius.*

27 DECEMBER

You'll enjoy feeling you're getting on better with someone you can tend to disagree with. A relationship could deepen. You'll enjoy relaxing and indulging in romance, good food and company. *Moon in Pisces.*

28 DECEMBER

Shared duties, space or responsibilities will be easier to navigate now the pressure of Christmas is off. Romance and fun events will appeal. If you're shopping, avoid overspending as you are likely to buy big. A spiritual interest could deepen. Try to get important paperwork completed before Mercury turns retrograde tomorrow. ***Moon in Pisces.***

29 DECEMBER

A trip home or a reunion and return to an old haunt could be more significant than meets the eye. This is a good day for a work or health appointment. Key news or a meeting may lead you to reconsider your position on various decisions, especially to do with work or health or a particular friend or group. ***Moon in Aries.***

30 DECEMBER

You may tend to be a little impulsive so take things in your stride. Avoid being drawn into an argument that isn't yours to be involved in. ***Moon in Aries.***

31 DECEMBER

Happy New Year! You'll enjoy the sense that you are turning a corner into the new year and can leave some of the trials of 2022 behind. You'll feel more settled as the day and evening go by. ***Moon enters Taurus.***

THE ESSENCE OF VIRGO

As an earth sign that is ruled by the planet Mercury you are quite the enigma: you are not only supremely practical and grounded, you are also a great communicator. You're adaptable and able to follow trends and can act as a mediator and connector between people and organisations. The biggest pitfall for you lies in being a perfectionist, not only because it's nigh on impossible to get things done absolutely perfectly, it's also a disadvantage because you can tend to be driven by the sound of your own wheels spinning rather than by your higher potential.

Your true calling is to be a wonderful help to others, and you love to serve a great cause. This isn't to say you can't help and be of service to yourself, which you must always do first otherwise you will quite often run yourself so far into the ground in an effort to be supportive and helpful that you end up exhausted and unable to help anyone.

You will be attracted to avenues that provide you with a sense of accomplishment through helping others, such as health services, hospitality, financial and social services and the military. You like to feel your unique skills are recognised and of use. You are able to blend your communication skills with your ability to implement ideas and negotiations in practical, reliable and constructive ways. This makes you cherished and fulfilled by those with whom you interact.

SELF-ESTEEM

You derive satisfaction, fulfilment and confidence from feeling valued by others, so much so that you risk failing to understand what you would ideally like to do with your own life regardless of what other people want, need and value in you. You risk being a martyr to a cause or being more interested in what others desire, yet the key to high self-esteem is feeling fulfilled through your own actions. It's vital that while being helpful and valued by others you also consider what provides you with a sense of accomplishment deep down, otherwise you can feel taken for granted and, worse, abused.

There are ways to be of service to others while also satisfying your own needs and fulfilling your own potential. To ensure your needs are being met it's important to recognise that you need to connect with people, to feel that you are an effective and important cog in the wheel of the bigger-picture network.

You are a people person who needs to communicate and interact in meaningful, positive relationships.

YOUR INNER LIFE

Being a perfectionist takes a great deal of your time and energy, so if you already knew that you are in essence perfect you'd realise that all you need do is act on this quality. It's a case of allowing your inner self to expand positive inner qualities such as your ability to help others, your kindness and compassion, your organisational skills and your interest in health and well-being, cleanliness and purity. Focus on developing these qualities outside your inner self and into your environment, allowing them to permeate your relationships with the calmness and completeness that kindness and compassion brings.

Focus on diminishing your negative qualities such as self-criticism and the tendency towards martyrdom. This can be done through yoga and meditation and by using cognitive behavioural techniques to keep the tendency towards compulsive perfectionism at bay. Your positive qualities will then flow.

It's important when much of your attention is on the outside world and your impact on it to focus on your inner world as well, on your peace of mind and a routine that can boost your sense of peace. It's from a harmonious and contented mind that true peace in the outer world will flow. When you combine your intention to create a calm mind with positive actions you'll see optimal results begin to crystallise inside your own mind and ripple outwards into the world. This may be opposite to the process you tend to follow, which is to see what is wrong in the outside world and what must be done to right it. When you turn the process around and work from inside, when you allow your inner light to expand into the world through recognising that you will utilise your unique way to bring positive results, you'll feel more valued and fulfilled.

HOW OTHERS SEE YOU

You are both sensitive and practical. Because you seem to have everything under control people can tend to overlook your sensitivity, and because you are so practical people tend not to offer you help but will expect your help. Your vulnerabilities can then kick in and you can become seemingly introverted or act like a martyr when in fact you are reacting to what seems to you to be an unfair circumstance. If you complain about the unfairness you'll be seen as being critical of others, when all you believe you are doing is stating a fact!

A real pitfall for Virgos is that other people view you as being critical, because you express what you see in the world as being imperfect. This becomes your stimulus to put things right, and all you are doing is seeking balance. And because we often get what we give you may be prone to being criticised by others, which will undermine your self-esteem and lead to you feeling undervalued and misunderstood.

This is a spiral that can lead to martyr-like behaviour, so it's important to break the cycle. Be ready to accept that other people's opinions and views of you are superficial, as they are seeing only the external manifestation of an internal process. You know the process is well meaning; they don't. Explain your ideas rather than simply diving into critical behaviour without preamble. There is no shame in explaining you are a sensitive character underneath the practical exterior and that you merely want what's best. Be ready to use your considerable communication skills to negotiate a balanced and mutually acceptable outcome.

HOW TO MAXIMISE YOUR POTENTIAL

It's important to monitor how self-critical you are. Are you being overly harsh on yourself or on others? It's vital you are clear about why you are critical: you want to make things better. You are perfect as you are, especially when you enhance your positive traits and minimise your negative ones. Remember to turn your compassionate mindset on yourself as well: you are doing your best, and that is just what you need for success!

Your recipe for happiness is to combine what you know other people need from you with what *you* need from you. Look for your true motivation and follow it no matter how impractical it may seem, as you know that as a supremely practical character you can get any plan or idea up and running. You will enhance your self-esteem and sense of being valued by expending your energy on activities, efforts and ideas that are useful and cherished by the people closest to you such as family and peers and by the society in which you live.

Whenever you find yourself taking on other people's problems as if they were your own, remember that their self-development is not yours and it doesn't directly concern you. You can help if you're able to, but don't actively assume a role in their lives that they have not asked you to assume as it will only lead to heartache. Look for ways to value your own actions as a reflection of your wish for a better world, happy relationships and an abundant and rewarding life.

VIRGO AND ITS ASCENDANTS

This chapter is about your sun sign, Virgo, and your predictions for the year ahead. The more you know about yourself the better you will be able to take advantage of opportunities, and also to avoid the pitfalls. It's critical to know as much about 'you' as possible.

In astrology your core self is represented by your sun sign, but your personality traits are represented by your ascendant (also known as your rising sign). The ascendant describes your personality, the way other people see you on first meeting you and the way you tend to filter life's events.

When you have intimate knowledge about your sun sign – your engine room or core being – you will be on the way to a happier life. When you add the knowledge about your personality – your ascendant – you will gain even deeper insight into what makes you tick.

Your ascendant sign is determined by the time of your birth on the date and year of your birth. Because the ascendant sign changes approximately every two hours, the best way to determine it is to ask an astrologer to calculate it for you. Certain apps will also calculate your ascendant sign (see page 873).

The following gives you more information about your abilities, characteristics and personality according to your sun sign Virgo in combination with your ascendant sign.

VIRGO SUN SIGN WITH ARIES ASCENDANT

You are a natural-born healer who wants to make the world a better place. Luckily this combination can lead to careful work that executes exactly that outcome, but sometimes the inner tension between the dynamic, outgoing Aries attitude and the careful, methodical, perfectionist Virgo temperament can create indecision or inaction. You will be attracted to healing modalities, teaching, being of service to others and activities that improve the circumstances of others and also of yourself. When you combine your dynamic energy levels with careful planning your efficiency and power cannot be ignored.

VIRGO SUN SIGN WITH TAURUS ASCENDANT

You will be seen by those who first meet you as being a careful, earthy and practical character, someone who is dependable and enjoys the good things in life and is able to methodically plan

ahead. You are a sensuous, loving and affectionate person, and as people get to know you better you'll also be seen as the wonderfully helpful character you are. You can tend to be meticulous to the point of perfectionism and to be critical of others who do not measure up to your high standards. In moments of self-doubt you can also be supremely self-critical and obstinate if you feel your values or ideas are being challenged. Find ways to be adaptable, and your earthy nature then becomes a trustworthy and positive quality rather than a stumbling block that holds you back from change and self-development.

VIRGO SUN SIGN WITH GEMINI ASCENDANT

You have a strong communications streak in you, as both Virgo and Gemini are ruled by communications maestro Mercury. As a highly mercurial character you have many different forms of expression: you may be constantly on the go, restless and hard to pin down and also be overly analytical on occasion and get caught up in your thoughts. It's important to release tension and your tendency to worry through action-oriented activities such as sport and nature rambles. Find ways to also disperse critical thoughts.

Gemini rising people often gesticulate with their arms and hands when they talk and can be wiry in appearance. The combination with the Virgo energy means you are unlikely to carry excess weight as you are constantly on the go. You need mental stimulation and enjoy travel, so follow your heart and engage in activities that provide information and learning opportunities.

VIRGO SUN SIGN WITH CANCER ASCENDANT

The earthy Virgo with the sensitive, intuitive Cancerian personality makes an effective combination and will help you to strive ahead with inspired ventures and projects in practical ways. You are unlikely to get caught up in thoughts and ideas and not put them into action. Your major stumbling block to happiness is that you are the ultimate caring personality who simply wishes the world to be one big contented, healthy and positive family, so you can become disheartened when faced with the reality that humans are not at all perfect. You'll work towards nurturing and caring for others in admirable ways, be this via your own family or in society in general. Self-care must come first so that you can then care for others.

VIRGO SUN SIGN WITH LEO ASCENDANT

The Leo ascendant can point to a dynamic, outgoing and upbeat personality, someone who likes being the centre of attention, yet the Virgo inner core is a more earthy, practical person who wishes to serve and help others. You want to make the world a better place. You do know how to execute careful, often meticulous work in a proactive, outgoing way, but sometimes the clash between the dynamic, outgoing Leo attitude and the methodical, earthy and perfectionist Virgo temperament can lead to inner tension. You may tend to charge ahead without forethought, only to then have to correct your mistakes. Work wholeheartedly with the intention not only to shine but to do so in practical, well thought out ways.

VIRGO SUN SIGN WITH VIRGO ASCENDANT

As a double Virgo you are doubly perfectionist, doubly practical and doubly good at communicating. Your meticulousness can be a real asset at work, especially where your job demands accuracy such as in accounting. However, in your personal life your meticulousness can be difficult to come to terms with as you have super-high standards and expectations of others. You are a good communicator and will be attracted to work in the media and to managerial and responsible positions. You are well organised and dependable, reliable and responsible. Negative traits can include obsessive-compulsive behaviour such as excessive cleaning and tidying.

VIRGO SUN SIGN WITH LIBRA ASCENDANT

You are looking for peace and harmony in life and are on a quest for a better world. While this may sound noble and enlightening, this quest may be disappointing or frustrating unless you temper your ideals and values with a sense of realism. The Virgo sun sign and Libra ascendant can lead to careful, harmonising work that executes a perfect outcome, but sometimes the clash between the perfectionist Virgo attitude and the sensitive yet steadfast Libran approach can lead to disappointment and a lack of self-belief. Allow your Virgo self to drive your ideals in practical, realistic ways and for your Libra ascendant to find time for self-expression through art, music, creativity and dance. You make a supportive partner and are a hard worker.

VIRGO SUN SIGN WITH SCORPIO ASCENDANT

The Scorpio persona is passionate, charming and intense, which is quite opposite to the classically reserved and reliable Virgo. You are an enigma! Under your charismatic and zealous exterior lies a super-organised, calm and diligent person. When you're under pressure you may even be a little confused by your own impulsive reactions, as these can be volatile and excitable and opposed to your well-ordered and analytical mind. As you mature and are able to work with your passionate, outgoing qualities and your super-organised approach you'll find that you are not only seen as being extremely charismatic but also capable and effective.

VIRGO SUN SIGN WITH SAGITTARIUS ASCENDANT

Your gregarious, outgoing personality takes the Virgo wish for a better world to the next level: you'll manage to implement your humanitarian ideals in proactive, exciting ways. You will be attracted to broadening your horizons through travel, study, art and technology and will soak up life's experiences while keeping your feet on the ground. In your love life you'll instigate relationships wherever your heart draws you, taking the person you fall in love with on exciting life experiences and being unafraid to explore new worlds and activities.

VIRGO SUN SIGN WITH CAPRICORN ASCENDANT

You are practical, methodical, diligent, reliable and well organised. Once you have found the right career you're a hard worker able to overcome any obstacle. You will be drawn to activities that demand your full attention such as health work, accountancy and banking. You may be seen as a staid and reliable traditionalist. A pitfall is that you can resist change and become stuck, so you should try to be more adaptable in life. As a double earth sign you are doubly sensuous and down to earth and you meet your own needs without problem. You may not need a partner as much as some sun signs do but can still suffer from loneliness. Be open to accepting someone wonderful in your life.

VIRGO SUN SIGN WITH AQUARIUS ASCENDANT

You are a quirky, upbeat character able to courageously strive forward into new territory, and you're able to make practical changes in your life as you are adaptable, realistic, sensible and inspired. You are a lovely combination of originality, individuality, dependability and strength. You are a loyal partner even if you are quirky or a little distracted at times. You are able to make long-term commitments, especially when you mature. As a youngster you may be keen to explore the world, which will lead to great wisdom and experience you'll wish to share with those you love.

VIRGO SUN SIGN WITH PISCES ASCENDANT

Your Pisces personality presents as a philosophical, imaginative and artistic individual. You are an inspired and meticulous person who is able to implement your ideas in real life; you are unlikely to suffer as an obscure artist working alone in an isolated place as you are able to bring your imaginative ideas to life. You are a reliable worker and profound thinker who is able to help those in life who are less gifted than you. You also have strong spiritual interests and may spend considerable periods of your life in devotion to a higher power.

VIRGO IN LOVE

You are a perfectionist and a practical character who is likely to be selective about who you spend time with in the long term. In this section you can check out your compatibility with other sun signs. Remember that we are all complex individuals, so the more you know about someone's astrological birth chart the better you can determine your compatibility. Consider having your astrological birth chart compared with that of a partner, friend or family member, as the compatibility – known as 'synastry' in astrology – goes even deeper than a comparison of sun signs, although this is a good place to begin.

VIRGO WITH ARIES

The upbeat Aries personality will feel attractive to the earthy Virgo, so much so that you may feel truly drawn to this dynamic sign. However, your Virgo make-up is essentially careful, prudent and meticulous and you can feel disoriented by the impulsive, spontaneous Aries character. And, of course, the dominance of the entrepreneurial and independent Aries personality can feel a little unsettling to the practical Virgo. If there are other aspects in your synastry that indicate you are a good match there are many ways you can work together harmoniously, as the earthiness of the Virgo acts to ground the fiery Aries rashness and the impulsive and spontaneous Aries feels revitalising and energising to the practical Virgo.

VIRGO WITH TAURUS

You'll appreciate the sensuality and outward calm of the Taurean. This relationship can be settling, grounding and comforting and can provide the earthiness you desire. One major stumbling block is that you can both be uncompromising in your views once you have decided on something, which can lead to a stalemate where neither of you will budge. Stubbornness and obstinacy could be a real bugbear in this union, but if you can agree to disagree on occasion there is every chance your Taurean partner will find you exciting if a perfectionist and you find your Taurean partner calming and sexy.

VIRGO WITH GEMINI

This is a lovely match, even if you both find yourselves so busy in your own lives that you spend more time missing each other's company than actually being together! When you make a commitment to spend time with each other you'll both profit from it, otherwise you could truly miss out on the benefits of this match. You'll appreciate the Gemini intellectual stimulation, freedom of movement and light-hearted attitude, and your partner will admire your independence and ability to take the lead when necessary.

VIRGO WITH CANCER

Your earthiness will initially appeal to the sensitive Cancerian, who'll see you as someone with whom they can feel empathy, while the Cancerian may enjoy the sense of safety, security and care emanating from you. You'll appreciate the Cancerian's emotional intelligence, tenderness and compassion. These signs can certainly gain much from each other and be mutually supportive. A pitfall may be that both can be cantankerous and that the Cancerian character will undoubtedly wish to take control over certain issues, something to which the Virgo may need to adapt.

VIRGO WITH LEO

The upbeat and outgoing Leo personality is likely to attract you, Virgo, as you will be enthralled by Leo's bright, dynamic and adventurous outlook. Your Leo partner will be intrigued and feel comfortable in your down-to-earth and sensual presence. You may fairly quickly find the Leo excitement unsettling, and the Leo's desire for the limelight in the relationship, their restlessness and occasional egocentrism, selfishness and impulsiveness can become frustrating for you. Eventually Leo may find you lacking in motivation and enthusiasm and your perfectionism a turn off. You both fundamentally come from different sides of the ring, but if you have a strong fire signature in your astrology chart and your Leo partner has strong earth this could still be a match as your different attributes can complement each other if you work at the partnership.

VIRGO WITH VIRGO

This match is quite possibly too much of a good thing! You are both such practical, analytical and careful characters that you may need a little push just to get things started. You are both earthy and sensual, and this pairing could be sexy and delightful as long as you both avoid over-analysing each other and pre-empting each other's thoughts and actions. You are both likely to be super organised and your shared space will be tidy. Make sure you have enough spontaneity in the relationship that you don't become too set in your ways.

VIRGO WITH LIBRA

Your Libran partner will admire the fact you are a good thinker and conversations are likely to be lively, while you'll admire your Libran partner's ability to be rational and analytical and also their penchant for creating beauty in their environment. However, there may be that special spark missing in this relationship unless you both make the effort to ignite passion in your love life and unless you have other aspects in your astrology chart that point to passion. Another real pitfall here is that you are both a little indecisive and may not be able to commit to a relationship that fulfils both in equal measures. If you look for that special spark you may be able to ignite it.

VIRGO WITH SCORPIO

Your Scorpio's lust for life may well set your heart on fire, but you'll need to ensure life's mundanities don't dampen their ardour. Your Scorpio may feel ignored unless you prioritise your relationship ahead of your work and daily duties, even though they will admire the fact you are so well organised and practical as it makes a grounding contrast to their fire and passion. Together you can make sweet music, although you may need to put yourself second to Scorpio's demands. If you feel playing a support role to someone else's main act is not your thing, this match may be tiring and demanding.

VIRGO WITH SAGITTARIUS

You'll be attracted to the adventurous spirit of the Sagittarian, their larger-than-life personality that sweeps you up into their world and whisks you off on an exciting trip through life. The Sagittarian will appreciate your down-to-earth and sensuous nature and will feel this complements their excitability, and that together you make a wonderful match – that is, as long as you don't feel overshadowed by the Sagittarian's flamboyant influence and penchant for taking charge. If you can plan activities and ideas together you do make a good match, but there must be give and take here or your plans will be at cross purposes.

VIRGO WITH CAPRICORN

You are both on the same page, which is a big plus point for compatibility! You have the same modus operandi in life and understand each other's motivation. You are both practical, realistic, down to earth and diligent and will admire these qualities in each other. The pitfall is that unless you make a concerted effort to be more outgoing and upbeat you will sink into a boring routine. If you plan exciting events and holidays this match will be a long-term commitment and is ideal for creating a solid base for family and home life.

VIRGO WITH AQUARIUS

The independent and slightly quirky Aquarian will initially attract you and will certainly create a sense of excitement in your life. The Aquarian partner will be attracted to your earthy sensuality and admire your ability to reason and analyse. You certainly complement each other's qualities. What unites you is your shared interest in humanitarianism, your inner calling to help others and make the world a better place. If you unite under these mutual aims this can be a happy combo, but if you find your interests vary you may find your character traits have no common ground in which to blossom.

VIRGO WITH PISCES

The inspired, imaginative and philosophical Piscean nature will certain attract you; this is a case of opposites attracting! Your Pisces partner will find your reasoning and practical skills grounding and that they earth their dreamy, abstract and spiritual approach to life. You need each other, so this relationship will be based on the other completing you. The pitfall is that it can be a co-dependent relationship, so care must be taken to delineate between personalities and not to fall into the victim-martyr roles associated with both signs. When you avoid this pitfall it can be a harmonious partnership in love.

THE YEAR AHEAD FOR VIRGO

Affirmation: *'Adventure beckons!'*

Heed the call to adventure in 2022, or you risk sitting on your laurels and feeling lacklustre as a result. Study, learning new skills and travel will all be attractive to you and could boost your relationships and communication abilities as a result.

The eclipses in 2022 represent major turning points for you and will be most potent regarding finances and shared commitments and duties. Personal relationships such as marriage could undergo considerable changes. It's also a year where multi-tasking and covering your bases with careful planning will be vital.

You are likely to be ready to step out of your comfort zone with regard to the areas you share such as your home life, joint finances and shared space at work. Be prepared to be adventurous and consider your options from a long-term point of view.

The key times when you find your values, principles and morals important to consult this year will be around the total lunar eclipses on 16 May and 8 November. Let your experience and heart do the talking when making major decisions at these times as they are likely to revolve around long-term commitments both financially and in your personal life. Consider what your true priorities are and use these as a guide.

Major developments are likely in your personal life and concerning property or family. Check early on in the year that you are on the same page as family, a partner or domestic circumstances so that you're able to navigate through tense times with all the more certainty that you are supported and seen.

HEALTH

Saturn will be in your health zone for the entire year, which will put the focus on your well-being and specifically on how you manage your health. January's events may ask that you look more closely at a progressive health routine and consider whether you could break out of a routine or bad habit that does not promote good health.

However, you may need to provide further scope for rest and relaxation in the second half of the year to avoid fatigue. Luckily, your home life should provide you with a sense of belonging in the winter months, allowing you to totally refuel energy levels and relax.

For all Virgos, 2022 will take much of your energy as you may need to make considerable decisions that affect not only your finances but also your home life and those close to you.

Thus it's vital this year to ensure you take time out and find ways to enjoy peace of mind and strength of spirit.

FINANCES

Prepare for major financial developments in 2022. If you tend to spend every penny of your income the minute it comes into your hand, consider preparing a slush fund for a rainy day. This isn't to say you will need it: on the contrary, you may be in a position to make a considerable investment such as a property investment, but even in this case you will need money to have greater freedom of movement.

You may also find that major developments concerning family arise and you may need to funnel more money into promoting their financial well-being. The more solid the agreements you make and the more wiggle room you provide yourself financially the better it will be for you.

It is likely that you will need to negotiate fairly and squarely with a business or personal partner, so prepare to get your negotiation skills up to scratch.

The partial solar eclipse on 30 April will be in your shared finance zone, as will the total lunar eclipse on 8 November. The latter eclipse could be pivotal, especially for mid-September Virgos. These eclipses predict major financial changes in 2022, so the earlier you get your thinking hat on the better for you. Your decisions will revolve around mutual interests such as property and income and how best to share or divide them.

HOME LIFE

If you find support is lacking from those you rely on this year you are best to play it safe concerning changes at home. If support is plentiful, however, 2022 could be the year you make changes at home you never look back on.

Mars in your home sector in January will give you the energy you need to make changes at home. If you've been contemplating a move, some DIY or a change such as fresh décor or a new house mate, January is a good time to get your plans up and running.

Later in the year, from mid-November to mid-December, you'll gain an additional boost of vitality at home with the benefit of Mercury helping with communications and Venus providing a feel-good factor.

As for the interim times, with so much focus on other people's well-being and on your work and finances you will do well to reserve extra time for yourself in your own home so you get the peace, quiet and happiness you deserve.

LOVE

Two eclipse seasons this year fall across your marriage zone, one from the end of April to mid-May and another from the end of October to early November. These will spotlight key changes in the way you share resources, including anything from money and duties to space at home.

Specifically in your love life these eclipses can suggest singles will change your status to married but also that partners will find new ways to share common ground and assets. This could mean exciting developments such as a move, but if you feel your relationship has reached a breaking point it can also mean the time is ripe for parting ways in 2022 and finding new ways to divide your assets, responsibilities and common space.

Hotspots to look out for regarding differences of opinion will be in January, mid-year and October. Keep an eye on what's most progressive yet most sensible and reasonable moving forward. You could reach mutually agreeable arrangements at these times, although a little soul searching may be necessary.

Peak times for romance will be in January, when you may even reunite with an ex or revisit an old haunt. In February Mars will ramp up your allure but could also bring out feisty tempers. November and December could also be ideal for more romance.

CAREER

Consider whether you could find more satisfaction in your work in 2022, otherwise your job may become a drudge and you suffer mentally as a result of doing the same thing every day if it has no meaning or rhyme to it.

Positive developments in your daily life including work are possible in the first quarter and then again in May and October, but if you have allowed your work situation to drift or to stagnate you may find that this situation continues and your career and work become a means to an end – in this case, a secure home life. This is all well and good for relaxing at home, but consider whether you might feel more fulfilled if your career offered you more satisfaction.

This is a good year to consider breaking into something new. If you have worked alone up until now perhaps a collaboration will be successful, and if you've only worked for other people perhaps being self-employed will appeal more.

You will be enticed to broaden your horizons in 2022 either through travel, study or learning new skills at work, so when new opportunities arise to engage more fully with your career ensure you accept the offers.

January

career	love	home	health	finance

Notes: the pie charts such as the one above listed for each month show energy distribution according to the stars for the month ahead. If you wish to make changes in the areas of your finances, health, career, love or home and you see there is a large amount of energy in that sector in the chart, your endeavours should succeed as long as you have prepared well in advance. The charts also show which areas will potentially have the most focus in your life during the month.

The moon sign listed for each day's entry in the diary is the position of the moon at the end of the day in Greenwich Mean Time (GMT). To gain the most information about a particular day's circumstances, read the day before and the day after for a complete picture.

1 JANUARY

Happy New Year! You'll enjoy being in the company of those you love and it'll certainly be a mixed crowd! Changes at home could be enjoyable. You'll appreciate the feeling of a new year beginning and doing something different for a change. ***Moon enters Capricorn.***

2 JANUARY

The new moon and supermoon in Capricorn will kick-start a fresh phase for you in a personal context, such as a new chapter in your personal life or at home. You'll be pleased to be able to establish more peace and harmony at home.

3 JANUARY

This is a good time to ask yourself how you could bring more stability and security into your personal life. This may involve breaking into new ground at work or reformulating the way you share duties or even space at home. ***Moon enters Aquarius.***

4 JANUARY

A change of pace or of place merits a patient approach, as the change of tempo may be a little unsettling. Aim to find ways to soothe nerves. ***Moon in Aquarius.***

5 JANUARY

This is an excellent day for romance and family time. Creative Virgos will be at your peak of artistic ability, so if you're feeling creative make time to really indulge in your abilities. ***Moon in Aquarius.***

6 JANUARY

The Pisces moon tends to put your focus more on the people close to you, either those you love or those you have in your environment such as at work. Today's developments may require you to focus a little more on the details, especially if you are returning to work after a break. ***Moon in Pisces.***

7 JANUARY

You'll enjoy a romantic end to the week, so if you have nothing planned yet organise a treat! Someone may even confide their true feelings to you. ***Moon in Pisces.***

8 JANUARY

This is a good day to get things shipshape at home and then to plan a trip or a relaxed get-together. You'll enjoy a reunion this weekend and the chance to catch up with chores and improve domestic décor. ***Moon in Aries.***

9 JANUARY

Creative Virgos will enjoy a little more beauty and love in your home, appearance and life in general. If you have a project you must complete this is a good day to get busy. ***Moon in Aries.***

10 JANUARY

The Aries moon during most of the day will bring someone's feistiness out, so watch out as sparks could fly. Aim to channel restlessness into productive activities and you'll achieve a great deal. *Moon enters Taurus.*

11 JANUARY

It's a mixed bag as romance could blossom but there may be a little tension around making arrangements, so you may need to attend to logistics more than usual. If you prefer your romantic life to be stress free, find the time to take breaks and avoid over-thinking your personal situation. *Moon in Taurus.*

12 JANUARY

The moon in Taurus brings your practical side out and, even if some matters are a mystery for now, you'll manage to get ahead regardless. Try to get loose ends to do with work tied up over the next two days before Mercury turns retrograde on Friday, to avoid delays or having to renegotiate agreements at a later time. *Moon in Taurus.*

13 JANUARY

You'll appreciate the opportunity to devote some time at least to your favourite pastimes, hobbies and people. Make a date with someone you love; you'll be glad you did. *Moon in Gemini.*

14 JANUARY

You may receive key news to do with work, health or someone close. You may need to reconsider a health or work schedule and could make changes in your usual routine so it suits you better. Someone may surprise you and delays may occur, so factor in extra time if you're travelling. *Moon in Gemini.*

15 JANUARY

You may be wearing your heart on your sleeve over the next two days, so if you're working remember to put your professional hat on. You'll enjoy a get-together with someone you love, but if arrangements fall through you'll appreciate some me time instead. *Moon enters Cancer.*

16 JANUARY

A get-together may be more intense than you'd expected. If you're single and meet someone new this could be a passionate relationship. Couples and family members may receive key news to do with long-term plans. A visit or change at home could be transformative. *Moon in Cancer.*

17 JANUARY

The Cancerian full moon will spotlight a change in your career, general direction or even status. This may be due to developments in your personal life or at home. Key changes will mean you must consider the big picture. Base decisions on practicalities and avoid allowing emotions to overwhelm reason.

18 JANUARY

The moon in Cancer will encourage you to think intuitively about your circumstances, which will enable you to make informed decisions. As the moon steps into Leo you'll feel more inclined to take action in areas you know you must. *Moon in Leo.*

19 JANUARY

This is a good day to get things done, especially regarding creative projects and domestic matters. You'll enjoy the sense that the changes you wish to see can take shape. *Moon in Leo.*

20 JANUARY

The sun in Aquarius for the next four weeks will bring your inspiration and imagination to the surface. You may feel it's time to approach a personal matter from a fresh perspective. If someone is behaving unpredictably, try to improve communication skills as these are the key to better relationships. *Moon in Leo.*

21 JANUARY

When the moon is in your sign you feel more in your own element. You're able to better deal with the practicalities and realities of circumstances. A domestic, personal or collaborative venture could fall into place; just keep an eye on the logistics. *Moon in Virgo.*

22 JANUARY

This is a good time for a beauty or health appointment. You may also enjoy a get-together with someone chatty or a healthy activity such as sports. A trip will be enjoyable. *Moon enters Libra.*

23 JANUARY

You'll enjoy a reunion and the chance to review a particular project or plan. You may bump into an old friend or hear from someone unexpectedly. It's a good time to review your plans moving forward, especially those that affect your personal life. *Moon in Libra.*

24 JANUARY

You'll be drawn to looking for fairness, will uphold your principles and may have more of a need to see value for money. If you're shopping you may be liable to overspend on sale items purely because of the good value, but ask yourself if you really need them. Avoid

stubbornness if your values clash with those of someone else. Maintain an open mind for the best results. *Moon in Libra.*

25 JANUARY

This is a good time to discuss new ideas, especially with family and someone close. If you're contemplating making changes at home or with family you may make progress. *Moon in Scorpio.*

26 JANUARY

As Mercury retrograde re-enters Capricorn you may review some of your ideas and will need to find alternative plans. Focus on the practicalities of what you're trying to do. Some travel or communications may be delayed, so factor in extra time to avoid frustration. *Moon in Scorpio.*

27 JANUARY

When the moon is in Sagittarius you may be more outspoken and wish to get things done more quickly. You'll feel motivated although not everyone else will, so you may need to be patient. *Moon in Sagittarius.*

28 JANUARY

You'll get a great deal done with your domestic and work matters. If you're travelling, double-check itineraries to avoid disappointment and mix-ups. You'll enjoy updating domestic décor but will need to check with those you share space with that everyone agrees on colour schemes and choices. *Moon in Sagittarius.*

29 JANUARY

A reunion or the chance to change an aspect of your domestic or personal life will go well but may be more intense than you'd imagined. Be prepared for change, but also to maintain perspective. *Moon in Capricorn.*

30 JANUARY

Someone may behave unpredictably. If it's you, try to explain to those concerned why you must change your plans to avoid misunderstandings. An impromptu get-together or a change of circumstance is best managed one step at a time. *Moon in Capricorn.*

31 JANUARY

This is a lovely day for talks, get-togethers and meetings. If you're renovating you'll appreciate the chance to spruce up your home. A change of environment or a fresh atmosphere at home or with family will suit you. *Moon in Aquarius.*

February

| career | love | home | health | finance |

1 FEBRUARY

The new moon in Aquarius signifies a fresh start for you in your personal life, and if you're a truly creative Virgo in a project. You may be ready to try something new or to bring more variety into your life. For some this new moon signals a fresh daily routine or work program.

2 FEBRUARY

You'll appreciate the opportunity to innovate and to bring your imagination to the table, especially at work. A different schedule or a fresh activity or program may seem obstructive at first, but you will gain the chance to get on top of it. *Moon enters Pisces.*

3 FEBRUARY

Someone close may be ready to confide their deeper emotions and thoughts to you. Someone may need your advice, help or support. If you need guidance, it is available. *Moon in Pisces.*

4 FEBRUARY

Key news to do with a personal matter or a decision will give you the green light to move forward with more insight and clarity. A work or health matter may be decided upon. It's a good day to make a decision or commitment as long as you have all the facts. It's a good day for research. *Moon in Pisces.*

5 FEBRUARY

You will feel more outgoing, upbeat, capable and positive about overcoming any obstacles that come your way. If domestic matters or your love life requires focus this is a good time to devote more energy to these important areas of your life. Avoid arguments as they may be hurtful. ***Moon in Aries.***

6 FEBRUARY

You like to see the best, most practical way forward but not everyone has your unique ability to be hands-on and grounded. You may find you need to encourage someone to see things your way. This aside, you'll enjoy a lovely reunion or favourite activity. ***Moon in Aries.***

7 FEBRUARY

As the moon aligns with Uranus you are ready for something different, especially in a shared circumstance or in your personal life. You'll feel motivated to make changes. ***Moon in Taurus.***

8 FEBRUARY

This is a good day to bring something or someone new into your life. If you are busy transforming important aspects of your life or ventures, consider how the expertise of someone with more experience than you might help. A spontaneous visit or change at home will be enjoyable. ***Moon in Taurus.***

9 FEBRUARY

When the moon is at the zenith of your chart, as it is today, your talkative, communicative side is stronger and you'll enjoy being chatty and sociable. It's a good time to tidy up loose ends with paperwork and to make long-overdue phone calls. ***Moon enters Gemini.***

10 FEBRUARY

You'll enjoy improving an aspect of yourself, such as your appearance or health. You may enjoy the company of someone you love more than usual, and romance can blossom. You may feel a little idealistic about lifeso be practical as well, especially at work. ***Moon in Gemini.***

11 FEBRUARY

You'll get the chance to review and reconsider important aspects of a key project or relationship. A meeting may be more significant than meets the eye. Communications may be intense, so ensure you maintain perspective. A trip or visit could be transformative. ***Moon in Cancer.***

12 FEBRUARY

Today's Cancerian moon could put your heart on your sleeve and you'll be tempted to indulge your senses. Avoid over-committing to activities, as this will tire you out. You'll enjoy a romantic get-together. A family or domestic matter could progress. *Moon in Cancer.*

13 FEBRUARY

Check that your emotions aren't leading you into feeling more sensitive than need be, especially concerning someone close or a domestic matter. You'll enjoy a meeting and romance could thrive, so take time out to savour life. *Moon in Cancer.*

14 FEBRUARY

Happy St Valentine's Day! This is always a quirky day when we hear unexpected news or have the chance to reveal our true feelings. You'll gain insight into how someone close truly feels, and a fun or romantic, creative, musical or artistic event will be enjoyable. *Moon in Leo.*

15 FEBRUARY

Be open to a new path, especially concerning work and/or health. You may be ready to embrace a fresh approach to someone close. *Moon in Leo.*

16 FEBRUARY

The Leo full moon will shine a light on your routine such as your work or a health or daily schedule. It's time to be more proactive about how you wish to see your everyday routine take shape. A domestic or personal matter will become much more solid and stable, so this is a good time to make a commitment to someone or to a venture. *Moon enters Virgo late in the day.*

17 FEBRUARY

This is another good day for decision making and for making a commitment to a person or project, for example, at work or at home. You may hear unexpected good news to do with work or a venture. *Moon in Virgo.*

18 FEBRUARY

As the sun enters the zodiac sign Pisces you are likely to feel more inspired by the people around you and will feel more drawn to romance and love as the days go by. However, you may also tend to feel a little head in the clouds, so ensure you are also practical and realistic over the next four weeks. *Moon in Libra.*

19 FEBRUARY

You like to know that you get value for money when you're shopping. You may find a true bargain, but if it doesn't feel quite right then trust your instincts. This is a good time to devise a new

financial budget if you have gone into the red. Someone may be feeling sensitive and need your support. ***Moon in Libra.***

20 FEBRUARY

This is a good day to focus on relaxation and reconnecting with someone you love. However, you may also feel you need to recharge your batteries, in which case this is the perfect day for rest! ***Moon in Libra.***

21 FEBRUARY

Trust your instincts, especially regarding someone close. If they seem a little vague or even evasive, give them space and look for common ground you can both agree on. ***Moon enters Scorpio.***

22 FEBRUARY

This is an excellent day for bringing more beauty and happiness into your personal life. Romance could truly blossom over the next two days. This is also a good time to focus on improving domestic dynamics as your efforts are likely to take. ***Moon in Scorpio.***

23 FEBRUARY

A family or personal project could flourish, so be inspired and put your energy into ventures you enjoy. If you're making key decisions to do with your home, ensure you engage expert help. ***Moon in Sagittarius.***

24 FEBRUARY

This is an excellent day for romance. Singles may meet someone new and couples will enjoy rekindling a little mystery and fun in your love life. You're likely to feel inspired about making changes at home or at work. Allow your imagination free rein as it has valuable insights for you. ***Moon in Sagittarius.***

25 FEBRUARY

Be prepared to be spontaneous as you may receive news that means you must be adaptable. If you must change your plans it will be for a good reason. Some matters may be delayed, so remain positive. Avoid misunderstandings. ***Moon enters Capricorn.***

26 FEBRUARY

Communications and travel are likely to be more straightforward so it's a good day to sort out problems. This is also a good day for beauty and health appointments. ***Moon in Capricorn.***

27 FEBRUARY

The earthy moon will encourage you to get down to brass tacks with plans and chores. Once the moon is in Aquarius you'll enjoy bringing something new to your day such as a change of routine or a fresh approach to getting Sunday chores done. *Moon enters Aquarius.*

28 FEBRUARY

Be careful where you place your focus: if you look only at what isn't working you'll be a little dismayed, but if you look at what is working in your life you'll see there are new opportunities and fun events on the way. Avoid arguments and misunderstandings for the best results. *Moon in Aquarius.*

March

career love home health finance

1 MARCH

You'll gain a sense that you are on the right track and will have more purpose and direction. Someone close may have an interesting approach to your long-term plans. ***Moon enters Pisces.***

2 MARCH

The Pisces new moon signals the chance to turn a corner, especially in your personal life if you were born in August and at work or health-wise if you're a September Virgo. A business or personal partner may have unexpected news for you. Look for inspired ways to move forward but keep your feet on the ground.

3 MARCH

The Venus-Mars-Pluto conjunction will be in your fifth house, signalling key developments in your personal life. For some Virgos this could mean a new suitable partner if you're single, and if you're super creative a project could become more serious or viable. Someone has key news. This could be an intense time so you must maintain perspective. Avoid being overcome by emotions and maintain a clear perspective. ***Moon in Pisces.***

4 MARCH

You'll feel more engaged and proactive, and if recent developments have brought out your vulnerabilities you'll find the inner strength in yourself. Your love life could turn a corner. If it's in the right direction congratulations, but if not there will be a silver lining. **Moon in Aries.**

5 MARCH

You'll gain insight into someone close to you, especially if you were born in early September. If you're working this will be a busy time and you'll do well to take regular breaks. You may be prone to misunderstandings, so ensure you get the facts straight. **Moon in Aries.**

6 MARCH

As both Mars and Venus step into Aquarius you will be prepared to forge into new territory, especially in your personal life and for some Virgos domestically. Some communications or relationships may be complex or difficult, so avoid making judgements until the dust has settled. **Moon in Taurus.**

7 MARCH

The Taurean moon will help you to be more practical about changes you'd like to make regarding the way you share various duties or even finances. This is a good day for planning, but avoid making snap decisions. **Moon in Taurus.**

8 MARCH

This is a good day to make changes, both in your personal life and at work. You may find you can take a little time off for a beauty or health appointment or to talk to someone you really need to straighten things out with. **Moon enters Gemini.**

9 MARCH

The Gemini moon brings out your inner chatterbox and you're able to better communicate, especially about important long-term plans. A trip or holiday may be appealing, and the logistics will determine the rest. **Moon in Gemini.**

10 MARCH

As your sign's ruler Mercury steps into mystical Pisces you may find that your interests turn increasingly over the coming weeks to philosophical matters and the rights and wrongs of certain events, be these to do with work or health. It's a good time to make plans but you must check facts and ensure those you make arrangements with are definitely on the same page for the best results. **Moon in Gemini.**

11 MARCH

You'll appreciate the chance to show just how caring and empathic you are, especially at work or in connection with a health matter. *Moon in Cancer.*

12 MARCH

When the moon is in Cancer you are more intuitive, so take note of your impressions and especially your first impressions if you meet someone new. You'll gain insight into someone close and may make plans for a work scenario or venture that could prove uplifting. *Moon in Cancer.*

13 MARCH

This is a romantic day, especially for Virgos born before mid-September. Those born later will enjoy a beauty or health boost and the chance to truly relax. Plan something beautiful you and those you love will enjoy. *Moon enters Leo.*

14 MARCH

This is a good day to for discussions, especially at work and concerning family. It's also a good day for a health, fitness or beauty appointment. *Moon in Leo.*

15 MARCH

Today's developments may bring inner frustrations out, so take a moment to gather your thoughts if you feel you are more bothered by circumstances than need be. A lovely connection with someone you love could flourish, so take the time to connect with them. *Moon in Leo.*

16 MARCH

The Virgo moon puts your feet firmly on the ground, enabling you to make decisions based on practicalities and not suppositions or hopes. Take a moment to work out how you'd like your projects and plans to move forward and then take them one step at a time. *Moon in Virgo.*

17 MARCH

You'll enjoy a lovely change of routine or an unexpected development that breathes fresh air into your day. You may hear surprise news from someone you love, and an impromptu invitation will be worth accepting. *Moon in Virgo.*

18 MARCH

The Virgo full moon shines a light on your personal life, bringing a fresh chapter your way. For some mid-September Virgos this full moon signals a fresh chapter in a work or daily schedule. You may be super romantic, so ensure you keep your feet on the ground. A surprise may be distracting, but if you maintain focus on your goals you will succeed with your plans.

19 MARCH

The Libran moon will bring your penchant for luxury, love and all things comfortable into the forefront of your mind. You may even be drawn to bringing more luxury in the shape of soft cushions or a new wardrobe into your life. If you're shopping avoid overspending, especially if you're already in debt. *Moon in Libra.*

20 MARCH

When the sun enters Aries it is the vernal equinox. During the next four weeks you may find that your collaborations both in your personal life and at work become more of a focus, and that you feel more proactive about your ventures and more upbeat about relationships. *Moon in Scorpio.*

21 MARCH

Key talks and a meeting could bring you closer to a work or personal partner. You may gain insight into how someone truly feels about you. Romance will blossom. A change of routine or of circumstance may require a little adaptation. *Moon in Scorpio.*

22 MARCH

This is a good day for discussions, both in your personal life and at work. It's also a good day for making agreements with someone special. You may experience a surprise or a change of routine that requires extra focus. If you're disappointed by delays and miscommunication, be patient and focus on good communication skills. *Moon enters Sagittarius.*

23 MARCH

Someone close may reveal more about themselves. A work project will require a little more research, and today's the day to find out more. A change of place or of pace will be inspiring; just avoid being forgetful. *Moon in Sagittarius.*

24 MARCH

You'll feel more practical and grounded, especially regarding your personal life, family or home. If you feel there is opposition to your plans take a moment to ensure you are on the same page, as misunderstandings could arise. You'll appreciate encouragement from someone you trust or admire. *Moon enters Capricorn.*

25 MARCH

No one is an island; everyone relies on everyone else to get things right. You may need to be a little patient with a person whose circumstances and viewpoints are different from yours. Someone close has your back. *Moon in Capricorn.*

26 MARCH

This is a lovely day for getting together with like-minded people. If you're considering making changes to an important aspect of your life such as a personal situation this is a good time to broach the topic. You'll enjoy immersing yourself in music, the arts, film and creativity. *Moon in Capricorn.*

27 MARCH

You'll find out more about how someone close feels: they may be more talkative or simply more demonstrative. You may enjoy being more independent and exploring different areas of your environment. *Moon in Aquarius.*

28 MARCH

This is a good day for making work agreements such as signing a new contract or taking interviews. If health has been a focus you are likely to hear conclusive news. It's a good day to bring more beauty into your environment, either at work or at home. *Moon in Aquarius.*

29 MARCH

The Pisces moon will bring out your emotions and you may feel a little nostalgic or simply tired. It's a good time to surround yourself with music and books you love in your spare time, and to get in touch with people who inspire you. *Moon in Pisces.*

30 MARCH

This is a good day for a beauty or health appointment. You may be feeling a little idealistic about a relationship or project at work, so be inspired but also realistic. *Moon in Pisces.*

31 MARCH

Once the moon is in Aries you may feel a little more focused. Beforehand the Pisces moon could contribute to forgetfulness, so focus a little more at work and on important details such as financial transactions. You'll enjoy taking the time to be with favourite people. *Moon in Aries.*

April

career   love   home   health   finance

1 APRIL

The Aries new moon spells a fresh chapter in a key relationship. For some this will be a love relationship and for others a professional one or even a legal matter. Your vulnerabilities may rise during this time, but this will be your chance to turn a corner and to leave something behind.

2 APRIL

You may receive key news from someone important in your life. There may be an unexpected benefit to developments. *Moon enters Taurus.*

3 APRIL

This is a good day to make changes, either at work or in your personal life or both! It's an excellent day for a makeover or a new look or to introduce fresh ideas to friends or family. *Moon in Taurus.*

4 APRIL

A plan or project such as a work or health venture can proceed rapidly, so if you're happy with the way things are going this is a good time to invest more heavily in them. But if you wish to apply the brakes as things are going too fast, you may need to act quickly before new agreements get underway. *Moon in Taurus.*

5 APRIL

Fresh ideas and plans, a new way to get on with a project or simply the chance to change dynamics in a relationship will present themselves. Be progressive. ***Moon in Gemini.***

6 APRIL

This is a good time for working out the details of some of your agreements, and to ensure the logistics are working well for you. A health or sports event will raise your mood. ***Moon in Gemini.***

7 APRIL

This is a good day for meetings and get-togethers, both at work and regarding your interests and activities. A travel plan could come together well, and if you are already travelling you'll enjoy discovering new places. It is a good day to persuade someone close of your plans. ***Moon in Cancer.***

8 APRIL

Your interest in the arts, dance, music, spirituality and everything your heart desires will be met by opportunities to indulge in these favourite activities; just clear the space so that you can. A work meeting is likely to be successful. ***Moon in Cancer.***

9 APRIL

Romance could flourish, so ensure you take time out to plan something special with someone special! If you're making travel plans, ensure you check the fine print to avoid misunderstandings. ***Moon in Cancer.***

10 APRIL

Communications and travel may be a little intense so avoid mix-ups and take the time to plan ahead. You or someone close may get the wrong end of the stick, so avoid firing up as you may not have all the details yet. ***Moon in Leo.***

11 APRIL

You may feel more practical and grounded about how you approach a thorny topic and this will help you to make progress, especially if you must negotiate with someone. ***Moon in Leo.***

12 APRIL

Before you make agreements with anyone ensure you have all the details. A prospective project or even romance may be appealing, but if you don't know yet who you are dealing with you risk making a mistake. That said romance could blossom, so make a date! ***Moon in Leo.***

13 APRIL

This is a truly productive day and you can make agreements now that will stick. Just ensure you have all the details before committing to any long-term plans to avoid making mistakes. *Moon in Virgo.*

14 APRIL

This is a time to be optimistic and to research new ideas and projects. However, you may be super idealistic so ensure you check the details, especially if you are making financial arrangements. *Moon enters Libra.*

15 APRIL

As Mars enters Pisces you'll be prone to being super idealistic, which will be positive for your ventures but could land you in hot water unless you also research your projects. You may be easily misled, so be careful if you are making choices with people you don't know well as yet. *Moon in Libra.*

16 APRIL

The Libran full moon will spotlight your personal life and, for some, your financial agreements. You'll be looking for more balance in either or both areas of your life, and this is a good time to find it!

17 APRIL

This is a good time to discuss areas in your life where you need other people's collaboration, as the better you get on with others at the moment the better for you personally. This is still a romantic time, so if you're single and are looking for love take action! *Moon in Scorpio.*

18 APRIL

You may bump into someone unexpectedly or receive an unusual message. You are communicating well, so avoid feeling you have given someone mixed messages. People may be volatile so avoid arguments. *Moon in Scorpio.*

19 APRIL

Finding the time to discuss some of your ideas with someone loyal who you trust as a sounding board will be useful and will help you to gain direction and confidence. Be ready to rise to challenges at work but avoid disgruntlement, as this will only distract you from your tasks. *Moon in Sagittarius.*

20 APRIL

As the sun enters Taurus certain agreements and arrangements will feel more settled, but if you feel cornered or a little stuck by developments find the time for some wiggle room and avoid the tendency to be obstinate. Find ways to move forward in the most realistic way. *Moon in Sagittarius.*

21 APRIL

Your practical and realistic side will be prevalent, and today's moon will help you to keep your feet on the ground with changes. You'll demonstrate just how capable you are. *Moon in Capricorn.*

22 APRIL

You'll gain ground once again by taking things one step at a time, especially in your personal life and with long-term projects. Aim for the top, and take the necessary steps to get there. You will. *Moon in Capricorn.*

23 APRIL

You'll enjoy a get-together with someone important to you that will bring a ray of sunshine into your life. If you have nothing planned yet, make a date. If you're studying, this is a good time to get ahead. A trip or meeting will be more significant than meets the eye. *Moon in Aquarius.*

24 APRIL

You'll find out whether you've over- or under-estimated a situation or a person. If you have done either, the good news is you'll get the chance to pave the way to a better path with the invaluable insights you gain. If you're travelling, ensure you organise extra time as there may be delays. Avoid misunderstandings. *Moon in Aquarius.*

25 APRIL

Your feelings about work and your well-being will bubble up. Perhaps a current project is frustrating or you'd prefer to be elsewhere. Avoid snap decisions, as this may just be a case of Mondayitis. A financial or work meeting could see progress, but you may see the world through rose-coloured glasses so ensure you maintain perspective. *Moon in Pisces.*

26 APRIL

You'll feel more motivated and on the ball and could complete important chores. If you have a difficult talk you must undertake this could be the day to do it. Be realistic and practical with new ideas. *Moon in Pisces.*

27 APRIL

This is an excellent day for romance and all things in life you love, so make a date if you haven't already! However, where work decisions are concerned you may be super idealistic and making choices will merit careful thought rather than supposition. Focus on the details and you'll succeed with your chores and duties. ***Moon enters Aries.***

28 APRIL

This is another excellent day to get together with people you love as you'll enjoy bonding over common aims and goals. If you're travelling, the trip could be transformative. It's a good time to initiate change. ***Moon in Aries.***

29 APRIL

You'll be increasingly drawn to broadening your horizons. For some Virgos this will include, for example, travel and study, and for others the chance to deepen ties with someone you love. ***Moon in Aries.***

30 APRIL

The partial solar eclipse in Taurus will represent a fresh chapter for you in a shared circumstance, such as communal space at home or shared finances or duties. You may wish to alter some of your legal agreements. This is a romantic time that is ideal for couples. If you're single you may meet someone who transforms your life. Avoid seeing the world through rose-coloured glasses; just check it really is rosy first.

May

career love home health finance

1 MAY

If you're looking for a commitment from someone, this is a good day to ask for it. A family or personal tie could deepen. *Moon in Taurus.*

2 MAY

As Venus enters Aries you'll feel more upbeat about your personal life and your opportunities moving forward. You may also notice your friends and those close to you are more dynamic and outgoing over the coming weeks. Make plans for something fun! *Moon in Gemini.*

3 MAY

This is another good day for making agreements with someone close to you. It's an excellent day for making changes that involve collaborations. If you have quarrelled with someone this is a good day to mend bridges. *Moon in Gemini.*

4 MAY

You'll enjoy a change of routine and simply being spontaneous. You may hear unexpected news at work or from someone close. A visit somewhere different will be refreshing. A favourite hobby such as sport may breathe fresh air your way. *Moon in Gemini.*

5 MAY

Expect a surprise. Someone close has unexpected news, and if you're in a position to make spontaneous changes to your activities you'll enjoy doing something different such as taking a trip somewhere beautiful with someone special. *Moon in Cancer.*

6 MAY

This is an excellent time for discussions and meetings. A favourite interest, venture or pastime is likely to go well. If you're looking for information that can help you advance, this is a good day for research. *Moon in Cancer.*

7 MAY

You'll enjoy being outgoing and upbeat, and together with someone you love or admire you could truly go places. Collaborations and joint ventures will be a particular focus. Sports, nature walks and work could all produce good results. *Moon in Leo.*

8 MAY

This is a good day to be outgoing and adventurous. Sports, physical exercise and organising your working week in advance will all get you feeling motivated. You'll also gain ground with chores and gardening and will feel good as a result of how much you achieve. *Moon in Leo.*

9 MAY

If you like a little tension to feel motivated you'll like today's vibe at work, but if you fall at the first hurdle when you sense unease you may need to take extra breaks. Aim to tie up loose ends at work and regarding communications before Mercury turns retrograde tomorrow. *Moon enters Virgo.*

10 MAY

As Mercury turns retrograde you're likely to receive key news regarding a favourite project, trip or study. If you are engaged in legal matters you may need to review your circumstances. Try to allow extra time for travel and communications to avoid frustration over the coming weeks. *Moon in Virgo.*

11 MAY

As Jupiter enters Aries you may notice that someone close takes more of your focus; they may be more talkative or upbeat. But if conflict is brewing, take steps to de-escalate it rather than adding to it for the best results. You may be ready to embrace fresh projects. *Moon in Virgo.*

12 MAY

You are a pragmatic soul and tend to look for solutions before you look for problems. It'll be in your interest to look for balance, especially if a partner's situation or a project is harder than you'd prefer. *Moon in Libra.*

13 MAY

Key news to do with shared matters or a favourite person or interest will be significant. You'll enjoy a reunion, and if you meet someone for the first time there may be a familiarity you can't quite explain. Singles may meet someone with a soul connection, so if you have nothing planned for an evening or day out now's your chance to arrange something! *Moon in Libra.*

14 MAY

You'll feel more passionate about life and someone in particular this weekend, so if all is well in your relationships you'll enjoy deepening ties. But if you feel tension is brewing, take a deep breath and find ways to move forward without conflict. *Moon in Scorpio.*

15 MAY

This is a good day to take that extra little bit of care with yourself and those you love. Someone may need your help. If you need support it will be available. A particular project or person may be more complex than you'd hoped and will need more work. Romance could blossom, so take time out for someone special. *Moon in Scorpio.*

16 MAY

The total lunar eclipse in Scorpio may feel particularly intense, as it will spotlight a situation that may seem inescapable. All things change, so if you feel you are stuck regain perspective. This eclipse suggests great change is on the way, either financially or in your personal life. You could make great headway with treasured projects.

17 MAY

Be practical and at the same time inspired, as you could make great progress within your work and personal life. An agreement could be ideal, so be proactive and reach out. *Moon in Sagittarius.*

18 MAY

There is a strong sense of romance around you. If it is bringing you everything you desire all well and good, but if you feel lost or disoriented by developments you must get your feet back on the ground. Be inspired to make valid, workable agreements with those you love and admire. *Moon in Capricorn.*

19 MAY

A plan or project or a visit or outing with family will go well even if there is a great deal of change or effort that must go into events. ***Moon in Capricorn.***

20 MAY

This is a good day for meetings, both regarding your interests in general and in your personal life. A trip will present the chance to go over old ground. A legal matter could advance, but you may need to first review some details. If some matters are delayed it will give you the chance to gain more research time. ***Moon in Aquarius.***

21 MAY

As the sun enters chatty Gemini a get-together or news will be important. A trip may take you back to a familiar place or you will enjoy a reunion. This is a good time to discuss your plans with those they concern. You may reconsider your position or ideas. ***Moon in Aquarius.***

22 MAY

This is an excellent time to deepen ties, especially with the people you must collaborate with on a daily or long-term basis. Not everyone will agree with you even though you're at your charming best! Find the time to relax. ***Moon enters Pisces.***

23 MAY

You will get the chance to shine. For some this will be in your personal life and for others with a project or interest such as sport. If you're travelling you'll enjoy the change of atmosphere. This is a good time to review some of your projects or goals. ***Moon in Pisces.***

24 MAY

This is a good time to make agreements as they are likely to last. Take the time to go over the terms and conditions and find out where you stand exactly, especially with work arrangements. A review will put you in a stronger position. ***Moon in Pisces.***

25 MAY

The green light you have been waiting for is on the way! If you have had to rearrange or renegotiate some personal arrangements you're likely to see progress with them. You'll enjoy a reunion or the chance to revisit an old haunt. ***Moon in Aries.***

26 MAY

This is a good day for research and to deepen your ties with people you love. If you'd like to alter some of your agreements, talks will be productive. ***Moon in Aries.***

27 MAY

If you love a little passion in life you'll enjoy today, but if you prefer your love life or personal life on an even keel ensure you maintain perspective and make arrangements you know you'll enjoy rather than simply going along with someone else's plans. Avoid conversations you know could be triggers, as today's stars could contribute to intense talks. *Moon in Taurus.*

28 MAY

Venus in Taurus for the next few weeks will contribute to your tendency to enjoy indulging in a little luxury and comfort. You'll enjoy being with someone you love and treating them to something special. *Moon in Taurus.*

29 MAY

You'll enjoy being spontaneous and upbeat. Your partner or someone close may suggest something different and active for a change this weekend. You'll enjoy sports, being in the outdoors and exploring new ideas. Romance could blossom, so make a date! *Moon enters Gemini.*

30 MAY

The Gemini new moon will spotlight your feelings about turning a new page in your ventures and projects. You may be contemplating a trip, study or a fresh approach to someone close and to look for more variety and spice in life. Key news could open new doors for you. It's a good time to begin a new project or collaboration.

31 MAY

You're communicating well even if you feel you are not fully understood by everyone. Those close to you understand you; however, if you feel mistakes or misunderstandings are occurring take the time to get back on common ground and establish more stability in your relationships, especially at work and concerning shared matters. *Moon in Gemini.*

June

career love home health finance

1 JUNE

The moon at the zenith of your chart could put your heart on your sleeve, so if you feel more sensitive than usual blame it on the moon! If you feel you're under pressure, take breaks to unwind when you can. **Moon in Cancer.**

2 JUNE

You're generally known as a practical, realistic character but you can also be super sensitive. If your inner doubts or vulnerabilities surface, ensure you maintain perspective. You can't always agree with everyone. You may be asked to help someone. If you need support ask for it as it is available. **Moon in Cancer.**

3 JUNE

Mercury ends its retrograde phase today and you may see over the coming weeks that communications and travel plans become easier, especially where they concern your personal life. You may receive key news that will merit close attention to a collaborative effort, joint finances or a relationship. **Moon enters Leo.**

4 JUNE

This is a good day for chats and more meaningful talks with those close to you. A financial matter is best looked at from the long-term perspective, especially if a heavy investment is involved. *Moon in Leo.*

5 JUNE

The Leo moon helps you to feel more sociable and outgoing. Today, however, if you feel at odds with other people's plans find the time to schedule activities you all love and can enjoy. That said, you may be surprised to see that someone else's plans bring you enjoyment and fulfilment. Someone may need your support. Avoid rash decisions. *Moon in Leo.*

6 JUNE

It's a definite case of Mondayitis as you wish to be doing something other than work! If you have a difficult project to do, rest assured you will manage to excel but you will need to focus that little bit harder than usual. Someone has your back. *Moon in Virgo.*

7 JUNE

Unexpected developments may take you by surprise, but if you're waiting for the green light you're likely to hear good news. A legal, financial, study or travel plan could move ahead well. *Moon in Virgo.*

8 JUNE

You'll appreciate the opportunity to invest more heavily in your projects, especially those you love such as family events and sports. If someone lets you down it will be for good reason. Use your considerable organisational skills for the best results. *Moon enters Libra.*

9 JUNE

An upbeat, dynamic character may take your focus and managing their energy levels could be taxing. Look for balance but avoid trying to control them. If indecision is one of your failings or you're unsure of a financial or personal matter, ensure you gain expert guidance. *Moon in Libra.*

10 JUNE

You'll appreciate seeing that some of your ventures and transactions and relationships are gaining a more even keel. If you have been formulating new ideas and plans they can take great strides forward. *Moon enters Scorpio.*

11 JUNE

Expect unanticipated news or a surprise. Financial matters could be a focus. If you're shopping or making a large investment, avoid impulse buys. You'll enjoy doing something different and may bump into an old friend. If you're reluctant to make changes, you may need to be more adaptable. **Moon in Scorpio.**

12 JUNE

You may be ready to invest in someone or a project. This is a good time to check that your values and principles coincide with theirs, as if you have argued it may be a case of different values. Avoid decisions based on emotions alone; take a moment to think things through. **Moon enters Sagittarius.**

13 JUNE

You'll enjoy a chattier, more upbeat few weeks ahead, where travel, meeting people and feeling you have more freedom of movement will appeal. **Moon in Sagittarius.**

14 JUNE

The full moon and supermoon in Sagittarius represents a fresh chapter for you in the level of freedom you experience. You may enjoy a new study course or trip or the chance to level up a relationship and be more outgoing and spontaneous. A legal matter may come to a conclusion.

15 JUNE

Someone close may share some of their deeper thoughts. You may tend to be impulsive with shared concerns such as joint finances, so be careful with spending. A teacher or adviser may prove particularly helpful to you. **Moon in Capricorn.**

16 JUNE

This is an excellent day to get ahead at work and to boost your profile or status or your direction in general. Just ensure everyone is on board with your plans first, as mistakes and misunderstandings could arise otherwise. A key meeting or news will be decisive. You may enjoy a reunion. **Moon enters Aquarius.**

17 JUNE

You'll enjoy an impromptu activity. A personal or business partner may surprise you, or you may decide to be spontaneous and surprise them! **Moon in Aquarius.**

18 JUNE

If you have been careful with your projects and with planning in particular you'll manage to get over logistical conundrums. But if you have been forgetful or, worse, reckless you may discover a spanner in the works, especially with work and personal projects. **Moon in Aquarius.**

19 JUNE

You are diligent and know how to work hard, and will focus on creating a positive outcome. Family get-togethers and romance could be exciting but may require more tact. *Moon in Pisces.*

20 JUNE

The Pisces moon will bring your creative side out and you'll enjoy adding a touch of beauty and charm to everything you do. A partner may also be more romantic. *Moon in Pisces.*

21 JUNE

As the sun enters Cancer, marking the solstice, you will feel more inclined to focus on family and on how to nurture someone close. If you're career minded you'll appreciate the opportunity to further your job prospects over the next four weeks. A positive development with a favourite pastime or in your family will be encouraging. *Moon in Aries.*

22 JUNE

Someone close such as a business or personal partner is likely to be more assertive. Avoid taking their feistiness personally, but if they fire up without due reason they may need to be reminded of boundaries. *Moon in Aries.*

23 JUNE

You'll feel a little more grounded and less likely to react to other people's mood swings or aggression. If a power struggle is underway try to avoid arguments as these could escalate. *Moon enters Taurus.*

24 JUNE

You'll enjoy planning a slower pace this weekend. There are many ways you can plan to relax, beginning right now! There are therapeutic aspects to the weekend, so why not plan a healthy treat or a walk in nature? *Moon in Taurus.*

25 JUNE

Calming and grounding activities and people you love will be a true drawcard this weekend, and you'll enjoy a change of routine even if the logistics aren't as straightforward as you'd prefer. *Moon in Taurus.*

26 JUNE

When the moon is in Gemini life is likely to be busier, and you'll appreciate the sense that you are a little more flexible and free with communications and meetings. You'll enjoy a get-together such as a sports event or a favourite hobby. *Moon in Gemini.*

27 JUNE

This is a good day for moving forward with business and personal relationships. Someone may need your help or advice. If you need guidance an expert or adviser could prove helpful. *Moon in Gemini.*

28 JUNE

You may be pleasantly surprised by a development, for some involving work and for others a favourite pastime or venture. You'll appreciate the sense that your projects are moving forward. You may hear unexpectedly from someone who can be a little quirky. *Moon enters Cancer.*

29 JUNE

The Cancerian new moon will kick-start a fresh chapter, for some in your career and in your general direction in life and for others with a favourite project. You may need to persuade someone of your keenness. A negotiation may be tough, but if you focus on the facts you'll gain ground. *Moon in Cancer.*

30 JUNE

Trust your instincts, especially with a social or personal matter. You are thinking intuitively and will pick up important information as a result. *Moon in Cancer.*

July

career   love   home   health   finance

1 JULY

The Leo moon brings out your feisty side. You'll enjoy socialising and may even gain the chance to get together with friends at lunchtime. If you feel there is a little tension in a social or work group it would be wise to sidestep it if possible. *Moon in Leo.*

2 JULY

This is a good day to get ahead at work and particularly with meetings. However, misunderstandings could arise so ensure you have all the facts at your fingertips. Be patient with delays too. Avoid allowing a difference of opinion to escalate, especially over finances. This is a good day for a health or medical appointment. *Moon in Leo.*

3 JULY

You are known as a hard worker and your abilities and skill sets will be in demand. Just avoid tiring yourself out. Find the time to overcome arguments, otherwise they could become long-term disagreements. *Moon enters Virgo.*

4 JULY

You will detect underlying disagreements and tensions, especially at work and regarding someone close. Be prepared to find common ground and to de-escalate tension if possible. *Moon in Virgo.*

5 JULY

You'll appreciate the chance to enter new territory with a venture, agreement or project. Be positive, as new collaborations or ventures begun now could be inspiring and constructive. *Moon enters Libra.*

6 JULY

This is a good day to mend bridges with people you have argued with. Someone may be feeling sensitive and may need to be handled with kid gloves. It's a good day to improve your appearance. *Moon in Libra.*

7 JULY

You will look for balance and harmony in your interactions and may act as a mediator at work. If finances have become an issue you'll find a more balanced budget. *Moon in Libra.*

8 JULY

You may be surprised by news or a get-together. Someone may feel particularly sensitive or vulnerable. If it's you, find ways to untangle your feelings and to boost your self-esteem. A little help from an expert or some guidance will be available if you need it. *Moon in Scorpio.*

9 JULY

An agreement may require a rethink. If you're travelling, prepare for delays. A misunderstanding is best handled carefully to avoid bruising someone's ego. *Moon in Scorpio.*

10 JULY

You'll appreciate doing something different or going somewhere new. A fun pastime or upbeat event will breathe fresh air into your day. *Moon enters Sagittarius.*

11 JULY

You'll enjoy a trip or conversation that shines a light on your abilities and gives you a sense of adventure. You'll feel more able to understand someone who seems unhappy at the moment, so be prepared to listen to their story. *Moon in Sagittarius.*

12 JULY

You'll enjoy a social or networking event. Be inspired, because many of your plans and relationships can gain ground. Just avoid being too idealistic with some of your plans. *Moon enters Capricorn.*

13 JULY

The full moon and supermoon in Capricorn will spotlight an important personal relationship or creative project. You may be ready to begin a new chapter at home or involving family or children. You can make a great deal of headway with a work project or business decision.

14 JULY

You'll discover whether your expectations have been unrealistic about a plan, person or project. Luckily, this will give you the chance to set your expectations straight and will help with planning moving forward. *Moon enters Aquarius.*

15 JULY

You'll feel motivated by your projects and the people they concern. However, there may be a little tension in the air or you may discover a spanner in the works. This could contribute to a mystery, but if stress is a real turn off for you you may wish to take things one step at a time. If an obstacle arises you will overcome it. *Moon in Aquarius.*

16 JULY

A social or networking venture will bring you in touch with inspired and imaginative people, but you may need to get on top of chores and duties at work first. You may simply wish to relax and avoid a busy crowd: the choice is yours! *Moon enters Pisces.*

17 JULY

This is a lovely day for get-togethers and romance. You may already be scheduled to meet a group or attend a meeting. If not, plan something lovely as you'll be glad you did. *Moon in Pisces.*

18 JULY

Conversations may be more intense than you'd hoped but at least you will know the lie of the land. You may hear key news to do with family or a project and may need to alter some arrangements to accommodate other people. *Moon enters Aries.*

19 JULY

As Mercury enters upbeat Leo a project or friendship can step into new territory. If you must find out more information about a group or organisation, this is your day! *Moon in Aries.*

20 JULY

This is a good day for making changes in your personal life, and if you're creative or artistic for truly immersing yourself in your abilities and projects. If you're single you may meet someone charming but intense. *Moon enters Taurus.*

21 JULY

The more practical you are about your various activities and projects the better for you. Avoid being rushed and ensure you cover ground thoroughly in your various ventures. *Moon in Taurus.*

22 JULY

As the sun enters Leo you will enjoy feeling more outgoing and sociable over the coming weeks. You may already have a social or networking event planned or will spend more time with someone you love. *Moon in Taurus.*

23 JULY

You'll enjoy touching base with someone close and talks and plans can go ahead well. If you're planning a trip this is an excellent time for research. You may enjoy a reunion or returning to an old haunt. *Moon in Gemini.*

24 JULY

Your chatty side will come out and you'll enjoy talking up a storm and reconnecting with favourite people and hobbies. *Moon in Gemini.*

25 JULY

Someone you know you must co-operate with may not be so easy to get along with at the moment. If you have shared duties or even finances this is a good time to tread carefully to avoid arguments. *Moon enters Cancer.*

26 JULY

This is another day to be diplomatic and choose your words carefully, as someone you must get on with may not agree with your views or the actions you take. Aim to establish common ground to avoid arguments. *Moon in Cancer.*

27 JULY

If you argued with someone recently this is a good time to build bridges with them. It's also a good day to consult an expert such as a medical professional or accountant. *Moon in Cancer.*

28 JULY

The Leo new moon points to a fresh chapter concerning a friend, group or organisation. If you've been quiet socially you may be more likely to kick up your heels over the coming weeks. A change of routine or an unexpected development will move ahead if you approach circumstances matter of factly. Keep those you know in the loop if you need to change plans abruptly.

29 JULY

You'll enjoy socialising and networking even if initially plans don't appeal to you. You may warm to the events and to someone in particular. Travel and communications may be subject to change, so be clear about your arrangements for the best results. *Moon in Leo.*

30 JULY

An assertive and compassionate approach to yourself and to others will work wonders. A little time out to recharge your batteries will also be beneficial. *Moon enters Virgo.*

31 JULY

You'll enjoy an impromptu get-together or a change of environment. Singles may meet someone who seems familiar and romance could blossom. You may enter a fresh agreement with someone that takes you somewhere new. Be spontaneous, but you must avoid snap decisions. *Moon in Virgo.*

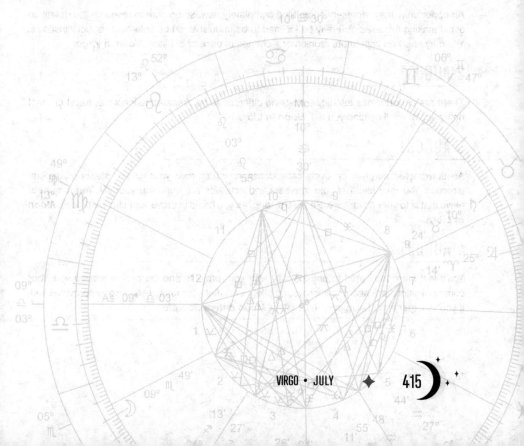

August

career   love   home   health   finance

1 AUGUST

An opportunity may represent something completely new, so be sure to research the details to avoid making mistakes. You may be inclined to be impulsive, so be bold but trust your instincts. You may enjoy an impromptu reunion or a change of pace or of place. ***Moon in Virgo.***

2 AUGUST

There are opportunities to enjoy something different so be prepared to innovate, travel or meet new people. You'll be glad you did. ***Moon in Libra.***

3 AUGUST

An unexpected surprise or lovely coincidence could improve your career, status or general direction. You may feel that your interests and activities are enriching your life. You may hear news that is to your advantage. Be enterprising, as you could improve your circumstances. ***Moon in Libra.***

4 AUGUST

You'll feel more motivated to engage fully with your projects and the people around you. Your communications are about to improve, so take heart that your relationships can improve as well if you've experienced disagreements lately. ***Moon enters Scorpio.***

5 AUGUST

Work or finances will require additional attention, especially if you feel a situation is unfair. Be tactful to overcome nerves and assertive so that your viewpoints are heard. *Moon in Scorpio.*

6 AUGUST

You'll feel outgoing and willing to meet people halfway with their ventures and activities this weekend. Trust your instincts if you're unsure of someone. *Moon enters Sagittarius.*

7 AUGUST

Work and chores are likely to soak up a lot of your attention, but if you organise your day well you'll get the chance to make the most of excellent stars for romance and delights. *Moon in Sagittarius.*

8 AUGUST

There is a positive aspect to your interactions, so if you need information from a group, organisation or friend it will be available. You may be asked to help someone, and if you need advice or expert help it will be available to you. *Moon enters Capricorn.*

9 AUGUST

Communications and interactions are likely to be more intense than you like. This could signal more passion in a relationship, but if you prefer romance on an even keel you may need to find ways to pace yourself. A work meeting or project is likely to go well. It's a good time for a health or medical appointment. *Moon in Capricorn.*

10 AUGUST

Your plans for a more settled personal life are likely to show promise as you gain a sense of stability and security. For some this will be domestically, and for others via a close relationship or project. *Moon enters Aquarius.*

11 AUGUST

A friend, group or organisation may surprise you with a change of plan. Be proactive with your activities but ready to be adaptable so that you can make the most of your circumstances. *Moon in Aquarius.*

12 AUGUST

The Aquarian full moon will highlight your personal life or family situation. Be prepared to be flexible as circumstances outside your control may have a bearing on your situation. Think laterally if an obstacle arises.

13 AUGUST

You'll appreciate the opportunity to relax and unwind. A health or beauty appointment will appeal. It's a good day to slow down if you can and to focus on creating a sense of wellness and happiness. ***Moon in Pisces.***

14 AUGUST

This is a good day to make a commitment to an idea, person or venture. Be proactive with your activities as you could make great and long-term change. ***Moon enters Aries.***

15 AUGUST

You'll enjoy a reunion, hearing from an old friend or visiting someone. A work project could be successful. This is a good day for a health appointment. ***Moon in Aries.***

16 AUGUST

A change of schedule or in your work routine may be unexpected or will take you into new territory that is exciting or unusual in some way. You'll enjoy being spontaneous but must avoid making snap decisions. ***Moon in Aries.***

17 AUGUST

You may need to find out more information before you make important decisions. Ensure you do your research. Someone may seem evasive or forgetful, and if it's you take a moment to recalibrate. ***Moon in Taurus.***

18 AUGUST

This is a super romantic day that is ideal for a get-together with your partner or for immersing yourself in art, music and your favourite activities. Social meetings are likely to go well, but some career matters will require more focus to make them work for you. ***Moon in Taurus.***

19 AUGUST

You may sense some tense undercurrents in developments so the best way forward is through using tact and diplomacy. You can make progress but must avoid power struggles. ***Moon in Gemini.***

20 AUGUST

Mars will now be in Gemini until the end of March 2023, which will help you to make great progress with your activities and ventures and at work. A travel plan, study or legal matter is likely to take shape. ***Moon in Gemini.***

21 AUGUST

You'll find out if you've misunderstood someone or have made an error in judgement. Luckily, you'll get the chance to rectify things if you have. Romance could flourish, so plan a day out or in! *Moon in Gemini.*

22 AUGUST

You're communicating well at the moment and a family or personal matter can advance as a result. A trip or domestic development can lead to further change down the road. *Moon in Cancer.*

23 AUGUST

Now that the sun is in Virgo you are likely to gradually feel more energetic over the next few weeks. You may need to listen to someone's opinions and take their feelings on board. *Moon in Cancer.*

24 AUGUST

A helpful person will extend the hand of friendship to you, so if you need to sort out personal or financial matters this is a good time to do so. There is a healing, therapeutic aspect to the day, so make an appointment if you feel you need to boost health and well-being. *Moon enters Leo.*

25 AUGUST

The moon in Leo may bring out your more upbeat, outgoing side and you'll enjoy connecting with like-minded people. *Moon in Leo.*

26 AUGUST

This is a good time to appraise your finances and personal situation and make adjustments if need be over the next few days and weeks. You'll aim for more balance and fair play. *Moon in Leo.*

27 AUGUST

The new moon in Virgo may bring a surprise or two your way. For some Virgos this will be in your personal life, but for many the new moon will be a good time to begin something fresh either in your health and fitness schedule or at work. Be prepared to adapt to circumstances, as stubbornness will only lead to a stalemate.

28 AUGUST

This is a good day for serious discussions and for making long-term commitments to a fresh course of action or even to a person. A financial decision could be successful as long as you have adequately researched the variables. *Moon in Virgo.*

29 AUGUST

You can tend to be a perfectionist, so if you find opposition to some of your plans ask whether or not you're trying too hard to achieve the impossible. You are looking for fair play and the best way ahead in practical terms but may need to adapt to something new. *Moon enters Libra.*

30 AUGUST

Put your back into your work as this will lead to success, especially if you rise to any challenges. If you succumb to arguments or difficulties you may find the day trying. *Moon in Libra.*

31 AUGUST

You may find you have misjudged a situation or person. If you feel disappointed find a more realistic approach to circumstances that will help you feel happier. *Moon enters Scorpio.*

September

career   love   home   health   finance

1 SEPTEMBER

This is a proactive day where you can achieve a great deal. A meeting, collaboration or project can get ahead. Avoid rushing, as you have what it takes to succeed. **Moon in Scorpio.**

2 SEPTEMBER

You'll gain a sense of achievement by avoiding conflict and intense undercurrents. Maintain a professional demeanour at work and avoid gossip. Your personal life will feel fulfilling if you avoid dramas. **Moon enters Sagittarius.**

3 SEPTEMBER

This is a good day to put important matters on the table for discussion. If finances have put you in the red, it's an excellent time to devise a new budget. **Moon in Sagittarius.**

4 SEPTEMBER

The Sagittarian moon will be motivational for you to get things done at home and to improve interpersonal dynamics. But if someone in particular proves enigmatic or difficult in some way, avoid making tension worse; find ways to co-operate if possible. **Moon in Sagittarius.**

5 SEPTEMBER

As Venus enters your sign your attention is likely to wander increasingly towards your love life and finding ways to better manage money. Just avoid over-analysing your circumstances and find practical ways forward. *Moon in Capricorn.*

6 SEPTEMBER

The moon in Capricorn will help you to be more practical, especially in your personal life and with your family and projects. Make the most of this phase to be productive and decisive. *Moon in Capricorn.*

7 SEPTEMBER

You are a capable and effective worker, and when the moon is in Aquarius you are inspired and more able to work around obstacles and difficulties. Be inspired and you'll enjoy finding new and better ways to get the same old things done. *Moon in Aquarius.*

8 SEPTEMBER

This is a good day to get health and well-being in tip-top shape, even if you feel a little lacklustre. Find the time to get help and advice about your fitness, and if you need relationship advice someone will be able to help you. *Moon in Aquarius.*

9 SEPTEMBER

Avoid taking other people's problems to heart and seeing their problems as yours. Find ways to be a shoulder to cry on while also maintaining your own peace of mind. If you need advice or help it will be available. *Moon in Pisces.*

10 SEPTEMBER

The full moon in Pisces will shine a light on your business and personal relationships, especially if you were born at the end of August and in early September. Mid-September Virgos will be ready for a fresh chapter in your work or health schedule. Be innovative but avoid seeing things through rose-coloured glasses.

11 SEPTEMBER

A surprise visit or trip will be enjoyable, and news could represent something fresh for you. If you're working you may experience something unusual. Now that Mercury is retrograde you may find some communications and financial matters could be a little more complex, so be patient. *Moon in Aries.*

12 SEPTEMBER

You are a logical and reasonable character and you're extra talented at finding innovative ways around problems. Your abilities may be in demand and you'll certainly overcome any hurdles that come your way. ***Moon in Aries.***

13 SEPTEMBER

The Aries moon for much of the day will help you maintain a dynamic approach to work and the people you interact with. Once the moon is in Taurus for the next few days you'll feel more grounded and able to make long-term plans, especially with ideas that have been in the making for a while. ***Moon enters Taurus.***

14 SEPTEMBER

This is a good time to be actively involved in creating a solid base for yourself, be this at work or at home or with a project you wish to advance such as a trip. ***Moon in Taurus.***

15 SEPTEMBER

This is another good day for progressing with your plans one step at a time. Avoid making snap decisions but take all the variables into consideration if you are making important determinations. ***Moon enters Gemini.***

16 SEPTEMBER

While you're a practical person you also can be romantic and idealistic, especially on days like today. If you feel you may be unclear about a decision, ensure you gather all the details before committing to a particular course of action. ***Moon in Gemini.***

17 SEPTEMBER

The moon in your 10th house of work will bring your talkative and capable sides out. You'll enjoy being with like-minded people but must avoid impulsiveness. ***Moon in Gemini.***

18 SEPTEMBER

You'll enjoy a reunion or the chance to touch base with someone close. If a financial matter needs to be rectified this is an ideal time to work on a clever budget. If work is complex, consider a fresh way to move forward. ***Moon enters Cancer.***

19 SEPTEMBER

This is a good day to make changes in your personal life, with family or at home. If you have plans to make changes at home or within your health or work life, these are likely to go well. ***Moon in Cancer.***

20 SEPTEMBER

It's all in the planning: if you have laid a solid foundation for your various plans they are likely to go well. You may enjoy being spontaneous and visiting somewhere new or doing something different. ***Moon enters Leo.***

21 SEPTEMBER

The moon in Leo will contribute to a more positive frame of mind as the day goes by. You'll enjoy organising socialising and networking and may feel more assertive. ***Moon in Leo.***

22 SEPTEMBER

You have a natural ability to put others at ease, but when other people are feeling tense you can also feel tense. Avoid contributing to strain and find fun ways to unwind. ***Moon in Leo.***

23 SEPTEMBER

As the sun steps into Libra it marks the equinox, a time when we collectively sense we can achieve more balance and harmony in our lives. Your attention is likely to go increasingly to managing finances and finding more peace at home and in your personal life over the coming weeks. ***Moon in Virgo.***

24 SEPTEMBER

A romantic day for most Virgos, although mid-September Virgos may be more focused on work or health. If you're having a health or beauty treatment ensure you are clear about what you want, as misunderstandings could occur. ***Moon in Virgo.***

25 SEPTEMBER

The new moon in Libra points to a fresh circumstance in a financial or personal situation. You'll be looking for fair play and to establish more peace and harmony in your home and relationships. Someone close may have key news for you.

26 SEPTEMBER

You'll receive important information or have a key get-together. Romance could truly blossom, so if you have nothing planned yet organise a treat. ***Moon in Libra.***

27 SEPTEMBER

Important developments could mean changes for you in your personal life and for some in your business life also. Be brave and prepared to discuss your options openly as this is a transformative time for you. ***Moon in Libra.***

28 SEPTEMBER

This is a good day for your work and projects to advance, so take the initiative. ***Moon in Scorpio.***

29 SEPTEMBER

You'll feel motivated to express yourself more passionately and may even take some people by surprise with your intense stance on various activities. You can make great progress with your ventures, so be positive. ***Moon in Scorpio.***

30 SEPTEMBER

This is a good time to spend with like-minded people. You'll feel communicative and may be prepared to deepen some relationships. You'll enjoy a change of place or of pace. Romance could blossom. ***Moon in Sagittarius.***

October

career   love   home   health   finance

1 OCTOBER

You'll enjoy reconnecting with someone special. You may also need to focus on spending and budgets, especially if a large invoice arrives on your desk. You will benefit from reviewing past agreements and finding positive ways forward. *Moon in Sagittarius.*

2 OCTOBER

You're in a position to reconsider an important agreement or to review how you feel about someone. Key news may arrive that steers you in the right direction. You'll enjoy discussing key changes you'd like to implement. *Moon in Capricorn.*

3 OCTOBER

You'll attend to all the practicalities at work and at home with your usual flair. You may need to review or oversee a change at work. Consider how you could be more practical and find ways to communicate with more sensitivity and compassion. *Moon in Capricorn.*

4 OCTOBER

This is a good day to clear chores, especially backlogs of work at home or that concern your personal life. You may find a health or fitness routine that you can implement at home is productive. *Moon enters Aquarius.*

5 OCTOBER

You're thinking clearly, which will enable you to make clever changes at work and financially. If you have projects that must be cleared quickly this is the day you'll do it. *Moon in Aquarius.*

6 OCTOBER

This is a good time to use your imagination as it will not let you down, especially at work and with health and well-being. Consider new and exciting ways to get your work done. A fresh way to save and invest money may appeal. *Moon enters Pisces.*

7 OCTOBER

Finances merit careful attention for those Virgos who have been tempted to overspend. An expert or adviser will be useful for you if you need help financially. If you have the opportunity, a little more focus on family and someone special will pay dividends. Someone may require your help. *Moon in Pisces.*

8 OCTOBER

You'll feel intuitive so listen to your gut, especially where someone's feelings are concerned. If you're unsure of how to proceed, take a moment to work out how to distinguish between your feelings and those of others. Romance could blossom, so organise a treat or simply relax! *Moon enters Aries.*

9 OCTOBER

The Aries full moon will spotlight how you feel about someone close, such as someone you love or share space with. You or they may be feeling particularly sensitive or health may be a concern, so take time out. For many, though, today's full moon will spotlight lovely plans for a happy future.

10 OCTOBER

This is a good day to focus on health and well-being, either your own or that of someone close. A new look or attention to your appearance may appeal. If money is tight it's time to look for ways to budget. You may receive a compliment or even a financial boost. *Moon enters Taurus.*

11 OCTOBER

This is a good day to discuss the logistics of your circumstances, especially regarding finances and your personal life. It's also a positive day to make headway at work and with health matters, so take the initiative! *Moon in Taurus.*

12 OCTOBER

Matters you have already discussed such as your finances or personal situation are likely to come up again and you'll see there has been progress. If not, it's time to rethink the situation.

Ensure you have all the facts and avoid rushing or feeling under pressure, as mistakes and misunderstandings could occur. *Moon in Taurus.*

13 OCTOBER

An unexpected development is best approached with a diligent and persistence attitude to ensure you get on top of anomalies and complexities. When you focus on your priorities you could make unexpected progress. *Moon in Gemini.*

14 OCTOBER

This is an excellent day for sorting out finances and for making work and financial commitments, as long as you have done adequate groundwork. You may receive a compliment. A beauty or health matter can progress with a diligent approach. You may gain a sense of security with a financial or work matter. *Moon in Gemini.*

15 OCTOBER

Your mind is sparking on all cylinders and general restlessness is best channelled into favourite pastimes or chores around the house as you'll complete a lot of goals. You're likely to be busy! *Moon enters Cancer.*

16 OCTOBER

You may prefer to relax and it will be a less stressful day than yesterday, but someone will catch your attention. A financial or personal mystery may be in the making. If so, now's the time for research! *Moon in Cancer.*

17 OCTOBER

This is another excellent day for getting things done, although you may be more awash with ideas than actual time to implement them so ensure you prioritise tasks. Avoid seeing someone through rose-coloured glasses as this could trip you up. *Moon in Cancer.*

18 OCTOBER

Your caring side will wish to find expression and you'll appreciate the time to devote to yourself or someone close. That is, if you can take some time out from a busy schedule. *Moon in Leo.*

19 OCTOBER

Life will progress well for you, especially as you can focus on your work and projects and on improving your financial circumstances and status. However, you may need to make a tough call in the process. Avoid conflict and find better ways to resolve disagreements. *Moon in Leo.*

20 OCTOBER

Your values are likely to differ from those of someone close. You may find that a debt needs to be repaid or simply that your thoughts clash. It's a good time to establish common ground and find ways forward. *Moon enters Virgo.*

21 OCTOBER

The Virgo moon brings your practical, realistic side out, which will be useful if you find you are in hot water over a financial or personal matter. Take things one step at a time to build an outcome you can live with. *Moon in Virgo.*

22 OCTOBER

Key talks or financial transactions could bring a good result your way. If you're working you'll enjoy the sense you are creating abundance. Avoid gambling, both financially and emotionally, as it'll backfire. *Moon in Virgo.*

23 OCTOBER

As the sun enters passionate Scorpio you will feel more ardent over the next four weeks. This will be expressed more through your values and principles and how these translate into your financial and personal situations. Discussions about money and/or work could be fruitful; just avoid annoying someone in a position of power. Be tactful. *Moon in Libra.*

24 OCTOBER

A shared situation such as space at home or joint finances will merit careful attention to avoid making mistakes that could be costly. *Moon in Libra.*

25 OCTOBER

The partial solar eclipse in Scorpio will spotlight your finances as you may be drawn to look for news ways to budget or earn money or to share what you already have. Your self-esteem may be under the spotlight, so if you feel disappointed in someone or in yourself find ways to boost confidence such as through positive self-talk.

26 OCTOBER

You are likely to be feeling more emotionally invested in actions you take now, so ensure you remain grounded. Trust in your excellent communication skills, as they will not let you down. *Moon in Scorpio.*

27 OCTOBER

This is a good time to boost your work and financial circumstances, so take the time to talk to your employer if you'd like to make changes and circulate your resume if you're looking for work.

Just avoid pressuring someone into seeing life your way. Avoid emotional and financial gambling. *Moon enters Sagittarius.*

28 OCTOBER

A partner or someone else who is close such as a work colleague may broach topics you believed had been resolved. Find a way to move forward and encourage them to do the same. ***Moon in Sagittarius.***

29 OCTOBER

You like to see life in its most practical and, preferably, perfect version, so when disagreements arise or developments seem out of sync with how you see them it can be frustrating. Take a moment to gather your thoughts and avoid reacting purely emotionally to events. Be practical. ***Moon enters Capricorn.***

30 OCTOBER

The Capricorn moon will help you to get things done, especially at home and with family. Find time for yourself and to spend with someone you know has your back. ***Moon in Capricorn.***

31 OCTOBER

Happy Hallowe'en! You'll appreciate the opportunity to get down to brass tacks with domestic or personal matters and with areas in your life you share. Expect a quirky day – so nothing unusual for the day of the year! If you're unsure of a project or a person ensure you research the situation. ***Moon enters Aquarius.***

November

career   love   home   health   finance

1 NOVEMBER

You'll feel very strongly about a principle or financial matter, so it's important to maintain perspective. Today's Aquarian moon will help you to think outside the box. Someone close has your back, so ensure you bounce your ideas off them. *Moon in Aquarius.*

2 NOVEMBER

You're a good communicator but people can get the wrong end of the stick sometimes and make mistakes. A financial or personal matter is best handled carefully to avoid further errors or misunderstandings. Someone may need your help. An expert or adviser could be helpful to you, so reach out. *Moon enters Pisces.*

3 NOVEMBER

This is a good time to go over old ground, especially to do with a financial or personal matter. A contract or agreement may need to be rethought. Consider a meeting or a talk as ways forward. If you're considering a large financial outlay ensure you consult experts. *Moon in Pisces.*

4 NOVEMBER

You are an intuitive person, and when the moon is in Pisces as it is until later today you can trust your instincts. However, you may be easily misled, so ensure you have covered your bases if you're making key decisions. A friend or colleague will be an attentive listener if you need to discuss ideas. *Moon enters Aries.*

5 NOVEMBER

You can improve your circumstances, especially through careful communications. However, you may feel that a karmic situation needs to be undergone first. You may need to rectify a situation or someone needs to do the same for you. *Moon in Aries.*

6 NOVEMBER

You'll feel more dynamic about tackling difficult tasks, which will put you in a stronger position to gain the results you want. A reunion or a trip to a familiar place may bring emotions to the surface, so ensure you focus on the positives. *Moon in Aries.*

7 NOVEMBER

A financial or personal situation will merit careful focus. You must see that you need to negotiate terms and conditions that suit you better, otherwise you could put yourself in a position of difficulty or in an insecure or unpredictable situation. Find ways to gain more stability. *Moon in Taurus.*

8 NOVEMBER

The total lunar eclipse in Taurus will spotlight how you share resources such as finances and also space at home or duties and responsibilities. It's a good time to consider how these could be fairer without becoming obstinate. You may receive key news or undergo financial developments.

9 NOVEMBER

Expect a surprise unless you already experienced one yesterday. Be prepared to discuss developments, especially if they do not suit you. Find ways to break into a more stable situation by being flexible and adaptable to change. *Moon enters Gemini.*

10 NOVEMBER

You are generally a good communicator, but you may wonder if this is still the case. Focus on good interactions and you'll gain ground with your various projects, especially at work and financially. Check that you have not been seeing someone or a situation idealistically and make the necessary changes. Romance could blossom, so make a date. *Moon in Gemini.*

11 NOVEMBER

Be prepared to work hard for your goals. You can achieve a great deal by being practical and grounded. However, you may tend to be stubborn, especially with a work or financial matter, and this could keep you in a rut. Be adaptable without compromising your values. *Moon in Gemini.*

12 NOVEMBER

Key news could be uplifting, but if it shows just how easily you've been misled avoid feeling disappointed and find ways to move forward. Lovely meetings will raise spirits. You will be drawn to art, creativity, romance and lovely people. A spiritual interest could flourish this weekend. *Moon in Cancer.*

13 NOVEMBER

This is a good day for talks with family members and those you love. If you need to make important decisions, avoid making them impulsively. Find ways to be more grounded and practical. *Moon in Cancer.*

14 NOVEMBER

You'll appreciate the sense that certain people have a caring and nurturing nature, and this will fuel you with inspiration. *Moon enters Leo.*

15 NOVEMBER

This is an excellent day for making progress with someone special and with your work and personal plans. It's also a good time for talks with someone you have had a rough patch with. Developments may snowball, so ensure you're happy with circumstances as they will gain their own momentum. *Moon in Leo.*

16 NOVEMBER

This is a good day for talks, trips and visits and for putting new plans and ideas in gear. If you'd like to do some home renovations or a little DIY or simply improve domestic dynamics, this is it! You'll enjoy planning a holiday, unless you're already on one! *Moon in Leo.*

17 NOVEMBER

As Mercury enters the zodiac sign Sagittarius expect more focus to be on proactive talks and less on deep emotions. You may even feel you are turning a corner with some talks and relationships. You'll feel more inclined to be upbeat and outgoing in pursuit of adventure and discovery. *Moon in Virgo.*

18 NOVEMBER

This is a good time for get-togethers with friends and family, and if you're considering spending money on projects and people you love you are likely to invest well. *Moon in Virgo.*

19 NOVEMBER

You are in a busy phase, but if some projects have stalled avoid feeling too frustrated. This phase will give you space to rethink some of your ideas and strategies. Find the time for research as this will fuel your inspiration and give you time to invest more wisely in your ventures. ***Moon enters Libra.***

20 NOVEMBER

The moon in Libra engages your analytical and intellectual mind, which will be helpful with planning, financial budgets and getting things shipshape at work. A new look may appeal. ***Moon in Libra.***

21 NOVEMBER

You'll enjoy a trip or get-together and news will be uplifting. If you feel disappointed look at the positives, of which there are many. ***Moon enters Scorpio.***

22 NOVEMBER

The sun in Sagittarius for the next few weeks will put the focus firmly on travel, communications and adventure! You'll feel motivated to get things done and to be more outgoing with your big-picture plans. You may consider a holiday or updating digital devices so communications are better. ***Moon in Scorpio.***

23 NOVEMBER

The Sagittarian new moon signals you're ready to embrace something new, such as an adventure, fresh agreement or even a new relationship. If you are beginning a fresh project this moon suggests you will find the project takes you into exciting territory.

24 NOVEMBER

The moon in Sagittarius will contribute to a feeling of optimism in your personal life. It's a good time to boost relationships and communications. Consider being more adventurous in life. ***Moon in Sagittarius.***

25 NOVEMBER

A therapeutic and healing influence will help you to feel more enthusiastic about life. A trip, conversation or meeting could be uplifting. It's a good time to gain expert help or advice. Someone close may have good news for you. ***Moon enters Capricorn.***

26 NOVEMBER

This is another good day to find the help and support you need and to offer it to someone else. It's an especially good day to boost your relationships and well-being. A trip or talk could have a healing influence. ***Moon in Capricorn.***

27 NOVEMBER

A talk or meeting may involve an unusual circumstance. If you're involved in legal matters you may experience a surprise. Avoid impulsive decisions. ***Moon enters Aquarius.***

28 NOVEMBER

This is a good day for indulging in your favourite activities such as sports and spiritual interests. Meetings and discussions are likely to go well. You'll enjoy making plans that will involve positive outcomes. ***Moon in Aquarius.***

29 NOVEMBER

Talks and meetings are likely to be upbeat albeit feisty, so ensure you maintain perspective. A trip will take you to an old haunt and a meeting may be unexpected. You will manage to get through developments, so be positive. ***Moon in Aquarius.***

30 NOVEMBER

This is a good day for talks, meetings and get-togethers, especially to do with work and your home life. You could make a long-term commitment or arrangement. ***Moon in Pisces.***

December

career   love   home   health   finance

1 DECEMBER

Key talks and meetings will provide more clarity about logistics moving forward, especially at work and with your projects. A trip or venture such as study or a legal matter may reach a turning point. Avoid arguments and look for common ground if your opinions differ from those of someone you must collaborate with. ***Moon in Pisces.***

2 DECEMBER

This is a good day for discussions and travel, so if you have a meeting it's likely to go well. However, you may find some travel delays or even computer or technical glitches get in the way of a smoothly running day, so ensure you leave yourself plenty of time. ***Moon in Aries.***

3 DECEMBER

There are therapeutic aspects about this weekend, so a healing or restorative activity will be beneficial. You could get closer to someone and deepen ties, and they may be more liable to open up to you about what is on their mind. You may be helpful to them or will find help from someone else. ***Moon in Aries.***

4 DECEMBER

This is a good day for making changes to your environment, such as your home or garden. Avoid misunderstandings by being super clear and listening hard to others. *Moon enters Taurus.*

5 DECEMBER

The Taurus moon will bring out your practical abilities and you'll be able to get down to the basics of what must be done, making this a good time to organise both your own itinerary and that of others. *Moon in Taurus.*

6 DECEMBER

Communications and travel may be subject to delays and misunderstandings. A trip or meeting may need to be rescheduled. Back up computers to avoid losing information. *Moon enters Gemini.*

7 DECEMBER

This is a good time to focus on domestic, personal and family matters so that you can come to mutually agreeable arrangements. However, some communications will require more tact and diplomacy to ensure you can reach agreements. A change of circumstance is best handled one step at a time to avoid making waves. *Moon in Gemini.*

8 DECEMBER

The Gemini full moon spotlights a fresh chapter for you in a particular relationship, project or agreement. You could make rapid progress but must avoid rushing ventures and being pressured into making agreements you're unsure of. Take a moment to decide how you would like to see your future. Avoid snap decisions, but be spontaneous if a fresh opportunity arises.

9 DECEMBER

You'll enjoy being spontaneous and may receive an unexpected invitation or news. You'll see where some of your options and new opportunities could have positive outcomes. *Moon in Cancer.*

10 DECEMBER

This is another day to be careful with communications, especially those with someone close such as a family member, partner or house mate. You may simply want different things at the moment. Try to find common ground and work from there to create an understanding. *Moon in Cancer.*

11 DECEMBER

As Venus joins Mercury in Capricorn you'll express yourself in a more practical, grounded and realistic way, especially within a domestic or travel-related plan. But you must avoid obstinacy, and if someone close is behaving stubbornly gently encourage them to be more adaptable. *Moon enters Leo.*

12 DECEMBER

This is an excellent day for planning and moving ahead at work and with your projects in general. A clever agreement could provide the framework for a workable plan. *Moon in Leo.*

13 DECEMBER

The Leo moon brings your social and networking talents out and you'll enjoy spending time with someone you understand well. However, some of your interactions will benefit from more tact and diplomacy to smooth the way forward. Avoid being stubborn. *Moon in Leo.*

14 DECEMBER

Communications and travel may be subject to delays or mix-ups, so ensure you're super clear with your communications. Factor in extra time for travel to avoid being late. *Moon enters Virgo.*

15 DECEMBER

The moon in your sign will help you to be more practical and hands-on with domestic and personal developments. You'll feel more grounded and understanding of recent domestic changes. *Moon in Virgo.*

16 DECEMBER

Some of your activities and interests may clash with domestic duties, so it's a case of prioritising where you place your attention. You'll enjoy a reunion. *Moon enters Libra.*

17 DECEMBER

You'll enjoy spending time with someone whose company you cherish. They may be an upbeat and slightly unpredictable character. A change at home is likely to go well. You may configure a better way to share space or duties at home. *Moon in Libra.*

18 DECEMBER

This is a good time to deepen your understanding of someone close. A trip may be beneficial as a visit will help you to bond. However, a fundamental disagreement with someone is best approached philosophically. Someone may be super sensitive, so avoid bruising their ego. Someone may need your help or vice versa. *Moon in Libra.*

19 DECEMBER

You'd love to relax and enjoy a slow Sunday, but a trip or visit will take some of your focus from relaxation. Try to get chores out of the way earlier in the day so you can enjoy relaxing later. *Moon in Scorpio.*

20 DECEMBER

When the moon is in Scorpio you may experience stronger emotions, especially regarding your values and principles. You'll find kindred spirits support your ideas but must avoid provoking someone you know has alternative views. *Moon in Scorpio.*

21 DECEMBER

The solstice is a time of reflection when you can gather your wits as you assimilate your progress this year. You may enter a fresh phase at home, with family or a property. You're likely to feel more secure and stable but must still contend with a difference of opinion. Avoid being stubborn. Be open to change or a trip or new circumstance. *Moon in Sagittarius.*

22 DECEMBER

You'll enjoy a change of pace or of place. A fun event will promote a sense of Christmas spirit and you'll enjoy being spontaneous and spending time with like-minded people. *Moon in Sagittarius.*

23 DECEMBER

The new moon and supermoon in Capricorn signals a fresh start for you in a domestic context. You may enjoy feeling you have created something new, or can bring more security into your personal life. You may begin a new chapter regarding family or someone close. It's a good day to make a commitment at work or in your personal life.

24 DECEMBER

You'll enjoy being with people who inspire you and who bring you a sense of togetherness. A creative, romantic, music-fuelled day will raise spirits. This is a romantic day for many Virgos, which you'll enjoy. *Moon in Capricorn.*

25 DECEMBER

Merry Christmas! You'll enjoy doing something different this year or will be with a new set of people. You may simply wish to strike out on your own in different circumstances. You'll enjoy a reunion or hearing from someone unexpectedly. *Moon in Aquarius.*

26 DECEMBER

A change of pace or in your environment will add a fresh tone to your usual Christmas. If you're missing someone you will gain the chance to be with people who are like-minded, which will be a treat. ***Moon in Aquarius.***

27 DECEMBER

This is a good day for get-togethers. If you're back at work there will be positives about the day you have, which you'll enjoy. ***Moon in Pisces.***

28 DECEMBER

This is an excellent day for romance and seasonal treats. You'll enjoy immersing yourself in music, good company, the arts, creativity and fine food. Try to get important paperwork completed before Mercury turns retrograde tomorrow. ***Moon in Pisces.***

29 DECEMBER

A reunion and the chance to reconnect with yourself will be a real treat. You may return to an old haunt or will receive key news from someone special. ***Moon in Aries.***

30 DECEMBER

A domestic matter is best treated carefully to avoid impulsive decisions. You may be travelling or returning to a favourite place. Avoid feeling too flustered by delays or frustrations. ***Moon in Aries.***

31 DECEMBER

Happy New Year! You'll enjoy the feeling of moving forward this New Year's Eve. Some lovely meetings and news will raise your spirits. ***Moon enters Taurus.***

LIBRA

23 September - 23 October

THE ESSENCE OF LIBRA

Your sign's symbol of the scales represents your wish for a balanced, harmonious and peaceful life. The scales tend to dip up and down – sometimes gently and sometimes quite severely – thus you can experience life as being disruptive and unbalanced. However, you are equipped to steady the scales and find balance when it is needed.

Many people with a strong Libran signature in their astrology chart have a heart- or round-shaped face with a pleasing form that invokes the notion of calmness and beauty. This is because Venus, the planet that rules Libra, bestows beauty on you both inside and out. Venus is also the planet that rules love and money, which are important to you: not only as currency to interact with other people but also as objects of desire. Your desire for love is strong, so you are unlikely to be a loner. Your desire for comfort and pleasant surroundings is equally as strong, so you are unlikely to live in a home that is ugly or worn down. To attain love and money you'll actively seek loving relationships and work hard to get the money to buy the comfort you need in life.

Venus rules art, music and all things related to beauty, so you are artistically inclined. You may enjoy good food and drink and must avoid overindulgence in all things that can be overindulged in: from money to sex to food to drink, from comfort to work to chocolate and social media.

Because you are constantly looking for balance in life you can be indecisive. You'll vacillate from one idea to the next, unable to make up your mind. This is a true pitfall for Librans but one that can be overcome by considering the practicalities first up and then meshing these with your ideals. Mix realities and dreams together and add a sprinkle of intuition and you will make the right decisions to excel in life.

SELF-ESTEEM

You need to feel passionate about your activities and beliefs in order to feel you are making a bold statement so that you gain a sense of achievement. Beneath your calm exterior rages a great deal of emotion and drive. Your passionate approach to life is revealed in your desire for relationships: the more passionate your romantic relationships are the more you'll feel you have accomplished a goal and the more you will feel fulfilled.

You will feel complete through relationships. Sometimes, though, your inner passion can boil over into tempers and tantrums – not necessarily in you, but in the people you surround yourself with or those you attract who seem to complement your inner drive. You will rely on your natural ability to create charm and for harmonising circumstances and act as a mediator and peacemaker.

Your self-esteem is contingent on feeling needed, not only by a partner but also by children, workmates and friends. You feel needed when you are seen as being the problem solver, the channel of reason and intellect. You also need to feel desired, so beauty in all its forms really does appeal to you as a way to boost self-esteem. The time you may spend perfecting your own looks isn't vanity but a ritual to make you feel more desirable.

Your self-esteem will be enhanced by feeling you have worked hard and developed a certain degree of luxury, but if you pursue money, luxury and relationships purely as goals you will fail to see the beauty in the essence of love and comfort. Your constant desire for desire itself can lead to a truly unfulfilled life unless you understand that the essence of beauty is love.

YOUR INNER LIFE

As an air sign you do think a great deal, to the extent that you can overthink your circumstances. Constantly weighing up your options until you no longer see any perspective in what you do is the source of some of your indecision. You also have a predilection for being easily misled because your mind is caught up in pros and cons rather than in planning and strategy, although you are aware of this. Your indecision can be crippling to the extent that nothing moves forward in your life.

To banish your fear of making the wrong decision it's important to break decisions down into bite-sized pieces. Aim to develop strong instincts and listen to your intuition, because relying purely on rationality can prevent you from taking meaningful action.

Your love for art and beauty in all its many forms, from flowers, music and romance to film and creativity, feeds your soul.

HOW OTHERS SEE YOU

You are a peacemaker and mediator, but beneath this exterior can lie a great deal of self-analysis and critique of the world around you that churns in your mind. You have perfected the art of external beauty and calmness, yet when people see the passion within it can come as a surprise. This is all well and good when the passion is expressed in positive ways, but sometimes when the volcano that smoulders just beneath your skin erupts in tempers and outbursts it can shock those close to you. Luckily you have charm on your side, and the object of your love attention is likely to be easily seduced by your Venusian qualities of beauty and outer calm.

In your quest for beauty you may be seen as being vain and self-absorbed, although to you this quest is undertaken purely so you are more desired. Likewise, your quest for money and comfort is simply an outward expression of your wish to be surrounded by beauty. Others may see you as being egotistical in your desire to be physically beautiful.

There is a cold, calculating element inherent in Venus, the Roman goddess of love after whom the planet is named. We usually associate Venus with love, beauty, sex, fertility and victory, although Venus was born from a violent altercation between her father and grandfather.

You can be cold, remote and calculating if people get on the wrong side of you. This is an element of Libra that you would be the first to deny, yet as you are an air sign ruled by Venus there is no doubt that your head can sometimes rule your heart. Other people admire your ability to think clearly, to cut through murky or imprecise talk to provide clarity and a level-headed appraisal. This ability to step back and provide perspective when the chips are down will surprise those who have been caught in the Libran web of charm.

A real pitfall for you is that you are adept at making decisions for others but not so much for yourself, as your objectivity can be clouded by your strong emotions, desires and passions. It's important to actively seek a calm mind through activities such as meditation.

HOW TO MAXIMISE YOUR POTENTIAL

To feel that you are moving forward in life and are not simply a harmoniser, balancing force and mediator for everyone else it's important to banish your fear of making the wrong decision by developing your intuition. When you combine your intuition with your keen intellect you will not only receive inner wisdom and celestial guidance, but you will also be crystal clear on which choices to make. A strong rational mind is there to guide you along with your strong intuition. Use your potent rational mind when your passionate desires take over and cloud your judgement.

When you manifest your best qualities of calmness, peace and balance you will gain superpowers that lead to the love, meaning and beauty you so crave in life.

LIBRA AND ITS ASCENDANTS

This chapter is about your sun sign, Libra, and your predictions for the year ahead. The more you know about yourself the better you will be able to take advantage of opportunities, and also avoid the pitfalls. It's critical to know as much about 'you' as possible.

In astrology your core self is represented by your sun sign, but your personality traits are represented by your ascendant (also known as your rising sign). The ascendant describes your personality, the way other people see you on first meeting you and the way you tend to filter life's events.

When you have intimate knowledge about your sun sign – your engine room or core being – you will be on the way to a happier life. When you add the knowledge about your personality – your ascendant – you will gain even deeper insight into what makes you tick.

Your ascendant sign is determined by the time of your birth on the date and year of your birth. Because the ascendant sign changes approximately every two hours, the best way to determine it is to ask an astrologer to calculate it for you. Certain apps will also calculate your ascendant sign (see page 873).

The following gives you more information about your abilities, characteristics and personality according to your sun sign Libra in combination with your ascendant sign.

LIBRA SUN SIGN WITH ARIES ASCENDANT

This can be a tricky combination, as your dynamism and brashness seem contradictory to your wish for peace and harmony. You can be impulsive rather than calm. There is inner tension between wishing to see the world as an ideal, beautiful place and wishing to be a dominant effective force, and the two approaches don't always meet in the middle. Your positive traits of being energetic, an independent thinker and bold are strong, but so too are your negative traits of impulsiveness, recklessness and bossiness. Aim to boost your favourable traits of patience and a balanced outlook with diligence, perseverance, loyalty and reason for the best results.

LIBRA SUN SIGN WITH TAURUS ASCENDANT

This is a combination made for love! Both Libra and Taurus are ruled by Venus, bringing your need for love, relationships, desire and comfort into sharp focus. You are unlikely to be single for extended periods and will enjoy the sensuality inherent in relationships. You love spending time with like-minded people and visiting beautiful places, have a keen eye for art and design and will appreciate fashion, poetry, film, dance and music.

The pitfalls with this sun sign and ascendant combination can be that you tend towards overindulgence because you love the good things in life and can be lazy. You may need to self-motivate more than some other signs, so take this into account if you ever feel your life is in a rut.

LIBRA SUN SIGN WITH GEMINI ASCENDANT

You are a double air sign, quick thinking and needing mental stimulation to avoid being bored. You are a mercurial character with many different forms of expression. You may be seen as being constantly on the go, fidgety, restless and hard to pin down. You can be overtly analytical and must learn to earth yourself in practicalities to avoid obsessive thoughts. You may be particularly attracted to people who are intense and sensual and who wish to settle into a routine but then you also wish to retain your individuality, which can be confusing for those you befriend.

LIBRA SUN SIGN WITH CANCER ASCENDANT

You are a force to be reckoned with, a strong character who can be stubborn if crossed. Your strong will may come as a surprise, especially as you are seen as being gentle and have a love for music, art, reading, writing and romance. Your inner resourcefulness and ability to stand your ground may be quite the surprise to those who get to know you better. Your Cancerian personality is as sensitive as your Libran core, and you may have artistic or psychic abilities. Combine this with your search for peace and harmony in life and you really are a gentle, perceptive yet strong and determined character.

LIBRA SUN SIGN WITH LEO ASCENDANT

Your fiery and bold exterior belies a much gentler yet more determined, steadfast and diligent character underneath. Your personality is very much the Leo type: preferring to be the centre of attention but also being a loving, generous and creative character. The Leo dynamic is able to overcome immense hurdles and is the king of the jungle. Your more negative traits are self-absorption, obstinacy and an inability to see other people's viewpoints, and you can be a powerful and disrespectful enemy. Channel your fiery energy into productive pursuits or the fighter in you will emerge, which will not only create trouble in your life but also inner tension as the Libra core wishes for peace and harmony above all else.

LIBRA SUN SIGN WITH VIRGO ASCENDANT

You are a natural-born healer in the sense of wishing to make the world a better place. Many Virgo-ascendant people are healers in the broader term, working in the medical and health fields; many are also drawn to teaching. The Virgo ascendant with Libra sun sign can lead to careful work that executes a perfect outcome, but sometimes this mix can lead to overly high expectations and a lack of self-belief. Aim for realistic and peaceful goals, even if they are far from the perfection you are looking for. You make a supportive partner and are a hard worker.

LIBRA SUN SIGN WITH LIBRA ASCENDANT

You are a double Libra and as such are doubly motivated to look for peace and harmony in your life. Whether or not you find it depends on the actions you take and if you can overcome indecision. Find ways to be practical and believe that the choices you make are for the best, even if there are mistakes along the way. As a double air sign you use your mind; your analytical brain tends to make the tough calls. This can lead to missteps, as your intuition is the inner compass that will always guide you to the right choices. Take time to get in touch with your invaluable intuition and allow it to lead you along life's path.

LIBRA SUN SIGN WITH SCORPIO ASCENDANT

Your outwardly charismatic and passionate demeanour belies a calm and intellectual mind. You initially appear to be an emotional, charming and even magnetic character often physically attractive and outgoing, yet your inner core is harnessed by your mind and not your passions. You may attract people who are drama magnets or you are a drama magnet yourself. Luckily your reason will steer you clear of the self-destructive behaviour associated with Scorpio rising, but you will nevertheless be attracted to highly emotional relationships, passionate pursuits and potentially extreme self-expression. On the plus side this is a supremely creative combination, and you'll find great expression in art, music and sport.

LIBRA SUN SIGN WITH SAGITTARIUS ASCENDANT

You're an adventurous and outgoing character likely to enjoy sport and physical activity, although your inner core is more attuned to art, music and creativity. You'll enjoy combining all of your interests through quiet times spent relaxing and undertaking musical, sporty and adventurous breaks. You are honest and can be blunt yet your inner core looks for harmony, diplomacy and tact, so you may be surprised at times by your own brash or upfront behaviour. In relationships you will wish to retain a sense of independence but will be diplomatic about it. You prefer a partner who is talkative and outgoing and has an appreciation for art and music.

LIBRA SUN SIGN WITH CAPRICORN ASCENDANT

You may be seen as being cautious, committed and reliable. You are level headed and tend to be a hard worker. In relationships you are loyal, trustworthy and earnest unless you have aspects in your astrology chart that indicate otherwise. You may seem slow to commit, yet once in a relationship you are unlikely to stray as you are loyal. You can be an uncompromising soul, which doesn't leave much room for spontaneity in interpersonal relationships. Partners will appreciate the settled nature of your character.

LIBRA SUN SIGN WITH AQUARIUS ASCENDANT

This is a quirky combination, and one where you may be seen as a trendsetter and innovator. You are a thinker, although you can be impulsive. You will work to a plan to the extent of sometimes

being seen as manipulative. You are certainly tenacious, until you tire of a plan and move on to the next one. Being analytical, you seem devoid of emotion at times (depending on your moon sign) and can be cold. However, your feelings run deep and you wish for a better world.

LIBRA SUN SIGN WITH PISCES ASCENDANT

You are a philosopher, dreamer and idealist: a genuine artist. Despite being a true creative you are also able to function in the real world, making money and building a strong foundation from which to launch your wonderful interests and ideas. You have a keen, practical mind that allows your imagination to take flight so you are unlikely to lose touch with reality, even when deep in the creative process. You make a loving and supportive partner despite being easily distracted and tending to let your mind wander. Your creativity enriches your life and that of your family.

LIBRA IN LOVE

You are on such a quest for love and balance, Libra, you actively search for the right partner. In this section you can check out your compatibility with other sun signs. Remember that we are all complex individuals, so the more you know about someone's astrological birth chart the better you can determine your compatibility. Consider having your astrological birth chart compared with that of a partner, friend or family member, as the compatibility – known as 'synastry' in astrology – goes even deeper than a comparison of sun signs, although this is a good place to begin.

LIBRA WITH ARIES

Aries and Libra will attract each other, but there is a predisposition in this match for disharmony principally because the Aries drive is at odds with what Libra desires. You will each frequently need and crave very different things in life and from each other; however, some matches thrive on a little tension and you may enjoy the fact that you must constantly keep up with each other's interests and projects, regularly feeding each other what you need. You are coming from different corners of the ring, and if you can meet in the middle you may find the rainbow at the end of the day.

LIBRA WITH TAURUS

Two very sensual and earthy individuals can make merry music together and are a great match, because you both love and appreciate the importance of having strong values and like to indulge in the good things in life such as food and comfort. However, you can both be predisposed towards stubbornness and deadlocks can develop unless you are able to focus on your common ground and on establishing solid foundations in the relationship. Depending on other planetary placements at the time of your birth, this combination can bring out either your worst characteristics or your best. If you are two individuals who are consciously working on being the best version of yourselves it can be a successful combination, but if you're not conscious of your worst attributes such as laziness and overindulgence the combination could be dissatisfying.

LIBRA WITH GEMINI

These two air signs will come together in mutual and everlasting understanding and harmony. Occasionally the spark necessary for romance to ignite will be missing, as too much air in a relationship can mean too much room to miss each other's relevance and extra effort to nurture the relationship may be needed. This relationship may become a companionship and less of a romantic liaison, although you are fundamentally compatible and the combo will have less drama and stress than some relationships as both individuals give each other freedom of movement.

LIBRA WITH CANCER

This is a double cardinal match, and while both these sun signs appear on the surface to be soft, gentle characters both will wish to take the lead. They will do so in different ways: the Cancerian will wish to be heard emotionally and be emotionally fulfilled, while the Libran will wish to be respected and to find peace and harmony. As both signs can be indecisive and constantly looking for emotional and mental support from each other, this match can tend to fall flat. This can be tiring, especially when both are looking for personal fulfilment from the other rather than from themselves or in their life. If the Cancerian has strong air in their chart and the Libran strong water, this match could work.

LIBRA WITH LEO

There is a fundamental match here: fire needs air to exist and air appreciates the excitement of fire! You provide your Leo partner with the analysis, intellect and reason they appreciate, and your Leo supplies you with the motivation you thrive on. You will appreciate your Leo partner's ability to take action, to initiate activities and feel excited about life, and your Leo partner will appreciate your ability to analyse and plan. You complement each other on many levels.

LIBRA WITH VIRGO

You are both likely to admire each other. Your Virgo partner will admire the fact you are a good thinker and conversations are likely to be lively, while you'll admire your Virgo partner's ability to be rational and analytical and also their penchant for creating beauty in their environment. However, there may be that special spark missing in this relationship unless you both make the effort to ignite passion in your love life and unless you have other aspects in your astrology chart that point to passion. Another real pitfall here is that you are both a little indecisive and may not be able to commit to a relationship that fulfils both partners in equal measures. If you look for that special spark you may be able to ignite it.

LIBRA WITH LIBRA

This is a lovely relationship for friendship and companionship but may lack the spark of passion necessary for romance. You are both rational, analytical characters who need a little fire to drive romance. In addition, you can both be indecisive and may be unwilling to commit to a relationship that lacks passion. It can be a fulfilling relationship if you have fire elements in your astrology charts as you are both looking for peace and harmony, although you may need to work hard at finding it.

LIBRA WITH SCORPIO

This is a romantic connection because the fire and passion in the Scorpio will most certainly appeal to your romantic Libran soul, while your peaceful, calm and balanced persona will complement the Scorpio passion. But will it last? You are likely to need each other, but this combo can lapse into co-dependency and you may therefore feel needy or unfulfilled. If you both work on self-fulfilment as opposed to seeking fulfilment from each other the relationship does have room to grow.

LIBRA WITH SAGITTARIUS

This is a fun-loving, upbeat, romantic pairing and has what it takes to be a fulfilling and mutually respectful relationship. The outgoing adventurousness of the Sagittarian and their larger-than-life personality will appeal as a counterpoint to your gentle, peace-loving approach. Together you will seek new experiences and be unafraid to step into new territory to discover life's riches. Together you will gain wisdom from being in a fulfilling relationship, so this combination is likely to be long lasting as you both seek depth in your experiences.

LIBRA WITH CAPRICORN

You may appear to be a match as you are both self-effacing, diligent and patient and you feel that quality is important via luxury, money and status, but there is a fundamental clash: you are both strong characters under your quiet and unassuming personalities and each is unlikely to play second fiddle to the other. You also approach life's challenges differently: Librans tend to analyse and then act whereas Capricorns will sense and feel your way through challenges. You are likely to reach different conclusions, which can lead to arguments. If you are both excellent at conflict resolution it can be a good match.

LIBRA WITH AQUARIUS

You both have a search for happiness in common: Librans are looking for balance in life and Aquarians are looking for a better world. This makes for a good match as long as you both appreciate that you tend to go about your goals very differently. You are fun loving and can be quirky, especially in each other's company, but you both have a deadly serious side that can kick in at a moment's notice. As long as you are in sync with your moods and momentarily serious at the same time it can be a lovely match.

LIBRA WITH PISCES

This is a romantic relationship and one that could be fulfilling, especially if you both express your artistic, creative attributes freely. The Piscean imagination and keen philosophising will appeal to you, but ultimately Pisceans may display less get up and go than you prefer in a partnership. This relationship will flourish best when founded on shared interests, so if there are none then you can seek common ground by making the effort to establish strong foundations.

THE YEAR AHEAD FOR LIBRA

Affirmation: *'I will excel as I build up resilience to change.'*

Considerable changes at home and in your personal life will merit careful focus this year. So, too, will health and well-being. The more you can boost your fitness on all levels – spiritual, mental, emotional and physical – the better for you, as you may find the year resembles a fitness challenge or obstacle course if you're not at peak fitness.

If you've been considering making wide-ranging changes such as a move or travel this is the year you're likely to embrace these projects. You will need to check that those your plans affect are all on board. If not there could be some tough calls to make, not only in the realm of compromise but also prospectively if no common ground can be found in the realm of taking separate paths.

The eclipses will be across your shared concerns such as joint finances, duties and responsibilities and, for later-born Librans such as those born in mid-October, your personal life. So it's the year to work out how to divide chores and assets, investments and resources equally and fairly among those you share responsibilities with.

As someone seeking balance, fair play and harmony you do like to feel you're a progressive person, and early in the year you'll gain insight into whether it's your home life or work or both that must provide more room to be creative and gain a more fulfilling life.

January, May and June will be months of major change, and from there until the end of August you'll gain a sense of direction even if you know already that making key changes in your life will be arduous. It will most likely be necessary but will be worth the effort.

In the second half of the year a busy time will put greater focus on how to collaborate and get on with significant people in your life. However, the eclipse season from October to November will once again demand that you're careful with your business and personal relationships, as doing so will enable you to make valid, long-term decisions.

HEALTH

It's a good time to state the intention to make health and well-being your priority in 2022. Chiron, the asteroid named after the Greek centaur, will be in your health zone all year if you were born in September, providing you with the opportunity to boost this important aspect of your life. For October Librans there will be more focus on the health of a partner or simply of the health of a key relationship.

In the second half of the year you may find that energy levels flag if you have overworked or overinvested in projects earlier in the year, so ensure you pay it forward in terms of your energy levels so you do not tire yourself out and must drag yourself through the last few months of the year.

There will be a great deal of change this year that will draw on your resilience, so opt for fitness training that builds stamina.

April will be a particularly busy month that will merit more care and attention to health and fitness. It will also provide the opportunity to seek expert health advice and to begin a new

schedule. A holiday at this time may be enjoyable but must fit into your work schedule.

You are liable to overwork this year so ensure you avoid taking on too much, especially in April to June. The end of July and early August could be ideal for a short break or simply to reconvene and check your health schedule is on track.

Beauty is important to you, and the end of August through to the end of the year will be ideal for adopting a new look or exploring a fresh wardrobe.

In terms of rushing too much and minor accidents, aim to slow down at the end of September and early October to avoid bumps and scratches.

Emotionally and work-wise, September through to the end of the year could bring significant developments, so look at your options carefully and avoid exhausting yourself.

FINANCES

There will be financial ups and downs this year, although the extent will depend to a large degree on your financial management in the past. If you've already created a slush fund all the better for you, but if you've entered into debt your arrangement may need focus now and especially concerning property, shared investments and joint projects.

Developments at work or concerning your personal life in the first two months will give you the heads-up about what is possible later in the year regarding investments and changes to your daily life that will affect your finances.

The eclipses in April-May and October-November will spotlight whether you have over-invested or, contrarily, under-invested in an area of your life or if a gamble you've made in the past will pay off.

You will feel enthused in 2022 to invest more of your time, energy and money into projects that have a deeper meaning for you than money alone, so be guided by what makes you happy and not only by what could make you rich.

Changes in your career and/or daily routine in May suggest you avoid impulsive investments, even if the tide seems to turn your way. Instead of reacting month by month to events, decide early on in the year to establish a stable financial plan to help you weather any storms and manage bonanzas realistically.

The eclipse on 16 May will spotlight important negotiations and the chance to alter how you share your funds with someone important. For some Librans there could be major developments at work or due to health matters.

HOME LIFE

Your home life will be the scene of considerable change in 2022. Consider how you'd like it to develop and put plans in place early in the year. If you need the co-operation of those you live with or of family and a partner, it's important to make agreements that will stick through good times and bad.

If you're making important changes to your home such as renovation or even a move, ensure your finances are secure. Various developments in 2022 could mean significant sums of money will pass through your fingers, so ensure these are sufficient for your plans for domestic developments. You may gain insight in January as to what kind of support, both moral and financial, your domestic plans will receive and may have to adjust your plans accordingly.

The times of the year that may be particularly stressful at home will be mid-February, mid-May, mid-June and November, so try to plan important moves or developments at other times of the year.

Positive times for making changes at home will be from January to May, although you may find emotions are exaggerated at this time so aim to keep things on an even keel. In mid-February you will gain insight into the best way forward domestically with family or someone close. Be prepared to make changes.

If you work from home you may need to restructure where duties rest in the various areas of your house, and leaving domestic issues at the kitchen sink as you enter the office would be wise.

You may find developments with family and/or at work dictate that developments at home must be catered to.

LOVE

Someone in your close proximity may already be behaving irrationally or erratically. Together you may simply be restless and looking for new ways to enjoy life or to broaden horizons. Flashpoints for key change in this scenario will be January, the end of February, mid-March and August through to October. If you wish to keep your love life on an even keel ensure you navigate through these hotspots carefully.

Singles may find that lovers seem to be unpredictable or on-again, off-again this year, so if you're looking for a commitment ensure you are clear about this early in the relationship.

The first quarter will be the most romantic this year and will provide ample opportunity to get close to someone special and for singles to look for amorous company, if not to find 'the one'. Travel or meeting up with people in fresh territory could open doors to new and exciting ways to connect.

The eclipse seasons in April-May and October-November will once again demand that you're careful about your business and personal relationships, as doing so will enable you to make valid, long-term decisions.

CAREER

There will be key financial developments this year, so unless these come about because of changes in your personal circumstances such as single to married these are likely to be due to events at work or at home because of a move or renovation, for example.

January is a good time to take stock of where your priorities lie work-wise and regarding family. How much time do you wish to spend throughout the year on work and how much on children, a partner or family? Aim to spare time for those you love or this year could become one you remember for having lost valuable time.

The full moon in Cancer on 17 January will spotlight which projects and career path will suit you best. Avoid making assumptions about potential outcomes; do your financial calculations and stick with the facts.

A great deal of focus will be on your home life and personal life this year, so keeping your work and career up and running may take extra focus. Luckily, Jupiter in your work zone until early May will keep you focused and may also bring in wonderful new opportunities. Keep an eye out for developments in mid-April, in particular, as these could be ideal, but you must check details and avoid making assumptions.

Work-wise, the eclipse season in October-November will once again ask that you're careful about your business and financial decisions, as doing so will enable you to make valid, long-term decisions.

January

career love home health finance

Notes: the pie charts such as the one above listed for each month show energy distribution according to the stars for the month ahead. If you wish to make changes in the areas of your finances, health, career, love or home and you see there is a large amount of energy in that sector in the chart, your endeavours should succeed as long as you have prepared well in advance. The charts also show which areas will potentially have the most focus in your life during the month.

The moon sign listed for each day's entry in the diary is the position of the moon at the end of the day in Greenwich Mean Time (GMT). To gain the most information about a particular day's circumstances, read the day before and the day after for a complete picture.

1 JANUARY

Happy New Year! You'll enjoy the diversity of company you have and you may be pleasantly surprised by a visit or call. A change at home will be enjoyable. *Moon enters Capricorn.*

2 JANUARY

The new moon and super moon in Capricorn will kick-start a fresh phase for you in a personal context, such as a fresh chapter at home, with family or in a different property. You may enjoy considering new ways to improve communications, such as updating devices or even a vehicle.

3 JANUARY

You'll appreciate the sense that you can create more stability and security at home and feel more relaxed. You may enjoy venturing out into fresh domain as a trip or visit takes you somewhere new. *Moon enters Aquarius.*

4 JANUARY

A change of pace or of place at home or with family will merit a patient approach, as the alteration in tempo may be a little unsettling. Aim to find ways to soothe nerves. *Moon in Aquarius.*

5 JANUARY

This is a good day for a change of pace or of place. You may enjoy entering a fresh environment via a trip or welcoming someone new into your home. If you've had visitors and they've now left you'll enjoy having space to yourself. *Moon in Aquarius.*

6 JANUARY

The Pisces moon tends to put your focus on romance, family and children. If you're artistic you'll appreciate the opportunity to indulge a little more in creativity. *Moon in Pisces.*

7 JANUARY

You'll enjoy a romantic end to the week, so if you have nothing planned yet organise a treat! However, you or someone close may be more forgetful than usual, so keep an eye on details. You won't automatically get on with everyone so take things one step at a time. Avoid misplacing valuables such as keys. *Moon in Pisces.*

8 JANUARY

This is a good day to invest in yourself and those you love such as family and friends. You may wish to spend some money on your home décor or on a change of scenery. If you're shopping, you may spy a bargain but must avoid overspending as you'll regret it. *Moon in Aries.*

9 JANUARY

A get-together at home or with family will be enjoyable. If you're drawn to DIY this is a good time to invest in your home décor to include a little more luxury in your life. *Moon in Aries.*

10 JANUARY

You won't always agree with everyone in your life, so be philosophical about a difference of opinion. You may have super-high expectations of someone, so ensure you remain realistic. *Moon enters Taurus.*

11 JANUARY

Today is a mixed bag, as you'll appreciate a change of pace but may also tend to be annoyed by a different pace that will take a little while to get used to. Take things one step at a time for the best measure. *Moon in Taurus.*

12 JANUARY

The moon in Taurus brings out your appreciation of luxury, sensuality and someone special. You'll enjoy investing in your home life and ensuring you have all the creature comforts you need. *Moon in Taurus.*

13 JANUARY

A shared situation may require a little more focus to ensure you're all on the same path, be this at home or at work. A little tact and diplomacy will work wonders. Try to get key paperwork and financial matters resolved before Mercury turns retrograde tomorrow to avoid delays over the next few weeks. *Moon in Gemini.*

14 JANUARY

You may receive key news to do with family, finances or someone close. Someone may surprise you. Take a moment to digest information before jumping to conclusions. Avoid gambling, both financially and emotionally. *Moon in Gemini.*

15 JANUARY

The moon at the zenith of your chart will put your emotions centre stage, and you may be feeling a little conflicted about a development. Find the time to discuss developments so you can get on top of things. *Moon enters Cancer.*

16 JANUARY

Key news or a meeting will be intense, so ensure you are ready for something big! For some this will be a romantic development, and if you're artistic you'll feel super creative. If you are disappointed find ways to process developments in a positive way. *Moon in Cancer.*

17 JANUARY

The Cancerian full moon will spotlight a change in your general direction or even status. This may be due to developments in your personal life or at home. Key changes will mean you must consider the big picture. Base decisions on practicalities and avoid allowing emotions to overwhelm your reason.

18 JANUARY

The moon in Cancer will encourage you to think intuitively about your circumstances, which will enable you to make informed decisions. As the moon steps into Leo you may feel a little more feisty and will wish to take action where more recently you have been reluctant to do so. Choose your actions wisely. ***Moon in Leo.***

19 JANUARY

This is a good day to discuss domestic matters and for meetings. If you're making changes at home or with family you will manage to get a lot done. A trip or talk could be transformative. ***Moon in Leo.***

20 JANUARY

The sun in Aquarius for the next four weeks will encourage you to be more adventurous in your personal life and at home. You may be ready to try something new in a personal relationship, especially if you recently hit a speed bump. ***Moon in Leo.***

21 JANUARY

When the moon is in Virgo it will bring your more practical and realistic sides out, which will enable you to make reasonable decisions. However, you may also feel a little stubborn with someone special, so ensure you are adapting to new circumstances well. ***Moon in Virgo.***

22 JANUARY

You'll appreciate the sense you are getting on better with someone close. A reunion or a little DIY at home is likely to go well. You'll enjoy receiving a visitor. ***Moon enters Libra.***

23 JANUARY

You may be drawn to return to an old haunt or to reconsider your domestic decisions and circumstances. A change at home could make you nostalgic or, alternatively, will convince you your decisions are correct. ***Moon in Libra.***

24 JANUARY

When the moon is in your sign you tend to feel more at peace with who you are. If you have a habit of being indecisive you may feel more so now, so ensure you have all the facts at your fingertips before making important decisions. If you are very proficient at decision-making you'll feel all the more convinced you're on the right track. ***Moon in Libra.***

25 JANUARY

This is a good time for a get-together and meetings and for domestic changes. Someone may wish to discuss their feelings more than usual and you'll lend an ear. ***Moon in Scorpio.***

26 JANUARY

Conversations and family matters may seem to go over old ground, but you will gain the opportunity to make some recent decisions more practical and actionable. *Moon in Scorpio.*

27 JANUARY

An upbeat approach to finances and to the people you share your home with will contribute to a more optimistic outlook. If you're investing in your home or in a project ensure you have adequately researched your situation. *Moon in Sagittarius.*

28 JANUARY

You'll enjoy feeling more proactive and outgoing, perhaps as the weekend begins. However, it's a good time to ensure your plans for the weekend are secure, so consider double-checking the arrangements. *Moon in Sagittarius.*

29 JANUARY

Key news or developments at home or in your personal life will merit careful attention. You may return to an old haunt or reunite with someone close and bond over important matters. *Moon in Capricorn.*

30 JANUARY

An unpredictable character will behave true to form. You may hear unexpected news or will need to adapt to an unusual circumstance. *Moon in Capricorn.*

31 JANUARY

This is a lovely day for talks and meetings. If you're making changes at home or in your personal life you'll appreciate the results of your actions. A trip may be enjoyable. *Moon in Aquarius.*

February

career love home health finance

1 FEBRUARY

The new moon in Aquarius will spotlight new ideas and innovative plans for your home, property or family. It's a good time to think outside the square but also to be realistic and practical about changes, especially concerning someone else.

2 FEBRUARY

You'll feel inspired to follow your instincts, especially at work and with someone special in your family. Creative Librans will be particularly inspired. You'll be drawn to art, music and dancing and may be super intuitive, so trust your instincts. ***Moon enters Pisces.***

3 FEBRUARY

This is a good time to devote to yourself, so look for ways to feel more invested in your daily routine. It's a good time for a health and well-being appointment, and if you're spiritually minded to gain a deeper understanding of yourself and others. ***Moon in Pisces.***

4 FEBRUARY

You may be ready to make an agreement with someone about a domestic, personal or financial matter. Just double-check details, especially if signing paperwork. Agreements made now could bring more stability and security your way. ***Moon in Pisces.***

5 FEBRUARY

When the moon is in Aries you may find that people are a little more feistier than usual and that you need to adjust to their moods and outspokenness. Avoid arguments but find fun ways to channel emotions into activities you all enjoy. *Moon in Aries.*

6 FEBRUARY

Find the time to ask for collaboration and support with your various projects and ideas, as working together and enjoying time together will feel fulfilling. Avoid being at counterpoint with someone who can be feisty. Try to establish common, peaceful ground instead. *Moon in Aries.*

7 FEBRUARY

You'll feel your collaborations and relationships can gain a more even keel. Be realistic and practical and take things one step at a time, especially with someone who can be unpredictable. *Moon in Taurus.*

8 FEBRUARY

A trip or unscheduled meeting will be uplifting, so find the time to meet someone whose company you enjoy as you'll be glad you did! Someone may surprise you. *Moon in Taurus.*

9 FEBRUARY

When the moon is in Gemini, as it is today, your analytical mind kicks into action and you may find you are better able to make decisions. If, however, you are uncertain about particular choices, this is a good time to seek information and/or advice. *Moon enters Gemini.*

10 FEBRUARY

You'll appreciate finding the time for a health or beauty treat. Romance or the chance to enjoy music, fun and time with someone special will appeal. *Moon in Gemini.*

11 FEBRUARY

A key meeting or news at home about property or family could signal important developments to do with someone special. A trip could bring you in touch with someone you love. If you make new arrangements they are likely to improve an aspect of your personal life. *Moon in Cancer.*

12 FEBRUARY

The Cancerian moon for the next two days will bring your inner nurturer out. You'll enjoy spending time on improving your sense of self-care and will help someone important to you. *Moon in Cancer.*

13 FEBRUARY

You'll appreciate the sense that your family, personal life or recent decisions can lead to positive outcomes. Take a moment to relax, especially if you feel your emotions are running away with your imagination. *Moon in Cancer.*

14 FEBRUARY

Happy St Valentine's Day! You may feel more outgoing than usual and may take a risk with sending someone your compliments or a love token. You'll hear good news from someone you love. *Moon in Leo.*

15 FEBRUARY

You may not always agree with everyone, so be open to a new path and especially concerning a shared duty or personal matter. You may be ready to embrace a fresh approach to someone close. *Moon in Leo.*

16 FEBRUARY

The Leo full moon will shine a light on your personal life. You may be ready to try something new at work or to sign a fresh financial agreement. It's time to be more proactive about how you wish to see your life take shape. This is a good time to make a commitment to someone or to a venture. A trip or meeting could be significant. *Moon enters Virgo late in the day.*

17 FEBRUARY

This is a good day for decision-making and especially in connection with your home or a trip. You may enjoy a visit. A business or personal partner may have good news. You'll enjoy a get-together. *Moon in Virgo.*

18 FEBRUARY

As the sun enters the zodiac sign Pisces you are likely to feel more inspired but also more idealistic about certain agreements and people in your life, so ensure you are practical and realistic over the next four weeks. *Moon in Libra.*

19 FEBRUARY

When the moon is in your own sign you'll appreciate feeling more in your element. A little extra focus on your home life and ways to make this more exciting may appeal. *Moon in Libra.*

20 FEBRUARY

While you like to feel that everyone can live in peace and harmony, this isn't always the case! You may discover that your feelings are at counterpoint with someone else's, but the good news is you'll find a way to work with this or around it. *Moon in Libra.*

21 FEBRUARY

You may feel more motivated about a work project and more passionate about a personal matter. Check you aren't seeing some things in life through rose-coloured glasses. If you aren't, enjoy the romance and fun. *Moon enters Scorpio.*

22 FEBRUARY

This is an excellent day to check your values and principles and ensure you are following them. If you discover you are not it's a good time to find ways to be more true to yourself. *Moon in Scorpio.*

23 FEBRUARY

A domestic project could flourish, so be inspired and put your energy into creating a more upbeat vibe at home. If you work from home you may find a valid way to boost your work and home life by sprucing up your home office. *Moon in Sagittarius.*

24 FEBRUARY

This is a good day to boost your own appearance, health and well-being. You'll be drawn to romance, music and art and to a little luxury, so why not treat yourself? *Moon in Sagittarius.*

25 FEBRUARY

Unexpected developments that affect your home life or someone close will mean you must be adapatable or spontaneous Avoid misunderstandings. *Moon enters Capricorn.*

26 FEBRUARY

You'll enjoy getting together with a friend or family member. A visitor may cheer up your home life. If you're feeling creative you may enjoy a little DIY or making other changes at home. *Moon in Capricorn.*

27 FEBRUARY

You'll appreciate being able to change some aspects of your domestic arrangements, and this is an excellent time to discuss ideas. You may hear unexpectedly from an old friend. *Moon enters Aquarius.*

28 FEBRUARY

Developments now will benefit from a careful and practical approach on your part, especially where you wish to make changes at home or in your environment. Be innovative but bear in mind your ideas may not suit everyone, so run them by those they concern. *Moon in Aquarius.*

March

career   love   home   health   finance

1 MARCH

You're thinking analytically, which will help you move ahead with your various projects and with planning. Avoid believing you need to get on with everyone all the time as it's not possible. Be tactful if someone seems disgruntled. ***Moon enters Pisces.***

2 MARCH

The Pisces new moon signals the chance to turn a corner in your personal life or with a creative project. For some Librans a new chapter is dawning in your home life involving a favourite activity or interest. Look for inspired ways to move forward.

3 MARCH

The Venus-Mars-Pluto conjunction will be in your fourth house of home, family and property; you may be ready to make considerable changes there. For some Librans this conjunction means changes in a key relationship and intense talks may be involved. Avoid being overcome by emotions and maintain a clear perspective. ***Moon in Pisces.***

4 MARCH

Today's Aries moon will encourage you to be more outspoken, especially at work and with matters to do with health and well-being. It's a good day for a health or beauty appointment. Avoid taking other people's problems as your own. It's a good time to be helpful but you must avoid getting caught in the dramas of others. *Moon in Aries.*

5 MARCH

An inspiring project such as a change at home including renovations or even a move will capture your attention. It's a good day for romance, but you or someone close may tend to exaggerate emotions so ensure you maintain an even keel. *Moon in Aries.*

6 MARCH

Expect changes as both Mars and Venus step into Aquarius in your fourth house of home and family. You may be entering new territory either literally or figuratively as you embrace the new dynamics at home or with family. For some a trip will be transformative. *Moon in Taurus.*

7 MARCH

The Taurean moon will help you to feel more grounded and practical, especially with circumstances that may be unusual or unexpected. Avoid obstinacy and ensure you are being open-minded for the best results. *Moon in Taurus.*

8 MARCH

This is a good day for talks and meetings, as these are likely to go well. Reach out to friends and family as you could build bridges if you've recently argued. A change at home or a trip will be exciting. *Moon enters Gemini.*

9 MARCH

The Gemini moon will help you to look at life from a fresh perspective, and you may also see someone close in a new light. Be open minded about people you collaborate with. *Moon in Gemini.*

10 MARCH

As Mercury enters Pisces you will feel increasingly inspired over the coming weeks, especially about a family, creative or personal circumstance. This is a good day to make commitments to a project or domestic development. *Moon in Gemini.*

11 MARCH

This is a good day to put your mind on things you love, which will encourage you to plan ahead with activities that are enjoyable and supportive of good relationships. A healing or therapeutic activity may appeal. *Moon in Cancer.*

12 MARCH

This is a good weekend for devoting at least some time to the feel-good factor in your life. If it has been lacking, this is a good time for more nurturance and inspiration. *Moon in Cancer.*

13 MARCH

This is an excellent day to enjoy the arts, creativity, music and dance and simply to relax. Spiritual interests could be particularly rewarding. Romance will blossom, so organise a treat for someone special! *Moon enters Leo.*

14 MARCH

Communications are likely to improve, especially in your personal life and concerning domestic matters. If you need to build bridges with someone today's your day! *Moon in Leo.*

15 MARCH

The Leo moon is motivating for you and you'll feel all the more ready to get things done. If you find not everyone is of the same mindset ensure you avoid distractions and you'll find you achieve a great deal. *Moon in Leo.*

16 MARCH

You have an eye for detail and beauty, and when others seem a little less bothered about their own surroundings and the quality of their work it can be frustrating for you. Check that your expectations haven't been too high and consider how to move forward in the best way possible. *Moon in Virgo.*

17 MARCH

You'll enjoy an impromptu get-together, and someone may even pleasantly surprise you with their news or an event. It's a good day to be versatile and spontaneous. *Moon in Virgo.*

18 MARCH

The Virgo full moon shines a light on your association with friends, groups and organisations. You may be ready to enter a new circle or to end an association with someone in particular. Check your expectations aren't unrealistic, and if that isn't the case this could be the start of something promising.

19 MARCH

The Libran moon will bring your intuition out and you'll gain insight into your personal life and especially your home life. You may enjoy a reunion and certainly will enjoy the chance to relax. Avoid taking someone's unpredictability personally. Dance, music and art will appeal. *Moon in Libra.*

20 MARCH

When the sun enters Aries it is the vernal equinox. During the next four weeks you may find that your work and the way you connect with someone special become more of a focus, and that you feel more proactive about your ventures and upbeat about relationships. *Moon in Scorpio.*

21 MARCH

Key talks and a meeting could be more significant than meets the eye. A romantic liaison could mark a turning point in your love life. Romance will blossom. A change of routine or of circumstance may require a little adaptation. *Moon in Scorpio.*

22 MARCH

Someone's unpredictability is likely to be a focus, and it's a good time to discuss ways this can be worked with more constructively to avoid disruptions. It's a good day to make fresh arrangements. *Moon enters Sagittarius.*

23 MARCH

Your connection with someone close such as a work colleague or family member can deepen as you gain insight into them. Creative Librans will find this a super-productive day. You'll be drawn to music, dance and romance. Spiritual Librans will enjoy deepening your beliefs. You'll appreciate the chance to reconnect with someone special. *Moon in Sagittarius.*

24 MARCH

A more practical and grounded approach both at work and in your personal life will reap rewards. It's a good day for health and beauty appointments. *Moon enters Capricorn.*

25 MARCH

This is a constructive day for talks with someone important in your life, especially where their behaviour may have been a little unpredictable. You'll gain ground with key talks. A health or well-being matter is best approached head-on. *Moon in Capricorn.*

26 MARCH

A trip or conversation will be constructive as you'll enjoy the company and change of pace or place. A visit or developments at home will be similarly uplifting. *Moon in Capricorn.*

27 MARCH

You'll feel less likely to mince your words while Mercury is in Aries for the next few weeks and some of what you say will be well received. However, the more sensitive people in your life may find your approach aggressive, so ensure you keep an eye on how you deliver important information. This aside, lovely developments at home will raise morale as you relax and enjoy your Sunday. *Moon in Aquarius.*

28 MARCH

You'll see the rewards of your hard work as developments in your personal life start to move forward. You can make new agreements at home or with family that will be binding. If you've done your groundwork the developments will be ideal, but if you've missed key details you may discover that more research needs to be done. *Moon in Aquarius.*

29 MARCH

The Pisces moon will bring your idealistic, inner dreamer out. You'll feel drawn to music and books you love in your spare time and to getting in touch with people who inspire you. *Moon in Pisces.*

30 MARCH

You'll appreciate the opportunity to spruce up your surroundings and to bring more beauty and harmony into your personal space, be this at home or at work. A meeting and romance will be inspiring. *Moon in Pisces.*

31 MARCH

You are motivated to get ahead at the moment at work and with your various chores. Just double-check now and then that your daily activities still align with your big-picture values and goals. *Moon in Aries.*

April

career love home health finance

1 APRIL

The Aries new moon spells a fresh chapter in a key relationship for September Librans and at work or health-wise for October Librans. If your birthday is in early October this will be a potent new moon for you as you have an opportunity to improve a key relationship. Your vulnerabilities may rise during this time, but this will be your chance to turn a corner and leave something behind.

2 APRIL

You may receive key news from someone important in your life, especially if you were born in early October. A health and well-being development is best approached from a practical point of view. Someone special will be unexpectedly helpful. *Moon enters Taurus.*

3 APRIL

This is a good day to make changes, either at work or in your personal life or both! It's an excellent day for a makeover or new look, or to introduce new ideas to friends or family. *Moon in Taurus.*

4 APRIL

A plan or project can proceed well so if you're happy with the way things are going this is a good time to invest more heavily in them. *Moon in Taurus.*

5 APRIL

You will feel moved to make changes at home but someone you rely on may seem less motivated than you'd hoped. Venus in Pisces will bring your artistic side out and you will also be feeling idealistic, yet circumstances suggest you remain grounded and practical. *Moon in Gemini.*

6 APRIL

You can make a great deal of progress with personal projects and domestic matters. Be practical and allow your vision for the future to take shape. Meetings will be productive. Romance and family time will blossom, so organise a fun event. *Moon in Gemini.*

7 APRIL

This is a good day for talks, especially with someone you share space at home with or who has a say about how things proceed domestically. It is a good day to persuade someone close of your plans. *Moon in Cancer.*

8 APRIL

Romance could blossom, so ensure you organise something special. Family fun times could take much of your focus. You'll be drawn to further expressing your appreciation for music, dance, beauty and luxury. *Moon in Cancer.*

9 APRIL

This is a productive weekend for you, especially where your home life and health are concerned. Take the time to plan your schedule so you make the most of this motivational time. *Moon in Cancer.*

10 APRIL

If you have recently argued with someone close such as a family member or partner, avoid escalating tension as otherwise discussions could ignite rapidly into conflict. *Moon in Leo.*

11 APRIL

Communications are likely to regain a more even keel, which you'll appreciate. Keep communication lines open, as stubbornness on either side will only delay inevitable discussions that must be undertaken. *Moon in Leo.*

12 APRIL

This is a super-romantic time when bridges can be built after difficult talks. However, you may be seeing the world through rose-coloured glasses so ensure you also are being practical. Someone close may have their own expectations that you must take into account. *Moon in Leo.*

13 APRIL

This is a truly productive day and thus a good one to make agreements, as they're more likely to take. Just ensure you have all the details before committing to any long-term plans to avoid making mistakes. **Moon in Virgo.**

14 APRIL

You or someone close is likely to feel optimistic about your ventures and the success of prospective projects. This approach will be infectious. However, you may be super idealistic, so ensure you check the details especially if you are making financial arrangements. **Moon enters Libra.**

15 APRIL

As Mars enters Pisces you'll see that some matters at home can move into new territory. If you have recently deepened your interest in all things spiritual and mystical, the following few weeks will be ideal for further research and deepening your understanding of life and existence. **Moon in Libra.**

16 APRIL

The Libran full moon will spotlight your personal life and signals a fresh chapter for you, especially if you were born in mid-October. If you were born later in October you will begin a fresh phase at work or a new health routine. You may discover more stability and security are possible at home or with family.

17 APRIL

You wear your heart on your sleeve when the moon is in Scorpio and may tend to be more passionate and feisty. If you're undergoing an argumentative phase, watch out for further conflict. Avoid contributing to it and find peaceful ways ahead instead. **Moon in Scorpio.**

18 APRIL

You may be surprised by someone's news or behaviour. People may be volatile, so avoid arguments. A conflict of interest or a difference of opinion needn't cause difficulties if you first look for common ground. **Moon in Scorpio.**

19 APRIL

You'll feel inclined to stick with your principles and morals and will find these are what enables you to move ahead constructively. If you're shopping, avoid impulse buys as you may regret them. It's a good day for a health or beauty appointment. **Moon in Sagittarius.**

20 APRIL

As the sun enters Taurus you will feel more stable and secure about certain agreements and arrangements. But if you feel a little stuck by developments, find some wiggle room and avoid the tendency to be obstinate. Source ways to move forward in the most realistic fashion. *Moon in Sagittarius.*

21 APRIL

Communications and relationships are more likely to flow in a way you like over the next two days, so it's a good day to make suggestions and plans for a more smoothly sailing situation both at work and at home. *Moon in Capricorn.*

22 APRIL

Be practical and take conversations and trips one step at a time to avoid having to rush and make mistakes. Avoid arguments with someone who can be stubborn as they are unlikely to give an inch. Romance could blossom, so organise a fun event. A family or creative project could also flourish. *Moon in Capricorn.*

23 APRIL

A meeting may be more significant than meets the eye. You'll appreciate the opportunity to share your ideas and thoughts with someone who has your back. This is a good day to work out a sound financial budget. *Moon in Aquarius.*

24 APRIL

Communications and arrangements may be more difficult than you'd prefer so take a moment to gather your thoughts and plan ahead, leaving lots of time for travel and to alter arrangements if necessary. Avoid misunderstandings. Romance and creative ventures, the arts and music will appeal. *Moon in Aquarius.*

25 APRIL

You could see progress with your various ventures although some logistics will still require focus, especially if you are seeing the world through rose-coloured glasses. *Moon in Pisces.*

26 APRIL

Someone special is a lovely positive influence over you at the moment. You'll enjoy feeling you have someone who has your back. *Moon in Pisces.*

27 APRIL

Romance could go off the dial, so organise an event if you didn't already! However, if you're undertaking key financial transactions ensure you have done adequate research to avoid mistakes. ***Moon enters Aries.***

28 APRIL

This is a good day for talks, especially to do with shared duties and responsibilities and joint finances or communal space at home. You could make significant changes. A trip could be transformative. ***Moon in Aries.***

29 APRIL

Be prepared to enter fresh territory with a financial or shared circumstance. You may be drawn to express yourself in new ways or to be more independent. Key news could mean changes to come. ***Moon in Aries.***

30 APRIL

The partial solar eclipse in Taurus signals you are ready for a fresh phase in a shared circumstance or a relationship. A legal agreement may require focus.

May

career love home health finance

1 MAY

A family or personal tie could deepen. Work around your home could be beneficial. You'll enjoy making changes at home and relaxing when you can. *Moon in Taurus.*

2 MAY

As Venus enters Aries you'll feel more outspoken and dynamic in your personal life and your work or daily activities moving forward. The next few days are ideal for making upbeat changes to your appearance and wardrobe. You may consider a fresh health and fitness routine. *Moon in Gemini.*

3 MAY

The effort you are putting into your daily life and home is paying off. You may receive good news to do with changes you've undertaken. A family or personal matter could go from strength to strength, so ensure you invest in the people you love. *Moon in Gemini.*

4 MAY

Someone may surprise you and it will provide news or a refreshing change of pace for most Librans. *Moon in Gemini.*

5 MAY

This is a good time to consider something new in your life such as a fresh agreement at work or at home. Someone may have unexpected news for you. You may be ready to enter fresh territory, so think outside the square about your various options. *Moon in Cancer.*

6 MAY

This is an excellent time for discussions and meetings, especially to do with work and shared interests such as duties, responsibilities and collaborations. You may hear good news at work or regarding health and well-being, either of your own or of someone close. *Moon in Cancer.*

7 MAY

Collaborations and joint ventures will be a particular focus, especially at work. Sports, nature walks and your efforts to get on well with someone close could all produce good results, so be positive. *Moon in Leo.*

8 MAY

This is a good day to be outgoing and adventurous. You may wish to take the lead with the organisation of events, so ensure you gain the support of those your plans affect to avoid disappointments. Sports, physical exercise and organising your working week in advance will all get you feeling motivated. *Moon in Leo.*

9 MAY

You can achieve a great deal but you may feel a little tense. If so, ensure you take breaks as you may simply be tired or have taken on too much at once. Aim to tie up loose ends at work and regarding communications before Mercury turns retrograde tomorrow. *Moon enters Virgo.*

10 MAY

As Mercury turns retrograde you're likely to receive key news regarding a shared or legal matter, a collaboration or joint finances. You may need to review your circumstances. Try to allow extra time for travel and communications to avoid frustration over the coming weeks. *Moon in Virgo.*

11 MAY

As Jupiter enters Aries you may see matters in their most exaggerated form, so it's important to maintain perspective especially at work and regarding your physical health and well-being. You will gain in energy over the coming weeks and months but may need to pace yourself for the best measure. *Moon in Virgo.*

12 MAY

When the moon is in your own sign you can tend to take things more personally, so find the time to ensure you have adequate perspective. Someone close will prove to be a true support. **Moon in Libra.**

13 MAY

You'll enjoy a reunion and the chance to catch up over important shared concerns. **Moon in Libra.**

14 MAY

You may feel more motivated to get things done this weekend, especially around the home and in your neighbourhood. You may enjoy a change of pace or of place. **Moon in Scorpio.**

15 MAY

If you attend to practicalities first thing you'll get a head start on circumstances that could involve delays or obstacles. Someone close may need your help or support. If you need advice it will be available. This is a good day to indulge in your favourite interests and in music, the arts and creativity. Romance could blossom, so organise a date. **Moon in Scorpio.**

16 MAY

The total lunar eclipse in Scorpio may feel particularly intense and will spotlight an important financial or legal agreement. Be practical and grounded and avoid snap decisions. **Moon enters Sagittarius.**

17 MAY

This is a good day to make agreements, especially with a family member or domestic circumstance. A lovely meeting or visit will be inspiring. **Moon in Sagittarius.**

18 MAY

This is a good day to be practical about creating the kind of life you want, as ideal agreements can be made with the people who count. Artistic Librans will be particularly creative. Singles could meet someone inspiring and couples could rekindle romance and passion. **Moon in Capricorn.**

19 MAY

You'll enjoy a meeting or trip or change of pace. If you are currently making changes at home they are likely to be for the best even if they involve some upheaval. **Moon in Capricorn.**

20 MAY

Talks and travel are likely to go well especially if you must re-evaluate an agreement or return to an old haunt. You could renegotiate some agreements, especially if you have all the facts at your fingertips. *Moon in Aquarius.*

21 MAY

Key news or a meeting will be significant. For some developments will involve new ways to share common ground, and for others romance and a sense of progress at home will be well received. This is a good day to sort out finances. *Moon in Aquarius.*

22 MAY

You'll enjoy being with like-minded people, either by way of a trip to visit them or via a meeting at your house or in a lovely place. You could make great progress with a venture or project. You'll enjoy family time, and if you're interested in starting a family the current times could be super conducive. *Moon enters Pisces.*

23 MAY

You'll enjoy a reunion and the chance to enjoy doing projects you enjoy. You're collaborating well and teamwork will put you in a good position at work. *Moon in Pisces.*

24 MAY

You may wish to reconfigure some of your agreements. It's a good time to find out where you stand if you have recently disagreed with someone in a position of authority. A review will put you in a stronger position. *Moon in Pisces.*

25 MAY

You may find that people are a little more boisterous and feisty today and over the coming weeks. You'll gain a sense of being more dynamic and proactive and could get a great deal done. *Moon in Aries.*

26 MAY

This is a good day to review some of your financial commitments and to discuss better ways to get ahead with someone you share duties with. A legal matter could see progress. *Moon in Aries.*

27 MAY

You or someone close or both of you may be feeling a little intense. If your arguments tend to spiral easily into conflict, try to avoid weighty talks as they could escalate quickly. *Moon in Taurus.*

28 MAY

Venus in Taurus for the next few weeks will contribute to you feeling more settled in a relationship and happier with the way you have handled your communications, but it may also be conducive to stubbornness either in yourself or someone close. Remember to be flexible and adaptable, especially with important personal and domestic matters. ***Moon in Taurus.***

29 MAY

You'll feel productive and can get a great deal done around the house and garden. Someone close may have key news for you. ***Moon enters Gemini.***

30 MAY

The Gemini new moon will spotlight a new chapter within a particular agreement. For some Librans a travel, study or legal matter may turn a corner.

31 MAY

This is a good day both for talks and meetings at work and for deepening your relationship with someone close. A health or beauty appointment could be enjoyable. ***Moon in Gemini.***

June

career   love   home   health   finance

1 JUNE

Certain aspects of your day are likely to annoy you, yet if you focus on what is working well for you at the moment you'll find you get around frustrations easily. If feel you're under pressure take breaks to unwind when you can. *Moon in Cancer.*

2 JUNE

When the moon is at the zenith of your chart you will feel more able to get on with the tasks at hand. Someone may need your help, and if you need some advice or support be sure to ask for it as it will be available. Just avoid over-working and, if you're exercising, over-stretching yourself. *Moon in Cancer.*

3 JUNE

Mercury ends its retrograde phase today and you may see over the coming weeks that communications and travel plans become easier. You may receive key news that will merit close attention to a collaborative effort, joint finances or a relationship. *Moon enters Leo.*

477

4 JUNE

You'll enjoy a change of pace and being more outgoing, perhaps even altering where you shop and what you'd usually do on a Saturday. A health or beauty treat will appeal. You may enjoy a get-together and romance could blossom, so organise a social event. ***Moon in Leo.***

5 JUNE

The Leo moon will encourage you to be more active and you'll enjoy a sports or fitness event. If you have nothing planned yet, consider a ramble in nature or a meeting that gets you out of the house. You may not agree with everyone, so maintain perspective to avoid arguments. ***Moon in Leo.***

6 JUNE

You are not afraid to put your back into your work when the moon is in Virgo, although you may tend to be a little perfectionist. Pay attention to details but be sure to take breaks to avoid over-tiring yourself. ***Moon in Virgo.***

7 JUNE

Someone may surprise you and you'll enjoy being spontaneous. An unexpected trip or visit will be pleasurable. Just be sure to keep everyone in the loop if you alter your routine abruptly. ***Moon in Virgo.***

8 JUNE

You are a practical soul at heart and are productive as a result. You'll be pleased with the outcome of your hard work, even if it has involved some ups and downs. ***Moon enters Libra.***

9 JUNE

While you may prefer to take a day off you will nevertheless rise to the demands of a busy day. Consider exercise as a way to improve energy levels and not as a waste of them. ***Moon in Libra.***

10 JUNE

You'll enjoy a meeting at work or at home that provides a sense of progress with your ventures and also your communications. You may hear good news regarding a trip or a visit. ***Moon enters Scorpio.***

11 JUNE

A friend, colleague or partner may have unexpected news or will surprise you. A financial matter may require a little extra focus. ***Moon in Scorpio.***

12 JUNE

You will enjoy investing in yourself and others. This could mean you are ready to buy something expensive or simply that you wish to spend more time with those you love. Avoid limiting your options too much. Think big, but do not over-invest. *Moon enters Sagittarius.*

13 JUNE

Communications with someone close are about to get a whole lot easier. You may have already received good news, either financially or to do with a shared interest. *Moon in Sagittarius.*

14 JUNE

The full moon and supermoon in Sagittarius represents a fresh chapter for you in a particular relationship. Key travel choices, negotiations, study or even legal matters may come to a head or will need more focus.

15 JUNE

Someone close may need your help or will express their vulnerabilities and may be hurtful, especially if you were born early in October. Avoid minor scrapes and bumps and be prepared to be the bigger person if someone is unkind towards you. You may need the help of an expert or adviser. *Moon in Capricorn.*

16 JUNE

You will gain the opportunity to find more stability and security at home and/or with someone close. You will enjoy a reunion or deepening a relationship. If you are making key financial or long-term decisions ensure you have all the details and avoid making assumptions. *Moon enters Aquarius.*

17 JUNE

A partner or colleague may surprise you or have good news. Take a moment to work on the best way forward if your usual routine changes unexpectedly. You may wish to do something different and will enjoy being spontaneous. *Moon in Aquarius.*

18 JUNE

You may discover a financial anomaly, and this is the right time to find out how to get around it. If someone you trust lets you down there will be a good reason. However, you may wish to review the arrangement. *Moon in Aquarius.*

19 JUNE

You may experience a little tension in a relationship, which will enable you to get over disagreements rather than leaving important matters undiscussed. Romance and family time could be enjoyable, so plan a treat. *Moon in Pisces.*

20 JUNE

The Pisces moon will bring your creative side out and you'll find this useful at work and with artistic ventures. A partner may be more romantic. *Moon in Pisces.*

21 JUNE

As the sun enters Cancer, marking the solstice, you will feel more inclined to focus on your favourite ventures and interests such as travel, art and music over the coming weeks. If you're career minded you'll appreciate the opportunity to further your job prospects. A positive development with someone you find charming and alluring will be enjoyable. A financial transaction could open doors. *Moon in Aries.*

22 JUNE

You'll feel more inclined to boost health and well-being and to be proactive at work and upbeat at home. Not everyone will agree with your ideas, but your enthusiasm will go a long way to paving the road to success. *Moon in Aries.*

23 JUNE

The Taurean moon will encourage you to see other people's viewpoints more readily, which will foster better relationships as long as they are not stubborn! *Moon enters Taurus.*

24 JUNE

The more practical and realistic you are with your various projects and chores the better it will be for you. You'll feel drawn to indulging in a little luxury and treats this evening. *Moon in Taurus.*

25 JUNE

You'll enjoy a slower pace this weekend, giving you the time to enjoy your home or someone else's. If arguments have been brewing, avoid being obstinate and find ways you can meet over common ground. *Moon in Taurus.*

26 JUNE

You may feel a little more chatty and sociable and will enjoy touching base with a colleague or someone close. A trip or get-together will be enjoyable, but if you decide you'd prefer to enjoy your own company it'll certainly recharge your batteries. *Moon in Gemini.*

27 JUNE

This is a good day to improve your relationships, both at home and at work, and for a health appointment. Someone may need your help or advice or vice versa. If you need guidance, an expert or adviser could prove helpful. ***Moon in Gemini.***

28 JUNE

You may be pleasantly surprised by a development. A favourite pastime or venture could advance well, so take the initiative. You'll enjoy a trip and being spontaneous. ***Moon enters Cancer.***

29 JUNE

The Cancerian new moon will kick-start a fresh chapter for you. For some Librans this will be in your career, and for others with a favourite project. A change in your family or status may impact on your situation. You may have to persuade someone of your plans, especially if you need their co-operation. A negotiation may be tough, but if you focus on the facts you'll gain ground. ***Moon in Cancer.***

30 JUNE

You are highly intuitive at the moment and may not realise that your insight is valid, so ensure you take notice of some of your impressions as they are spot on. ***Moon in Cancer.***

July

career	love	home	health	finance

1 JULY

This is a proactive day for you and you'll relish the feeling of being productive. It's a good time to clear backlogs of work. *Moon in Leo.*

2 JULY

You'll enjoy the freedom that weekends bring, although a trip or visit may take much of your attention. If you're making important changes at home or with a project, ensure you pay attention to details to avoid mistakes. Emotions could run high, so maintain perspective as someone may be feeling outside their comfort zone. *Moon in Leo.*

3 JULY

Your organisational skill sets will be in demand and you'll manage to get on top of chores and also keep an eye on health and well-being. Find the time to overcome arguments, otherwise they could become long-term disagreements. *Moon enters Virgo.*

4 JULY

Tense undercurrents in conversations could be distracting, so ensure you maintain a professional outlook at work. A trip, study or legal matter may bring strong emotions out in you, so be prepared to find common ground and to de-escalate tension if possible. *Moon in Virgo.*

5 JULY

You'll appreciate the chance to feel you are on a more even keel with a relationship or personal matter over the coming weeks, even if there are still disagreements in the air. A project, trip or meeting is likely to advance. *Moon enters Libra.*

6 JULY

This is a good day to build bridges with people you have argued with. It is also a good time for beauty and health appointments. *Moon in Libra.*

7 JULY

When the moon is in your own sign you will look for balance and harmony in your life. Paradoxically, this can make you more demonstrative and proactive as you feel motivated to set things straight; just avoid making waves in the process. Use your intuition, as it's spot on. *Moon in Libra.*

8 JULY

You may be pleasantly surprised by news or a get-together. If you generally need to tiptoe around someone's feelings you may find that today is just another day as someone may be feeling vulnerable or unwell and will require added focus. If you need support there is help available from an expert or adviser. *Moon in Scorpio.*

9 JULY

Certain talks and meetings will require additional focus to avoid misunderstandings and mistakes being made. If you're travelling ensure you leave enough time in case of delays. Back up computers as you may experience technical problems. *Moon in Scorpio.*

10 JULY

You'll enjoy a reunion. Someone may be in touch with you from out of the blue and you'll enjoy doing something different such as taking a trip somewhere beautiful. *Moon enters Sagittarius.*

11 JULY

A sociable day will take your mind off any disappointments. You may be drawn to undertaking some retail therapy. If you tend to overspend leave the credit card at home, especially if you're already in debt. *Moon in Sagittarius.*

12 JULY

You'll enjoy feeling proactive at work and could get a great deal done. If you have a day off you'll enjoy boosting health and vitality. There is a therapeutic aspect to the day, which you'll appreciate. You may receive good health news. *Moon enters Capricorn.*

13 JULY

The full moon and supermoon in Capricorn will spotlight an important change that affects your status or domestic or personal life. You may be ready to make a key decision regarding any of these areas and they will all impact on each other. Look for security and stability. A project, study course or trip could be productive.

14 JULY

While the full moon is shining a light on your potential for success you'll discover whether your expectations have been unrealistic, which will give you the chance to set them straight. You may be prone to misunderstandings and delays, so be patient. *Moon enters Aquarius.*

15 JULY

There may be a little tension in the air, so a little more work especially with your interactions and relationships will benefit you. If an obstacle arises you will overcome it. *Moon in Aquarius.*

16 JULY

Key news to do with a project, trip or domestic matter will provide you with direction. You'll enjoy a sense that your projects are coming together, even if work is still required to ensure you are all happy. *Moon enters Pisces.*

17 JULY

This is a lovely day for romance and to enjoy the company of those you love. You may enjoy a trip somewhere beautiful or receiving guests. Music, the arts and creativity will all appeal. *Moon in Pisces.*

18 JULY

A key change either at work or at home or regarding a trip will impact on an important relationship. Some conversations may be intense, so maintain an even keel. *Moon enters Aries.*

19 JULY

As Mercury enters upbeat Leo you'll feel more outspoken and proactive about your feelings and your ability to get things done, both at work and in your personal life. Be positive! *Moon in Aries.*

20 JULY

This is a good day for making changes in your personal life and at work. You may be ready to enter new territory, either literally via travel or figuratively in your projects and work. However, some communications may be intense, so ensure you maintain solid ground. *Moon enters Taurus.*

21 JULY

You'll find the going a little easier as you gain ground in your situation and work out the best way to tackle unpredictable or intense people. ***Moon in Taurus.***

22 JULY

As the sun enters Leo you will enjoy feeling more outgoing and upbeat, especially at work and with your own personal projects. This is a good time to trust that your confidence and experience put you in a strong position. ***Moon in Taurus.***

23 JULY

This is an excellent day for communications, meetings and decision-making, especially at work and where your decisions could impact health and well-being and someone close such as a business or personal partner. Plans for a trip should go well. ***Moon in Gemini.***

24 JULY

Your chatty side will come out and you'll enjoy talking up a storm and reconnecting with favourite people and hobbies. ***Moon in Gemini.***

25 JULY

One of your projects or plans may be a little more complex than you'd hoped. Someone you rely on may not be available or as amenable to helping you. This is a good time to tread carefully to avoid arguments. ***Moon enters Cancer.***

26 JULY

This is another day to choose your words carefully, as someone you must get on with, for example at work or at home, may not agree with your views or the actions you take. Aim to establish common ground to avoid arguments turning into conflict. ***Moon in Cancer.***

27 JULY

This is a much better day for communications, and if you have recently had disagreements you could build bridges. Those in the medical profession may be busy but will receive good news. It's a good day for a health appointment. Take the time to discuss your ideas with someone who may feel a little vulnerable. ***Moon in Cancer.***

28 JULY

The Leo new moon points to a fresh chapter at work or with a project. You may be ready to reveal a new aspect of yourself or alter your status: from single to married, for example. If you have been considering legal or long-term decisions you are likely to make a choice. You may also receive unexpected news or will need to alter your plans.

29 JULY

While your plans can go ahead at a fast pace, especially at work and health-wise, not everyone will agree with your choices. Be tactful and diplomatic where necessary for the best results. *Moon in Leo.*

30 JULY

You'll appreciate the sense that the spotlight is off you and you have the chance to gather your thoughts. A little time out to recharge your batteries will be beneficial. *Moon enters Virgo.*

31 JULY

You'll enjoy a change of pace or of place. A decision is likely to be made that affects your status or home life. You may hear unexpectedly from an old friend. If you're single, you may bump into someone new. Be spontaneous, but you must avoid making snap decisions. *Moon in Virgo.*

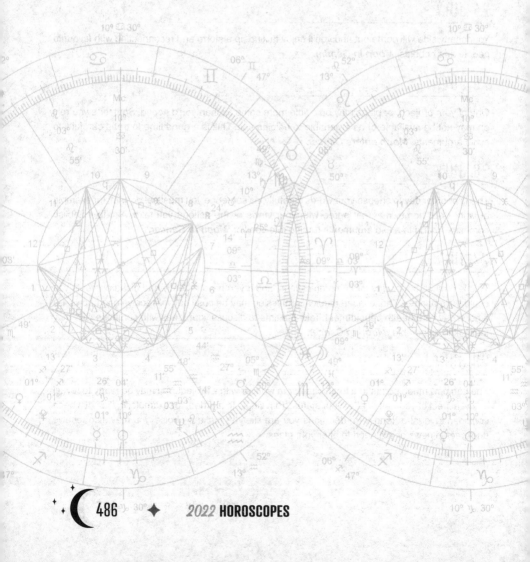

August

career   love   home   health   finance

1 AUGUST

You'll enjoy an impromptu reunion or the chance to float a fresh idea with a business or personal partner. Just be sure you have all the information if you are making long-term decisions. *Moon in Virgo.*

2 AUGUST

You'll appreciate the chance to be spontaneous but may tend to make snap decisions. A lovely meeting or the chance to enjoy a favourite activity will raise spirits. Singles may bump into someone unexpectedly or hear from an ex. *Moon in Libra.*

3 AUGUST

An unexpected surprise or lovely coincidence could boost your morale. You may enjoy a meeting or interview to do with a special project or venture such as sports or study. Be enterprising, as you could improve your circumstances. *Moon in Libra.*

4 AUGUST

The Scorpio moon brings out your intuition, helping you to make important calls about decisions. Rely on your instincts with a work or personal matter. *Moon enters Scorpio.*

5 AUGUST

A project at home or at work may be more complex than you'd hoped. Find the time to overcome obstacles and you'll find you'll succeed. Avoid an oppositional approach and find ways to collaborate for the best results. ***Moon in Scorpio.***

6 AUGUST

You'll feel more positive about your ventures, especially financially and regarding your long-term plans. Trust your instincts with personal matters. ***Moon enters Sagittarius.***

7 AUGUST

This is a lovely day for romance and you'll enjoy spending time doing activities you love, such as creative projects and meeting friends and family. If a difficult topic must be discussed, ensure you are diplomatic and tactful. Making changes at home will require careful planning. ***Moon in Sagittarius.***

8 AUGUST

There is a therapeutic aspect to your day, especially concerning work and health. It's a good day for a health appointment and to improve dynamics with someone close such as a business or personal partner. Someone may need your help. If you need advice it will be available. ***Moon enters Capricorn.***

9 AUGUST

Key talks and decisions may bring out your emotions, so ensure you remain level-headed. A trip or venture could transform your environment as you enter new territory. If you are travelling or undertaking complex discussions, ensure you remain patient as there may be delays. You will succeed with a diligent approach. ***Moon in Capricorn.***

10 AUGUST

Your interactions and conversations may be more emotionally charged than you'd prefer, so take things one step at a time. Be prepared to enter new agreements and learn something new. ***Moon enters Aquarius.***

11 AUGUST

The better you are at collaborating the better will be the outcome. Take time to work with an unexpected or unusual change at work or with someone you must collaborate with for the best results. You may discover a clever way to get on with daily chores. For some Librans love will blossom, so take the initiative and organise a treat. ***Moon in Aquarius.***

12 AUGUST

The Aquarian full moon will highlight your personal life or family situation. Changes at work or within your status may alter some of your domestic decisions. Be prepared to be flexible as circumstances outside your control may have a bearing on your situation. Think laterally if an obstacle arises. *Moon enters Pisces.*

13 AUGUST

Be inspired by people and activities you love this weekend, as this will be the path to relaxation. Avoid seeing someone through rose-coloured glasses as this could undo all your hard work. *Moon in Pisces.*

14 AUGUST

This is a good day to make a commitment to an idea, person or venture, but be aware that you won't necessarily agree with someone you need to be on the same page with. Find the common ground. Be proactive as you could make great and long-term change, especially with shared projects and at home. *Moon enters Aries.*

15 AUGUST

A meeting will put you in line for new ideas and will spotlight your ability to communicate well. You may be drawn to work with a fresh plan of action or to a new group or activity. You'll enjoy a reunion or hearing from an old friend. *Moon in Aries.*

16 AUGUST

You'll enjoy a surprise or impromptu get-together. Socialising and networking will appeal. If you must sort out a conundrum at work or with a group, organisation or friend your efforts should pay off. Think outside the square for the best results. *Moon in Aries.*

17 AUGUST

Pay extra attention to the details, especially at work and with important agreements or activities, as you may be a little forgetful or head in the clouds. *Moon in Taurus.*

18 AUGUST

This is another day to be careful with your interactions and transactions as you may be prone to making mistakes or being forgetful. This aside, you could make great progress at work or with a personal project. You may be drawn to a new look or outfit. *Moon in Taurus.*

19 AUGUST

There may be some intensity surrounding some of your talks and meetings. Take extra time for conversations and transactions to avoid arguments and mistakes. If you're travelling, arrange spare time to avoid delays. *Moon in Gemini.*

20 AUGUST

Mars will now be in Gemini until the end of March 2023, which will help you make great progress with your various plans and especially those that affect people you share activities, chores and duties with. A financial matter may gain more attention and it's in your interest to avoid overspending. *Moon in Gemini.*

21 AUGUST

Communications are likely to be busy and you may be prone to glossing over some details or being forgetful as a result, so focus on the details to avoid mistakes. You'll find out whether you've misjudged a situation, and luckily you'll get the chance to rectify things if you have to. *Moon in Gemini.*

22 AUGUST

Communications and meetings are likely to go well. It's a good day for a trip and to improve health circumstances and your environment at home or at work. *Moon in Cancer.*

23 AUGUST

Now that the sun is in Virgo you are likely to gradually feel more focused and less distracted, especially at work. However, today's circumstances may require you to be more patient with someone whose opinions differ from yours. *Moon in Cancer.*

24 AUGUST

There is a healing, therapeutic aspect to the day, so make an appointment if you feel you need to boost health and well-being. A new outfit, hairstyle or beauty treatment may appeal. It's a good day to mend bridges if you have recently argued with someone. *Moon enters Leo.*

25 AUGUST

The moon in Leo may bring out your more assertive side and you'll enjoy being more proactive about your own ideas and values. However, some people may find this aspect of you aggressive, so ensure you are diplomatic. *Moon in Leo.*

26 AUGUST

You'll be more inclined to speak your mind and even to share secrets over the coming weeks. The next few weeks are ideal for focusing on health and vitality as your efforts are likely to take. *Moon in Leo.*

27 AUGUST

The new moon in Virgo may bring a surprise or two your way. For some Librans this will spell a new agreement with a group, friend or organisation and for others the need to renegotiate a personal arrangement. Be practical and avoid arguments, as they could lead to a Mexican stand-off.

28 AUGUST

This is a good day for serious discussions and for making long-term commitments to a fresh course of action, especially at home and at work. You may need to agree to disagree with someone about how to run shared arrangements, so try to come to a workable agreement. *Moon in Virgo.*

29 AUGUST

Your feelings are likely to be strong at the moment, so maintain perspective. However, your ability to charm and persuade others of your ideas and plans is also very strong, so be prepared to make solid agreements with someone who has been oppositional in the past. *Moon enters Libra.*

30 AUGUST

A group or organisation may have ideas that are different from yours. For some, the difference of opinion will revolve more around your personal life. If you find ways to get ahead collaboratively you'll be pleased with the outcome. If you succumb to arguments or difficulties you may find the day trying. *Moon in Libra.*

31 AUGUST

Be open to seeing a work or personal situation in a new light. You may find you have misjudged a situation or a person. Aim for a realistic approach to circumstances and avoid seeing life through rose-coloured glasses for the best results *Moon enters Scorpio.*

September

career · love · home · health · finance

1 SEPTEMBER

Your collaborations and joint efforts will reap rewards. You may make great headway with a work or health venture, so take the initiative. **Moon in Scorpio.**

2 SEPTEMBER

You may need to focus a little more than usual on your interactions and talks as there may be an intense undercurrent to events. Pace yourself and be diligent for the best results. **Moon enters Sagittarius.**

3 SEPTEMBER

Important discussions and meetings are best approached with an optimistic but also careful attitude. Someone may have their own opinions and you'll do well to persuade them of yours if necessary. This is a good day for a health or work meeting, especially if you were born in October. **Moon in Sagittarius.**

4 SEPTEMBER

The Sagittarian moon will be motivational for you as you'll feel more outgoing, especially with your communications and discussions. You may even surprise yourself with how bold you are! **Moon in Sagittarius.**

5 SEPTEMBER

As your sign's ruler Venus enters Virgo, where it will be for the next three weeks, you may find you become increasingly preoccupied with the details and practicalities of some of your plans. This will be beneficial at work, but you must avoid over-analysing your personal circumstances. *Moon in Capricorn.*

6 SEPTEMBER

The moon in Capricorn will help you to make practical plans, especially in your personal life and with collaborations, groups and organisations. It's a good time to get paperwork shipshape. *Moon in Capricorn.*

7 SEPTEMBER

You'll appreciate the opportunity to think outside the box regarding some of your personal and domestic options. Take a moment to consider how you could improve domestic dynamics and décor to provide more comfort. *Moon in Aquarius.*

8 SEPTEMBER

You may experience a schedule clash or will try to fit too much into one day. It's a good day to slow down and pay attention to your health and fitness or that of someone close. *Moon in Aquarius.*

9 SEPTEMBER

Take a moment for yourself and the people in your life whom you prioritise or you may find you will be chasing your own tail and feel tired as a result. Try to tie up loose ends with paperwork and key discussions before Mercury turns retrograde tomorrow to avoid delays further down the line. *Moon in Pisces.*

10 SEPTEMBER

The full moon in Pisces will shine a light on your personal relationships, especially your family and loved ones. Take a moment to decide who and what your priorities are and focus on these to avoid being distracted. For some Librans this full moon will spotlight a healthier and more vibrant daily routine that could involve an inspiring work or health schedule.

11 SEPTEMBER

You'll enjoy a change in your usual Sunday routine and may also be pleasantly surprised by a development. Someone close may have good news. A social event may be out of the ordinary or exciting. *Moon in Aries.*

12 SEPTEMBER

If you organise your day well you'll be able to schedule in all your activities and duties so that nothing and no one feels forgotten. Take a moment to focus on a domestic or personal matter even if it seems challenging. You will overcome hurdles. *Moon in Aries.*

13 SEPTEMBER

This is a good time to be proactive with your various activities, especially at home and with someone close. Just avoid firing up at the first hurdle. Once the moon is in Taurus you'll feel more settled and life may seem less intense, but be wary of obstinacy. *Moon enters Taurus.*

14 SEPTEMBER

You'll appreciate the co-operation of a friend, group or organisation. You may also enjoy the company of someone special, so organise a mid-week treat! *Moon in Taurus.*

15 SEPTEMBER

You'll get on well with someone you have no option but to co-operate with, although some matters may still be a bone of contention at home or with family. Aim to focus on the tasks at hand and avoid being distracted by disagreements, otherwise you could find this a stressful day. *Moon enters Gemini.*

16 SEPTEMBER

Ask yourself if your expectations have been exaggerated if you experience a disappointment. You will get the time to put things right if they have been. Find the time for talks and meetings with someone you find inspiring but forgetful or vague. You may not agree with everyone but try to find the middle ground. *Moon in Gemini.*

17 SEPTEMBER

The Gemini moon will bring out your ability to view the world objectively, which will help you to overcome differences, However, you may appear uncaring as a result so ensure you are tactful. You'll enjoy being with like-minded people but must avoid impulsiveness. *Moon in Gemini.*

18 SEPTEMBER

This is a good time to review a health or work matter. If you were born at the end of September you may appreciate the opportunity to discuss important matters with someone close. Plans for a trip or reunion could shape up well. *Moon enters Cancer.*

19 SEPTEMBER

You'll enjoy the chance to reconnect with someone special. You may enjoy a trip or a meeting that could even deepen your relationship. If you have key matters to discuss with an organisation this could be a good day to do so. *Moon in Cancer.*

20 SEPTEMBER

Making changes at home and with your various arrangements at work and socially may take some of your focus, but you will get to make progress with careful attention to logistics and planning. You'll enjoy a spontaneous get-together and the chance to do something exciting or different. *Moon enters Leo.*

21 SEPTEMBER

An outgoing and optimistic approach to your day will help you to make the most of circumstances. You may be busy and will appreciate the chance to relax this evening. *Moon in Leo.*

22 SEPTEMBER

You are likely to be busy and must avoid over-tiring yourself. Ensure you pay adequate attention to your own health and well-being. *Moon in Leo.*

23 SEPTEMBER

As the sun steps into your sign it marks the equinox, a time when we collectively sense we can achieve more balance and harmony in our lives. Your attention is likely to go increasingly to managing work and finding more peace in your daily life over the coming weeks. *Moon in Virgo.*

24 SEPTEMBER

You'll be drawn to all the elements in life that make you happy. Romance and good times with the people you love could flourish, so organise a treat. If health has been under the weather this is a good time to consider a new fitness routine or diet. You may also be drawn to a new look. *Moon in Virgo.*

25 SEPTEMBER

The new moon in your own sign points to a fresh chapter in your personal life, especially if it's your birthday, so be prepared to turn a corner in your personal life and/or home. If you were born later in September or in October you're ready for a fresh start in a work or health routine. You may receive key news.

26 SEPTEMBER

You'll receive important information or will enjoy a key get-together. You may relish a reunion or the chance to go over old ground and review some of your arrangements at home or at work. *Moon in Libra.*

27 SEPTEMBER

A work meeting or the chance to review some of your work practices will be productive. If you're looking for work this is a good time to circulate your resume. It's a good day for a health or beauty appointment. You'll enjoy a reunion. If it's your birthday you're likely to receive important news or will enjoy a trip or event at home. *Moon in Libra.*

28 SEPTEMBER

Your projects and interests can make great progress. If you're welcoming people to your house or making changes at home these are likely to go well. *Moon in Scorpio.*

29 SEPTEMBER

You'll feel motivated to express your ideas, and you may also be drawn to a little retail therapy. Spending on your home or household bills may be adding up, so ensure you avoid overspending at the shops. *Moon in Scorpio.*

30 SEPTEMBER

A project at work and the opportunity to do something different will be inspiring, and you'll enjoy the chance for some 'me' time at the end of the week. *Moon in Sagittarius.*

October

career   love   home   health   finance

1 OCTOBER

A reunion and the chance to slow down a little will both appeal. An occasion will call for a new outfit or more attention to your appearance. You'll enjoy boosting the feel-good factor in your life. *Moon in Sagittarius.*

2 OCTOBER

A return to an old haunt or news from someone from your past will signal the chance to make changes, either in your day's schedule or due to a change of location. You'll enjoy a trip or meeting. *Moon in Capricorn.*

3 OCTOBER

The more practical you are with your various talks, meetings and chores the better you'll progress. Someone may be in touch unexpectedly. An unpredictable character will benefit from a calm response. *Moon in Capricorn.*

4 OCTOBER

Some communications will feel revitalising as they may introduce you to new ideas. If you need to smooth things over with a social group or an organisation this could be a good day to do so. *Moon enters Aquarius.*

497

5 OCTOBER

You are a compassionate and kind person, but you can be analytical as well. If a conundrum arises you'll find an innovative way around it. *Moon in Aquarius.*

6 OCTOBER

A change of pace or of atmosphere at home will be enjoyable, as you get the time to spend some quality moments with someone special. If you have nothing planned yet consider something new or different. *Moon enters Pisces.*

7 OCTOBER

You are going to be in demand today. Someone who can be a little taxing emotionally may need your help. If you need support or advice it will be available. It's a good day for a health or fitness appointment. A reunion or the chance to work at home will appeal. *Moon in Pisces.*

8 OCTOBER

You'll feel inspired by your activities, but if health matters have been on your mind you may find you are a little emotional. Take a moment to centre yourself and you'll find you'll feel uplifted by a dynamic, upbeat character. *Moon enters Aries.*

9 OCTOBER

The Aries full moon will spotlight how you feel about someone close such as a business or personal partner, especially if you were born in early October. You or they may be feeling particularly sensitive. If health is a concern, take time out. There is a therapeutic aspect to the day, so aim to find pleasant and calming activities.

10 OCTOBER

A strong focus on health and well-being will surround you, especially if it's your birthday earlier in October. You may find this is an excellent time for a health or fitness appointment. Someone close will need attention, and if it's you ensure you ask for support. A work matter may need extra focus. *Moon enters Taurus.*

11 OCTOBER

This is a good day to discuss the logistics of your circumstances, especially regarding your home life. If you experience a disappointment, rest assured there will be a silver lining. *Moon in Taurus.*

12 OCTOBER

Matters you have already discussed are likely to come up again and you'll see there has been progress. If not it's time to rethink the situation, especially to do with work and health. You may need to travel to return to an old haunt. *Moon in Taurus.*

13 OCTOBER

An unexpected development is best approached with a practical and optimistic attitude. When you focus on your priorities you could make unexpected progress. **Moon in Gemini.**

14 OCTOBER

This is an excellent day for getting ahead with personal matters, especially to do with your home, travel and, for some, work. A health matter is best attended to carefully. **Moon in Gemini.**

15 OCTOBER

You are an analytical thinker and your ability to think outside the square will be useful. You can make great progress with your activities, especially at home and with areas such as sports, travel and study. **Moon enters Cancer.**

16 OCTOBER

Even if you are a good thinker, not everyone else is! You'll appreciate the opportunity to relax, but if some arrangements need to be changed or some people are forgetful avoid taking it personally. **Moon in Cancer.**

17 OCTOBER

You are proactive and able to get things done, however, not everyone is as capable as you. Avoid being impatient with those who aren't as dynamic, and go easy on yourself if you're forgetful or head in the clouds. **Moon in Cancer.**

18 OCTOBER

The moon at the zenith of your chart is bringing your inner superhero out. However, you may appear a little impatient as a result. You'll get a great deal done and will enjoy the results of your hard work. **Moon in Leo.**

19 OCTOBER

You are focused on results at the moment, especially to do with favourite projects. If you're on holiday, studying or travelling you'll feel dynamic and accomplished. However, if you feel conflict is brewing give it a wide berth. **Moon in Leo.**

20 OCTOBER

Your values are likely to differ from those of someone close, and unless you're careful you could find arguments arise quickly. Avoid allowing them to escalate into conflict. **Moon enters Virgo.**

21 OCTOBER

The Virgo moon brings out your innovative side and your ability to look outside the square. You may enjoy socialising and being in the company of like-minded people. A hobby could take off. *Moon in Virgo.*

22 OCTOBER

You may be drawn to a new look or a new outfit or hairstyle. A sense of beauty and luxury will appeal and you may be inclined to overspend or overindulge as a result. Your efforts with a hobby such as sports will pay off. There's a lot you'll enjoy about today. Singles could meet someone new. You may hear from someone from your past unexpectedly. *Moon in Virgo.*

23 OCTOBER

While this is good day for discussions in general, it would be an error to assume everyone will be on the same page. You may need to explain some of your projects and ideas in more detail to see them through. *Moon in Libra.*

24 OCTOBER

Someone from your past who you do not always see eye to eye with may bring out your vulnerabilities. Take a moment to centre yourself and avoid allowing sensitivities to run your day. You may need to help someone. *Moon in Libra.*

25 OCTOBER

The partial solar eclipse in Scorpio will be intense and changes in your personal life or finances are best processed carefully. If you feel disappointed in someone or in yourself, find ways to boost confidencesuch as positive self-talk. Avoid misunderstandings.

26 OCTOBER

Your emotions may be strong, and you'll feel motivated to express your values and principles. Avoid taking things personally if your ideas fall on deaf ears with someone in your personal life or at work. A favourite activity or hobby will be enjoyable. *Moon in Scorpio.*

27 OCTOBER

You are communicating clearly and can make your feelings felt. A trip, venture, study or legal matter can proceed well. However, people won't automatically agree with you. Take a moment out to avoid allowing disagreements to turn into arguments. *Moon enters Sagittarius.*

28 OCTOBER

Be prepared to review some of your work or health or personal matters. You may feel you're going over old ground but there will be benefits to rearranging some of your duties or schedules. ***Moon in Sagittarius.***

29 OCTOBER

Over the next few weeks you will feel more strongly about your principles and ideas, which may be frustrating as you prefer life on an even keel. Find ways to dissipate restless energy to ensure you do not find life too frustrating. ***Moon enters Capricorn.***

30 OCTOBER

The Capricorn moon will help you to see life and relationships in their most practical light. You'll appreciate the chance to touch base with people you know have your back. ***Moon in Capricorn.***

31 OCTOBER

Happy Hallowe'en! You'll appreciate the opportunity to spend quality time with someone you love. Expect a quirky day – so nothing unusual for the day of the year! If you're unsure of a project or a person ensure you research the situation. ***Moon enters Aquarius.***

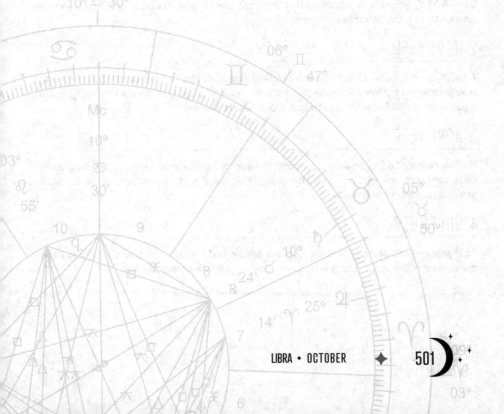

November

career · love · home · health · finance

1 NOVEMBER

You're thinking analytically and this will be helpful, especially if challenges arise. Today's Aquarius moon will help you to think outside the box. Someone close has your back, so ensure you bounce your ideas off them. *Moon in Aquarius.*

2 NOVEMBER

A health or work matter or both is best approached carefully and sympathetically. Someone who is vulnerable or sensitive will require delicate handling. If finances have been a little shaky, this is a good time to find better ways to budget. *Moon enters Pisces.*

3 NOVEMBER

You'll appreciate finding the time to reconnect with someone you love. You may hear unexpected news from someone who can be a little erratic. Find ways to process information in the most practical way. *Moon in Pisces.*

4 NOVEMBER

Trust your instincts as they will help you to find ways to understand a personal situation. You'll be drawn to relax through music, good food and company. *Moon enters Aries.*

5 NOVEMBER

Your romantic and optimistic sides will seek expression, and you will enjoy a reunion and the chance to go over old ground with someone special. However, an unpredictable person may behave true to form. It's a good day for a health or beauty appointment. *Moon in Aries.*

6 NOVEMBER

Someone close may be a little more outspoken, and if a mystery has been in the making you may find out more information. A health or financial matter is best approached delicately. *Moon in Aries.*

7 NOVEMBER

A financial or personal situation may represent a stalemate, yet if you apply logic and insight to the situation you will find a way to succeed. Avoid gambling, both emotionally and financially, as it will backfire. *Moon in Taurus.*

8 NOVEMBER

The total lunar eclipse in Taurus will spotlight someone's opinions and circumstances. You may need to consider their feelings above all else and consider how you share resources such as finances and also space at home or duties and responsibilities. You may receive key news or undergo financial developments.

9 NOVEMBER

Key financial matters are best negotiated with a calm approach, especially as you may be going through unexpected circumstances. If you're engaged in legal matters ensure you maintain perspective. *Moon enters Gemini.*

10 NOVEMBER

You may be tempted to throw good money after bad, yet if you maintain a strong sense of values and principles you could gain the moral high ground. Avoid being pressured into spending too much on domestic matters. You may receive a financial, work or ego boost. Avoid overspending and overindulging as you'll regret it. *Moon in Gemini.*

11 NOVEMBER

Your ideas are likely to be different from those of someone you must collaborate with on a domestic or personal level. To ensure you can both move forward without too many problems it's a good idea to set new arrangements in place if possible, especially financially. Avoid snap decisions, but be prepared to think on your feet. *Moon in Gemini.*

12 NOVEMBER

You'll appreciate the chance to indulge in your senses this weekend, and romance, music and love will all appeal. Just avoid overspending, especially if you're already in debt. *Moon in Cancer.*

13 NOVEMBER

You'll enjoy cocooning, either at your own house or at someone else's. Good food, fine wine and pleasant company will all appeal. Just avoid overindulging as you'll regret it tomorrow! *Moon in Cancer.*

14 NOVEMBER

Trust your gut instincts as they are spot on. If a work or personal matter requires a little more insight, care and attention, your efforts will not go to waste. *Moon enters Leo.*

15 NOVEMBER

This is an excellent day for making progress with someone special and with your work and personal plans. It's also a good time for talks with someone you have had a rough patch with. Developments may snowball and gain momentum, so ensure you're happy with circumstances. *Moon in Leo.*

16 NOVEMBER

This is a good day for romance and also for getting ahead with your various projects. You may need to focus a little harder than usual as you may be easily distracted. *Moon in Leo.*

17 NOVEMBER

As Mercury enters the zodiac sign Sagittarius expect there to be more focus on getting things done in the best possible way, especially regarding finances and your personal life. You may even experience a financial or ego boost. *Moon in Virgo.*

18 NOVEMBER

This is a good time to plan how to get ahead both with your financial situation and domestically. Some Librans will be excited about organising a trip or receiving a visitor. *Moon in Virgo.*

19 NOVEMBER

Attention to details will dispel misunderstandings and mistakes, especially at work and regarding long-term plans such as travel, study or legal matters. *Moon enters Libra.*

20 NOVEMBER

The moon in Libra for most of the weekend will encourage you to enjoy your spare time in ways only you know how. You'll appreciate the opportunity to get things shipshape in your environment so that you can relax and enjoy the company of like-minded people. *Moon in Libra.*

21 NOVEMBER

A change of pace or of place will be enjoyable. If you're travelling you'll enjoy the sense of freedom. You'll be drawn to invest in your happiness and a meeting will be the icing on the cake. If you're shopping ensure you avoid overspending, especially if you're already in debt. *Moon enters Scorpio.*

22 NOVEMBER

The sun in Sagittarius for the next few weeks will put your focus firmly on adventure and discovery. You may be drawn to make a large investment, either financially or emotionally. Some Librans will be drawn to travel and exploration. You may consider a holiday or updating digital devices so communications are better. *Moon in Scorpio.*

23 NOVEMBER

The Sagittarian new moon signals that you're ready to embrace something new such as a fresh agreement or even a new relationship. Financial matters will benefit from careful appraisal.

24 NOVEMBER

The moon in Sagittarius will contribute to a feeling of expansion in your personal life. You may enjoy a sense that your horizons are about to open up. If you're planning a trip, this will be a cue to a change of routine. For some Librans a new chapter at work or in your daily life will begin. *Moon in Sagittarius.*

25 NOVEMBER

Today's therapeutic and healing aspect will help you to feel more enthusiastic about life. A financial decision or meeting could represent a fresh arrangement that suits you well. This is a good day for a health or beauty appointment. *Moon enters Capricorn.*

26 NOVEMBER

You'll be drawn to improving your appearance and well-being and to helping someone who may benefit from an ego boost. You may be tempted to undertake a little retail therapy and may even find that a fresh outfit lifts spirits! Spiritual Librans will deepen your understanding of yourself and your own spirituality. *Moon in Capricorn.*

27 NOVEMBER

You may receive unexpected news from a business or personal partner. If finances have been a little up in the air, this is a good time to sort through them. *Moon enters Aquarius.*

28 NOVEMBER

This is a good day for making agreements about your long-term ventures and goals, both at work and at home. You'll enjoy making a commitment to someone specialor to a clever financial plan. *Moon in Aquarius.*

29 NOVEMBER

Talks and meetings are likely to be upbeat if not feisty, so ensure you maintain perspective. A trip will take you to an old haunt and a meeting may be unexpected. You may need to make considerable financial outlays but must avoid impulse spending. If problems arise you will manage to get over them, so be positive. *Moon in Aquarius.*

30 NOVEMBER

This is a good day for making financial agreements that are realistic and that you can stick to. Someone at home or in your family may have upbeat news. *Moon in Pisces.*

December

career love home health finance

1 DECEMBER

Developments are likely to gain their own momentum, especially in connection with finances and for some travel and agreements. If you're happy with a financial or personal matter you'll find current developments rewarding, but if they seem to progress too quickly it's time to gently apply the brakes if necessary. *Moon in Pisces.*

2 DECEMBER

This is a good day for discussions and for making agreements but only if you have all the details you need at hand, otherwise mistakes can be made. However, you may find some travel delays or even computer or technical glitches get in the way of a smoothly running day, so plan ahead and be patient. *Moon in Aries.*

3 DECEMBER

There are therapeutic aspects about this weekend; a healing, spiritual or restorative activity will be beneficial. You may deepen ties. Someone may need your help, and if you need expert advice or guidance it will be available. *Moon in Aries.*

4 DECEMBER

This is a good day for talks and meetings. If you have blown your budget this is a beneficial time to discuss how to get back on track. Avoid making assumptions; find ways to gain the information you need. ***Moon enters Taurus.***

5 DECEMBER

The Taurus moon will bring out your ability to be practical and down to earth about key decisions and plans. However, it may also bring out a partner's obstinacy, so be prepared to work constructively with them. A little more patience may be required! ***Moon in Taurus.***

6 DECEMBER

You are known to be a peace seeker and your diplomatic skills will be useful, as communications and travel may be subject to delays and misunderstandings. A trip or meeting may need to be rescheduled. Back up computers to avoid losing information. ***Moon enters Gemini.***

7 DECEMBER

Once again your ability to be tactful and diplomatic will be useful, especially if you find you must alter your plans at the drop of a hat. An unpredictable character will behave true to form. ***Moon in Gemini.***

8 DECEMBER

The Gemini full moon spotlights a fresh chapter for you in a particular relationship, project or agreement and urges you to undertake conversations and make agreements that suit you. It's a constructive time to make changes financially and especially at home.

9 DECEMBER

You may be pleasantly surprised by a development or by a spontaneous event or gathering. ***Moon in Cancer.***

10 DECEMBER

The key to your happiness this weekend lies in good communication skills. Take the time to explain your ideas and values carefully to avoid allowing a difference of opinion to escalate into an argument. A trip or get-together may be delayed. ***Moon in Cancer.***

11 DECEMBER

As Venus joins Mercury in Capricorn you'll feel more secure and solid about some of your arrangements over time. However, you must avoid obstinacy, and if someone close is behaving stubbornly try encouraging them to be more adaptable. ***Moon enters Leo.***

12 DECEMBER

This is an excellent day for discussions to do with your home, finances and general prospects. Take the time to configure a positive plan to do with these areas of your life. You may experience an uplifting development in one or more of these matters. *Moon in Leo.*

13 DECEMBER

The Leo moon will motivate you to be more outspoken and outgoing, especially at work. Your ability to collaborate and co-operate will still be a valuable asset, so avoid feeling you need to carry the can. *Moon in Leo.*

14 DECEMBER

You'll be drawn to the mystical, musical, romantic aspects of life, yet when you need to focus at work this could be a hindrance so find the time for your interests outside work or mistakes could be made. Avoid misunderstandings and gambling, both financially and emotionally. *Moon enters Virgo.*

15 DECEMBER

You'll feel a lot more able to focus than you were yesterday so it's a good time to get ahead with your projects and chores. You'll also be drawn to spend time with a group, friend or organisation that provides you with a sense of stability or security. *Moon in Virgo.*

16 DECEMBER

While communications are likely to improve over time you may nevertheless speak before you think, so remember to keep your tactfulness in full operational mode! Someone may similarly speak up in an unguarded moment; avoid taking their opinions personally. *Moon enters Libra.*

17 DECEMBER

You'll enjoy an impromptu event or a get-together that takes you outside your usual sphere. A trip or a new communications device may well be just what you want. *Moon in Libra.*

18 DECEMBER

It's a mixed bag today: on the one hand you'll enjoy the company of someone you love, and on the other there may be some matters that need to be dealt with such as chores. If health has been a little on your mind it's a good time to focus more on well-being and fitness. Avoid misunderstandings, delays and digital glitches. *Moon in Libra.*

19 DECEMBER

This is another good day for getting together with someone you share similar values with. You may experience a financial or ego boost. However, some conversations may be tense so using your diplomatic skills will be a useful skill set to employ. *Moon in Scorpio.*

20 DECEMBER

When the moon is in Scorpio you like to spend time with someone close to you. Romance could flourish but so could intense, destructive feelings, so ensure you feed the positive emotions and starve the more negative ones. *Moon in Scorpio.*

21 DECEMBER

The solstice is a time of reflection when you can gather your wits as you assimilate your progress this year. You may enter a fresh understanding of someone or a new agreement. A trip or change in your environment will bring a more stable and secure atmosphere into being. *Moon in Sagittarius.*

22 DECEMBER

You'll enjoy a meeting with someone upbeat and a little quirky. You will also enjoy a change of pace or of place, so if you have nothing planned yet it's a great day to view the Christmas lights! *Moon in Sagittarius.*

23 DECEMBER

The new moon and supermoon in Capricorn signals a fresh start for you in a particular relationship or even environment. You may be ready to travel or to receive a guest. Be positive about changes even if a little upheaval must accompany your day.

24 DECEMBER

There is an ideal atmosphere to the day as a domestic or family development brings your romantic self out. A change of pace or of place could be ideal, even if some of the logistics are complex or annoying. *Moon in Capricorn.*

25 DECEMBER

Merry Christmas! A lovely get-together will warm your heart. You'll enjoy doing something different this year or you may simply wish to strike out on your own in different circumstances. A lovely message or meeting will be therapeutic. *Moon in Aquarius.*

26 DECEMBER

A quirky or different pace will provide a fresh context and bring some of your frustrations to the surface. Avoid arguments, as these are likely to escalate. A diversion or distraction will bring a welcome change of focus if you're missing someone. *Moon in Aquarius.*

27 DECEMBER

You'll enjoy feeling more relaxed and taking the time to enjoy the company of people you love and the activities you like. *Moon in Pisces.*

28 DECEMBER

There is a romantic aspect to your day and you'll enjoy the opportunity to spend time with someone you love in a beautiful location. If you have nothing planned yet consider a trip to a beautiful place. Try to get important paperwork or talks summed up before Mercury turns retrograde tomorrow, or some of your plans may be delayed. *Moon in Pisces.*

29 DECEMBER

A key meeting, talk or trip will be more significant than meets the eye. Avoid making snap decisions, as these are likely to need a review further down the line. *Moon in Aries.*

30 DECEMBER

A trip or conversations my be more complex than they need be. Give yourself extra time if you're travelling and avoid feeling too flustered by delays or frustrations. *Moon in Aries.*

31 DECEMBER

Happy New Year! You'll enjoy seeing that someone you love seems more settled than they have been. If it's you who feels more settled you'll appreciate the sense that everything has its place, just as you have yours in life. Some lovely meetings and news will raise spirits. *Moon enters Taurus.*

♏ SCORPIO

23 October - 22 November

THE ESSENCE OF SCORPIO

You're smouldering hot and you know it, and if you don't it's time to recognise you have a magnetic effect on others. They see you as being charismatic, charming and seductive but not in a showy way; your magnetism smoulders just beneath the surface of your skin. You don't need to show off, as you are naturally charming and attractive. It's who you are, and no effort is required to be beautiful, potent and intense. You may not recognise this yourself, which adds to your charm. Your charisma is natural, as if it were a fragrance that wafts from your pores. You attract people the way flowers attract bees.

Make no mistake: your attraction is extremely potent and you can weave a web of beauty and charm without even knowing it. People who are caught in your web will be inexplicably drawn to you, not realising they are in so deep with you they cannot extract themselves from your charming world. If they try to do so it will illicit an intense reaction from you, which is where your reputation for being intense and having a scorpion's sting in the tail arises. You feel you're the innocent party, that you had no part in their circumstance. You're not to blame, as you didn't even realise you were spinning a web and had no intention of doing so.

You attract people and circumstances unconsciously, which is something to be aware of. You are a dream weaver with insight beyond the norm, and you do like to draw people to you. Don't be surprised when you draw people in who you don't actually want to have close. Anticipate that you may need to let them down when they begin to relate to you in a more familiar way than you intended. As a water sign you have a strong intuition, and you can rely on this and your instincts to decipher who you should be spending your time with and who you wish to keep at arm's length.

With your activities it's important to be discerning about what you choose to do and not do in life. Once you mature this won't be a problem, as you'll know where your loyalties lie and will be discerning about who you draw close. As a youngster though you may be surprised by the intensity of the people and circumstances you seem to attract, which can be attributed to the planets that rule your sign: power-packed Mars and potent Pluto. You have energy beyond your own belief, and when you channel this into productive pursuits you will scale mountains.

SELF-ESTEEM

You derive self-esteem from feeling that you generate adventure and excitement in your life. You need to feel you have a goal and that you are effective in creating the life you desire; that you are not only the actor in your story but also the writer, director and producer. In this way your adventures become truly meaningful experiences and provide a sense of fulfilment, as they are the result of your vision, hard work, lust for life and productivity.

Because your sign is ruled by fiery and weighty Mars and Pluto you need to feel you are the person who has the power, the one with the most proactive and dynamic personality. Rarely will you feel comfortable playing second fiddle in relationships: for you to thrive and feel valued and confident relationships would need to be fair and equal.

If you feel disrespected your potent passion will turn against those who disrespect you and potentially even against yourself. The sting in your tail will emerge if you perceive you are under attack, but often in the process you can sting yourself through your actions more than you do others. The sting can be self-destructive unless care is taken to channel your strong emotions, passions and impressions into productive outcomes as opposed to harmful endings.

On the positive side, you are never down for long. Another symbol for Scorpio is the phoenix, the bird that rises from the flames of destruction. You always emerge from adversity intact even if your ruffled feathers are a little singed at the edges.

You naturally possess high self-esteem, which forms part of your charm. However, when life throws you a curve ball you can all too easily throw up your hands in surrender and your self-esteem evaporates and is replaced by your more negative traits of self-doubt, insecurity and anger. You have a tendency to lash out at those who seem to block your way.

When your self-esteem is dented it can take a while for you to rebuild it, so it's important to take time to find ways to do so. If you're a volatile Scorpio, the more quickly you learn to restore your self-esteem the better for you so you remain in control of your better qualities of loyalty, effectiveness and passion for all you experience in life.

YOUR INNER LIFE

While on the outside you're a charismatic character you may not be able to see this yourself, so your tendency is to think you need to work hard at your abilities or you will be ineffective in life. Avoid feeling you are lacking in any way as you have the wherewithal to create the life you want and to charm people along the way!

Inevitably you will attract drama or will be part of some form of intense transformation in your life, which can again lead to the sense you're not as effective as you'd like to be. When drama occurs you must find ways to overcome hurdles in a peaceful, calm way because otherwise the tendency will be to leap to intense reactions and aggressive behaviour as your go-to modus operandi. This default response to stress is clearly not in your best interests, so the more you can work at developing impulse control and overcoming strong, self-destructive tendencies the better you will work your way through life.

As you are such a passionate character and have a strong lust for life you can tend to overindulge in the good things, not only food and drink but also narcotics and sex. You have a tendency towards co-dependent behaviour as you rapidly identify with others, and you can tend to exhibit other addictive behaviour such as obsession and gambling. To avoid these tendencies it's vital you seek balance and find out how to overcome impulses that are addictive and self-destructive.

HOW OTHERS SEE YOU

You are seen as being a powerful, intense character, and all the more so as people get to know you when you move forward in your relationships. You may initially be seen as someone who is shy or retiring, but once people become closer to you they will find an undeniable magnetic quality. In intimate relationships you can be seen as a really passionate character whose will is hard to resist once you are truly entwined in a relationship.

As a parent you can be fiercely protective of your children and partner, which may be seen as domineering rather than caring. Be aware that your potency can be easily misconstrued as dominance rather than nurturance and protectiveness.

When you are crossed the sting in your tail can emerge, which can make you appear spiteful, vengeful and destructive. People will think you have little self-control and see you as being dangerous. To enhance the image you project aim to show your loyal side and your wish to nurture and transform others more often, and demonstrate your ability to rise above drama and intrigue. In these ways you will rise ever stronger like a phoenix from the ashes.

HOW TO MAXIMISE YOUR POTENTIAL

With Mars and Pluto at the helm you have power at your disposal. To enjoy your life and make the most of your potential it's important to channel your power into activities that have meaning for you and that resonate with your highest potential. Otherwise you can tend to be easily seduced into activities that pander to your more base desires and could, if you take a wrong turn, lead to drama-fuelled events and destructive and self-destructive behaviour.

Aries and Scorpio, both of which are ruled by fiery Mars, are the most volatile signs. If you feel anger is an emotion you have little to no control over then anger management will be useful. If other impulses such as addictive behaviour and gambling seem to get the upper hand, the sooner you can find out how to manage impulse control the better.

Your true abilities lie in self-transformation and the transformation of others. You are an ideal coach who is able to work with the self-transformation of other people. All this begins with work on yourself from a young age and from understanding how to turn negative situations into positive outcomes.

SCORPIO AND ITS ASCENDANTS

This chapter is about your sun sign, Scorpio, and your predictions for the year ahead. The more you know about yourself the better you will be able to take advantage of opportunities, and also to avoid the pitfalls. It's critical to know as much about 'you' as possible.

In astrology your core self is represented by your sun sign, but your personality traits are represented by your ascendant (also known as your rising sign). The ascendant describes your personality, the way other people see you on first meeting you and the way you tend to filter life's events.

When you have intimate knowledge about your sun sign – your engine room or core being – you will be on the way to a happier life. When you add the knowledge about your personality – your ascendant – you will gain even deeper insight into what makes you tick.

Your ascendant sign is determined by the time of your birth on the date and year of your birth. Because the ascendant sign changes approximately every two hours, the best way to determine it is to ask an astrologer to calculate it for you. Certain apps will also calculate your ascendant sign (see page 873).

The following gives you more information about your abilities, characteristics and personality according to your sun sign Scorpio in combination with your ascendant sign.

SCORPIO SUN SIGN WITH ARIES ASCENDANT

Both these signs are ruled by Mars, the planet of fire and war. Passion is your middle name and you'll find your life and relationships take you on many a rollercoaster of change and excitement.

You may appear bolder and more courageous than you are. Underneath that bravado there is intense passion that smoulders and takes its time to achieve goals. The Scorpio and Aries combination is a force to be reckoned with, but you can be predisposed to fiery outbursts, temper tantrums and conflict. You may need to engage in anger and impulse control. You will be a huge success if you channel your high energy into sport and physical activities and pursuits you're passionate about.

SCORPIO SUN SIGN WITH TAURUS ASCENDANT

You will be seen initially as a careful and methodical character, someone who is well organised and practical. Yet beneath the earthy, calm exterior rages an intense heartbeat that smoulders. You have passion in bucketloads, and when you combine your passion with the earthy sensuality of the Taurean ascendant you're an attractive, charismatic and magnetic personality who is prone to mood swings and outbursts. Another pitfall is that you can be the most obstinate person, unwilling to change aspects of your personality and activities unless there is a valid reason such as health and well-being.

SCORPIO SUN SIGN WITH GEMINI ASCENDANT

You are a complex character with many different forms of expression. You may be constantly on the go, restless and hard to pin down, yet you may also be quiet, moody, passionate and loyal once you commit to a relationship. Gemini-rising people often gesticulate with your arms and hands when you talk and can be wiry in appearance. When combined with the Scorpio energy you are a sensual, active personality. You are likely to be upbeat, outgoing, adventurous and home-loving, a romantic character who is self-possessed yet intense.

SCORPIO SUN SIGN WITH CANCER ASCENDANT

You are a double water sign and as such are intuitive and emotional and can be super moody! Being moody is no surprise to you as you sense your way through life and are a truly empathic character. Your mood swings are in line with the atmosphere or event you're experiencing. You will seek expression in intense ways and may be volatile. As a youngster these qualities may be confusing: you may be easily misled, perplexed by your actions and distracted. You have artistic, even psychic, abilities. You may tend to overindulge in the good things in life and must avoid co-dependent and addictive behaviour. You'll find balance by seeing the world instinctively and through practical eyes.

SCORPIO SUN SIGN WITH LEO ASCENDANT

The Leo ascendant is the most outgoing and dynamic of all and is exciting but can be egocentric. Combined with your Scorpio magnetism you are the centre of attention, whether you consciously draw people to you or not! You must guard against being led by your passions and desires above all else, as these impulses could lead you astray or into dramas and negativity. Your upbeat Leo personality needs to find positive expression, so allow it to display your kind, compassionate heart and drive your passions into productive pursuits.

SCORPIO SUN SIGN WITH VIRGO ASCENDANT

You are quite the enigma: you are passionate, charming and intense, which is quite opposite to your classically reserved and reliable Virgo exterior. Under your super-organised, calm and diligent personality lies a charismatic and zealous character. When you're under pressure you may be a little confused by your own impulsive and volatile reactions, as these can be in contrast to your well-ordered and analytical mind. As you mature you'll manage your abilities well, being both charming and a hard worker. You are a natural-born healer who wishes to make the world a better place.

SCORPIO SUN SIGN WITH LIBRA ASCENDANT

Beneath your outwardly calm and intellectual mind lies a charismatic and passionate character. You may attract people who are drama magnets or be a drama magnet yourself. Luckily your reasoning abilities and wish for peace will steer you clear of the self-destructive behaviour associated with Scorpios. Your interest in the arts, music and creativity makes an ideal outlet for your strong feelings. You'll also find great expression in sport and other exciting activities. Psychology and a deeper understanding of the mysteries of life may appeal.

SCORPIO SUN SIGN WITH SCORPIO ASCENDANT

You are a double Scorpio and as such are doubly passionate, charismatic and powerful! You are a strong character and must be aware you appear intense, or you will wonder why people feel overshadowed or overwhelmed by you. You are supremely creative and artistic; music, the arts and film are likely to appeal. You are also a drama magnet, and your relationships may be tempestuous as your feelings run deep. Aim to find balance in life and you will be a force of nature.

SCORPIO SUN SIGN WITH SAGITTARIUS ASCENDANT

Your upbeat, adventurous approach to life is fuelled by deep, passionate desires and the need to express yourself, and to be recognised as a force to be reckoned with. You have a larger-than-life personality and a marked sense of humour, even if at times it seems dark or sarcastic. You're willing to take risks and may seem to have little control over your emotions and exuberance. Sport and adrenaline-filled activities will appeal to you, along with the need to understand the depth and complexities of people and life.

SCORPIO SUN SIGN WITH CAPRICORN ASCENDANT

Your outer calm and diligent character hides the intense will and passion of your Scorpio inner wild child. Your deep feelings may surprise even you on occasion, let alone those who get to know you better; your methodical, reliable and trustworthy qualities can be overcome by emotions, especially when you're under pressure. If you harness your strong emotions and channel these into mighty feats you will excel. You're a good worker but must avoid being easily distracted by fads and other people's dramas.

SCORPIO SUN SIGN WITH AQUARIUS ASCENDANT

A quirky and complex character, you're both highly emotional and highly philosophical. As you're able to compartmentalise your attributes you may alternate between them: emotional in relationships and analytical and effective at work. You can present as a complex character. You have a fun sense of humour that may be extremely dry or dark. You have inner strength and resourcefulness that help you to overcome and rise above life's challenges.

SCORPIO SUN SIGN WITH PISCES ASCENDANT

You are a seeker, mystic and philosopher. You have a natural love of music, the arts and books. When young you may seem easily distracted and influenced. You are intuitive and instinctive and may be swayed by the emotions of others. As you mature you'll find your own ground and build stronger foundations for yourself. Your creativity is a wonderful outlet for deep emotions and sensitivity. You are inspired and mystical and may feel drawn to develop your psychic abilities.

SCORPIO IN LOVE

You are such a passionate individual, Scorpio, love is a huge motivator in your life. In this section you can check out your compatibility with other sun signs. Remember that we are all complex individuals, so the more you know about someone's astrological birth chart the better you can determine your compatibility. Consider having your astrological birth chart compared with that of a partner, friend or family member, as the compatibility – known as 'synastry' in astrology – goes even deeper than a comparison of sun signs, although this is a good place to begin.

SCORPIO WITH ARIES

Watch out: sparks will fly in this match as both signs are ruled by Mars, the god of war, indicating fireworks and conflict. Scorpio is co-ruled by intense Pluto, contributing to the sense of drama and potential explosiveness. This is a high-energy, potentially high-maintenance relationship as you are both dominant personalities. Scorpio is likely to dampen Aries' fire, which Aries will resent, feeling smothered by Scorpio's ardour. Passion will abound at first in a love match; it will be an engaging relationship full of zest and charm, but all too often end as quickly as it begins. Daily care must be taken to channel intense energy into positive and constructive compatible pursuits.

SCORPIO WITH TAURUS

You'll appreciate the outward calm and composure of Taurus, although you may be frustrated on occasion by the lack of comparative fire and dynamism unless there is a strong fire element in the Taurus chart. This relationship can be grounding and comforting for both of you and can provide you with the sensuality you desire in relationships. One major stumbling block could be stubbornness on both parts, but if you can agree to disagree on occasion there is every chance that Taurus finds you exciting if moody and you find your Taurean partner attractive, calming and sexy.

SCORPIO WITH GEMINI

This is a lovely match, even if you both find yourselves so busy in your own lives that you spend more time missing each other's company than actually being together! You may need to make a conscious effort to spend quality time together or you could truly miss out on the benefits of this match. You'll appreciate the Gemini intellectual stimulation, freedom of movement and light-hearted attitude, and your partner will feel excited by your independence and ability to take the lead when necessary.

SCORPIO WITH CANCER

Two water signs make for a passionate, emotional and intense relationship; however, both partners may feel overwhelmed by the other so it's important to maintain healthy boundaries and focus on self-care or this combination can be co-dependent. This is one of the best matches as both signs are on the same page emotionally; both have similar outlooks in life as you are intuitive and passionate about your activities. This relationship goes much deeper than many others; if you are both willing to explore the wonders of love and of each other this is a fulfilling match.

SCORPIO WITH LEO

Scorpio and Leo together are a passionate combination, although with this kind of fire sparks will fly! If you both have good anger and impulse control you'll manage to channel passion into self-fulfilling and mutually enhancing activities. Come to terms with past issues in your lives or else the match may be too hot to handle. There may also be ego battles: Leo will wish to be the peacock in the relationship, and Scorpio can take this as a personal insult. Both signs may wish to control or lead the other, so a pecking order will need to be established or there will be fireworks.

SCORPIO WITH VIRGO

Your lust for life may well set your Virgo on fire! You'll admire the fact that your Virgo partner is so well organised and practical as this makes a grounding contrast to your fire and passion, but you may come to find the Virgo's focus on work and daily duties soon dampens your ardour. Together you can make sweet music, although you must avoid forcing your Virgo partner to play second fiddle to your demands. They may not take kindly to playing a support role to your main act, which would make this match tiring and demanding.

SCORPIO WITH LIBRA

The romance, calm and balance of the Libran persona will complement the fire and passion in you; this is a romantic connection although it may not necessarily last. You are likely to need each other, but this combo can lapse into co-dependency and therefore you may feel needy or unfulfilled. Your emotions could seesaw, but if you both work on self-development as opposed to seeking fulfilment from each other this relationship does have room to grow.

SCORPIO WITH SCORPIO

This is a hot, steamy relationship: passionate, powerful and tempestuous! You are both strong characters, and while mutual physical attraction is likely you risk burning each other out. If you work at establishing personal boundaries and maintaining a healthy approach to each other's abilities, and if you avoid co-dependency, alcohol and substance abuse this could be a deep, penetrating, mystical relationship. You must work at finding balance in your relationship or this can be a tumultuous match.

SCORPIO WITH SAGITTARIUS

You are both vying for attention from each other in different ways. The outgoing Sagittarian character needs freedom and independence to feel fulfilled, whereas Scorpio requires deep commitment and an earthy, almost supernatural connection. If you're able to give each other what you crave you'll find this a worthy match, otherwise you'll feel unfulfilled by the other's inability to provide what you need.

SCORPIO WITH CAPRICORN

While initially the emotional Scorpio may be attracted to the earthy, settled persona of the Capricorn, the attraction risks running out of steam fairly quickly as the Capricorn pace of life – which is slow compared to the Scorpio's – will soon lose its allure. For Capricorn, while the initial allure of the charismatic Scorpio may feel exciting, the depth of emotions and confusion expressed by Scorpio can soon be off-putting for the stable Capricorn character. This match is not ideal unless there are solid moon connections in the astrological chart.

SCORPIO WITH AQUARIUS

This relationship can quickly turn to game, set and match because it may have neither the staying power nor the commitment necessary for a happy partnership. This is because both signs are so stubborn, especially when together! Both people are so obstinate there can be little middle ground and certainly no willingness to adapt or change, let alone to bend to another's will. At first both partners may find the other exciting, as both have the tendency to push boundaries and explore life. This is a match as friends and companions, less so romantically.

SCORPIO WITH PISCES

As water signs you both have fundamental compatibility: you lead from the heart and are intuitive and instinctive. You'll enjoy romance, art, music and dance together, and may also have a mutual interest in spiritual development. This can be a truly deep connection, but unless you are adept at drawing the line between your path and another's you may easily become lost in each other's lives and lose yourselves.

THE YEAR AHEAD FOR SCORPIO

Affirmation: *'I've got this!'*

This year will be one to remember, and you may already have begun to experience some radical changes at the end of 2021 as the eclipse on 19 November was in your opposite sign Taurus and will have altered at least some important aspects of your life. Eclipses are turning points, and this year Scorpios with birthdays at the end of October and mid-November will be the most impacted by considerable change.

For some Scorpios these changes will take place principally at work; for others concerning your health or that of someone close. If your birthday falls on an eclipse (25 October or 8 November) you may experience significant developments in an important relationship or in your personal life.

While your birthday may not fall on either of the eclipse dates this will still be a year in which you can make long-overdue changes, so where you have been procrastinating or did not find the motivation to make changes last year you will find the opportunity to do so. It will be in your interest to avoid being stubborn or fearful about making necessary changes, as otherwise events this year will have a tendency to nudge you forward in directions you may not wish to go. It is far better to guide your life down avenues you wish to pursue than be shunted along by unexpected developments that take you on a detour or the slow road to where you want to be and what you want to do.

HEALTH

Your health is the most important aspect of your life and it's vital this is in good condition as all else stems from here. January presents the perfect time to make a year-long plan to prioritise your health. Astrologically, the sixth house is associated not only with health but also with work because one co-exists with the other.

If your work routine is exhausting you it's vital you change this and find more balance in your life. The moon's north node, Chiron and Jupiter will travel through your sixth house at varying intervals depending on when you were born and will provide the information and opportunity to do so. However, with Uranus very strong in your sixth house if you were born in November there may be events during the year that are hotspots that remind you how important your health is. These hotspots will occur during the first quarter and from July to October.

A healing phase in April and October will encourage you to make any necessary changes at home or within your pastimes and habits that will further boost your health. The eclipses in April-May and October-November will spotlight further what you must do to boost health. Patience, repetitively keeping to a regime and a nutritious diet will all serve this purpose.

FINANCES

The earlier in the year you can put in place a solid and reliable financial plan the better for you. Circumstances may be chaotic or will merit professional help with your financial planning but you will gain the chance to regulate your spending early in the year, which will put you in a strong position for the entire year.

The total lunar eclipse on 25 October will open new parameters for your work, and you must be fully aware of the consequences of actions you take and agreements you make now. Do not gamble; seek the advice of trusted professionals if you're considering a major investment. If a health circumstance or change of routine at this time takes your focus, ensure your finances are covered.

There is an attraction to speculation and gambling in 2022 that will be hard to ignore. In March, developments at home will ask that you rearrange finances or agreements with family, but you must be careful about how you do so. Mars in your eighth house of investment, inheritance and debt from August to the end of the year suggests you may be prone to reckless spending then.

HOME LIFE

Changes at work, in your personal life or health-wise will produce changes at home. The times of most change are likely in the first quarter and during the eclipse seasons of April-May and October-November. Saturn in your home zone all year will put the focus very much on your domestic responsibilities. If you decide to build or renovate it will put additional pressure on relationships, so be sure to factor extra care and attention for loved ones into the work you carry out. You will gain the help and support you need from friends and family to make long-overdue changes at this time.

Flashpoints when you may find you need to co-operate more with those you live with will be in early January, mid-March and at the end of October, but if you feel your relationships really have hit rock bottom these could be the times you decide to alter how you share space.

In this light, the new moon in your home sector on 1 February will be a good opportunity to invest more time in your home life or family. If you are making long-term financial decisions, ensure these have been well researched.

LOVE

Key changes to your love life will arise, as the eclipses span both your personal life and relationships. You relish adventure but above all to feel you are close and loyal with your loved ones, so if you feel your closest relationships are in any way stagnant or uncomfortable you can begin to yearn for more signs of commitment. Couples who work and play together will enjoy infusing your relationships with more of a sense of togetherness, including travel and sports, but if these activities are not possible then in mutually enjoyable activities such as exercise routines, art, music and creativity.

This is a good year for singles to consider a commitment if you have spent so many years being solitary and carefree. Someone who is upbeat and has a sense of independence and individuality could catch your eye.

The eclipses at the end of April, in early May, at the end of October and in early November signal key turning points for you in your love life. The second half of the year is likely to be more fiery than the first, so aim to look for ways to channel strong emotions and passions rather than disruptive outburst and tempers into projects.

CAREER

Mars will spark up your daily work calendar from mid-May onwards and could bring you closer to a sense of purpose and fulfilment at work. However, you will also need to hone your communication skills as collaborations and agreements will need to be made and not everyone will see eye to eye with you at work.

The partial solar eclipse on 30 April could signal the chance to change aspects of your career you no longer feel fulfilling. Take the opportunity. You may even want to investigate a fresh avenue of work and a surprise or unexpected development at this time could open doors to something new.

The Leo new moon on 28 July will enable you to see yourself and your career in a new light. This together with the eclipses in October-November will place enormous focus on your daily schedule, including your home life, enabling you to work out what and who take the highest priority in your life.

The most important aspect of your career is that you are happy and feel fulfilled. If you do not, this year you will gain the opportunity to change this. Avoid resting on your laurels, as you'll be glad you made changes in retrospect.

January

career love home health finance

Notes: the pie charts such as the one above listed for each month show energy distribution according to the stars for the month ahead. If you wish to make changes in the areas of your finances, health, career, love or home and you see there is a large amount of energy in that sector in the chart, your endeavours should succeed as long as you have prepared well in advance. The charts also show which areas will potentially have the most focus in your life during the month.

The moon sign listed for each day's entry in the diary is the position of the moon at the end of the day in Greenwich Mean Time (GMT). To gain the most information about a particular day's circumstances, read the day before and the day after for a complete picture.

1 JANUARY

Happy New Year! You already know that variety is the spice of life, so you'll enjoy your start to the new year. An unanticipated visit or trip will bring a little spontaneity your way. ***Moon enters Capricorn.***

2 JANUARY

The new moon and supermoon in Capricorn will kick-start a fresh phase for you in a personal context, especially if you were born in October, and in a financial sense if you were born in November. You'll enjoy a meeting or get-together involving family or a change at home.

3 JANUARY

The new year sales are likely to have already drawn your attention, and you'll be enticed to invest in your home. A little investment in yourself and someone special will add to a sense of change and will spice up some relationships. *Moon enters Aquarius.*

4 JANUARY

The Aquarian moon will motivate you to be a little more outgoing. If you're back at work you may need to find ways to communicate with a different set of people or to adapt to a fresh routine. *Moon in Aquarius.*

5 JANUARY

A little luxury and beauty in your surroundings certainly raises morale, and you'll enjoy a trip to somewhere beautiful or the time to indulge in a friend or family member. *Moon in Aquarius.*

6 JANUARY

You may find out whether you've miscalculated a domestic or personal matter. If so, you will get the chance to reorganise your priorities and to adapt to circumstances. *Moon in Pisces.*

7 JANUARY

There's a dreamy quality about the day, so if you're on holiday you'll love the vibe and will enjoy being by the sea and with people you love. If you're at work or must undertake important negotiations you may be head in the clouds, so you must be prepared to focus that little bit extra. *Moon in Pisces.*

8 JANUARY

This is a good day for get-togethers, be these via a short trip or a receiving visitors. You'll feel drawn to spending time and money on those you love, including yourself. You may receive a financial or ego boost. If you're shopping you must avoid overspending as you'll regret it. *Moon in Aries.*

9 JANUARY

A reunion or trip will be enjoyable. If you're undertaking DIY or improving your home in some way this is a good day to make progress. However, you must avoid overspending and overindulging as you'll regret it tomorrow. *Moon in Aries.*

10 JANUARY

An unexpected or unusual change of circumstance such as a long trip or an alteration in your schedule is best handled calmly to avoid contributing to the upheaval. Be practical and avoid firing up if arguments seem likely. ***Moon enters Taurus.***

11 JANUARY

It's a mixed bag today: on the one hand you'll appreciate the comfort of certain arrangements and the connection you have with some people, but on the other a difference of opinion or in values could disturb the peace unless you're willing to see another's point of view. Consider your options carefully, and if arguments seem likely ensure you have the facts, especially financially. ***Moon in Taurus.***

12 JANUARY

The moon in Taurus brings out your more practical side, and you'll gain a sense of possibility especially with someone you love and with a favourite project. However, you may also tend to be a little stubborn when the moon is in Taurus and may see others as also being obstinate, so aim to find common ground. ***Moon in Taurus.***

13 JANUARY

You'll appreciate a more light-hearted atmosphere, especially within a complex relationship. Try to get key paperwork and financial matters resolved before Mercury turns retrograde tomorrow to avoid delays over the next few weeks. ***Moon in Gemini.***

14 JANUARY

You may receive key news or will undertake a trip. Certain negotiations could progress as long as you all take a moment to avoid being obstinate. Find the time to digest information before jumping to conclusions if a development takes you by surprise. ***Moon in Gemini.***

15 JANUARY

When the moon is in Cancer your intuition becomes strong, so ensure you trust your instincts and especially regarding someone close or a transaction or agreement. Find the time to discuss developments so you can get on top of things. ***Moon enters Cancer.***

16 JANUARY

Key news, a trip or a meeting will be intense, so ensure you are ready for change. For some Scorpios developments will revolve more around financial matters and the need to work out your own values and what you are prepared to spend. ***Moon in Cancer.***

17 JANUARY

The Cancerian full moon will spotlight a financial or personal transaction that could put a new shine on an agreement or legal matter. Your finances could be a focus, and you may also appreciate the sense that you can work more constructively with the assets and money you already have.

18 JANUARY

The moon in Cancer will encourage you to intuit the feelings of those close to you, so trust your instincts. Once the moon is in Leo you'll feel more outgoing, and undertaking projects, sports, travel and exciting ventures will appeal. *Moon enters Leo.*

19 JANUARY

This is a good time to meet people who can be helpful and supportive. A financial or personal interaction could even alter the way you see yourself and your sense of self-confidence, as you may receive a compliment or ego boost. *Moon in Leo.*

20 JANUARY

The sun in Aquarius for the next four weeks will bring out your quirkier side, and you'll be more outgoing socially and will enjoy travel and meeting new people. *Moon in Leo.*

21 JANUARY

The moon in Virgo at the zenith of your chart brings out the hard worker in you. You'll be feeling practical and able to get things done in the most efficient ways. You'll enjoy a reunion. *Moon in Virgo.*

22 JANUARY

You'll appreciate the opportunity to go over finances and agreements and to meet an old friend. There may be a nostalgic ambience to the day but you'll enjoy reconnecting. *Moon enters Libra.*

23 JANUARY

News or a get-together will be enjoyable. If you're shopping you may be tempted to purchase something unusual or unexpected. It may be appealing, but just check its longevity. It's a good day to get on top of finances if you need to. *Moon in Libra.*

24 JANUARY

It's likely to be a busy day. If you feel a little conflicted about a project, group or friend, find the best way forward by researching circumstances more. *Moon in Libra.*

25 JANUARY

You'll manage to be productive so take the initiative with your projects. You may also tend to overspend or over-invest, so if you're making a large purchase double-check its merits. *Moon in Scorpio.*

26 JANUARY

A financial review will be beneficial for you. You may need to go over old ground with personal agreements. Someone close will be in touch or you may enjoy a reunion. *Moon in Scorpio.*

27 JANUARY

You'll enjoy the sense of revitalised energy you have, which will be motivating in your personal life and provide an upbeat approach to work. However, you may also feel more impassioned about your ideas, so remember not everyone will feel the same way and you may need to persuade them of the worth of your ideas. *Moon in Sagittarius.*

28 JANUARY

A proactive stance certainly gets things done, but it's in your interest to check you are not seeing life through rose-coloured glasses. Important news, for many to do with finances, is on the way. Just avoid gambling, both financially and emotionally. *Moon in Sagittarius.*

29 JANUARY

Key news or developments in your personal life or financially could be transformative. You may wish to reconsider a decision or may reunite with an ex or revisit an old haunt. The news you receive and developments could signal more change to come, so be aware of the implications of circumstances. *Moon in Capricorn.*

30 JANUARY

A change of schedule or unexpected news could be a surprise. For some this will concern work and for others someone you love. Take a moment to recalibrate and consider your best option moving forward. *Moon in Capricorn.*

31 JANUARY

This is a good day to consider your circumstances in a positive light and to take time out to talk to and meet the people you love. A financial matter could be positive and a trip or meeting will be productive. You may receive a compliment or an ego boost or will wish to give one. *Moon in Aquarius.*

February

career   love   home   health   finance

1 FEBRUARY

The new moon in Aquarius will spotlight new agreements and negotiations. You may have bright and upbeat ideas, but someone close may need persuading of their merit. A trip or change of environment will be progressive but potentially disruptive, so plan ahead well.

2 FEBRUARY

This is a good time to think outside the box and to consider how you'd best like to move forward, especially with your commitments, domestically and with family. You'll enjoy relaxing with someone special. ***Moon enters Pisces.***

3 FEBRUARY

Your intuition is powerful when the moon is in Pisces, so ensure you listen to your gut instincts. Music, romance, flowers, dancing and all things beautiful will appeal to you, so feed your senses. Spiritual Scorpios may be particularly inspired. ***Moon in Pisces.***

4 FEBRUARY

This is a good day to make a commitment to a transaction, be it in your business or personal life. You may need to crack a few eggs to make your omelette but the effort will be worthwhile. Key news to do with someone close, travel or finances will be worth looking at carefully. ***Moon in Pisces.***

5 FEBRUARY

The moon in Aries can tend to fire you up, which is conducive to getting a lot done but could also put other people's backs up. You may feel vulnerable yourself and are best to take things one step at a time. A gamble may not pay off, so be careful with finances and feelings. *Moon in Aries.*

6 FEBRUARY

You cannot get on with everyone all the time, and today is one such an example. You're generally on a good path with most of the people you need to get on with, but someone may exhibit different values to yours. Avoid gambling, both financially and emotionally, as it will backfire. *Moon in Aries.*

7 FEBRUARY

Your earthy, practical qualities will come out, which will be useful at work and with general day-to-day logistics. However, you may also tend to feel a little obstinate, so double-check whether or not you could be a little more adaptable. *Moon in Taurus.*

8 FEBRUARY

You'll welcome a change of routine and the chance to do something different. A friend or colleague, partner or business associate may suggest a new way of going about things. You may make ground at work or will receive a financial boost. This is a good day for something different. *Moon in Taurus.*

9 FEBRUARY

You'll feel sympathetic with someone you hold dear, but is your loyalty at cross purposes with your values? Find ways to be loyal both to your own principles and to those you love. *Moon enters Gemini.*

10 FEBRUARY

A lovely get-together will warm your heart. If domestic matters have been strained you'll find a way to enjoy better relationships there. A trip will take you somewhere lovely. *Moon in Gemini.*

11 FEBRUARY

This is a good day for talks and especially for financial discussions. A trip or meeting is likely to be transformative. If you find events intense, take time out to unwind when you can. *Moon in Cancer.*

12 FEBRUARY

The Cancerian moon for the next two days is ideal for spiritual work, psychic development and meditation. You may feel more introspective or intuitive. Just avoid escapism and overindulgence, which you'll regret! *Moon in Cancer.*

13 FEBRUARY

You'll relish the chance to deepen your ties with someone special. A domestic or family matter may catch your attention. It's a good time to consider how to zhuzh up your daily life and to alter your usual schedule to bring more fun into your life. *Moon in Cancer.*

14 FEBRUARY

Happy St Valentine's Day! You'll enjoy treating someone special to something lovely. You'll hear good news from someone you love and will enjoy a get-together, so organise a treat if you didn't already. *Moon in Leo.*

15 FEBRUARY

While you may still feel the love vibe after tomorrow, things may not necessarily go to plan today. Take a moment out of your busy day if you feel some conversations are at cross purposes, and find ways to get them back on track. *Moon in Leo.*

16 FEBRUARY

The Leo full moon will shine a light on your favourite activities and plans. You may be ready for something new: travel, embracing study or a fresh project. You may receive key financial or personal news that will either provide the green light or will mean you must do a little more research to bring logistics up to date. *Moon enters Virgo late in the day.*

17 FEBRUARY

This is a good day for getting together with someone you love and also for business meetings. You'll find that agreements can be made relatively straightforwardly. A financial negotiation could also be agreed upon. *Moon in Virgo.*

18 FEBRUARY

As the sun enters the zodiac sign Pisces you'll appreciate the opportunity over the next four weeks to be more inspired by what you do and who you meet. It's a good time to plan a holiday, to take a trip and to put new ideas into place. *Moon in Virgo.*

19 FEBRUARY

While the moon is in Virgo you will find the time to complete chores. When the moon is in Libra you may be more inclined to look for peace at all costs, which may surprise the people who know how hard you can fight for your ideas and plans. You'll enjoy the creature comforts of home later in the day. *Moon in Libra.*

20 FEBRUARY

Your sociable side will come out just in time for a friendly day. You'll enjoy being with the people you feel most comfortable with and will wish to avoid crowds. ***Moon in Libra.***

21 FEBRUARY

Your more boisterous side is likely to emerge and you'll appreciate the opportunity to feel engaged at work and with your everyday chores. You'll also enjoy getting things done at home. ***Moon enters Scorpio.***

22 FEBRUARY

You'll enjoy connecting more deeply with someone you love and a trip or social event will be uplifting. A financial matter could be ideal, so investigate options to invest or to do business. You may spy a bargain at the shops. ***Moon in Scorpio.***

23 FEBRUARY

This is a lovely day for romance, and you'll be inspired by the people you love the most. A financial or personal domestic matter could go well. ***Moon in Sagittarius.***

24 FEBRUARY

This is another lovely day for romance, and you'll also enjoy beautifying your home and environment. You may also enjoy investing in yourself for a change, improving your appearance and well-being. ***Moon in Sagittarius.***

25 FEBRUARY

You may be surprised by a message or news. Someone you already know can be unpredictable will behave true to form. It's a good day to be adaptable but also to hold firm to your principles without being obstinate, or a stalemate could arise. ***Moon enters Capricorn.***

26 FEBRUARY

A trip or visit will be enjoyable and will take you somewhere different or refreshing. A trek to the ocean or to meet a family member will fit the bill. ***Moon in Capricorn.***

27 FEBRUARY

You're known for your passion and charm but few people realise you can be as unpredictable as anyone; today, you may simply feel like doing something different. Avoid rocking the boat by keeping everyone in the loop. Back up computers as technical glitches could arise, and be patient with travel delays. ***Moon enters Aquarius.***

28 FEBRUARY

You'll enjoy being super expressive. Take a fresh development in your stride, as otherwise you may be drawn to make a mountain out of a molehill. Health and fitness are best approached one step at a time. You'll enjoy getting together with someone you love or with someone who shares your values. ***Moon in Aquarius.***

March

career   love   home   health   finance

1 MARCH

You're thinking analytically, which will help you to move ahead with your various projects and also with planning. However, not everyone will have the same insight as you so be tactful if someone seems disgruntled. *Moon enters Pisces.*

2 MARCH

The Pisces new moon signals the chance to turn a corner in your home or family or a domestic situation. However, you may be seeing life through rose-coloured glasses so ensure you have all the details and trust your instincts.

3 MARCH

The Venus-Mars-Pluto conjunction signals important conversations and, for some, financial transactions. A key relationship could be deepened. Be inspired, but above all ensure facts have been adequately researched to avoid mistakes being made as this could be an intense turning point for you. *Moon in Pisces.*

4 MARCH

You may need to provide a shoulder for someone to cry on or at least have broad shoulders to help support someone who may have grievances or is simply sensitive. If you are feeling vulnerable there will be someone to help you, so ensure you look for support. *Moon in Aries.*

5 MARCH

Developments at home or due to a change of environment will be enjoyable and uplifting, so ensure you reach out and make upbeat plans. *Moon in Aries.*

6 MARCH

As both Mars and Venus step into Aquarius you'll enjoy doing something different and may even be ready to plunge into new terrain via a trip or a change of routine. You may gain new perspective over a financial or personal matter. *Moon in Taurus.*

7 MARCH

The Taurean moon will help you to feel more grounded and practical, especially with circumstances that may be unusual or unexpected. Avoid obstinacy and ensure you are being open minded, especially regarding negotiations and travel. *Moon in Taurus.*

8 MARCH

This is a good day for discussions, as these are likely to go well. A financial matter may be decide upon or you may receive a financial boost or compliment. *Moon enters Gemini.*

9 MARCH

The Gemini moon will bring out your appreciation for having a sense of freedom and you may even appear a little non-committal. If you have important arrangements to make ensure you are committed to a course of action and show that you are. *Moon in Gemini.*

10 MARCH

As Mercury enters Pisces you will feel increasingly inspired over the coming weeks, and artistic, creative and inspired projects will move forward. This is a good day to make a commitment or an agreement as it's likely to take. *Moon in Gemini.*

11 MARCH

It's important to you that you feel inspired, so you'll enjoy the Cancer moon as you'll look for invigorating company and activities. However, you must always ensure you're being practical when the moon is in Cancer or you can tend to be easily distracted or misled. *Moon in Cancer.*

12 MARCH

This is a good weekend for your favourite activities, from sports to spirituality. You'll enjoy connecting more deeply with those you love, so organise a treat. *Moon in Cancer.*

13 MARCH

This is an excellent day to enjoy the arts, creativity, music, dance and simply to relax. If you've been considering a little DIY or to spruce up décor you'll feel inspired. Spiritual interests could be particularly rewarding. Romance will also blossom. *Moon enters Leo.*

14 MARCH

You'll enjoy the chance to beautify or improve your surroundings, either at home or via a change of environment. A meeting or trip will be productive. *Moon in Leo.*

15 MARCH

The Leo moon is motivational and you'll feel enthusiastic about getting things done. If you find not everyone is in the same frame of mind, ensure you avoid appearing bossy. Someone close has your back. *Moon in Leo.*

16 MARCH

Your attention to detail both at work and in your personal life will be rewarding. If you disagree with someone, find a way to get down to brass tacks to establish common ground. *Moon in Virgo.*

17 MARCH

You'll enjoy a change of routine and the chance to dive a little deeper into projects you enjoy. An impromptu visit will be enjoyable. Someone close may surprise you. *Moon in Virgo.*

18 MARCH

The Virgo full moon shines a light on your personal life. A romantic or domestic situation may require a little more focus as you may be seeing things through rose-coloured glasses. Talks with a group or organisation could signal the start of a new agreement.

19 MARCH

You may be surprised by a situation that exposes someone's unpredictability. A change of routine may involve complex logistics, so ensure you plan ahead well in advance to avoid annoyances. *Moon in Libra.*

20 MARCH

When the sun enters Aries it is the vernal equinox. During the next four weeks you may find that your work and projects become a greater focus and that you feel more upbeat and proactive with your relationships. *Moon in Scorpio.*

21 MARCH

Key talks and a meeting could mean changes at home, with family or within your personal life. You may enjoy planning or undertaking a trip. *Moon in Scorpio.*

22 MARCH

To make changes there is inevitably a little upheaval involved, and today may be a case in point. Find ways to earth your projects so that you can work with the unpredictability of some variables in a practical way. *Moon enters Sagittarius.*

23 MARCH

This is a good time to be making changes at home, with family or with property. Creativity and changes in décor or even a move may be successful as long as you have planned well in advance. If you are spiritually inclined you may reach an epiphany. *Moon in Sagittarius.*

24 MARCH

You are feeling optimistic and outgoing, and while this will be uplifting, as the day goes by a more practical and grounded approach both at work and in your personal life will reap rewards. *Moon enters Capricorn.*

25 MARCH

This is a constructive day for talks with someone important in your life, especially where situations have been up in the air. You prefer to be passionate and spontaneous yet the moon in Capricorn could slow things down, so be patient. *Moon in Capricorn.*

26 MARCH

This is another good day for talks, especially about matters in which you'd like to see change at home over time. Business and work discussions could be constructive, and a trip could be transformative. *Moon in Capricorn.*

27 MARCH

You may surprise yourself with how expressive you are at the moment, as you are much bolder than you have been for a while. Just avoid delicate topics as these may cause argumentative responses. *Moon in Aquarius.*

28 MARCH

This is a good day to come to a workable agreement either at home, with property or with someone you have made a commitment to, so take the initiative. ***Moon in Aquarius.***

29 MARCH

The Pisces moon will bring out your intuitive side, so ensure you trust your gut instincts. You'll know what the best way forward is, especially domestically. ***Moon in Pisces.***

30 MARCH

Focus on allowing beauty and harmony to prevail as this will reap positive rewards, especially in your personal life and with creative or family matters. Avoid allowing deep disagreements to dominate your day. Focus on being with people you know love you. ***Moon in Pisces.***

31 MARCH

You are motivated to get ahead and can make great headway both in your personal life and at work. Just avoid appearing too feisty as your efforts could backfire. ***Moon in Aries.***

April

career   love   home   health   finance

1 APRIL

The Aries new moon spells a fresh chapter in a work or health context; you are ready for something untried. For some Scorpios this new moon is ideal for beginning a fresh chapter in a key relationship. Your vulnerabilities may rise during this time, but this will be your chance to turn a corner and to leave something behind.

2 APRIL

You may receive unexpected news from someone important or at work. A health and well-being development is best approached from a practical point of view. Someone special will be unexpectedly helpful or will need your help. ***Moon enters Taurus.***

3 APRIL

You'll find conversations and improvements you initiate particularly transformative, especially at home. You may be drawn to visit a beautiful place or to improve your home life. ***Moon in Taurus.***

4 APRIL

Be inspired by your dreams as you could make headway with your projects, especially at home or with family and someone special. ***Moon in Taurus.***

5 APRIL

Developments at home will be definitive, as you'll get the chance to make agreements that stick. If you're travelling or making key decisions ensure you have all the details and that your goals align with your values and wishes. ***Moon in Gemini.***

6 APRIL

This is a good day for talks, especially regarding matters that may seem out of your hands. Take the time to discuss your ideas with someone you know has your back. ***Moon in Gemini.***

7 APRIL

You can make great progress with a health and work project, which will certainly help you to see that you are on the right track. A trip or conversation could be ideal. ***Moon in Cancer.***

8 APRIL

Creative and spiritual Scorpios will see that the more you invest in your projects the better the outcome for you. That is unless your expectations have been super high or unrealistic, in which case you may need to correct some of them. ***Moon in Cancer.***

9 APRIL

This is a productive weekend, and whether you're working at the office or at home, outside in the garden or on your favourite project your initiatives can go far. ***Moon in Cancer.***

10 APRIL

Communications will merit a little extra care and attention as there may be misunderstandings. If you're travelling, ensure you give yourself enough time to factor in delays. Avoid tense topics as these will escalate quickly. ***Moon in Leo.***

11 APRIL

You'll appreciate the opportunity to get down to brass tacks with key communications both at work and at home. Avoid allowing a difference of opinion to become a stalemate. ***Moon in Leo.***

12 APRIL

You'll enjoy deepening your connection with someone close and romance could flourish. Creative, artistic and spiritual Scorpios will be particularly inspired. ***Moon in Leo.***

13 APRIL

This is a good day to make agreements, both at home and at work as it is a truly productive day. Just ensure you have all the details before committing to any long-term plans to avoid making mistakes. *Moon in Virgo.*

14 APRIL

You'll enjoy indulging in love, romance, music and being creative. A family matter may catch your attention. You may be excited about a fresh work incentive. It's a good day to boost health and vitality. *Moon enters Libra.*

15 APRIL

As Mars enters Pisces your personal life is likely to become a focus. However, you may tend to be highly idealistic, so ensure you keep your feet on the ground if you are making key decisions over the next month. *Moon in Libra.*

16 APRIL

The Libran full moon signifies the start of a fresh cycle for you such as a fresh phase at work or a new health routine. You may discover you want more harmony, balance and peace in your life. Stability and security are possible at home or with family, so this is a good time to look for ways to achieve it.

17 APRIL

You'll feel more passionate about your ideas and ventures and will feel motivated to spend time with those you love and on activities you adore. If you sense a little tension in the air, avoid escalating it and find peaceful ways to enjoy your day. *Moon in Scorpio.*

18 APRIL

You may hear unexpected news or will be engaged in an unusual circumstance. A health matter can progress, so take the initiative. Avoid contributing to stress and drama and find peaceful ways to overcome hurdles and enjoy your day. *Moon in Scorpio.*

19 APRIL

The Scorpio moon will encourage you to speak your mind when necessary and to take the time to engage in projects you're passionate about. When the moon is in Sagittarius you may feel more inclined to be boisterous and outspoken but others may see you as blunt, so if storm clouds are brewingtake things one step at a time. *Moon in Sagittarius.*

20 APRIL

As the sun enters Taurus you will feel more stable and secure about certain agreements and arrangements, either at work or in your personal life. This is a good time to find ways to move forward in the most realistic way. ***Moon in Sagittarius.***

21 APRIL

This is a good time to gain traction with your work and creative ideas. Your family and those close to you will draw much of your attention. ***Moon in Capricorn.***

22 APRIL

Spending time on projects and with people you love really does soothe the soul, so if you're feeling the tiredness of the week plan some lovely events for this evening or tomorrow. ***Moon in Capricorn.***

23 APRIL

A get-together or talk with someone important to you could open doors to a deeper understanding of them, so take the time for meetings and chats. ***Moon in Aquarius.***

24 APRIL

You'll find out whether you've over- or under-estimated a project or a person. Luckily, you'll get the chance to put things right if you avoid being obstinate. ***Moon in Aquarius.***

25 APRIL

You're thinking creatively, which will help you to get over logistical matters and think outside the box. However, you may also be a little idealistic, so take things one step at a time. ***Moon in Pisces.***

26 APRIL

This is a romantic time for you and you'll enjoy family time and/or being with someone special. A creative, musical or inspiring project can blossom. ***Moon in Pisces.***

27 APRIL

A lovely time for the arts, romance and music will raise your spirits. If you're single you may meet someone charming and couples will enjoy rebooting romance. ***Moon enters Aries.***

28 APRIL

There is a transformative quality to events, and you'll appreciate the opportunity to discuss your plans with those they concern. It's a good time for a trip or visit. ***Moon in Aries.***

29 APRIL

A meeting could be important and will provide you with insight into someone special. If you're travelling it will be a particularly memorable trip. Business and negotiations could be particularly significant, so ensure you are happy with the details. ***Moon in Aries.***

30 APRIL

The partial solar eclipse in Taurus signals you are ready for a fresh phase in a work or health situation. If it's your birthday in October you may begin a fresh agreement in a business or personal partnership. Avoid gambling, both financially and emotionally. A situation that arises could be ideal.

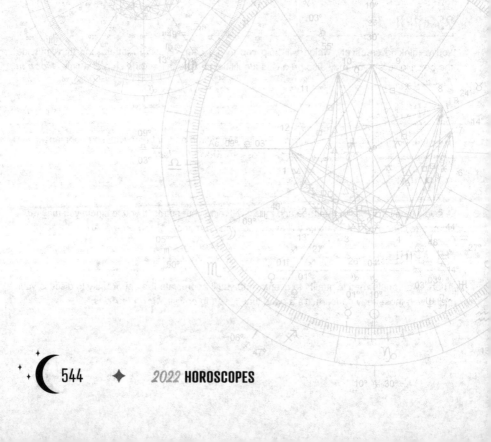

May

career   love   home   health   finance

1 MAY

This is a good day to deepen personal and family ties. Work around your home could be a success. A trip or meeting will bring you closer to family. Romance could blossom, so organise a treat! *Moon in Taurus.*

2 MAY

As Venus enters Aries you'll feel more dynamic and outspoken and also more passionate! You'll enjoy pursuing favourite pastimes and interests such as music and spirituality. *Moon in Gemini.*

3 MAY

The changes you wish to see in your life can certainly take effect, but if you feel a little overwhelmed by developments ensure you take time out. *Moon in Gemini.*

4 MAY

Someone may surprise you and it will be a pleasant surprise for most Scorpios, such as a refreshing change of pace or news. For some, news from a partner will merit careful attention. Romance could take you somewhere different. Singles may unexpectedly meet someone, especially if you were born from 5 to 7 November. *Moon in Gemini.*

5 MAY

You may be surprised by news or developments such as a change of schedule at work or a fresh interest or activity that takes you in new directions. A partner or someone close may have a surprise. *Moon in Cancer.*

6 MAY

This is a good day to discuss recent developments and for meetings, especially romantic ones. A financial matter will improve your mood. *Moon in Cancer.*

7 MAY

This is a productive weekend, and whether you're working or at home you can complete a great many chores. Collaborations and joint ventures will be a particular focus. Sports, nature walks and your efforts to improve domestic dynamics could all produce good results. *Moon in Leo.*

8 MAY

You'll enjoy being outgoing and adventurous. Sports, physical exercise and organising your working week in advance will all get you feeling motivated. However, someone close may not feel the same way, so avoid overwhelming them. *Moon in Leo.*

9 MAY

If you like a little tension in the air as you find it motivating you'll like today, but if you prefer life on an even keel ensure you take things one step at a time. Aim to tie up loose ends at work and regarding communications before Mercury turns retrograde tomorrow. *Moon enters Virgo.*

10 MAY

As Mercury turns retrograde you're likely to receive key news that means you will need to review your circumstances. For some this will mean a fresh negotiation, and for others changes at home or with family. Try to allow extra time for travel and communications to avoid frustration over the coming weeks. *Moon in Virgo.*

11 MAY

As Jupiter joins Venus and Chiron in Aries you will feel more outspoken and may also tend to feel more passionate, especially in your personal life and about domestic matters. You will gain in energy over the coming weeks and months but may need to pace yourself to avoid feeling over-tired. *Moon in Virgo.*

12 MAY

When the moon is in Libra you are looking for more peace and harmony in your life. However, to find it some matters always need to be set straight. A little tact and diplomacy will work wonders. *Moon in Libra.*

13 MAY

You'll enjoy a reunion and the chance to catch up over important work matters. *Moon in Libra.*

14 MAY

The Scorpio moon puts you in a positive mindset but can also bring intense emotions to the surface. Find ways to channel emotional energy into productive, fun activities as you will get a lot done this weekend. You may enjoy a change of pace or of place. *Moon in Scorpio.*

15 MAY

As a determined individual there is little that takes you off course unless you become caught in a situation where there is no wiggle room. You will gain the chance to renegotiate some matters that will enable you to move forward. Romance could blossom, so organise a date. *Moon in Scorpio.*

16 MAY

The total lunar eclipse in Scorpio marks considerable changes for you, especially in your personal life if you were born from 15 to 17 November. It will spotlight an important agreement or negotiations. If you were born later a health or work matter will be in the spotlight. Be practical and grounded and avoid snap decisions.

17 MAY

This is a good day to check that the agreements you're hoping to make hold water. You may tend to be a little idealistic, so ensure you double-check figures. It's a good day to make a commitment. *Moon in Sagittarius.*

18 MAY

You'll enjoy a domestic or family-related event. For some Scorpios a meeting or trip will be ideal and could spotlight your spiritual, artistic or personal interests. *Moon in Capricorn.*

19 MAY

A change you'll enjoy is in full swing and you'll appreciate the help of someone close such as a business or personal partner. You could make positive changes within your relationships so take the initiative. *Moon in Capricorn.*

20 MAY

You'll appreciate the sense that some of your relationships and agreements are moving into fresh territory, and this is a good day to discuss how the new arrangements will work for you. *Moon in Aquarius.*

21 MAY

Key news or a meeting will be significant. For some, developments will involve new ways to agree upon arrangements that are already in place, and this weekend's get-together will foster a reunion and the chance to deepen your understanding of someone. *Moon in Aquarius.*

22 MAY

A trip somewhere exciting or the chance to improve your domestic circumstances will be a drawcard this weekend. You'll appreciate the opportunity to improve your environment in some way. It's also a good time to invest in your own well-being. *Moon enters Pisces.*

23 MAY

This is a good time to reconfigure or review an arrangement. It may mean that you must renegotiate, but the review will put you in a stronger position. You may be returning to an old haunt, which you'll enjoy. *Moon in Pisces.*

24 MAY

This is an excellent day for talks. If you're trying to make progress with a particular plan or project you'll find today's stars will help you do just that. *Moon in Pisces.*

25 MAY

You'll be feeling increasingly dynamic over the coming weeks but if you have ever been called bossy watch out, as you may seem increasingly so unless you are careful. You could certainly get a great deal done and negotiations and travel will go well. *Moon in Aries.*

26 MAY

If you need someone's agreement for a plan to get ahead this is a good day to ask for it. You may benefit from reviewing how you see a project or idea, especially regarding love, health and/or work. *Moon in Aries.*

27 MAY

You are a passionate character and can sometimes have trouble holding back your true thoughts, even when they're destructive. For the sake of peace you will need to avoid arguments, as these could escalate quickly. *Moon in Taurus.*

28 MAY

Venus is in Taurus for the next few weeks will encourage you to enjoy life more, and a little extra comfort, sensuality and romance will go a long way to putting a smile on your face. *Moon in Taurus.*

29 MAY

You'll feel productive and can get a great deal done around the house and garden. A creative, family or sports venture could be enjoyable. Someone close may have key news for you. *Moon enters Gemini.*

30 MAY

The Gemini new moon will spotlight a new agreement or arrangement. Key developments, for some to do with work and for others family, will signal this is a good time to be flexible and adaptable to changes.

31 MAY

This is a good day both for a health or beauty appointment. You'll also feel motivated to beautify your home or office. Be prepared to make changes so that you feel more positive. *Moon in Gemini.*

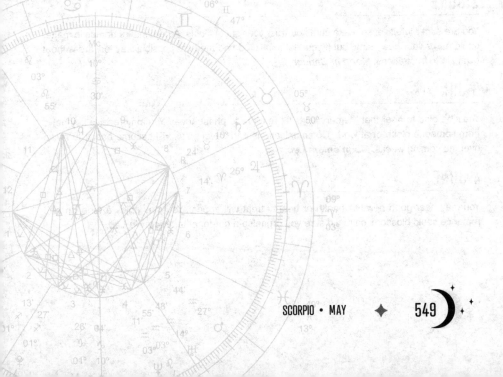

June

career   love   home   health   finance

1 JUNE

The moon in Cancer brings your caring and nurturing side out, yet certain aspects of your day are likely to annoy you so focus on self-nurturance first up. If feel you're under pressure take breaks to unwind when you can. *Moon in Cancer.*

2 JUNE

You are super intuitive, so make sure you trust your gut instincts. A personal or domestic matter could make your heart sing, but if you feel conflicted find the best possible way forward without giving in to frustrations. *Moon in Cancer.*

3 JUNE

You'll be glad to hear that Mercury ends its retrograde phase today. You may receive key news from someone close or at work. Communications and travel plans will become easier to make over the coming weeks. *Moon enters Leo.*

4 JUNE

You may hear good news. A health or beauty treat will appeal. You may enjoy a meeting and romance could blossom, so make sure you organise a get-together. *Moon in Leo.*

5 JUNE

The Leo moon brings out your feisty side and you may be inclined to believe everyone is feeling as bold and dynamic as you are. They aren't! Delays and a sense of annoyance needn't get in the way of your plans; just be patient and you'll be super productive. *Moon in Leo.*

6 JUNE

This is a good day to pay attention to the details, especially at work and with your long-term plans, as you could make great headway with your projects. Just avoid being super demanding as this could backfire. *Moon in Virgo.*

7 JUNE

You'll enjoy a spontaneous event or a surprise get-together. News may be uplifting and could introduce something different into your usual day. *Moon in Virgo.*

8 JUNE

Be practical and you could get a great deal done. Meetings, trips, negotiations and financial matters will all benefit from a level head. *Moon enters Libra.*

9 JUNE

The Libra moon can bring out your inner perfectionist. If you find the day is easy going you'll enjoy being with like-minded people, but if events are annoying and it seems as though you're having to re-invent the wheel take some time out just to savour people and situations that are going well. *Moon in Libra.*

10 JUNE

You'll see that your hard work and relationships are regaining a more even keel. You may find meetings are dynamic and that you make great headway. A trip or talk could be transformative. *Moon enters Scorpio.*

11 JUNE

A friend, colleague or personal partner may have unexpected news or will surprise you, especially if it's your birthday from 7 to 9 November. Mid-November Scorpios will experience a change of routine at work or due to a health or beauty appointment. *Moon in Scorpio.*

12 JUNE

You'll enjoy a lovely reunion with someone who makes your heart sing. If some communications are not on track, take time out to find ways you can get on without stirring the pot. *Moon enters Sagittarius.*

13 JUNE

Communications with someone close are about to get a whole lot lighter. You may be in a less serious mood as you begin the week. You may receive good news from a partner, financially or regarding a shared interest. ***Moon in Sagittarius.***

14 JUNE

The full moon and supermoon in Sagittarius represents a fresh chapter for you in a particular agreement. For some this will mean a fresh financial situation, and for others a new way to share key areas such as duties or space at home.

15 JUNE

Avoid rushing as you may make mistakes or, worse, have a bump or a scrape. If you are meeting someone sensitive or have undergone arguments, try to be tactful to avoid bruising egos. ***Moon in Capricorn.***

16 JUNE

This is a good day to organise a special event for someone such as a catch-up at your home or at theirs. You may be ready to make a commitment to a new way of doing things at home, at work (especially if you work from home) or regarding shared responsibilities such as finances. ***Moon enters Aquarius.***

17 JUNE

You're proactive and dynamic and can certainly achieve a great deal. A business or personal partner may have surprise news for you. Be spontaneous but avoid impulsiveness. ***Moon in Aquarius.***

18 JUNE

A difference of values could be at the root of differences of opinions. Take things one step at a time, especially with domestic and personal matters, to avoid arguments as these could turn into a Mexican stand-off. ***Moon in Aquarius.***

19 JUNE

You tend to communicate in many different ways and not only verbally. An element of tension in the air can be dispelled with friendly gestures and attention to details. ***Moon in Pisces.***

20 JUNE

The Pisces moon will bring out your intuition, which you'll find useful at work and at home. Just avoid being moody and having super-high expectations as you'll be disappointed. ***Moon in Pisces.***

21 JUNE

As the sun enters Cancer, marking the solstice, you will feel inclined to focus more on family and shared duties such as finances. Trust your instincts and you could get a lot done. Romance could blossom, so organise a date or a night in! ***Moon in Aries.***

22 JUNE

You'll feel more inclined to be busy and upbeat and may be a little short-tempered if people don't match your speed. Be positive but avoid putting pressure on others as they won't like it. ***Moon in Aries.***

23 JUNE

You'll feel more in tune with other people's needs and may also feel drawn to gaining extra stability and comfort in your own life. Just avoid being stubborn and feisty as this will ruffle people's feathers! ***Moon enters Taurus.***

24 JUNE

While you may see other people as unpredictable, they may see you in the same light. Aim to establish common ground for the best results. ***Moon in Taurus.***

25 JUNE

You'll enjoy slowing down this weekend and engaging in some creature comforts. A visit or trip will be enriching. Romance could blossom, so organise a treat. Singles should mingle; you may meet someone romantic. ***Moon in Taurus.***

26 JUNE

You'll be drawn to doing something different or simply getting out of the house, and travel, sports and being in nature will appeal. It'll certainly recharge your batteries. ***Moon in Gemini.***

27 JUNE

There is a therapeutic quality to the day, and you'll enjoy being with like-minded, uplifting people. Negotiations and talks could be productive. However, you may also feel a little sensitive or vulnerable. If you need guidance, an expert or adviser could prove helpful. ***Moon in Gemini.***

28 JUNE

You may be pleasantly surprised by a development. A negotiation or project could advance well, so take the initiative. You'll enjoy a change of routine. ***Moon enters Cancer.***

29 JUNE

The Cancerian new moon will kick-start a fresh chapter in a shared venture. You may need to persuade someone of your plans, especially if you need their co-operation. A development with family or regarding a project may be tough, but if you focus on the facts you'll gain ground.

30 JUNE

Trust your intuition, as it will not let you down. You'll enjoy indulging in your favourite pastimes and activities, as these will raise morale. *Moon in Cancer.*

July

career   love   home   health   finance

1 JULY

There is a great deal of tension building in the skies and this could contribute to arguments, so be calm. Aim to channel energy into productive activities. Some communications may be confusing, so ensure you double-check details. ***Moon in Leo.***

2 JULY

You'll enjoy a trip or a get-together but must ensure you pay attention to details to avoid mistakes. Emotions are running high, so maintain perspective as someone may be feeling feisty and oppositional. ***Moon in Leo.***

3 JULY

Your organisational skills are peaking and you could certainly get a lot done. However, you may also be demanding of others and they could see you as putting pressure on them. Find a balanced approach for the best results. ***Moon enters Virgo.***

4 JULY

Tense undercurrents in talks could bring out your worst side. A financial matter may require a little more research before you can commit. ***Moon in Virgo.***

5 JULY

Communications are likely to move into new territory. It's worth your while to be adaptable and to do your own financial research. Avoid being stubborn. ***Moon enters Libra.***

6 JULY

This is a good day to build bridges with people you have argued with, and also for remedial work at home or on domestic dynamics. ***Moon in Libra.***

7 JULY

You'll appreciate the opportunity to spend a little time on yourself and on your health and well-being. A get-together may be therapeutic. Just avoid rushing, as you may be a little accident prone. ***Moon in Libra.***

8 JULY

You may be pleasantly surprised by news or a get-together. Be careful with some communications, as someone may take your comments personally. If you need expert advice it will be available. ***Moon in Scorpio.***

9 JULY

This is another day to be careful with communications and also to be super focused with financial transactions, as mistakes can be made. Avoid misunderstanding and do your own research. A change at home could be more complex than you'd hoped. ***Moon in Scorpio.***

10 JULY

You'll enjoy a change of routine and a reunion. A new look or fitness routine may appeal, and this is a good day to research one. ***Moon enters Sagittarius.***

11 JULY

When the moon is in Sagittarius you will feel more adventurous and outgoing. However, you may also feel inclined to splurge at the shops and overindulge, so keep an eye on overspending. ***Moon in Sagittarius.***

12 JULY

Your practical and capable sides will come out and you'll enjoy getting things done. If finances need a minor overhaul, this is a good day to consider a fresh budget. ***Moon enters Capricorn.***

13 JULY

The full moon and supermoon in Capricorn will spotlight an important financial matter. You are ready to consider how to share or distribute your resources in a new way. This full moon can also spotlight changes in your personal circumstances, which will be transformational. Look for security and stability but avoid stubbornness.

14 JULY

You'll discover whether your expectations have been unrealistic, especially regarding a personal matter. If you discover a financial anomaly this is a good time to set things right. You may be prone to misunderstandings and delays, so be patient. ***Moon enters Aquarius.***

15 JULY

Some interactions and relationships may be intense, so ensure you keep things on an even keel in your communications. If an obstacle arises you will overcome it. ***Moon in Aquarius.***

16 JULY

A key meeting will be delightful. Spiritually minded Scorpios will enjoy deepening your understanding. A visit at home or a trip will take you somewhere beautiful. Just avoid delicate topics and traffic delays by planning well ahead. ***Moon enters Pisces.***

17 JULY

This is a lovely day for romance and to enjoy the company of those you love. Music, the arts, spirituality and creativity will all appeal. You may enjoy receiving guests or a trip somewhere beautiful. ***Moon in Pisces.***

18 JULY

Key interactions and transactions could be transformative, so ensure you keep an eye on the details. You may receive a financial or ego boost. ***Moon enters Aries.***

19 JULY

As Mercury enters upbeat Leo you'll feel more outspoken and proactive over the coming weeks. Your own interests, be these involving sports or study, will gain ground. Be positive! ***Moon in Aries.***

20 JULY

If you tend to fire up easily take breaks, as you may find this is an intense time. It's a good time for research, especially into finances and projects, but you may tend to take other people's news personally. ***Moon enters Taurus.***

21 JULY

You'll find that there is a more even playing field, which will enable you to feel practical and grounded and which you'll like. *Moon in Taurus.*

22 JULY

As the sun enters Leo you will feel more expressive and will wish to spend extra time pursuing personal projects and pastimes. This is a good day to trust that your confidence and experience put you in a strong position. *Moon in Taurus.*

23 JULY

This is an excellent day for a trip and for study, domestic matters and indulging more in sports, spirituality and your favourite activities. *Moon in Gemini.*

24 JULY

Your more light-hearted side comes out when the moon is in Gemini, and you'll enjoy being chatty and sociable. A fun activity with people you love will appeal. *Moon in Gemini.*

25 JULY

You won't get on with everyone and trying to match your values with theirs may not work, so ensure you establish common ground first if you have no alternative but to collaborate and co-operate. *Moon enters Cancer.*

26 JULY

This is another day to choose your words carefully as someone you must get on with, for example at work, may not agree with your views or the actions you take. Travel, study, work and communications may be delayed, so be patient. *Moon in Cancer.*

27 JULY

Communications and travel may proceed with less obstacles, but for some developments may snowball. If so, take time out and seek the advice of a trusted friend or expert. *Moon in Cancer.*

28 JULY

The Leo new moon points to a fresh chapter regarding shared circumstances such as those at work or at home. A new financial agreement may be put in place. Expect an unforeseen development. Back up computers and plan extra time for travel as there may be disruptions.

29 JULY

While your plans can go ahead at a fast pace, not everyone will agree with your choices. Be tactful and diplomatic where necessary for the best results, but if you are convinced of your stance you could make great progress even if you undergo stress. ***Moon in Leo.***

30 JULY

You'll appreciate the sense that the spotlight is off you as the day progresses and that you can relax a little. Time out to recharge your batteries will be beneficial. ***Moon enters Virgo.***

31 JULY

You'll enjoy a get-together with like-minded people. Romance can blossom, so organise a treat. However, some decisions will merit careful attention. A legal, business, study or financial matter may require a commitment. ***Moon in Virgo.***

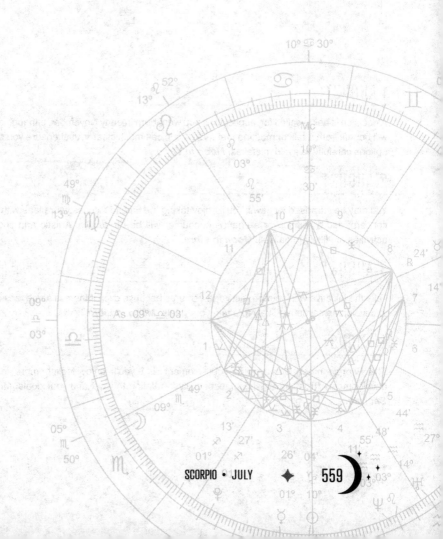

August

| career | love | home | health | finance |

1 AUGUST

A decision is being called for, especially if you were born in early November, although all Scorpios will benefit from a talk or meeting that makes choices much clearer. Just ensure you search your options carefully to avoid mistakes. *Moon in Virgo.*

2 AUGUST

You may be surprised by news. You'll enjoy taking the time to discuss your plans with those they concern, and a reunion or a chance encounter will be productive. Artistic and sports-related activities are likely to go well. *Moon in Libra.*

3 AUGUST

Take the initiative with your projects and ventures because even if there is some tension involved in developmentsyou are likely to attain your goals. *Moon in Libra.*

4 AUGUST

The Scorpio moon puts you in your element and you'll enjoy feeling more in tune with developments. Trust your instincts, especially in relation to work and your goals. *Moon enters Scorpio.*

5 AUGUST

You can gain ground with a personal venture or creative project through sheer hard work and determination. You'll get ahead with financial budgets by ensuring you have a cash flow. Avoid an oppositional approach and find ways to collaborate for the best results. ***Moon in Scorpio.***

6 AUGUST

You're collaborating well, even if some of your ideas don't match those of other people. You'll be willing to see their point of view. An outgoing, upbeat approach to family and home life will be productive. ***Moon enters Sagittarius.***

7 AUGUST

This is a lovely day for romance and for improving domestic circumstances. However, you won't automatically agree with everyone and common ground will need to be found to avoid arguments. ***Moon in Sagittarius.***

8 AUGUST

This is a good day to undertake activities and projects that everyone enjoys. A physical activity such as walking in nature will be therapeutic. It's also a good time to spruce up your domestic life and to welcome visitors. ***Moon enters Capricorn.***

9 AUGUST

Mercury at the zenith of your chart suggests key talks will provide a turning point. For many this will be to do with money, and for others love. Be patient if you are travelling or undertaking complex discussions as there may be delays. You will succeed with a diligent approach. ***Moon in Capricorn.***

10 AUGUST

Your conversations may be more emotionally charged than you'd prefer, so be practical and realistic. Be prepared to enter fresh agreements and to learn something new. Avoid obstinacy. ***Moon enters Aquarius.***

11 AUGUST

A change of focus and the chance to do something different will be enjoyable but may involve having to overcome some logistics, so ensure you plan ahead. Abrupt changes to your schedule are best navigated carefully. You'll enjoy relaxing this evening. ***Moon in Aquarius.***

12 AUGUST

The Aquarian full moon will spotlight key negotiations and may also bring to light the importance of a trip or a change of environment. Be prepared to make changes. Think laterally if an obstacle arises.

13 AUGUST

Artistic and creative Scorpios will find today's atmosphere is ideal for work, but you need to focus on the details as you may be a little forgetful and should double-check facts for the best results. **Moon in Pisces.**

14 AUGUST

You are ready to make a commitment to a project, idea or person. A financial transaction or personal interaction could be beneficial and boost morale. A trip or meeting will set a new situation in motion, so be sure you're happy with it. **Moon enters Aries.**

15 AUGUST

You'll be in touch with people you understand well, which will enable you to make progress with your ventures. You may be drawn to work with a fresh plan of action or to a new group or activity. You'll enjoy a reunion or hearing from an old friend. **Moon in Aries.**

16 AUGUST

Be open to fresh ideas and to changing your usual schedule, as you'll enjoy meeting new people and discussing interesting ideas. A trip could take you somewhere unexpected. **Moon in Aries.**

17 AUGUST

Pay extra attention to the details, especially at home and in connection with your projects and activities such as sports and spirituality. You will feel inspired but may be a little forgetful or head in the clouds. **Moon in Taurus.**

18 AUGUST

A trip and some communications may be delayed, so factor in extra time to avoid feeling frustrated. You'll enjoy romance and cocooning. Domestic improvements will delight. **Moon in Taurus.**

19 AUGUST

You'll appreciate the sense that you are making progress and are happier with your general situation, but some interactions and activities will merit careful attention to avoid misunderstandings. If you're travelling, arrange spare time to avoid delays. **Moon in Gemini.**

20 AUGUST

Mars will now be in Gemini until the end of March 2023, which will help you to make great progress with your negotiations and bring a lighter feeling to relationships. A financial matter may require more attention, and it's in your interest to avoid overspending. **Moon in Gemini.**

21 AUGUST

You'll enjoy socialising and relaxing and may even feel a little escapist. You'll appreciate a change of environment or at home. Just avoid over-indulging as you'll regret it tomorrow. *Moon in Gemini.*

22 AUGUST

This is a good day for discussions and negotiations at work. If you must impress someone this is the day to do it! A trip will take you somewhere potentially transformational. *Moon in Cancer.*

23 AUGUST

Now that the sun is in Virgo for the next four weeks you are likely to gradually feel more focused and less distracted, especially at work. However, you may also be more demanding of others so ensure you maintain perspective. *Moon in Cancer.*

24 AUGUST

You'll appreciate finding the time for your own interests and activities. A lovely get-together with family or a friend will be therapeutic. You may enjoy sprucing up your appearance or helping someone. If you need some advice it will be available. *Moon enters Leo.*

25 AUGUST

The moon in Leo may bring out your more assertive side and you'll be more expressive about your own ideas and values. However, some people may find this aspect of you aggressive, so ensure you are diplomatic. *Moon in Leo.*

26 AUGUST

You'll be more inclined to look for ways to collaborate and find common ground over the coming weeks, especially in relation to friends, groups and organisations. The next few weeks are ideal for improving relationships as your efforts are likely to take. *Moon in Leo.*

27 AUGUST

The new moon in Virgo may bring a surprise your way. Developments at work, in your personal life and with people you love are likely to be a focus, and these will require you to be practical and hands-on. Avoid reactive behaviour as this could lead to a Mexican stand-off. Try to be proactive instead.

28 AUGUST

Serious discussions and long-term commitments may be necessary, especially regarding study, money and your principles in general. You may need to agree to disagree with someone about how to run shared arrangements. Try to come to a workable agreement. *Moon in Virgo.*

29 AUGUST

You'll feel driven to communicate how you feel yet you may feel a little conflicted, so take things one step at a time to avoid speaking before you've thought things through. ***Moon enters Libra.***

30 AUGUST

You can achieve a great deal but will need to be focused and must avoid biting off more than you can chew. Be realistic and optimistic. ***Moon in Libra.***

31 AUGUST

Be inspired by your dreams and goals, but aim for a realistic approach to circumstances and avoid seeing life through rose-coloured glasses for the best results. ***Moon enters Scorpio.***

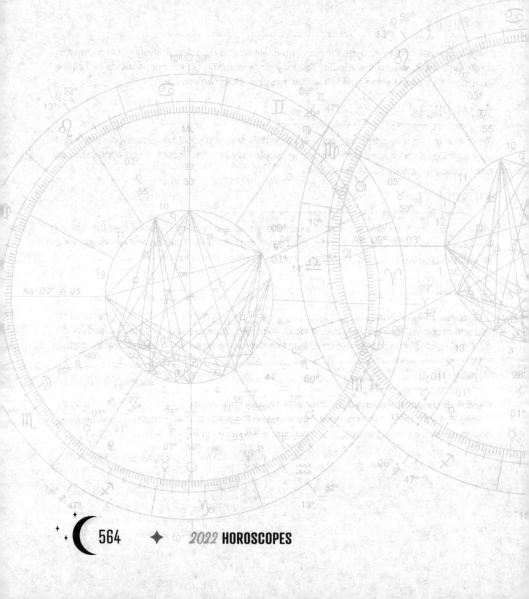

September

career love home health finance

1 SEPTEMBER

You'll feel drawn more so than usual to be with people you love, even if you don't always agree with them! An instinctive approach towards fixing problems will work the best for you. ***Moon in Scorpio.***

2 SEPTEMBER

A difference of opinion may boil down to a difference in values. If you are considering a financial investment, ensure you have double-checked the details. ***Moon enters Sagittarius.***

3 SEPTEMBER

Key talks will provide you with the chance to get down to brass tacks about circumstances. You may be contemplating or undertaking travel or considerable commitments, and these could take you somewhere memorable. ***Moon in Sagittarius.***

4 SEPTEMBER

An outgoing and upbeat approach to someone who can be fiery will be motivational for both of you as you'll gain the chance to appreciate the sense of progress you are experiencing in your relationship and in life in general. ***Moon in Sagittarius.***

5 SEPTEMBER

The next few weeks you'll appreciate approaching your projects and activities with a little more attention to detail. You're unlikely to jump into a venture without adequate research, and this trend starts now! *Moon in Capricorn.*

6 SEPTEMBER

The moon in Capricorn will bring your practical and realistic sides out, which will help you to organise your work life and domestic matters. It's a good time to get paperwork shipshape. *Moon in Capricorn.*

7 SEPTEMBER

You'll appreciate the opportunity to look at someone in a new light. You may notice they are more independent and able to get on with projects themselves, which will give you more independence and quality time. *Moon in Aquarius.*

8 SEPTEMBER

You are a confident and passionate character and those people who aren't can tend to find your intensity overwhelming. You may experience this as someone close may be feeling vulnerable, so give them extra consideration and a wide berth. You may discover a vulnerability of your own or a soft spot for someone! *Moon in Aquarius.*

9 SEPTEMBER

You are a generous and giving character, but you can also realise when you've been a little over-generous and must pull back the reins. Try to get the loose ends of important paperwork tied up before Mercury turns retrograde tomorrow. *Moon in Pisces.*

10 SEPTEMBER

The full moon in Pisces will shine a light on your personal and home life and, for some, travel and your environment. You may receive key information or news at work or concerning your status and general direction in life that will alter how you see yourself.

11 SEPTEMBER

You'll enjoy a change in your usual routine, and socialising and networking will appeal. You may receive an unexpected visitor or invitation. Someone close may have good news. *Moon in Aries.*

12 SEPTEMBER

Someone who can be stubborn and unwilling to discuss matters may be a thorn on the rose, but if you stick with your plans and are persistent without being obstinate you could make great headway, especially at home and with your various projects and friendships. *Moon in Aries.*

13 SEPTEMBER

You'll feel productive and motivated even if it's purely because you need to get on top of chores. Once the moon is in Taurus you'll feel more settled and life may seem less intense. Just avoid obstinacy. *Moon enters Taurus.*

14 SEPTEMBER

You'll enjoy the company of like-minded people, and if you're looking for the green light with a project or venture you may get it. Look for stability and security and you'll find it. *Moon in Taurus.*

15 SEPTEMBER

There is a sensual mood to the day and you'll appreciate getting the time to indulge in activities you love. If you need an excuse to spend time on yourself, for some shopping or a beauty treat, you have it! *Moon enters Gemini.*

16 SEPTEMBER

This is another romantic day and you'll enjoy making time for yourself and the people and activities you love. However, someone may have other plans for you, and work and duties may well keep you busy. *Moon in Gemini.*

17 SEPTEMBER

The moon will bring out your ability to see the world objectively. This will help you to overcome differences, but you may appear to be less motivated than usual as a result so be tactful. You'll enjoy being with like-minded people but must avoid impulsiveness. *Moon in Gemini.*

18 SEPTEMBER

This is a good time to review a health or work matter. If you were born at the end of September you may appreciate the opportunity to discuss important matters with someone close. Plans for a trip or reunion could shape up well. *Moon enters Cancer.*

19 SEPTEMBER

You'll enjoy a reunion and the chance to review some matters you let go a while back, especially to do with family or a creative project such as music or dance. You may enjoy a trip or a meeting that could deepen a relationship. If you have key matters to discuss with an organisation this is a good day to do so. *Moon in Cancer.*

20 SEPTEMBER

You'll enjoy a lovely meeting and can make progress at work. If you're looking for work, circulate your resume and make calls as you may find something by chance. Be diligent with plans at home and these will succeed. *Moon enters Leo.*

21 SEPTEMBER

A sporting event or upbeat activity will encourage you to be more outgoing. You'll enjoy a trip or conversation that brings more variety into your usual routine. *Moon in Leo.*

22 SEPTEMBER

You are likely to be busy and conversations will be lively. You won't always agree with everyone, especially not at home, but you could bring a fresh agreement into being that everyone can live with. *Moon in Leo.*

23 SEPTEMBER

As the sun steps into Libra it marks the equinox, a time when we collectively sense we can achieve more balance and harmony in our lives. Your attention is likely to go increasingly to socialising and networking and a reunion or the chance to deepen some relationships will appeal. *Moon in Virgo.*

24 SEPTEMBER

Romance will blossom this weekend and you'll enjoy surrounding yourself with like-minded people and indulging in good food and a lovely ambience. Creative and spiritual Scorpios will be in your element and will enjoy being relaxed. You may tend to be a little escapist, so avoid overindulging as you'll regret it on Monday! *Moon in Virgo.*

25 SEPTEMBER

The new moon in Libra signals a fresh chapter in your personal life. Be prepared to turn a corner in your personal life and/or with your family. You may be drawn to update your health and well-being schedule.

26 SEPTEMBER

You'll receive important news or will enjoy a key get-together. You may enjoy a reunion or the chance to go over old ground and to review some of your arrangements at home or at work. *Moon in Libra.*

27 SEPTEMBER

You'll enjoy socialising and networking. This is a good time to review a health and well-being plan and to improve your appearance and wardrobe. A trip could be transformative. *Moon in Libra.*

28 SEPTEMBER

You'll feel motivated to lock some of your plans into a workable schedule so you can make concrete decisions moving forward, especially regarding your home and personal lives. *Moon in Scorpio.*

29 SEPTEMBER

A reunion and the chance to go over some of your work decisions to ensure you're on the right track will appeal. You may be drawn to updating domestic décor and to boosting interpersonal dynamics at home. *Moon in Scorpio.*

30 SEPTEMBER

A positive plan of action will bring good results for you in a personal situation. Just avoid gambling, both financially and emotionally. *Moon in Sagittarius.*

October

career   love   home   health   finance

1 OCTOBER

You'll enjoy reconnecting with friends and family this weekend. A trip will be enjoyable but you may find there are delays, so be patient. *Moon in Sagittarius.*

2 OCTOBER

Key news or meetings may involve a slightly nostalgic element. Friends or family will be a large part of your weekend, and if someone is delayed avoid taking this personally. If you prefer being creative rather than socialising you'll find a project can advance. *Moon in Capricorn.*

3 OCTOBER

Today's Capricorn moon will help you to be more hands-on with developments, especially where your organisational skills are concerned. It's a good day to double-check financial circumstances. *Moon in Capricorn.*

4 OCTOBER

Discussions and meetings will be productive, so take the initiative if you must sort out invoices, bills and work logistics. *Moon enters Aquarius.*

5 OCTOBER

Your analytical mind will be strong and is perfect for making key business and personal decisions as your emotions won't get in the way! However, you may appear a little distant, so avoid putting anyone offside. ***Moon in Aquarius.***

6 OCTOBER

A change of pace or of atmosphere at home will be enjoyable, as you will get the time to spend quality moments with someone special. ***Moon enters Pisces.***

7 OCTOBER

You'll gain the chance to review and put right any paperwork or agreements that need extra focus. It's a good day for a health or fitness appointment. Someone may need your help. If you need expert advice ask for it, as it will be available. Creative projects can flourish. Avoid being forgetful and idealistic. ***Moon in Pisces.***

8 OCTOBER

You'll appreciate the weekend to focus on people and activities you love. Discussions about shared duties and finances could be productive, but you must have the facts at your fingertips. Someone may be stubborn and will to wish to change their plans. You'll enjoy socialising and beautifying your home. ***Moon enters Aries.***

9 OCTOBER

The Aries full moon will spotlight a personal, work or health matter. There is a therapeutic aspect to the day, so aim to find the best way forward if obstacles arise. Look for pleasant and calming activities. It's a good day for health and fitness appointments. Consider putting in place a more balanced health and work routine.

10 OCTOBER

This is another good day to put in place a solid health and well-being schedule. You may be drawn to a new look. Work-wise, a fresh artistic project or health-related focus will appeal. ***Moon enters Taurus.***

11 OCTOBER

A strong and stable work ethic will serve you well, both at home and at work – all the more so as you may experience unexpected news or an unusual change of schedule will be necessary. ***Moon in Taurus.***

12 OCTOBER

Important decisions are likely to be on the table, and the more information you can gather the better for you. Avoid making decisions without adequate research. *Moon in Taurus.*

13 OCTOBER

Be practical and base decisions on reasonable expectations as an unexpected development will benefit from a level-headed response. *Moon in Gemini.*

14 OCTOBER

This is a good day to make practical changes at home and with family. You'll discover the benefits of working from home if you have a home office. Commitments you make today are likely to be productive. *Moon in Gemini.*

15 OCTOBER

You'll appreciate the sense that your projects are coming together. Talks and meeting are likely to go well, especially to do with your work, shared duties and home. Someone unpredictable may behave true to form. *Moon enters Cancer.*

16 OCTOBER

Spiritual and artistic endeavours will prove motivational. You'll gain a deeper understanding of someone if you look more closely at their values and ideas. You or someone close may be a little head in the clouds, so be patient. *Moon in Cancer.*

17 OCTOBER

There is a dynamic flavour to the day, and unless you have chores to do you may feel restless. Aim to channel restlessness into productive activities. If you're unsure of someone's feelings ask them, but be prepared for the answer! *Moon in Cancer.*

18 OCTOBER

The moon at the zenith of your chart will bring out your inner superhero. However, you may appear a little impatient as a result. You'll get a great deal done and will enjoy the results of your hard work. *Moon in Leo.*

19 OCTOBER

You are focused and motivated, especially concerning work and health. A domestic or spiritual activity will gain momentum. However, if you feel conflict is brewing, give it a wide berth. *Moon in Leo.*

20 OCTOBER

A difference of opinion in a work or personal context may arise out of a difference of fundamental values. Some interactions will flow and others will be intense. Avoid allowing disagreements to escalate into conflict. ***Moon enters Virgo.***

21 OCTOBER

The Virgo moon brings out your practical and reasonable sides, and you'll manage developments well as a result. Just keep an eye on misunderstandings and mistakes for the best measure. ***Moon in Virgo.***

22 OCTOBER

This is a good day to consider a new look and for a health or beauty appointment. You will enjoy a reunion or news from someone from your past. Romance could sizzle, so organise a date. Singles may met someone who is romantic, and this relationship will be passionate but may also entail a battle of egos at some point. Avoid mix-ups as you may be surprised by developments. ***Moon in Virgo.***

23 OCTOBER

Now that the sun will be in your sign for the next four weeks prepare to shine! Today's astrological aspects suggest that the better organised you are, especially at work and at home, the better your weekend will flow. Avoid taking hiccups personally. You can make great progress at home. ***Moon in Libra.***

24 OCTOBER

A circumstance from your past that still niggles may make waves again. You may hear from someone and must offer help or advice. If you need expert guidance it will be available, so reach out. ***Moon in Libra.***

25 OCTOBER

The partial solar eclipse in your sign signals the start of a brand new phase in your life. If it's your birthday this will entail a new chapter in your personal relationships, and for all other Scorpios a chance to turn a corner in your daily schedule, including your work life and health. If you feel disappointed in someone or in yourself find ways to boost confidence such as positive self-talk. Avoid misunderstandings.

26 OCTOBER

Your emotions may be strong as you gain perspective over a change that seems inevitable. Avoid taking things personally if your ideas fall on deaf ears. Someone supportive has your back. A reunion with someone could motivate you to make changes in your work or personal life. ***Moon in Scorpio.***

27 OCTOBER

Be proactive with your plans, especially at work and with people you know will collaborate with you as communications with them will go well. However, some negotiations may be more complex so take talks one step at a time. *Moon enters Sagittarius.*

28 OCTOBER

This is a good time to review some of your work, health or family matters. You may feel you're going over old ground but there will be benefits to rearranging some of your priorities and schedules. *Moon in Sagittarius.*

29 OCTOBER

Over the next few weeks you will place more focus on health, well-being and family. Some communications may present difficulties, but if you stick with your aims you will succeed. Find ways to dissipate restless energy to ensure you do not find life frustrating. *Moon enters Capricorn.*

30 OCTOBER

The Capricorn moon will help you to be realistic and hands-on, especially about developments in your life that will mean considerable change. You'll appreciate the chance to touch base with people you know have your back. *Moon in Capricorn.*

31 OCTOBER

Happy Hallowe'en! There's a progressive atmosphere at work and with your various projects, and approaching change with a dynamic attitude will work for you. If you're unsure of a project or a person ensure you research the situation. *Moon enters Aquarius.*

November

career   love   home   health   finance

1 NOVEMBER

You're thinking laterally and this will be helpful, especially if challenges arise. Today's Aquarian moon will help you to think outside the box, especially with logistics at home. ***Moon in Aquarius.***

2 NOVEMBER

Be practical and mindful that all obstacles can be overcome, especially with a health or work matter or both. Someone who is vulnerable or sensitive will require delicate handling. ***Moon enters Pisces.***

3 NOVEMBER

You'll reconnect with someone important to you. This is a good day for health and well-being appointments and to seek the advice of an expert. You may be asked to provide expert help yourself. Find ways to process information in the most practical way. ***Moon in Pisces.***

4 NOVEMBER

Your usual dynamic and upbeat approach to life will resurge once the moon is in Aries, but beforehand and for much of the day the Piscean moon will bring forth your imaginative, creative side and you'll enjoy letting out your inner romantic. ***Moon enters Aries.***

5 NOVEMBER

Meetings and talks may push your buttons, so it'll be wise to think before you speak or you may cause increased tension in an already tense circumstance. Be ready to look for solutions to problems. An expert will be invaluable. *Moon in Aries.*

6 NOVEMBER

A tense situation in your personal or family life is best approached with an understanding attitude, or you may find you end up arguing. Stand your ground, but be prepared to also give a little. *Moon in Aries.*

7 NOVEMBER

A personal situation may present a stalemate unless you are willing to carefully discuss terms and conditions. Be prepared to negotiate in financial matters as a flat-out 'no' could lead only to further obstacles. *Moon in Taurus.*

8 NOVEMBER

The total lunar eclipse in Taurus will spotlight a key change in an agreement, especially if it's your birthday. For some this will mean a new chapter in your personal life, and for others at work or regarding your health routine. You may receive key news that signals new developments.

9 NOVEMBER

You may be surprised by the reaction to some of the more recent events, especially from a business or personal partner. Avoid making snap decisions yourself as these could backfire. *Moon enters Gemini.*

10 NOVEMBER

It's a mixed bag today: on the one hand romance can flourish and you will be able overcome so many obstacles, and on the other certain conversations and developments will challenge you and especially ask that you communicate well. If you discover your expectations have been unrealistic, you will get the chance to correct your course. *Moon in Gemini.*

11 NOVEMBER

With hard work and perseverance you will attain your goals, even if your ideas are different from those of someone you must collaborate with on a domestic or personal level. Avoid snap decisions, but be prepared to think on your feet. *Moon in Gemini.*

12 NOVEMBER

This is a good day to get your ideas across to those you wish to influence. On the other hand, you may be easily influenced yourself so be discerning. Romance, the arts, music, film and dance will all appeal, so make a date! *Moon in Cancer.*

13 NOVEMBER

Your relationships with the people who truly matter to you can improve and you'll gain the chance to deepen your understanding of each other. However, some communications and negotiations may still be a little tense, so take things one step at a time. *Moon in Cancer.*

14 NOVEMBER

Trust your gut instincts as they are spot on, especially to do with work, your favourite projects and someone close. Romance and interests such as hobbies can all flourish, so ensure you organise some you time. *Moon enters Leo.*

15 NOVEMBER

This is an excellent day for personal matters, especially family and romance, so organise a lovely event or a special meal. Creative and spiritual Scorpios may be particularly inspired. Work may be busy, so ensure you spare some time for those you love and for yourself. *Moon in Leo.*

16 NOVEMBER

You'll notice a slight change in atmosphere as you gain a sense of dynamism and adventure, especially in your personal life. You may feel more optimistic and outgoing, so enjoy this upbeat phase. *Moon in Leo.*

17 NOVEMBER

As Mercury enters the zodiac sign Sagittarius your attention is likely to go to travel and study and ways to express yourself more and broaden your horizons. You may experience a financial or ego boost. *Moon in Virgo.*

18 NOVEMBER

While many conversations and developments will flow more easily than they have for a while you may still need to focus on the details or misunderstandings and mix-ups can arise, especially with those you must collaborate and interact with this weekend. *Moon in Virgo.*

19 NOVEMBER

Ensure you have done adequate research if you have to make key decisions. You may easily misunderstand someone and vice versa, so ensure you are on the same page. *Moon enters Libra.*

20 NOVEMBER

The moon in Libra will provide you with the chance to adapt to changes in your work and health or developments with family. **Moon in Libra.**

21 NOVEMBER

You'll gain a sense you are more on track with your various projects. Personal and family developments will take you into new territory, which will be exciting on many levels. Key news, meetings or a trip will be uplifting. **Moon enters Scorpio.**

22 NOVEMBER

The sun in Sagittarius for the next few weeks will encourage you to enjoy a greater sense of freedom, adventure and discovery. You may be planning a holiday or taking one. Key financial matters could take giant leaps forward, but as always the key to success is to research details. Avoid gambling. **Moon in Scorpio.**

23 NOVEMBER

The Sagittarian new moon signals a more dynamic phase that is up and coming and which will involve improving health, well-being and dynamism in your daily life. You may be prepared to invest more in yourself and those you love. A key financial investment will involve work and research but could be profitable.

24 NOVEMBER

The moon in Sagittarius will contribute to a feeling of expansion in your personal life and, for some, this will also involve finances. You may enjoy a sense that your horizons are about to open up and there is a sense of excitement about your plans. **Moon in Sagittarius.**

25 NOVEMBER

A therapeutic and healing aspect to the day is ideal for a health or beauty appointment. If you have personal matters that need to be worked on this is the time to find an ideal way ahead. A financial decision or a meeting could represent a fresh arrangement that suits you well. **Moon enters Capricorn.**

26 NOVEMBER

This is another excellent day for personal improvement. Spiritual and artistic Scorpios may find this a particularly productive time. If health has been on your mind, this is a great time to boost health. This is also a good time to improve your appearance and to bring more beauty into your life. **Moon in Capricorn.**

27 NOVEMBER

A change of routine or an unexpected development may throw the spanner in the works of your usual Sunday routine, but you'll find that the extra effort you put into events will pay off. **Moon enters Aquarius.**

28 NOVEMBER

A constructive, practical approach to getting things done both at home and at work will reap rewards. If you'd like to make changes in either areas these are likely to progress slowly but surely. **Moon in Aquarius.**

29 NOVEMBER

Talks and meetings are likely to be upbeat and could also get heated, so ensure you maintain perspective. For some the topic will revolve around investments, especially financial matters. If you have all the facts at your fingertips you will achieve a positive result. **Moon in Aquarius.**

30 NOVEMBER

This is a good day for making financial arrangements, especially those that involve family, a property or your home. Someone at home or in your family may have positive news. **Moon in Pisces.**

December

career love home health finance

1 DECEMBER

Personal and financial matters are likely to gain momentum, so if you have important things to discuss and transactions to undertake ensure you are clear about the consequences or find the time to research your decisions. *Moon in Pisces.*

2 DECEMBER

This is a positive and proactive time for you. However, if you are unclear of your options and uncertain of your choices it's vital you look more deeply into matters to avoid making mistakes. Someone close may be forgetful. *Moon in Aries.*

3 DECEMBER

This is an excellent weekend to relax and recuperate, especially if you have found recent times stressful. You'll enjoy a health or beauty treat. If you need to build bridges with someone, this is the time to do it! *Moon in Aries.*

4 DECEMBER

This is a good day for talks, meetings and financial decisions. If you're shopping ensure you are not going to blow your budget as you may be prone to overindulge and overspend. *Moon enters Taurus.*

5 DECEMBER

The Taurus moon will bring out your practical and down-to-earth qualities, enabling you to plan better and accommodate circumstances that may be outside your control. A little more patience may be required. ***Moon in Taurus.***

6 DECEMBER

Communications and financial transactions may be tense, but if you know you have done adequate research at work or financially you will overcome hurdles. Just avoid making snap decisions and gambling. Back up computers to avoid losing information. ***Moon enters Gemini.***

7 DECEMBER

This is a good day to implement changes you wish to see financially and in your personal life, as communications are likely to improve. However, you may experience an out-of-the-ordinary or unexpected change of plan, so the more adaptable you are the better for you. ***Moon in Gemini.***

8 DECEMBER

The Gemini full moon spotlights a fresh chapter for you in a particular agreement or shared financial arrangement. Take a moment to work on the best outcome. You may wish to seek expert help.

9 DECEMBER

You may be pleasantly surprised by news from a business or personal partner and could make headway with a financial matter or at work, so be positive and spontaneous. ***Moon in Cancer.***

10 DECEMBER

An important matter is coming to a head this weekend and the calmer and more assertive you are the better for you. Otherwise, disagreements could swiftly turn into arguments. A financial or personal matter is best discussed from the long-term point of view. If you're shopping, avoid overspending if you're already in debt; you may be tempted to splurge! ***Moon in Cancer.***

11 DECEMBER

As Venus joins Mercury in Capricorn you'll feel more certain about your opinions, especially with regard to finances and investments. Avoid obstinacy both in yourself and others and look for clever, inspired ways forward. ***Moon enters Leo.***

12 DECEMBER

This is an excellent day to get ahead both with work and personal matters. If a financial investment has been on your mind, this is a good day to make a commitment if you've researched the facts. ***Moon in Leo.***

13 DECEMBER

The Leo moon will bring out your inner lion and you'll feel ready to roar, but you must question whether a softly-softly approach might work better, especially if you have experienced arguments of late. Be positive and optimistic, as your work and health projects will succeed. *Moon in Leo.*

14 DECEMBER

You'll discover whether you have misjudged someone or a situation. Avoid taking things personally if you experience a disappointment. You will gain the chance to put things straight. *Moon enters Virgo.*

15 DECEMBER

This is a good day to build from the ground up, in other words, to take things one step at a time, especially if you feel under pressure at work. Build solid relationships and your success will come from good communication skills. *Moon in Virgo.*

16 DECEMBER

Communication skills are the key to success with negotiations. Whether you're at work or on a shopping trip you'll find you can make great progress with finances and investments while you look for good value. A trip or discussion may be delayed so factor extra time into your schedule. *Moon enters Libra.*

17 DECEMBER

A lovely event or get-together will be enjoyable and will raise morale. If you are looking for a health boost you may find something new or out of the ordinary that enhances your mood and well-being. *Moon in Libra.*

18 DECEMBER

On the one hand you'll enjoy the chance to deepen some relationships and will enjoy a trip or get-together. On the other you may need to be sensitive to someone's feelings and appointments may need rescheduling. Avoid misunderstandings, delays and digital glitches. *Moon in Libra.*

19 DECEMBER

You'll enjoy boosting your self-esteem and being with like-minded people. A festive event may be just what you want, and you may be surprised by some developments. *Moon in Scorpio.*

20 DECEMBER

When the moon is in Scorpio you feel empowered and passionate, and you'll enjoy a get-together with like-minded people or someone you love. *Moon in Scorpio.*

21 DECEMBER

The solstice is a time of reflection when you can gather your wits as you assimilate your progress this year. You may enter a fresh understanding or agreement with someone. You may learn something new. Avoid seeing only obstacles but be aware that gambling, both financially and emotionally, will be counterproductive. *Moon in Sagittarius.*

22 DECEMBER

You'll enjoy a change of pace and a get-together and the chance to socialise and collaborate with people in a different environment. You'll also enjoy a trip and a change of scenery. *Moon in Sagittarius.*

23 DECEMBER

The new moon and supermoon in Capricorn signals a fresh start for you in a personal situation. For some Scorpios this new moon indicates a fresh financial chapter in your life where looking for stability and security is paramount. Be positive about changes, even if a little upheaval must accompany your day. A trip or visit will bring you together with family or friends.

24 DECEMBER

You'll enjoy today and the lovely, calmer feeling it brings. It is ideal for get-togethers, romance and trips. Creative Scorpios may feel particularly inspired. *Moon in Capricorn.*

25 DECEMBER

Merry Christmas! You'll feel warmed by being with people you admire, and this year you may experience a slightly different atmosphere at home and with the company you keep. *Moon in Aquarius.*

26 DECEMBER

A change of pace will be relaxing and you'll find the time to do the activities you love. Art, reading, music and relaxation will all appeal. *Moon in Aquarius.*

27 DECEMBER

You'll enjoy a short trip and being in a beautiful place. If your home seems a little confined, you'll enjoy walks and meetings with people outside in the fresh air and in nature. *Moon in Pisces.*

28 DECEMBER

A reunion or return to an old haunt will be inspiring. You may feel particularly inspired or romantic about the place you are in at the moment. Try to get the loose ends of important paperwork tied up by the end of the day before Mercury turns retrograde tomorrow, to avoid delays down the line. *Moon in Pisces.*

29 DECEMBER

Key meetings or financial transactions could be significant. Avoid making snap decisions, as these are likely to need a review further down the line. Also avoid being easily led. A romantic development will be uplifting. *Moon in Aries.*

30 DECEMBER

Your plans and projects may be subject to abrupt change or simply be more complex than you'd prefer. Take a moment to gather your thoughts and plough on. You'll overcome any hurdles with diligence and persistence. *Moon in Aries.*

31 DECEMBER

Happy New Year! Being with the people you love is what raises your spirits and you'll enjoy some lovely get-togethers. As the day progresses you'll feel more inclined to settle into the new year in a relaxed way, without too much hullabaloo! *Moon enters Taurus.*

SAGITTARIUS

22 November - 21 December

THE ESSENCE OF SAGITTARIUS

You aim high in life and generally reach your target. You use your skills to serve a fulfilling purpose. Your generosity of spirit, optimism and sense of adventure all combine to paint a positive picture. You are adept at learning and keep up to date with new developments, unless you lose track of your goals or allow yourself to be easily distracted.

One of your biggest pitfalls is being easily led and focusing on unimportant aspects of other people's lives. When you remain focused you have the key to great success and your path is an adventurous one that follows a learning curve into fresh terrain. This will stretch your capabilities, imagination and understanding in life so that you feel you live an exciting life of discovery, exploration and reward.

Your penchant for learning will begin at a young age; for a few it will kick in when you're a little more mature. Long-distance travel, the conduit for learning about other cultures and peoples, will appeal to you. You'll be the one in high school who wishes to see more of the world, to travel and to study through higher education to assimilate as much as you can in terms of wisdom, experience and education. You'll also enjoy teaching in a learning institution or more broadly by sharing your experiences in life with those you love.

You love the camaraderie of like-minded people but will also seek out the company of those who have had a different upbringing or cultural heritage. You're a curious character, and curiosity can kill the cat. Luckily, cats have nine lives and you'll learn from your mistakes and gain increasingly in wisdom and knowledge.

Any form of challenge will serve to pave the way to a deeper understanding of who you are and of your capabilities. You are the true alchemist of the zodiac, as you transform even negative experiences into positive ones purely through your inherently positive mindset.

YOUR SELF-ESTEEM

Your self-esteem is derived from feeling secure, which will come to you from all kind of sources and at varying times of your life. For some the sense of security will come via a financial safety net; for others via a relationship; and for yet others via success at work or in your status.

The strong foundation is necessary for you because you like to have your feet on the ground and to feel that you can be daring in other areas of your life through your hobbies, travel, ideas and beliefs. A solid foundation is what will give you the chance to be adventurous and try new and different ideas and courses of action, all of which will enable you to complete sometimes hazardous tasks and boost your self-esteem.

It may initially appear counter-intuitive to look for a sound base and security in life, especially when what truly boosts your sense of self is aiming high and being an adventurous character. Yet once you have that sense of security – be it financial, emotional or status driven – it becomes your springboard for success.

You also gain self-esteem from good relationships and feeling you can get traction in life through sharing your wisdom and experience and helping others to enjoy life as you do. You love grand schemes such as planning long-distance travel and daredevil experiences such as mountain climbing, snowboarding, skydiving and speed racing. You are likely to be sporty and to have had the chance at school to show just how athletic you are.

YOUR INNER LIFE

You have a great deal of zest and lust for life, which fuels your ambitions and projects. You have a need to succeed that comes from an emotional core that motivates you to leave your comfort zone and be gregarious and bold beyond your own understanding. You may even wonder sometimes where your strong motivation comes from. It's an emotional need, one that will be hard to suppress. It's impossible to subdue the kind of drive and desire that is at the seat of your lust for life, so your best course of action is to channel it into upbeat projects.

You revel in boosting your experiences through travel, study and broadening your horizons through various interests and experiences. Because your true sense of strength comes from having a solid foundation in life, it's important to establish a sense of security so that your need for adventure doesn't leave you vulnerable and without a safety net.

You have a strong sense of justice and also of fair play. You'll frequently be drawn into inner debate about what would be the most moral or beneficial course of action for you to take and what action may be morally questionable. Legal matters may concern you at various times in your life, as you're not afraid to stand up for your values and beliefs and will fight hard for those you see as being oppressed or hard done by.

The archer is the symbol for your sign, and the meaning here is clear: you'll aim high in life, although there may be tension involved in the process. You need to stretch your resources to their limits so that you can reach your target – and a bull's eye.

HOW OTHERS SEE YOU

Your joviality is a real credit to you; you know you're able to see life in a good-natured, positive light and to see the brighter side when necessary. Your good sense of humour enables you to maintain an optimistic approach to life, and people see in you a confident, accomplished person.

As the alchemist of the zodiac, the person who can turn adversity into success, you understand that a positive mindset can absolutely free the mind. You can appear to others as being carefree and that nothing in life brings you down, yet you are human; to be successful you must make as much of an effort as anyone else.

Your success depends on working out how you can shoot a bull's eye. As you mature you will see that your ideas play out through the actions you take, so when you have positive ideas it's important to take action; very little results from an idea alone. This may seem obvious yet you must always remember to give yourself an extra little push, which will enable the arrow – your intention and projects – to fly so much further.

You may appear to others to find the process of attainment simple, but there may well be sweat and tears behind your success. Don't be afraid to ask for the support and advice you need to make your endeavours a success; people are less likely to offer you help as you seem so accomplished and capable.

HOW TO MAXIMISE YOUR POTENTIAL

You are seen initially as a larger-than-life, bold character who is happy to take on herculean tasks, someone who is basically happy and ready to take a good bite out of the cherry of life. You have a playful side to your character that people admire and enjoy.

People view you as being honest and keen to see that fair play is done. Your main pitfall in your relationships, at work and in your interactions in general is that you are so honest you can be blunt or uncaring and even uncompromising. Knowing that your honesty – which is a positive aspect – can be seen on occasion as a negative trait will encourage you to consider being more tactful and diplomatic.

You enjoy fun sports activities and a night out on the town, but your ebullience can be mistaken for insincerity and a lack of seriousness. To counteract this impression, always be clear to delineate when you're joking and when you're serious, when you're playing and when you're working. To you the difference is clear but to others it's less so; some people simply won't know the difference until they get to know you better.

Your larger-than-life character comes predominantly from your ruling planet Jupiter, the largest planet in our solar system and one that bestows a gregarious personality and a wish to broaden horizons, both in self-expression and through experiences in life. Be aware that sometimes people can find your influence overbearing or invasive and that you sometimes transgress personal boundaries.

Your largesse translates well into generosity, both financially and of spirit. You also have a keen mind, one that rarely lets you down and enables you to learn and subsequently teach subjects for which you have a passion. Your generosity of spirit adds to the general impression that you are a kind-hearted individual.

You love freedom of movement and independent thought. As a partner you can seem difficult to tie down, being constantly on the go or perpetually planning new adventures. You do appreciate a bright and chatty partner, which gives you the intellectual connection you crave with others. Good communication skills and a meeting of minds are hallmarks of a successful relationship for archers, and you'll attract like-minded people for this reason.

SAGITTARIUS AND ITS ASCENDANTS

This chapter is about your sun sign, Sagittarius, and your predictions for the year ahead. The more you know about yourself the better you will be able to take advantage of opportunities, and also to avoid the pitfalls. It's critical to know as much about 'you' as possible.

In astrology your core self is represented by your sun sign, but your personality traits are represented by your ascendant (also known as your rising sign). The ascendant describes your personality, the way other people see you on first meeting you and the way you tend to filter life's events.

When you have intimate knowledge about your sun sign – your engine room or core being – you will be on the way to a happier life. When you add the knowledge about your personality – your ascendant – you will gain even deeper insight into what makes you tick.

Your ascendant sign is determined by the time of your birth on the date and year of your birth. Because the ascendant sign changes approximately every two hours, the best way to determine it is to ask an astrologer to calculate it for you. Certain apps will also calculate your ascendant sign (see page 873).

The following gives you more information about your abilities, characteristics and personality according to your sun sign Sagittarius in combination with your ascendant sign.

SAGITTARIUS SUN SIGN WITH ARIES ASCENDANT

You're a double fire sign so you're doubly fiery! You're the zodiac's daredevil adventurer and you're brave and energetic beyond your own understanding. You love competition and the outdoors, and if you're just as comfortable indoors you'll crave fresh air and physical activity to work off excess energy. You're an honest, straightforward character to the point of being blunt, but at least everyone knows where they stand. You may wear out earth signs and find water signs are damp squibs! Air signs will match your restlessness, but may find your impulsiveness confronting. Fellow fire signs are your closest match.

SAGITTARIUS SUN SIGN WITH TAURUS ASCENDANT

Your down-to-earth, practical personality hides your larger-than-life buoyant character. You'll love sport, study and upbeat activities but are also family oriented and a lover of life, good food and pleasant company. You love to create a sense of stability and security. You may experience different phases in life when you wish to be outgoing, unattached and adventurous, and others where you wish for close family and to provide balance and security above all else.

SAGITTARIUS SUN SIGN WITH GEMINI ASCENDANT

Your Gemini adaptability and desire for freedom and independence enhance your adventurous, daring, outgoing and upbeat Sagittarian core self. You're a strong, active person and are one of the most loyal characters in the zodiac, as long as you're able to retain your identity and not feel caged by circumstances. You'll enjoy writing, reading, travel and sport and will usually not suffer with weight gain as you remain so active. You may appear to have a nervous disposition that belies your inner composure and strength.

SAGITTARIUS SUN SIGN WITH CANCER ASCENDANT

The Cancerian personality can seem gentle and introspective, yet underneath your sense of adventure and drive cannot be ignored. You have a kind of extrasensory perception, as your Cancerian personality enables you to gain insight into people and circumstances. Combine this with your inner dynamo and you possess drive and insight. Your gregarious Sagittarian qualities will take the lead. You'll enjoy travelling, absorbing information, being chatty and upbeat. There is likely to be a strong interest in writing, publishing, study and storytelling.

SAGITTARIUS SUN SIGN WITH LEO ASCENDANT

You're a double fire sign and quite the optimistic, fiery, independent, extroverted character. You're active and love to instigate upbeat, exciting and fun ventures. You present to others as confident, capable and individualistic. The worst-case scenario is that you appear selfish, egotistical and overbearing; you are competitive, after all. Even if you present as the shy, kitten type of Leo you'll always draw attention.

SAGITTARIUS SUN SIGN WITH VIRGO ASCENDANT

You're a natural-born humanitarian and healer: you wish to make the world a better place. You're also a good worker. Sometimes the clash between the dynamic, outgoing Sagittarius attitude with your careful, methodical and perfectionist Virgo temperament can point to inner tension. You'll manage to implement your humanitarian ideals in proactive, exciting ways. In your love life you may appear reserved initially, but your earthy sensuality with underlying fire and passion will be attractive to others.

SAGITTARIUS SUN SIGN WITH LIBRA ASCENDANT

You are an enigma: on the one hand you look for peace and harmony in the world and evaluate life's events through this filter, while on the other you're an adventurous, risk-taking and outgoing character. Some of the riskier activities and interests that bring little peace to your life may even surprise you. You're honest and can be blunt, and your frankness may be at counterpoint to your personality which appears, especially on first meeting, to be gentle and passive.

SAGITTARIUS SUN SIGN WITH SCORPIO ASCENDANT

You have deep, passionate desires and can be extremely charismatic. You are inquisitive and feel driven to gain experiences in all areas of life; few experiences will seem off limits. Your emotions can be intense and you rarely shy away from risk taking, which can lead you into deep water unless you set strict boundaries for yourself. Music, dance, physical activity and creative expression will be important in your self-development. Meditation and yoga will be beneficial.

SAGITTARIUS SUN SIGN WITH SAGITTARIUS ASCENDANT

You are a double Sagittarian and are doubly bold, honest and straightforward, but also doubly blunt. You are a gregarious, outgoing character and little will deter you from your next big adventure. You're generous and can be demanding of others, even appearing overbearing unless you implement respectful distance when necessary. You are optimistic and will rarely understand anyone who is not as positive as you are. Travel, study, teaching and broadening your horizons will appeal.

SAGITTARIUS SUN SIGN WITH CAPRICORN ASCENDANT

You may appear initially as a careful, reserved and quiet character. You are diligent and able to complete tasks in a measured, step-by-step way, yet your Sagittarian daring and penchant for excitement lie just beneath the surface. You may compartmentalise your abilities, combining a good work ethic during the week with wild weekends! You're generally trustworthy and able to strategise and plan ahead well and are an energetic and enthusiastic worker. You may be good with money but must avoid gambling.

SAGITTARIUS SUN SIGN WITH AQUARIUS ASCENDANT

You are the life and soul of the party when you're not scaling a mountain or running a mindfulness retreat! You're an eccentric character who can run through a gamut of personalities: sometimes super quiet, then other times dancing on chairs! What infuses you with enthusiasm is your lust for life and thirst for knowledge. You may well be changeable, but underneath you're as honest and transparent as the day is long.

SAGITTARIUS SUN SIGN WITH PISCES ASCENDANT

Your thirst for knowledge and wisdom knows no bounds. You'll enjoy being up with the news and down with the local gossip. You'll enjoy an exciting life and spending time pursuing an ideal or a spiritual goal. Travel that is fuelled by spiritual or humanitarian interests will appeal. You're a seeker who will leave few stones unturned in your quest for answers. You are a romantic soul but also crave excitement, needing freedom of movement along with loyal friends and supporters.

SAGITTARIUS IN LOVE

You are such an independent person, Sagittarius, and so freedom loving you are likely to be fairly selective about who you decide to settle down with. In this section you can check out your compatibility with other sun signs. Remember that we are all complex individuals, so the more you know about someone's astrological birth chart the better you can determine your compatibility. Consider having your astrological birth chart compared with that of a partner, friend or family member, as the compatibility – known as 'synastry' in astrology – goes even deeper than a comparison of sun signs, although this is a good place to begin.

SAGITTARIUS WITH ARIES

A fire sign match: both sun signs are comfortable in each other's company as your fundamental approach to life is similar. This is an adventurous, outgoing and upbeat relationship where both signs give each other space and encouragement. This is a happy partnership unless there are incompatibilities elsewhere in the chart, as both bring each other's playfulness and action-oriented lust for life out in full bloom. There may be some element of competitiveness, but it's unlikely to deter the basic underlying harmony when both are invested in the relationship.

SAGITTARIUS WITH TAURUS

Taurus will be attracted to your outgoing nature but you may be more daring and competitive than Taurus feels comfortable with in a long-term relationship, largely because Taurus is looking for stability and security and you're looking for adventure and excitement. However, both signs can complement each other; for you, the Taurean caution and reason can lessen your tendency towards risk taking, and your larger-than-life personality and predilection for excitement and risk taking may be a breath of fresh air for Taurus.

SAGITTARIUS WITH GEMINI

This is a fun, adventurous and upbeat match that could be perfect for long-term commitment. You both understand how important it is to live life to the fullest, and both enjoy travel and broadening your understanding of life. You'll appreciate how important independence and mental stimulation is for Gemini, and Gemini understands you cannot be caged or dominated. The mutual understanding and respect for each other's self-expression makes for fundamental compatibility, and the lust for life you both have in common spells a happy union.

SAGITTARIUS WITH CANCER

It's a case of opposites attracting: Cancer will admire the fire and excitement you embody, and you'll be intrigued and seduced by the tenderness and allure of the Cancerian. However, Cancer, driven by emotions, can swamp your get up and go, seemingly clipping your wings albeit unintentionally unless, that is, care is taken to understand each other. Cancer is principally a caring, nurturing person and Sagittarius is principally an outgoing adventurer. Embrace your differences and allow them to complement each other and you have a good match.

SAGITTARIUS WITH LEO

There is fundamental compatibility, as you are both fire signs. You will automatically understand where the other is coming from and will enjoy active, adventurous pursuits such as travel and sport. You both have strong personalities and are keen to take the lead, but instinctively know when the other should lead and you should take the back seat. Your lust for life makes for light-hearted, fun and giggly moments together, and you're able to pull together to mutually support each other in times of need.

SAGITTARIUS WITH VIRGO

You'll appreciate the Virgo's down-to-earth and sensuous nature as this complements your excitability and larger-than-life personality. If you can plan mutually exciting activities together you do make a good match, but there must be give and take otherwise your plans could be at cross purposes as your fundamental interests are likely to differ. Common ground includes humanitarian interests, health and well-being, so if you base activities and interests around these areas this match may flourish.

SAGITTARIUS WITH LIBRA

This is a fun-loving, upbeat romantic pairing and can be a fulfilling relationship. Libra will be attracted to your outgoing adventurousness, and your gregarious personality will be appealing as a counterpart to their gentle, peace-loving approach to life. You both seek new experiences and gain wisdom from being in a fulfilling relationship. This combination is likely to be long lasting, as you both seek depth in your experiences.

SAGITTARIUS WITH SCORPIO

You are both vying for attention from each other in different ways: you need freedom and independence to feel fulfilled in a relationship, while Scorpio requires deep commitment and an earthy, almost supernaturally strong connection. If you're able to give each other what you crave you'll find this a worthy match, but otherwise you'll feel unfulfilled by the other's inability to provide you with what you need.

SAGITTARIUS WITH SAGITTARIUS

You are both larger-than-life personalities, and while you may initially feel you mirror each other this partnership may be too much of a good thing! Your fundamental qualities of honesty and

transparency are exactly what you need as the foundation for a strong relationship. Depending on your levels of self-development and ability to see past your own ego, this could be a good match as you'll appreciate your similarities and enjoy common interests and goals.

SAGITTARIUS WITH CAPRICORN

You will be attracted to the practical, reserved and level-headed Capricorn as a contrast and rock to your risk-taking and adventurous approach to life. You both have strong opinions and can be at counterpoint unless you are both prepared to see the other's opinion. Together you're able to complete herculean tasks without breaking a sweat and are able to concentrate under pressure. You have big hearts and true love will prosper.

SAGITTARIUS WITH AQUARIUS

This is an upbeat and fun match: you both motivate each other to enjoy life's merry-go-round and to explore new experiences. Neither of you is afraid to step into new territory, and together you make a fearless team. Long-distance travel, study, research and learning about all manner of wisdom will provide hours of conversation and fun. You may feel the Aquarian ability to roll their sleeves up when the pressure is on attractive, and Aquarius will match your eagerness for escapades one hundredfold.

SAGITTARIUS WITH PISCES

You may initially be intrigued by the deep, philosophical mind of the Pisces, and together you'll certainly enjoy exploring life's experiences and gaining wisdom. However, Pisces may come to feel overloaded by your strong personality and you may find, ultimately, that Pisces pours cold water on your fire. Unless Pisces has a strong fire element in their astrological chart and you have strong water elements, this match may serve as good companionship only and passion may be lacking.

THE YEAR AHEAD FOR SAGITTARIUS

Affirmation: *'It's full steam ahead!'*

You'll be pleased to hear that 2022 will not have the intensity of 2021 for you personally, even if in January it still feels as though there is a motser of a mountain to climb. Rest assured, you will gain the opportunity to change your daily life, work and health schedules so they suit you better, and without the extreme drama of 2021. This will to a degree depend on how well you managed circumstances last year: if you felt you were behind with your targets, this year you'll get to catch up.

The square aspect between Saturn and Uranus in January and the influence of these two astrological heavyweights will once again become prominent in the last quarter of the year. The upshot? You will gain the opportunity to make the lasting changes in your life you have been looking for but it will mean considerable upheaval, especially in your daily life.

In January you will be able to put in place a clever plan for stable growth that allows you to make fundamental changes in your personal and everyday life. The key to success here lies in avoiding assumptions; do not gamble on an outcome.

If you research your circumstances carefully, 2022 could be a breakout year in that it enables you to move ahead into fields that suit you far more than those in 2021. You will gain the chance this year to pursue a path that suits you increasingly, providing a sense of purpose and fulfilment as you reach milestones.

HEALTH

The dramas of 2021 can take a toll on your health, so it's important to be conscious of the fact that you're not a superhero. You will need to gain the upper hand with your health right at the start of the year, and luckily the new moon and supermoon on 2 January will provide you with ample opportunity to do so. This is an excellent start to the year as you'll have the chance to boost your looks, health and relationships, which will enable you to feel more positive moving forward.

The eclipses in 2022 will be across your health zones, so it's vital you take time out when possible to feed your mind, body and soul. How do you nurture your soul? By being kind not only to others but also to yourself, by generosity of spirit and heart and by honouring the fact you are not perfect!

Feeding your mind will involve learning, not only academically or a skill set but by learning through life's events and gaining in wisdom and knowledge.

The eclipses on 30 April and 8 November will be the most powerful turning points for you in your health. From the end of August onwards will be excellent to put your health first as Mars in your health sector will help you to boost energy levels.

FINANCES

Saturn in your finance sector brings the sense that you have financial responsibilities you cannot avoid. The good news is that as long as you plan and invest wisely you can create financial security and stability. That is, as long as you avoid gambling on certain investments and outcomes. The key to success in 2022 rests firmly in the lap of reason, strategy and calculation. Stress points financially will be the first and third quarters, when key decisions will need to be made at work or regarding investments.

As you will gain the chance this year to pursue a path that increasingly suits you at work you will have a sense of purpose and fulfilment as you reach milestones. Your finances will ebb and flow in line with the changes you make at work, so it's vital you avoid counting on particular financial outcomes. It's far better to plan ahead carefully to avoid shortfalls during times of peak change in your daily working life.

Saturn will remain in your finance sector all year, and will on the one hand provide security and on the other will magnify your need to have more money.

The lesson in 2022 will be that you cannot have abundance without fear of loss and you cannot have security without going outside your comfort zone, and both scenarios are not ideal. This year, finding the balance between these paradoxes will be the secret to financial happiness.

HOME LIFE

Your personal life could be subject to a stop-start or restless feeling this year, as you will gain the chance to make long-overdue changes in your home life but may find life is more mercurial than you bargained for.

You appreciate adventure and are happy to be dynamic at home and go with the flow, which is all the more reason to put down a plan of action for the year and follow this to create more

freedom and exploration in your life with the intention of changing tack if need be.

However, with Chiron in your fourth house of home, property and family there will be a strong element of healing and potentially even the need to convalesce at home as either you or someone close will benefit from additional downtime.

The first half of the year will be the most go ahead with regard to making changes at home, and the plans you put in place in the first six months will be acted upon in the second half.

Jupiter in your home sector will bring a sense of change at home in the second half of the year. You may be drawn to inviting more people to stay at your home or to changing your living situation considerably. If you're lucky to be travelling, the second half of the year will change at home due to travel and time spent in new horizons.

LOVE

Your love life is the scene of much of the change going ahead this year, as someone and perhaps even you has an unpredictable state of mind or can be super stubborn. And while you may be in the position to set in motion a fresh set of circumstances that will suit you better such as changes at home that facilitate a more relaxed scenario or even a move, the influences of the erratic behaviour that impact on your love life may be considerable.

The 28 July new moon is a revitalising time in your love life when you are likely to feel more outgoing and sociable. However, if your partner does not experience the same feelings you may need to make a tough call about spending time with your separate interests.

A rollercoaster situation may not be an exaggeration this year, but it will depend a great deal on your own reaction to events. If you must contend with a stubborn partner, one of you – you! – will need to be the flexible partner. If you really cannot see that as a possibility, a stubborn relationship will reach a crossroads this year. Potential breaking points will be the first and third quarters. Take time out to re-consider your priorities.

Luckily, the second and fourth quarters will involve better communications and the chance to overcome differences.

CAREER

Saturn in your second house of finances spells a need to earn money and invest in yourself, and you can make a great deal of progress if you're careful, plan ahead and are prepared to step into new territory in your career if need be. Be open to dreaming, even if the odds seem stacked against you. October will be particularly conducive to new projects and ideas.

Furthermore, the new moons on 27 August and 25 September will be conducive to a fresh focus on your career progress. However, developments in October will also tie in with changes in your personal life and interests, so it'll be vital to keep both aspects of your life in balance or you may tend to sacrifice one for the other.

This aside, you can build on the skill set you already have this year and great progress can be made. You'll gain the chance to alter your career path if you wish to so that it aligns more closely with your sense of purpose and leads to a sense of achievement.

January

career   love   home   health   finance

Notes: the pie charts such as the one above listed for each month show energy distribution according to the stars for the month ahead. If you wish to make changes in the areas of your finances, health, career, love or home and you see there is a large amount of energy in that sector in the chart, your endeavours should succeed as long as you have prepared well in advance. The charts also show which areas will potentially have the most focus in your life during the month.

The moon sign listed for each day's entry in the diary is the position of the moon at the end of the day in Greenwich Mean Time (GMT). To gain the most information about a particular day's circumstances, read the day before and the day after for a complete picture.

1 JANUARY

Happy New Year! Starting the year with the moon in your sign will bring a sense of optimism, even if life isn't exactly perfect quite yet! A quirky or unusual start to the new year will add to the upbeat vibe. ***Moon enters Capricorn later in the day.***

2 JANUARY

The new moon and supermoon in Capricorn will kick-start a fresh phase for you in a personal context and, for some, financially. You may be prepared to make a financial or personal investment and may improve your finances this month. A trip or news will be uplifting for you.

3 JANUARY

A change of pace or of place will boost morale, even if it involves a little upheaval. Take a moment to decide where you'd like to put your priorities this year; it's a good day to consider a new venture or project. ***Moon enters Aquarius.***

4 JANUARY

The Aquarian moon will motivate you to embrace something new. You may find conversations and meetings take you into fresh territory. Be open to change and avoid being stubborn about making changes this year. If you're back at work you may need to find ways to communicate with a different set of people or to adapt to an altered routine. ***Moon in Aquarius.***

5 JANUARY

A pleasant development at home or in your environment will please you. A little luxury and beauty in your surroundings certainly raises morale and you'll enjoy a trip to somewhere beautiful or simply the time to indulge in with a friend or family member. ***Moon in Aquarius.***

6 JANUARY

You may find out whether your expectations of an event have been unrealistic. If so, you will get the chance to reframe your plans and to adapt to circumstances. ***Moon in Pisces.***

7 JANUARY

You'll enjoy being more creative and imaginative as there's a dreamy quality to the day. You may also tend to be forgetful, so if you're at work or must undertake important negotiations be prepared to focus that little bit extra. ***Moon in Pisces.***

8 JANUARY

Energetic and proactive Mars in your sign for the next three weeks will create a more dynamic environment and mindset for you, ideal for getting things done, but you may also be prone to impatience so take things one step at a time, especially today. ***Moon in Aries.***

9 JANUARY

A key financial or personal matter will be on your mind. You'll enjoy a get-together, and for some this will be a romantic day. However, you must avoid overspending and overindulging as you'll regret it tomorrow. ***Moon in Aries.***

10 JANUARY

This is likely to be a busy day and the more focused you are on the details the better, as you may experience a surprise change of schedule or the need to be spontaneous. Negotiations will go well if you're open to change. *Moon enters Taurus.*

11 JANUARY

It's a mixed bag today: on the one hand you'll appreciate the sense that some relationships are blossoming, but on the other you may discover a mistake or realise you have been labouring under a delusion. Consider your options carefully, and if arguments seem likely ensure you have the facts at hand to avoid further misunderstandings. *Moon in Taurus.*

12 JANUARY

The moon in Taurus brings out your sensual and creative side, and you'll enjoy being imaginative with work projects and spending time with someone whose company you enjoy. However, you may also tend to be a little stubborn and may see others as being obstinate, so aim to find common ground. *Moon in Taurus.*

13 JANUARY

You'll appreciate the opportunity to dig down and get work done. You may also be more motivated to boost your appearance, health and well-being. Try to get key paperwork and financial matters resolved before Mercury turns retrograde tomorrow to avoid delays over the next few weeks. *Moon in Gemini.*

14 JANUARY

You may receive key news regarding an important trip, decision or finances. Certain negotiations could progress as long as you all take a moment to look for positive ways ahead, as unexpected developments will require some focus. *Moon in Gemini.*

15 JANUARY

A change of plan or the need to be more adaptable will lead you to rethink a commitment or investment, which will give you the time to organise a Plan B if necessary. *Moon enters Cancer.*

16 JANUARY

Key developments will signal deep-rooted change so ensure you see developments now from a long-term perspective, especially your financial and personal investments. Strong emotions may arise, so find ways to channel them into happy outcomes. *Moon in Cancer.*

17 JANUARY

The Cancerian full moon will spotlight a financial or personal transaction that could put a new shine on an agreement or relationship. This will be an intense full moon, so ensure you find the time to ground and earth yourself. Developments could be transformational.

18 JANUARY

The moon in Cancer will encourage you to follow your instincts and be strong, even if intense emotions emerge. Once the moon is in Leo you'll feel more outgoing and will enjoy dissipating excess energy through sports, travel and exciting projects. *Moon in Leo.*

19 JANUARY

You are intrinsically a proactive person and Mars in your sign will bring out your dynamism and sense of adventure. You'll appreciate the chance to be progressive, either with a personal or financial opportunity, so be open to change. *Moon in Leo.*

20 JANUARY

The sun in Aquarius for the next four weeks will bring out your chatty, pioneering aspects and you'll feel more inclined to travel, socialise and engage with the community, which you'll enjoy. You may also be drawn to new projects and ideas. *Moon in Leo.*

21 JANUARY

The moon in Virgo at the zenith of your chart brings out your inner perfectionist. You'll feel motivated to get things wrapped up for the weekend so you can find some time to relax. *Moon in Virgo.*

22 JANUARY

You'll enjoy a reunion and/or a return to an old haunt. A visit or trip will be enjoyable, so be sure to organise something fun. *Moon enters Libra.*

23 JANUARY

This is another good day for get-togethers and for reunions. You may feel drawn to spruce up your domestic décor or to enjoy a little domestic me time. It's also a good day to get on top of finances if you need to. *Moon in Libra.*

24 JANUARY

It's likely to be a busy day. You may feel under pressure due to a deadline and will be in a positive frame of mind to get things done. A financial review or the need to go over certain communications will bear fruit. *Moon in Libra.*

25 JANUARY

You'll be productive so take the initiative with your projects. A meeting or the need to review some decisions will have a positive outcome. *Moon in Scorpio.*

26 JANUARY

This is a good time to go over paperwork and agreements to ensure everyone involved is still on the same page. You will enjoy a reunion and may get the time to spruce up your appearance or a work station. *Moon in Scorpio.*

27 JANUARY

Trust your intuition as you'll gain insight into a domestic or work matter. You may be repaid a debt or will repay one yourself. *Moon in Sagittarius.*

28 JANUARY

When the moon is in your sign you will gain additional courage and feel more in your element. You'll appreciate the opportunity to review and reorganise some of your agreements, both financially and at work or regarding health schedules. *Moon in Sagittarius.*

29 JANUARY

Key news or developments in your personal life or financially could be transformative. You may wish to reconsider a decision. The news you receive and developments could signal more change to come, so be aware of the implications of your circumstances. *Moon in Capricorn.*

30 JANUARY

Be prepared for changes, some of which may come about unexpectedly. Avoid gambling if you are making large financial or personal investments. Ensure you do your research instead. *Moon in Capricorn.*

31 JANUARY

You may hear positive news. It is a good day for talks and meetings, especially to do with personal matters and money. Romance could flourish, so organise a treat! *Moon in Aquarius.*

February

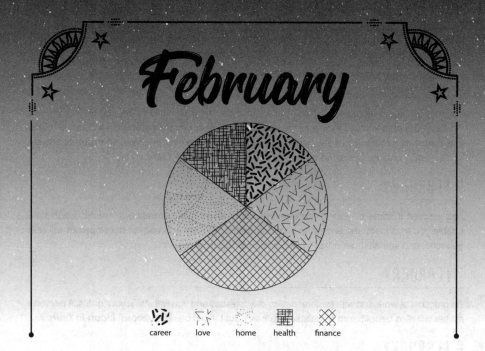

career love home health finance

1 FEBRUARY

The new moon in Aquarius will spotlight fresh agreements and negotiations for some Sagittarians and a fresh financial phase for others. You may have bright and upbeat ideas, but someone close may need persuading of their merit. Circumstances will progress but will need careful planning.

2 FEBRUARY

Consider the feelings of someone close, especially if they have already voiced that their opinions differ from yours; they may have a valid point. Careful negotiations and talks will reap rewards. ***Moon enters Pisces.***

3 FEBRUARY

You are persuasive when the moon is in Pisces as you are more able to listen to others and discuss matters from their point of view. A change of pace or of place will be inspiring and will bring new ideas into being. Spiritual Sagittarians may be particularly inspired. ***Moon in Pisces.***

4 FEBRUARY

Key news will arrive and you may be ready to make a commitment. For some the news will be in connection with financial matters, and for others due to personal circumstances. It's a good time to reconsider your thoughts if necessary and to adapt to developments. Avoid gambling, both financially and emotionally, as it'll backfire. *Moon in Pisces.*

5 FEBRUARY

You may feel more emotional or fiery than usual while the moon is in Aries, and as it aligns with Chiron your vulnerabilities may emerge. Avoid taking other people's problems as your own. You may be asked for help, and if you need some support it will be available from an expert or adviser. You'll enjoy a change of routine or an impromptu visit. *Moon in Aries.*

6 FEBRUARY

Ask yourself if some of your disagreements come down to a difference in values, as this will enable you to understand someone so much better. A lovely and upbeat development will help you relax and see life from a fresh perspective. *Moon in Aries.*

7 FEBRUARY

Be practical at work and with general day-to-day logistics and you will attain your goals. A personal matter will also benefit from a realistic approach. Just avoid being stubborn. *Moon in Taurus.*

8 FEBRUARY

This is a good time to be proactive with the changes in your life that are inevitable. Be positive, as you will find that new ideas steer you in the right direction. A personal or family matter may surprise you. *Moon in Taurus.*

9 FEBRUARY

You'll enjoy being with like-minded people and a reunion or at least a chat on the phone will help ground you if you feel a little disoriented by events. *Moon enters Gemini.*

10 FEBRUARY

You'll enjoy a compliment and may also receive a financial boost. If you're shopping avoid splurging, as something beautiful may catch your eye! *Moon in Gemini.*

11 FEBRUARY

This is a good day for talks with someone close, as you will gain deeper insight into each other and yourself. A key financial matter could lead to further developments, so ensure you are clear about the value of your transactions. Avoid overspending. If you find events intense, take time out to unwind when you can. *Moon in Cancer.*

12 FEBRUARY

The Cancerian moon for the next two days is ideal for you to gain a deeper understanding of someone who can sometimes seem difficult to comprehend. It's also good for spiritual work, psychic development and meditation. Just avoid escapism and overindulgence, which you'll regret! *Moon in Cancer.*

13 FEBRUARY

You'll relish the chance to deepen your ties with someone special. Trust your instincts, as they are spot on. You'll be drawn to music, art and a beautiful place. *Moon in Cancer.*

14 FEBRUARY

Happy St Valentine's Day! You'll enjoy a romantic time and someone special will certainly let their feelings be known. You may be drawn to get there first! Feelings could be intense, so maintain perspective. *Moon in Leo.*

15 FEBRUARY

While you may still feel the love vibe not everyone will be feeling the same way. Take a moment out of your busy day if you feel some conversations are at cross purposes, and find ways to get them back on track. You may need to carve out a fresh path for yourself if you feel you are on a different trajectory to someone close. *Moon in Leo.*

16 FEBRUARY

The Leo full moon will shine a light on your shared duties and responsibilities such as communal space at home or finances. A key decision may be necessary regarding a financial or personal matter. You may need to do a little more research to get things on track. *Moon enters Virgo late in the day.*

17 FEBRUARY

You may be surprised by developments. This is a good day for getting together with someone you love and also for business meetings. A financial negotiation could be agreed upon. *Moon in Virgo.*

18 FEBRUARY

As the sun enters the zodiac sign Pisces you'll appreciate the opportunity over the next four weeks to follow more closely your own sense of purpose and your values and principles. Be inspired but also be practical. *Moon in Virgo.*

19 FEBRUARY

While the moon is at the zenith of your chart you will find the means to get things done. Domestic chores and practicalities may need to take second place to your favourite activities such as sports and time spent with those you love. ***Moon in Libra.***

20 FEBRUARY

This is again a constructive and proactive day, although you may need to prioritise between fun and family and chores. As the moon is in Libra you'll manage to find the balance. ***Moon in Libra.***

21 FEBRUARY

You'll enjoy being inspired by your activities and will notice more than usual if you're unhappy with any aspect of your life. It'll give you the insight you need to make changes. Your more boisterous side is likely to emerge and you'll appreciate the opportunity to channel energy into work and everyday chores. ***Moon enters Scorpio.***

22 FEBRUARY

Trust your instincts when the moon is in Scorpio, as you will see more clearly the underlying dynamics of various interactions. This will provide insight into your various decisions. However, you may feel fairly idealistic, so be inspired but maintain perspective. ***Moon in Scorpio.***

23 FEBRUARY

This is a good day for talks, meetings and a trip somewhere beautiful such as the ocean. A key financial matter could progress and you may experience a financial boost or receive a compliment. Romance could flourish, so organise a treat! ***Moon in Sagittarius.***

24 FEBRUARY

This is another lovely day for get-togethers and talks. You may also enjoy investing in yourself for a change by improving your appearance and well-being. ***Moon in Sagittarius.***

25 FEBRUARY

You may be surprised by developments. Someone who can be unpredictable may behave true to form and you may need to think on your feet. Avoid making snap decisions, especially financially, as you may regret them. Avoid financial and emotional gambling. ***Moon enters Capricorn.***

26 FEBRUARY

You'll enjoy a trip or a visit and a beautiful place or great company will lift your moods. A little retail therapy may appeal but you must avoid overspending, especially if you're already in debt. ***Moon in Capricorn.***

27 FEBRUARY

You'll enjoy cocooning this weekend if life has been too busy, as a sensual, earthy mood will encourage you to slow down. You'll also enjoy the company of someone you love. A family get-together will be grounding. *Moon enters Aquarius.*

28 FEBRUARY

A change of pace or of focus will bring out your inner resourcefulness. You'll enjoy meeting people but may need to prioritise between work and home as you'll be in demand at home. *Moon in Aquarius.*

March

career love home health finance

1 MARCH

You're thinking both analytically and creatively, which will help you to move ahead with finances and planning. But if you feel a little like a fish out of water ensure you remain grounded and practical. ***Moon enters Pisces.***

2 MARCH

The Piscean new moon signals the chance to turn a corner in a relationship or negotiation or financially. Take the time to make a wish: as long as it's inspired but also practical you'll be happy with the outcome. Trust your instincts.

3 MARCH

The Venus-Mars-Pluto conjunction signals important news and, for some, key financial transactions. You may be surprised by news and developments. Be sure to align your actions with your higher purpose; in other words, avoid taking action in ways that could jeopardise your good name and compromise your pleasant nature. ***Moon in Pisces.***

4 MARCH

You'll feel more outgoing and proactive about your actions but may need to be sensitive to someone's feelings. If you are feeling vulnerable there will be someone to help you, so ensure you look for solid advice and guidance. A meeting could be therapeutic, even if it's intense. *Moon in Aries.*

5 MARCH

Key meetings and news will be decisive and could mean further opportunities will open up. You may meet someone chatty and optimistic. For some, travel will be important and a trip will take you somewhere new, while for others the big news will involve money or changes at home. *Moon in Aries.*

6 MARCH

As both Mars and Venus step into Aquarius you'll enjoy being proactive and adventurous, and ready to step into new terrain via a personal or business agreement. You may be drawn to a new look and activity this weekend. Singles could meet someone new who seems outgoing yet earthy, and couples could re-ignite the passion in your relationship so plan a treat! *Moon in Taurus.*

7 MARCH

The Taurean moon will help you to feel more grounded and practical, especially with circumstances that may take you outside your usual sphere of reference. Avoid obstinacy and ensure you are being open-minded, especially regarding negotiations and new experiences. *Moon in Taurus.*

8 MARCH

This is a good day for negotiations as they are likely to go well. A trip or meeting will be enjoyable and could contribute to raised morale or self-esteem. *Moon enters Gemini.*

9 MARCH

The Gemini moon will provide a lighter atmosphere, especially at work and with a sporting or health matter. Someone close may be chattier or more willing to see your perspective. *Moon in Gemini.*

10 MARCH

As Mercury enters Pisces you will feel increasingly inspired over the coming weeks and may be drawn to planning travel and improving close relationships through activities you have in common. This is a good day to make a commitment or an agreement as it's likely to take, especially at home or regarding finances. *Moon in Gemini.*

11 MARCH

Someone you share duties or space with at home or at work may inspire you to spend more time together, as you seem to be on a better footing now even if you don't always see eye to eye. *Moon in Cancer.*

12 MARCH

This is a good weekend to spend time with the people you love and on sprucing up your home life or domestic dynamics. You'll enjoy connecting more deeply with those you love, so organise a treat. *Moon in Cancer.*

13 MARCH

This is an excellent day to invest in your home and family and in your favourite interests such as music, dance and romance. You may deepen your spiritual interests. Romance will blossom, and a beautiful romantic setting will be conducive to love. *Moon enters Leo.*

14 MARCH

This is a good time to consider how you could boost your finances and relationships. Good communication skills will improve your circumstances in both areas. *Moon in Leo.*

15 MARCH

The Leo moon brings your inner adventurer out. You'll appreciate the opportunity to let off some steam doing something you love such as sports. Someone close has your back. *Moon in Leo.*

16 MARCH

Attention to detail and a practical approach will put you in a strong position with someone who can be a little erratic or unpredictable. If you disagree with someone, find a way to get down to brass tacks and establish common ground. *Moon in Virgo.*

17 MARCH

Someone close may surprise you. You'll enjoy doing something different such as taking a trip somewhere unexpected. Be spontaneous, as you'll enjoy the change of mood. *Moon in Virgo.*

18 MARCH

The Virgo full moon shines a light on your career, general direction and status. You may be beginning or ending a particular phase in your life that means changes at home or with family. Talks with a group or organisation could signal the start of a new agreement.

19 MARCH

You may be surprised by a situation that involves someone's unpredictability. A change of circumstance will benefit from a spontaneous approach. Just avoid gambling, both financially and emotionally, as it will backfire. *Moon in Libra.*

20 MARCH

When the sun enters Aries it is the vernal equinox. During the next four weeks you're likely to feel revitalised, especially in your personal life, enjoying being more spontaneous and willing to engage in family and creative ventures. **Moon in Scorpio.**

21 MARCH

This is a good time to make changes at home and to receive visitors. You may be drawn to discussing key family and creative projects that involve personal investment of time or money. **Moon in Scorpio.**

22 MARCH

On the one hand conversations and meetings are likely to go well, and on the other you may experience a surprise that involves having to alter your plans. Avoid being tempted to gamble on outcomes. Find ways to earth your projects so you can work with the unpredictability of some variables in a practical way. **Moon enters Sagittarius.**

23 MARCH

This is a good time to spruce up your home through DIY or a splash of fresh colour in the décor. You will enjoy a visit, and if you are spiritually inclined you may reach an epiphany. Romance could blossom so organise a treat, or a visit to somewhere beautiful could bring romance into your life. **Moon in Sagittarius.**

24 MARCH

You'll enjoy a reunion and the chance to touch base with someone special. You won't necessarily see eye to eye with everyone, so be sure to keep an open mind and be tactful to avoid arguments. **Moon enters Capricorn.**

25 MARCH

You are an adventurous and outgoing person but the moon in Capricorn could slow things down, so be patient. If a difference of opinion occurs find ways to re-establish common ground for the best results. **Moon in Capricorn.**

26 MARCH

You'll enjoy touching base with someone who has a strong influence over you. A trip or change at home could be transformative. If you're shopping or considering a large outlay, ensure you gain expert advice to avoid mistakes. **Moon in Capricorn.**

27 MARCH

This is a lovely day for get-togethers and a short trip or visit. You'll find people are more sympathetic to your views, so if you have important ideas to discuss today's the day! *Moon in Aquarius.*

28 MARCH

This is a good day to come to a workable agreement, whether in your personal life or at work or financially. Just ensure you have all the correct information to avoid mistakes, as you may be easily led. You'll enjoy a lovely get-together. *Moon in Aquarius.*

29 MARCH

Trust your gut instincts, as these will not lead you astray. You may tend to be a little escapist, so avoid ignoring important matters that you know must be attended to. *Moon in Pisces.*

30 MARCH

Let beauty, love and harmony into your life, as you'll find this uplifting. You may be drawn to a beautiful place or to beautifying your home environment. Romance could blossom, so be prepared to deepen relationships. *Moon in Pisces.*

31 MARCH

You are motivated to get ahead and can make great headway in your personal life, especially at home and with family. Just avoid appearing feisty as your efforts to bring more peace into your life could backfire. *Moon in Aries.*

April

career   love   home   health   finance

1 APRIL

The Aries new moon spells a fresh chapter within a key relationship. If you find your vulnerabilities rise during this time, this will be your chance to strengthen your ability to be assertive and to turn a corner and leave a chapter behind. Someone may need your help. If you need advice it will be available, so find an expert. A health or travel matter may need attention.

2 APRIL

You may by surprised by news. A health development is best approached from a practical point of view. Someone special will be unexpectedly helpful or will need your help. A trip could take you somewhere especially healing. This is a good time to make domestic improvements. ***Moon enters Taurus.***

3 APRIL

This is a good day to take the initiative with changes you'd like to see; your finances and self-esteem could improve as a result. A change of pace or of place will be therapeutic. ***Moon in Taurus.***

4 APRIL

You can make headway with your projects by using your excellent communication skills. Avoid being dragged into arguments and find inspired ways to get on with others. *Moon in Taurus.*

5 APRIL

Key agreements and commitments may be made, and as long as they resonate with you on a deep level you will succeed with your tasks. If you feel that some aspects of the agreements you wish to make go against the grain, it's important to speak up assertively and without recourse to arguments. *Moon in Gemini.*

6 APRIL

This is a good day for talks, especially regarding your personal life and finances. Take the time to discuss your ideas with someone you know has your back. *Moon in Gemini.*

7 APRIL

You can make great progress with domestic and personal matters. If financial agreements need to be made you'll appreciate the opportunity to get these up and running. A trip could be ideal. *Moon in Cancer.*

8 APRIL

Creative and spiritual Scorpios will see that the more you invest in your projects the better the outcome for you. That is, unless your expectations have been super high or unrealistic, in which case you may need to correct some of your expectations. *Moon in Cancer.*

9 APRIL

This is a productive weekend, and making changes at home, outside in the garden or on your favourite project initiatives can go far. You'll enjoy investing more in yourself and your environment and on those you love. *Moon in Cancer.*

10 APRIL

Communications will merit care and attention as there may be misunderstandings. If you find you are prone to arguments, as you are sensitive to underlying tension, find ways to disperse frustrations and consider if tensions come from different values. Avoid tense topics, as these will escalate quickly. *Moon in Leo.*

11 APRIL

You'll feel matters get onto a more even keel as you gain a sense of progress, especially in your personal life and with creative and imaginative projects. Your home life will also gain a

more even keel, especially if you approach differences with a practical stance to get things shipshape. *Moon in Leo.*

12 APRIL

You'll enjoy giving full rein to your imagination, creativity and inspiration. You'll also enjoy a lovely get-together or a trip somewhere beautiful. However, someone may not share your point of view, so avoid allowing this to upset the apple cart and look for constructive ways to get ahead, especially financially. *Moon in Leo.*

13 APRIL

This is a good day to make agreements, especially financially and regarding your home life. If you are planning a meeting or a trip some arrangements may need to be rethought, but if you have checked the details travel could take you somewhere useful. *Moon in Virgo.*

14 APRIL

You'll enjoy indulging in love, romance, music and being creative. This is a good day to engage in your true interests and to infuse your ideas and projects with inspiration that comes from your own expeirence and knowledge. Romance could blossom, so plan a treat! *Moon enters Libra.*

15 APRIL

As Mars enters Pisces for the next few weeks you may be surprised by a change of focus. The arts, spirituality, romance and music will all appeal more to you. However, you may tend to be idealistic, so ensure you keep your feet on the ground if you are making key decisions over the next month. *Moon in Libra.*

16 APRIL

The Libran full moon signifies the start of a fresh cycle for you, and you may already be considering how to alter your general direction and your projects and activities. You may be experiencing changes at work or within your status. You may wish to find more time for your own interests, so now is a good time to reconfigure your schedule so you are able to do this.

17 APRIL

You'll feel more passionate about your ideas and ventures and will feel motivated to spend time with those you love and on activities you adore. If you sense a little tension in the air, avoid escalating it and find peaceful ways to enjoy your day. *Moon in Scorpio.*

18 APRIL

You may hear unexpected news or will be engaged in an unusual circumstance. A health matter can progress, so take the initiative. Avoid contributing to stress and drama and find peaceful ways to overcome hurdles and enjoy your day. *Moon in Scorpio.*

19 APRIL

The Scorpio moon will bring out your inner passions and you'll appear dynamic and focused. Just avoid appearing more aggressive than need be, especially at work, or your efforts will be counterproductive. Once the moon enters your sign you'll feel more in your own element and comfortable about how you express yourself. ***Moon enters Sagittarius.***

20 APRIL

As the sun enters Taurus you will feel more stable and secure about certain agreements and arrangements, especially in your personal life. This is a good time to find ways to move forward in the most realistic way. Beforehand, if you feel a little feisty find ways to disperse nervous energy. ***Moon in Sagittarius.***

21 APRIL

This is a good time to gain traction with your relationships, especially at home and with property and family. It's also a good time to socialise and network. ***Moon in Capricorn.***

22 APRIL

You'll enjoy investing time and energy in your favourite projects and people. If you have any logistics to overcome, you will manage to do so by paying extra attention to the practicalities of your situation. ***Moon in Capricorn.***

23 APRIL

A reunion will be enjoyable this weekend. You may also appreciate the time to boost health and well-being. A beauty or fitness treat will raise your spirits. ***Moon in Aquarius.***

24 APRIL

A personal or financial situation may require more focus. Take a moment to work out the best-case outcome. Good communication skills will help you to move forward. Avoid gambling, both financially and emotionally. ***Moon in Aquarius.***

25 APRIL

You're thinking philosophically, which will help you to get over logistical matters and to think calmly and clearly. However, you may be a little idealistic, especially about some relationships, so take things one step at a time. ***Moon in Pisces.***

26 APRIL

This is a sociable time for you and you'll enjoy being more outgoing and artistic. A trip, get-together or creative venture could flourish under these stars. ***Moon in Pisces.***

27 APRIL

This is a good time for a trip to somewhere lovely. Meetings both at work and socially are likely to go ahead well. If you're single you may feel more outgoing and enthusiastic about people in a friendly or creative environment. *Moon enters Aries.*

28 APRIL

This is a good time to initiate long-term change as your efforts are likely to take hold. Work and financial transactions are likely to go well. It's a good day for a health and well-being appointment. Meetings in all shapes and sizes are likely to take you somewhere inspiring. *Moon in Aries.*

29 APRIL

Talks could take you somewhere new. A trip or the chance to begin a fresh project will be inspiring. Domestic, property-related and family matters can step to a new level, so take the initiative with discussions and ideas. *Moon in Aries.*

30 APRIL

The partial solar eclipse in Taurus signals you are ready for a fresh phase in a personal situation. A family matter will benefit from a solid, practical approach as you may be ready to embrace an adventure. A domestic development is best handled realistically and from a logistical viewpoint. Avoid gambling, both financially and emotionally.

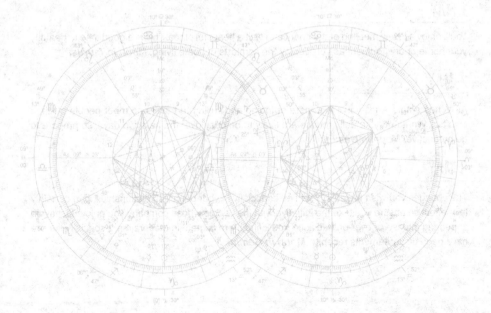

May

| career | love | home | health | finance |

1 MAY

You'll enjoy a lovely meeting or the chance to visit a beautiful place. This is a good time to beautify your home or environment as you'll enjoy the comforts of home living. ***Moon in Taurus.***

2 MAY

As Venus enters Aries you'll feel more outgoing and willing to travel and meet people on their own turf. Work and your daily routine are likely to be busy over the next two days, so prepare to be productive. ***Moon in Gemini.***

3 MAY

The changes you wish to see in your life, especially in your personal relationships, can certainly take effect so ensure you take the initiative with the people whose company you enjoy. Just avoid appearing intense or over-enthusiastic. You'll find there is merit in moderation, especially if there have been disagreements recently. ***Moon in Gemini.***

4 MAY

Someone may surprise you, and it will be a pleasant surprise such as a refreshing change of pace or news. For some it will be news from family. Developments could take you somewhere different. Singles may meet someone unexpectedly, so be prepared to mingle! *Moon in Gemini.*

5 MAY

You may be surprised by news or developments such as a fresh interest or activity that takes you in new directions. A domestic development may be unexpected. You may receive an impromptu visitor. *Moon in Cancer.*

6 MAY

An upbeat change of routine and the chance to blow off some steam this evening will cheer up your usual schedule. This is a good day for meetings, especially at work and regarding health and well-being. A financial matter will improve your mood. *Moon in Cancer.*

7 MAY

This is a productive weekend and you'll enjoy activities that provide a sense of purpose. Family and friends will be available for talks and visits, so ensure you reach out. You'll gain the chance to boost domestic dynamics. *Moon in Leo.*

8 MAY

You'll enjoy indulging in calming and relaxing activities such as walks in nature and a visit to the coast. A personal or financial matter is best viewed from a long-term perspective. Avoid making snap decisions and finding only short-term solutions to problems. *Moon in Leo.*

9 MAY

You'll feel motivated to get things done, especially with shared duties and chores. However, those you must collaborate with may not share your motivation and you may need to encourage them to be as optimistic and productive as you are. Aim to tie up loose ends at work and regarding communications before Mercury turns retrograde tomorrow. *Moon enters Virgo.*

10 MAY

As Mercury turns retrograde you're likely to receive key news that means you will need to review your circumstances. For some this will mean a change at work and for others a fresh approach to health, and if you were born in late November a new attitude to a business or personal partner. Try to allow extra time for travel and communications to avoid frustration over the coming weeks. *Moon in Virgo.*

11 MAY

As Jupiter joins Venus and Chiron in Aries you will feel more outgoing and willing to make changes in your environment, be this via travel or due to changes at home. You will gain energy over the coming weeks and months but may need to pace yourself to avoid being over-tired. *Moon in Virgo.*

12 MAY

When the moon is in Libra your rational side comes out and you can tend to be more analytical where usually you would be spontaneous. Avoid allowing an over-busy mind to get in the way of your usual enthusiasm. A little tact and diplomacy will work wonders. *Moon in Libra.*

13 MAY

You'll enjoy a meeting with like-minded people and romance could flow. If you're single you'll enjoy the chance to socialise and may meet someone who seems familiar but who you haven't actually met before. Couples will enjoy reigniting romance. *Moon in Libra.*

14 MAY

The Scorpio moon brings out your passionate, adventurous side and you'll relish socialising and engaging in favourite activities. You'll enjoy a trip and channelling energy into productive, fun activities. You will get a lot done this weekend. *Moon in Scorpio.*

15 MAY

If you're working this weekend it will be a super-productive time ideal for getting chores around the house and garden completed. Financial matters will deserve some focus. If you're shopping avoid overspending, and if you're contemplating a large outlay ensure you have researched your options carefully. Someone may need your help or vice versa. Rest assured support will be invaluable. *Moon in Scorpio.*

16 MAY

The total lunar eclipse in Scorpio marks considerable changes for you, especially in your personal life. It will spotlight an important agreement and the level of loyalty that is present or, in some cases, missing. For some this eclipse points to a fresh daily or work schedule.

17 MAY

This is a good day to check that the agreements you're hoping to make hold water. You may tend to be a little idealistic, so ensure you double-check financial arrangements. It's a good day to make a commitment if you have checked everything. *Moon in Sagittarius.*

18 MAY

You can attain important goals, be these financial ones or personal aims you have worked at for some time. Be proactive with your plans as your efforts are likely to pay off. *Moon in Capricorn.*

19 MAY

You'll appreciate the sense that your work and general arrangements in life are panning out, and this is a good day to discuss how to continue to improve your circumstances. You may enjoy a reunion. A work, health or financial matter will be looking up. *Moon in Capricorn.*

20 MAY

A reunion will be enjoyable and you'll enjoy a trip or visit. You may return to an old haunt. If you need to renegotiate some agreements you're likely to reach a good outcome. A trip may be delayed, so ensure you factor in extra time to avoid disappointment. *Moon in Aquarius.*

21 MAY

A fun and exciting project could come together. You may enjoy the fact that someone close is communicating better, enabling you to deepen your understanding of each other. *Moon in Aquarius.*

22 MAY

You'll enjoy developments that boost your self-esteem and belief in yourself this weekend. This is a good time to consider learning self-developmental techniques and ways to boost communications to deepen relationships. *Moon enters Pisces.*

23 MAY

This is a good time to reconfigure or review arrangements. It may mean that you must renegotiate, but a review will put you in a stronger position. You may return to an old haunt or welcome a visitor, which you'll enjoy. *Moon in Pisces.*

24 MAY

This is an excellent day for talks, both at home and at work. If you need to rethink a budget this is the time to do it, as you'll manage to work out something viable. *Moon in Pisces.*

25 MAY

You could certainly get a great deal done and negotiations will go well, but if you feel some matters are progressing under their own steam without your necessarily agreeing with the direction they are going in this is a good time to slow things down or they could snowball. *Moon in Aries.*

26 MAY

If you need someone's agreement for a plan to succeed this is a good day to ask for it. A social or work event will be enjoyable, but you must avoid overindulging or you'll regret the headache tomorrow! *Moon in Aries.*

27 MAY

You are an adventurous character and can be seen as so brutally honest that you're blunt on occasion. For the sake of peace you will need to avoid arguments, so be tactful and diplomatic for the best results. A financial or personal disagreement could quickly escalate to conflict. *Moon in Taurus.*

28 MAY

You're not known for being obstinate yet when the mood takes you you can be as stubborn as an ox. Over the next four weeks, for your best interests, just double-check that you're not being stubborn if you get into hot water. You'll enjoy focusing more on the creature comforts over the coming weeks, such as a little more luxury at home and good food and company. *Moon in Taurus.*

29 MAY

You'll feel productive and can get a great deal done. You'll enjoy a key meeting and may feel a little restless, so engaging in sports and a visit to the ocean or forest will feel fulfilling. Someone close may have key news for you. *Moon enters Gemini.*

30 MAY

The Gemini new moon will spotlight a new agreement or arrangement for November Sagittarians in a personal or business partnership, and for December Sagittarians at work or regarding health. This a good time to be flexible and adaptable to changes.

31 MAY

This is a good day for meetings, especially those to do with agreements and financial budgets. Be prepared to make changes so that you feel more positive. *Moon in Gemini.*

June

career love home health finance

1 JUNE

The Cancerian moon brings out your caring and nurturing side, but you may become more easily distracted by other people's agendas so ensure you focus, especially at work. **Moon in Cancer.**

2 JUNE

It's a good day to trust your intuition, as it's spot on. You may be drawn to expressing yourself more than usual, especially your emotions, and may be surprised by them. Someone may confide their feelings in you. Take time out if you can, as you'll enjoy a trip to the sea or to somewhere else beautiful. **Moon in Cancer.**

3 JUNE

You'll be glad to hear that Mercury ends its retrograde phase today. You may receive key news concerning work or health. Communications and travel plans will become easier to make over the coming weeks. **Moon enters Leo.**

4 JUNE

You may hear good news. You'll enjoy getting together with like-minded people and will feel motivated to make the first move. **Moon in Leo.**

5 JUNE

The Leo moon brings out your adventurous side and you'll enjoy being more active and blowing off steam via sports and your hobbies. However, some people may wish for a quiet, relaxing day so just be patient as you'll also enjoy feeling more relaxed as the day goes by. *Moon in Leo.*

6 JUNE

There is a healing or therapeutic quality about today that will help you to get things done, especially with the help of someone such as a work colleague or family member. You can make progress at work and with your long-term plans. *Moon in Virgo.*

7 JUNE

You'll enjoy a spontaneous event or a surprise. Someone close has news for you. A change of routine may breathe fresh air into your usual day. *Moon in Virgo.*

8 JUNE

This is a good day to get things done, especially at work and regarding health and well-being. You may feel more motivated about your projects and tasks so take the initiative. *Moon enters Libra.*

9 JUNE

The Libra moon can bring out your inner analyst, and you'll tend to look for rational and balanced ways to get ahead. This will be useful at work and to sort out any conundrum that comes your way. A change in your usual routine or a feeling that you are making progress will provide excellent motivation to pursue your goals. *Moon in Libra.*

10 JUNE

You'll see that your hard work is paying off as meetings and news show that you're making headway. You may also experience a financial or work improvement. *Moon enters Scorpio.*

11 JUNE

You'll enjoy doing something different and an impromptu get-together or invitation will be fun. However, you may need to prioritise between chores and duties on the one hand and fun on the other. If you're well organised you'll manage to do both! *Moon in Scorpio.*

12 JUNE

A reunion will take you back into the past in more ways than one, and you may unearth feelings you'd forgotten you had. Take the time to enjoy your evening, but you'll know when to call it quits. *Moon enters Sagittarius.*

13 JUNE

Communications are about to get more light-hearted, especially at work and regarding health and well-being. You may be in a lighter mood as you begin the week. You may receive good news at work. ***Moon in Sagittarius.***

14 JUNE

The full moon and supermoon in your sign represents a fresh chapter for you in your personal life. If you were born after mid-December you may begin a new daily schedule including a fresh approach to health. Take a moment to work out where your priorities lie and then make decisions from there.

15 JUNE

A personal matter is best approached carefully, even if you must act swiftly or feel under pressure. Avoid rushing, as you may make mistakes or, worse, have a bump or scrape. If you are meeting a sensitive character and you feel vulnerable or have been involved in arguments, try to be tactful to avoid bruising egos. ***Moon in Capricorn.***

16 JUNE

This is a good day to make a commitment to a new agreement, such as a financial budget or a practical way to approach your differences with someone. Avoid repeating the same old mistakes. Someone you love or respect will be a true help. ***Moon enters Aquarius.***

17 JUNE

You'll enjoy an impromptu get-together and the chance to touch base with someone whose company is uplifting. You may receive unexpected news or a guest at home. Be spontaneous but avoid impulsiveness. ***Moon in Aquarius.***

18 JUNE

A financial matter is best faced head-on to avoid making mistakes. If you are in debt it's a good idea to consider a fresh budget. A difference of values could be at the root of differences of opinions. Take things one step at a time, especially with domestic and personal matters, to avoid arguments. ***Moon in Aquarius.***

19 JUNE

You may have a slightly escapist approach to life and will enjoy being somewhere exciting and with like-minded people. Avoid overspending and overindulging, as you'll regret it tomorrow. Romance could flourish. An element of tension can be dispelled with friendly gestures and attention to details. ***Moon in Pisces.***

20 JUNE

The Piscean moon will excite your creativity, and if you work in the arts this will be useful but you may also feel a little idealistic about how things should be in your personal life. Just avoid being moody and having super-high expectations, as you could be disappointed. *Moon in Pisces.*

21 JUNE

As the sun enters Cancer, marking the solstice, you will feel more inclined to focus on the people you love and on shared projects. You may feel there has been much progress in your relationships but know you will not always automatically agree with everyone. Be proactive, as you could get a lot done. You may be drawn to a new look or outfit. *Moon in Aries.*

22 JUNE

You'll feel more inclined to be outspoken and positive, especially at home and regarding domestic matters. Be positive but avoid putting pressure on others, as they won't like it. *Moon in Aries.*

23 JUNE

You'll feel drawn to gaining more stability and comfort in your own life, and the opportunity to relax at home will appeal. *Moon enters Taurus.*

24 JUNE

You may be drawn to altering some aspects of your home life so that you feel more at home and at ease. Just ensure you run your ideas past those they will affect to avoid arguments. Aim to establish common ground for the best results. *Moon in Taurus.*

25 JUNE

You'll enjoy being practical about making changes in your life, especially at home and in your personal life. You may invest in more comfort at home or in someone you love such as a partner or family member. Romance could blossom, so organise a treat. Singles should mingle; you may meet someone romantic. *Moon in Taurus.*

26 JUNE

You'll enjoy feeling more outgoing and upbeat, and a visit or get-together with someone you love will have a healing quality to it. It's a good day to recharge your batteries through your own interests, such as walking, running, meditation or yoga. *Moon in Gemini.*

27 JUNE

This is an excellent day for meetings and for talks where you need people to know how you feel so you can make changes, especially in your personal life and health. However, you may feel

a little sensitive or vulnerable. If you need guidance, an expert or adviser could prove helpful. *Moon in Gemini.*

28 JUNE

This is a good day for health and beauty appointments. You may be drawn to a new look or to alter your usual health routine. You may be surprised by news or an impromptu meeting. *Moon enters Cancer.*

29 JUNE

The Cancerian new moon will kick-start a fresh chapter in a shared venture or relationship. You may need to persuade someone of your plans, especially if you need their co-operation and especially regarding travel or money. A negotiation may be tough, but if you focus on the facts you'll gain ground. *Moon in Cancer.*

30 JUNE

Talks and meetings will go well even if you feel a little at odds with someone's ideas or viewpoints. Trust your intuition, as it will not let you down. Avoid allowing emotions and expectations to run your life; look at the practicalities of your circumstances first. *Moon in Cancer.*

July

career love home health finance

1 JULY

There is growing tension in the skies that could contribute to arguments, especially over personal and financial matters, so take things one step at a time. If some communications are confusing, double-check the details. **Moon in Leo.**

2 JULY

This is a good time for a trip or get-together but you must pay attention to details to avoid mistakes and factor in extra time to avoid travel delays. Developments may feel intense, so maintain perspective to avoid arguments. **Moon in Leo.**

3 JULY

There is still tension in the air, so if you know someone's vulnerabilities avoid contributing to their sensitivity. This is a good day to get organised, especially with your plans moving forward for travel or a lovely project. **Moon enters Virgo.**

4 JULY

Avoid allowing tense undercurrents to bring your worst side out in talks and relationships. A financial matter may require a little more research before you can commit and a little tact and diplomacy to avoid arguments. **Moon in Virgo.**

5 JULY

This is a good day to consider how you could take some factors that are stuck into a new pattern so you can get out of a rut. It's a good day for romance, so if you have nothing planned yet organise a treat! A family get-together is likely to provide a sense of stability. ***Moon enters Libra.***

6 JULY

This is a good day for health and beauty appointments. If you'd like to improve domestic dynamics your efforts will go well, but you must factor in someone's feelings if you are making key decisions. ***Moon in Libra.***

7 JULY

Your analytical mind is in full form and you won't miss a beat at work, so take the initiative with your projects. A domestic matter may require more focus to ensure your improvements are as you'd like them to be. ***Moon in Libra.***

8 JULY

An unexpected change of plan or a surprise get-together will be enjoyable. However, you must avoid misunderstandings, especially with someone at home or someone you share duties or finances with. ***Moon in Scorpio.***

9 JULY

Be careful once again with communications as misunderstandings can arise. Also, financial transactions will merit careful focus as mistakes can be made in that area. If you're travelling you may experience delays, so factor in extra time. A vehicle or device may require repair. Back up computers for the best measure. ***Moon in Scorpio.***

10 JULY

Someone will surprise you and you'll enjoy breathing fresh air into your usual Sunday routine. You'll enjoy getting together with someone special, and romance could blossom unexpectedly. You may enjoy a reunion. ***Moon enters Sagittarius.***

11 JULY

When the moon is in your sign you feel more optimistic and therefore more likely to take action in areas you may generally be a little shy in. You'll enjoy moving some relationships into fresh territory, but if you're uncomfortable ensure you take things one step at a time. ***Moon in Sagittarius.***

12 JULY

This is a good day to get things done. You'll be productive at work, and if health, well-being or personal matters need a little focus you will manage to set things on track. ***Moon enters Capricorn.***

13 JULY

The full moon and supermoon in Capricorn will spotlight an important personal matter. You are ready to consider how to share duties or resources in a new way. This full moon can also spotlight changes in your finances, which could be transformational. Look for security and stability and avoid making decisions based on assumptions.

14 JULY

You'll discover whether or not your expectations have been unrealistic, especially regarding someone in particular such as a business or personal partner. The good news is this is a good time to set things right. You may be prone to misunderstandings and to delays, so be patient. You may also be easily misled. ***Moon enters Aquarius.***

15 JULY

Some talks will be intense, as you may need to discuss important financial or personal matters. Rest assured that if an obstacle arises you will overcome it. ***Moon in Aquarius.***

16 JULY

This is a lovely day for romance, home improvements and generally spending time with someone you care about. If you're shopping or considering a large investment ensure you do adequate research. Spiritually minded Sagittarians will enjoy deepening your understanding. A financial or legal matter will need to be clarified. ***Moon enters Pisces.***

17 JULY

You'll enjoy a get-together or trip somewhere beautiful, such as to the sea. Romance and family time will appeal. ***Moon in Pisces.***

18 JULY

Key talks could spell a change in the way you go about a financial or personal matter. If you are undertaking legal matters you may receive concrete news. You may receive a financial or ego boost. ***Moon enters Aries.***

19 JULY

As Mercury enters upbeat Leo you'll feel more adventurous about your plans over the coming weeks. Your own interests and the amount of time you can spend with the people you love are likely to increase. Be positive! *Moon in Aries.*

20 JULY

Expect important meetings or news, and decisions that have to be made. It's a good time for research, especially into finances and commitments. You may be ready to take a project or relationship in a new direction. *Moon enters Taurus.*

21 JULY

You like circumstances to move forward quickly so you may be slightly impatient and feel restless, especially with ventures that are moving more slowly than you'd like. You'll find ways to spend more time with the people you love as a result, so plan some lovely events. *Moon in Taurus.*

22 JULY

As the sun enters Leo you will feel more optimistic and active. You'll appreciate the chance to organise upbeat events such as a trip or fun activity with someone whose company you like. *Moon in Taurus.*

23 JULY

This is an excellent day for a trip and your favourite activities. If you're shopping avoid overspending as you'll regret it, but you will love a treat! You'll enjoy a meeting and the chance to move forward with domestic repairs and also to improve interpersonal dynamics. *Moon in Gemini.*

24 JULY

You'll enjoy being chatty and sociable and someone fun will be great company. You'll savour a change in your usual Sunday routine, so consider what you'd like to do and organise it! *Moon in Gemini.*

25 JULY

A difference of opinion needn't turn into a full-blown argument. Look at ways to establish common ground if you have no alternative but to collaborate and co-operate with someone whose values are different from yours. *Moon enters Cancer.*

26 JULY

Choose your words carefully, as someone you must get on with may not agree with your views or the actions you take. Avoid snap decisions, as these are likely to backfire. A financial decision or agreement may be delayed, so be patient. *Moon in Cancer.*

27 JULY

Communications are likely to proceed on a much more even keel. A vehicle or device may need to be fixed, and if you're travelling you may be delayed. You may be asked to help someone, and if you need advice or support it will be available. ***Moon in Cancer.***

28 JULY

The Leo new moon points to a fresh chapter regarding shared finances or duties. You may decide that recent disagreements don't add up and that you must research your options more deeply. Someone who tends to be unpredictable may behave true to form and set a new ball in motion. Avoid snap decisions and look for solid ways to move forward.

29 JULY

Good communication skills are the key to your success. Be tactful and diplomatic where necessary and willing to see another's viewpoint. ***Moon in Leo.***

30 JULY

Once again your success lies in how well you present your ideas and yourself. Take a moment to gather your thoughts and be prepared to think outside the box about methods of moving forward in the most delightful way. You'll enjoy a more relaxing time and the chance to recharge your batteries. ***Moon enters Virgo.***

31 JULY

This is a good time to make a commitment to someone or to a financial investment. Just ensure you have done adequate research if you are making financial investments. Avoid snap decisions. Someone may surprise you. Romance can blossom, so organise a treat. ***Moon in Virgo.***

August

career   love   home   health   finance

1 AUGUST

Key meetings or news may come about unexpectedly and could move a significant relationship forward. However, if you must make a bold statement such as a work presentation or inform someone of a decision, ensure you carefully research your options to avoid mistakes. Some meetings or travel may be delayed, so be patient. *Moon in Virgo.*

2 AUGUST

You may be surprised by news. You'll enjoy taking the time to discuss your plans with those they concern, and a reunion or a chance encounter will be productive. Artistic, domestic and sports-related activities are likely to go well. *Moon in Libra.*

3 AUGUST

Think outside the square as your initiatives will succeed with a little lateral thinking. Romance could flourish, and you may be surprised by developments in a personal situation such as at home. *Moon in Libra.*

4 AUGUST

The moon at the zenith of your chart puts your emotions upfront in your mind, and you may feel a little less certain of some of your plans. Trust in the research you've done and aim to work methodically towards your goals. ***Moon enters Scorpio.***

5 AUGUST

You can gain ground with a personal venture or financial project through sheer hard work and determination. Avoid giving up at the first hurdle; be diligent with your work and personal plans and you'll succeed. ***Moon in Scorpio.***

6 AUGUST

Be inspired this weekend by the people you admire and the activities you enjoy. You may need to put in a little extra hard work, especially with domestic matters and financial decisions, but when you do you'll see positive results for your hard work. ***Moon enters Sagittarius.***

7 AUGUST

This is a lovely day for romance and for spending time in a pleasant setting. Consider a short trip somewhere beautiful or inviting friends into your own environment. ***Moon in Sagittarius.***

8 AUGUST

This is a good day to build bridges with someone you don't always see eye to eye with. It's also a good day to seek expert advice, for example from an accountant or another expert. You may also be asked for help. ***Moon enters Capricorn.***

9 AUGUST

A personal matter is best dealt with carefully, as intense emotions may otherwise bubble up. If you must make an agreement or a commitment, ensure you have researched your options well. A trip will be transformational, but there may initially be delays or communication difficulties so be patient. A financial matter is best approached from a long-term point of view. ***Moon in Capricorn.***

10 AUGUST

Be practical with personal and domestic decisions even if it seems that matters are up in the air or cannot be decided upon quite yet. Manage your responses carefully. ***Moon enters Aquarius.***

11 AUGUST

A change in a situation such as at home or regarding shared duties will mean you must be adaptable. You will find that there is merit in being inspired by changes to look for solutions rather than taking an adversarial approach. You'll enjoy relaxing this evening. ***Moon in Aquarius.***

12 AUGUST

The Aquarian full moon will spotlight key negotiations and relationships and may put the focus on finances and your expectations of a work or health matter. Be prepared to make changes. Think laterally if an obstacle arises.

13 AUGUST

You'll feel more inclined to look for solutions and talks will be productive if you take a realistic and practical stance. Look for ways to build a solid platform for yourself and your ventures. *Moon in Pisces.*

14 AUGUST

A financial transaction or personal interaction could be beneficial and boost morale, but if you feel things are moving too quickly it's time to apply the brakes. A work or personal agreement could be lucrative, but if it limits your movements too much you may need to rethink your options. *Moon enters Aries.*

15 AUGUST

Communications will flow. If you are a good communicator you'll relish the chance to find out more about your circumstances, either at work or with a venture, but if you find someone can be unpredictable you may need to be super adaptable as changes could speed things up. You'll enjoy a meeting or fun activity such as sport or a trip. *Moon in Aries.*

16 AUGUST

A trip or study will go well and will introduce you to new ideas or people. A sports activity or a legal matter could open your eyes to new possibilities. *Moon in Aries.*

17 AUGUST

Ensure you have all the facts at your fingertips or you may be prone to making assumptions that could get you into hot water. You will feel inspired but may be a little forgetful or head in the clouds. *Moon in Taurus.*

18 AUGUST

This is a good day for get-togethers and for romance, so take the initiative and plan a date! If you discover a project has been put on the back-burner avoid feeling disappointed, as you will gain the chance to focus on other matters in the meantime. This is a good time to consider a fresh budget. *Moon in Taurus.*

19 AUGUST

Some activities will merit careful attention to avoid misunderstandings, especially those in which you must collaborate well with others. Avoid a battle of egos and focus on common ground to avoid arguments. *Moon in Gemini.*

20 AUGUST

Mars will now be in your opposite sign Gemini until the end of March 2023, which will help you to make great progress with relationships as you'll find these a little more light-hearted and you may feel more sociable yourself. That doesn't mean you'll automatically get on with everyone, though. *Moon in Gemini.*

21 AUGUST

A trip somewhere beautiful will be inspiring. You may enjoy deepening your understanding of someone or of yourself. Your interest in the arts, spirituality and music may deepen. You'll enjoy a trip but may be forgetful, so avoid misplacing keys. *Moon in Gemini.*

22 AUGUST

This is a potentially transformational time for you. Travel, study, sports and work could all take you somewhere new, so be inspired! *Moon in Cancer.*

23 AUGUST

Now that the sun is in Virgo for the next four weeks you are likely to gradually feel more focused and serious about your long-term plans. It's a good time to put together a rough idea of how you'd like to see the next four weeks shape up. *Moon in Cancer.*

24 AUGUST

There is a therapeutic quality to events, and meetings and talks could propel you into a more nurturing phase for yourself and for someone close. It's a good time to seek expert advice. *Moon enters Leo.*

25 AUGUST

The Leo moon brings out your more outgoing and upbeat side and you'll be more expressive about your ideas and vales. You'll enjoy socialising, however, some people may find this aspect of you aggressive so ensure you are diplomatic. *Moon in Leo.*

26 AUGUST

Your ideas and plans have merit, so look for ways to see them take shape. The next few weeks are ideal for improving your circumstances, especially regarding travel, study and legal matters. *Moon in Leo.*

27 AUGUST

The new moon in Virgo may bring an event your way that you didn't see coming. This could be a change in your schedule or circumstances that will merit more focus. This is a good weekend to work out your priorities and plan ahead so your life revolves more around these. If someone's behaviour surprises you avoid reactive behaviour, as this could lead to a Mexican stand-off. Try to be proactive instead.

28 AUGUST

Serious discussions and long-term commitments may need to be discussed, including financial matters and shared arrangements. A commitment can be made. If disagreements arise, try to come to a workable agreement. *Moon in Virgo.*

29 AUGUST

You'll feel driven to communicate your long-term plans but may also feel a little conflicted, so take things one step at a time to avoid speaking before you've thought things through. *Moon enters Libra.*

30 AUGUST

You can achieve a great deal through a diligent and careful approach, but you will need to be focused, realistic and optimistic. *Moon in Libra.*

31 AUGUST

You may discover whether or not your expectations have been unrealistic. Be inspired by your dreams and goals and adopt a realistic approach to circumstances for the best results. *Moon enters Scorpio.*

September

career   love   home   health   finance

1 SEPTEMBER

A proactive, energetic approach to work and communications will reap rewards. You may feel more inclined to plan travel, get-togethers and fun events. A reunion may also appeal. *Moon in Scorpio.*

2 SEPTEMBER

You can't always agree with everyone, and today's tension in a relationship may be a case in point. If you're considering a financial investment ensure you have double-checked the details. A project will succeed with persistence and diligence. *Moon enters Sagittarius.*

3 SEPTEMBER

A trip, reunion or return to an old haunt will be enjoyable, but some talks may require more tact and diplomacy. This is a good day for building bridges with people you don't always see eye to eye with and a sensitive approach will reap rewards. *Moon in Sagittarius.*

4 SEPTEMBER

You'll enjoy leaving your comfort zone to do something different with someone you love or admire. A favourite activity such as sport or creative interests will be refreshing. *Moon in Sagittarius.*

5 SEPTEMBER

Over the next few weeks you'll appreciate approaching your projects and activities with a little more attention to detail. You'll see the wisdom in tempering your usually impulsive attitude with a little forethought, especially at work. ***Moon in Capricorn.***

6 SEPTEMBER

The Capricorn moon will bring out your practical and realistic sides, which will help you to get organised at work. However, you may feel frustrated by a lack of momentum so ensure you are patient. It's a good time to get paperwork shipshape. ***Moon in Capricorn.***

7 SEPTEMBER

A fresh approach to a project will be beneficial for you and you'll see that a work or financial venture could move forward with a rational and analytical approach. ***Moon in Aquarius.***

8 SEPTEMBER

This is a good day to better schedule in your spare time with your work and domestic duties so you can engage in activities that raise morale. Someone at home may need your help, and if you need expert advice about a project or venture it will be available. ***Moon in Aquarius.***

9 SEPTEMBER

You are a generous and giving character but you can be over-generous, especially with your time and especially for those you love, so ensure you get the balance right between your time and the time you spend on other people's concerns. Try to get the loose ends of important paperwork tied up before Mercury turns retrograde tomorrow. ***Moon in Pisces.***

10 SEPTEMBER

The full moon in Pisces shines a light on your travel plans and on changes in your neighbourhood or immediate environment. Someone close may provide key information or news. You may receive critical news at work or concerning a change of direction. This is a good time to plan to broaden your horizons and to learn something new.

11 SEPTEMBER

You'll enjoy doing something different this weekend and may receive an unexpected visitor or invitation. Someone close may have good news or will wish to take you somewhere new. ***Moon in Aries.***

12 SEPTEMBER

You may not be your usual enthusiastic self, especially due to activities you'd rather not have to undertake, but if you stick with your plans and are persistent without being obstinate you could make great headway. ***Moon in Aries.***

13 SEPTEMBER

Focus on your favourite activities and people and you'll find that chores and difficult logistics take second place and you'll whizz through chores so much more quickly and efficiently. *Moon enters Taurus.*

14 SEPTEMBER

You'll enjoy the company of like-minded people, and if you're looking for the green light with a venture or for someone's agreement you may get it. Seek stability and security and you'll find it. *Moon in Taurus.*

15 SEPTEMBER

This is an excellent day to set goals for yourself and attain them, so ensure you take the initiative. Plough steadily forward and be practical for the best results. *Moon enters Gemini.*

16 SEPTEMBER

A trip somewhere beautiful and the chance to indulge in a favourite interest or activity will raise your morale. This is a romantic day and you'll enjoy making time for yourself and the people and activities you love. However, you may need to take someone's demands into account, and work and duties will keep you busy first. *Moon in Gemini.*

17 SEPTEMBER

The Gemini moon will bring out someone's chattiness and you may be surprised by some of what they have to say. If you agree with their opinions you'll enjoy a constructive day, but otherwise some disagreements may need to be ironed out. You'll enjoy being with like-minded people but must avoid impulsiveness. *Moon in Gemini.*

18 SEPTEMBER

A key trip or meeting will take you back in time. You may enjoy a reunion or will be feeling nostalgic. If you're travelling, factor in extra time as there may be delays. *Moon enters Cancer.*

19 SEPTEMBER

You'll enjoy deepening your interest in a project, person or venture. If you wish to make changes to a key plan today's your day, as your intentions are likely to take shape even if you do have some key discussions to get through first. *Moon in Cancer.*

20 SEPTEMBER

Your projects and ideas are likely to succeed, although you will need to be persuasive and diligent. Take a moment to ensure your values and principles align with those of someone you

must collaborate with and iron out any differences in a pleasant way to gain ideal results. *Moon enters Leo.*

21 SEPTEMBER

Be positive and show that you are practical and dependable, especially at work and financially. You may feel more confident and upbeat about your plans. *Moon in Leo.*

22 SEPTEMBER

This is another proactive day when you can make changes you wish to see with your various plans and ventures. You won't always agree with everyone, especially not at home, but you could bring a fresh agreement into being that everyone can live with. *Moon in Leo.*

23 SEPTEMBER

As the sun steps into Libra it marks the equinox, a time when we collectively sense we can achieve more balance and harmony in our lives. Your attention is likely to go increasingly to relationships, both in business and in your personal life. Find ways to enjoy common aims for the best results. You may hear key news about a study, travel or legal matter. *Moon in Virgo.*

24 SEPTEMBER

This is a lovely time to truly immerse yourself in your activities, be these related to sports, travel, education or spirituality. The arts and romance will blossom this weekend. You may tend to be a little escapist, so avoid overindulging as you'll regret it on Monday! *Moon in Virgo.*

25 SEPTEMBER

The new moon in Libra signals a fresh chapter for you, and the way you tend to see the world is likely to be changing largely because your values are changing. Be prepared to turn a corner with a key venture, interest or financial or personal investment. For some this new moon points to changes at work and in your status.

26 SEPTEMBER

A get-together, trip or venture will claim your attention as you get the chance to do something you love. Romance could go off the dial, so singles ensure you socialise and couples will enjoy deepening your connection. You may be a little forgetful, so avoid misplacing valuables such as house keys. *Moon in Libra.*

27 SEPTEMBER

You'll enjoy a change of environment or of pace. If you are planning on making changes in your personal life or financially this is an excellent time to get the ball rolling. *Moon in Libra.*

28 SEPTEMBER

Work projects are likely to gather steam. You could make a strong statement in your projects. A health and well-being incentive could flourish, so ensure you take the initiative. You may receive a financial or ego boost. *Moon in Scorpio.*

29 SEPTEMBER

You'll appreciate the time to review some of your decisions to ensure you're on the right track. You may also be drawn to socialise and network. *Moon in Scorpio.*

30 SEPTEMBER

You'll enjoy being your usual optimistic and outgoing self. You'll appreciate the opportunity to show just how capable you are and meetings are likely to go well, so be positive. Just avoid gambling, both financially and emotionally. *Moon in Sagittarius.*

October

career love home health finance

1 OCTOBER

You'll enjoy making changes at home and in your environment. You may enjoy a trip, and a reunion will bring you in touch with favourite people and activities. *Moon in Sagittarius.*

2 OCTOBER

You may receive key news to do with your work or home. A project or travel may take your focus as you decide more seriously where your priorities and loyalties lie. *Moon in Capricorn.*

3 OCTOBER

The Capricorn moon will help you to be more hands-on about developments, although you may be disappointed due to delays. It's a good day to double-check your plans both at work and at home to ensure you're on the right track where logistics are concerned. *Moon in Capricorn.*

4 OCTOBER

This is a good day to discuss your plans, especially if you feel new ideas and options could be important factors to take into account, so take the initiative. *Moon enters Aquarius.*

5 OCTOBER

You're thinking pragmatically, which will help you to overcome any logistical conundrums. You may receive good news at work or will feel more on track with your various projects and plans. Avoid being distracted by people who wish to put you under pressure but speed up if you're being extra slow! *Moon in Aquarius.*

6 OCTOBER

You'll appreciate a lighter feeling in the working day and may also enjoy a change of pace or of atmosphere socially, as you may get to spend some quality moments with someone special if you can. *Moon enters Pisces.*

7 OCTOBER

This is a good day for repairs and to renew appliances, for example, and to look after aspects of your domestic life that need care and attention. Someone may need your help. If you need expert advice ask for it, as it will be available. You'll enjoy a reunion or news from a group or friend. *Moon in Pisces.*

8 OCTOBER

You'll appreciate finding the time for your family and home this weekend. Discussions about plans for holidays will be enjoyable, and you'll also enjoy spending time being creative and taking part in group activities. You'll enjoy socialising and beautifying your home. *Moon enters Aries.*

9 OCTOBER

The Aries full moon will spotlight a personal and domestic matter. You may need to find the time for someone special and to consider their feelings above your own. If you need support it will be available. A group or friend may be particularly helpful. A health matter is best approached head-on to avoid delay.

10 OCTOBER

This is a good day to put in place a solid health and well-being schedule. You may be drawn to a new look or to research a little more about your circumstances. A group, friend or organisation may be particularly helpful to you. For some changes at work will mean changes at home or in your personal life. *Moon enters Taurus.*

11 OCTOBER

An important decision that could affect your personal life is best taken carefully to avoid making mistakes. You may find that a friend or organisation is particularly helpful or informative. A relationship could deepen. Talks and meetings at work are likely to be successful even if they are stressful. *Moon in Taurus.*

12 OCTOBER

Key talks and meetings are best entered into with all the facts at your fingertips. If you are unsure of your position it's vital you find out more before making important agreements. A trip could take you back to a previous circumstance. *Moon in Taurus.*

13 OCTOBER

A change of routine or a surprise circumstance is best approached in a practical way. Base decisions on reasonable expectations. Be adaptable for the best results. *Moon in Gemini.*

14 OCTOBER

You'll enjoy being with people who have their feet on the ground, as those who can be flighty may make you nervous. You'll appreciate the chance to discuss your ideas and to socialise with like-minded people. *Moon in Gemini.*

15 OCTOBER

You'll enjoy socialising and being light-hearted about life. Talks and meeting are likely to go well. Someone unpredictable may behave true to form and you'll avoid allowing them to upset your peace of mind. *Moon enters Cancer.*

16 OCTOBER

A mystery or conundrum needn't get the better of you. Spiritual and artistic endeavours will prove motivational. You'll gain a deeper understanding of someone if you look more closely at their values and ideas. You may be a little escapist or forgetful, so avoid misplacing valuables and overindulging as you'll regret it tomorrow. *Moon in Cancer.*

17 OCTOBER

There is a dynamic flavour to the day that you'll enjoy. You can make great progress with projects and also in your personal relationships, as you'll feel motivated and upbeat. *Moon in Cancer.*

18 OCTOBER

The Leo moon brings out your inner adventurer. You'll enjoy being active and outgoing. You'll feel more confident than you have for some time and could get a great deal done, so take the initiative. *Moon in Leo.*

19 OCTOBER

You are focused and motivated but not everyone else is. You may notice more than usual that some people have different values or opinions to you, and if you feel conflict is brewing give them a wide berth. *Moon in Leo.*

20 OCTOBER

A difference of opinion may arise out of a difference of fundamental values. A financial dispute is best settled early rather than allowing it to fester. Some interactions will flow and others will be intense. Avoid allowing disagreements to escalate into conflict. *Moon enters Virgo.*

21 OCTOBER

The Virgo moon will help you to manage intense developments well. However, there may still be strong feelings around either in you or in other people, so ensure you avoid arguments for the best measure. *Moon in Virgo.*

22 OCTOBER

A lovely get-together will raise morale. Romance could truly blossom, so ensure you organise a treat. A social event could be ideal. If you're single this is a good day to meet new people. Couples will enjoy reigniting love. However, some communications may be complex, so avoid misunderstandings. Travel may be delayed so factor in extra travel time. *Moon in Virgo.*

23 OCTOBER

Now that the sun will be in Scorpio for the next four weeks you'll enjoy socialising and networking more. You may also feel more passionate about work and your projects. You can make great progress with meetings and work, so be productive. *Moon in Libra.*

24 OCTOBER

You may hear from an old friend. A circumstance from your past may require a little more attention. Your help or advice may be appreciated. If you need expert guidance it will be available, so reach out. *Moon in Libra.*

25 OCTOBER

The partial solar eclipse in Scorpio signals the start of a new chapter for you at work and in your health routine. You may find you'll be particularly busy over the coming weeks and months. A personal situation or collaboration could blossom, but if you experience a disappointment and must take things more slowly, rest assured you will find a silver lining to any clouds that arise. Avoid misunderstandings.

26 OCTOBER

Your emotions may be strong as you gain perspective over a change that may seem unavoidable. Avoid taking things personally if your path seems blocked. Someone has your back. Someone from your past could motivate you to make changes in your work or personal life. *Moon in Scorpio.*

27 OCTOBER

You'll enjoy spending time with a business or personal partner as communications with them will go well. However, some negotiations may be more complex than you'd hope so take talks one step at a time, especially regarding finances. ***Moon enters Sagittarius.***

28 OCTOBER

This is a good time to review your domestic decisions and, for some, to reconsider a trip or negotiation. You may feel you're going over old ground but there will be benefits to rearranging some of your priorities and schedules. ***Moon in Sagittarius.***

29 OCTOBER

Over the next few weeks you may feel more passionate about your ideas and communications may be intense, so ensure you are definite about your opinions and the facts. Find ways to dissipate restless energy so you do not find life frustrating. You may need to tread carefully with discussions. ***Moon enters Capricorn.***

30 OCTOBER

You're proactive and effective, so take the time in the morning to get chores done. You'll appreciate the chance to relax and to boost energy levels. ***Moon in Capricorn.***

31 OCTOBER

Happy Hallowe'en! You're efficient and productive so this is a good time to put work and personal initiatives into action. If you're unsure of a project or a person research the circumstances adequately. ***Moon enters Aquarius.***

November

career   love   home   health   finance

1 NOVEMBER

You're thinking analytically, which will be helpful especially if challenges arise. Today's Aquarian moon will help you to think outside the box, especially with logistics to do with finances and your involvement with a group or organisation. *Moon in Aquarius.*

2 NOVEMBER

Do you tend to take other people's opinions personally when they differ from yours? Avoid taking events outside your control to heart; be practical and mindful that all obstacles can be overcome, especially with matters to do with work or a group, friend or organisation. Someone who is vulnerable or sensitive will require delicate handling. *Moon enters Pisces.*

3 NOVEMBER

A reunion may be intense, so give yourself room for movement and avoid feeling stuck in a situation. This is a good day for health and well-being appointments and to seek the advice of an expert. You may be asked to provide expert help yourself. *Moon in Pisces.*

4 NOVEMBER

You're thinking intuitively and can absolutely trust your gut instincts. A personal or work matter is best approached from the long-term point of view. Avoid making snap decisions. An expert or adviser's help will be invaluable. *Moon enters Aries.*

5 NOVEMBER

Meetings and talks may push your buttons, so take a moment to let developments sink in before being reactive and impulsive. A personal situation can be overcome with diligence and a compassionate approach both to yourself and others. *Moon in Aries.*

6 NOVEMBER

You may feel restless or emotional, so ensure you dissipate energy with upbeat activities such as sports. Someone close may need your help. If you need some advice or support, rest assured it will be available. *Moon in Aries.*

7 NOVEMBER

A work or financial situation may represent a difficult decision, so ensure you gain expert advice if possible. Be prepared to discuss options with those they concern to avoid hard feelings. *Moon in Taurus.*

8 NOVEMBER

The total lunar eclipse in Taurus will spotlight a key change at work or regarding your health routine. You may receive news that signals new developments and an important decision will be necessary. For some, decisions will cause change in your personal life.

9 NOVEMBER

An unexpected development at work or a change of routine will mean you must look more closely at what you're doing and how you're trying to accomplish your goals. Avoid snap decisions as these could backfire. *Moon enters Gemini.*

10 NOVEMBER

You'll find out whether or not your expectations have been unrealistic, and the good news is you will get the chance to correct your course. News, a trip or a negotiation may represent a restriction for you, but you will find there will be a ray of sunshine at home and in your personal life. Romance could blossom, and you'll find someone special has your back. *Moon in Gemini.*

11 NOVEMBER

With hard work and perseverance you will attain your goals, even if your ideas are different from those of someone you must collaborate with. Avoid snap decisions, but be prepared to think on your feet. *Moon in Gemini.*

12 NOVEMBER

This is a good day to talk so ensure you arrange meetings and get-togethers, especially at work. It's also a good day for health and well-being, so organise a treat as a way to round off your week. You'll enjoy a reunion and the chance to spruce up your home life. *Moon in Cancer.*

13 NOVEMBER

Your communications at work and regarding finances are likely to improve, so set wheels in motion if you need to get key information across. However, not all communications and negotiations will be productive, so take things one step at a time. *Moon in Cancer.*

14 NOVEMBER

Trust your intuition, especially to do with work and your home life. This is a good day to discuss shared duties and finances as your ideas are likely to be heard. *Moon enters Leo.*

15 NOVEMBER

This is an excellent day for making improvements at home, be these to décor or interpersonal dynamics. You will enjoy a reunion or a catch-up by phone with someone special. You may receive a financial or ego boost. *Moon in Leo.*

16 NOVEMBER

As Venus enters your sign you'll notice an increased sense of dynamism and adventure, especially in your personal life. You may feel more optimistic and outgoing so enjoy this upbeat phase, although nothing can be taken for granted and especially in your personal life and with collaborations. *Moon in Leo.*

17 NOVEMBER

As Mercury enters your sign you are likely to wish for an increased sense of freedom to discover new horizons, either at work or literally via travel. You may experience a financial, work or health boost. *Moon in Virgo.*

18 NOVEMBER

You'll enjoy a more sociable end to the week and will appreciate the time to touch base with like-minded people. Just avoid overindulging this evening, as you may experience mix-ups and loss of respect due to tiredness or inebriation as a result. *Moon in Virgo.*

19 NOVEMBER

While you're communicating well, others may not be as clear as you'd prefer. Keep en eye out for bad drivers and for misunderstandings to avoid mix-ups and mistakes. ***Moon enters Libra.***

20 NOVEMBER

The Libran moon will motivate you to look for ways to feel more nurtured and to establish more balance in your life. You may be drawn to treat yourself or someone close to a special event. Avoid misunderstandings and fast cars, as mistakes can be made. ***Moon in Libra.***

21 NOVEMBER

This is a lovely day for a reunion and to spend time with like-minded people. A trip or get-together will be enjoyable. A work meeting will be productive. It's also a good day for health, beauty and well-being appointments. ***Moon enters Scorpio.***

22 NOVEMBER

The sun in Sagittarius for the next few weeks will encourage you to be more optimistic and outgoing. Avoid getting bogged down in the past and make tracks to create the life you want. ***Moon in Scorpio.***

23 NOVEMBER

The Sagittarian new moon signals a perfect time to reinvent yourself, so consider what you need to do to be happier. You could turn a corner in a key relationship and at work. Make a wish, but as always be careful as it will come true.

24 NOVEMBER

The Sagittarian moon brings out your inner adventurer and optimist. You may enjoy a sense that your horizons are about to open up and there is a feeling of excitement about your plans, especially to do with your love life, travel, family and home. ***Moon in Sagittarius.***

25 NOVEMBER

A therapeutic and healing aspect to the day is ideal for a health or beauty appointment. If you have domestic matters that need to be ironed out this is an ideal time to do so. Be prepared to adopt a positive approach to making changes that will last. ***Moon enters Capricorn.***

26 NOVEMBER

This is an excellent day for personal improvement, especially improvement to your appearance, health and well-being. Working Sagittarians born in December may find that work will go particularly well, so take the initiative. This is a good weekend to do a little DIY and improve domestic dynamics. ***Moon in Capricorn.***

27 NOVEMBER

You may be surprised by news, a change of routine or an unexpected development. You may enjoy an impromptu get-together or event even if it seems disruptive at first. ***Moon enters Aquarius.***

28 NOVEMBER

This is a good day for talks and meetings, especially to do with finances and collaborations. If you're looking for a business or personal commitment from someone you may receive it. ***Moon in Aquarius.***

29 NOVEMBER

Talks and meetings are likely to be animated but you could achieve your goals if you remain practical and focused, otherwise arguments may arise. Someone's behaviour or opinions may surprise you. ***Moon in Aquarius.***

30 NOVEMBER

This is a good day to make financial agreements, especially those that involve family, a property, your neighbourhood or your home. Avoid arguments and look for solutions if problems arise. You may receive good news at work or a compliment. ***Moon in Pisces.***

December

career   love   home   health   finance

1 DECEMBER

Discussions are likely to be animated unless you've reached an impasse. Try to keep communication channels open to avoid a stalemate. Romance could flourish if you like some tension in your relationships, but if there's too much stress events could be a real passion killer. *Moon in Pisces.*

2 DECEMBER

This is a good day for negotiations and making agreements. If financial matters must be decided upon you're likely to reach acceptable agreements: that is, as long as you have all the facts. It's vital you look more deeply into matters to avoid making mistakes. Someone close may be forgetful. *Moon in Aries.*

3 DECEMBER

This is an excellent weekend to find the time to relax and recuperate, and you'll enjoy a visit, guest or a trip. If you have recently argued with someone you could make amends. It's a good day for a health treat. *Moon in Aries.*

4 DECEMBER

This is a good day for financial decisions, especially if you're looking for ways to improve your budget. You may be forgetful, so ensure you keep an eye on the house keys, for example. You may be inclined to overspend if you're shopping so ensure you set a ceiling. You may be prone to misunderstandings, so check you're on the same page if arguments arise. ***Moon enters Taurus.***

5 DECEMBER

Events may seem to slow you down, and this could be frustrating as you'd rather the pace was quick and lively. Avoid feeling stymied and be patient. ***Moon in Taurus.***

6 DECEMBER

Communications, travel and financial transactions may be slow and frustrating, so ensure you have a way to blow off steam so you don't become too annoyed. Back up computers to avoid losing information. ***Moon enters Gemini.***

7 DECEMBER

An unexpected development needn't get the better of you if you are willing to be resourceful and look outside the square at your options. You may experience a financial or ego boost. ***Moon in Gemini.***

8 DECEMBER

The Gemini full moon spotlights a fresh chapter for you in a particular personal or business relationship, especially if you were born in late November and early December. Those born later are likely to begin a fresh work or health routine. Developments may arise rapidly, so think on your feet.

9 DECEMBER

You may be surprised by news from a business or personal partner and could make headway at work, so be positive and spontaneous. You can also make progress with a health matter. You'll enjoy an impromptu get-together. ***Moon in Cancer.***

10 DECEMBER

This is a good day for serious discussions, especially those that will affect your personal life or finances. It's a good time for a mini financial review. Some talks may be difficult, so be prepared to listen and to communicate clearly. Avoid minor bumps and scrapes. ***Moon in Cancer.***

11 DECEMBER

As Venus joins Mercury in Capricorn you'll feel more obstinate about some of your ideas and opinions, especially with regard to finances and investments. Be prepared to listen to others,

within reason. You may need to stand your ground but must avoid being obstructive, or arguments will arise. Avoid minor accidents by being super self-aware, especially while travelling. *Moon enters Leo.*

12 DECEMBER

This is an excellent day for financial and work discussions. Be practical with your plans and you'll make great headway. This is a good day to make a commitment if you've researched the facts. *Moon in Leo.*

13 DECEMBER

The Leo moon will bring out your inner adventurer and you'll enjoy being more outgoing and outspoken. Be positive and optimistic, as your work and collaborations will succeed. If your health has been down in the dumps this is a good time to improve it with fitness training. *Moon in Leo.*

14 DECEMBER

You'll discover whether you have miscalculated an arrangement or agreement. If someone lets you down, avoid taking things personally; you will gain the chance to put things straight. Put aside extra time for travel and communications as these may be delayed. *Moon enters Virgo.*

15 DECEMBER

Your practical abilities are in peak form, and you'll manage to get a great deal done. You'll get ahead with collaborations due to good communication skills and a talent for planning. *Moon in Virgo.*

16 DECEMBER

Avoid putting the cart before the horse and believing an agreement is in the bag without solid confirmation. Be prepared to adjust to unexpected circumstances. A trip or discussion may be delayed, so factor extra time into your schedule. *Moon enters Libra.*

17 DECEMBER

You'll enjoy an impromptu get-together or a change at home and with family. You may hear unexpected news or will take a trip to somewhere different such as a fresh environment, which you'll enjoy. *Moon in Libra.*

18 DECEMBER

You'll appreciate the chance to deepen your connection with someone close and a reunion could be ideal. However, some travel and communications may be a little complex and delays and digital glitches may occur. Ensure you back up computers and avoid misunderstandings and arguments. *Moon in Libra.*

19 DECEMBER

A change of routine may be delayed or a little more complex than you'd prefer but it will be worthwhile as you will touch base with someone important to you. You'll enjoy boosting your self-esteem and may be surprised by some developments. *Moon in Scorpio.*

20 DECEMBER

When the moon is in Scorpio you may experience life more intensely. If you feel some developments are a little over the top ensure you take time out. You'll enjoy a get-together with like-minded people or someone you love. *Moon in Scorpio.*

21 DECEMBER

The solstice is a time of reflection when you can gather your wits as you assimilate your progress this year. You may get a fresh understanding of someone or enter a fresh agreement. You may learn something new or feel that you are in a more stable or secure position. However, if you feel circumstances are limiting find ways to breathe fresh air into your schedule. Travel and communications may be delayed so be patient. *Moon in Sagittarius.*

22 DECEMBER

You'll enjoy a spontaneous get-together and a change of atmosphere at home or in your personal life. You'll enjoy being with an upbeat group of people and feeling more outgoing. *Moon in Sagittarius.*

23 DECEMBER

The new moon and supermoon in Capricorn signals a fresh chapter for you in a personal situation or financially. For some, this new moon signals more stability and security. A trip or visit will bring you together with family or friends.

24 DECEMBER

You'll enjoy shopping and finding ways to brighten up your appearance and surroundings. You may enjoy visiting someone or sprucing up your environment. If you're shopping avoid overspending; you may be prone to overindulgence. *Moon in Capricorn.*

25 DECEMBER

Merry Christmas! You'll feel inclined to be with people who make you feel safe and secure, and will enjoy a change in your usual schedule or the way you would normally go about Christmas Day. *Moon in Aquarius.*

26 DECEMBER

You may feel a little conflicted about some of your feelings and will do well to keep them to yourself for the sake of peace and relaxation. You'll appreciate the creature comforts of home and the company you keep, but if arguments seem to loom avoid allowing them to escalate. *Moon in Aquarius.*

27 DECEMBER

You'll enjoy a boost in self-esteem via a compliment or a meeting. If you're shopping you'll be drawn to the value of sales items and may find a real bargain. *Moon in Pisces.*

28 DECEMBER

You may be drawn to overindulging or overspending so keep an eye on your budget. Romance could thrive, so ensure you organise a special treat. Try to get the loose ends of important paperwork tied up before the end of today before Mercury turns retrograde tomorrow, to avoid delays down the line. *Moon in Pisces.*

29 DECEMBER

Key meetings and financial transactions could be significant. You may be drawn to making a considerable personal or financial investment. Ensure you have all the details you need to do so to avoid mistakes. *Moon in Aries.*

30 DECEMBER

A change of environment may suit you but you must avoid being impulsive with your decision-making. If you're returning to work it may be hard on you but you will adapt well; you'll overcome any hurdles with diligence and persistence. *Moon in Aries.*

31 DECEMBER

Happy New Year! You'll enjoy doing something you know everyone in your life enjoys for New Year's Eve. You tend to enjoy busy days out, but as the day progresses you'll feel more inclined to enjoy a relaxed event with like-minded people. *Moon enters Taurus.*

CAPRICORN
21 December - 20 January

THE ESSENCE OF CAPRICORN

You are essentially a goal-oriented person, so very little will get in your way as you strive towards your desired outcomes. In order to achieve your goals you're unlikely to rush your activities or feel pressured; instead, you'll appear to progress slowly and methodically. However, your measured progress belies your tenacity: your sign's symbol is the mountain goat, and you'll reach the summit of the mountain just as they do. You attain the summit of your own goals and do so unfailingly and regardless of any obstacles that may stand in your way.

You are diligent and will procure your aims even if your projects take forever. You're focused, and it's very hard to put you off your stride once you have a goal in mind. You have a calm, understated demeanour even if excitement and motivation linger just beneath the quiet exterior. You're adventurous and unafraid to enter fresh territory and love to try new ideas, especially in the health field. It's partly this underlying drive and thirst for untried experiences and adventure that feed your ability to remain focused, as you need exciting experiences as much as you need air.

Capricorns are often seen as being boring and staid due to their diligence, but excitement and drive sizzles just below the surface. Those who get to know you intimately realise this and appreciate your depth.

You are a sensuous, earthy character who is not afraid to show affection, even if you appear reserved or shy at first. You are dependable and will not let people down unless you have a restless moon sign or ascendant. You're the most dependable character in the zodiac, even if you do seem focused on career, status and earnings at various times in your life. You're a traditionalist at heart, so family and upholding values will be important to you.

SELF-ESTEEM

You're an earthy, practical and diligent person able to realistically embrace the steps you must take to succeed in life. Your self-esteem increases in measure with your perceived success, so the more successful you are in the world you inhabit the higher will be your self-esteem. As the modern world's idea of success revolves around money and career, so too does your idea of success revolve around money, status and career and you'll seek to improve these areas. However, if you were raised in a culture where kindness, compassion and companionship are the most valuable and seemingly successful qualities you will embrace them so you can feel you are a success.

You are at heart adaptable; it's just that when you have a goal in mind very little will deter you so you have a reputation for being inflexible. You feel your self-esteem is dented when your ability to succeed is unappreciated. You take the opinions of others personally, which can be a real pitfall as you'll react according to other people's values. This is something you can work on to provide yourself with an enduring sense of worth regardless of what other people feel is valuable. Be guided by your heart, love, compassion and mutual respect and you'll stay on the path of contentedness.

YOUR INNER LIFE

You have an adventurous, outgoing, fun-seeking underbelly, which can surprise those who see you as being thoroughly staid and traditional in the pursuit of your goals. Capricorn is the sign that is often related to tradition, status quo, history and authority; it is the sign of reliability and dependability, although you may see yourself as someone quite different: someone who is driven to succeed and who upholds traditions, but you are never boring! You have an adventurous streak and are not afraid to take a risk.

You're careful with money and can be seen as a miser, but when exciting quests beckon you're not afraid to invest in activities that appeal to your sense of adventure. You are careful with your actions, which adds to your sense of authority and the respect that others show you. You may find you are more respected later in life as you earn the status you value so highly. Knowing that your success may only come after considerable effort does not deter you from your projects and ventures, and your tenacity, diligence, hard work and application will get you where you want to go.

Your sense of fulfilment is immeasurable, as you know you are a self-made success. You also know how to schmooze and work the social scene and are likely to be a social climber, but you'll see networking as an element of work and as a skill.

HOW OTHERS SEE YOU

You can be seen as being supremely focused to the point of obstinacy in the pursuit of your goals and may resultingly be seen as being inflexible, even if your dependability is acknowledged. You can be unrelenting in the pursuit of your goals and uncompromising when your path is blocked or your will opposed.

You can also be seen as being reserved or even distant because you are slow to commit to ideas, people and ventures, but once you do you're one of the most steadfast and loyal individuals. Your reputation for reliability, constancy and dependability will grow the more you hang on to your self-respect and stand your ground; it may just take people a while to see the positive aspects of your methods.

You can be seen on occasion as a social climber or someone who focuses on wealth and outer forms of success rather than on inner spiritual fortitude. You are the sign most likely to follow in your father's footsteps unless you have a prominent Aquarian, Scorpio or Aries signature in your chart. Money, status and authority seem to appeal to you, although they are mere by-products of your hard work ethic. You're often seen as a hard worker, and this is certainly true.

HOW TO MAXIMISE YOUR POTENTIAL

Your staid, fuddy-duddy personality can be seen as being obstinate and unable to go with the flow and adjust to circumstances. However, you have a quirky understanding of life and a streak of adventure that when engaged and expressed will give you a more open frame of mind. Don't be afraid to express the bubbly personality that fizzes just beneath the surface of your persona, as people who know you appreciate your sense of humour and love of life.

You possess a well-developed dry humour that few people understand. Find ways to express your unconventional take on life and you'll find that you are seen less as a one-dimensional, serious work horse and more as the rounded, understanding, understated and upbeat individual you are.

Take the time to develop and express your loving, earthy side, your affectionate, down-to-earth regard for others and for the life you lead and people will respond accordingly.

CAPRICORN AND ITS ASCENDANTS

This chapter is about your sun sign, Capricorn, and your predictions for the year ahead. The more you know about yourself the better you will be able to take advantage of opportunities, and also to avoid the pitfalls. It's critical to know as much about 'you' as possible.

In astrology your core self is represented by your sun sign, but your personality traits are represented by your ascendant (also known as your rising sign). The ascendant describes your personality, the way other people see you on first meeting you and the way you tend to filter life's events.

When you have intimate knowledge about your sun sign – your engine room or core being – you will be on the way to a happier life. When you add the knowledge about your personality – your ascendant – you will gain even deeper insight into what makes you tick.

Your ascendant sign is determined by the time of your birth on the date and year of your birth. Because the ascendant sign changes approximately every two hours, the best way to determine it is to ask an astrologer to calculate it for you. Certain apps will also calculate your ascendant sign (see page 873).

The following gives you more information about your abilities, characteristics and personality according to your sun sign Capricorn in combination with your ascendant sign.

CAPRICORN SUN SIGN WITH ARIES ASCENDANT

You are a double cardinal sign and have strength of character beyond the norm; you have inner resourcefulness that springs up when under duress. You may appear outwardly fiery and impulsive although you may have been shy as a youngster, but once people get to know you they see your dependable and practical qualities. Your positive traits are strong: energetic, entrepreneurial, independent and reliable. However, your negative traits are also quite strong – impulsive, reckless, bossy, domineering, obstinate and uncompromising – unless you work on self-improvement.

CAPRICORN SUN SIGN WITH TAURUS ASCENDANT

You are a double earth sign and are seen as being careful, methodical, practical, dependable and earthy, someone who enjoys the good things in life and is able to methodically plan ahead. You can be intense and sensual and wish to settle into a routine. At times you can appear distant or preoccupied because you like to immerse yourself in work, music, art and beauty. You succeed in combining your need for comfort and love with your need for prestige and status and can establish positive relationships, especially with fellow earth signs.

CAPRICORN SUN SIGN WITH GEMINI ASCENDANT

Gemini-rising people often gesticulate with arms and hands when you talk and can be wiry in appearance. You appear restless and as having a nervous disposition, although underneath you are staid, steady and reliable. A risk is that you can be overly analytical. It's important to release tension and a tendency to worry through action-oriented activities that disperse excess energy and reconnect you with the earth such as nature rambles. You need mental stimulation but you also need peace and quiet. You can experience inner tension, so it's important to meditate. You can get caught up in managing other people's lives rather than your own.

CAPRICORN SUN SIGN WITH CANCER ASCENDANT

You are a force to be reckoned with: two cardinal signs in such prominent positions point to a strong character. You can be stubborn, especially if you're opposed, but you have resilience that lies beneath a personality that can be sensitive and your resoluteness can surprise those who get to know you. You are earthy and gentle and have a kind of sixth sense that comes from your Cancer ascendant. Combine this with the steadfastness of the Capricorn character and you are both astute and trustworthy.

CAPRICORN SUN SIGN WITH LEO ASCENDANT

The raging heart of Leo the lion masks your practical, reasonable and sensible core. Your personality is dynamic and daring, although your sense of duty and responsibility is quite the contrast and you may experience inner conflict. You can be impulsive and must avoid hopping from activity to activity. Your fun-loving Leo personality will wish for constant stimulation, and your Capricorn core will wish for peace. Try to compartmentalise these aspects: be outgoing at the weekend and a hard worker during the week and you will be hugely successful.

CAPRICORN SUN SIGN WITH VIRGO ASCENDANT

You are practical, diligent, reliable, well organised and meticulous. You are also adaptable and able to bend with the needs of others. You're a hard worker and will be drawn to activities that demand your full attention and offer a service or product such as health work, landscaping and agriculture. As a double earth sign you're doubly sensuous, down to earth and resourceful; you are also self-sufficient but do enjoy the company of others.

CAPRICORN SUN SIGN WITH LIBRA ASCENDANT

Art, music, beauty and comfort appeal to you; you have an automatic appreciation of quality and value. You enjoy the company of others and will prefer a settled personal life to a chaotic or supremely disruptive one. You may be seen as being cautious, committed and reliable, and are level headed and tend to be a hard worker. In relationships you are romantic, trustworthy and earnest unless you have aspects in your astrology chart that indicate otherwise.

CAPRICORN SUN SIGN WITH SCORPIO ASCENDANT

You are a combination of passion and intense willpower, calmness and determination. Your core strengths are reliability and trustworthiness, although your outer wild child and depth of emotions may surprise even you on occasion. If you harness your strong emotions and channel these into mighty feats you will excel. You're a good worker but must avoid being easily distracted from your goals by fads and other people's dramas and self-destructive behaviour.

CAPRICORN SUN SIGN WITH SAGITTARIUS ASCENDANT

Your persona projects a sense of generosity, adventure and daring, although underneath you're a careful, reserved, quiet character. You're diligent and able to complete tasks in a measured way, but you are also drawn to upbeat ventures; you are no shrinking violet! You're generally trustworthy and able to strategise and plan ahead well. You are an energetic and enthusiastic worker and may be good with money, but you must avoid gambling.

CAPRICORN SUN SIGN WITH CAPRICORN ASCENDANT

As a double Capricorn you are doubly earthy, practical, serious and diligent. You'll feel a sense of achievement and success through status, money, marriage or work. You prefer a settled, calm life, although once you have a goal in mind you'll turn heaven and earth to accomplish feats. You are reliable and loyal but can easily get stuck in a rut. Ensure you feel fulfilled by your activities rather than following tradition prescribed by society, culture or family.

CAPRICORN SUN SIGN WITH AQUARIUS ASCENDANT

Yours is a quirky and changeable personality although underneath you are steady, focused and reliable. You are an independent character who is objective and clear thinking even while under pressure. You are a humanitarian, and will enjoy creating a strong foundation for yourself and others. You may go through phases where you wish to explore other cultures and countries and alternative ideas and ways of living life. You are progressive yet have a solid approach to practicalities, and are able to derive from life what you and those close to you need.

CAPRICORN SUN SIGN WITH PISCES ASCENDANT

You are both inspired and practical, a dreamer and a do-er, an artist and a creator, a worker and a poet. Your gifts span many skills, but fundamentally you are capable and effective. While being artistic, musical and creative, you also have a business mind; this rare combination of artist and businessperson puts you streets ahead of those who only work in one modality. Yours is a romantic soul with the ability to make things happen in concrete terms.

CAPRICORN IN LOVE

You are such a prudent individual, Capricorn, you are likely to be fairly selective about who you decide to spend long-term time with. In this section you can check out your compatibility with other sun signs. Remember that we are all complex individuals, so the more you know about someone's astrological birth chart the better you can determine your compatibility. Consider having your astrological birth chart compared with that of a partner, friend or family member, as the compatibility – known as 'synastry' in astrology – goes even deeper than a comparison of sun signs, although this is a good place to begin.

CAPRICORN WITH ARIES

Aries may be attracted to your Capricorn ability to be calm and measured in your approach to life but may come to the conclusion that your Capricorn staid, traditional stance is in stark contrast to the Aries style of dynamic leadership. There is a fundamentally different approach to life here, where Capricorn seeks carefully attained status and financial gain and Aries seems foolhardy and impetuous. The Capricorn partner may tend to be older or is seen as being older, and may wish to teach, guide or protect the Aries sun sign, which Aries may see as patronising and limiting. This match could provide both with the chance to experience their very different approaches to life through each other's eyes but both people would need to be super patient.

CAPRICORN WITH TAURUS

You'll appreciate the sensuality and the outward calm of Taurus, but you may tend to be a little frustrated by their relative lack of motivation and inability to take the lead. This relationship can be settling, grounding and comforting and can provide the earthiness you enjoy and appreciate in life. Stubbornness could be a real problem in this union, but if you can agree to disagree on occasion there is every chance that Taurus finds you dependable if traditional and you find Taurus sensual, calming and sexy. You'll need to establish mutual ground and find ways to enjoy your life outside the relationship or you may tend to feel limited or potentially stuck.

CAPRICORN WITH GEMINI

In contrast to your measured approach to life you'll find Geminis intellectually stimulating and will appreciate their freedom of movement and light-hearted attitude. Gemini will feel excited by your independence and air of authority and may appreciate the sense of stability and security you can provide. But there the compatibility could end, unless you have other aspects in your astrological charts that are more compatible than these two chalk-and-cheese sun signs. Gemini may become easily frustrated by Capricorn's plodding approach to life, and Capricorn can see Gemini as being superficial, changeable and unreliable.

CAPRICORN WITH CANCER

This is a case of opposites attracting, although you have more common ground than initially meets the eye. As you are both cardinal signs you are strong characters who understand each other's approach to life: it's direct and often goal oriented. You represent safety and security to Cancer, and you are attracted to Cancer's sensitivity and charm. Cancer's gentleness and intuition represent completion for you as you are essentially practical, reasonable and intellectual. This is a match for partnership as long as you are both willing to give in to the other on occasion and in equal measures.

CAPRICORN WITH LEO

Your resolute, measured and serious demeanour is quite the contrast to the average Leo, who is outgoing, upbeat and spontaneous. You are fundamentally at odds, so if there are no other signs of compatibility in the natal astrology chart it can be a difficult match unless Leo finds a way to complete you and vice versa. Leo may express the feistiness you can be lacking and you may provide Leo with a deeper sense of responsibility, but you'll prefer a slow pace of life even while being determined to succeed and shine. Leo may feel restricted or limited by your slow pace, and you can feel unsettled by the fiery spontaneity of Leo.

CAPRICORN WITH VIRGO

You are both on the same page, which is a big plus for compatibility! You have the same modus operandi in life and therefore understand each other's motivation. You are both practical, realistic, down to earth and diligent and will admire these qualities in each other. The pitfall is that unless you make a concerted effort to be more outgoing and upbeat you sink into a routine that becomes boring. Plan exciting events and holidays, and this match will make for a long-term commitment and is ideal for creating a solid base for family and home life.

CAPRICORN WITH LIBRA

You may appear to be a match as you are both self-effacing, diligent and patient and you both feel that quality is important, such as in luxury, money and status. But there is a fundamental clash: you are strong characters under your quiet and unassuming personalities and are each unlikely to play second fiddle to the other. You approach life's challenges differently: Libra tends to analyse and then act whereas you sense and feel your way through life. You are likely to reach different conclusions, which can lead to arguments. If you're both excellent at conflict resolution it can be a good match.

CAPRICORN WITH SCORPIO

While initially you may be attracted to the passionate yet emotional Scorpio, the early attraction may quickly run out of steam as the drama and intrigue of the Scorpio lifestyle (especially when young) will disrupt your preferred calm pace of life. The allure of the charismatic Scorpio may feel exciting, but intense events that so often accompany Scorpios can become off-putting and Scorpio can quickly lose interest in your comparatively ponderous demeanour. This match is not ideal unless there are strong moon connections in the astrological chart.

CAPRICORN WITH SAGITTARIUS

You may be attracted to the risk-taking and adventurousness of Sagittarius, who will be attracted to your practical, reserved and level-headed self as a contrast and potential rock. You both have strong opinions and can be at counterpoint unless you are both prepared to see the other's point of view. Together you are able to complete herculean tasks without breaking a sweat, and you are both able to concentrate under pressure. You have big hearts and true love could flourish.

CAPRICORN WITH CAPRICORN

There is compatibility with this match, but you may be two peas in a pod and potentially limit the other's growth unless you make a conscious effort to allow each other space to be your own person. You also need to actively enjoy events that allow growth, both independently and within the relationship. You'll feel settled, loyal and mutually supportive as you have the same basic values in life: to feel secure and enjoy a degree of comfort and sense of achievement from shouldering responsibilities.

CAPRICORN WITH AQUARIUS

The Aquarian quirky, upbeat approach to life will attract you initially. You'll appreciate the revitalising sense of freedom in the relationship, yet you may wish to commit to a steady relationship sooner than Aquarius or will wish for a more traditional role in the partnership. Aquarius fundamentally wishes to retain independence even if able to commit to a relationship, and this could grate on your traditional view. While initially attracted to your sense of duty, reliability and earthiness, Aquarius may come to see you as being staid and unwilling to learn; however, as they mature they will come to value your dependability.

CAPRICORN WITH PISCES

You are fundamentally different: you are a doer, a pragmatist, a thinker and an organiser, while Pisces is a poet, creative, romantic and an artist. This relationship is able to span the divide between the Piscean artist and the Capricorn analyst, but you must be prepared to see the other's perspective or your fundamentally different approaches spell zero mutual ground. If you find ways to work together you'll complement each other; the Pisces inspiration combined with the Capricorn sense of practicalities could scale mountains.

THE YEAR AHEAD FOR CAPRICORN

Affirmation: *'I will build something new.'*

You have never been afraid of hard work and are one of the most determined and successful of the zodiac signs, but as an earth sign there is a deeper sense of disruption when you're faced with long-term change that can cause restlessness and melancholy.

This year it's as well to consider how to manage the deep changes of 2021 and the ways these impact on 2022. Setting in place a solid health and well-being schedule will help boost the health of mind, body and spirit.

You have an inbuilt inner tension between wanting to be successful and pushing yourself to new heights and wanting to keep things on an even keel, embracing on the one hand progressive principles but wishing also to keep life in balance to the point of stubbornness.

In 2022 this inner tension could become a source of stress unless you are able to work on ways to adapt to new circumstances without digging your heels in, to adapt and embrace a new way of going about your work and your daily life without feeling you are compromising your own principles and values.

Sometimes this is difficult, but to ensure you walk seamlessly through the year it's vital at stress points such as May and November to have valid stress-busting techniques in place so you avoid ignoring important opportunities (which can come about as you can be so set in your ways). On the flip side, you can be blind to the risks you undertake when you are tempted to throw caution to the wind in moments of stress.

The year of 2022 is the year to find the almost impossible balance between being progressive on the one hand and being secure and stable on the other, between being open to change and open-minded while also honouring tried and trusted traditions.

HEALTH

Pluto will be in your sign all year and can help you to find ways to feel more vibrant and alive, but if you have a bad habit you have been combating for some time the second half of the year is a time to avoid returning to negative behaviour. You will gain the first half of the year to review your health strategy to build well-being and vitality if you feel you have fallen into a lifestyle that is counterproductive to good health.

The supermoon and new moon in your sign on 2 January is particularly potent and ideal for kick-starting the year the way you mean to carry on. The stellium of planets at this time will encourage you to put your self-esteem and principles first and to follow up with action that will determine your happiness, especially at home, for some time to come.

You will appreciate the opportunity to consider complementary health strategies that will support your usual health practices and will be more open to trying something new. You may also be drawn to combine mind, body and spiritual health in a holistic approach that includes deeper understanding of your own psyche through psychological analysis or interests.

You'll benefit from focusing on establishing a healthy routine. January and then mid-year will be optimum times to remind yourself of the importance of a balanced day in mind, body and spirit. Exercise, good diet, social interaction and emotional hygiene will be key to good health then.

FINANCES

As two total lunar eclipses this year will be in your career sector expect to see financial changes, especially in mid-May and early November as your status and potentially also your earning power take a turn. This may be due to changes at work or at home, the one area of your life impacting on the other.

As Saturn will be in your second house of money and belongings you will be looking for ways to accrue at least some financial stability, so it's important in 2022 to seek expert advice at all major decision-making times. The first quarter and from September to November will contain the most change and may be critical turning points where the more research you do the better, especially if you're planning to share resources such as joint income in a new way.

Neptune will have a potent effect over your finances, bringing a sense of uncertainty, which is all the more reason to ensure you have expert advice this year and especially if you are planning major investments or must tighten your belt. In addition, Jupiter traversing your second house of money will encourage you to spend big, especially in mid-April. You may be a lucky Capricorn and earn particularly well at this time. When spending, ensure your money is going on something that has meaning and purpose or you may be inclined to fritter away hard-earned cash in 2022.

HOME LIFE

Uranus, the celestial game changer, is in your home sector and will preside over changes here, with major change likely in January and September-October. These may be periods when you realise that more work will need to be done, either on domestic relationships or on the nuts and bolts of décor and structure. If you've been considering a move for a while this year may see your plans come to fruition, with the first and third quarters being times when making changes could be most productive even if they are topsy turvy.

The eclipses will be across your career and domestic zones, suggesting that a change at work will impact on your home life or a change at home will mean fresh work opportunities. The eclipses on 16 May and 8 November may be particularly significant for developments at home and begin a new set of circumstances for you either at home regarding property or with family.

You will be looking for stability at home yet there will also be restlessness that comes from the year's developments. An area to watch out for is trying to compensate for changes through being overly controlling. Be adventurous too; this is the year to bring something new into your home life.

You may be drawn to altering your environment. If you can travel you'll love altering the status quo at home by letting out your house or renting someone else's.

LOVE

For the first half of the year any relationships you do engage in will be truly meaningful: whether family based or those that you feel drawn to on a deep level. Halfway through the year you will be looking for more spontaneity and freedom of movement in your relationships.

You're already known as independent and capable, and this year singles are likely to wish to remain so: that is, apart from a strong draw to someone special around Valentine's Day! A new meeting or relationship that escalates at this time will be a fated link and could change your life. Couples will enjoy deepening ties, and if starting a family has been a goal this year could be it!

The conjunction of Jupiter and Neptune in April could be a turning point in your love life. You will be looking at who you love and how much you're invested in new terms. If you're single you may meet someone who has the same values as you this year, but you must ensure you are not looking at them through rose-coloured glasses.

In addition, the eclipses at the end of April and in mid-May and once again at the end of October and in early November will lead to a fresh understanding of your commitments. These could be intense times, so be prepared for a little soul searching and be true to yourself.

CAREER

Pluto in your first house has been urging you to develop a deeper understanding of the importance of being happy in your life for many years. If you're happy with the field you are in at work, changes this year will revolve more around ensuring your daily life – in which your career plays a major part – is fulfilling.

In 2022 you get the chance to make life as satisfying as possible, even if in the throes of making changes drama and disruption have to take place. In January and February and then again during the last quarter of the year you may feel this call to satisfaction at work the most powerfully. You will gain opportunities to respond to the call all year.

The new moons on 2 January and 30 May and the total solar eclipse on 25 October will propel your ideas to step into new areas or embrace new skills or, if you're in the mindset, to change tack altogether.

Saturn in Aquarius will urge you to embrace something new, and you are most likely to embrace diversity within a pre-set plan that has been some time in the making. You have diligence and perseverance on your side and will meet the goals you set yourself.

January

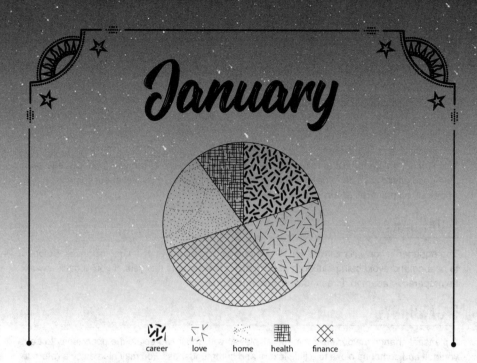

| career | love | home | health | finance |

Notes: the pie charts such as the one above listed for each month show energy distribution according to the stars for the month ahead. If you wish to make changes in the areas of your finances, health, career, love or home and you see there is a large amount of energy in that sector in the chart, your endeavours should succeed as long as you have prepared well in advance. The charts also show which areas will potentially have the most focus in your life during the month.

The moon sign listed for each day's entry in the diary is the position of the moon at the end of the day in Greenwich Mean Time (GMT). To gain the most information about a particular day's circumstances, read the day before and the day after for a complete picture.

1 JANUARY

Happy New Year! You may experience a pleasant surprise or a quirky or unusual start to the new year that will add to an upbeat vibe. You'll enjoy a change at home or a difference in your usual routine. **Moon enters Capricorn.**

2 JANUARY

The new moon and supermoon in your sign will kick-start a fresh phase for you in a personal context if it's your birthday or if you were born in December. If you were born in January, a fresh work or health schedule is about to start.

3 JANUARY

This is a good time to take a moment to decide where you'd like to put your priorities this year; it's a good day to consider a new venture or project and how you truly feel about someone close. Above all, be practical. *Moon enters Aquarius.*

4 JANUARY

The Aquarian moon will motivate you to look outside the square at your circumstances. Be open to change and avoid being stubborn about making adjustments this year. If you're back at work be prepared to adapt to a fresh routine. *Moon in Aquarius.*

5 JANUARY

A pleasant change in your environment will please you. You'll appreciate the opportunity to treat yourself and someone close to a little luxury and sumptuousness. You may also enjoy a return to an old haunt or a reunion. *Moon in Aquarius.*

6 JANUARY

If you're shopping avoid overspending if you're already in debt. Leave the credit card at home if you are! You'll get the chance to reframe some of your plans if you discover your expectations have exceeded reality. *Moon in Pisces.*

7 JANUARY

Your instincts and intuition are in top form, so be sure to use them if you're in doubt about your decisions. You may also tend to be forgetful so be prepared to focus that little bit extra, especially at work. *Moon in Pisces.*

8 JANUARY

You'll enjoy a reunion or a return to an old haunt. It's a good day for romance, so organise a treat. *Moon in Aries.*

9 JANUARY

Romance could go off the dial, especially if it's your birthday or you were born earlier in January or in December. Capricorns born later in January may find work matters and chores around the house take your focus. You'll enjoy boosting your health and appearance. A reunion could be ideal. *Moon in Aries.*

10 JANUARY

You'll enjoy feathering your own nest and finding ways to be more comfortable either at home or at work. Be open to change and to new ideas. *Moon enters Taurus.*

11 JANUARY

It's a mixed bag today: on the one hand you'll enjoy certain meetings and talks, but on the other you may need to review or revise some of your projects or ideas. Avoid misunderstandings by being super clear with communications. Travel may be delayed, so factor in extra travel time for the best measure. *Moon in Taurus.*

12 JANUARY

You'll enjoy being with someone whose company you enjoy and making changes at home. However, you may tend to be a little stubborn and unwilling to see someone else's opinion. Try to find common, stable ground, especially if someone appears erratic. *Moon in Taurus.*

13 JANUARY

You may feel a little restless or at a loose end, so find ways to feel more grounded. Try to get key paperwork and financial matters resolved before Mercury turns retrograde tomorrow to avoid delays over the next few weeks. Back up computers and files for the best measure. *Moon in Gemini.*

14 JANUARY

You may receive key news regarding finances, travel or a domestic matter. Be careful with negotiations and communications as unexpected developments will require some focus. *Moon in Gemini.*

15 JANUARY

You'll enjoy a sense of freedom of movement, and if you haven't yet you will find ways to achieve it! This is a good time to be adaptable and to rethink a domestic decision or investment if necessary. *Moon enters Cancer.*

16 JANUARY

Key developments will signal long-term change, especially if it's your birthday. You will enjoy good company and could deepen your ties with the people you love. Avoid taking someone's erratic behaviour personally. Strong emotions may arise so find ways to channel them into happy outcomes. *Moon in Cancer.*

17 JANUARY

The Cancerian full moon will spotlight a personal transaction that could put a new shine on an agreement or relationship, especially if it's your birthday. This will be an intense full moon, so ensure you find the time to ground and earth yourself. Developments could be transformational.

18 JANUARY

Trust your intuition, as your emotions may be strong and could overpower your better reason. You'll feel clearer and more positive once the moon is in Leo and will appreciate the opportunity to do a little soul searching. *Moon in Leo.*

19 JANUARY

You'll enjoy socialising and networking and the opportunity to catch up with an old friend or colleague. It's a good day to focus on improving your own health and well-being. *Moon in Leo.*

20 JANUARY

The sun in Aquarius for the next four weeks will bring out your proactive side and you'll enjoy considering tasks and projects that may be a little quirky or different. You may enjoy a change of routine that brings you together with someone whose values you feel aligned with. *Moon in Leo.*

21 JANUARY

The moon in Virgo at the zenith of your chart will prompt you to get chores done, to be proactive about your various projects and interests and to find the time to be with people you admire and love. *Moon in Virgo.*

22 JANUARY

You'll enjoy a trip or visit. You may hear from an old friend. If you're shopping avoid overspending as you may be prone to overindulge, which you'll regret tomorrow. *Moon enters Libra.*

23 JANUARY

This is a good day for get-togethers and reunions. It's also a good day to get on top of finances if necessary and to establish a fresh budget that works for you and your family. If you're shopping, avoid overspending and check your purchases are practical. *Moon in Libra.*

24 JANUARY

You have an eye for what's fair and equal, and at work your fair-mindedness may be in demand. *Moon in Libra.*

25 JANUARY

If you're in business you will find your meetings and talks go relatively well. You may feel more inclined to take the lead in talks. If you need to review some previous decisions, ensure you trust your intuition. *Moon in Scorpio.*

26 JANUARY

This is a good time to review paperwork, decisions and agreements to ensure everyone involved is still on the same page, especially at work and regarding health and well-being. You may receive news that is to your benefit and may get the time to spruce up your appearance. *Moon in Scorpio.*

27 JANUARY

A networking or social event will be enjoyable and your talkative and outgoing nature may surprise you. *Moon in Sagittarius.*

28 JANUARY

You'll gain insight into a work matter, which will provide the chance to renegotiate or review your circumstances. This is a good time to consider a more active and outgoing sports and fitness routine. *Moon in Sagittarius.*

29 JANUARY

A meeting could be transformative or will bring out strong emotions. You'll enjoy getting together with someone you feel a strong connection with. A trip may take you to an old haunt. *Moon in Capricorn.*

30 JANUARY

You may be surprised by a development. For some this will be personal in nature and for others it ill be financial. Be prepared to adapt but avoid getting caught up in someone else's dramas if possible. *Moon in Capricorn.*

31 JANUARY

You may hear positive news. This is a better day for conversations and meetings, especially to do with personal matters and finances. Romance could flourish, so organise a treat! *Moon in Aquarius.*

February

career love home health finance

1 FEBRUARY

The new moon in Aquarius will kick-start a fresh financial phase and, for some, a fresh way to approach your personal life. You may have bright and upbeat ideas, especially on ways to tackle a personal, domestic or logistical issue.

2 FEBRUARY

This is a good time to trust your intuition and to observe your circumstances as if from the outside to obtain a sense of objectivity. Careful negotiations and talks will reap rewards. ***Moon enters Pisces.***

3 FEBRUARY

You are intuitive when the moon is in Pisces and more likely to listen to your instincts. If your gut tells you that a financial or personal matter is best viewed a certain way, trust it. However, equally, you must avoid being easily misled by a charming character, especially if a financial matter is at stake. ***Moon in Pisces.***

4 FEBRUARY

Key financial news is best approached carefully as you may make a great deal of progress but you could also be prone to making mistakes, especially if you tend to gamble. You may be ready to make a commitment to a work or personal venture. It's a good time to reconsider your thoughts if necessary and to adapt to developments. ***Moon in Pisces.***

5 FEBRUARY

Your vulnerabilities and doubts may emerge, especially in connection with your domestic and personal life. Someone may need your help or will appear vulnerable themselves. If you need a little reassurance that your decisions are correct, take a moment to validate them. You'll enjoy a change of routine or an impromptu visit. ***Moon in Aries.***

6 FEBRUARY

This is a lovely day to take time out, especially if you have been overworking or are stressed. A pleasant change of atmosphere at home or in a new environment will boost your mood, so organise a treat if you haven't already. ***Moon in Aries.***

7 FEBRUARY

The more practical you are at work and with health and well-being the better for you, as you may otherwise tend to rush or be influenced by other people's restlessness. A personal matter will benefit from a realistic approach; just avoid being stubborn. ***Moon in Taurus.***

8 FEBRUARY

This is a good time to go with upbeat and exciting changes in your life, especially at home. You may find that a change of circumstance brings new opportunities into being. A personal or family matter may surprise you. ***Moon in Taurus.***

9 FEBRUARY

You'll enjoy a lovely midweek get-together and at the very least a catch-up by phone with someone close. This is a good time to consider how your personal life, self-esteem and budget could be better managed. Be inspired! ***Moon enters Gemini.***

10 FEBRUARY

This is a good day to improve your appearance and self-esteem, so look for inspiring ideas, platforms and talks that help you improve yourself. It's also a good day for meetings and romance. A key financial development could boost morale but you must avoid overspending. ***Moon in Gemini.***

11 FEBRUARY

You may receive good news at work or in your personal life, but if you are disappointed by events take a moment to recalibrate. A trip or meeting could be transformational. If you're single you may meet someone you feel a predestined link with especially if you were born after mid-January. If you find events intense, take time out to unwind when you can. ***Moon in Cancer.***

12 FEBRUARY

The Cancerian moon for the next two days is ideal for a little introspection and to ensure you're on the right track, both at work and in your personal life. You may feel inspired by work projects and ideas to boost your health and well-being. It's also a good day for spiritual work, psychic development and meditation. Just avoid escapism and overindulgence, which you'll regret! *Moon in Cancer.*

13 FEBRUARY

You'll relish the chance to deepen your understanding of someone special. Trust your instincts, as they are spot on. You may, however, feel a little emotional and channelling feelings into productive activities will be uplifting. You'll be drawn to music and art and a beautiful place. *Moon in Cancer.*

14 FEBRUARY

Happy St Valentine's Day! You'll enjoy a romantic day, and if you're single you may hear from someone special. Couples will enjoy deepening your ties. Feelings could be intense so maintain perspective. *Moon in Leo.*

15 FEBRUARY

You won't get on with everyone, and you may sense that someone close is not in a brilliant frame of mind. Perhaps you yourself have issues to iron out. A financial or personal matter will take on a more positive outlook if you approach matters fairly and squarely and with the willingness to learn something new. *Moon in Leo.*

16 FEBRUARY

The Leo full moon will shine a light on your relationships in which you have shared duties and responsibilities such as communal space at home or at work. You may be preparing to make changes. Key developments romantically could mean the start of a new phase. A meeting will be significant, especially if you were born on 7 or 8 January. *Moon enters Virgo late in the day.*

17 FEBRUARY

This is a good day for making agreements and arrangements, especially those that concern work and health. Finances may be looking up and you may receive a compliment or ego boost. *Moon in Virgo.*

18 FEBRUARY

As the sun enters the zodiac sign Pisces you'll appreciate the opportunity over the next four weeks to feel more inspired about your projects and recent changes that have occurred at home and in your personal life. It's a good time to start planning a trip or get-together with someone special. *Moon in Virgo.*

19 FEBRUARY

While the moon is at the zenith of your chart you will be efficient, so it's a great time to get things shipshape at home and in the garden. You'll enjoy some lovely time spent with someone you love, so organise a treat if you haven't already. *Moon in Libra.*

20 FEBRUARY

This is an inspired time for you so take note of your ideas and impressions, as they could lead to some lovely projects and plans for the future. *Moon in Libra.*

21 FEBRUARY

You're looking for balance and a fair go in life, so where you see it is missing you'll feel motivated to make changes, especially at work and in your personal life. Tune in to music, the arts and a beautiful environment if you feel your peace of mind is disturbed to regain a sense of contentment. *Moon enters Scorpio.*

22 FEBRUARY

As a practical and realistic person you tend to dislike drama and intrigue, yet life does include these qualities from time to time. Trust your instincts as these will guide you down the right path if some situations seem more intense than they need to be. *Moon in Scorpio.*

23 FEBRUARY

This is a good day for talks and meetings. You'll appreciate the chance to boost your self-esteem, looks or health. A financial matter could progress and you may experience a financial boost or receive a compliment. Romance could flourish over the next two days, so organise a treat! *Moon in Sagittarius.*

24 FEBRUARY

This is another lovely day for romance and also a good time for business and work. If you've been considering a new look you may find just the outfit or haircut today. This is a good time for a health or beauty appointment. *Moon in Sagittarius.*

25 FEBRUARY

Someone unpredictable may behave true to form. You may be surprised by a domestic development and will need to think on your feet. Travel and communications may be delayed or erratic, so ensure you give yourself adequate time to get from A to B. Back up computers for the best measure. *Moon enters Capricorn.*

26 FEBRUARY

A meeting or financial transaction will raise your mood. Communications are better than yesterday, so this is a good day to organise an event. A little retail therapy may appeal but you must avoid overspending, especially if you're already in debt. *Moon in Capricorn.*

27 FEBRUARY

You'll enjoy a trip somewhere beautiful or a get-together with a like-minded person. A spending spree will be enjoyable but you may still be inclined to overspend or overindulge, which you'll regret tomorrow. A family gathering will be grounding. *Moon enters Aquarius.*

28 FEBRUARY

A sense of togetherness and support from those you love warms the depths of your heart. You may be distracted by personal matters, so if you're working you'll need to focus a little harder than usual. *Moon in Aquarius.*

March

career   love   home   health   finance

1 MARCH

This is a good day for socialising and networking. You may meet someone whose ideas match your own and you'll get on well. But some talks may be less successful. Take a moment to order your thoughts. *Moon enters Pisces.*

2 MARCH

The Pisces new moon signals a good time to seek inspiration. A coincidence and the chance to enjoy a change of pace could be just what you want. A holiday or an inspired project will be motivational. Think laterally. Trust your instincts.

3 MARCH

The Venus-Mars-Pluto conjunction signals great change for you, especially if you were born around 20 January. You have the chance to put in place clever ideas and plans. Be sure to align your actions with your higher purpose. *Moon in Pisces.*

4 MARCH

Your creative and inspired qualities are coming out and you may feel more inclined to socialise as a result. However, you may tend to be a little idealistic so ensure your plans are also practical. *Moon in Aries.*

5 MARCH

You'll enjoy a trip or get-together with someone who can be a little larger than life. You may be contemplating long-distance travel. News could be just what you want to hear, but if not maintain perspective and look for constructive ways forward. ***Moon in Aries.***

6 MARCH

As both Mars and Venus leave your sign you'll be looking at life from a fresh perspective. You may be ready to step into new terrain via a personal or business agreement. You may be drawn to new interests and activities. Singles could meet someone new who seems outgoing yet earthy, and couples could re-ignite the passion in your relationship so plan a treat! ***Moon in Taurus.***

7 MARCH

The Taurean moon will motivate you to be practical and hands-on, especially with domestic and personal matters. Avoid obstinacy and ensure you are being open-minded, especially regarding finances and new experiences. ***Moon in Taurus.***

8 MARCH

This is a good day for work and health appointments. You may benefit from a financial boost or a compliment. A debt may be repaid. You'll enjoy a reunion or hearing from an old friend or colleague. ***Moon enters Gemini.***

9 MARCH

The Gemini moon will provide a lighter atmosphere, especially in your personal life. You may need to find new ways to approach someone who may be a little unpredictable. Someone close may be chattier or more willing to see your perspective. ***Moon in Gemini.***

10 MARCH

As Mercury enters Pisces you will feel increasingly drawn to look at life from an idealistic point of view, especially finances and personal relationships. You may also be drawn to travel and will enjoy giving full rein to your imagination and creativity. Just ensure you keep your feet on the ground! ***Moon in Gemini.***

11 MARCH

A partner or someone close may be more communicative and may ask for more support over the next two days, so be prepared to offer help. A change in your usual routine could be inspiring. ***Moon in Cancer.***

12 MARCH

You'll enjoy paying more attention to someone you love and finding the time to be in a beautiful environment. You'll enjoy getting together with people who have similar interests and may enjoy an ideal circumstance. Romance could flourish, so ensure you organise a lovely evening. Avoid believing everything will be perfect; there may be some delays or misunderstandings. *Moon in Cancer.*

13 MARCH

This is an excellent day to invest in yourself and in those you love. You may be drawn to shopping and may find perfect treats but will also be prone to overspending, so avoid overindulgence as you'll regret it tomorrow! You may deepen your spiritual interests. Romance will blossom. *Moon enters Leo.*

14 MARCH

You're communicating well, so if you have important discussions to undertake this is the day! Just avoid misunderstandings by being super clear. You may experience a financial or ego boost. *Moon in Leo.*

15 MARCH

The Leo moon may bring out other people's feistiness, so avoid taking their behaviour personally if you find someone a little overbearing or even oppositional. You'll see that someone close has your back and that you can rely on them. *Moon in Leo.*

16 MARCH

Attention to detail and a practical approach will put you in a strong position with circumstances that are up in the air, but if you disagree with someone find a way to get down to brass tacks to establish common ground. *Moon in Virgo.*

17 MARCH

You'll enjoy a change of pace or of place. Someone close may surprise you. You'll enjoy doing something different. Be spontaneous but avoid impulse spending, as you may end up with something you don't want. *Moon in Virgo.*

18 MARCH

The Virgo full moon shines a light on the areas of life you share, such as your joint finances and duties or space at home. Find practical ways to agree on matters to avoid arguments or, worse, legal disagreements. Talks with a group or organisation could signal the start of a new agreement.

19 MARCH

An unexpected development will spotlight the difference in attitude between you and someone whose opinions can be erratic. A change of circumstance will benefit from a spontaneous but also realistic approach. *Moon in Libra.*

20 MARCH

When the sun enters Aries it is the equinox. During the next four weeks you're likely to feel revitalised, especially in your personal life, enjoying more spontaneity and the chance to be more outgoing. However, you may feel inclined to take uncalculated risks, so ensure you also maintain perspective. *Moon in Scorpio.*

21 MARCH

Key financial or travel decisions are likely to be made. You may feel drawn to visit someone or to put in place new ideas at work. Your investments are likely to pay off if you've done adequate research. You must avoid gambling and impulsiveness. *Moon in Scorpio.*

22 MARCH

This is a good time for communications and financial transactions, but if you rush your plans or take risks you may make mistakes. A trip, meeting or event may be delayed, so be patient. Misunderstandings are likely. Avoid losing digital information by backing up computers. *Moon enters Sagittarius.*

23 MARCH

You will enjoy a get-together and meetings could point to considerable changes. If you're making an investment, ensure you have done adequate research. The spiritually inclined may reach an epiphany. Romance could blossom, so organise a treat. *Moon in Sagittarius.*

24 MARCH

You'll enjoy socialising and networking although you won't necessarily see eye to eye with everyone, so be sure to keep an open mind and be tactful to avoid arguments. *Moon enters Capricorn.*

25 MARCH

The Capricorn moon brings out your earthy qualities and your ability to take things one step at a time. However, it may also bring out your obstinate traits, so ensure you are keeping an open mind about developments. *Moon in Capricorn.*

26 MARCH

You'll enjoy connecting with someone you see eye to eye with. A short trip or a shopping spree will raise your spirits. If you find some events intense, take time out to recalibrate your thoughts. *Moon in Capricorn.*

27 MARCH

Financial and personal decisions may seem easy to make but you may be tempted to throw caution to the wind, so ensure you have researched circumstances especially if you're planning long-term investments of your time or money. *Moon in Aquarius.*

28 MARCH

You may be prepared to make a commitment or will need to state your true feelings and opinions to those who they affect. A situation may seem ideal and it may well be, but you must double-check you are not being misled. *Moon in Aquarius.*

29 MARCH

You may be drawn to new horizons or new ideas, and while this will be exciting it's in your interest to check that your activities align with your deeper sense of purpose and aims and goals. A meeting will bring your inner romantic out. *Moon in Pisces.*

30 MARCH

You'll feel drawn to see the beauty and love in your life as a true positive, which it is. However, you may also tend to see life through rose-coloured glasses. If making long-term decisions, ensure you have adequately researched the circumstances. Romance could blossom, so be prepared to deepen relationships. Singles may meet someone charming. *Moon in Pisces.*

31 MARCH

You are motivated to get ahead at the moment and can make great headway with projects that are important to you. Just avoid being eager to overlook circumstances that aren't ideal, as these could prove to be difficult down the line. *Moon in Aries.*

career love home health finance

1 APRIL

The Aries new moon suggests a fresh approach to communications, travel or finances will be beneficial for you. You may be drawn to update a digital device or vehicle. If you find your vulnerabilities rise during this time it will be your chance to strengthen your communication skills. Someone may need your help. If you need advice it will be available, so find an expert. A health or travel matter may need attention.

2 APRIL

You may by surprised by news. A health or financial development is best approached from a practical point of view. You may bump into an old friend unexpectedly. Someone special will be surprisingly helpful or will need your help. A trip could take you somewhere extremely healing. *Moon enters Taurus.*

3 APRIL

This is a good day to make changes, especially in your appearance and personal life; your self-esteem could improve as a result. You may receive a compliment or ego boost. *Moon in Taurus.*

4 APRIL

The next two days are good for making decisions and headway with your ideas and plans, especially those involving a financial or personal investment. Just avoid being impulsive. **Moon in Taurus.**

5 APRIL

Be inspired by ideas and people; you'll find you can create increasingly productive pathways for yourself both at work and in your personal life. Key agreements and commitments may be made, as long as they resonate with you on a deep level. **Moon in Gemini.**

6 APRIL

This is a good day for talks and undertaking agreements, especially financially. You may experience a financial or ego boost. Take the time to discuss your ideas with someone you know has your back. **Moon in Gemini.**

7 APRIL

You can make great progress with a financial and personal matter. A trip could be ideal. If making large investments, be these in your personal life or financially, just ensure you have all the facts to avoid making mistakes. Also avoid making assumptions. **Moon in Cancer.**

8 APRIL

You'll enjoy a get-together or a trip somewhere beautiful. If you're shopping avoid being seduced by bling, as you may decide at a later date that all that glitters is not gold. **Moon in Cancer.**

9 APRIL

You'll enjoy investing more time and money in yourself, your environment and those you love. If you are making a large financial or emotional investment, ensure the area you're investing in supports your values and aims and goals wholeheartedly to avoid disappointment down the line. **Moon in Cancer.**

10 APRIL

An important matter will demand your attention over the next two days. Communications and transport will merit care and attention as there may be misunderstandings or delays. Avoid tense or sensitive topics if possible as these will escalate quickly into arguments. **Moon in Leo.**

11 APRIL

There is still likely to be tension surrounding a personal or financial matter, so ensure you avoid obstinacy and try to find common ground and a calm way out of difficulties. Communications will get onto a more even keel as you gain a sense of progress, especially in your personal life. **Moon in Leo.**

12 APRIL

A meeting or news will be significant. You could boost your status, self-esteem, career and finances, so ensure you take steps to focus on any or all of these areas as you could make headway. Romance could blossom. **Moon in Leo.**

13 APRIL

This is a good day to make a commitment, especially financially and in your personal life. Emotions may be strong, and you'll feel motivated to do your best to make steps in the right direction. **Moon in Virgo.**

14 APRIL

You'll enjoy indulging in romance, music and being creative. You may be inclined to overindulge and overspend, so if you're already in debt leave the credit card at home if you're shopping. Romance could blossom, so plan a treat! **Moon enters Libra.**

15 APRIL

As Mars enters Pisces for the next few weeks the arts, spirituality, romance and music will all appeal more to you. However, you may also tend to be idealistic, so ensure you keep your feet on the ground if you are making key decisions over the next month. **Moon in Libra.**

16 APRIL

The Libran full moon signifies the start of a fresh cycle for you, and you may already be in a position to begin something new in your general direction, projects or activities. For some this full moon signals the opportunity to consider how to organise your shared duties, collaborations or joint finances in a more balanced or equal way.

17 APRIL

You'll feel motivated by your ideas, plans and ventures with the aim of being able to spend more time on activities you adore. You may feel passionate about a trip or project, so this is a good time to invest more energy into it. A visit or change at home may be spontaneous or unexpected. **Moon in Scorpio.**

18 APRIL

This is a good day to put your energy into your projects. A trip or communications may be a little tense, so avoid escalating stress if you see it is already a factor. A financial and personal matter can progress, so take the initiative. **Moon in Scorpio.**

19 APRIL

Be positive about your ventures as you can make great progress. Just avoid being easily distracted by the demands of everyday life and remain focused on your goals. Once the moon enters Sagittarius you'll feel more outgoing and able to express yourself. ***Moon enters Sagittarius.***

20 APRIL

The sun in Taurus for the next four weeks will bring more of a sense of stability and security your way, especially in your personal life. This is a good time to find ways to move forward in the most realistic way. ***Moon in Sagittarius.***

21 APRIL

You'll enjoy an increased sense of direction and purpose over the coming days, so this is a good time to concentrate on your deeper aims and goals and find ways to attain them. You may enjoy socialising and networking. ***Moon in Capricorn.***

22 APRIL

This is a good time to invest in yourself, including your appearance, health and well-being. You'll enjoy socialising with friends and family. If you have any logistics to overcome, you will manage to do so through paying extra attention to the realities of your situation as opposed to what you wish for. ***Moon in Capricorn.***

23 APRIL

You'll enjoy a reunion and the chance to get things shipshape at home. Some Capricorns will enjoy a trip and the chance to improve your environment. This is a good time to avoid worrying about things you can't change. Instead, focus on the areas you can change. ***Moon in Aquarius.***

24 APRIL

A personal or financial situation may require more focus. It may be time to put in place a better budget, especially if you have a large outlay or debt to pay. Good communication skills will help you to move forward. Avoid misunderstandings. Back up computers to avoid losing information. Travel may be delayed. ***Moon in Aquarius.***

25 APRIL

You're thinking creatively and philosophically, which will help you to think calmly and clearly and overcome logistical conundrums. However, you may also be a little idealistic, especially about some relationships and finances. ***Moon in Pisces.***

26 APRIL

You're communicating well, making this an excellent time to build bridges with people you've argued with. A trip, get-together or domestic event could flourish under these stars. **Moon in Pisces.**

27 APRIL

This is a good time for meetings, romance and financial transactions. Just ensure you have researched circumstances adequately if you are making considerable investments. If you're single, you may feel more outgoing and enthusiastic about people in a friendly or creative environment. **Moon enters Aries.**

28 APRIL

You can make great progress with the long-term changes you'd like to make in your personal life, so take the initiative. You'll gain more direction as a result. It's a good time to discuss plans with those they concern. **Moon in Aries.**

29 APRIL

A change in circumstance will encourage you to discuss your options. It's a good day to decide whether you are on the right track, and if you feel you have veered away from your goals and have lost a sense of purpose it's a good time to consider how you could get back on track. A trip or the chance to do something different will be inspiring. **Moon in Aries.**

30 APRIL

The partial solar eclipse in Taurus signals you are ready for a fresh phase in a personal situation. For some this will involve a domestic, family or property situation and for others a travel, neighbourhood or community matter. A financial matter can flourish, but you must avoid gambling.

May

| career | love | home | health | finance |

1 MAY

This is a good time to enjoy your home or environment and to invest in yourself. It's also a good time for a little DIY and to beautiful your home. *Moon in Taurus.*

2 MAY

As Venus enters Aries you'll feel more upbeat and dynamic, especially in connection with domestic matters, family and your personal life. Your self-esteem is likely to improve. *Moon in Gemini.*

3 MAY

You'll enjoy doing something different and breathing fresh air into your life. A quirky new project or interest will grab your attention. If you're single you may feel motivated to meet new people and try new activities. Couples may find your relationship becomes more dynamic and upbeat. *Moon in Gemini.*

4 MAY

A visit or a change of environment will be enjoyable. Someone may surprise you and you may receive unexpected news. *Moon in Gemini.*

5 MAY

Unexpected developments and the chance to spend more time with upbeat and fun people will be inspiring. You may bump into old friend. Singles may meet an eccentric character and couples will enjoy infusing your relationship with more variety. You may have an unexpected visitor. *Moon in Cancer.*

6 MAY

You'll enjoy being with upbeat, likeable people and a lovely event will boost your mood. Creative Capricorns could be busy as you lean into your artistic abilities. *Moon in Cancer.*

7 MAY

This is a creative and entertaining weekend and you'll enjoy being with like-minded people in fun places. Family and friends will be available for talks and visits, so ensure you reach out. You'll also gain the chance to boost domestic dynamics. *Moon in Leo.*

8 MAY

This is a good time to get outstanding chores and paperwork done to do with domestic matters so you're shipshape for the next few weeks and months. Someone close may seem more upbeat but may also be a little feisty, so avoid arguments if you feel conflict is brewing. *Moon in Leo.*

9 MAY

You'll feel motivated to get things done, especially with shared duties such as paying off bills and getting things in order. However, people you collaborate with may not share your motivation and you may need to galvanise them to get things done. Aim to tie up loose ends at work and regarding communications before Mercury turns retrograde tomorrow. *Moon enters Virgo.*

10 MAY

As Mercury turns retrograde you're likely to receive key news from someone close, at home or regarding a key project. For some this will mean a change at home, and for others the need for a fresh approach to family or those you share space with. Try to allow extra time for travel and communications to avoid frustration over the coming weeks. *Moon in Virgo.*

11 MAY

As Jupiter joins Venus and Chiron in Aries communications are likely to be busy over the coming weeks, and you may feel motivated to take a trip or make changes at home and in your immediate environment. *Moon in Virgo.*

12 MAY

You like to make decisions based on facts as opposed to supposition, and when the moon is in Libra you are able to make fair-minded decisions. Base your choices on research and fair play for the best results. ***Moon in Libra.***

13 MAY

A meeting or news could propel a favourite project or relationship onto more stable ground. Take the initiative if you're single to find someone suitable; you may be surprised by who you meet. Couples will enjoy re-igniting romance. ***Moon in Libra.***

14 MAY

The Scorpio moon brings out a sense of motivation and you'll enjoy feeling engaged in your many ventures this weekend. You'll get a lot done, so ensure you organise some treats. ***Moon in Scorpio.***

15 MAY

You'll enjoy spending time in a beautiful place. Romance could blossom, so ensure you reserve time for someone special. If you're working this weekend you'll be super productive. This is a good time to organise a realistic budget. You may not agree with everyone, so find ways to establish common ground if possible. Someone may need your help or vice versa. Rest assured support will be invaluable. ***Moon in Scorpio.***

16 MAY

The total lunar eclipse in Scorpio is an intense full moon as it will spotlight how you feel about someone close and about your general direction. You may feel more aligned and supported than ever, but if you feel the opposite this is a good time to find greater direction for yourself so you feel more fulfilled.

17 MAY

This is a good day to be practical, especially about finances and personal developments. Avoid allowing your imagination to run away with you and seeing life through rose-coloured glasses. Be inspired but also realistic about your various personal and financial investments. ***Moon in Sagittarius.***

18 MAY

You can attain important goals. Be proactive with your plans as your efforts are likely to pay off. However, if you discover you have over-estimated your circumstances you will gain the opportunity to set things right. ***Moon in Capricorn.***

19 MAY

You're likely to see progress with your projects, especially those to do with creativity, family and your personal life. This is a good day to discuss how to continue to improve your circumstances. It's a good day to boost your appearance and for romance. **Moon in Capricorn.**

20 MAY

You'll enjoy a meeting, trip, reunion or visit. It's a good time to plan a trip and to repair devices or vehicles. **Moon in Aquarius.**

21 MAY

The sun in Gemini will add a little fun and excitement to your daily life over the coming weeks. You may be busier than usual and you'll get a taste of the kind of pace you'll be setting. **Moon in Aquarius.**

22 MAY

Meetings and discussions will go well. You'll enjoy getting together with like-minded people. This is a good day to consider how to improve some relationships, especially if you feel you have reached a stalemate. **Moon enters Pisces.**

23 MAY

This is a good time to boost relationships. A creative, family or personal interest can flourish. A trip or reunion will go well. If you're shopping, avoid overspending and overindulging as you'll regret it tomorrow. **Moon in Pisces.**

24 MAY

A commitment and investment are likely to be paying off for you now, especially in your personal life. However, if you feel disappointed this is a good time to discuss your differences and to try to reach common ground. **Moon in Pisces.**

25 MAY

This is another good day to make alterations in your personal life as negotiations, trips and talks will go well. If some matters are progressing quickly without your agreement this is a good time to slow things down, otherwise circumstances could snowball. **Moon in Aries.**

26 MAY

A domestic event will be enjoyable, and if you're renovating or doing a little DIY you're likely to see positive results. A visit will go well and romance could blossom, so organise a date! **Moon in Aries.**

27 MAY

You are a rational character and are seen as practical and realistic. You may be caught in a little drama, so if you prefer life on an even keel be tactful and diplomatic for the best results as a personal disagreement could quickly escalate to conflict. *Moon in Taurus.*

28 MAY

You'll appreciate the sense that over the next four weeks matters will begin to regain a little more of an even keel, especially at home and in your personal life. You'll enjoy focusing more on creativity, your interests and creature comforts over the coming weeks, such as a little more luxury at home and good food and company. *Moon in Taurus.*

29 MAY

You'll appreciate being a little spontaneous and being with outgoing and upbeat people. Sports or a trip or visit will be enjoyable. Someone close may have key news for you. *Moon enters Gemini.*

30 MAY

The Gemini new moon will spotlight a new agreement or arrangement in your personal life or at home. For some this new moon is an ideal time to launch a project or personal initiative. If you're considering starting a family this could be the time to do it! Be flexible and adaptable to changes. *Moon in Gemini.*

31 MAY

You'll feel motivated to put your best foot forward and to invest both in yourself and those you love. You may feel the need to invest more financially in a project, trip or domestic matter. *Moon in Gemini.*

June

career love home health finance

1 JUNE

You can accomplish a great deal, especially with work and health matters. You'll appreciate the opportunity to discuss or research a health or fitness schedule so you feel more energetic. The moon in Cancer brings out your caring and nurturing side, and someone close may show their support for you. *Moon in Cancer.*

2 JUNE

It's a good day to discuss your long-term plans, especially if you have already decided to make some changes in your personal life. Someone close such as a colleague or business or personal partner may wish to share their thoughts. Be prepared to listen. *Moon in Cancer.*

3 JUNE

You'll be glad to hear that Mercury ends its retrograde phase today. You may receive key news concerning a creative or family venture. A domestic matter may be reviewed. Communications and travel plans will become easier to make over the coming weeks. A financial matter is best reviewed and attended to before it becomes a problem. *Moon enters Leo.*

4 JUNE

This is a good day for meetings and trips and generally enjoying good company. You may feel motivated to beautify your immediate environment such as your home and garden. *Moon in Leo.*

5 JUNE

The Leo moon brings out your upbeat side and you'll enjoy being more active with people whose company you enjoy such as friends and family. *Moon in Leo.*

6 JUNE

This is a good day to put in place a fresh health and well-being schedule. You will be feeling more practical about getting things shipshape in your diet, health and home. This is also a good time to make progress with your long-term plans. *Moon in Virgo.*

7 JUNE

A change at work or in your usual schedule may involve a surprise turnaround. You'll enjoy an impromptu get-together and being spontaneous. Be adaptable, especially if some matters have been stuck. *Moon in Virgo.*

8 JUNE

You're at your efficient and practical best, so take advantage of this time when your best qualities are peaking. You may need to take control of a venture or project that has gone off track. Your organisational skills are peaking. *Moon enters Libra.*

9 JUNE

You may need to act as a mediator or peacemaker, especially with domestic matters. If emotions become heated, look for ways to establish calm and balance. Someone may confide their deeper thoughts to you. *Moon in Libra.*

10 JUNE

It's a good day for talks and visits, especially those that have a long-term implication. Meetings and news indicate you're making headway. Romance could blossom, so singles should mingle and couples will enjoy re-igniting passion. *Moon enters Scorpio.*

11 JUNE

A lovely get-together may come out of the blue or will be spontaneous. You may experience a surprise at home or with a family matter. You'll enjoy doing something different. Avoid impulsiveness. *Moon in Scorpio.*

12 JUNE

Someone from your past may bring out strong emotions. A social or networking event may be enjoyable, but if it seems to take up more energy than you're willing to give you'll know when to call it quits. ***Moon enters Sagittarius.***

13 JUNE

Those you love such as family and friends will take up more of your time and energy over the coming weeks. You may be busy at work. This is a good time to consider new ways to make your daily routine more varied and exciting. ***Moon in Sagittarius.***

14 JUNE

The full moon and supermoon in Sagittarius represents a fresh chapter for you regarding your past; in other words, you're turning over a new leaf. For some this will mean a new daily schedule including a fresh approach to health. Take a moment to work out where your priorities lie and make decisions from there.

15 JUNE

Someone may need your help, such as a family member or sibling. Avoid rushing and erratic drivers, as you may make mistakes or, worse, have an accident. Choose your words carefully as you may speak before you've thought things through and regret hastily spoken words. Avoid taking other people's random remarks personally. ***Moon in Capricorn.***

16 JUNE

This is a good day to make a commitment to a fresh agreement, such as a new work contract or financial budget. If you're looking for work this is a good day to circulate your resume and for interviews. It's also a good day to commit to a new health schedule or fitness routine. Just check contracts carefully. Romance could blossom, so organise a date. You may hear from an old friend. ***Moon enters Aquarius.***

17 JUNE

You'll enjoy being spontaneous and may bump into an old friend or hear unexpectedly from someone. Avoid snap decisions, as you may regret them. Do your research instead. ***Moon in Aquarius.***

18 JUNE

You may need to carefully tackle a thorny topic as a difference of opinions may be due to a fundamental disparity in values. Be prepared to negotiate to avoid arguments. Avoid gambling, both financially and emotionally. ***Moon in Aquarius.***

19 JUNE

You'll enjoy clearing your head via a visit to somewhere beautiful or discussing your thoughts with someone sympathetic to your views. Romance could blossom, and you'll enjoy indulging in music, relaxation, reading, film and dance. *Moon in Pisces.*

20 JUNE

The Pisces moon may bring out your idealistic side, leading to disappointment in someone or in a development. Just avoid seeing the world through rose-coloured glasses or you could be disappointed. *Moon in Pisces.*

21 JUNE

As the sun enters Cancer, marking the solstice, you will feel inclined to focus more on work, health and well-being. You may feel drawn to romance and feel the need to find more stability and security in life. Be proactive, as you could get a lot done. You may be drawn to a new look or outfit. *Moon in Aries.*

22 JUNE

You'll feel inclined to be more outspoken and demonstrative, especially at home and regarding important decisions. Be positive but avoid being obstinate or bossy, as it could get you into hot water. *Moon in Aries.*

23 JUNE

You'll feel drawn to being more in control of your life, and will strive to gain more influence both at work and at home. Use your charm rather than appearing domineering for the best results. *Moon enters Taurus.*

24 JUNE

You may be drawn to altering some aspects of your home life so that you feel more at home and at ease. Just ensure you run your ideas past those they will affect to avoid arguments. Aim to establish common ground for the best results. *Moon in Taurus.*

25 JUNE

You'll enjoy bringing more comfort into your home and spending extra time on projects you love. Dance, music and the arts will appeal. Romance could blossom, so organise a treat. Singles should mingle; you may meet someone romantic. *Moon in Taurus.*

26 JUNE

A change in your usual Saturday schedule will raise morale. You'll enjoy being more active and may even feel restless initially. Channel energy into fun activities, and if you have outstanding chores into housework. You'll be pleased with the result. *Moon in Gemini.*

27 JUNE

This is an excellent day for health and well-being appointments. Someone close such as a family member or housemate may need help and you'll be there to offer it. If you need guidance, an expert or adviser could prove helpful to you. *Moon in Gemini.*

28 JUNE

An upbeat change in your usual routine will be enjoyable. You may decide to add a little more diversity to your usual schedule. A sports- or arts-related event will be fun. Romance could blossom. You may be surprised by news or an impromptu meeting. *Moon enters Cancer.*

29 JUNE

The Cancerian new moon will kick-start a fresh chapter in a business or personal relationship for December-born Capricorns and a new work or health routine for January Capricorns. You may need to come to a fresh personal or domestic arrangement in the process.

30 JUNE

Talks and meetings will go well as long as you avoid taking an oppositional approach. Someone close may be feeling emotional and could trigger a reaction in you, so avoid allowing emotions and expectations to run your life. Look at the practicalities of your circumstances first. *Moon in Cancer.*

July

career love home health finance

1 JULY

There is mounting tension in the skies that could contribute to arguments, especially over domestic, family and financial matters, so take things one step at a time. If some communications are confusing, double-check the details. ***Moon in Leo.***

2 JULY

Communications regarding chores and your finances are likely to improve over the next few days as long as you have laid solid groundwork and have prepared for developments in these areas. If you feel you haven't, this is a good time to do some research and earth your plans. If some developments feel intense, ensure you maintain perspective to avoid arguments as you may well encounter strong opinions that differ from yours. ***Moon in Leo.***

3 JULY

There is still likely to be tension in the air, so it's a good time to consider ways you can dispel the tension through fun activities such as sports and spiritual interests. This is a good day to get organised for the week ahead. ***Moon enters Virgo.***

4 JULY

Intense talks at work or regarding your daily routine may bring out stress, so take a moment to order your thoughts about your projects and avoid arguments with a little tact and diplomacy. A health matter may require a little more research before you can commit to a plan such as a new diet or fitness schedule. *Moon in Virgo.*

5 JULY

This is a good day to consider how you could take some factors that are stuck into a new pattern so that you can get out of a rut. It's a good day for romance, so if you have nothing planned yetorganise a treat! A family get-together is likely to provide a sense of stability. *Moon enters Libra.*

6 JULY

This is a good day to consider how you could better manage your work/life balance or, more precisely, your daily routine so you can fit in your domestic chores and/or family time. *Moon in Libra.*

7 JULY

This is a good day for health and beauty appointments. It's also a good time to find more space in your diary for your domestic and personal lives as someone may need your help or support. *Moon in Libra.*

8 JULY

An unexpected development may take you by surprise. Someone may express their vulnerabilities and you may need to ask for help yourself, especially regarding personal or domestic matters. Rest assured advice or help will be available. A trip or meeting may need to be postponed. *Moon in Scorpio.*

9 JULY

Travel and communications may be delayed or postponed, so aim to be flexible and adaptable to big-picture developments. A vehicle or device may require repair. Back up computers for the best measure to avoid losing important information. This is a good time to check fitness and health schedules to ensure they support your needs. *Moon in Scorpio.*

10 JULY

A surprise get-together or visit will be enjoyable. Romance could blossom, so take the time to develop a lovely connection. You may enjoy a reunion. *Moon enters Sagittarius.*

11 JULY

When the moon is in Sagittarius you may surprise yourself, as you are more outgoing and active and willing to take calculated risks and express yourself more. ***Moon in Sagittarius.***

12 JULY

This is a good day to be practical and realistic, especially with work, personal and health matters. Consider your big-picture goals and aim for them. ***Moon enters Capricorn.***

13 JULY

The full moon and supermoon in your own sign will spotlight an important personal matter, especially if you were born in mid-January. If you were born later you may consider a fresh daily health or work routine. A business or personal partner may have important news for you. Look for security and stability and avoid making decisions based on assumptions.

14 JULY

You prefer life to be black and white yet decisions often take you into grey territory. If you need more information to make a choice or to feel you are certain of your position, it's important you do your research. You may be prone to misunderstandings and to delays, so be patient. You may also be easily misled. ***Moon enters Aquarius.***

15 JULY

You'll make great headway by being adaptable and willing to try something new. However, some talks will be intense, as you may need to discuss important work, financial or personal matters. ***Moon in Aquarius.***

16 JULY

Consider whether a fresh approach to someone in your personal life or at work could be useful. You may receive key news that may mean you must reconsider a personal or financial situation. ***Moon enters Pisces.***

17 JULY

This is a lovely day for get-togethers and for indulging in your favourite activities. If you're shopping you may be tempted to splurge, so ensure your finances are watertight before you overspend. Romance and family time will appeal. ***Moon in Pisces.***

18 JULY

This is a good time for important talks, especially regarding how you share duties either in your personal life or at work. You may find some talks are intense, so avoid conflict by taking things one step at a time. You could make key changes in a situation by being thorough and researching your circumstances well. *Moon enters Aries.*

19 JULY

As Mercury enters upbeat Leo you may begin to more easily understand someone else's points of view. Someone close may simply voice their feelings more, enabling you to better hear their side of the story. You may feel more adventurous about your plans over the coming weeks. Be positive! *Moon in Aries.*

20 JULY

Key news and developments will signal a change in the circumstances of someone close, and these may impact your circumstances. It's a good time to discuss important long-term decisions as those you must discuss these with are likely to listen. You may be ready to take a project or relationship in a new direction. *Moon enters Taurus.*

21 JULY

You like circumstances to move forward quickly so you may be slightly impatient and feel restless, especially with ventures that are moving more slowly than you'd like. You'll find ways to spend more time with the people you love as a result, so plan some lovely events. *Moon in Taurus.*

22 JULY

As the sun enters Leo someone close is likely to feel more optimistic and active. They may also be more expressive and generous. You'll enjoy being with like-minded people, so why not organise an event? *Moon in Taurus.*

23 JULY

You'll enjoy a trip and your favourite activities this weekend. A meeting and at least a chat with someone whose values you share will be uplifting. If you're shopping you may be inclined to overspend, so check you budget first. *Moon in Gemini.*

24 JULY

You'll relish a sense of freedom of movement and may enjoy a visit or trip somewhere different. If you feel arguments are brewing, take time out to avoid allowing them to gain momentum. Organise a fun event to bring a little light-heartedness into the day. *Moon in Gemini.*

25 JULY

You have a strong character and when opposed you can be super stubborn, yet a difference of opinion needn't turn into a full-blown argument. A work or financial matter is best tackled in practical ways to avoid emotions getting the upper hand. ***Moon enters Cancer.***

26 JULY

An oppositional approach to someone who is a little feisty will only lead to more anger being ignited, so try to find ways to be firm in gentle ways. Good communication skills are the secret to success. Avoid snap decisions, as these are likely to backfire. A financial decision, trip or meeting may be delayed, so be patient. ***Moon in Cancer.***

27 JULY

This is a good day to review some of your decisions and agreements and to put in place more manageable and agreeable arrangements. A vehicle or device may need to be fixed, and if you're travelling you may be delayed. A financial matter is best approached in a business-like manner to avoid allowing emotions to overrule your better sense. ***Moon in Cancer.***

28 JULY

The Leo new moon points to a fresh chapter in an agreement or personal or business partnership. For some this will mean a fresh way to share finances or duties or even space at home. You may receive unexpected news or will travel somewhere new. Someone who tends to be unpredictable may behave true to form. Avoid snap decisions and look for solid ways to move forward. Travel and meetings may be delayed, so allow for extra time.

29 JULY

Unexpected developments or news will deserve a patient approach; good communication skills are the key to your success. Be tactful and diplomatic where necessary and willing to see another's viewpoint. ***Moon in Leo.***

30 JULY

The more attention you pay to details and to getting things right, especially financially, the better the outcome as mistakes could be made. You'll appreciate catching up with someone whose company you truly enjoy. ***Moon enters Virgo.***

31 JULY

You may be surprised by developments. Someone may be in touch from out of the blue or you may bump into someone. You'll enjoy being spontaneous but must avoid making snap decisions. Romance can blossom, so organise a treat. ***Moon in Virgo.***

August

career   love   home   health   finance

1 AUGUST

The clearer you are with communications the better will be the outcome of your day, as otherwise you may be prone to making mistakes largely through making assumptions. Some meetings or travel may be delayed, so be patient. ***Moon in Virgo.***

2 AUGUST

You may be surprised by news. A spontaneous get-together will be enjoyable. You'll enjoy taking the time to discuss your plans with those they concern, especially at work and regarding changes at home. Artistic, domestic and sports-related activities are likely to go well. ***Moon in Libra.***

3 AUGUST

Romance could flourish, and you may be surprised by developments in a personal situation such as at home. You may need to think on your feet, and a little lateral thinking will encourage you to see circumstances from a fresh perspective. ***Moon in Libra.***

4 AUGUST

You'll feel motivated by your projects and ideas and will enjoy putting your energy into your ventures. Avoid allowing distractions to deter you from your big-picture goals. ***Moon enters Scorpio.***

5 AUGUST

Your hard work will begin to show signs of success. You may need to overcome a hurdle, but if you're diligent your efforts will be worthwhile. *Moon in Scorpio.*

6 AUGUST

Are you a glass half full person? If so, your efforts will pay off this weekend as you'll feel more inclined to be optimistic and proactive with your ventures and projects. You may need to put in a little extra hard work, but when you doyou'll see positive results. *Moon enters Sagittarius.*

7 AUGUST

This is a lovely day for socialising and romance. You may be asked for help from someone or will need some support yourself, and this will be available. You may find a shopping spree has a therapeutic effect but must avoid overspending, as you'll regret it. *Moon in Sagittarius.*

8 AUGUST

This is a good day to consider how you could help along a circumstance that has become tense. Avoid taking someone's random comments personally. Expert advice may be useful. You may be asked for help. *Moon enters Capricorn.*

9 AUGUST

If you like a little tension in your romantic life as it adds spice and variety you'll appreciate current circumstances, but if tension leads to stress this could be a real passion killer. Avoid allowing a difference of opinion to lead to arguments. You could make considerable changes in your life. Singles may meet someone passionate yet intense. Some matters may be delayed, so be patient and avoid misunderstandings. *Moon in Capricorn.*

10 AUGUST

Be practical and your projects will succeed, both at work and at home. There may still be a little tension in the air, so manage your responses carefully. *Moon enters Aquarius.*

11 AUGUST

If circumstances are shaping up the way you want them to go with the flow and avoid rocking the boat, but if you experience an annoying change of plan or unexpected and frustrating news find a way to tactfully get things back on track. Avoid overspending and overindulging as you'll regret it tomorrow. You'll enjoy relaxing this evening. *Moon in Aquarius.*

12 AUGUST

The Aquarian full moon will spotlight finances for some Capricorns and a personal decision for others. Be prepared to make a commitment to a certain course of action and to be proactive about making changes in your personal life and/or at home.

13 AUGUST

You'll enjoy giving your imagination full rein and relaxing. You may be drawn to music, spirituality, film and dance. You'll enjoy immersing yourself in a creative atmosphere. On a partnership and work level, look for ways to build a solid platform for yourself and for your ventures. *Moon in Pisces.*

14 AUGUST

You may be prepared to make a commitment or a decision, and the more you base this on facts rather than on expectationsthe better the outcome. A financial or personal agreement could be productive, but if it limits your movements too much you may need to rethink your options. *Moon enters Aries.*

15 AUGUST

You'll enjoy a reunion or a trip to a familiar place. Communications will flow. You'll enjoy a meeting or a fun activity such as sports, the arts and creativity. *Moon in Aries.*

16 AUGUST

A change of place or of pace will breathe fresh air into your usual Tuesday routine. You may be surprised by news or by someone's change of mind. *Moon in Aries.*

17 AUGUST

If you're making long-term decisions and investments, ensure you have all the facts at your fingertips or you may be prone to making assumptions. You will feel inspired but may be a little forgetful or head in the clouds. You may also be easily misled. *Moon in Taurus.*

18 AUGUST

This is an excellent day for romance, so organise a treat if you haven't already. Key financial matters are likely to go well as long as you have adequately researched the circumstances. Avoid committing to a plan, trip or agreement without reading the fine print. Some travel may be delayed, so factor in extra time for the trip. *Moon in Taurus.*

19 AUGUST

You can be obstinate once you have your mind set on a particular outcome. While your projects can progress well, if you find some are delayed avoid being stubborn in your response to delays.

Be adaptable and consider fresh logistics. Avoid a battle of egos and focus on common ground to avoid arguments. **Moon in Gemini.**

20 AUGUST

Mars will now be in Gemini until the end of March 2023, which will help you to make great progress with your work projects and also with your own personal ventures such as those you undertake with family and your creative projects. You may be willing to see other people's points of view but that doesn't mean you'll automatically get on with everyone, so avoid a battle of egos. **Moon in Gemini.**

21 AUGUST

Romance could blossom, and you'll be drawn to immerse yourself in your interests such as spirituality, the arts and writing. You'll enjoy deepening your understanding of someone or of yourself. You'll enjoy a trip but may be forgetful, so avoid misplacing keys. **Moon in Gemini.**

22 AUGUST

Your ability to be practical and reasonable will be in demand. You may be asked to help sort out the logistics of a personal or domestic matter. A trip and the chance to discuss your long-term plans will be enjoyable. **Moon in Cancer.**

23 AUGUST

Now that the sun is in Virgo for the next four weeks you will appreciate the opportunity to get down to the basics with practical matters, such as those at home. You'll enjoy the sense that life has more reason and rhyme. It's a good time to plan for the next four weeks, especially regarding travel. **Moon in Cancer.**

24 AUGUST

There is a therapeutic quality to events and you'll appreciate the opportunity to boost your health and that of those you love. A trip somewhere beautiful will be uplifting. It's a good time for a visit to a medical or beauty appointment. It's also an ideal time to seek expert advice. **Moon enters Leo.**

25 AUGUST

The moon in Leo brings out your more upbeat side but it may also bring out your combativeness and obstinacy, so avoid putting people's backs up. **Moon in Leo.**

26 AUGUST

People are very likely to see your point of view, as your charm and persuasiveness are more pronounced than usual. Take a moment to communicate your ideas and plans with those they affect. The next few weeks are ideal for improving your situation, especially within collaborations. **Moon in Leo.**

27 AUGUST

The new moon in Virgo may create a few waves: it's ideal for beginning a new chapter in a shared venture such as a collaboration at work or regarding joint finances at home, for example. This may come about due to a surprise event or a change of priority in you or someone else. If someone's behaviour surprises you, avoid a Mexican stand-off by being diplomatic yet also proactive.

28 AUGUST

You may discover that someone close has very different viewpoints to yours. You may even be surprised by them and may need to come to a fresh arrangement. It's a good day to reach new terms and conditions for agreements. *Moon in Virgo.*

29 AUGUST

This is a good day for talks, You may need to be a mediator or must find the middle ground in a dispute. You'll feel motivated to communicate your long-term plans, but if you feel a little conflicted take things one step at a time to avoid impulsive decisions you'll regret. *Moon enters Libra.*

30 AUGUST

You can achieve a great deal through a diligent and careful approach but will need to be optimistic. A difference of opinions may stem from a fundamental disparity in values, so consider whether new circumstances would merit an adjustment in values. *Moon in Libra.*

31 AUGUST

Romance and all things artistic and beautiful will draw your attention, so ensure you make time for a little luxury and sumptuousness. However, you may discover that your expectations have been unrealistic. If so, consider adopting a more realistic approach to circumstances. *Moon enters Scorpio.*

September

career   love   home   health   finance

1 SEPTEMBER

This is a good time to be proactive and energetic as you will reap rewards for your hard work. You may feel more inclined to get things done at work and to better organise your budget. A reunion may appeal. ***Moon in Scorpio.***

2 SEPTEMBER

You can't always agree with everyone, and today's tension in a relationship may simply be a case in point. If you're considering a personal or financial investment ensure you have double-checked the details. You will succeed with your projects with persistence and diligence. ***Moon enters Sagittarius.***

3 SEPTEMBER

Important discussions are best approached matter of factly to avoid overly high expectations. A financial agreement could be advantageous but you may be inclined to be impulsive, so ensure you are prudent with the facts. A trip, reunion or return to an old haunt will be enjoyable but may also bring out strong feelings. ***Moon in Sagittarius.***

4 SEPTEMBER

You'll enjoy leaving being active and outgoing this weekend; socialising and networking will appeal. A favourite activity such as sport or creative interests will be refreshing. ***Moon in Sagittarius.***

5 SEPTEMBER

Over the next few weeks you'll appreciate the sense that some matters are beginning to settle down, especially in your financial life and personally. You'll see the wisdom in a practical, realistic and grounded approach both to finances and your personal life. *Moon in Capricorn.*

6 SEPTEMBER

The moon in Capricorn is an excellent time for you to get organised at work and at home. You're likely to feel motivated by a sense of purpose or duty. It's a good time to get paperwork shipshape. *Moon in Capricorn.*

7 SEPTEMBER

You'll see the wisdom in a fresh approach to a work project or personal matter such as health and well-being. Adopting a rational and analytical approach while also being flexible about inevitable changes will help you to proceed. *Moon in Aquarius.*

8 SEPTEMBER

As a generally diligent character you can take difficulties in communications personally, yet sometimes you will be misunderstood through no fault of your own. Someone you share duties and responsibilities with may need your help, and if you need expert advice about a project or venture it will be available. *Moon in Aquarius.*

9 SEPTEMBER

A little extra care and attention with communications and travel will put you in a solid place for progress. Be patient if some communications or travel are delayed. Try to get the loose ends of important paperwork tied up before Mercury turns retrograde tomorrow. *Moon in Pisces.*

10 SEPTEMBER

The full moon in Pisces shines a light on your finances and personal life. You may receive key information or news from someone close that signals change at home or with family. This is a good time to keep your feet on the ground with your plans while also adopting an inspired approach.

11 SEPTEMBER

You'll enjoy a change of routine, for many concerning your home life and for some due to a change of environment. A visit or trip will be refreshing. Someone close may have good news or will wish to take you somewhere new. *Moon in Aries.*

12 SEPTEMBER

A project or venture will deserve careful attention to ensure it goes the way you prefer. Rest assured that your hard work will be worthwhile. A financial matter will also need close scrutiny. It's a good day to consider a fresh budget or a trip somewhere beautiful. *Moon in Aries.*

13 SEPTEMBER

Avoid getting stuck in worrying about other people's expectations of you and trust that your best intentions will be sufficient for getting projects done. Ensure you have the facts as well, though, to avoid confusion and letting anyone down. *Moon enters Taurus.*

14 SEPTEMBER

You'll appreciate the sense that you are making progress with your ventures and relationships, both at home and at work. Look for stability and security and you'll find it. *Moon in Taurus.*

15 SEPTEMBER

You're well known for your organisational abilities, and these will certainly put you in a good position to get things done. Trust you can get the results you want and you will. *Moon enters Gemini.*

16 SEPTEMBER

You'll appreciate finding the time for a favourite interest or activity. You'll enjoy a get-together or talk. This is also a romantic day and could be ideal for couples to rekindle romance. Singles may meet someone charming. If you're considering a substantial financial outlay ensure you have done your research. Avoid gambling, both financially and emotionally. *Moon in Gemini.*

17 SEPTEMBER

You'll embrace the chance to do something different this weekend and a family event or favourite hobby will be enjoyable. However, you must avoid impulsiveness as it will backfire. *Moon in Gemini.*

18 SEPTEMBER

A reunion or return to an old haunt may be significant. Today's talks and negotiations could open doors, but if you're unsure of your plans and feelings give yourself time to think. You may be picking up threads of conversations and ideas from earlier in the month. If you're travelling, factor in extra time as there may be delays. *Moon enters Cancer.*

19 SEPTEMBER

You'll enjoy making significant changes in your life, and this is an ideal time to embrace something different. A trip, interest or project could be transformative. If you're single you may meet someone new. You may be drawn to a fresh look or outfit. *Moon in Cancer.*

20 SEPTEMBER

Take a moment to ensure your values and principles align with those of someone you must collaborate with. If they don't, find out if you can overcome the differences before committing further to the circumstance. Your projects and ideas can succeed, although you will need to work hard at them. If you're considering a major financial investment there may be delays or you may reconsider some of the terms. *Moon enters Leo.*

21 SEPTEMBER

An inspired and upbeat approach to your day will reap rewards. Be clear about your intentions both at work and at home to avoid misunderstandings. *Moon in Leo.*

22 SEPTEMBER

This is another proactive day although you may need to explain or negotiate some of your ideas and plans. You won't always agree with everyone, especially not at home, but you could bring a fresh agreement into being that everyone can agree with, especially if you are enthusiastic and practical. *Moon in Leo.*

23 SEPTEMBER

As the sun steps into Libra it marks the equinox, a time when we collectively sense we can achieve more balance and harmony in our lives. Your attention is likely to go increasingly to your projects and ventures as you'll wish to gain more of a sense of purpose at work and peace in your life over the next four weeks. *Moon in Virgo.*

24 SEPTEMBER

You may hear key news, for some in relation to work and for others in relation to your general direction in life or your status. You may need to review some of your ideas. A reunion or visit may be inspiring, but if you experience a disappointment this weekend see it as a way to move forward. You'll be inspired by the arts, music and romance. *Moon in Virgo.*

25 SEPTEMBER

The new moon in Libra signals a fresh chapter for you, and the way you see your own position in the world is likely to be changing. Be prepared to turn a corner with your career and general direction in life, which may come about due to changes at home.

26 SEPTEMBER

It's all change for you, and the more grounded and practical you are the better for you. Look for ways to bring balance and peace into your life. You may be a little forgetful, so avoid misplacing valuables such as house keys. *Moon in Libra.*

27 SEPTEMBER

A change in your activities could take you somewhere different or to an old haunt or familiar circumstance. This is a good time to get the ball rolling with changes in your personal life or at work. Initiate meetings and talks to discuss your options. *Moon in Libra.*

28 SEPTEMBER

Work projects are likely to gather steam. For many this is a constructive and lucrative time, but if you find your options are becoming limited find ways to broaden your scope. Avoid impulsiveness, even if circumstances are moving quickly. A health or personal venture could flourish, so ensure you take the initiative. You may receive a financial or ego boost. *Moon in Scorpio.*

29 SEPTEMBER

You'll enjoy a meeting or the chance to gather your thoughts. This could be an intense day, so ensure you take breaks. *Moon in Scorpio.*

30 SEPTEMBER

You'll enjoy being proactive and initiating talks and meetings that are necessary so you can gain the information you need. Just avoid presupposing everyone is on the same page as you. You may need to explain your thoughts and plans to those they affect. *Moon in Sagittarius.*

October

career love home health finance

1 OCTOBER

You'll enjoy meeting someone important who can help you with a project. Romance could blossom. If you're making financial decisions, avoid making sentimental choices; get expert advice instead. You may enjoy a trip and a reunion. *Moon in Sagittarius.*

2 OCTOBER

Key news or developments will help you to plan ahead far more constructively, even if you must revise a previous plan. You'll enjoy creature comforts and relaxing. *Moon in Capricorn.*

3 OCTOBER

Today's Capricorn moon will help you to organise your week and be practical about work and meetings. It's a good day to review your work plans and meetings to ensure you're logistically on the right track. *Moon in Capricorn.*

4 OCTOBER

Your plans and projects will gather pace over the next few days, so ensure you're on the right path. If you feel you need to discuss more of your ideas with someone, take the initiative. *Moon enters Aquarius.*

5 OCTOBER

You are very good at logistics and strategy and your bright ideas will certainly do you credit, especially with collaborative efforts. You may enjoy the slightly faster pace of life. *Moon in Aquarius.*

6 OCTOBER

Double-check you're on the same page as the people you need to collaborate with both at home and at work to ensure your plans will go ahead as expected, otherwise you may discover you have been talking at cross purposes. It's best to find out now rather than when it's too late to make changes. *Moon enters Pisces.*

7 OCTOBER

This is a good day for talks, meetings, travel and especially where your efforts are intended to bring about positive changes. There may be a health-related or therapeutic aspect to the day's events. A financial matter will deserve more focus. If you are considering a large outlay or must budget differently, consider the help of an expert. You may be asked for help or advice yourself. Avoid erratic drivers. *Moon in Pisces.*

8 OCTOBER

You'll appreciate finding the time to seek inspiration and gather the information you need. Discussions about important matters such as finances and travel will be productive. Just ensure you are clear about what you need. *Moon enters Aries.*

9 OCTOBER

The Aries full moon will spotlight a personal or financial matter. If you feel vulnerable about circumstances it's important to find the expert advice you need. You may need to find the time for someone special and to consider their feelings above your own. A trip or vehicle may require more attention so that it works as it should. A health matter is best approached head-on to avoid delay.

10 OCTOBER

Your ideas and values may differ considerably to those of someone else. If you find the common ground you can establish an agreement. However, you may find the differences are too great to overcome. Avoid taking circumstances personally. It's in your interest to gain expert advice in relation to finances and/or your personal life. *Moon enters Taurus.*

11 OCTOBER

This is a good day to make progress with your ventures and especially your collaborations. Your efforts are likely to lead to success; just avoid restricting your options too much. You may be surprised by someone's news or a visit. Prepare to be adaptable. *Moon in Taurus.*

12 OCTOBER

Personal and financial matters deserve careful analysis. You may experience an uplifting development in either or both areas, but if you proceed without adequate information you could make mistakes. Avoid gambling, both financially and emotionally. *Moon in Taurus.*

13 OCTOBER

You may be surprised by someone's news or circumstances. Be adaptable, but avoid being thrown off your stride. Base decisions on reasonable expectations. Avoid making assumptions. *Moon in Gemini.*

14 OCTOBER

This is a good day for making a commitment to a particular idea or venture. A financial agreement could work out well, but you must research it adequately. You may experience a financial or ego boost. *Moon in Gemini.*

15 OCTOBER

You'll appreciate having extra free time and will enjoy doing something fun with like-minded people. Talks and meeting are likely to go well. If you do something different you may be forgetful or absent-minded due to the change of circumstance, so ensure you avoid misplacing valuables such as keys. *Moon enters Cancer.*

16 OCTOBER

If you have been feeling restless you'll appreciate the opportunity to slow down and enjoy a calmer pace. Romance, music, the arts, dance and film will all appeal. You'll gain a deeper understanding of someone if you look more closely at their values and ideas. *Moon in Cancer.*

17 OCTOBER

A lovely connection with a like-minded person will feel refreshing. You may enjoy being more creative and trying new activities. You can make great progress with projects and also in your personal relationships. *Moon in Cancer.*

18 OCTOBER

The moon in Leo brings out a sense of adventure in you and also in those close to you. You may feel more confident than you have for some time and could get a great deal done, so take the initiative. However, you or someone close may feel a little more feisty, so avoid needless arguments. *Moon in Leo.*

19 OCTOBER

You are inspired and outgoing and keen to immerse yourself in your projects and ventures. If you're on holiday you'll enjoy relaxing. Romance can blossom, so ensure you organise a treat. A difference of opinion or simply feelings of restlessness could get in the way, so ensure you pace yourself and avoid allowing arguments to turn into conflict. *Moon in Leo.*

20 OCTOBER

This is another intense day, so if conflict was brewing yesterday ensure you avoid a tinderbox today. A dispute is best settled early rather than allowing it to fester. Some interactions will flow and others will be problematic, so maintain perspective. *Moon enters Virgo.*

21 OCTOBER

There is still a feisty or restless atmosphere around you. This is ideal for getting things done, but you may feel at a loose end if you're not working. Find ways to channel strong energy into something productive. *Moon in Virgo.*

22 OCTOBER

The arts, music and a favourite activity will all inspire you, so ensure you organise something enjoyable. A lovely get-together will raise morale, and some Capricorns may experience a boost at work or in your career. Romance could truly blossom. If you're single this is a good day to meet new people. Couples will enjoy deepening your ties, but if you find some interactions are tense ensure you take the pressure off them. *Moon in Virgo.*

23 OCTOBER

Now that the sun will be in Scorpio for the next four weeks you'll feel more motivated by your career and your activities and will feel the need to express yourself in these areas. This is a good time for travel and to make agreements with people in authority. You may experience a financial or ego boost. *Moon in Libra.*

24 OCTOBER

A circumstance from your past may require a little more attention. A repair may need to be carried out at work or at home. Your help or advice may be appreciated. If you need expert guidance it will be available, so reach out. *Moon in Libra.*

25 OCTOBER

The partial solar eclipse in Scorpio signals the start of a new chapter for you that will affect your general direction in life. You may reconsider your career, for example, or a particular venture. Avoid making impulsive decisions and ensure you get the full details of circumstances before making choices. If you experience a disappointment you will find a silver lining to any clouds that arise. Avoid misunderstandings.

26 OCTOBER

The moon in Scorpio is motivational, but you may feel strong emotions. Avoid taking things personally if developments are challenging. Be practical and logical about your decisions. *Moon in Scorpio.*

27 OCTOBER

It's a good day for meetings and travel. Work and health matters are likely to move forward quickly, so take the initiative as your efforts will be worthwhile. However, if you experience difficulties and delays, work methodically toward a better circumstance. Communications could be intense. *Moon enters Sagittarius.*

28 OCTOBER

You may need to review some of your ideas. A trip could take you to somewhere from your past. Avoid feeling you're going backwards, as you will get the chance to move forward soon enough. *Moon in Sagittarius.*

29 OCTOBER

Over the next few weeks you and those around you may feel more passionate about ideas and communications may be intense, so ensure you are positive about your opinions and the facts. Find ways to dissipate restless energy so you do not find life frustrating. You may need to tread carefully with discussions. *Moon enters Capricorn.*

30 OCTOBER

Be constructive and proactive about changing your routine so you get time for sports, relaxation and me time. Some get-togethers may need to be delayed so you can relax. Avoid feeling too disappointed by difficult conversations. You'll appreciate the chance to relax and boost your energy levels. *Moon in Capricorn.*

31 OCTOBER

Happy Hallowe'en! You're efficient and productive and will impress people close to you with your organisational skills and being able to be grounded when needed. This is a good time to put work and personal initiatives into action. Avoid rushing and making snap decisions. *Moon enters Aquarius.*

November

career   love   home   health   finance

1 NOVEMBER

Clear, analytical and strategic thinking will help you to get on top of important matters, especially in connection with a friend, group or organisation. Be prepared to put emotions aside if a conundrum arises at work. *Moon in Aquarius.*

2 NOVEMBER

A logistical matter is best dealt with matter of factly to avoid anyone's feelings being hurt. Be compassionate but avoid taking someone's thoughts and sensitivities personally if you feel you are being criticised. Someone who is vulnerable or sensitive will require delicate handling. *Moon enters Pisces.*

3 NOVEMBER

A reunion may be as enjoyable as it is intense. Travel delays will benefit from a patient attitude. If you are asked for help, the more practical you are the better; avoid letting sentimentality get the better of you. This is a good day for health and well-being appointments and to seek the advice of an expert. You may be asked to provide expert help yourself. *Moon in Pisces.*

4 NOVEMBER

With so much focus on everything that's going on around you you'd be excused for forgetting to think about yourself, yet this is the time to take a break and ask yourself if you're happy with the direction your life is moving in. If you are, you'll enjoy continuing on the same path. If not, this is a good time to find remedies for the situation. **Moon enters Aries.**

5 NOVEMBER

Meetings and talks will put the spotlight on you and you may feel vulnerable as a result. Sudden or unexpected developments at home, in your personal life or regarding your general direction are best handled one step at a time. **Moon in Aries.**

6 NOVEMBER

Avoid feeling you must agree with everyone all the time. You will find a way to discuss your plans with someone you know may not agree with them. Someone close may need your help. If you need some advice or support, rest assured it will be available. **Moon in Aries.**

7 NOVEMBER

A circumstance will benefit from careful appraisal and a little negotiation will be needed. Be prepared to discuss options with those they concern to avoid hard feelings on both sides. **Moon in Taurus.**

8 NOVEMBER

The total lunar eclipse in Taurus will spotlight a key development in your personal life. For some this will be at home or with family, a property or someone special. You may receive key news that could alter your direction at work or with a special project. A trip or visit could be particularly significant.

9 NOVEMBER

An unexpected development will mean you must look more deeply at the long-term ramifications of your current decisions. Avoid snap decisions as these could backfire, but be prepared to consider your best step forward and be prepared to embrace something new. **Moon enters Gemini.**

10 NOVEMBER

Conversations and meetings may require a little extra attention on your part, especially if they concern finances, so that there are no mistakes or misunderstandings. You may receive good news, but if it seems too good to be true double-check the facts. **Moon in Gemini.**

11 NOVEMBER

There is a lot that can go right for you, especially if you're keen to succeed. If obstacles arise, see them as opportunities to excel. Avoid making snap decisions and getting involved in arguments with someone in a position of authority. ***Moon in Gemini.***

12 NOVEMBER

This is a good day to discuss your long-term plans and ambitions. You may be tempted to overindulge and overspend, so if you're shopping avoid impulse buys. You'll enjoy socialising and networking and may also meet someone like-minded if you're single. ***Moon in Cancer.***

13 NOVEMBER

This is a good time to make changes in your personal life and health. You may be drawn to a new look or to improving your fitness schedule. A get-together or social or work event may cut into your free time, but if you organise your day well you'll still get time to relax. ***Moon in Cancer.***

14 NOVEMBER

You are better known for your practical and organisational skills but you, like everyone, have intuition, which can be trusted. Your gut instincts will steer you in the right direction, so if in doubt trust your intuition. ***Moon enters Leo.***

15 NOVEMBER

You have charm and influence on your side, and you'll notice that socialising and group events feel more relaxing for you. You'll enjoy being able to spend time with like-minded people and to make progress with your various projects. A beauty or health treat is likely to go well. ***Moon in Leo.***

16 NOVEMBER

As Venus enters Sagittarius your values are likely to be a little more progressive and you may feel more expressive. Meetings and a trip are likely to go well even if you don't necessarily agree with everyone. A change of routine or the need to be well organised will reap rewards if you remain practical. ***Moon in Leo.***

17 NOVEMBER

As Mercury joins Venus in Sagittarius you are likely to feel drawn to new groups, ideas and organisations. Travel and fresh experiences will appeal to you. You may feel more inclined to socialise and network and will enjoy meeting a different social circle over the coming days and weeks. ***Moon in Virgo.***

18 NOVEMBER

Some lovely get-togethers will be enjoyable. A short trip or a visit will raise morale, so ensure you organise something special as you'll be glad you did! *Moon in Virgo.*

19 NOVEMBER

This is a good day to take things easy as you may be tired or will wish to take time out. Avoid misunderstandings and gambling, both financially and in your personal life. *Moon enters Libra.*

20 NOVEMBER

The moon at the zenith of your chart will motivate you to look for ways to gain more of a sense of balance and peace in your life. You may need to act as a mediator or bring balance and harmony to a circumstance. This is another day to avoid gambling and cutting corners. *Moon in Libra.*

21 NOVEMBER

You'll enjoy meetings and discussions. If you are undertaking a key financial transaction you're likely to see the benefit in so doing as you may see your finances increase. Just ensure you have double-checked the facts to avoid mistakes. *Moon enters Scorpio.*

22 NOVEMBER

The sun in Sagittarius for the next few weeks will encourage you to be more optimistic, outgoing and upbeat, especially at work but also regarding your health and fitness regime. *Moon in Scorpio.*

23 NOVEMBER

The Sagittarian new moon signals a perfect time to be more positive about your work and personal goals. Consider what you need to do to be happier as you could turn a corner in either or both areas. Make a wish, but as always be careful as it will come true. You may enjoy being more outgoing and sociable.

24 NOVEMBER

The moon in Sagittarius brings your inner adventurer and optimist out. You may sense that new horizons are about to open for you. Travel, networking and meeting new people will all appeal over the coming weeks. *Moon in Sagittarius.*

25 NOVEMBER

A therapeutic and healing aspect will motivate you to make positive changes in your life. For some these will be in your personal life such as in your home life. Others may be drawn to make changes in your health as you find ways to embrace a more productive fitness schedule or diet, for example. *Moon enters Capricorn.*

26 NOVEMBER

This is a good day for a health or beauty appointment. It's also a good time to build bridges with anyone you have recently argued with. A short trip or meeting will raise morale. An expert or adviser may have positive news for you. ***Moon in Capricorn.***

27 NOVEMBER

You may be receive unexpected news. Someone who can be unpredictable will behave true to form. You may enjoy an impromptu get-together or event even if it seems disruptive at first. ***Moon enters Aquarius.***

28 NOVEMBER

This is a good day to get things done, especially at work. You may receive an unexpected financial or ego boost. A trip or agreement could be constructive. ***Moon in Aquarius.***

29 NOVEMBER

Talks and meetings are likely to be animated but you could achieve your goals if you remain practical and focused, especially at work. This is a good day for a health appointment. Avoid making snap decisions, even if you must be spontaneous and think fast. ***Moon in Aquarius.***

30 NOVEMBER

This is a good day for work and financial agreements, so ensure you look at all the variables and commit to a plan or project if it ticks the boxes. Avoid arguments and look for solutions if problems arise. You may receive good news at work or a financial boost or compliment. ***Moon in Pisces.***

December

career   love   home   health   finance

1 DECEMBER

This is a good day to get things done, including work and financial matters. Meetings are likely to be animated. Romance could flourish, and you'll enjoy indulging in your favourite activities. Creativity could blossom. The arts, film, dance and music will all appeal. ***Moon in Pisces.***

2 DECEMBER

If making long-term agreements, ensure you have done adequate research before jumping in feet first. Someone close or you may be forgetful, so avoid distractions and consider ways to be more focused. Avoid misplacing valuables such as keys. You'll enjoy a reunion. ***Moon in Aries.***

3 DECEMBER

This is therapeutic day ideal for relaxing and spending time with like-minded people. You will enjoy a trip or visit. Health and well-being could blossom. You may be asked for help, and if you need some guidance or support it will be available so reach out. ***Moon in Aries.***

4 DECEMBER

A reunion or news from someone from your past will be uplifting. It's a good time to boost your health and well-being and to improve your appearance. If you are making long-term decisions ensure you have the facts, especially financially, to avoid mistakes as misunderstandings could occur. **Moon enters Taurus.**

5 DECEMBER

You'll appreciate the opportunity to get your feet on the ground with various negotiations, talks and meetings, especially if some matters have been up in the air. **Moon in Taurus.**

6 DECEMBER

Just before communications maestro Mercury steps into your sign it will make a tough aspect with Jupiter, which could spell difficult conversations, delays and potentially financial conundrums or even losses so ensure you avoid risky behaviour. Travel may be slow and frustrating, so factor in extra time for trips. Back up computers to avoid losing information. **Moon enters Gemini.**

7 DECEMBER

Surprising news, an impromptu meeting or a change in your usual routine needn't set the mood for the day. A lovely relationship with a group, friend or organisation will be productive. It's a good day for health and beauty appointments. **Moon in Gemini.**

8 DECEMBER

The Gemini full moon spotlights a fresh chapter for you at work as a new project or venture will gain ground. You may be prepared to begin a different health routine. Developments may arise rapidly, so think on your feet. For some, today's developments will revolve more around your personal life as a fresh chapter begins there.

9 DECEMBER

You may be surprised by news that could mean a fresh and livelier circumstance both at work and at home. A change of routine or a spontaneous meeting could be refreshing. **Moon in Cancer.**

10 DECEMBER

This is a good day to take talks and financial transactions carefully, as you may need to rethink a plan or there will be delays and mistakes can be made. Some interactions may be difficult, so be prepared to communicate clearly. Avoid trying to push your ideas on someone and avoid being pressured yourself for the best results. **Moon in Cancer.**

11 DECEMBER

As Venus joins Mercury in Capricorn you'll feel increasingly able to take matters in your stride, but you must avoid obstinacy. You may need to stand your ground or to express yourself more clearly but must avoid being argumentative, as conflict could arise quickly. Avoid minor accidents by being careful while travelling. **Moon enters Leo.**

12 DECEMBER

This is an excellent day for making agreements and commitments, especially in your personal life, financially and with a group or organisation. Be practical and plan ahead as this is a productive day. *Moon in Leo.*

13 DECEMBER

The Leo moon will encourage you to be a little more daring and assertive. This is a good time to try something new, both at work and at home. *Moon in Leo.*

14 DECEMBER

You'll discover whether or not your expectations have been realistic. If you find they have been unrealistic you will get the chance to put things straight by being clear and concise with communications. Aim to unravel a mystery and avoid being easily misled. *Moon enters Virgo.*

15 DECEMBER

When the moon is in Virgo you tend to be super productive and able to use your organisational abilities to the max. You're grounded and practical and can achieve a great deal, so get busy! *Moon in Virgo.*

16 DECEMBER

You're in a productive phase but may tend to be a little impulsive, so while you'll get a lot done avoid making snap decisions and cutting corners as you'll regret having rushed important matters. *Moon enters Libra.*

17 DECEMBER

This is a lovely day for socialising and networking. Work and health meetings are likely to go well too, even if some developments are unexpected. You will enjoy an impromptu get-together and you may be surprised by developments at home or with family. *Moon in Libra.*

18 DECEMBER

You'll appreciate the chance to socialise and network with people at work. However, some conversations may be a little more difficult than others, so use your discernment. A health or beauty appointment may appeal. If you're asked for help, your support will be appreciated. Avoid gambling, both financially and emotionally, as it's likely to backfire. *Moon in Libra.*

19 DECEMBER

A change of place or of pace will be welcome, although some aspects of your day may be more complex than you'd prefer. Avoid rushing into decisions but find the time to enjoy circumstances and the time of the year. *Moon in Scorpio.*

20 DECEMBER

A reunion and the chance to go somewhere that has emotional significance for you will appeal. You may be surprised by news or developments. Factor in extra time for travel as there may be delays or a surprise along the way. *Moon in Scorpio.*

21 DECEMBER

The solstice, when the sun enters your sign, is a time of reflection when you can gather your wits as you assimilate your progress this year. Over the next four weeks you will feel increasingly in your own element, and may experience some pleasant surprises over the coming days. Travel and communications may be delayed so be patient for the best results. *Moon in Sagittarius.*

22 DECEMBER

You'll enjoy a get-together with family or someone whose company you love. You may be surprised by today's developments. A change of routine or of pace and a trip will be refreshing. *Moon in Sagittarius.*

23 DECEMBER

The new moon and supermoon in your sign signals a fresh chapter for you in a personal situation, especially if it's your birthday or it was in the previous two days. You may receive good news to do with work or will experience a boost in self-esteem. For many Capricorns the new moon represents a fresh daily routine, and for others a new work phase. If you're shopping avoid overspending, as you'll regret it!

24 DECEMBER

As a traditionalist you relish this time of year and are likely to feel a little sentimental. You'll enjoy shopping but may be prone to overspend or overindulge, so be careful! Romance will blossom and you'll enjoy being with someone you love. *Moon in Capricorn.*

25 DECEMBER

Merry Christmas! You'll appreciate a sense of togetherness. You may experience something different about your Christmas Day this year but rest assured, you'll find the way to adapt. Just avoid taking personally any developments that are not to your liking. *Moon in Aquarius.*

26 DECEMBER

A little restlessness will encourage you to be more active, and you'll enjoy getting together with like-minded people or indulging in your favourite activities. The arts, music, film and dance will all appeal. You'll also enjoy relaxing. *Moon in Aquarius.*

27 DECEMBER

You'll appreciate the creature comforts, and if you're shopping you are likely to find some bargains. Just avoid overspending on items you don't need. You'll enjoy a boost in self-esteem via a compliment or a meeting. ***Moon in Pisces.***

28 DECEMBER

Romance could blossom, so ensure you organise a special treat. You may be drawn to reconnect with an ex or with an old friend. Try to get the loose ends of important paperwork tied up before Mercury turns retrograde tomorrow to avoid delays down the line. ***Moon in Pisces.***

29 DECEMBER

You may be ready to return to a familiar circumstance or to meeting an old friend. Romance could blossom, especially if you were born in mid-January. Key meetings and financial transactions could be significant. You may be drawn to reconsider a financial or emotional investment. Ensure you have all the details you need to do so to avoid mistakes. ***Moon in Aries.***

30 DECEMBER

You are not known for being impulsive, yet you may be tempted to behave out of character. Avoid making snap decisions as they could backfire. You may be asked to make a fast decision, so ensure you are not pressured into something you do not wish to do. You'll overcome any hurdles with diligence and persistence. ***Moon in Aries.***

31 DECEMBER

Happy New Year! There is a strong romantic flavour to your new year and you'll enjoy being with someone you love and/or with like-minded people. Just avoid making snap decisions as these may not sit well with you in retrospect. You may be inclined to overspend, so keep an eye on your budget. ***Moon enters Taurus.***

THE ESSENCE OF AQUARIUS

You are independent, inventive, quirky, unique and imaginative, yet paradoxically you can also be very traditional. You have a strong social conscience that will drive much of your work and activities. You are a people person: you see yourself as a vital member of the social fabric rather than only as an individual and will at some time in your life fight for a cause even if it's played out in your personal life. Your fight for justice, and humanitarian causes will have cultural and social implications.

Your sign is co-ruled by two planets, Saturn and Uranus. In ancient mythology, Saturn (or Kronos in Greek) is the son of Uranus. These two gods fought and Saturn overthrew his father, discarding his body into the ocean. Venus was born from the discarded body parts. This symbolic myth shows the new order, embodied in the son, Saturn, who overthrows the old order in the shape of the father, Uranus. Your sign, Aquarius, is the repository of this constantly evolving fight in the human condition: how to evolve and move forward in innovative ways without recourse to completely overthrowing and destroying what has been before.

This battle can lead to great inner tension and indecision that comes from weighing up the relative merits of embracing the new and discarding the old. It's as if you have the two gods in constant raging conflict inside you. You'll frequently need to decide whether to hold on to the past or welcome the new, which must often occur in radical ways. You can seem to others to be irrational and quirky, changing your mind at the drop of a hat, yet your decisions will have emerged from the inner battle of choosing which way to go.

If you are indecisive or changeable you do have your reasons. You have a need to innovate and bring the new into being, and to overcome the past in some way. If you can reconcile with the fact that change is a constant you'll always be able to move forward and overthrow the past, and not necessarily in a destructive way.

SELF-ESTEEM

Your self-esteem can take a battering due to the conflicting inner tension that pulls you this way and that. Luckily, the inner tension is often unconscious and only emerges when you're under pressure.

To boost your self-esteem you'll find reward in the study of philosophy, spirituality, art, music, creativity and similar activities that build a sense of collaboration and team spirit such as sport and volunteer work; you'll feel less alone in your existential struggle. When you focus on the outside world you will gain a sense of achievement from having directed restless energy into form and function.

YOUR INNER LIFE

The inner tension that is inherent in Aquarius revolves around the inevitable human condition symbolised by the conflict between Saturn and Uranus: the constant need to review and reset, to progress and yet to value what is time honoured and works well. You are often subconsciously

in the process of trying to reconcile the existing, accepted norms of society, relationships and behaviour with an understanding of the new order to come. On occasion you feel conflicted about what you should do and may even wonder who you are, as you have two such opposing impulses running concurrently inside you: the old order and the new.

Your internal turmoil can be confusing, as you will not be able to choose between wishing to discard the old when there is so much value in it yet knowing you must move forward. This can lead to inaction, especially in loving relationships that provide status quo. If it feels as though the relationship is not progressing you can feel frustrated. The inner debate will arise about the relative value between stability and security versus the new and moving forward.

As a progressive, inventive and eccentric character you need stimulation and can sometimes let excellent situations go because you need change or mental stimulus. It's vital to have a set of checks and balances so you don't allow one particular dominant characteristic to take the lead. Avoid wishing things could stay the same, especially regarding security and stability, rather than wishing for freedom and independence. It's possible for the two to co-exist.

HOW OTHERS SEE YOU

Your quirkiness and independence seem to be at counterpoint to your ability to take charge, make rational decisions and keep a tidy ship. Some Aquarians will vacillate between the two, one week being supremely well organised and the next being all at sea. Other Aquarians will assimilate both the quirkiness and the rationality into your personality and seem a little out there on occasion. You can be a truly eccentric character, behaving in quite unconventional ways. Many Aquarians, though, seem no more oddball than anyone else, but people may often point out anomalies in your rationale where you see none at all. Bear in mind you are a bit of an enigma, so if you prefer to project dependability take the time to present yourself in a stable light to reassure others of your constancy.

You like to retain your independence within relationships, which can feel frustrating for those you hold dear, but depending on your moon sign you can be as affectionate and sensual as anyone else. There is a degree of independence you will not surrender, which can make you hugely attractive to some partners or conversely frustrating to others in your seeming lack of commitment.

HOW TO MAXIMISE YOUR POTENTIAL

Embrace a way to be a traditionalist and an innovator: to be secure and stable on the one hand and outgoing and eccentric on the other, to be both spontaneous and dependable. This is who you are! Embrace your inner tension rather than allowing it to become a problem.

You are a maverick, and it's important to use your innovative abilities and imagination. You like to immerse yourself in pursuits that switch your mind off such as technical and digital media, but you can be prone to repetitive behaviour and bad habits such as alcohol or drug abuse as these may seem to be easy paths to a calm mind.

The true path to a calm mind and one that provides you with a platform from which to gain strength is stability, which is best reached through meditation, visualisation techniques and other calming activities that produce clarity. A real pitfall for you is over-stimulation of your mind to the degree you become confused or frustrated by additional input over and above the already raging undercurrent of deep-down tension.

You are an air sign, and there's no doubt you have a smart mind. Feed and nurture your mind with interesting and diverse activities and it will work at its optimum capacity, opening doors to rewarding insights and experiences.

AQUARIUS AND ITS ASCENDANTS

This chapter is about your sun sign, Aquarius, and your predictions for the year ahead. The more you know about yourself the better you will be able to take advantage of opportunities, and also to avoid the pitfalls. It's critical to know as much about 'you' as possible.

In astrology your core self is represented by your sun sign, but your personality traits are represented by your ascendant (also known as your rising sign). The ascendant describes your personality, the way other people see you on first meeting you and the way you tend to filter life's events.

When you have intimate knowledge about your sun sign – your engine room or core being – you will be on the way to a happier life. When you add the knowledge about your personality – your ascendant – you will gain even deeper insight into what makes you tick.

Your ascendant sign is determined by the time of your birth on the date and year of your birth. Because the ascendant sign changes approximately every two hours, the best way to determine it is to ask an astrologer to calculate it for you. Certain apps will also calculate your ascendant sign (see page 873).

The following gives you more information about your abilities, characteristics and personality according to your sun sign Aquarius in combination with your ascendant sign.

AQUARIUS SUN SIGN WITH ARIES ASCENDANT

You are a fun character, and there will certainly never be a dull moment! Your feisty, upbeat and outgoing personality belies a quirky character beneath: you can appear to be both traditional and authoritarian and a little oddball at the same time. Your positive traits such as being energetic, entrepreneurial and independent are strong, although your negative traits of being unpredictable, reckless, bossy, domineering and obstinate are also strong unless you work on self-improvement. You can be difficult to know because your personality seems straightforward, yet you can tend to change your mind at a whim.

AQUARIUS SUN SIGN WITH TAURUS ASCENDANT

You will be seen by those who first meet you as being a careful, methodical and practical character, someone who is dependable and earthy and enjoys the good things in life and is able to plan ahead one step at a time. When people get to know you you can be quirky, oddball and a little unreliable, which can be confusing. You may be particularly attracted to people who are intense and sensual, people who wish to settle into a routine, and then you may also wish to retain your independence. Find ways to combine your need for freedom with your need for comfort and love and you'll establish positive relationships.

AQUARIUS SUN SIGN WITH GEMINI ASCENDANT

You are a double air sign and tend to initially approach life analytically rather than sensually or intuitively. You have a bright mind and can be a worthy opponent in debate. You can appear as a mercurial, hard-to-pin-down character with many different forms of expression. You may be seen as being constantly on the go, fidgety and restless. Relaxation techniques such as meditation and yoga will help you to avoid over-stimulating your mind, which could lead to indecision, inflexibility and unreliability.

AQUARIUS SUN SIGN WITH CANCER ASCENDANT

You are an enigma: you can appear to be truly sensitive and gentle, introspective and caring, yet when you scratch the surface you are strong willed and stubborn, especially if your will is opposed! The strength of character and inner resourcefulness that lie beneath your gentle personality can surprise those who get to know you. You do have a kind of extrasensory perception, as your Cancerian traits enable you to pick up information about people and circumstances. Combine this with the eccentricity of your Aquarian personality and you really are a unique character with inner strength.

AQUARIUS SUN SIGN WITH LEO ASCENDANT

Your personality is very much the Leo type: preferring to be the centre of attention but also being a loving, creative character. You are a determined person able to overcome immense hurdles and are the king of the jungle. This Aquarius–Leo combination can make for a powerful but potentially also disrespectful character unless you harness the Aquarian intellect and channel it into productive pursuits that celebrate togetherness and compassion. This combination can tend to bring inner tension between wishing to work with others and wishing to put yourself first. When you work out that both are possible you will overcome this dichotomy.

AQUARIUS SUN SIGN WITH VIRGO ASCENDANT

You are a natural-born healer and humanitarian who wishes to make the world a better place. Your perfectionist attitude belies a rebel who is willing to change things beyond the norm, to radically make your life a work of art in the sense that almost nothing is off limits in your pursuit of an ideal. You can be a solid worker, especially when you believe in your career, but you can be a potent foe when your circumstances don't match your mindset or opinions: you will fight methodically and unrelentingly for the outcome you want. Your worst traits are rebelliousness and a repressed mindset that leads to manipulative or self-defeating introspective behaviour.

AQUARIUS SUN SIGN WITH LIBRA ASCENDANT

This is a quirky combination: you are creative and a trendsetter and innovator. You're a thinker yet you can be changeable, going against your own plans and ideas on occasion. Once you have a goal in mind you can work to a plan, even if you seem to be easily distracted. As you're ruled by Venus, love, luxury, art and money are important to you. Your feelings run deep: you wish for a better world but ultimately you are self-sufficient and independent, even if you crave love.

AQUARIUS SUN SIGN WITH SCORPIO ASCENDANT

Your smouldering personality is attractive, charming and on occasion intense. You're drawn to activities that have purpose, and are unlikely to linger long in a relationship that lacks depth or meaning. You're a complex character, being both highly passionate and highly philosophical to the point of detachment. You may alternate between these attributes: emotional in relationships and analytical at work. You have a quirky or dry sense of humour, and inner strength and resourcefulness that help you to overcome and rise above life's challenges.

AQUARIUS SUN SIGN WITH SAGITTARIUS ASCENDANT

You are the life and soul of the party when you're not being serious at work, such as teaching, leading a humanitarian effort or running a mindfulness retreat. You have a sobre message to bring through your life's work regarding compassion and humility, but when the time is right you are an eccentric, fun-loving character. What infuses you with enthusiasm is your lust for life and thirst for knowledge. You may well be changeable, but underneath you're as honest and transparent as the day is long.

AQUARIUS SUN SIGN WITH CAPRICORN ASCENDANT

Yours is a steady, focused and reliable personality, yet underneath you have a quirky and changeable character. You are seen as being quite a surprising individual, able to knuckle down at work when necessary and then dance on tables when the mood takes you. You can certainly aim for a goal and reach it. You may go through phases where you wish to explore other cultures and countries and alternative ideas and ways of living,and then other phases where you wish to be traditional and live life behind a white picket fence.

AQUARIUS SUN SIGN WITH AQUARIUS ASCENDANT

You are a double Aquarius and doubly quirky, humanitarian, practical and fun. You are inventive, resourceful and progressive but you can be doubly stubborn, and your stubbornness can thwart your progressiveness. Be careful with long-term decisions: make sure you're choosing the wise path rather than the open-minded path for the sake of it. If you feel stuck, remember you are the most resourceful of all signs and banish obstinacy.

AQUARIUS SUN SIGN WITH PISCES ASCENDANT

Your ability to combine both an inspired and rational outlook to life may be confusing to some people, but for you there is no paradox: you are an individual! You straddle the creative, spiritual, rational and intellectual in one giant leap, but you can feel confused at times yourself as you are gentle and inspired yet forward-looking and rebellious, able to take a back seat yet wishing to push yourself onward. You are creative, so art, music, teamwork, film, collaborations and inspired spiritual and humanitarian pursuits will nurture your soul.

AQUARIUS IN LOVE

You are such an independent and outgoing character, Aquarius, you are likely to meet many people in your lifetime. In this section you can check out your compatibility with other sun signs. Remember that we are all complex individuals, so the more you know about someone's astrological birth chart the better you can determine your compatibility. Consider having your astrological birth chart compared with that of a partner, friend or family member, as the compatibility – known as 'synastry' in astrology – goes even deeper than a comparison of sun signs, although this is a good place to begin.

AQUARIUS WITH ARIES

You both enjoy excitement and diversity in life but in different ways. Aries is entrepreneurial, dynamic and outgoing whereas you are fundamentally group and community oriented and socially conscious and humanitarian. Aries may appreciate your ability to collaborate and you may appreciate the entrepreneurial approach of Aries; however, you may appear too out there for Aries and Aries too bossy for you. Each sign seems to the other to be unpredictable, which could create a gulf in the partnership unless you make the effort to collaborate on common ground.

AQUARIUS WITH TAURUS

You'll appreciate the sensuality and outward calm of the Taurean, but you may tend to be frustrated by their relative lack of motivation and dynamism unless there is a strong fire element in the Taurus chart. This relationship can be settling, grounding and comforting and can provide the earthiness you sometimes lack. You can both be uncompromising in your view – obstinacy could be a real problem – but if you can agree to disagree on occasion there is every chance that Taurus finds you exciting if impulsive and you find Taurus relaxing and supportive.

AQUARIUS WITH GEMINI

There is fundamental compatibility: your quirkiness will appeal to Gemini's sense of humour and you both give the other the space you need to express yourself. You understand each other's need for independence, as both are free spirits. You are most likely to need stability in the relationship and Gemini's sense of loyalty will respond to your need, as long as you respect their individuality as Gemini can easily feel boxed in. This is generally a favourable combo because both signs appreciate uniqueness and independence and have a fun sense of humour.

AQUARIUS WITH CANCER

Cancerians look for safety, security and emotional contentment in a partnership while you look for excitement, independence and learning, so you are looking for different qualities. While this match may be enticing and exciting at first, unless there are other indicators in your astrology charts such as sun-moon compatibility neither partner is likely to feel fulfilled by the other. Cancer could feel unsupported by you and you may feel beleaguered by Cancer's strong emotions. As companions and friends, however, this can be a light-hearted, fun relationship as both approach life with such different attitudes and each can teach the other much about life.

AQUARIUS WITH LEO

Each sun sign complements the other with this love match. You are eccentric and independent and present Leo with a willing partner for madcap escapades. Leo completes your penchant for spontaneity and excitement. This is a good match as both signs are freedom loving and individualistic. You will enjoy exciting and quirky activities together, sharing an offbeat sense of humour. However, you can both be serious and will wish for a settled family life, although this desire may kick in a bit later in life than for most sun signs.

AQUARIUS WITH VIRGO

You will be attracted to Virgo's earthy sensuality and will admire their ability to reason and analyse. Virgo will initially be attracted to your quirkiness as it creates a sense of excitement. You certainly complement each other's qualities, but fundamentally you are quite different: Virgo is down to earth and sensitive while you can be eccentric and excitable. Your shared interest in humanitarianism and inner calling to help others will unite you, but if your interests vary your character traits may find no common ground in which to blossom.

AQUARIUS WITH LIBRA

You are both searching for happiness: Libra is looking for balance in life and you're looking for a better world. This makes for a good match as long as you appreciate that you go about your goals very differently. You are both fun loving and can be quirky, especially in each other's company, but you both have a deadly serious side that can kick in at a moment's notice. As long as you are in sync with your moods and can be serious for a moment at the same time, this is a match.

AQUARIUS WITH SCORPIO

Both partners may find the other exciting at first as both have the tendency to push boundaries and explore life, but this combination can quickly turn to game, set and match because it may have neither the staying power nor the commitment necessary for a happy partnership. Both signs are stubborn, especially when together! When both are so obstinate there can be little middle ground, and certainly no willingness to adapt or to change let alone to bend to another's will. This is a match as friends and companions, less so romantically.

AQUARIUS WITH SAGITTARIUS

This is an upbeat and fun match: you motivate each other to enjoy life's merry-go-round and explore new experiences. Neither of you is afraid to step into new territory, and together you make a fearless team. Long-distance travel, study, research and learning about all manner of wisdom will provide hours of conversation and fun. You may feel attracted to the Sagittarian eagerness for escapades, and Sagittarius will admire your ability to roll your sleeves up when the pressure is on.

AQUARIUS WITH CAPRICORN

Capricorn is attracted to your quirky, upbeat approach to life and will appreciate the revitalising sense of freedom in the relationship, but may wish to commit to a steady relationship sooner than you are willing to. Capricorn may wish for a more traditional role in the partnership while you prefer to retain independence even if you are able to commit to a relationship, and this may grate on Capricorn. While you may be initially attracted to Capricorn's sense of duty, reliability and earthiness, you may come to see Capricorn as staid and uncompromising. However, as you mature you'll come to value their dependability.

AQUARIUS WITH AQUARIUS

Together you are stronger, especially if you both develop your better qualities such as humanitarianism, compassion and ingenuity, but if you both operate from your negative qualities of obstinacy, rebellion, changeability and extremism you may rebel against each other. Your ability to emotionally detach from circumstances and from each other may also spell an inability to form a close bond, but if you unite under your common aim to make the world a better place and operate from your greater selves this a potential match.

AQUARIUS WITH PISCES

You are both creative, ingenious, inventive and dreamers. You are idealists but also pragmatic. If both partners have integrated their better qualities and operate without difficulty at full potential this makes a wonderful match, as you can support each other's projects, creativity and goals in life. If either partner doesn't know how to approach life both creatively and rationally this match could be confusing if not frustrating.

THE YEAR AHEAD FOR AQUARIUS

Affirmation: *'I'll follow a deeper calling.'*

The year starts with the very real opportunity to make changes in your personal life that will alter the way you are seen and how you see yourself. Saturn in your sign all year wishes to bring change into being in small, bite-sized pieces, and Uranus will help in this endeavour.

You are in a strong position this year to find security and stability via the change that occurs, so aim to manage your position and your circumstances will support you. Consider also that you may be underestimating your abilities. If so, and you do nothing to improve your life by using your skill sets, life will make change happen to you and you may not like it! It is far better to instigate changes in the way you wish them to be by responding to a sense of calling or finding out more about your own purpose.

You are likely to be drawn to new organisations early in the year and to explore new friendships and groups. The eclipses in 2022 will be across your communications and travel sectors, suggesting the way you interact with others will be a true turning point for you. If you're interested in study and boosting various skill sets, 2022 is your year to improve your circumstances.

The conjunction of Venus and Mars in February suggests this year's Valentine's Day may be more poignant than many. You may meet a long-lost friend or reunite with an ex. This illustrates the kind of growth you achieve this year: a combination of reviewing the past to break into something new. In the process of this reshaping of your life you may find that obstacles seem to block your way. Know that you will gain strength from overcoming hindrances as you move forward and reshape the things to come.

HEALTH

Pluto in your 12th house of health suggests you have some way to go to transform your daily routine so that it better promotes your health and well-being. You'll find that 2023 will help you to do just this in many adventurous ways, and that 2022 is very much about allowing yourself to let go of the bad habits that hinder good health in preparation for a new you in 2023.

It may prove particularly difficult to shed certain ingrained routines and habits that have formed over many years and created a pattern, so asking for professional help would assist you this year if you find your health suffers due to changes that are outside your control.

Peak stress points health-wise will be in January and September, although the eclipse seasons in April-May and October-November could bring out your reluctance to alter your health routines. Take this stubbornness as an indication that you need to make change.

FINANCES

Neptune will be in your money sector all year, so this is a year to be super careful with investments, planning and spending as you may be easily misled to undertake financial incentives that may not be exactly right for you.

You may be particularly inclined to overspend in the first six months of the year and will need the second six months to adjust repayments. It is better to avoid overspending in the first place and to work on a sustainable budget in January.

Luckily, the moon's north nodes in Taurus will help you to keep your feet on the ground with your spending habits. Nevertheless, do not underestimate the power of Neptune in your second house to mislead you financially, even if you do have good prospects for improved earning capacity this year.

HOME LIFE

Be prepared to adapt to new domestic circumstances this year. Once the sun enters your fourth house of home, family and property at the mid/end of May, followed by Venus at the end of June and Mars at the end of August, you will find change takes place at a fast pace.

You may feel restless and will wish to travel. You may also feel more neighbourly and will place extra focus on your home during these months. However, you may feel ready to make changes at home such as a little DIY or a move, but avoid making changes for the sake of them. You'll gain the chance in the last quarter of the year to reconsider in a better light any of your decisions to do with your home life.

LOVE

The eclipses in 2022 will alter how you communicate with those who are important to you, which will mean that your relationships will change. You may be surprised by revelations and perhaps even by your own responses to other people's communications and circumstances. Stress points for communications will be in January, April-May and October-November. During these times, bear in mind that those you have a strong bond with may be finding life particularly difficult and therefore a compassionate approach will work wonders.

Your values and interests are likely to change this year, which means you will be relating with others from a different baseline. If you're aware that this process is occurring, then the more you can communicate the better so those close to you can also adapt.

Singles may find that you begin to look for company that is as diverse as the changes in your own life. You'll enjoy meeting people from various backgrounds and learning more about their values and principles, informing yourself as you progress.

CAREER

This year you'll find it increasingly difficult to follow a career that has little meaning to you other than funding your lifestyle. In other words, you are going to be more drawn to expressing your true interests in your everyday life, including your career. While this may appear difficult initially and at various stress points during the year, you will find a way to break into a new mould should you wish to.

Major stress points and opportunities to diversify in your career will fall at similar times in April-May and October-November. It is only by realising that the troubling circumstances of the path you're on no longer suit you that you'll find a new path.

Of course, if you're happy with your career the likelihood is that you'll continue to follow your chosen path, and new opportunities, especially in the first quarter and in the October-November phase, will arise.

At mid-year you may discover an interest and aptitude for something that catches your attention and that may also be lucrative.

As you embrace an adventurous attitude to what you can do in your career you'll find that new doors open. Good times for launching fresh ideas and projects are the new moons on 2 January and 1 February, as long as you check your financial situation carefully. The second half of the year will be ideal for reviewing your progress so far in 2022 and deciding whether or not you wish to tweak some of your plans and projects. If so, the new moon on 28 July will be ideal for beginning something fresh.

Remember that if you experience difficulties in September-October it will alert you to the fact that what you do must have more significance to you than money alone, so think big picture and not small potatoes!

January

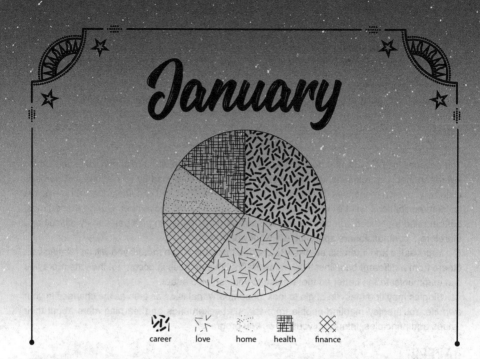

career love home health finance

Notes: the pie charts such as the one above listed for each month show energy distribution according to the stars for the month ahead. If you wish to make changes in the areas of your finances, health, career, love or home and you see there is a large amount of energy in that sector in the chart, your endeavours should succeed as long as you have prepared well in advance. The charts also show which areas will potentially have the most focus in your life during the month.

The moon sign listed for each day's entry in the diary is the position of the moon at the end of the day in Greenwich Mean Time (GMT). To gain the most information about a particular day's circumstances, read the day before and the day after for a complete picture.

1 JANUARY

Happy New Year! You'll enjoy a pleasant surprise or sociable start to the new year that will add to a fun vibe. Be prepared to embrace something new this year. *Moon enters Capricorn.*

2 JANUARY

The new moon and supermoon in Capricorn will kick-start a fresh phase for you in a social context, especially if you were born in February, and at work or regarding health and well-being if you were born in January. You'll be ready for something new in either area or in both. You may experience an ego or financial boost. If you're shopping in the sales you may spy a bargain!

3 JANUARY

This is a good time to decide how you'd like to see your work life and general well-being develop this year. You may be drawn to something new but must ensure your ideas are practical as well as inspired. *Moon enters Aquarius.*

4 JANUARY

The Aquarian moon will encourage you to be innovative and imaginative with your various projects and plans, especially to do with work and your personal life. Avoid being deterred by aspirations that may seem to cause upheaval. The end result will be worthwhile if you plan ahead well and keep those your plans will affect in the loop. *Moon in Aquarius.*

5 JANUARY

You'll enjoy a pleasant change of pace. If you're back at work there will be benefits you'll enjoy of being in a familiar routine. If you're socialising you'll appreciate the time to catch up with favourite people. Romance could blossom, so organise a treat! *Moon in Aquarius.*

6 JANUARY

If you're shopping avoid overspending if you're already in debt. Leave the credit card at home if you are. You'll get the chance to reframe some of your plans if you discover your expectations have exceeded reality. *Moon in Pisces.*

7 JANUARY

You're feeling creative and may also feel more romantic than usual, so why not organise a treat? Your instincts and intuition are in top form, so be sure to use them if you're in doubt about decisions. You may also tend to be forgetful so be prepared to focus, especially at work. *Moon in Pisces.*

8 JANUARY

This is an excellent day to get things done, so plan to complete chores so that you also have time for socialising and enjoying yourself. You'll appreciate the chance to catch up with someone you admire. *Moon in Aries.*

9 JANUARY

You'll enjoy a reunion and spending time with your favourite people and on your favourite activities. Music, the arts, dance and film will all appeal. If you're shopping avoid overspending, as you may be a little overindulgent. *Moon in Aries.*

10 JANUARY

You'll appreciate the opportunity to get things shipshape both at home and at work. You may be drawn to an old haunt and will enjoy a reunion. ***Moon enters Taurus.***

11 JANUARY

Meetings and talks are likely to go well, especially at work and concerning health and well-being. However, it's important to focus on the facts or you may tend to gloss over the details and could make mistakes or be misled as a result. ***Moon in Taurus.***

12 JANUARY

The Taurus moon brings out your practical and realistic qualities and you'll appreciate the opportunity to be hands-on with your projects and make progress as a result. However, some developments may proceed more slowly than you'd prefer, so be patient and keep working towards your goals. ***Moon in Taurus.***

13 JANUARY

You'll appreciate a lighter feel to proceedings and will manage to make changes to your circumstances if necessary. Try to get key paperwork and financial matters resolved before Mercury turns retrograde tomorrow to avoid delays over the next few weeks. Back up computers and files for the best measure. ***Moon in Gemini.***

14 JANUARY

You may receive key news that may be unexpected or signals you will need to reconsider or review your position. Be careful with negotiations, finances and communications as unexpected developments will require some focus. ***Moon in Gemini.***

15 JANUARY

The Gemini moon enables you to be analytical and reasonable about your decisions and activities, making this an excellent time to strategise, especially with work and domestic matters. You'll enjoy a sense of freedom of movement, and if you haven't yet you'll find ways to do so. ***Moon enters Cancer.***

16 JANUARY

A reunion or a return to an old haunt may bring intense memories to the surface. If you are working you may be busy or will need to bring on board changes into your usual routine. This is a good time to consider how to improve your health and well-being. ***Moon in Cancer.***

17 JANUARY

The Cancerian full moon spotlights a new chapter. For some this will be at work, for others concerning health and for some there is a new chapter concerning a creative project or family. If you've been considering starting a family or a new era is beginning in your personal life this full moon will spotlight your feelings. Developments could be transformational.

18 JANUARY

The full moon is likely to bring out strong emotions, so be prepared to take time out if necessary. It's a transformational time for you, so get ready to take action. A partner may have key news. *Moon in Leo.*

19 JANUARY

You'll enjoy having the opportunity to boost your circumstances, especially at work and socially. A get-together will be encouraging and motivating. *Moon in Leo.*

20 JANUARY

The sun in your own sign of Aquarius for the next four weeks will be motivational and you'll appreciate feeling more in your element. You may enjoy a change in the air that provides a sense of progress and optimism. *Moon in Leo.*

21 JANUARY

The moon in Virgo brings your practical can-do qualities to the surface, enabling you to socialise and network effectively. You'll enjoy the chance to organise events for the weekend, and work and your personal activities are likely to go well with careful planning and diligence. *Moon in Virgo.*

22 JANUARY

You'll enjoy a reunion or a return to an old haunt. You may hear from an old friend. A debt may need to be repaid, so find ways to balance your budget. You may be repaid a debt yourself. If you're shopping avoid overspending, as you may be prone to overindulging. *Moon enters Libra.*

23 JANUARY

This is a good day for get-togethers and reunions, especially if it's your birthday. You may enjoy a trip down memory lane. Key news is on the way that could encourage you to be more adventurous in your personal life. *Moon in Libra.*

24 JANUARY

You understand the importance of reasonable and logical thinking and have an eye for what's fair and equal, which will help you to make balanced decisions. You may be called on to mediate or help someone. *Moon in Libra.*

25 JANUARY

This is a lovely day for meetings and get-togethers, especially at work. It's also a good day for a health appointment. If you need to review a project or an idea this is a good day to gather information and for research. *Moon in Scorpio.*

26 JANUARY

You may be drawn to revisit past circumstances or an old haunt. It's a good day to review paperwork, decisions and agreements, especially at work and regarding health and well-being. You will enjoy a reunion and may get the time to spruce up your appearance and well-being. *Moon in Scorpio.*

27 JANUARY

You may be motivated to take action with a project or idea that has been simmering in the back of your mind for a while. It's a good day for research, learning and travel. *Moon in Sagittarius.*

28 JANUARY

The moon at the zenith of your chart will bring out your inner adventurer. You may even surprise yourself with the projects and plan you formulate. Be bold! *Moon in Sagittarius.*

29 JANUARY

You may hear news from your past that could be from an old friend, colleague or family member. You may return to an old haunt. This is a good day for a health appointment. News may be intense but also potentially transformative. *Moon in Capricorn.*

30 JANUARY

You may be surprised by news, a change of plan or an impromptu get-together. For some a financial situation will require additional focus. Avoid gambling. *Moon in Capricorn.*

31 JANUARY

You may hear positive news. This is a good day for a health or beauty appointment. Romance could flourish, so organise a treat! You'll enjoy a reunion. *Moon in Aquarius.*

February

career love home health finance

1 FEBRUARY

The new moon in Aquarius will kick-start a fresh phase in your personal life, especially if it's your birthday: happy birthday! If you were born later in February be prepared for a fresh work or health routine to kick in soon. You'll enjoy some impromptu get-togethers or surprises, but if you are disappointed put it down to experience and avoid taking someone's situation personally.

2 FEBRUARY

This is a good time to consider your long-term aims and goals and to avoid getting too attached to the fact you haven't attained them all yet. Pace yourself and be patient with someone who can be emotional. Careful negotiations and talks will reap rewards. *Moon enters Pisces.*

3 FEBRUARY

You are creative and romantic when the moon is in Pisces and will be drawn to music, good food and company. You may tend to be a little emotional and will appreciate exploring your emotions, but if you feel they are more exaggerated than usual blame it on the stars! Trust your intuition if you're unsure of someone. *Moon in Pisces.*

4 FEBRUARY

This is a good day to make a commitment to a certain path or plan of action. For January-born Aquarians this is likely to be in your personal life, and for those born later at work or regarding a health plan. Be prepared to knuckle down and fulfil duties. You may receive key news that spotlights your best approach, but may also be easily influenced. You'll enjoy a reunion. *Moon in Pisces.*

5 FEBRUARY

This is a good day to press pause and take time out. You may simply be tired and will require some time to recharge your batteries. Your vulnerabilities and doubts may emerge, so take things one step at a time. Someone may need your help or vice versa. You'll enjoy socialising or spending time with someone who inspires you. *Moon in Aries.*

6 FEBRUARY

There is a therapeutic atmosphere to the day, one where taking time out makes sense especially if you have been overworking or stressed. That said, a lovely social event, catch-up by phone or meeting will be uplifting. *Moon in Aries.*

7 FEBRUARY

A practical approach to your workload and the people you must collaborate and get on with will work well for you. Avoid taking other people's personal problems personally, but you may be asked for help or will be in a position to offer guidance. If you need help with a personal or work matter it will be available. *Moon in Taurus.*

8 FEBRUARY

You'll enjoy an exciting change of routine and may be surprised by some developments or by a chance meeting. You may find that a change of circumstance brings new opportunities into being. An impromptu get-together is likely to be refreshing. *Moon in Taurus.*

9 FEBRUARY

A considerable amount of focus on your past may create a nostalgic mood, yet there is a lot to be positive about at present. A tough matter is best approached from a realistic perspective, especially if you feel some matters could be improved. *Moon enters Gemini.*

10 FEBRUARY

This is a good day to improve both your appearance and self-esteem, so look for inspiring ideas, platforms and talks that help you improve yourself. This is an ideal time to improve your finances, so if you are in line for a promotion or are considering a fresh investment look into it a little more. It's also a good day for meetings and romance; just avoid overspending. *Moon in Gemini.*

11 FEBRUARY

You may receive good news at work or regarding health and well-being. A reunion could be pivotal or will bring you in touch with someone you feel you have a fated link with. If you find events intense or disappointing, take time out to unwind and recalibrate when you can. **Moon in Cancer.**

12 FEBRUARY

The Cancerian moon for the next two days is ideal to do a mini review about how far you've already come this year, both at work and in your personal life. You could go a long way with a personal or family project, especially if you feel truly invested in the outcome. If not, it's time to rethink your plans. **Moon in Cancer.**

13 FEBRUARY

You'll feel motivated by your work or a personal project. You may feel more emotional about a situation than usual, so ensure you maintain perspective. **Moon in Cancer.**

14 FEBRUARY

Happy St Valentine's Day! You'll enjoy reconnecting with someone from your past. You may experience strong emotions and could deepen your understanding of someone. Couples will enjoy bolstering your ties. **Moon in Leo.**

15 FEBRUARY

You are generally a progressive character but you can be obstinate if you're unsure of yourself or of someone close. Find the time to research your options more deeply if you're uncertain and avoid having an oppositional approach. **Moon in Leo.**

16 FEBRUARY

The Leo full moon will shine a light on your relationships, especially if you were born in January or before today. You may be ready to alter a key business or personal partnership. Key romantic developments could mean the start of a fresh phase. Singles may meet someone new and exciting. Couples could deepen your relationship or, if you've been on different tracks for some time, may realise you are better apart. A meeting will be significant at work or socially. **Moon enters Virgo late in the day.**

17 FEBRUARY

You may be surprised by news. This is a good day for making agreements and arrangements, especially those that concern work, health or finances. You may receive an unexpected compliment or an ego boost. **Moon in Virgo.**

18 FEBRUARY

As the sun enters the zodiac sign Pisces you'll appreciate the opportunity over the next four weeks to take more time for yourself and your personal life. Consider who and what mean the most to you and find ways to incorporate these elements into your life. *Moon in Virgo.*

19 FEBRUARY

You'll appreciate the opportunity to find more balance, peace and harmony in your life this weekend. If that involves socialising you'll love reconnecting with friends and meeting new people, but if peace and balance equal a quiet, healing time you'll find this truly satisfying as well. *Moon in Libra.*

20 FEBRUARY

This is a sociable time for you and you'll enjoy being with inspiring people and in beautiful environments. Tune in to music, the arts and pleasant surroundings to regain a sense of contentment if you feel your peace of mind has been disturbed. *Moon in Libra.*

21 FEBRUARY

You're more motivated by your projects and the people you look up to, so ensure you stride out and make headway towards projects and activities that have meaning for you. *Moon enters Scorpio.*

22 FEBRUARY

You're inspired but may also tend to have less patience for people who are obstructive and uncompromising, so avoid being similarly uncompromising in reaction. Trust your instincts as these will guide you down the right path if some situations seem more intense than they need be. *Moon in Scorpio.*

23 FEBRUARY

This is a good day for get-togethers and for indulging in the people and activities you love. A social or work meeting is likely to go well. A financial matter could progress and you may experience a financial boost or receive a compliment, but if you're investing in something ensure you have researched it adequately to avoid mistakes. Romance could flourish over the next two days, so organise a treat! *Moon in Sagittarius.*

24 FEBRUARY

This is another lovely day for romance, socialising and getting projects off the ground that will lead to success. Be positive. If you've been considering a new look you may find just the outfit or haircut today. This is also a good time for a health or beauty appointment. *Moon in Sagittarius.*

25 FEBRUARY

You may receive unexpected news and may need to reconsider a project, financial matter or personal investment. Avoid taking things personally, looking instead at productive ways to get ahead. Travel and communications may be delayed or erratic, so ensure you give yourself adequate time for travel. Back up computers for the best measure. *Moon enters Capricorn.*

26 FEBRUARY

A meeting or financial transaction will raise your mood. You may receive a financial or ego boost. If you're shopping avoid overspending, as you may be inclined to impulse buy. Communications will be better than yesterday, so this is a good day for get-togethers. *Moon in Capricorn.*

27 FEBRUARY

You'll appreciate the chance to get your feet on the ground and catch your breath. Gardening, being in nature and generally reconnecting with people you love will be enjoyable. *Moon enters Aquarius.*

28 FEBRUARY

The moon in your own sign brings out your inner quirkiness. You'll enjoy doing something different from your usual schedule, and could also kick a key goal. You'll enjoy a reunion or the chance to reconnect with someone lovely. *Moon in Aquarius.*

March

career   love   home   health   finance

1 MARCH

While you aim to be professional at work and supportive at home you can't always please everyone! This is one such day when you may notice that some people are not going to be pleased with your ideas or communications. However, other talks will be upbeat and enjoyable. ***Moon enters Pisces.***

2 MARCH

The Pisces new moon signals a good time to seek inspiration, especially in your personal life. Find the time to be with those you love and to minimise contact with those whose influence is annoying or oppositional. You'll enjoy being spontaneous and may receive unexpectedly good news. Think laterally and trust your instincts.

3 MARCH

The Venus-Mars-Pluto conjunction signals great change for you, especially at work and in your health routine for some. You have the chance to put in place clever ideas and plans, especially in these two areas of your life. Be inspired by those you love. Make appointments that will fully inform your decisions. Be sure to align your actions with your higher purpose. ***Moon in Pisces.***

4 MARCH

You will feel inspired by your big-picture plans and goals and may feel drawn to people and places that reflect your principles and values. However, you may also tend to be a little idealistic so ensure your plans are practical. ***Moon in Aries.***

5 MARCH

You'll enjoy a get-together with someone whose presence can be a little larger than life. You may be contemplating long-distance travel or a project that will broaden your horizons. Be positive and inspired. Romance could blossom. News could be just what you want to hear, but if not maintain perspective and look for constructive ways forward. ***Moon in Aries.***

6 MARCH

As both Mars and Venus enter your sign you'll be looking at life with more zest and optimism over the coming weeks and months. You may be ready to step into new terrain at work or regarding health and well-being. A personal matter may be truly motivational and you'll feel ready to invest more in yourself and in someone special. ***Moon in Taurus.***

7 MARCH

A get-together is likely to propel you forward into a more optimistic phase. If you feel a little tense or ill at ease, find ways to relax and focus on your goals and the reason you are doing what you are doing. The Taurean moon will motivate you to be practical and hands-on. Be open-minded, especially regarding new work and personal experiences. ***Moon in Taurus.***

8 MARCH

This is a good day for discussions, meetings and work and health appointments. A debt may be repaid or you may repay one. You'll enjoy a reunion or hearing from an old friend or colleague. ***Moon enters Gemini.***

9 MARCH

The Gemini moon is invigorating for you, especially mentally. You'll feel stimulated by upbeat company and will enjoy get-togethers, both at work and in your personal life. You may feel chattier and more adaptable and willing to see other people's perspectives. ***Moon in Gemini.***

10 MARCH

As Mercury enters Pisces you will feel increasingly drawn to look at life from a romantic point of view, especially your personal relationships. You may also be drawn to considering fresh ways to invest your time, energy and money. Just ensure that you adequately research your investments over the next few weeks to avoid disappointments. This is a good day to make a commitment to a new project or investment if you've already done your research. ***Moon in Gemini.***

11 MARCH

You'll appreciate finding the time for someone special and for a favourite interest, activity or hobby. You'll also enjoy blowing off steam after a busy week. **Moon in Cancer.**

12 MARCH

Trust your gut instincts at work and with personal and health matters, as they are working well for you. You'll enjoy getting together with people who have similar interests and may enjoy an ideal circumstance. Avoid delays and misunderstandings by planning ahead and being super aware. **Moon in Cancer.**

13 MARCH

You may hear positive work, financial or personal news. Romance could blossom over shared interests and pastimes. You may experience a compliment or ego boost. This is an excellent day to invest in yourself and in those you love. You may be tempted to overindulge or overspend, which you'll regret tomorrow! **Moon enters Leo.**

14 MARCH

It's a good day for work meetings and financial matters, especially if you are super clear about your aims and goals. You may experience a financial or ego boost. It's also a good day for a health or beauty treat. **Moon in Leo.**

15 MARCH

The Leo moon will be motivational for you but may bring out other people's feistiness, so avoid arguments especially if you feel someone is restless or spoiling for a fight. **Moon in Leo.**

16 MARCH

Keep an eye on your goals, especially in your personal life and at home, to avoid being distracted by other people's agendas. An important meeting or financial decision could work to your advantage as long as you have checked all the details. **Moon in Virgo.**

17 MARCH

You may experience a surprise, and for some this will involve your home life or family and for others your finances. Someone you like may pleasantly surprise you. Be open to change. **Moon in Virgo.**

18 MARCH

This is a good time to work out what your priorities are, not only at work and in your general direction in life but also in your personal relationships. The Virgo full moon shines a light on the

areas of life you share such as your joint finances and responsibilities. You may be ready to make fresh agreements with someone but must be sure of the variables.

19 MARCH

An unexpected development will spotlight the difference in attitude between you and someone who can be unpredictable. A change of routine at home or at work will benefit from a spontaneous but also realistic approach. You may need to adapt to a new environment. *Moon in Libra.*

20 MARCH

When the sun enters Aries it is the equinox. During the next four weeks you will feel more motivated to change the way you conduct some of your relationships and communications. You may be drawn to invest more heavily in yourself and in someone special. Just avoid impulsiveness and ensure you maintain perspective of your big-picture goals. *Moon in Scorpio.*

21 MARCH

Key financial or personal decisions are likely to be made. You may feel drawn to invest more heavily in your work and personal life. Your investments are likely to pay off if you've done adequate research. However, some changes may involve the need to be more careful with your self-expression, as an unpredictable circumstance deserves careful focus. *Moon in Scorpio.*

22 MARCH

Today is a mixed bag. On the one hand it's a good time for communications and especially for financial transactions, but if you take risks you may make mistakes. On the other hand you may not get on with everyone and misunderstandings could occur. Avoid losing digital information by backing up computers and factor in extra time for travel to avoid delays if possible. Someone may surprise you or you will need to rethink a plan. *Moon enters Sagittarius.*

23 MARCH

You will gain insight into a personal or financial situation. It's a good day for financial matters as long as you have done adequate research, otherwise you will be open to losses. The spiritually inclined may reach an epiphany and an interest in art and music will blossom. A romantic tie could deepen, so plan a treat. *Moon in Sagittarius.*

24 MARCH

You'll gain more clarity about a work or personal investment, but some situations will still merit a careful approach. Avoid ignoring red flags. You'll enjoy socialising and networking, although you won't necessarily see eye to eye with everyone so be tactful to avoid arguments. *Moon enters Capricorn.*

25 MARCH

Mars, Venus and Saturn in your sign are encouraging you to try new ideas, and there's no time like the present! Be bold and enjoy being free to choose who you spend your time with as you'll enjoy socialising and networking. Keep an open mind about developments rather than getting bogged down in arguments. *Moon in Capricorn.*

26 MARCH

You'll relish the change of pace. A reunion will be fun and you may also enjoy some retail therapy. A change of place will be refreshing, but if you find some events are intense take time out to recalibrate your thoughts. *Moon in Capricorn.*

27 MARCH

This is a good day for boosting your relationships with those you love. Romance could flourish. Financial and personal decisions may seem easy to make but you may be tempted to overestimate circumstances, so ensure you do your research and especially if you're planning large investments of your time or money. *Moon in Aquarius.*

28 MARCH

A key meeting or financial transaction could alter how you go about your work or home life, especially if you were born on 9 or 10 February. You may be prepared to make a commitment or will need to state your true feelings and opinions to those who they affect. A situation may seem ideal and it may well be, but you must double-check the details to be sure. *Moon in Aquarius.*

29 MARCH

You are prepared to invest in yourself and your plans and projects and this is a good time to look at the positives. However, you may tend to be idealistic and must check that your activities align with your deeper sense of purpose and your aims and goals. A meeting will bring out your inner romantic. *Moon in Pisces.*

30 MARCH

This is a good day for a beauty or health treatment. You may have a financial or ego boost. Romance is alive, so singles may meet someone charming and couples could rekindle passion. If you are making long-term decisions, ensure you have adequately researched the circumstances. *Moon in Pisces.*

31 MARCH

The Aries moon can bring out your inner hero and you may even surprise yourself with some of the actions you take. Be bold but avoid impulsiveness, as it could land you in hot water. *Moon in Aries.*

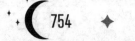

April

career   love   home   health   finance

1 APRIL

The Aries new moon suggests a meeting, new environment or trip will take you somewhere different and could alter how you go about your relationships. A fresh approach to communications, travel or finances will be beneficial for you. You may be drawn to update a digital device or vehicle. Someone may need your help. If you need advice it will be available, so find an expert. A health or travel matter may need attention. For some this new moon points to a fresh financial circumstance that will have to be negotiated.

2 APRIL

An impromptu get-together, surprise news or spontaneous trip somewhere different will be enjoyable, so be bold and try something new! Someone special will be unexpectedly helpful or may need your help. ***Moon enters Taurus.***

3 APRIL

This is a good day to make changes to your circumstances, especially your personal life and the way you go about your usual daily routine. Consider how you might improve your self-esteem. You may receive a compliment or ego boost and will be drawn to improving your appearance and health. A reunion will be enjoyable. ***Moon in Taurus.***

4 APRIL

The next two days are good for making headway with your ideas and plans, especially those involving a financial or personal investment. Work, sports and generally feeling more energetic will boost your morale; just avoid being impulsive. *Moon in Taurus.*

5 APRIL

You'll gain clarity about your circumstances. A commitment may be made, especially if you were born from 10 to 12 February, and you will be prepared to take your plans to the next level. *Moon in Gemini.*

6 APRIL

This is a good day for talks and making agreements, especially financially. You may experience a financial or ego boost. Personal matters can also thrive, so if you're looking for more romance in your life this is it! Take the time to discuss your ideas with someone you know has your back. *Moon in Gemini.*

7 APRIL

You can make great progress with meetings, and travel is likely to go well. Again, romance could blossom. Just avoid making assumptions and both financial and emotional gambling. *Moon in Cancer.*

8 APRIL

You'll enjoy a get-together or a trip somewhere beautiful. The arts, music, dance and romance will all thrive under these stars, so be sure to organise something fun. *Moon in Cancer.*

9 APRIL

You'll relish a change of environment and get-togethers. You may enjoy investing in your own environment, such as your garden or neighborhood. This is a good time to beautify your surroundings and yourself. You'll enjoy investing more in yourself and in those you love. *Moon in Cancer.*

10 APRIL

A powerful character at work or in your personal life will demand your attention over the next two days. Communications may not be as positive as you might hope, as someone and perhaps even you will not agree with the way things are done. There may be misunderstandings or travel delays, so be patient. Avoid tense or sensitive topics if possible as these will escalate quickly into arguments. Back up computers for the best results. *Moon in Leo.*

11 APRIL

There is still likely to be tension surrounding a personal or work matter, so ensure you keep communications channels open to avoid a Mexican stand-off. Communications will get onto a more even keel as you gain a sense of progress, especially regarding travel, your neighbourhood and environment. There may still be travel delays so be patient. *Moon in Leo.*

12 APRIL

You may find you need to agree to disagree with some people, or you could reach a stalemate. This aside, you could boost your status, self-esteem, career and finances so ensure you take steps to focus on any or all of these areas as you could make headway. Romance could blossom, but you must check you're not seeing life through rose-coloured glasses. *Moon in Leo.*

13 APRIL

This is a good day to make a commitment, especially financially and at work. If health has been an issue this is a good time to devise a new and practical health and fitness routine. *Moon in Virgo.*

14 APRIL

You'll enjoy getting together with inspiring people and will appreciate music and dance and being creative. If you're shopping you may be inclined to overindulge and overspend, so if you're already in debt leave the credit card at home. A lovely meeting with someone you're attracted to could turn to romance. *Moon enters Libra.*

15 APRIL

As Mars leaves your sign you may notice a change in energy levels over the next few days. You may feel more in need of rest and recuperation and your mind may turn to spirituality and the feel-good factors in life such as relaxation and self-care. However, you may also tend to be idealistic, so ensure you keep your feet on the ground if you are making key decisions over the next month. *Moon in Libra.*

16 APRIL

The Libran full moon signifies the start of a fresh cycle for you, and you'll be drawn to find more balance and harmony in your life and especially in your projects or activities. A study, legal, travel or personal matter may require a little extra attention. For some this full moon signals the opportunity to consider how to organise your shared duties, collaborations or joint finances in a more balanced or equal way.

17 APRIL

The moon at the zenith of your chart will put your focus more firmly on your activities and general direction, and you're likely to feel more motivated by your ideas, plans and ventures. This is a good time to invest extra energy into favourite activities. A visit or change at home may be spontaneous or unexpected. *Moon in Scorpio.*

18 APRIL

You may be surprised by a spontaneous get-together at home or a visit. You may hear from the past and a trip or communications may be a little tense, so avoid escalating stress if you see it is already a factor. A financial and domestic matter can progress, so take the initiative. *Moon in Scorpio.*

19 APRIL

You're likely to feel increasingly motivated by what you do and to get good results, but if you are not this is a good time to change this situation! Once the moon enters Sagittarius you'll feel more outgoing and able to express yourself. *Moon enters Sagittarius.*

20 APRIL

The sun in Taurus for the next four weeks will bring out your ability to be strategic and grounded, which will help improve your communications and relationships. This is a good time to find ways to improve your communications and travel matters in the most realistic way. *Moon in Sagittarius.*

21 APRIL

This is a good time to consider how you can bring about the results you want both at work and in your health. If you are looking for a promotion this is a good time to talk to your employer, and if you are looking for work to circulate your resume. *Moon in Capricorn.*

22 APRIL

You'll enjoy making time for yourself and those you love such as family and friends. If you have any logistics to overcome you will manage to do so through paying extra attention to the realities of your situation as opposed to what you wish for. *Moon in Capricorn.*

23 APRIL

A meeting or a trip will take you into familiar territory, which you'll enjoy. You may wish to make changes at home and will gain insight into the best way to do this. Avoid seeing obstacles as insurmountable as they may be opportunities in disguise. *Moon in Aquarius.*

24 APRIL

It's a good idea to take things one step at a time as you may be inclined to leap feet first into a situation that could merit a little restraint. This is mostly because right now you may be easily misled. Avoid arguments with someone who can be obstinate as conflict will only get you stuck. A trip may be delayed or postponed. *Moon in Aquarius.*

25 APRIL

Your diligence is a real credit to you but sometimes it can spill over into obstinacy. Double-check that a work or personal situation isn't stuck due to your own stubbornness or someone else's, and find ways to keep things moving. *Moon in Pisces.*

26 APRIL

Communications could improve so consider making headway with domestic and personal matters if they're stuck. However, you must avoid being a little idealistic, especially about some relationships and finances. *Moon in Pisces.*

27 APRIL

You'll enjoy a trip or a meeting as it's likely to be productive if not lucrative. Financial transactions could be profitable and you may enjoy a financial or ego boost. Just ensure you have researched circumstances adequately if you are making considerable investments. If you're single you may feel positive about meeting people in a friendly environment. *Moon enters Aries.*

28 APRIL

This is a good day for making changes, both at work and at home and especially if you work from home. For some Aquarians this is a good day for travel and for improving your health and well-being. *Moon in Aries.*

29 APRIL

You may receive key news at work or regarding health. A domestic or personal matter will enter a new phase in which you may feel a little restless or in need of more freedom of movement. A trip or the chance to do something different will be inspiring. *Moon in Aries.*

30 APRIL

The partial solar eclipse in Taurus signals you are ready to make a new agreement. For some this will be financial in nature and for others in your personal life, such as the beginning or the end of a key relationship. Before committing to a fresh path ensure your principles and values are in sync with the new circumstances. If not it may be time to alter some aspects of proposed agreements or embrace a fresh set of values.

May

career love home health finance

1 MAY

This is a good time to invest in yourself via your health, well-being and appearance. You may enjoy a reunion and/or the time to spend relaxing and enjoying being with someone you love. Romance could blossom. *Moon in Taurus.*

2 MAY

As Venus enters Aries you'll feel more upbeat and dynamic, especially in connection with finances and your personal life. Your self-esteem is likely to improve. However, you may be inclined to overspend or overindulge, so if you're already in debt be careful. Keep a check on your emotions, too, as you may be prone to being a little impulsive. *Moon in Gemini.*

3 MAY

A change of focus at work could be ideal as you'll get the chance to spend more time on activities you like. You may enjoy a reunion and having time to spend on yourself and your health and well-being. *Moon in Gemini.*

4 MAY

A change of place or of pace will be enjoyable. You may receive unexpected news or will go somewhere different. You'll enjoy being spontaneous but must avoid making snap decisions. *Moon in Gemini.*

5 MAY

A surprise message, meeting or phone call will merit some focus. You'll enjoy learning something new or meeting new people. *Moon in Cancer.*

6 MAY

This is a good day for meetings and get-togethers. You'll enjoy being with like-minded people and could make great financial progress. *Moon in Cancer.*

7 MAY

You'll feel more active and outgoing this weekend and will enjoy letting off steam through sports or simply socialising. This is a good day for getting chores done at home and for organising events. You may be prone to impulse buying, so if you're shopping get a second opinion. *Moon in Leo.*

8 MAY

This is a good time to get outstanding chores and paperwork done regarding domestic matters so that you're shipshape for the next few weeks and months. Someone close may seem more upbeat but may also be a little feisty, so avoid arguments if you feel conflict is brewing. *Moon in Leo.*

9 MAY

You'll enjoy being with upbeat and motivated people. A trip or sociable activity will be fun. Aim to tie up loose ends at work and regarding communications before Mercury turns retrograde tomorrow. *Moon enters Virgo.*

10 MAY

As Mercury turns retrograde you're likely to receive key news from someone close, at home or regarding a trip or key project. For some this will mean reviewing several of your plans. Try to allow extra time for travel and communications to avoid frustration over the coming weeks. *Moon in Virgo.*

11 MAY

As Jupiter joins Venus and Chiron in Aries you are likely to be busy over the coming weeks. You may feel motivated to travel or make changes in your personal life or financially. *Moon in Virgo.*

12 MAY

You like to make decisions based on facts as opposed to supposition, and this is certainly a good time to reconsider the facts surrounding an important situation such as your personal life or finances. Base your choices on research and fair play for the best results. *Moon in Libra.*

13 MAY

You'll enjoy a meeting and news could bring forward some of your plans and projects. A close relationship or interest could deepen. Take the initiative if you're single to find someone suitable; you may be surprised by who you meet. Couples will enjoy re-igniting romance. *Moon in Libra.*

14 MAY

Being with like-minded people and engaging in favourite activities will make your heart soar this weekend, so if you have nothing planned yet organise an event! A trip or reunion will make your heart sing. *Moon in Scorpio.*

15 MAY

You'll be inspired by someone special or by an activity but must avoid being too aggravated by delays and obstacles. A trip or meeting could be ideal, but you may not agree with everyone so find ways to establish common ground if possible. Someone may need your help or vice versa; rest assured support will be available. A little retail therapy will appeal, but if funds are tight keep it to window shopping if possible! *Moon in Scorpio.*

16 MAY

The total lunar eclipse in Scorpio is an intense full moon as it will spotlight how you feel about your activities and interests. You may feel more aligned and supported than ever by those around you, but if you feel the opposite this is a good time to find better direction for yourself so you feel more fulfilled. A trip could be pivotal. *Moon enters Sagittarius.*

17 MAY

Be inspired but also practical and you could move mountains. Avoid allowing your imagination to run away with you but, equally, strive for your ideals and you may be surprised by what you can achieve. *Moon in Sagittarius.*

18 MAY

Current developments are demanding you bring out your inner strategist and intellect. Your efforts are likely to pay off. However, if you discover you have over-estimated your circumstances you will gain the opportunity to set things right. You may experience a financial or ego boost but must avoid making impulsive decisions. *Moon in Capricorn.*

19 MAY

This is a good day to make changes, both to your domestic environment and at work. A trip or meeting is likely to be successful. You'll enjoy a reunion. It's a good day to boost your health and appearance. *Moon in Capricorn.*

20 MAY

A financial matter is likely to be a focus. If you have recently overspent it's a good time to consider a fresh budget. You may wish to return to an old haunt or reconnect with someone fun. You'll enjoy an ego boost or financial improvement. *Moon in Aquarius.*

21 MAY

The sun in Gemini for the next four weeks will encourage you to be more outgoing and chattier. You'll enjoy a sense of freedom of movement and a trip could be exciting. A meeting will take you back to the past or incur nostalgic feelings. *Moon in Aquarius.*

22 MAY

You are likely to be driven by your passions. If these are constructive and uplifting you'll appreciate the sense of well-being you gain, but if you are resuming bad habits take a moment out of your day to get back into a more positive daily and weekend schedule. *Moon enters Pisces.*

23 MAY

You may need to review a particular idea, plan or relationship. A trip or reunion will go well and will offer the chance to see your circumstances in a new light. If you're shopping avoid overspending and overindulging, as you'll regret it tomorrow. *Moon in Pisces.*

24 MAY

This is a good day to make a commitment or investment as long as you are clear about the terms and conditions. You may find a work or financial matter can progress, but if you feel disappointed this is a good time to consider new ways to move forward. *Moon in Pisces.*

25 MAY

On the one hand some aspects of your life will be progressing quickly, but on the other there may be an element of déjà vu or of history repeating itself. If you feel some matters are progressing too quickly this is a good time to discuss your feelings before it's too late to make changes. *Moon in Aries.*

26 MAY

A debt may be repaid and you may be ready to repay one yourself. Finances could be looking up, especially if you find ways to budget better. A trip or get-together will be enjoyable as long as you avoid sensitive topics that always lead to arguments. *Moon in Aries.*

27 MAY

You may need to review a decision or your stance about a work or health matter. It's a good time to research the facts so the decisions you make are watertight. Avoid disagreements as these could quickly escalate to conflict. *Moon in Taurus.*

28 MAY

If you have overspent recently this is a good time to consider a fresh budget and find other ways to enjoy yourself without needing to spend money – there are many! You may be more drawn to enjoying creature comforts such as relaxing at home. If you feel arguments are brewing, avoid allowing these to become the new normal and find a way to nip them in the bud. *Moon in Taurus.*

29 MAY

A spontaneous event will be fun and you'll appreciate the chance to be free and have an adventure. You'll enjoy being physically active via sports, walking or gardening and getting domestic chores done. Someone close may have key news for you. *Moon enters Gemini.*

30 MAY

The Gemini new moon will spotlight something new at home. For some this new moon is an excellent time to consider travel, updating technology, repairing a vehicle and refreshing interpersonal dynamics. Be bold and upbeat!

31 MAY

Be practical and you may surprise yourself with what you can accomplish. You may enjoy a personal compliment, ego boost or financial improvement. *Moon in Gemini.*

June

career   love   home   health   finance

1 JUNE

The moon in Cancer brings out your emotions and you will be motivated to spend some time with someone special. If you feel at odds with someone's ideas look for constructive ways to take yourself out of difficult circumstances. ***Moon in Cancer.***

2 JUNE

It's a good day to discuss your ideas such as plans for travel or to make changes at work. This is a good time to renegotiate some of your agreements or contracts. ***Moon in Cancer.***

3 JUNE

You'll be glad to hear that Mercury ends its retrograde phase today. You may receive key news concerning a work, health or personal matter. Communications and travel plans will become easier to make over the coming weeks. Take the time to consider your views and engage in practical steps to move forward. ***Moon enters Leo.***

4 JUNE

This is a good day for getting together with like-minded people. You may be drawn to expressing yourself more and will feel more outgoing. Shopping or another expense will need to be paid for and you may be prone to impulse buying. If you're in debt aim to curb expenses and devise a more foolproof budget. *Moon in Leo.*

5 JUNE

The Leo moon motivates you to get things done, especially at work. You may even surprise yourself with your level of productivity. *Moon in Leo.*

6 JUNE

This is a good day to focus on improving your health, well-being and interpersonal relationships. You may be a little perfectionist at the moment, and while this will be useful at work it may not be as successful an approach at home if you become critical of others. *Moon in Virgo.*

7 JUNE

A change at home or with family may be surprising. You'll enjoy an impromptu get-together and being spontaneous. Be adaptable and prepared to make changes in your everyday environment. *Moon in Virgo.*

8 JUNE

You may need to take control of a situation or project that has gone off track. Your organisational skills are peaking, so don't be afraid to take charge. *Moon enters Libra.*

9 JUNE

While you're not generally known for your impulsiveness, you do like freedom of movement and so tend not to get too involved in other people's dramas. However, you may be asked to act as a mediator so look for ways to establish calm and balance in a situation that isn't necessarily of your own making. *Moon in Libra.*

10 JUNE

Matters and discussions that have been stuck, slow to develop or difficult to decide will begin to move forward. You may be asked to commit one way or another to an opinion, project or venture. Meetings and news will indicate that you're making headway. *Moon enters Scorpio.*

11 JUNE

A surprise or spontaneous get-together may be enjoyable, but if you feel you are leaving your comfort zone you may wish to think twice. You'll enjoy doing something different or an impromptu meeting or trip. Avoid impulsiveness. *Moon in Scorpio.*

12 JUNE

The moon at the zenith of your chart suggests you'll enjoy feeling a sense of freedom. Whether you take a trip, deepen your spirituality or spend more time with someone you love you'll enjoy a sense of lightness, so ensure you make space for it. ***Moon enters Sagittarius.***

13 JUNE

As Mercury enters its own sign of Gemini you will appreciate an increasing sense of mental clarity. If you have felt muddled or confused, prepare for the fuzziness to lift. You may be busy, and travel could be exciting. ***Moon in Sagittarius.***

14 JUNE

The full moon and supermoon in Sagittarius represents a fresh chapter for you in your status, general direction or interests. You're turning over a new leaf, and adventure and a sense of possibility will be motivational for you. Take a moment to work out where your priorities lie and make decisions from there.

15 JUNE

A meeting will have a therapeutic or healing effect. This is a good day for a health or beauty appointment. Someone may need your help, and if you need help from an expert or adviser it will be available so reach out. Avoid making snap decisions, especially financially and in your personal life, as you may make mistakes. Avoid taking other people's random remarks personally. ***Moon in Capricorn.***

16 JUNE

This is a good day to make a commitment to a new agreement, especially in your personal life, at home or with family. Just check contracts carefully if you are signing a new lease, for example. Romance could blossom so organise a date. Singles may meet someone who seems remarkably familiar. ***Moon enters Aquarius.***

17 JUNE

Be open to new experiences and you'll find you enjoy the company of someone who has a therapeutic effect on you or who has interesting viewpoints. Just avoid making snap decisions that could get you into hot water such as gambling, both financially and emotionally. ***Moon in Aquarius.***

18 JUNE

You like to be accountable for your actions but sometimes your love of freedom and adventure can mean you forget your responsibilities and act rashly. Consider your options carefully as you are prone to making errors in judgement. ***Moon in Aquarius.***

19 JUNE

This is a lovely day for romance and you'll enjoy indulging in music, relaxation, reading, good food, film and dance. However, you may also need to get things done at work or around the house, so try to get the chores done first and then you can relax! *Moon in Pisces.*

20 JUNE

The Pisces moon may bring out your idealistic side, and you'll be inspired to follow your dreams. If you're looking for work, circulate your resume as you may strike gold. Just avoid seeing the world through rose-coloured glasses or you could be disappointed. *Moon in Pisces.*

21 JUNE

As the sun enters Cancer, marking the solstice, you will feel inclined over the coming weeks to focus more on your personal life and on creature comforts at home. You may feel drawn to romance and feel the need to find more nurturance. Be proactive, as you could get a lot done and could deepen your understanding of someone close either at home or at work. *Moon in Aries.*

22 JUNE

You'll feel inclined to be more active and will get a great deal done. Some people may find you a little feisty under the Aries moon, so if you experience adverse reactions consider whether you're appearing a little bossy without necessarily meaning to be controlling. *Moon in Aries.*

23 JUNE

You'll feel drawn to investing more in yourself, both at work and at home. Show just what you have at work by being efficient and effective. You'll enjoy indulging in good food and company over the next two days, so organise a treat. *Moon enters Taurus.*

24 JUNE

A reunion will remind you just how many people are in your corner, so ensure you reach out to friends and family. You'll enjoy a fun get-together with like-minded people. *Moon in Taurus.*

25 JUNE

Be practical about organising your activities this weekend to avoid feeling you are having to work to get things done. A working bee will get things shipshape at home. A lovely trip or get-together will be enjoyable. *Moon in Taurus.*

26 JUNE

A busy time at home or travelling to somewhere new will breathe fresh air into your day. You'll appreciate the sense that you can change your usual Sunday without too many logistical problems and will enjoy the sense of freedom it provides. *Moon in Gemini.*

27 JUNE

You'll find you can be super productive at work and may reap the rewards of an ego boost or financial improvement. You'll enjoy bringing a feeling of relaxation and fun into your home. If you are doing a little DIY or domestic work it will pay off. A little retail therapy will boost your mood and could improve home décor. *Moon in Gemini.*

28 JUNE

You're creative and imaginative, and these qualities can help you to make progress with your work and at home. Romance could blossom. You may be surprised by news, an unexpected visitor or an impromptu meeting. *Moon enters Cancer.*

29 JUNE

The Cancerian new moon will kick-start a fresh chapter in your daily schedule, for example at work or in your health routine. You may decide you wish to have more of a sense of togetherness at home or with family and will invest more time in these areas of your life. Just avoid arguments otherwise a difference of opinion could turn into a long-standing feud. *Moon in Cancer.*

30 JUNE

You may feel strongly about your viewpoints, which could lead to a Mexican stand-off if you take an oppositional approach. Look at the practicalities of your circumstances and at how you could nurture a more caring or inclusive approach, both in yourself and in others. *Moon in Cancer.*

July

career   love   home   health   finance

1 JULY

The key to success over the next few days lies in good communication skills. You may be liable to take some discussions or events personally, and with mounting tension in the skies this could contribute to arguments. Double-check details, especially financially and with domestic matters to avoid mistakes. ***Moon in Leo.***

2 JULY

You'll enjoy a change at home or with someone in your family. You may be ready to make a commitment to a certain path with family or a property. You may feel daring or under pressure, so if some developments feel intense ensure you maintain perspective. You may feel escapist, so avoid overspending on a trip and overindulging as you'll regret it tomorrow. ***Moon in Leo.***

3 JULY

A realistic and sensible (if boring!) approach to a circumstance or relationship will work out better for you than an oppositional or drama-fuelled attitude. This is a good day to get organised for the week ahead. ***Moon enters Virgo.***

4 JULY

You may experience strong emotions and will manage to keep a lid on these, but a better way to deal with strong feelings is to find healthy ways to channel them into productive pursuits such as sports or by blowing off steam through work that motivates you. A domestic or personal matter will require careful handling. *Moon in Virgo.*

5 JULY

This is a good day to take things one step at a time, especially with personal and family matters. You may experience a boost in self-esteem or financially by taking the initiative. *Moon enters Libra.*

6 JULY

A healing and therapeutic quality will help you to get things on a more even keel in your personal life. If finances or domestic matters have been difficult, an expert or professional guidance will be helpful. *Moon in Libra.*

7 JULY

Your ability to see the balanced side of all perspectives will help avert arguments. Look for the most constructive way to get ahead with collaborations both at home and at work. *Moon in Libra.*

8 JULY

You'll appreciate seeing a domestic or personal matter take a step in the right direction. If finances or your self-esteem have been at a low ebb, you may find an unexpected way to move forward. Just avoid taking on people's personal problems as your own. Someone may express their vulnerabilities and may need your help or vice versa; it will be available. *Moon in Scorpio.*

9 JULY

This is a good time to ensure your communications, be these in writing or verbal, are being received in the exact way you mean them to be. In other words, misunderstandings are likely so be extra clear for the best results. Travel may be delayed or postponed so be patient. Domestic repairs may be necessary. Avoid financial and emotional gambling. *Moon in Scorpio.*

10 JULY

You'll enjoy an impromptu get-together or a surprisingly upbeat development. You may enjoy a reunion. You'll gain comfort from cocooning or being with someone you love. *Moon enters Sagittarius.*

11 JULY

When the moon is in Sagittarius you'll enjoy being outgoing and upbeat and socialising and networking will appeal, although you may need to first attend to matters such as bills and chores. *Moon in Sagittarius.*

12 JULY

This is a good day to be practical and realistic, especially with personal and financial matters. You may benefit from considering your circumstances from a fresh perspective if you feel a little stuck. *Moon enters Capricorn.*

13 JULY

The full moon and supermoon in Capricorn will spotlight a fresh daily health or work routine. This is a good day for making a new personal or work commitment. Look for security and stability and avoid making decisions based on assumptions.

14 JULY

You prefer life to be uplifting yet it all too often presents difficulties. To make a choice or to feel certain about your position it's important you do your research. You may be prone to misunderstandings and delays, so be patient. You may also be easily misled so avoid gambling, both financially and emotionally. *Moon enters Aquarius.*

15 JULY

You're looking for an ideal weekend to relax, yet you have chores or duties to perform first! Avoid being disappointed by the fact that someone close has different ideas from yours and aim to find the relaxation you need and you will. *Moon in Aquarius.*

16 JULY

You'll appreciate a change in your usual routine and the chance to recharge your batteries. You may receive key news that means you must reconsider a work or health situation. Sports and being more outgoing will appeal. You'll enjoy deepening your understanding of spiritual matters. A meeting could be supportive so reach out! *Moon enters Pisces.*

17 JULY

This is a lovely day for promoting your work interests. A meeting could yield positive results that could boost finances and/or self-esteem. You may also enjoy being near the ocean and feel more in tune with your activities. *Moon in Pisces.*

18 JULY

This is a good time for important talks, especially regarding work and health. You may find some talks are intense, so avoid conflict by taking things one step at a time. You could make key changes in a situation by being thorough and researching your circumstances well. It's also a good day for a health or beauty appointment. *Moon enters Aries.*

19 JULY

As Mercury enters upbeat Leo you may feel more expressive and willing to share your ideas and plans with those they concern. You may also appear a little feisty, so if you have adverse reactions to some of your discussions you may wish to consider adopting a more even tone. You may feel more optimistic and enthusiastic about your plans over the coming weeks. *Moon in Aries.*

20 JULY

Key news and developments will signal a change in your circumstances. This is a good day to be active with work projects. You could change a lot about how you work. If you're looking for work, circulate your resume. A beauty or health appointment could point to a transformative process. *Moon enters Taurus.*

21 JULY

The Taurean moon will encourage you to be practical and realistic abut your plans and projects. If you encounter opposition to some of your plans or ideas, find ways to move forward one step at a time. *Moon in Taurus.*

22 JULY

As the sun enters Leo you may find work and your daily schedule is busy over the coming days and weeks. Someone close may be more expressive and outspoken. You'll enjoy being with upbeat and fun people, so why not organise an event? *Moon in Taurus.*

23 JULY

You'll enjoy a lovely get-together or a trip this weekend. A change of routine will be fun. This is a good time for discussing your plans with someone special as you're likely to be on the same page. If you're shopping you may be inclined to overspend, so check your budget first. *Moon in Gemini.*

24 JULY

A sociable and carefree feeling will be a lovely way to relax. However, if you feel arguments are brewing take time out to avoid allowing them to gain momentum. *Moon in Gemini.*

25 JULY

Perhaps it's just a case of Mondayitis, but underlying tension may distract from otherwise positive stars for getting things done and a productive day. It's unwise to tease someone who has a zero sense of humour, so avoid tense situations and aim instead for a smoothly running day. ***Moon enters Cancer.***

26 JULY

Once again good communication skills are the secret to success. Avoid adopting an oppositional approach to someone who is a little feisty. Also avoid making snap decision as these are likely to backfire. A meeting or talk may be tense, so look for ways to de-escalate stress. ***Moon in Cancer.***

27 JULY

There is a therapeutic aspect to the day, so this is a good time to build bridges with someone you have argued with. A financial matter could progress, but if you find yourself deeper in debt find ways to put in place a solid budget. ***Moon in Cancer.***

28 JULY

The Leo new moon points to a fresh chapter in a personal or business partnership if you were born today or earlier in July and a fresh work or health schedule if you were born later. Someone who tends to be unpredictable may behave true to form, so be careful with communications to avoid arguments. Avoid snap decisions and look for solid ways to move forward. Travel and meetings may be delayed, so allow for extra time.

29 JULY

Unexpected developments or news will deserve a patient approach. A change of pace or of place is best navigated one step at a time. Maintain good communication skills as otherwise disagreements are likely to escalate. Be tactful and diplomatic where necessary and willing to see another's viewpoint. ***Moon in Leo.***

30 JULY

You'll appreciate the time to sort out some of the thoughts in your mind. Pay attention to someone close and to getting things right to avoid mistakes. You'll appreciate catching up with someone whose company boosts the feel-good factor in your life. ***Moon enters Virgo.***

31 JULY

This is a good day to call a truce or reach an agreement with someone close. You'll enjoy a reunion and may be drawn to boost your health and fitness. A shopping trip may be expensive, so if you're in debt already avoid using the credit card. Romance can blossom, so organise a treat. ***Moon in Virgo.***

August

career   love   home   health   finance

1 AUGUST

You may hear from an old friend or colleague from out of the blue. A meeting with someone new may be more significant than meets the eye. The clearer you are with communications the better the outcome of your day, as otherwise you may be prone to making mistakes largely through making assumptions. Some meetings or travel may be delayed, so be patient. *Moon in Virgo.*

2 AUGUST

This is a good day to take the initiative both at work and with health matters. You may be surprised by news and developments. A trip or meeting could take you someplace exciting or different. *Moon in Libra.*

3 AUGUST

You may be surprised by developments at work or with family via particular news or a meeting. Romance could flourish, so take the initiative. Singles may meet someone as if by coincidence who seems curiously familiar. *Moon in Libra.*

4 AUGUST

Trust your instincts as you have curiously deep insight, especially to do with someone special. Avoid allowing distractions to deter you from your big-picture goals. *Moon enters Scorpio.*

5 AUGUST

You may need to focus extra hard on your goals, especially at work or with a creative project, to overcome a hurdle. But if you're diligent your efforts will be worthwhile. *Moon in Scorpio.*

6 AUGUST

An optimistic and outgoing approach will pay off this weekend as your activities will be motivational. Sports, outdoor activities and deepening spirituality or creative abilities will appeal. *Moon enters Sagittarius.*

7 AUGUST

If you're working, rest assured your hard work will pay off; you may just need to give projects that extra last push. This is a good day for beautifying your environment such as your home or office. A change of routine or a family get-together will be enjoyable. You'll enjoy music, dance and romance. *Moon in Sagittarius.*

8 AUGUST

There is a powerful healing and therapeutic quality to the day. It's a good day for a health or beauty appointment. You may find you are asked for help, and if you need guidance it is available. *Moon enters Capricorn.*

9 AUGUST

This is a good day to consider a fresh budget if you discover you've blown it! Find ways to gain more leeway or cash flow. You may need to negotiate fresh terms at work. A discussion may be intense, so avoid allowing it to escalate to conflict. *Moon in Capricorn.*

10 AUGUST

You may feel particularly intensely about a principle, work matter or health situation. Find ways to maintain perspective and be practical. *Moon enters Aquarius.*

11 AUGUST

You are expressing yourself well but may tend to be a little idealistic. If an event adds to confusion, take things one step at a time. Avoid making assumptions and find ways to get the information you need. You may have to back up computers or find ways to stay patient with matters that are frustrating. *Moon in Aquarius.*

12 AUGUST

The Aquarian full moon will spotlight your personal life, especially if it's your birthday on or before 8-10 February. If you were born later you will be ready to turn a corner at work or with a health situation. Be prepared to make a commitment to a certain course of action but avoid making snap decisions, as these are likely to backfire. ***Moon enters Pisces.***

13 AUGUST

You'll enjoy relaxing and finding ways to infuse your daily life with more peace and harmony. Meditation, music and the arts will all appeal. It's a good time to look for ways to build a solid platform for yourself and those close to you and for your ventures. ***Moon in Pisces.***

14 AUGUST

You may be prepared to make a commitment or decision, and the more you base this on facts rather than on expectations the better the outcome, especially in relation to a business or personal commitment. This is a good day to put your back into domestic chores, and if you work from home to tidy up paperwork. A trip or meeting could be transformative. ***Moon enters Aries.***

15 AUGUST

You'll enjoy a meeting or a trip somewhere familiar. Communications will flow and you could come to a significant financial arrangement or agreement. ***Moon in Aries.***

16 AUGUST

You'll enjoy a change of place or of pace. Finances could improve unexpectedly, and you'll appreciate the sense that someone has your back. You may bump into an old friend. ***Moon in Aries.***

17 AUGUST

There may be a mystery in the making, so it's best to research the circumstances. Avoid being misled and making mistakes by being completely sure of your actions and clear with your communications. You will feel inspired but may be a little forgetful or head in the clouds. ***Moon in Taurus.***

18 AUGUST

This is an excellent day for making progress at work. You may be drawn to a new look or a beauty treat. You may also feel drawn to invest more heavily in a personal situation. Financial investments are best analysed carefully to avoid mistakes. Romance could blossom, so organise a treat. ***Moon in Taurus.***

19 AUGUST

A tug of war at work needn't get in the way of your happiness. An intense situation may be distracting, but if you focus more on your tasks at hand you will succeed. Avoid a battle of egos and focus on common ground to avoid arguments. *Moon in Gemini.*

20 AUGUST

Mars will now be in Gemini until the end of March 2023, which will bring your focus on to communications and travel. You may be busy in either or both areas and today's developments will give you insight into the kinds of fields that will catch your attention over the coming months. *Moon in Gemini.*

21 AUGUST

You'll be drawn to music, the arts, dance, film and romance, but you may also be a little head in the clouds and forgetful so avoid misplacing keys. Romantically and in your personal life you may tend to be idealistic, so ensure you keep your feet on the ground. *Moon in Gemini.*

22 AUGUST

This is a good time to discuss work, finances and shared duties and responsibilities, as you're likely to progress with arrangements and agreements. You could make positive changes in all these areas. *Moon in Cancer.*

23 AUGUST

Now that the sun is in Virgo for the next four weeks you will appreciate the opportunity to focus more on someone special and on your joint responsibilities. You'll enjoy the sense that life has more reason and rhyme but must avoid being perfectionist, especially about money, work and someone close, as you may be disappointed. *Moon in Cancer.*

24 AUGUST

There is a therapeutic quality to events. This is a good day for a health and beauty treat. It's also a good day to discuss your ideas and plans with someone close at home or at work. It's a good time to seek expert advice; you may be asked for advice yourself. Avoid taking someone's problems to heart and taking random comments personally. *Moon enters Leo.*

25 AUGUST

The moon in Leo motivates you to be more productive at work and around the house but may also bring out your combativeness and obstinacy, so avoid putting people's backs up. *Moon in Leo.*

26 AUGUST

Finding the perfect middle ground so that you can agree with someone in your life is important to you, but you are unlikely to compromise your values. Take a moment to communicate your ideas and plans with those they affect. The next few weeks are ideal for improving your collaborations. *Moon in Leo.*

27 AUGUST

The new moon in Virgo suggests you're ready to make a fresh agreement with someone close. This time is ideal for beginning a new chapter in a shared venture such as a collaboration at work or in your personal life, but to rush into something new would be inadvisable. Take your time and consider your best path forward Events may surprise you, and developments could mean more changes to come.

28 AUGUST

You could make a commitment to a fresh course of action. You may agree to a new arrangement, but ensure it doesn't limit you too much moving forward. *Moon in Virgo.*

29 AUGUST

You are more likely to see someone else's viewpoints than your own. Double-check you are not being easily led into an agreement or arrangement. You may need to be a mediator or must find the middle ground in a dispute. Take things one step at a time to avoid impulsive decisions you'll regret. *Moon enters Libra.*

30 AUGUST

You can achieve a great deal by being optimistic but you must also be careful. A difference of opinion needn't be a hindrance to your plans but may spotlight important matters that need to be taken into account. *Moon in Libra.*

31 AUGUST

Someone you love will capture your attention and romance could thrive, especially if you like a little mystery in your love life. But if stress is a factor in your love life it could be a passion killer. Find ways to unwind. If you doubt someone either at home or at work it's your cue to find out more and do some research. *Moon enters Scorpio.*

September

career	love	home	health	finance

1 SEPTEMBER

A pleasant development will encourage you to boost your self-esteem. You may enjoy a financial or ego boost. A change at home or in your personal life could be advantageous. *Moon in Scorpio.*

2 SEPTEMBER

Your work may contain an intense element or a colleague may be feeling the pressure. If you are under the weather, find ways to be productive and organise something enjoyable for later on in the day or the weekend. You will succeed with your projects with persistence and diligence. *Moon enters Sagittarius.*

3 SEPTEMBER

You'll enjoy a get-together and the chance to discuss important matters. A financial agreement could be advantageous, but if you're making a large investment ensure you have the facts. A reunion or news from the past may be bittersweet. *Moon in Sagittarius.*

4 SEPTEMBER

You'll enjoy being outgoing and upbeat, and socialising or networking will appeal. Active hobbies such as sports and fitness training will keep you in high spirits. **Moon in Sagittarius.**

5 SEPTEMBER

Over the next few weeks you'll appreciate the sense that some matters are beginning to settle down, especially in your personal life and concerning financial arrangements. You may be asked for help, or if you need some support or advice yourself it will be available so reach out. **Moon in Capricorn.**

6 SEPTEMBER

The Capricorn moon brings out your practical, sensible side so this is a good day to make plans and agreements and arrangements both at home and at work. It's a good time to get finances shipshape. **Moon in Capricorn.**

7 SEPTEMBER

Once the moon is in your sign you'll feel increasingly in your element and able to look outside the box at your circumstances and find fresh perspective. Be innovative and imaginative if you feel some matters are more difficult than they need be. **Moon in Aquarius.**

8 SEPTEMBER

Your approach to life is fairly analytical, which can be beneficial when difficulties arise. Take a moment to work out how best to proceed, especially if someone close or you is feeling slightly vulnerable. Someone may ask for your help, and if you need expert advice about a project or venture it will be available. **Moon in Aquarius.**

9 SEPTEMBER

A difference of opinion and the need to proceed carefully to avoid treading on someone's feelings may revolve around a fundamental difference of opinions. If you're making a considerable investment, ensure you are not over-committing. Try to get the loose ends of important paperwork tied up before Mercury turns retrograde tomorrow. **Moon in Pisces.**

10 SEPTEMBER

The full moon in Pisces shines a light on your finances, values and/or personal life. You may receive key news about a shared project, investment or financial matter and you may need to reconsider or review your position. You may feel super romantic. Be inspired, but be practical above all else.

11 SEPTEMBER

You'll enjoy an uplifting development such as a trip somewhere lovely or different or an unexpected visit or progress at home. Someone close may have good news. **Moon in Aries.**

12 SEPTEMBER

The key to success lies in good negotiation skills: if you have key financial matters to discuss take these one step at a time. Rest assured that your hard work will be worthwhile. Romance could blossom, so ensure you plan a treat. **Moon in Aries.**

13 SEPTEMBER

There are likely to be several distractions yet if you can focus on your priorities, especially at work and at home, you will be productive. Just concentrate on being realistic, practical and methodical. **Moon enters Taurus.**

14 SEPTEMBER

You'll appreciate the sense that you are making progress at home and with someone special. A trip or meeting is likely to go well. You'll enjoy a change of environment. **Moon in Taurus.**

15 SEPTEMBER

Romance, love and all things related to creature comforts will appeal to you, so once you've allocated time to chores, duties and work you'll enjoy organising something special with someone special. **Moon enters Gemini.**

16 SEPTEMBER

You'll enjoy a get-together and romance could truly blossom. However, you may be tempted to overindulge or overspend so ensure you keep a cap on spending, especially if you're already in debt. You may receive a financial or ego boost. It's a good day to initiate a fresh budget. Singles may meet someone charming. There is a degree of tension in the skies, so avoid arguments as these will escalate quickly. **Moon in Gemini.**

17 SEPTEMBER

You're communicating well this weekend and will enjoy boosting family and personal relationships. You may also enjoy working at homeon your décor or garden. **Moon in Gemini.**

18 SEPTEMBER

Talks and negotiations could open doors, but if you're unsure of your plans and feelings give yourself time to think. A financial investment could be ideal, but you must do your research to ensure you are not overextending yourself if you are making a large purchase. It's a good time to discuss your plans with someone close. **Moon enters Cancer.**

19 SEPTEMBER

This is a good time to plan an investment or a change in the way you share various joint aspects of your life, such as communal space at home or shared investments. A work project may be transformative and you're likely to see the merits of a change of routine. **Moon in Cancer.**

20 SEPTEMBER

An upbeat if unexpected development will put you in a positive frame of mind. Someone at home may be particularly surprising. A change with family or property may be fortunate. Some developments will merit hard work, but rest assured your efforts will pay off. If you're considering a major financial investmentensure you have checked the details. **Moon enters Leo.**

21 SEPTEMBER

You'll reap the rewards of being proactive at work. A partner may have bright ideas to discuss with you. Be open to something new but avoid making snap decisions that could have long-term consequences. **Moon in Leo.**

22 SEPTEMBER

You'll get a great deal done but may need to list chores to ensure you get everything covered, as you may be easily distracted. You won't always agree with everyone and may be surprised by some people's ideas. **Moon in Leo.**

23 SEPTEMBER

As the sun steps into Libra it marks the equinox, a time when we collectively sense we can achieve more balance and harmony in our lives. Your attention is likely to go increasingly to shared projects and ventures both at home and at work, and today's news or developments will give you a heads-up about the areas that will take much of your focus over the coming weeks. **Moon in Virgo.**

24 SEPTEMBER

This is a key day for romance. Couples could deepen your understanding of each other, and if you're single this is an excellent time to look for love if you are seeking romance and commitment. You'll be inspired by the arts, music and romance. **Moon in Virgo.**

25 SEPTEMBER

The new moon in Libra signals a fresh chapter in a shared situation. You may be ready to commit to someone or to a project or job. If you've been single for a while you may look for a partner, and if you're a couple but have been finding the going tough you may choose to go your separate ways. A change in your daily schedule could be a large part of changes to come.

26 SEPTEMBER

It's all change for you, and the more grounded and practical you are the better for you. Look for ways to bring balance and peace into your life. A legal or personal matter will take much of your focus. A key meeting could signal considerable change to come. *Moon in Libra.*

27 SEPTEMBER

This is a good time for talks and negotiations, especially to do with work and health matters. If you are a little forgetful, avoid misplacing valuables such as house keys. *Moon in Libra.*

28 SEPTEMBER

This is a constructive time to make plans in your personal life and be positive that your efforts will pay off. You can accomplish a great deal so be optimistic and proactive, especially at home and with your personal ventures. *Moon in Scorpio.*

29 SEPTEMBER

A meeting or trip may be more significant than meets the eye. Legal, work and personal matters could change rapidly. *Moon in Scorpio.*

30 SEPTEMBER

You'll enjoy being motivated by your projects and ventures, so if you do feel you are at a loose end ensure you channel your energy into activities that have meaning for you to avoid feeling frustrated. A get-together could be important and may boost your personal or financial situation. *Moon in Sagittarius.*

October

career love home health finance

1 OCTOBER

Key personal or financial matters will grab your focus. Romance could blossom. If you're making financial decisions, be clear about what you want and obtain expert advice if necessary. You may be inclined to overspend or overindulge, so maintain perspective. *Moon in Sagittarius.*

2 OCTOBER

You may receive key news from a business or personal partner. For some, news will be of a financial nature and you may need to negotiate fresh terms. *Moon in Capricorn.*

3 OCTOBER

You may need to review some of your work or personal agreements to ensure you're on the right track. Conversations will be productive. A health matter could see progress. It's a good day to organise your week. *Moon in Capricorn.*

4 OCTOBER

You are practical and logical when the moon is in Capricorn, and once it enters your own sign you'll pick up some of your more innovative and adventurous ideas, bringing a little lightness to your working week or your day. *Moon enters Aquarius.*

5 OCTOBER

This is a good day to be practical both at work and at home to ensure your plans can get ahead. You may notice some of your projects and collaborations begin to speed up or even take off. *Moon in Aquarius.*

6 OCTOBER

Saturn in your sign is helping you to take the most reasonable paths in life and avoid being too erratic and restless, but if you find current circumstances are a little limiting take a moment out of your schedule to contemplate how you could spruce up your daily routine so it's more to your liking. *Moon enters Pisces.*

7 OCTOBER

This is an excellent day for talks and meetings and for making positive changes both at work, in your personal life and within your usual daily routine. You may discover that your health and well-being are on the up and that you feel more sure of the outcome of some of your ventures. If you do experience a disappointment or are feeling sensitive, take a moment out of your schedule to regroup. Avoid taking other people's random comments personally. *Moon in Pisces.*

8 OCTOBER

Be inspired by developments but avoid being too idealistic as this could turn out to be your Achilles heel, especially in a personal situation. *Moon enters Aries.*

9 OCTOBER

The Aries full moon will spotlight a personal or financial matter. Your vulnerabilities may surface, so find the time to gain perspective and be practical. If you feel you need expert advice, ensure you seek it. Someone may ask for your help.

10 OCTOBER

A personal or financial matter may attract your focus. Your ideas and values may differ considerably from those of someone else. Look for common ground, and you could establish an agreement. A personal or financial matter could have a therapeutic effect, especially if a debt is repaid, but if you feel vulnerable ensure you seek guidance. *Moon enters Taurus.*

11 OCTOBER

If you feel that fair play or more balance needs to be an active part of your life and your agreements, this is a good day to look for ways to seek more peace. Your efforts are likely to lead to success as long as you avoid gambling, both financially and emotionally. *Moon in Taurus.*

12 OCTOBER

You could make progress with your talks and negotiations, especially in connection with money and in your personal life, so take the initiative. A trip or meeting will signal progress in either your personal life or financially. Avoid making assumptions and ensure everyone is on the same page if you are making key agreements. *Moon in Taurus.*

13 OCTOBER

You may be surprised by someone's news or a development. You may enjoy a trip or a talk, but if you feel tense rest assured that your efforts will be worthwhile if you maintain a positive outlook. *Moon in Gemini.*

14 OCTOBER

This is an excellent day for making agreements, for changing your work role if you like and improving domestic circumstances. A work development could go well. You may be ready to make a personal, financial or work agreement. *Moon in Gemini.*

15 OCTOBER

You'll enjoy a sense of freedom and will appreciate the chance to do something different or that resonates with you. You're thinking analytically, so if you need to make a key decision this is a good day to weigh the pros and cons. Meetings are likely to go well. *Moon enters Cancer.*

16 OCTOBER

You'll appreciate the creature comforts but may tend to be a little escapist, so ensure you avoid overindulging in the finer things in life. If you do make a great escape in a vehicle, make sure you don't get lost. If someone's behaviour is mysterious you'll gain a deeper understanding of them if you look more closely at their values and ideas. *Moon in Cancer.*

17 OCTOBER

This is a good time to improve your home life and domestic dynamics. You may be drawn to doing a little DIY or to improving décor. You can make great progress with projects and personal relationships. If you need to collaborate with someone just ensure you're on the same page and avoid making snap decisions. *Moon in Cancer.*

18 OCTOBER

You'll appreciate feeling extra energetic and that you can get more done. You may also feel more confident, so take the initiative. However, you or someone close such as at work may appear a little feisty, so avoid needless arguments. *Moon in Leo.*

19 OCTOBER

This is still a good time for making changes at home, although not everyone is likely to agree with your ideas. Someone at work may have their own projects or ideas to complete, and if they need your help you may tend to overload your workload so choose your duties carefully. This could be an intense day, so pace yourself. ***Moon in Leo.***

20 OCTOBER

You can make a great deal of headway with your projects. However, this is another day where a power struggle or intense talks will need to be defused so that you avoid arguments and rapid changes that may not be what you want. If conflict was brewing yesterday, ensure you avoid a tinderbox today. A dispute is best settled earlier rather than later. ***Moon enters Virgo.***

21 OCTOBER

There is still a restless atmosphere around you. If you find a little stress is motivational you could be super productive, but if you find tension, especially at work, is debilitating it's important to take things one step at a time. Find ways to channel strong energy into something productive. ***Moon in Virgo.***

22 OCTOBER

This is a lovely day for a get-together and romance could flourish. The arts, music and a favourite activity will all inspire you. If you're single this is a good day to meet new people. Couples will enjoy deepening your ties. Some news and interactions may be surprising, so if you find some interactions are tense ensure you take time out when needed. ***Moon in Virgo.***

23 OCTOBER

Now that the sun will be in Scorpio for the next four weeks you'll feel more motivated by your collaborations, both at work and in your personal life. You may feel more passionate and romance could go off the dial this weekend! Just avoid making assumptions about someone's feelings and take things one step at a time. It's a good time for making travel and work plans. You may experience a financial or ego boost, and if you're working this could be a lucrative time. ***Moon in Libra.***

24 OCTOBER

A circumstance may remind you of the past in some way, and you may need to repair a situation or even a relationship. Your help or advice may be appreciated. If you need expert guidance it will be available, so reach out. ***Moon in Libra.***

25 OCTOBER

The partial solar eclipse in Scorpio signals the start of a new chapter for you that will affect your collaborations and general activities in life. You may be ready to commit to someone or something

new. If a relationship or project has run its course, this eclipse could signal the time to move forward. Avoid making impulsive decisions and ensure you get the full details of circumstances before making choices. If you experience a disappointment you will find a silver lining to these clouds. Avoid misunderstandings.

26 OCTOBER

The moon in Scorpio will bring out strong emotions either in you or in someone close. Be prepared to manage emotions and avoid making snap judgements, especially about your work and long-term prospects. Be practical and logical about your decisions. *Moon in Scorpio.*

27 OCTOBER

This is another good day to get things done at home, with property or family. You are communicating well despite the fact that some talks and interactions may be intense or difficult. A work or health matter may require more focus and attention to details. Find expert advice if you're unsure of your next step. *Moon enters Sagittarius.*

28 OCTOBER

You may tend to be a little nostalgic or idealistic, so ensure you aren't looking at life through rose-coloured glasses. A trip somewhere familiar or a reunion could be enjoyable. *Moon in Sagittarius.*

29 OCTOBER

Over the next few weeks you'll be drawn to being more expressive and involved in activities you're passionate about; you may enjoy being extra sporty or involved in family matters, for example. Find ways to dissipate restless energy if you find life frustrating. A trip or meeting may appear to be difficult, but if you are diligent you will overcome delays, difficulties and obstacles. *Moon enters Capricorn.*

30 OCTOBER

You'll enjoy a reunion and the chance to truly relax. This is a good time to focus on well-being and health. *Moon in Capricorn.*

31 OCTOBER

Happy Hallowe'en! You'll enjoy a fun or different schedule and will appreciate the chance to touch base with family or friends. However, some talks may be a little out of the ordinary or challenging, so ensure you keep an eye out for tricks and avoid them! *Moon enters Aquarius.*

November

career   love   home   health   finance

1 NOVEMBER

You're thinking clearly but you may be tempted to over-analyse circumstances and be a little self-critical and critical of others, so maintain a balanced outlook and seek clever ways to enjoy your me time. *Moon in Aquarius.*

2 NOVEMBER

Keep your goals uppermost in your mind as you may be inclined to resume bad habits or be easily distracted by other people's goals and agendas. If you're feeling sensitive, take time out. Someone else who may feel vulnerable or sensitive will require delicate handling. *Moon enters Pisces.*

3 NOVEMBER

A reunion may be enjoyable but also intense. This is a good day for deepening your understanding of someone and of yourself and your relationship. Take a few moments to gather your thoughts and avoid making snap decisions. *Moon in Pisces.*

4 NOVEMBER

The moon in Pisces is inspiring but can also create an idealistic mindset in which your imagination gets the better of you. Be practical, especially if difficult talks arise, and be prepared to see another's point of view. *Moon enters Aries.*

5 NOVEMBER

Meetings and talks will put the spotlight on your relationship with someone who can be intense. If you feel vulnerable as a result, find ways to boost your self-esteem with some positive self-talk, for example. Sudden or unexpected news, for some to do with finances and for others in a collaboration at work or in your personal life, are best handled one step at a time although you should be prepared to embrace change. *Moon in Aries.*

6 NOVEMBER

The Aries moon will bring out a feisty attitude in you that will help you to get things done but may also incline you towards being impulsive. Someone may need your help or vice versa. Rest assured it will be available. *Moon in Aries.*

7 NOVEMBER

Be prepared to discuss options with those they concern to avoid hard feelings on both sides. Keep communications open, or you could end up with a stalemate. For some this will concern a financial or work matter and for others a personal issue. *Moon in Taurus.*

8 NOVEMBER

The total lunar eclipse in Taurus will spotlight a key development. For some this will be at home, with family, a property or someone special. You may also receive key news that could alter your direction at work or with a special project. A trip or visit could be particularly significant. You must maintain a broad but practical view of how you will both fund and manage new plans and ideas.

9 NOVEMBER

You may be surprised by news at home or from someone close. An unexpected development will mean you must look more deeply at the long-term implications of your circumstances. Avoid snap decisions as these could backfire, but be prepared to consider your best step forward and to embrace something new. *Moon enters Gemini.*

10 NOVEMBER

Be prepared to think outside the box at your various options and considerations at the moment, especially in connection with work and your home life, to ensure there are no mistakes or misunderstandings. You may receive good news, but if it seems too good to be true double-check the facts. You could boost finances and your status, so take the initiative. *Moon in Gemini.*

11 NOVEMBER

If you are prepared to work hard you could make considerable progress with your many projects. There is a lot that can go right for you, but if obstacles arise see them as opportunities to excel. Avoid arguments with someone in a position of authority or in your personal life, as these could spring up spontaneously. *Moon in Gemini.*

12 NOVEMBER

This is a good day to increase your finances and status. If you're working it could be a lucrative day, although you may be tempted to spend as quickly as you earn! It's a good day to boost your appearance and self-confidence. You may be tempted to overindulge and overspend, so if you're shopping avoid impulse buys. *Moon in Cancer.*

13 NOVEMBER

You'll enjoy socialising and networking and your natural charm will shine through. However, you won't be able to charm everyone: there will be at least one person you may need to persuade if you have some solid plans you'd like to implement. This is a good time to improve your health and appearance. You may be drawn to a new look or to improve your fitness schedule. *Moon in Cancer.*

14 NOVEMBER

Your intuition is firing on all cylinders and you'll find this particularly useful at work and regarding key decisions. You may be asked to look after someone else's worries, and your caring nature will respond to calls for help should they arise. *Moon enters Leo.*

15 NOVEMBER

This is an excellent day to make progress with your various projects, especially at work and regarding your finances. You could boost your self-esteem and status. A beauty or health treat is likely to go well; just be clear about what you need. *Moon in Leo.*

16 NOVEMBER

As Venus enters Sagittarius you'll enjoy feeling more adventurous and outgoing, especially at work and regarding your general direction and projects. Meetings are likely to go well, even if you don't necessarily agree with everyone. *Moon in Leo.*

17 NOVEMBER

As Mercury joins Venus in Sagittarius you are likely to feel more self-expressive, especially at work and regarding your interests and activities. Travel and new experiences will appeal to you. You may feel more inclined to socialise and network over the coming weeks and will enjoy meeting a new social circle. *Moon in Virgo.*

18 NOVEMBER

This is a good day for get-togethers, especially at work and concerning your long-term plans. It's also a good day to boost your health, well-being and appearance and also your image and self-confidence. ***Moon in Virgo.***

19 NOVEMBER

Someone you tend not to get on too well with or who you need to work harder at understanding than other people may be the cause of misunderstandings, but it's important you check you're being super clear. If you're shopping, avoid overspending. You may be forgetful, so be wary of misplacing valuables such as house keys. Also avoid gambling, both financially and emotionally. ***Moon enters Libra.***

20 NOVEMBER

You're looking for balance in your relationships, so the more you feather your nest and make room for someone special in your life the more you'll enjoy your day. It's a good day to recharge your batteries and look after health – either yours or that of someone close. ***Moon in Libra.***

21 NOVEMBER

This is an excellent day for meetings and discussions. You may receive key news at work. If you are undertaking a key financial transaction you're likely to see the benefit in doing so as you may see your finances increase. Just ensure you have double-checked the facts to avoid mistakes. A personal project or undertaking could go well, and key news will point you in the right direction. ***Moon enters Scorpio.***

22 NOVEMBER

The sun in Sagittarius for the next four weeks will spotlight your ability to be outgoing and productive, especially at work. You may find that your status, career and general circumstances improve over the coming weeks. Take the initiative with your projects and plans, as these are likely to take off. A travel plan could be ideal. Sports and well-being projects will also thrive. ***Moon in Scorpio.***

23 NOVEMBER

The Sagittarian new moon signals a perfect time to turn a corner in your general direction in life. Consider what you need to do to be happier as you could also turn a corner in your career or boost your status. Make a wish, but as always be careful as it will come true. You may enjoy a more outgoing and sociable phase over the coming weeks.

24 NOVEMBER

The moon in Sagittarius brings out your inner adventurer and optimist, but it will also encourage you to take more risks. Just ensure these are calculated risks, as impulsive behaviour could get you into hot water. *Moon in Sagittarius.*

25 NOVEMBER

There is a therapeutic and healing aspect that will motivate you to make positive changes in your life. For some these will be within your general projects and path in life. For others there will be improvements at work or financially. You may be drawn to improving your health and appearance. *Moon enters Capricorn.*

26 NOVEMBER

This is a good day to boost your status and general direction in life. If you're looking for a job or seeking a promotion be proactive! A health or beauty appointment may appeal as a way to boost your self-esteem and energy levels. It's also a good time to build bridges with someone you have recently argued with. An expert or adviser may have positive news for you. *Moon in Capricorn.*

27 NOVEMBER

An unexpected change of circumstance or surprise news is best handled front on. Be prepared to adapt to new circumstances but maintain an eye on your goals and you will succeed. Travel and communications may be delayed or unusual, so be patient. *Moon enters Aquarius.*

28 NOVEMBER

This is a good day to get things done, especially at home and in your personal life. You'll feel more motivated and grounded about changes you know must be made. If you work from home you'll get a great deal done. Avoid rushing and take things one step at a time. *Moon in Aquarius.*

29 NOVEMBER

Talks and meetings are likely to be animated but you could achieve your goals if you remain practical and focused, especially at work. This is a good day for a health appointment. Avoid making snap decisions, even if you must be spontaneous and think fast. *Moon in Aquarius.*

30 NOVEMBER

This is a good day to make work and financial agreements and to make progress with your various projects, so take the initiative if you need to discuss some of your plans. If your ideas differ from those of someone else, avoid arguments and look for solutions if problems arise. *Moon in Pisces.*

December

career   love   home   health   finance

1 DECEMBER

This is a good day to get things done and meetings are likely to be animated. You may enjoy socialising and networking but may be inclined to over-extend yourself, so choose activities wisely. Romance could flourish, and you'll enjoy indulging in your favourite activities and creativity could blossom. Just avoid an oppositional approach either in yourself or someone else as arguments could arise. ***Moon in Pisces.***

2 DECEMBER

While this is a proactive time for you you could make great progress, especially with your personal interests and ventures. But if you are tempted to enter into agreements or to do activities you are not familiar with, ensure you do adequate research first or mistakes could be made. Avoid misplacing valuables such as keys. You'll enjoy socialising or a meeting at work. ***Moon in Aries.***

3 DECEMBER

This are therapeutic aspects to the day, so if you have argued with someone recently this is a good day to mend bridges. You will enjoy a trip or visit. It is a good day for health and well-being appointments and to seek expert advice if needed. You may be called upon to provide information or guidance yourself. ***Moon in Aries.***

4 DECEMBER

You'll enjoy a reunion or news from your past. It's a good time to boost your health and well-being. You may be forgetful, so avoid misplacing valuables such as keys. You may also tend to be easily influenced or to resume a bad habit and overindulge, so if any of these are your Achilles heel be careful! *Moon enters Taurus.*

5 DECEMBER

You'll feel more practical about personal and domestic matters and will find the way forward with your various projects, even if some matters are still up in the air. *Moon in Taurus.*

6 DECEMBER

While you're more known for your quirky ability to be innovative and your good sense for strategy, you are also very practical when you must be. It's in your interest to find the most grounded and reasonable way forward, especially with finances and groups and organisations you must be able to get on with. There could be delays and potentially misunderstandings. Back up computers to avoid losing information. *Moon enters Gemini.*

7 DECEMBER

If you tend to excel with logistical conundrums and even enjoy sorting them out, today's developments may surprise you and will merit a careful approach. A lovely link with a group, friend or organisation will be productive. It's a good day for health and beauty appointments. *Moon in Gemini.*

8 DECEMBER

The Gemini full moon spotlights a fresh chapter in your personal life. You may tend to be more outgoing and upbeat but may also be a little impulsive about your decisions, so ensure you gain expert advice if you are making long-term changes. Developments may arise rapidly to do with family or your home, so think on your feet. For some, today's developments will involve a creative project, group, friend or organisation.

9 DECEMBER

An unexpected development at home or with family will merit a careful approach. You may be pleasantly surprised by a visitor or news you receive. You may be drawn to update décor or to move furniture to create a better flow at home. *Moon in Cancer.*

10 DECEMBER

Find ways to relax in your own way. Avoid being pressured into a situation you don't want to be a part of. Approach talks and financial transactions carefully, as you may otherwise regret a purchase or an interaction. There may be delays and mistakes can be made. Some interactions may be difficult, so be prepared to communicate clearly. *Moon in Cancer.*

11 DECEMBER

As Venus joins Mercury in Capricorn you'll feel increasingly inclined to create more stability and security in your life, but you must avoid obstinacy when your views differ from someone else's. Try to find common ground instead. ***Moon enters Leo.***

12 DECEMBER

This is an excellent day for making headway with your work and with the people you must collaborate with, for example groups and organisations. If you're looking to make a fresh commitment or find a new way ahead in a relationship, this is a good day to be practical and make agreements. ***Moon in Leo.***

13 DECEMBER

This is a good day to focus on boosting self-esteem, especially at work. It's also a good day for a health or beauty appointment. You may begin to feel more upbeat and proactive at work as the day goes by. ***Moon in Leo.***

14 DECEMBER

You may discover whether you have misjudged a circumstance. If you find you have it's a good time to make changes to improve your situation. It's an ideal day to devise a better budget. If you're shopping, avoid overspending. You won't always agree with everyone, so be clear and concise with communications to avoid misunderstandings. A mystery is worth unravelling. ***Moon enters Virgo.***

15 DECEMBER

You'll feel practical and capable and will enjoy the sense that you are getting on well on a realistic level with groups, friends and organisations. A family, property or personal matter could progress; just avoid taking someone else's problems personally. You may be asked to help a group or organisation. ***Moon in Virgo.***

16 DECEMBER

A feisty or even frustrated end to the week needn't create problems for you. Maintain your sight on your goals and avoid being sidetracked by other people's agendas. That said, you may be asked to help and will be willing to accommodate the needs of others. If you need advice it will be available, so reach out. ***Moon enters Libra.***

17 DECEMBER

You'll enjoy a trip or visit and will appreciate the option to do something different. An uplifting social circumstance will feel refreshing. You may be surprised by developments at home or with family. ***Moon in Libra.***

18 DECEMBER

You'll enjoy a reunion, and a trip somewhere different will be enjoyable. If a work social event occurs you'll appreciate the chance to network. *Moon in Libra.*

19 DECEMBER

A return to an old haunt will be enjoyable, although some preparations and travel may be more complex that you'd like. Avoid rushing into decisions, especially at home and socially, but find the time to enjoy circumstances and the seasonal cheer. *Moon in Scorpio.*

20 DECEMBER

The Scorpio moon will bring strong emotions to the surface. You may have mixed feelings about a trip or gathering. If you're Christmas shopping, avoid overspending and keep an eye on your budget. Factor in extra time for travel as there may be delays or a surprise along the way. *Moon in Scorpio.*

21 DECEMBER

The solstice is when the sun enters the zodiac sign of Capricorn. It is a time of reflection when you can gather your wits as you assimilate your progress this year. Over the next four weeks you will increasingly focus on creating a solid base for yourself via stable work and health routines. Meanwhile, some interactions may be difficult so be relaxed and find comfortable ways to express yourself more fully. *Moon in Sagittarius.*

22 DECEMBER

You'll enjoy a get-together with someone whose company you love. A trip may have surprising elements or will take you somewhere different. A change of routine or of pace and a trip will be refreshing. *Moon in Sagittarius.*

23 DECEMBER

The new moon and supermoon in Capricorn signals a fresh chapter in your daily routine. You may be ready to turn a corner at work or to leave some aspects of the past behind. A health situation will merit a stable approach to ensure you maintain health and avoid over-indulgence during the festive season.

24 DECEMBER

You'll enjoy a reunion and the chance to touch base with someone special. If you're celebrating avoid overindulgence, as you'll regret it tomorrow! You'll enjoy shopping but may be prone to overspending, so be careful! Romance could blossom, so organise a treat. *Moon in Capricorn.*

25 DECEMBER

Merry Christmas! You'll appreciate a sense of tradition and will enjoy being with someone you love. Once the moon enters your sign you'll feel more in your element and may enjoy doing something different this year. **Moon in Aquarius.**

26 DECEMBER

You'll enjoy relaxing and being able to find a little more time for yourself. You may appreciate a change of atmosphere at home. The arts, music, film and romance will all appeal. **Moon in Aquarius.**

27 DECEMBER

A change of environment and the chance to socialise will raise your morale. You'll enjoy a reunion or a return to a familiar place. **Moon in Pisces.**

28 DECEMBER

Another sociable day will see you enjoying time with like-minded people. Romance could blossom, so ensure you organise a special treat. If you're shopping avoid overspending if you're already in debt and avoid being drawn into bargains, as they may not be what you actually want! Try to get the loose ends of important paperwork tied up before Mercury turns retrograde tomorrow to avoid delays down the line. **Moon in Pisces.**

29 DECEMBER

You'll enjoy a get-together, and particular news may have a nostalgic aspect to it. You may be inclined to overindulge right now, so if this is a long-term tendency ensure you have a cut-off point that is already preset. Romance could blossom, and singles may meet a like-minded character. You may be drawn to reconsider a financial or emotional investment; ensure you have all the details you need to avoid mistakes. **Moon in Aries.**

30 DECEMBER

A development that alters your usual routine either at home or at work will require a little extra attention, but rest assured the effort will be worthwhile. Avoid making snap decisions, as these could backfire. **Moon in Aries.**

31 DECEMBER

Happy New Year! You'll be drawn to spending time on meaningful relationships and may wish to avoid crowds. However, with the right encouragement from friends and family you'll be in the mood to celebrate, no matter how! **Moon enters Taurus.**

PISCES

18 February - 20 March

THE ESSENCE OF PISCES

Your sign's symbol is two fish, but more specifically two fish swimming in opposite directions. This juxtaposition characterises the inner tension Pisces embodies: tension between the need for an anchor and the sense of limitless direction and possibilities.

Your inner tension concerns your lust for life, drive to achieve and wish for expansion and knowledge versus your desire to let things be, to float away in the eternal waters of existence. This characterises the Piscean pitfall: you would ideally float through life irrespective of realities, duties and demands, which can contribute to an escapist mindset because life involves challenges, responsibilities and difficulties that are a part of your learning curve.

You have a lust for knowledge, experience and wisdom. You also have an innate sense of what is right and what is wrong and will fight a worthy cause zealously once it invokes your sense of justice and idealism. You are therefore attracted to philosophy, literature, debate, human rights, social work and creativity, areas that involve a sense of appraisal of the human condition and offer an ideal to work with.

You can tend to be vague as a result of the strong water element in your make-up – the water element representing the realm of the intuitive, sensitive and receptive nature that brings idealism into being. You love to daydream, to be inspired and to create. You are the zodiac's true artist and creator, able to bring into being ideas that are beyond the understanding of many people as you allow your mind to plumb the depths and heights of human existence.

You are also a practical character when you need to be. Jupiter, your sign's co-ruler with Neptune, keeps your feet on the ground even in the process of reaching out to increase your knowledge and experience in mind-expanding and heart-warming ways.

SELF-ESTEEM

Often the initial impression is that Pisces is a sensitive character prone to inner conflict between ideals and realities in life and with a tendency towards daydreaming, but the picture wouldn't be complete without mention of Pisces' go-getting self-esteem. You're not afraid to put yourself in a position of vulnerability, chiefly because of the appeal of expansion and knowledge but also because there is a boldness present in you that is not always apparent on first meeting. The Pisces self-esteem, despite a sensitive persona, is generally high.

Pisces is the 12th sign of the zodiac and is at the perimeter of the life cycle preparing esoterically for the next realm, so there is great courage and boldness in the Piscean make-up: courage to face the inevitable in life and to sail fearlessly into unknown territory.

Co-ruled by Neptune, the Roman deity named after the Greek god of the sea Poseidon, Pisces has a noble heart that rules the emotions and is symbolised by water. When the pressure is on Pisces will deliver, as there is an innate mastery over fear and emotions. Neptune was a wrathful god able to command thunderbolts and lightning, and Pisces can brave the high seas of drama and turbulence without fear of loss.

Pisces is also the sign associated with the cycle of learning through adversity, victimisation and sacrifice. A real pitfall for Pisces is falling into the victim-martyr role, which will really dampen self-esteem. When adversity strikes – and adversity is your chief bridge to learning – it is vital that you bolster self-esteem and avoid buying into other people's opinions of you as a victim or martyr. Be bold and strong, and seek always to expand your horizons.

YOUR INNER LIFE

You have a vivid imagination and artistic and creative abilities. When you develop these you'll open up a new world that facilitates your learning and development in beautiful and soul-nourishing ways.

You are inherently spiritual, whether you join an organised religion or movement or are conscious of the existence of higher powers. You will be innately aware of your connection with nature, the universe and god consciousness, and for many Pisces this will suffice. Religious practice may appeal to you, although spirituality is your own true nature and outward religious ritual merely a symbol of what is within. Religious practise such as observance of moral rights and wrongs will be a vital part of your life.

You are intuitive and instinctive, faculties that will flourish as you indulge in your creativity and artistic endeavours. Meditation, yoga, visualisation and mindfulness will all feel supportive of your generally intuitive mindset. You are also a sensitive character and this is not to be ignored, as you can especially when young feel easily influenced by the company you keep. You must be vigilant that you don't become caught up in the vagaries of other people's opinions of you and must tap into your own abilities.

HOW OTHERS SEE YOU

You're an inspired, gentle character who knows their own mind and is not afraid, when under pressure, to speak up. You're a creative individual, and if art is something that doesn't appeal to you then music and peaceful activities such as nature walks, fishing and swimming will express your appreciation for beauty.

You can on occasion be seen as an oddity, as your ideas can be light years ahead of those of other people. Because you are instinctive and intuitive you can pick up subtle undercurrents, and you may be seen as being unusual in your uncanny understanding of circumstances. Other people may view you as being different and may marginalise or alienate you. This can lead to martyr-like behaviour that will further marginalise you as you'll then be seen as being weak or a victim.

To gain confidence and avoid being seen as a victim or martyr it's important you work towards your ideals and expand your understanding of your role in life. Your unique ability is to rise above the kind of behaviour that would marginalise or shame you, to become wiser, more accomplished and compassionate than those who would seek to discredit you.

HOW TO MAXIMISE YOUR POTENTIAL

Remember you are a unique character with an ocean of possibilities. Your understanding of life, people, learning, wisdom and experience spans oceans and millennia; it is far deeper than the experiences of other zodiac signs. You stand at the precipice of the greater consciousness and are therefore ready for more responsibility, knowledge and wisdom.

Do not shrink from the additional responsibilities life will offer you. Embrace them and find ways to enhance abilities and skills that may initially seem overbearing or burdensome; you may be surprised by your own capabilities. You must equally avoid playing the martyr, weighing yourself down with duties that are not your responsibility and of no personal spiritual benefit.

Use your considerable intuitive abilities. Your intuition links you with spirit, great wisdom and knowledge; it is a fundamental Piscean quality that many other zodiac signs don't know how to use. Use your intuition in your everyday life, as it won't let you down if you clear your mind to allow this invaluable quality to guide you.

When you go through difficult times in life, drugs, alcohol and other addictive substances and behaviours may appeal to you as an easy way to dull your heightened sensitivity. However, when you dull your senses you mute your intuition, which is your true source of wisdom and support. This is clearly counterproductive. Avoid addictive behaviour both via substance abuse and co-dependency as they will rob you of your ability to fight for basic human rights, one of which is the right to personal freedom and individuality. If you enter or maintain co-dependent relationships you'll negate your own spark of creativity.

PISCES AND ITS ASCENDANTS

This chapter is about your sun sign, Pisces, and your predictions for the year ahead. The more you know about yourself the better you will be able to take advantage of opportunities, and also to avoid the pitfalls. It's critical to know as much about 'you' as possible.

In astrology your core self is represented by your sun sign, but your personality traits are represented by your ascendant (also known as your rising sign). The ascendant describes your personality, the way other people see you on first meeting you and the way you tend to filter life's events.

When you have intimate knowledge about your sun sign – your engine room or core being – you will be on the way to a happier life. When you add the knowledge about your personality – your ascendant – you will gain even deeper insight into what makes you tick.

Your ascendant sign is determined by the time of your birth on the date and year of your birth. Because the ascendant sign changes approximately every two hours, the best way to determine it is to ask an astrologer to calculate it for you. Certain apps will also calculate your ascendant sign (see page 873).

The following gives you more information about your abilities, characteristics and personality according to your sun sign Pisces in combination with your ascendant sign.

PISCES SUN SIGN WITH ARIES ASCENDANT

Initially you're seen as being an action-oriented, proactive character, someone who isn't afraid to get things done and to initiate new and bold ventures. Deeper down you're a soft, sensitive character. When your attributes work well together you're effective and competent; however, you can also be impulsive, domineering and uncompromising. It's important you always have your feet on the ground, then the Aries drive combined with the Pisces idealism can lead to excellent work and happiness.

PISCES SUN SIGN WITH TAURUS ASCENDANT

You will be seen by those who first meet you as being careful, earthy, sensuous and dreamy and also practical, dependable and trustworthy, someone who enjoys the good things in life and is able to methodically plan ahead. When people get to know you better they will see a sensitive, perceptive, artistic and wise person. A routine and regular life may appeal so you are left in peace with your own projects and thoughts. You do crave sensuality, comfort and love, so reach out for it.

PISCES SUN SIGN WITH GEMINI ASCENDANT

You're a good communicator on many different platforms, including the arts such as design, film and music. You may appear restless or mercurial and hard to pin down, and can be overly analytical and get caught up in your thoughts and imagination. You can be a contradiction: seemingly edgy on the outside yet inwardly possessing wisdom and peace. You need mental, artistic and spiritual stimulation, so follow your heart and study and grow in areas that provide room to expand your consciousness and experience.

PISCES SUN SIGN WITH CANCER ASCENDANT

You're an emotional and intuitive character, a sensitive person with deep perception. Your willpower and determination are rock solid, so your outward gentleness belies inner strength. You do have a kind of extrasensory perception, as both your Cancerian and Piscean psychic abilities make for a supremely intuitive individual. Sometimes this sensitivity can lead you to being easily misled and easily fooled, so ensure you base important decisions on facts and avoid being easily influenced.

PISCES SUN SIGN WITH LEO ASCENDANT

Your personality is very much the Leo type: preferring to be the centre of attention but also being a loving, creative character. The Leo dynamic is able to overcome immense hurdles and is the king of the jungle. When this is combined with kindness the Leo–Pisces character is adorable, but when steely determination creeps in the Pisces–Leo combination can make for an ambitious and immensely competitive character driven by the victim-martyr tendencies so prevalent in Pisces.

PISCES SUN SIGN WITH VIRGO ASCENDANT

You're meticulous and have good organisational skills, and your creative, philosophical, imaginative and inspired abilities find expression through carefully executed work and planning. You make a reliable worker and profound thinker, even if you do seem distant at times. You have strong spiritual interests and may be attracted to labour in service to others via health or social work. You do have a tendency towards victim-like behaviour when under pressure and must trust that your reason and logic will pull you through adversity.

PISCES SUN SIGN WITH LIBRA ASCENDANT

You're romantic and looking for peace and love in the world, principally through close relationships. You have a keen, practical mind that allows your inspiration to take flight in pursuit of the ideal.

Human rights and humanitarian pursuits will attract you, as will art, music, creative expression and film. You make a loving and supportive partner even if you are easily distracted and tend to let your mind wander.

PISCES SUN SIGN WITH SCORPIO ASCENDANT

You are intuitive, mystical and charming and can be passionate and zealous, attracting drama and chaos. Your intense personality belies the true peace in your heart. You're creative and instinctive and may be charismatic beyond even your own understanding. As you mature your kindness shines through, and you'll be seen for the creative and capable character you are. You're inspired and may feel drawn to develop your psychic abilities.

PISCES SUN SIGN WITH SAGITTARIUS ASCENDANT

Your thirst for excitement, adventure and knowledge knows no bounds, and you'll enjoy being up with the latest avant-garde thoughts and philosophy. You want an exciting life, yet deep down you're looking for peace, tranquillity and Zen-like fulfilment. You'll enjoy spending time pursuing an ideal or a spiritual goal. You're a seeker who will leave few stones unturned in your quest for answers. You need freedom of movement yet also wish for stability, which you'll find in your own unique way.

PISCES SUN SIGN WITH CAPRICORN ASCENDANT

You're inspired and practical, both a dreamer and a doer, an artist and a creator, a worker and a poet. Your gifts span many skills, but fundamentally you're capable and effective. While being artistic, musical and creative you also have a business mind; this rare combination of artist and businessperson puts you streets ahead of those who only work in one groove. Yours is a romantic soul with the ability to make dreams a reality.

PISCES SUN SIGN WITH AQUARIUS ASCENDANT

You're an individual who will be hard to miss: you're likely to be quirky in appearance or in mannerism or will pursue a life that is unusual or progressive. You're inspired and may be rebellious, pushing your ideas and those of society forward into avant-garde territory. Yours is a creative mind: art, music, film and humanitarian pursuits nurture your soul. You may be sensitive as a child, yet as you mature you'll make bold, radical changes in your life to uphold your strong sense of values.

PISCES SUN SIGN WITH PISCES ASCENDANT

You're highly creative, a dreamer and inspired. Your task will be to harness your talents and make good use of your skills rather than letting them remain dormant. Aim to be grounded and practical to allow your gifts to take flight. You may have a tendency to be easily influenced, especially when young. Spiritual and religious interests will infuse your life with meaning, but you must avoid victim-martyr roles in relationships. Trust your intuition.

PISCES IN LOVE

You are such an inspired individual, Pisces, you're likely to be fairly intuitive about who you decide to spend time with long term but may also tend to be idealistic. In this section you can check out your compatibility with other sun signs. Remember that we are all complex individuals, so the more you know about someone's astrological birth chart the better you can determine your compatibility. Consider having your astrological birth chart compared with that of a partner, friend or family member, as the compatibility – known as 'synastry' in astrology – goes even deeper than a comparison of sun signs, although this is a good place to begin.

PISCES WITH ARIES

Your dreamy, philosophical approach to life contrasts with Aries' action-oriented approach. While you can provide spiritual insight and support to Aries, the Aries' gung-ho approach to life may be anathema to you. There is a tendency here for both signs to miss the point of the other's mindset. The action-driven Aries can seem foolhardy to your more intuitive, instinctive approach, and your philosophical, gentle and forgetful nature can be annoying to impulsive, impatient Aries.

PISCES WITH TAURUS

Your soft, dreamy, philosophical approach to life can seem counter-intuitive to Taurus' rationale, which is always based on reason, facts and reality and not conjecture. While you can provide spiritual insight and inspiration to Taurus, the Taurus predilection for reason above all else can seem foolhardy to you. However, both Pisces and Taurus are sensual signs and there can be mutual enjoyment of each other's company. You will find common ground and rewarding enjoyment in art, music and companionship.

PISCES WITH GEMINI

You find Gemini's chattiness and joie de vivre appealing, yet as time goes by you may wish for more depth of character. If you want a long-term relationship there is certainly depth to be found, but all too often Gemini's restlessness can be a turn off for you. Gemini is attracted to your dreamy, inspired and yet philosophical intelligence, but you can unintentionally dampen their spirit. This union would need a strong air component in your astrology chart and a strong water signature in the Gemini's chart for it to work well.

PISCES WITH CANCER

This is a recipe for success as you are both water signs and have innate understanding of each other. You are intuitive, sensitive and tender partners, although your tendency for daydreaming may be frustrating for the more centred, strong-willed Cancer, who will wish to take the lead in the relationship. Your true pitfall would be playing the victim-martyr role. Both signs are complex, so you must give each other space for introspective time alone. This is, however, a mutually supportive partnership and can work for long-term commitment.

PISCES WITH LEO

You are drawn to Leo's larger than life personality but may subsequently feel overshadowed by their strong views and willpower. Leo must ensure they avoid stepping on your delicate ego. Leo is attracted to your sensitive personality, as your insight adds depth to the relationship and to their understanding of the world. This match can feel strained as you are both likely to operate in different worlds unless you learn more about the other's viewpoints and mindset.

PISCES WITH VIRGO

This is a case of opposites attract! You'll find Virgo's reasoning and practical skills grounding as Virgo earths your dreamy, abstract and spiritual approach to life. Virgo will be attracted to your inspired, imaginative and philosophical nature. This relationship will be based on the other completing you but it can be a co-dependent relationship and you must avoid playing victim-martyr roles. When you avoid this pitfall it can be a harmonious partnership in love.

PISCES WITH LIBRA

This is a romantic relationship that could be fulfilling, especially if you both express your artistic, creative attributes freely. Libra is attracted to your imagination and keen philosophising, but unless your particular Libra is proactive and decisive they will fall short of your high expectations. This relationship will flourish best when founded on common interests, so if there are none initially aim to find common ground by establishing strong emotional foundations.

PISCES WITH SCORPIO

As you are both water signs you have fundamental compatibility. You lead from the heart and are intuitive and instinctive, and enjoy romance, art, music and dance together and may also have mutual interests in spiritual development. This can be a truly deep connection, but unless you're adept at drawing the line between your path and your partner's you may easily become lost in each other's lives and consequently lose yourselves.

PISCES WITH SAGITTARIUS

Together you enjoy exploring life's experiences and gaining wisdom. You may initially be attracted to the upbeat, outgoing Sagittarian nature, and Sagittarius will be intrigued by your deep philosophical mind. You may in time come to feel overwhelmed by the strong personality of Sagittarius and intentionally or not pour cold water on their fire. Unless you have a strong fire

element in your astrological chart and Sagittarius has strong water elements, this match may serve as good companionship but enduring passion may be lacking.

PISCES WITH CAPRICORN

You're fundamentally different: you're a poet, creative, romantic and artistic, while Capricorn is a doer, pragmatist, thinker and organiser. This relationship is able to span the divide between your creativity and Capricorn's reasoning, but you must be prepared to see the other's perspective or your fundamentally different approaches spell no connection. If you find ways to work together as a team you could scale mountains, as your inspiration complements Capricorn's sense of practicalities.

PISCES WITH AQUARIUS

You're both creative, ingenious and inventive and are dreamers. You're idealists but also pragmatic. If you have both integrated your better qualities and operate without difficulty at your full potential this makes a wonderful match, as you can support each other's projects, creativity and goals. If either partner is unsure how to approach life both creatively and rationally this match could simply be confusing if not frustrating.

PISCES WITH PISCES

While seeming to be a romantic and ideal combination because like attracts like you can easily become lost in each other's lives, which then becomes confusing and frustrating especially if neither of you is clear about your own purpose or goals. Spiritually oriented Pisces may find this match rewarding; the pitfall is that unless you both have clear boundaries either partner can feel disoriented and become co-dependent, and thus risk playing a victim-martyr role.

THE YEAR AHEAD FOR PISCES

Affirmation: *'I'm worthy!'*

Good communications are the key to your success in 2022, as you'll get the chance to express yourself and your values so much more not only at work but also in your general interests and personal life. Communications can be non-verbal as well as verbal, so keep an eye on your body language and the message your actions give others this year as there is an opportunity for you to boost an element of sincerity and well-meaningness in your life that will be appreciated by many.

Sounds easy? It is, except that your values and beliefs are likely to change this year, meaning you will find new ways to express yourself and will therefore be seen differently. You may feel vulnerable as you emerge from your cocoon and begin to speak more fully with authority and persuasion, but those who know you as a certain person may be challenged to peg you into a new hole.

Being adaptable to new environments and circumstances will therefore be a true skill to learn and express in 2022.

Jupiter in your sign until mid-May will buoy your self-confidence but may also make you appear to have more swagger and bluster, so ensure you do not fall into the trap of grandstanding your ideas and believing your own hype during this time.

Turning points that will affect not only your self-esteem but also prospectively your finances and work will come in April-May and October-November. Aim to make decisions at these times with your head and not your emotions, with your heart (that is, with compassion) and not your mind. You could break into a new mould this year, benefiting from the chance to advance your status, career and standing and therefore also the way you are seen and the way you see yourself. So be brave; believe in your own abilities and that you deserve happiness. You are, after all, the most believing and spiritual of the zodiac signs, so decide early in the year that a loving heart deserves love!

HEALTH

Chiron, the celestial wounded healer, will transit your second house of self-esteem and values for the next six years, offering plenty of scope to improve your outlook towards others and yourself. Until July you are likely to feel on form health-wise but may suffer from seasonal flus and colds, especially in mid-July, late August, early October and mid-December.

Chiron in your second house this year presents the ideal opportunity to boost your immune system in the first half of the year and to increase your health and well-being on all levels: physically, spiritually, mentally and emotionally. Pisces born in late February and early March are most likely to need to slow down in the second half of the year and at least to be active about boosting your health then.

There is a truly go-ahead atmosphere for you in 2022, but a key pitfall would be that you overwhelm yourself with overwork and unrealistic expectations. On an emotional level, you may be inclined to keep challenges to yourself when those who love you would be happy to shoulder some of the burden.

Spiritually, this is an excellent year for a little soul searching as Chiron will help you to unearth your own innate abilities.

FINANCES

This year's eclipses on 30 April and 25 October will be across your finance sector and represent considerable changes in your fortunes, especially for March-born Pisces. Which way the changes will go will depend to a degree on your own decisions and financial planning. The partial solar eclipse on 30 April will present a fresh agreement or spotlight the way you share some of your resources such as tax debts and investments. The key to positive money management lies in adequate research and a little trust in your own instincts. Above all, avoid trends that dictate you must undertake one or another investment; be sure the organisations you invest with provide guarantees and have tried and tested track records.

The partial solar eclipse on 25 October will highlight your spending power and, more crucially, what and who you wish to spend your money on. You have a wonderful opportunity at this time to boost your circumstances financially but must be aware that extreme risk taking will not be a good idea in the financial climate.

However, work opportunities towards the end of the year are likely to boost your work and status and as a result you will manage to boost your finances, especially if you avoid gambling and risk taking.

HOME LIFE

With so much focus on your work, personal development and staying ahead of financial demands you will find time spent relaxing at home a real haven, but you are unlikely to make dynamic changes at home or with family unless you are drawn either through necessity or due to external circumstances or visitors to make changes such as a little DIY. If necessary, due to work developments, for example, there may be a move during the second half of the year.

Venus is more likely to bring a sense of cocooning in July and August and a wish to express your artistic and creative side in your décor and furnishings. However, if redecorating or even a move are necessary you are likely to most appreciate being able to make changes towards the end of June. An intense period may involve considerable changes, and the more patient you are with those in your home the better for you.

The sun in your fourth house for most of July will once again bring a sense that your home is your castle, so woe to anyone who tries to disturb the peace! Developments during July could be pivotal with regard to your long-term domestic plans and key decisions made then will have much chance of success even if choices prove to be stressful in the making.

LOVE

July is a turning point of the year for you, so watch out! It's likely to be a sizzling month. Before then it's a year to remind yourself that a good love life is based on excellent communication skills, so if you've ever felt you're not on the same page as your partner or prospective partner this is your year to work on your skills.

As the eclipses in May and November will be across your communications sector this suggests you'll be super busy and in demand at work, and will be required to express yourself better so everyone at work and at home understands you better.

The conjunction of the sun and Mercury in mid-July in your fifth house of fun will bring love and romance to centre stage in your life. If you've been planning a family you may find this is a turning point in your ventures. Aim to adapt to the prevailing winds when it comes to decision-making in your love life as a rigid response to matters that are outside your control could lead to stagnancy and an unwillingness to collaborate.

For the rest of the year you will enjoy spending more time on your health, well-being and self-development, which will reflect well on your love life and bring more calm and serenity, sexiness and passion into being.

CAREER

The new year begins with a new moon in your 10th house of work, career and status on 2 January, which will very much set the pace for the year. Keep an eye on the kinds of changes occurring in January as these will provide you with an indication of the developments that will occur for you in the bigger picture throughout the year, especially at key turning points in February, May and November.

You'll feel drawn to breaking fresh ground and may even be surprised by some of the opportunities that come your way, especially in February. Aim to embrace being busy. If you are involved in the health sector you may be particularly in demand with health and well-being concerns early in the year.

A real pitfall this year would be to focus so much on your career and status that you forget all other aspects of your life, especially early in the year. Aim to take breaks or you will suffer from fatigue.

The new moon in your sign on 2 March could bring new opportunities your way at work, so if you missed out on opportunities in January you will gain more then. Be prepared to negotiate and put your best foot forward as you could raise your game at this time.

In mid-April you may experience a degree of tension regarding your general direction and interests. Avoid giving in at the first hurdle and aim to make the changes that are necessary for you to progress.

A group, friend or organisation may be particularly helpful at this time. Tune in to your sense of purpose and the meaning you gain from this and you will not put a foot wrong.

Study and a chance to reconfigure how you see your finances will all contribute to a dramatic change in your career. Be brave, but do not take uncalculated risks.

January

career   love   home   health   finance

Notes: the pie charts such as the one above listed for each month show energy distribution according to the stars for the month ahead. If you wish to make changes in the areas of your finances, health, career, love or home and you see there is a large amount of energy in that sector in the chart, your endeavours should succeed as long as you have prepared well in advance. The charts also show which areas will potentially have the most focus in your life during the month.

The moon sign listed for each day's entry in the diary is the position of the moon at the end of the day in Greenwich Mean Time (GMT). To gain the most information about a particular day's circumstances, read the day before and the day after for a complete picture.

1 JANUARY

Happy New Year! You'll gain a sense this new year that your status, general direction and activities are changing, and you may experience a surprise change in your usual activities. You'll enjoy an impromptu get-together or a trip. *Moon enters Capricorn.*

2 JANUARY

The new moon and supermoon in Capricorn will kick-start a fresh phase for you in a social context and for some Pisceans at work. You'll be ready to embrace something different in either area or in both. Be practical about how you'll go about improving your status and embracing a fresh direction. You'll enjoy a reunion or altered daily routine.

3 JANUARY

You'll enjoy get-togethers that take you somewhere new, and if you're resuming your work schedule there will be uplifting elements and a social atmosphere you'll enjoy. ***Moon enters Aquarius.***

4 JANUARY

The Aquarian moon will encourage you to be more outgoing and upbeat about your various activities, especially in your personal life. You may feel more sociable and willing to embrace new and imaginative ideas and projects. ***Moon in Aquarius.***

5 JANUARY

You'll enjoy a reunion and the chance to touch base with like-minded people. Romance could blossom, so organise a treat. You'll be drawn to art, music and dance; a little luxury and a treat won't go astray! ***Moon in Aquarius.***

6 JANUARY

You'll feel in your element when the moon is in your own sign. You'll enjoy giving your goals and aspirations your full focus but you must be practical as well as inspired. Avoid being overly self-critical if you realise your plans are not quite as reachable as you'd like. Be diligent and you could attain a great deal. ***Moon in Pisces.***

7 JANUARY

When the moon is in your sign you'll feel creative, romantic, imaginative and artistic, but you may also tend to be idealistic so ensure your plans and ideas are feasible. You may be forgetful so be prepared to focus, especially at work. ***Moon in Pisces.***

8 JANUARY

This is a good time for meetings and for socialising, and you'll enjoy a reunion. A group or organisation may be particularly influential. Just ensure you are not being overly influenced by others. ***Moon in Aries.***

9 JANUARY

You'll enjoy spending time with your favourite people and activities. Music, the arts, dance and romance will all appeal. This is a good day for a health or beauty treat. If you're shopping avoid overspending, as you may be a little overindulgent. ***Moon in Aries.***

10 JANUARY

You're better known for your mystical, philosophical and spiritual interests yet you are also one of the most magnanimous of the zodiac signs and can make things happen in a big way! Remember that you can be practical and hands-on, and when the moon is in earth signs as it is today you can move mountains. *Moon enters Taurus.*

11 JANUARY

Meetings and talks are likely to go well, especially at work and concerning health and socially. However, you won't automatically get on with everyone and must guard against making assumptions, especially at work, or you could make mistakes or be misled. *Moon in Taurus.*

12 JANUARY

Be practical, realistic and hands-on with your projects and you'll make progress as a result, even if you feel matters are slow moving or represent hurdles. Be patient and diligent. *Moon in Taurus.*

13 JANUARY

The Gemini moon will provide a lighter feel to conversations and interactions providing there is room to move in negotiations. Try to get key paperwork and financial matters resolved before Mercury turns retrograde tomorrow to avoid delays over the next few weeks. Back up computers and files for the best measure. *Moon in Gemini.*

14 JANUARY

You may receive unexpected news at work or regarding a personal or financial commitment. Be prepared to renegotiate and reconsider some of your agreements and arrangements. *Moon in Gemini.*

15 JANUARY

The Gemini moon can sometimes spotlight areas of your life that are changing and elusive. If you discover that some matters need to be looked at in a new light see this as a positive, as it will enable you to subsequently move ahead with more insight and focus. *Moon enters Cancer.*

16 JANUARY

A get-together may be more relevant than meets the eye. You may meet someone who is intense or charismatic and has a transformative effect on you. A group, friend or organisation will be influential at the moment, so double-check that their influence is a positive one. *Moon in Cancer.*

17 JANUARY

The Cancerian full moon spotlights a new chapter concerning your personal life. For some this may involve a creative project and for others someone special such as a friend or family member.

If you've been considering starting a family or a new era is beginning in your personal life this full moon will spotlight your feelings. Developments could be transformational.

18 JANUARY

This is a good time to channel strong emotions or excess energy into productive activities as you could make a difference in many areas of your life. Be prepared to take action in concrete, practical and hands-on ways. ***Moon in Leo.***

19 JANUARY

An influential person or group could help boost your circumstances, especially at work and socially. A meeting or news will be encouraging and motivating. ***Moon in Leo.***

20 JANUARY

The sun in Aquarius for the next four weeks will provide the necessary insight and ability you need to make the necessary changes in your daily life. You may already feel a change in the air that provides a sense of possibility. It's a good time to ask yourself how to improve those areas of your life you feel are stagnant. ***Moon in Leo.***

21 JANUARY

The moon in Virgo is an excellent time to get organised, especially at work. It's also a good time for health and well-being appointments. Some emotions may be stronger than usual, but if you aim to pace yourself you could accomplish a great deal at work and in your personal life. ***Moon in Virgo.***

22 JANUARY

You'll enjoy socialising and networking, and there is a nostalgic atmosphere to the day. You may hear from an old friend or colleague. ***Moon enters Libra.***

23 JANUARY

This is another good day for get-togethers and reunions. A group, friend or organisation may catch your attention and you'll find you gain a sense of direction, purpose or meaning in your activities. Key news could encourage you to be more outgoing and adventurous with your enterprises. ***Moon in Libra.***

24 JANUARY

You may need to act as a mediator in meetings and talks, providing the voice of reason and understanding. Avoid taking someone's feelings or random comments personally. Maintain perspective. ***Moon in Libra.***

25 JANUARY

You can make great progress at work, so if you're looking for a promotion or for a job ensure you make an appointment with your employer or circulate your resume. This is a good day to gather information and for research into new projects and ideas. Be proactive about setting up meetings and about socialising and networking. *Moon in Scorpio.*

26 JANUARY

You may be drawn to reviewing a work or personal decision. You'll feel more aligned with your sense of purpose and a close friend or loyal family member will provide invaluable insight into your best step moving forward. *Moon in Scorpio.*

27 JANUARY

You may feel loyal to someone you love yet there is also benefit in being your own person and embracing new ideas. It's a good day for research and learning and for travel. *Moon in Sagittarius.*

28 JANUARY

The Sagittarian moon will encourage you to be more active in the areas of your life you love such as mysticism, spirituality and travel; you may even surprise yourself with the projects and plans you entertain. This is a good time to spruce up your appearance, health and fitness. *Moon in Sagittarius.*

29 JANUARY

You'll enjoy a reunion and the chance to deepen your relationship. However, some news or get-togethers may be a little intense, so ensure you maintain perspective. You may enjoy meeting a fresh social group or networking with people interested in self-development. *Moon in Capricorn.*

30 JANUARY

An unexpected change of plan or a surprise visitor needn't get in the way of an otherwise pleasant day. A financial matter will benefit from additional focus to ensure you are on the right track. You may need to rethink a financial budget, and there's no time like the present! *Moon in Capricorn.*

31 JANUARY

You may hear positive news at work or from a friend, group or organisation. This is a good day to boost your status, kudos and profile. Romance could flourish, so organise a treat! *Moon in Aquarius.*

February

career   love   home   health   finance

1 FEBRUARY

The new moon in Aquarius will kick-start a fresh phase in your daily routine such as a new work or health schedule. Be prepared to think outside the box about your options.

2 FEBRUARY

This is a good time to consider how you could move things around in your usual daily schedule so you find more time for your favourite activities and people. Careful negotiations and talks will reap rewards. *Moon enters Pisces.*

3 FEBRUARY

You may be particularly intuitive when the moon is in Pisces and will be drawn to music, good food and company. Trust your intuition if you're unsure about a health or work situation. *Moon in Pisces.*

4 FEBRUARY

This is a good day to make a commitment at work or to a health routine. You may be prepared to commit to a project that is ambitious but also innovative. You may hear from someone from your past or an authority figure. *Moon in Pisces.*

5 FEBRUARY

You can tend to take other people's random comments and challenges that are outside your control personally. If your vulnerabilities and doubts emerge, take things one step at a time and ask for expert guidance if necessary. Someone may need your help. *Moon in Aries.*

6 FEBRUARY

This is a good day for relaxing and recharging your batteries. If you feel you may be stressed, find ways to improve your nerves. Avoid taking matters personally unless they are clearly directed at you. If criticism is merited, find ways to improve yourself. If not, avoid those who wish to diminish you. *Moon in Aries.*

7 FEBRUARY

You'll gain the opportunity to set a few things straight, not only at work but also in your personal life. A practical and reasonable approach will work well. *Moon in Taurus.*

8 FEBRUARY

You may be surprised by some developments at work or a change in your usual activities. A new opportunity may arise. Being spontaneous or a change of environment and a chance encounter will be enjoyable. *Moon in Taurus.*

9 FEBRUARY

You're generally better known for your interests in the arts and philosophical, mystical and spiritual matters, yet currently travel, meetings and being more outgoing and sociable will also appeal. While the moon is in Gemini, why not combine all the above and plan some fun get-togethers over the next few days? *Moon in Gemini.*

10 FEBRUARY

You'll enjoy a reunion and the chance to touch base with someone at work, to add a more enlightened look at some of your projects. You may also be drawn to improving your health, appearance and well-being. *Moon in Gemini.*

11 FEBRUARY

A key meeting may be a little intense but will put you together with someone of like mind who you know you can collaborate with well. If you're single you may meet someone charismatic. A reunion could be pivotal or bring you in touch with someone you feel you have a fated link with. If you find events intense or disappointing, take time out to unwind and recalibrate when you can. *Moon in Cancer.*

12 FEBRUARY

The Cancerian moon for the next two days is ideal for cocooning and spending a little more time on your home and family and with the people you really resonate with. *Moon in Cancer.*

13 FEBRUARY

Your interest in the arts, mysticism and spirituality will blossom. A creative or personal venture could flourish. You'll be drawn to music and romance, so plan a treat! *Moon in Cancer.*

14 FEBRUARY

Happy St Valentine's Day! There is a slightly more intense feeling than usual to this iconic day. You'll enjoy hearing from and meeting those who are close to you, whether romance is a part of your connection or not. Couples will enjoy deepening your ties. *Moon in Leo.*

15 FEBRUARY

News from your past, such as from an employer, an authority figure or an old friend, may put into stark perspective how you feel about your current goals. You may not get on with everyone but you will gain perfect perspective about your priorities. *Moon in Leo.*

16 FEBRUARY

The Leo full moon will shine a light on your work and/or health schedules. Consider how you might work better in keeping with a routine you know not only promotes better working conditions but also better health. Be bold! Singles may meet someone new and exciting socially. Couples could deepen your relationship. A meeting will be significant at work or socially.

17 FEBRUARY

This is a good day to make solid plans and build strong foundations, either at work or in a personal relationship. Discuss your plans with those they concern as your ideas are likely to be appreciated. You may receive unexpected news such as a work, financial or ego boost. *Moon in Virgo.*

18 FEBRUARY

As the sun enters your sign you'll appreciate over the next four weeks feeling more in your element. You may feel extra energised and will find the time for yourself and your favourite activities. You may also feel more positive about your personal life. *Moon in Virgo.*

19 FEBRUARY

You'll enjoy spending a little time on your own health and well-being this weekend. If someone needs your help or advice you'll be sure to offer it. You'll gain a sense of more peace and calm in a close relationship or within a group. *Moon in Libra.*

20 FEBRUARY

This is a sociable time which you'll enjoy, and you may meet an attractive group of people or be involved in activities you enjoy. If you're working you'll appreciate being able to spend time doing what you love. You'll be drawn to the arts and a beautiful environment. *Moon in Libra.*

21 FEBRUARY

A sense of passion is going to feature in your interactions over the next two days. This will fire up romance but could also cause heated arguments at work, so avoid jumping to conclusions and think things through first. *Moon enters Scorpio.*

22 FEBRUARY

You're inspired and intuitive but not everyone else is. People may simply not understand what motivates you. Trust your instincts but be prepared to listen to other people's ideas and explain yours to them. *Moon in Scorpio.*

23 FEBRUARY

This is a good day for self-improvement and for enjoying time with someone special. Romance could flourish, so plan a treat. You may also enjoy socialising and networking. Avoid mistakes, as you may be a little idealistic. *Moon in Sagittarius.*

24 FEBRUARY

This is another lovely day for romance and socialising. Be positive. You'll be drawn to the arts, self-expression and creativity. *Moon in Sagittarius.*

25 FEBRUARY

You may be surprised by a development, especially to do with work or health. A financial or personal matter may require a little further thought. Communications may be mixed so avoid misunderstandings and plan extra time for travel to mitigate delays. *Moon enters Capricorn.*

26 FEBRUARY

This is a better day for communications although you may be tempted to overshare or exaggerate your feelings, so take things one step at a time. It's a good day for get-togethers and a health or beauty boost, and for taking a short trip. *Moon in Capricorn.*

27 FEBRUARY

You'll gain a sense of belonging in an important context and will enjoy the company of like-minded people. Romance could flourish, so plan something special. *Moon enters Aquarius.*

28 FEBRUARY

The moon in Aquarius is a good time to consider how best to move forward in areas of your life that need a little extra care and attention. Take a moment to organise your thoughts and put a plan of action in place that could take you somewhere new or fun. *Moon in Aquarius.*

March

| career | love | home | health | finance |

1 MARCH

Be innovative and consider new ways of going about your usual day. Alter your routine to add an element you enjoy. Find ways to boost your feel-good factor; you'll be glad you did! *Moon enters Pisces.*

2 MARCH

The new moon in your own sign signals a new chapter in your personal life, especially if it is your birthday on or before today. If your birthday is later in March you'll begin a fresh daily routine either at work or concerning health if you haven't already. Be inspired. You may receive unexpected news or will be surprised by developments.

3 MARCH

Expect news. The Venus-Mars-Pluto conjunction signals a change for you in a friendship group or via a group or organisation. You may simply feel more inclined to be sociable, or if you've been super sociable of late to take things a little more slowly. *Moon in Pisces.*

4 MARCH

The Aries moon brings out your inner feistiness and you may be productive as a result. However, you may also tend to be a little rash so ensure your plans are practical and avoid making snap decisions. *Moon in Aries.*

5 MARCH

You'll enjoy a get-together with someone whose is a little larger than life. Be positive and inspired. You may consider a new look, so this is a good day for a health or beauty appointment. Romance could blossom. News could be just what you want to hear, but if not maintain perspective and look for constructive ways forward. *Moon in Aries.*

6 MARCH

You'll enjoy socialising and may meet a progressive or different social circle. You may also be drawn to something new in your usual activities. You may be ready to step into different terrain. A personal matter may be truly motivational and you'll feel ready to invest more in someone special. *Moon in Taurus.*

7 MARCH

This is a good time to give yourself a reality check. Get your feet on the ground and ask yourself if all is at it seems in your life. If it is all the better, but if you discover some anomalies take steps to find out more. *Moon in Taurus.*

8 MARCH

This is a good day for research and meetings. Find ways to boost your circumstances at work through networking and hard work. You'll enjoy a reunion. It's also a good day for a health appointment. *Moon enters Gemini.*

9 MARCH

The Gemini moon will bring out your chatty, inquisitive side. You'll be interested in other people's opinions and a trip or a reunion will be refreshing. *Moon in Gemini.*

10 MARCH

As Mercury enters your sign your communication skills will improve over the coming weeks, and you may tend to be busy. Spiritual Pisces will enjoy delving more deeply into your beliefs and gaining a better understanding. You may be drawn to meditation, art and crafts. This is a good day to make a commitment to a work project or to make a personal commitment to better health or to someone special. *Moon in Gemini.*

11 MARCH

You'll feel super intuitive and in tune when the moon is in Cancer, so ensure you trust your instincts. You may be drawn to spend more time at home, with family or someone special. *Moon in Cancer.*

12 MARCH

This is a lovely weekend to spend boosting your appearance, wardrobe and well-being. You may also be drawn to updating your décor at home or to adding more luxury through sumptuous cushions, beautiful flowers or thick rugs. You could deepen your understanding of someone in your family. Spirituality and psychic work could flourish. ***Moon in Cancer.***

13 MARCH

You'll enjoy a get-together. Love and romance could flourish, so plan a date or to stay at home! However, you may be tempted to overindulge or overspend, which you'll regret tomorrow. ***Moon enters Leo.***

14 MARCH

This is a good day for work. You're likely to be productive and meetings should go well. However, you may tend to be idealistic so avoid being easily misled, especially financially. A meeting may be more significant than meets the eye. ***Moon in Leo.***

15 MARCH

The Leo moon will keep you busy so be prepared to work hard. If you're looking for work this is a good time to circulate your resume and for work interviews. ***Moon in Leo.***

16 MARCH

Keep an eye on your goals, especially at work and with regard to your health. Your eye for detail will be invaluable at work. Just avoid taking unwarranted criticism personally or being super critical yourself, as it will backfire. ***Moon in Virgo.***

17 MARCH

You may receive unexpected news or an unexpected visitor. You may bump into an old friend or will have a debt repaid. You may also receive an unexpected compliment or financial boost. ***Moon in Virgo.***

18 MARCH

The Virgo full moon signals a fresh chapter in your personal life or within a partnership if your birthday is today or before, and a fresh work or health situation if you were born later in March. Be prepared to put health and well-being first.

19 MARCH

An unexpected development will demand that you are adaptable – within reason. You may need to alter your views about a work or personal matter. If money is an issue, ensure you research your options carefully. ***Moon in Libra.***

20 MARCH

When the sun enters Aries it is the equinox. During the next four weeks you will feel more motivated to be upbeat, outgoing and positive. You may find that your finances or your self-esteem improve. You may also tend to overspend during the next four weeks, so it's a good time to put in place a fresh budget. You may be drawn to investing more heavily in yourself and in someone special; just avoid impulsiveness. *Moon in Scorpio.*

21 MARCH

A key trip or news will be important to you, especially if you were born between 5 and 7 March or before. A work or health situation will require a little focus if you were born later in March. This is a good time to plan travel, a meeting or a health or work venture. *Moon in Scorpio.*

22 MARCH

You may be surprised by news, and the more adaptable and practical you are the better otherwise misunderstandings could occur. It's a good day for meetings and talks, so be realistic and organise ways to move forward should a spanner be thrown in the works. *Moon enters Sagittarius.*

23 MARCH

A meeting will be ideal and may also be more significant than meets the eye. You may meet someone influential, and if you're single you may meet someone who seems familiar but whom you have never met before. The spiritually inclined may reach an epiphany, and an interest in art and music will blossom. A work meeting may be ideal but you must check the details if you're unsure of anything. *Moon in Sagittarius.*

24 MARCH

The moon at the zenith of your chart may put your heart on your sleeve, and you may also feel feistier. Channel energy into work and your projects to avoid getting caught in arguments. You could make a great deal of progress with your projects by being realistic and optimistic. *Moon enters Capricorn.*

25 MARCH

Mercury, Jupiter and Neptune in your sign are encouraging you to be inspired and take the initiative with projects and people that resonate. You may tend to be a little idealistic, so ensure you are also being practical. *Moon in Capricorn.*

26 MARCH

You'll enjoy relaxing and socialising with like-minded people. Certain meetings and talks could be transformative or will inspire you to make changes in your personal life. *Moon in Capricorn.*

27 MARCH

You may find that conversations become more upbeat or even feisty, so take a moment to adjust to a fresh pace. You'll enjoy a reunion and may be drawn to update your looks through a new outfit or haircut. ***Moon in Aquarius.***

28 MARCH

A key meeting or reunion could be significant. If you're looking for work this is a good time to make calls, circulate resumes and schedule interviews. It's also a good day for health and beauty appointments. If you're looking for love you may find romance. A situation may seem ideal and it may well be, but you must double-check the details to be sure. ***Moon in Aquarius.***

29 MARCH

The moon in your sign will bring out your inner romantic and you may be seeing life through rose-coloured glasses. If you're unsure about whether you're being idealistic, do a little more research before committing to certain plans or ideas. ***Moon in Pisces.***

30 MARCH

This is a good day for boosting your appearance and for a reunion. If you're an artist you are likely to feel inspired. Spiritual Pisces may gain deep insight. It's a good time for psychic development. Romance is alive, so singles may meet someone charming and couples could rekindle passion. ***Moon in Pisces.***

31 MARCH

The Aries moon can bring out people's fiery and antagonistic sides, so be careful with interactions if someone seems angry. Be bold but avoid impulsiveness, as it could land you in hot water. ***Moon in Aries.***

April

career love home health finance

1 APRIL

The Aries new moon will kick-start a fresh phase in your personal life, financially or at work. There may be a strong health-related theme to this new phase, as a therapeutic option will become clear. Be courageous but avoid jumping to conclusions. You may contemplate a new financial investment but must do your research to avoid losses.

2 APRIL

Surprise news and the chance to turn a corner with a personal or financial matter may be unexpected. Be prepared to try something new. If you need guidance or expert help it will be available. ***Moon enters Taurus.***

3 APRIL

You'll enjoy a reunion, the chance to boost your interests and altering your usual Sunday routine to bring more romance and love into your personal life. A beauty or health appointment may appeal. ***Moon in Taurus.***

4 APRIL

A work meeting or health appointment will go well. You may be drawn to undertaking considerable changes in your personal or work life, so this is a good time to research your options more fully. *Moon in Taurus.*

5 APRIL

As Venus enters your sign you'll be more drawn to expressing your deeper values and ideas, especially in your personal life. At work you may wish to gain more fulfilment and satisfaction in your daily routine. It's a good day for meetings with someone significant such as an employer or teacher, as you'll gain clarity about your options. *Moon in Gemini.*

6 APRIL

This is another good day for talks and making agreements, especially at work and in your personal life. Take the time to discuss your ideas with someone you know has your back. *Moon in Gemini.*

7 APRIL

You can make great progress at work and with health matters. Take the time to discuss arrangements and plans with those they concern. A financial agreement could be advantageous, but you must ensure you have researched the variables well. *Moon in Cancer.*

8 APRIL

You may be a little idealistic, and in this frame of mind you could tend to be a little impressionable, so ensure you keep your feet on the ground. The arts, music, dance and romance will all thrive under these stars, so organise an activity you'll enjoy. *Moon in Cancer.*

9 APRIL

You'll enjoy a reunion and the chance to invest a little more in the relationships and people who are truly dear to you. You may enjoy a health boost such as a trip to the ocean and the chance to improve your appearance and fitness. *Moon in Cancer.*

10 APRIL

Communications may not be as straightforward as you might hope, as someone and perhaps even you will not agree with everyone. A trip, financial transaction or disagreement may create an intense atmosphere, so be prepared to be patient. Avoid tense or sensitive topics if possible as these will escalate quickly into arguments. Back up computers to avoid losing information. *Moon in Leo.*

11 APRIL

There may be tension surrounding a personal or financial matter, so try to keep the communication channels open to avoid intense interactions. You may gradually feel the tension ease but must avoid becoming impatient or stubborn as this will delay important matters. *Moon in Leo.*

12 APRIL

Key discussions or financial transactions will provide a sense of direction, but if they further cloud your progress it's important to regain a sense of perspective as you may be super idealistic. Romance and the arts could blossom. You may find that you need to agree to disagree with some people. *Moon in Leo.*

13 APRIL

You are productive and work and your general projects are likely to advance as a result. It's a good day to make a commitment to someone or to a project; just avoid rushing decisions. *Moon in Virgo.*

14 APRIL

You'll be inspired by music and dance and being creative. A personal situation could flourish, and this is a good day for romance so organise a treat or get-together. *Moon enters Libra.*

15 APRIL

As Mars enters your sign you may notice your energy levels increase over the next few days and weeks. However, you may also feel rushed and under pressure, so ensure you take things at your own pace unless you must meet deadlines. *Moon in Libra.*

16 APRIL

The Libran full moon signifies the start of a fresh cycle in your shared duties, collaborations or joint finances. Consider distributing these in a more balanced or equal way, and if you are already doing the lion's share ask someone you perform these duties with if they'd consider making your arrangements fairer. You may begin a fresh agreement with a business or work partner.

17 APRIL

The Scorpio moon tends to bring people's passionate sides to the surface. You may find someone you share space with at home is more vocal and expressive, but if they are disgruntled encourage them to channel their energy into something productive such as sports. *Moon in Scorpio.*

18 APRIL

You may be surprised by news and developments. A financial situation may require more focus. Find the time to look for balance in an agreement and you are likely to be successful in your endeavours. Ask for help in a collaboration if it is needed. *Moon in Scorpio.*

19 APRIL

This is a good time to research your ideas and plans as you'll find the information you need. You may feel more expressive and outgoing, and a trip, study course or the chance to be more creative will appeal. *Moon enters Sagittarius.*

20 APRIL

The sun in Taurus for the next four weeks will encourage you to improve communications and travel in the most realistic way. You may also find that the practicalities of finances – how you spend your money and earn your living – will require extra attention to ensure you gain more stability in life. *Moon in Sagittarius.*

21 APRIL

This is a good time to be practical about your various projects and how you spend your spare time. Allocate decent amounts of time to your health and well-being, which involves having a social life. *Moon in Capricorn.*

22 APRIL

Your work and daily lives are likely to be busy, but if you haven't yet found your niche at work or in life this is an excellent time to find ways to do just that. Start with research into courses and/or organisations that can help you. *Moon in Capricorn.*

23 APRIL

You may meet someone important to you, and if you meet someone new this encounter may be more significant than meets the eye. A key financial situation may catch your eye. Avoid seeing obstacles as being insurmountable as they may provide opportunities for change. *Moon in Aquarius.*

24 APRIL

You may take the easy way rather than face obstacles head-on. If you delay some matters that need your attention you will need to tackle them at some point. A talk or meeting may be difficult, but rest assured if you tackle it now you'll be glad you did. Avoid obstinacy. *Moon in Aquarius.*

25 APRIL

You'll get ahead by being super focused on priorities and getting chores done. Find new ways to get ahead with matters that are stuck at work or in your personal life. ***Moon in Pisces.***

26 APRIL

You'll feel more in tune with developments and it's a good time to trust your instincts, especially regarding work, health and finances. Find the time to relax with favourite activities such as music, film and dance. ***Moon in Pisces.***

27 APRIL

You'll enjoy getting together with someone inspiring. A trip or meeting will be productive. Romance could flourish, especially if you were born in mid-March. If you're single you may meet someone, so take the initiative. Just ensure you have researched circumstances adequately if you are making considerable financial or personal investments. ***Moon enters Aries.***

28 APRIL

This is a good day for socialising and making changes in your life that you've had on the drawing board for some time. You may be drawn to travelling or to meeting a group of inspiring people. ***Moon in Aries.***

29 APRIL

You'll enjoy getting together with an inspiring or in some way different crowd of people. You may be ready to step into a new territory, either through travel or via your social life or personal interests. ***Moon in Aries.***

30 APRIL

The partial solar eclipse in Taurus signals a fresh understanding with someone. You may find that romance is intense, so this is a good time for singles to meet someone new and for couples to rekindle romance. You may experience the beginning or end of a key relationship. Your finances may improve or you must make a key financial decision. Take your priorities and values into account.

May

career	love	home	health	finance

1 MAY

You'll enjoy socialising and making changes where you need to regarding paperwork such as keeping up to date with filing and invoices. Romance could blossom, so organise a date! *Moon in Taurus.*

2 MAY

As Venus leaves your sign you will feel more inclined to consider your values and principles as you move forward over the coming weeks, especially concerning finances and your personal life. You may be prone to being impulsive, so take things one step at a time. *Moon in Gemini.*

3 MAY

Be inspired by your ideas and opinions and you will be more likely to inspire others either at work or at play! You could make considerable changes in both fields, so be proactive. You may be drawn to changing your appearance or to improving domestic or work décor. *Moon in Gemini.*

4 MAY

You may receive an unexpected call or visitor. If you've been considering a change of job or a new investment you may discover something to your advantage. You'll enjoy being spontaneous but must avoid making snap decisions. *Moon in Gemini.*

5 MAY

A surprise get-together or financial development will merit a little focus. You can get ahead at work so take the initiative. You'll appreciate the opportunity for a reunion. *Moon in Cancer.*

6 MAY

This is a good day for a short trip somewhere beautiful and for meetings, both at work and in your personal life. You could also make progress financially. *Moon in Cancer.*

7 MAY

You'll feel more active and outgoing this weekend and will appreciate the opportunity to focus on yourself and your interests. You may enjoy shopping, sports or favourite activities. If you're considering a large investment, avoid impulse buys by getting a second opinion from a friend or relative. *Moon in Leo.*

8 MAY

You'll feel outgoing and sociable, especially with family or someone close. Music, the arts and being creative and chatty will appeal. You may also enjoy sprucing up your home environment. *Moon in Leo.*

9 MAY

If you're working you may have a slight case of Mondayitis as you'd rather be anywhere but work! However, as the day proceeds you'll gain a sense of motivation and could accomplish a great deal. Aim to tie up loose ends at work and regarding communications before Mercury turns retrograde tomorrow. *Moon enters Virgo.*

10 MAY

As Mercury turns retrograde you're likely to receive key news that will merit a little focus. You may need to reconsider an agreement, financial investment or even a trip. Try to allow extra time for travel and communications to avoid frustration over the coming weeks. *Moon in Virgo.*

11 MAY

As Jupiter joins Venus and Chiron in Aries you are likely to notice a shift in pace and may be busy over the coming weeks. You may feel motivated to make changes in your personal life or financially and to be more adventurous. You may consider a trip or visit in more detail. *Moon in Virgo.*

12 MAY

You'll accomplish a great deal both at work and in your personal life by being practical and reasonable. It's a good time to consider whether you could find more balance and harmony in your daily routine and to make changes if you find you could. *Moon in Libra.*

13 MAY

You'll enjoy a reunion with someone close, and if you meet someone new your meeting may be more significant than meets the eye. A close relationship or interest could deepen. Take the initiative if you're single to find someone suitable. Couples will enjoy reigniting romance. Base your choices on research and fair play for the best results. *Moon in Libra.*

14 MAY

This is a good day for deepening your relationship with someone close, especially if you or they have been absent or if you have had disagreements recently. You'll enjoy finding more peace and harmony in your life this weekend. *Moon in Scorpio.*

15 MAY

You'll enjoy the company of an inspiring character. A trip or a meeting could be ideal even if it seems to clash with your usual routine. Someone may need your help or vice versa. Rest assured, support will be available. A little retail therapy will appeal, but if funds are tight avoid getting into debt. *Moon in Scorpio.*

16 MAY

The total lunar eclipse in Scorpio is an intense full moon as it will spotlight how you feel about your activities and interests and also about your investments, be these of your time, love, finances or energy. You may feel supported by those around you, but if you feel let down this is a good time to invest more fully in yourself and find new ways ahead. A trip could be pivotal. *Moon enters Sagittarius.*

17 MAY

You may discover whether you've over-estimated your circumstances. You may also discover you've been realistic and that your plans can work, especially in connection with work and health. Strive for your ideals and you may be surprised by what you can achieve. *Moon in Sagittarius.*

18 MAY

This is a good day to let your imagination do the talking, especially if you have felt your plans are working for you. If you've discovered you've made an error of judgment this is an ideal time to reconsider your situation and prepare to make changes, especially relating to your work, health and appearance. *Moon in Capricorn.*

19 MAY

This is a good day to make changes both in your personal life and environment. A trip or meeting is likely to be successful. Take a moment to decide how you'd like to spend your spare time and organise something special. *Moon in Capricorn.*

20 MAY

You'll enjoy a reunion, trip or return to an old haunt. You may hear from an old friend. It's a good day to consider a fresh budget, especially if you're in debt. ***Moon in Aquarius.***

21 MAY

The sun in Gemini for the next four weeks will encourage you to be more outgoing and chattier, and also to focus a little more on maintaining balance in your relationships and financially. You'll enjoy a sense of freedom of movement, and a trip or meeting could be exciting. ***Moon in Aquarius.***

22 MAY

You'll feel motivated to meet a group of like-minded people. You may return to a situation that is familiar or will find merit in going over old plans and ideas so you gain a sense of direction. ***Moon enters Pisces.***

23 MAY

You may see merit in reviewing an idea or project. You may feel drawn to reconnecting with someone. A trip or reunion is likely to go well. If you're shopping, avoid overspending and overindulging as you'll regret it tomorrow. It's a good time to review spending habits if you're in debt. ***Moon in Pisces.***

24 MAY

This is a good day to make a commitment to a project or to a person. You may feel more inclined to negotiate and find common ground in certain arrangements, especially if you have disagreed on terms in the recent past. It's a good time for discussions. ***Moon in Pisces.***

25 MAY

As Mars leaves your sign and enters Aries you may experience a shift in energy towards a more proactive and busier phase. In the process you may be busy and will need to think on your feet. If some matters are progressing too quickly this is a good time to apply the brakes before it's too late to make changes. ***Moon in Aries.***

26 MAY

This is a good day to consider how best to manage your finances. You may experience a financial or ego boost but you may be inclined to spend as quickly as you earn. A debt may be repaid to you and you may be ready to repay one yourself. A return to an old haunt or a visit may boost morale. ***Moon in Aries.***

27 MAY

How do you feel about someone in charge? If you feel they overshadow you it may be time to reconsider how you interact with them and whether they are too domineering in your relationship. You may need to review a decision or your stance about a work or financial matter. Avoid arguments, as these could escalate to conflict quickly. *Moon in Taurus.*

28 MAY

You'll feel drawn to investing in yourself over the coming weeks and will enjoy creature comforts such as simply relaxing at home. You may also wish to consolidate your financial situation to gain more of a sense of security and stability. If conflict is brewing, find a way to nip it in the bud to avoid arguments. *Moon in Taurus.*

29 MAY

A spontaneous event will be fun and you'll appreciate the chance to enjoy the company of an upbeat character. You'll enjoy being physically active via sports, walking or gardening. Someone close may have key news for you, especially if you were born in February. You may be prone to overspending or overindulging, which it's best to avoid if you're already in debt. *Moon enters Gemini.*

30 MAY

The Gemini new moon will spotlight something new in your personal life such as a fresh development at home or regarding travel and changes in a key relationship. For some this new moon points to the need to update technology or repair a vehicle, including fresh tyres, for example.

31 MAY

You'll be drawn to investing more in yourself or your work. If a large expense is looming take the time to put a clever budget in place. Romance could blossom, so organise a treat. You may enjoy a personal compliment, ego boost or financial improvement. *Moon in Gemini.*

June

career   love   home   health   finance

1 JUNE

The moon in Cancer motivates you to spend more time with those you love and cocoon. You're also likely to be more spot on with your intuition, so take the time to tune in to your instincts. ***Moon in Cancer.***

2 JUNE

This is a good time to renegotiate some of your arrangements, especially at home and with those close to you. You may not agree with everyone, so find clever ways to negotiate to avoid arguments. ***Moon in Cancer.***

3 JUNE

You'll be glad to hear that Mercury ends its retrograde phase today. You may receive key news concerning a personal or financial matter. Communications and travel plans will become easier to make over the coming weeks. Take the time to consider your views and take practical steps to move forward. Travel or communications may be delayed, so be patient. ***Moon enters Leo.***

4 JUNE

This is a good day to focus on your finances and find ways to boost your self-esteem if you've felt a little lacking in confidence lately. Try some positive self-talk. You may receive a compliment or financial or ego boost. It's a good day to devise a ffoolproof budget. ***Moon in Leo.***

5 JUNE

The Leo moon motivates you to get things done, especially with chores and your favourite projects. You may also feel more inclined to spend time with someone you love in your family. You may surprise yourself with your level of productivity. *Moon in Leo.*

6 JUNE

This is a good day to get things done in the most efficient way, as you may otherwise feel frustrated with chores and work load. Make a list and move ahead one step at a time. You may be asked for help or your advice. If you need guidance it will be available. *Moon in Virgo.*

7 JUNE

You may be surprised by news or a spontaneous event and will enjoy an impromptu get-together. Be adaptable and prepared to make changes. There is a healing or therapeutic aspect to the day that makes it ideal for a health appointment. *Moon in Virgo.*

8 JUNE

The more practical you are with events the better for you, especially at work and financially. Avoid being obstinate about changes that are long overdue. Your organisational skills are peaking, so don't be afraid to take charge. *Moon enters Libra.*

9 JUNE

The more you see the good in a current situation the better for you. You may be asked to mediate between two people or at work and will need to look for ways to establish calm and balance in a financial or personal situation. *Moon in Libra.*

10 JUNE

This is a great day for socialising and networking. You'll enjoy the company of like-minded people. You may also find that you receive a financial or ego boost. *Moon enters Scorpio.*

11 JUNE

Unexpected developments may bring you in touch with a deeper sense of synchronicity and will also deepen your spiritual or personal beliefs. You'll enjoy doing something different or an impromptu meeting or trip. Avoid impulsiveness as it could be counterproductive. *Moon in Scorpio.*

12 JUNE

You'll enjoy deepening your understanding of someone close or of yourself. If you're a spiritual Pisces you'll enjoy bolstering your beliefs. This is a good time for psychic and mediumship development. *Moon enters Sagittarius.*

13 JUNE

As Mercury enters its own sign of Gemini life and communications are likely to speed up once again. You may be super busy or find that some communications are complex or difficult. It's a good day to plan a trip. ***Moon in Sagittarius.***

14 JUNE

The full moon and supermoon in Sagittarius at the zenith of your chart represents a fresh chapter in your interests, activities and pastimes. You may be ready to alter how you go about some of your projects and will embrace more learning and travel and broadening your horizons. For some this full moon points to legal matters or a contract that will require focus. You may be ready to take a business or personal relationship to a new level. Changes at home may also feature.

15 JUNE

A meeting will have a therapeutic or healing effect. Avoid rushing and making snap decisions. Also avoid cutting corners literally as you or someone close may be accident prone. Someone may need your help, and if you need help from an expert or adviser it will be available so reach out. ***Moon in Capricorn.***

16 JUNE

This is a good day to make a commitment to a new agreement, especially at home or at work. Just check contracts carefully if you are signing a new lease, for example. A trip could take you somewhere inspiring or constructive although there may be delays, so be patient. A financial or personal matter could lead to promising developments. ***Moon enters Aquarius.***

17 JUNE

You may discover the benefits of a personal or financial matter and will enjoy being spontaneous and outgoing. Just avoid making snap decisions that could get you into hot water, such as gambling both financially and emotionally. It is better to research important matters first. ***Moon in Aquarius.***

18 JUNE

Take a moment to consider your circumstances, especially if you have been disappointed by a financial or work matter. If a situation has made you feel less than you are it is not worth your worry, as you must be respected above all else. A financial matter must be looked at in practical terms to avoid deepening debt. ***Moon in Aquarius.***

19 JUNE

You'll enjoy socialising and indulging in life's luxuries and romance. However, you may tend to be escapist and will be drawn to overindulging or overspending. If you're already in debt leave the credit card at home if you're shopping. ***Moon in Pisces.***

20 JUNE

The Pisces moon will be inspiring and you'll feel more inclined to follow your dreams than you usually do on a Monday! Take a moment to set your priorities and you'll find this is a productive week. You may be forgetful, so avoid misplacing valuables such as door keys. *Moon in Pisces.*

21 JUNE

As the sun enters Cancer, marking the solstice, you will feel inclined to focus more on your domestic and personal life over the coming weeks and on self-nurturance and the nurturance of those you love. A meeting at work could be super productive. Romance could flourish, so organise a treat. *Moon in Aries.*

22 JUNE

The Aries moon is motivational for you and you'll feel productive and more proactive. Some people may appear a little feisty under the Aries moon, so if you experience adverse reactions blame it on the moon and avoid contributing to tension. *Moon in Aries.*

23 JUNE

This is a good day to get things on a more even keel, especially at work and in your personal life. You may feel more grounded and practical about your projects and less flighty. Show just what you have at work by being efficient and effective. *Moon enters Taurus.*

24 JUNE

You'll enjoy indulging in good food and company over the next two days, so organise a treat for this evening or the weekend. *Moon in Taurus.*

25 JUNE

A trip or meeting will be productive and you could accomplish a great deal if you're working. A reunion or return to an old haunt could show you just how far you have come this year. *Moon in Taurus.*

26 JUNE

You'll enjoy being active and outgoing. You may enjoy a trip or a visit and meeting similarly minded people. If you're shopping, you may find just what you're looking for. *Moon in Gemini.*

27 JUNE

There is a therapeutic aspect to the day. You'll manage to clear a backlog of work, and good communication skills will pave the way for better relationships. Take the initiative at work and with health matters. You could attain a lot. *Moon in Gemini.*

28 JUNE

A change of routine or a spontaneous event will breathe fresh air into your day. You'll enjoy hearing from a friend or receiving a surprise guest. You may be surprised by news, an unexpected visitor or an impromptu meeting. *Moon enters Cancer.*

29 JUNE

The Cancerian new moon will kick-start a fresh chapter in your personal life. You could improve dynamics at home or with family and will invest more time in your home or a property. Avoid feeling that Rome was built in a day; current changes may take a little while to be finalised.

30 JUNE

Your intuition is very strong so ensure you trust it. If you're inclined to be irrational take a moment to settle your nerves and look for the most practical way to get ahead, especially at home and in your personal life. *Moon in Cancer.*

July

career love home health finance

1 JULY

The key to success over the next few days lies in solid decision-making and steering clear of impulsive behaviour. You may be liable to take some discussions or events personally, and with mounting tension in the skies this could contribute to arguments. *Moon in Leo.*

2 JULY

You'll appreciate the chance to get your feet on the ground and complete chores around the home and garden. You may also enjoy a return to an old haunt or a reunion. However, some developments will feel intense so ensure you maintain perspective with personal matters, and if some meetings or communications are delayed avoid taking things personally. *Moon in Leo.*

3 JULY

This is another good day to get your feet on the ground, especially with household chores. If a relationship has been strained, take practical and grounded steps to improve circumstances. You may be forgetful, so avoid misplacing valuables such as house keys. *Moon enters Virgo.*

4 JULY

There may be intense meetings or discussions, so polish up your communication skills to avoid misunderstandings and fraught interactions. If you focus on having a positive outcome to a trip or meeting your work and efforts won't go unnoticed. A domestic or personal matter will require careful handling. ***Moon in Virgo.***

5 JULY

This is a good day to practise what you preach, especially if you're looking for a better way ahead in your personal life. It's a good day to establish firmer relationships and find ways to move ahead with a deeper and clearer understanding. ***Moon enters Libra.***

6 JULY

There is a healing and therapeutic quality to the day that will help you to get things on a more even keel in your personal life. If certain interactions have been difficult you're likely to be able to establish some form of common ground. Someone may need your help, and if you need guidance it'll be available. It's a good day for a beauty treat. ***Moon in Libra.***

7 JULY

This is a good day to consider how you can better express yourself, especially if you have recently experienced arguments. You may feel inspired to gain a deeper understanding of someone close, and talks could move forward with a stronger appreciation of each other. ***Moon in Libra.***

8 JULY

Take a moment to consider how you'd best like your personal life to move forward. If you feel vulnerable or sensitive at the moment, ensure you take time out to regain perspective. Avoid minor bumps and scrapes and avoid taking other people's random comments personally. You may be drawn to doing a little DIY or home renovation. You may be surprised by some news or a positive remark. ***Moon in Scorpio.***

9 JULY

The key to success lies in good communication skills. You may not see eye to eye with someone at home or at work, but this doesn't mean you can't find common ground in some ways. Travel and communications may be delayed, so be patient. ***Moon in Scorpio.***

10 JULY

You'll enjoy improving your home or environment and a little DIY or splash of colour at home will feel refreshing. A surprise at home or the chance to do something different will be delightful. You may enjoy a reunion. ***Moon enters Sagittarius.***

11 JULY

The moon at the zenith of your chart will provide a more upbeat and outgoing atmosphere to your day. You may feel conflicted between wishing to be at home as opposed to doing things out in the world, but you will find a therapeutic aspect to being busy so take the initiative. ***Moon in Sagittarius.***

12 JULY

This is a good day to get organised and look for practical ways you can move forward with your plans. A group, organisation, family member or friend may be particularly useful as a sounding board. *Moon enters Capricorn.*

13 JULY

The full moon and supermoon in Capricorn will spotlight a fresh chapter in your personal life. For some this will be particularly to do with family and for others to do with your home life or a fresh social group. You'll feel more inclined to be with like-minded people and to establish extra stability and security in your life.

14 JULY

You are known for your spiritual and mystical abilities yet you can tend to look at life through rose-coloured glasses. You'll find out whether you've over- or under-estimated a circumstance, and the good news is you'll be able to set things right. Avoid being forgetful and mislaying valuables such as car keys. *Moon enters Aquarius.*

15 JULY

The lure of your home, cocooning, family and simply relaxing may be stronger than your sense of duty and social obligations. Choose your activities carefully, but if you need to devote some time to a friend, work or organisation rest assured your efforts will be worthwhile. *Moon in Aquarius.*

16 JULY

A lovely get-together with someone you love such as a family member or a partner will be enjoyable, even if you must overcome logistics such as getting the house shipshape, gardening or work schedules you must complete first. Romance could blossom but you may be short on relaxation time, so ensure you schedule it in or you'll miss the window! *Moon enters Pisces.*

17 JULY

This is a lovely day for romance and creativity. Artistic, spiritually minded and creative Pisces will appreciate the opportunity to get busy with your projects. A family get-together could be ideal. However, you may be feeling escapist and may tend to overindulge, so spare a thought for your bank balance and health. *Moon in Pisces.*

18 JULY

You may encounter deep feelings, either your own or of someone you interact with. Avoid intense stand-offs if arguments are brewing, as these could escalate into conflict. A trip or meeting could be transformative. *Moon enters Aries.*

19 JULY

As Mercury enters upbeat Leo you may feel more outgoing and positive about communicating some of your plans and ideas with those they concern. Just be sensitive to other people's feelings if you see that some of your plans may cause a rift. *Moon in Aries.*

20 JULY

This is another day when news that has long-term consequences is best handled carefully. You'll enjoy a get-together, but if you feel tension is increasing find ways to defuse stress rather than contribute to it. Creative Pisces may be particularly inspired and productive. A family or personal circumstance may change rapidly. *Moon enters Taurus.*

21 JULY

The moon in Taurus brings your practical and reasonable qualities into being, and you'll manage to communicate and express your desire for more stability and security in your life. However, you may tend to overindulge or overspend so be wary of accruing debt. *Moon in Taurus.*

22 JULY

As the sun enters Leo you'll gain a sense of connectedness with someone special in your life. You may also be prepared to be more light-hearted in your personal life over the next four weeks and to welcome extra fun and creativity in your life. *Moon in Taurus.*

23 JULY

This is a lovely day for deepening your relationship with someone special and also for spending more time on favourite activities. A trip or meeting will be enjoyable. *Moon in Gemini.*

24 JULY

You'll appreciate a sense of freedom and may be drawn to travelling or meeting people you haven't seen for a while. A domestic or personal matter may be tense, and you'll gain more ground by being communicative than burning bridges. *Moon in Gemini.*

25 JULY

You have a great deal of get up and go, especially where work and generally improving your motivation and health are concerned. However, not everyone will necessarily agree with you and a difference of opinion is best approached carefully. Your differences may well rest with a disparity in values and expectations, so find ways to establish common ground. *Moon enters Cancer.*

26 JULY

You may tend to be a little impulsive, especially if you're busy and under pressure. Avoid rushing into decisions. Do your research first, especially financially and at work. *Moon in Cancer.*

27 JULY

A therapeutic aspect to the day will encourage you to look at how you could improve your daily routine and health schedule so you feel revitalised. A change in your usual routine could also perk you up, so organise something different. This is a good day for a health appointment. You may be asked for help, and if you need it guidance is available so reach out. *Moon in Cancer.*

28 JULY

The Leo new moon points to a fresh chapter at work or regarding your health or that of someone close. For some this new moon points to a fresh chapter in your personal life, especially with your family. If you've been considering starting a family or adding to it, this could be it! Avoid making snap decisions and do your research. Travel and meetings may be delayed, so be patient.

29 JULY

This is a good time to consider your values, principles and key aims and goals, especially if you have an important decision to make. Be tactful and diplomatic where necessary and willing to see another's viewpoint. *Moon in Leo.*

30 JULY

This is a good weekend to consider the details of your various plans and ideas, especially regarding work, a change of routine or health matters. You'll get a lot done around the house and garden and will enjoy catching up with someone fun. *Moon enters Virgo.*

31 JULY

You'll enjoy a fun change of routine and the chance to boost your relationships, health and well-being. A key work, financial or health decision is best taken carefully, so ensure you gain expert advice if you're unsure. *Moon in Virgo.*

August

career love home health finance

1 AUGUST

The clearer you are with communications, both at work and in your personal life, the better will be the outcome of your day, as otherwise mistakes and misunderstandings may occur. Rest assured, though, that your efforts will be worthwhile, so aim to overcome any hurdles that arise. Some meetings or travel may be delayed, so be patient. *Moon in Virgo.*

2 AUGUST

You may be surprised by news and developments. For some this will be principally financially and for others in your personal life. Romance could blossom, and the arts, music and dance will all appeal. *Moon in Libra.*

3 AUGUST

Someone may surprise you with their good news, which may involve family or a financial matter. Singles may meet someone alluring by coincidence who seems curiously familiar, so keep an eye out! *Moon in Libra.*

4 AUGUST

While a great deal in your life seems written in stone, you will find there is room for movement so trust your instincts and take the initiative with your projects. *Moon enters Scorpio.*

 848

5 AUGUST

Your hard work will pay off, so ensure you maintain a structured and diligent approach to your work and duties. You may hear mixed news from someone from your past or from an authority figure. Again, being diligent and hard working will pay off. *Moon in Scorpio.*

6 AUGUST

You'll enjoy a sense of freedom this weekend and may be drawn to sports, the arts or simply connecting with like-minded people. Trust your instincts if you're unsure of the intentions of someone new. Romance can blossom this weekend, so make a date! *Moon enters Sagittarius.*

7 AUGUST

'The path of true love never runs smoothly' could apply today. If you encounter a hiccup in the love stakes avoid taking this personally and look for ways you can make your personal circumstances work. Romance, love, music and dance will all appeal but you may need to work a little harder on improving your self-esteem or finances. *Moon in Sagittarius.*

8 AUGUST

This is a good day for health and well-being appointments. If you have recently argued with someone this is a good day to overcome differences. You may find you are asked for help, and if you need guidance it is available. *Moon enters Capricorn.*

9 AUGUST

Good communication skills are the key to success and you'll find that work and your personal life proceed on a more even keel if you choose your words carefully. Some projects, communications or travel may be delayed, so be patient. A key meeting either at work or socially could be intense or will bring change to your life. *Moon in Capricorn.*

10 AUGUST

You'll appreciate the opportunity to look at a personal matter in a new light. Avoid feeling too intensely about a principle or personal matter. Find ways to maintain perspective and be practical. *Moon enters Aquarius.*

11 AUGUST

You will feel increasingly motivated about work and your daily routine, wishing to fit more of the activities you love into each day. You may be easily influenced by someone you tend to disagree with on some counts, which may largely be due to a surprise that takes you off guard so maintain perspective. *Moon in Aquarius.*

12 AUGUST

The Aquarian full moon signals the start of a fresh situation in your daily life, as you will be ready to turn a corner at work or with a health situation. Be prepared to make a commitment to a certain course of action but avoid making snap decisions, as these are likely to backfire.

13 AUGUST

You'll appreciate the moon in your own sign this weekend, as you'll find ways to relax and enjoy the company of inspiring people. Meditation, music and the arts will all appeal. It's a good time to look for ways to build a solid platform for yourself and those close to you and for your ventures. *Moon in Pisces.*

14 AUGUST

You may be prepared to make a commitment or a decision, and the more you base this on facts rather than on expectations the better will be the outcome, especially in relation to work and health. This is a good day to get on top of domestic chores, and if you work from home to tidy up paperwork. You'll also enjoy socialising. *Moon enters Aries.*

15 AUGUST

You'll enjoy a meeting that could bring changes at work, financially and in your personal life. Communications will flow and you could come to a significant financial arrangement or agreement. *Moon in Aries.*

16 AUGUST

You'll enjoy doing something different and will gain the opportunity to refresh your usual schedule. You may also appreciate a financial or ego boost. A business or personal matter may surprise you. *Moon in Aries.*

17 AUGUST

There is a tendency to be drawn into mysteries and to be a little introspective, so where you need to be practical ensure you take things one step at a time, especially at work and regarding a creative project. Avoid being misled and making mistakes. You will feel inspired but may be a little forgetful or head in the clouds. *Moon in Taurus.*

18 AUGUST

This is a lovely day for romance, creative projects and family time, so all these activities will bring happiness your way . . . take your pick! You may tend to be a little idealistic, however, so ensure you keep your feet on the ground. *Moon in Taurus.*

19 AUGUST

The key to success lies in good interpersonal skills, especially with a group, organisation or friend. You may need to overcome a misunderstanding or work super hard. Rest assured, your efforts will be worthwhile. *Moon in Gemini.*

20 AUGUST

Mars will now be in Gemini until the end of March 2023, which will encourage you to be more adaptable to new ideas and notions, plans and projects. You may have already noticed that your day is busier or that you're restless and willing to embrace something new. *Moon in Gemini.*

21 AUGUST

A key get-together, especially if you were born before mid-March, could be music to your ears. You'll be drawn to music, the arts, dance, film and romance. If you were born later in March a key work or health situation will grab your attention. If you're working, focus on the details as you may be prone to absent-mindedness. *Moon in Gemini.*

22 AUGUST

Collaborations and meetings are likely to go well and you will gain a sense of direction as a result. But if you feel some matters are progressing too quickly, take a moment to gain perspective and find more stable and secure ways to move ahead. You'll welcome a positive change in a relationship or at work. *Moon in Cancer.*

23 AUGUST

Now that the sun is in Virgo for the next four weeks you will appreciate the opportunity to focus more on work, getting things shipshape in your usual daily routine and on improving health. The next four weeks will provide the opportunity to deepen a close relationship. Avoid being super self-critical and critical of others for the best results. *Moon in Cancer.*

24 AUGUST

This is a good day for a health or beauty treat. If you need to tidy up your home or garden you'll get a lot done. A friend or family member may have a therapeutic effect on you. Romance, the arts, music and dance will also have a healing effect. It's a good time to seek expert advice, and you may be asked for advice yourself. *Moon enters Leo.*

25 AUGUST

You'll appreciate the opportunity to get ahead with your various chores this weekend, although you are likely to be more focused on wishing to rest, play and relax. However, your work may need more attention as chores will require focus. *Moon in Leo.*

26 AUGUST

You may need to act as a mediator between people who cannot find common ground. If you have recently had disagreements, consider acting as a mediator yourself to try to overcome differences. The next few weeks are ideal for improving your collaborations and relationships, so why not start now? *Moon in Leo.*

27 AUGUST

The new moon in Virgo suggests you're ready to make a fresh agreement with someone close. If you were born at the end of February you may be beginning a fresh chapter in a personal or business relationship, and if you were born in March get set for a fresh work or health schedule. Look for ways to find more balance in your life.

28 AUGUST

You could make a commitment or a binding agreement at work or in a personal context. It's a good time to commit to a health and well-being plan; just ensure it isn't too strict or limiting. It's a good time for a major tidy up at home or at the office. *Moon in Virgo.*

29 AUGUST

Someone is likely to ask you to see their viewpoint more clearly, especially if you have recently argued or tension is bubbling in your relationship. You may need to be a mediator between people or must find the middle ground in a dispute. You may discover a bright solution to issues, so think laterally. *Moon enters Libra.*

30 AUGUST

Work will merit careful focus, as you could make a great deal of progress with your projects and chores although you may feel the odds are against you. Be positive, and you may surprise yourself with how much you can achieve. *Moon in Libra.*

31 AUGUST

This is a good day to focus on your well-being; there will be nothing selfish in doing so. Take a moment to gain perspective, especially if you feel you have been taken advantage of or could do better in any area of your life. You'll appreciate finding the time to unwind later today. If you doubt someone either at home or at work it's your cue to find out more and do some research. *Moon enters Scorpio.*

September

career   love   home   health   finance

1 SEPTEMBER

This is a good day for a get-together or trip and to broaden your friendship circle. You may enjoy an ego boost. A change could be advantageous. ***Moon in Scorpio.***

2 SEPTEMBER

Sometimes to be motivated there has to be a little tension in the air or you simply don't feel the need to take action. There is motivation in bucketloads, which can point to a little stress either at work or in your personal life. Find ways to channel strong feelings into constructive activities such as work. A beauty or health matter can move forward with the right advice. ***Moon enters Sagittarius.***

3 SEPTEMBER

A meeting, trip and news will be advantageous, even if you feel your vulnerabilities rise or that a reunion brings out your sensitivities. You will nevertheless gain insight into your circumstances. A business or personal partner may have news. A financial matter is best negotiated carefully. ***Moon in Sagittarius.***

4 SEPTEMBER

The moon at the zenith of your chart brings out your proactive side, and you'll enjoy sports and being more active and outgoing. You may be drawn to travelling and at least to planning a trip or project. *Moon in Sagittarius.*

5 SEPTEMBER

Over the next few weeks you'll appreciate the opportunity to spend more time looking after yourself or someone close. A health or work situation is best navigated carefully to ensure you cover your bases. You may be asked for help, or if you need some support or advice yourself it will be available so reach out. *Moon in Capricorn.*

6 SEPTEMBER

Focus on the practicalities of your situation, especially in relation to a group, organisation or friend. Avoid making snap decisions and being impulsive. It's a good time to get your finances shipshape. *Moon in Capricorn.*

7 SEPTEMBER

An analytical and practical approach both to work and your personal life will work well for you. Information may come to light that provides insight into a positive path forward for you financially or in your personal choices. *Moon in Aquarius.*

8 SEPTEMBER

Take a moment to decide how best to proceed at work and regarding health and well-being. You can tend to put other people's concerns above your own, so ensure you think about your own well-being first. In that way you'll be better able to help others if need be. *Moon in Aquarius.*

9 SEPTEMBER

A critical person needn't get the better of you. If you feel arguments are brewing, double-check you are not being super critical of someone. Maintain a good mood to ensure you enjoy your day. If you're making a considerable emotional or financial investment, ensure you are not over-committing. Try to get the loose ends of important paperwork tied up before Mercury turns retrograde tomorrow. *Moon in Pisces.*

10 SEPTEMBER

The full moon in Pisces shines a light on your personal life. You may receive key news from someone close and may need to review a circumstance. You may discover whether you have over- or under-estimated someone. Be inspired and practical above all else.

11 SEPTEMBER

Someone will pleasantly surprise you. You may enjoy a boost in self-esteem or a financial improvement. Someone close may have good news or you will enjoy a spontaneous event or get-together. Be open to trying something new. *Moon in Aries.*

12 SEPTEMBER

You may have a case of Mondayitis. Nevertheless, you may receive unexpectedly good news from a work colleague or personal partner. You'll enjoy the chance to do something different and uplifting. Romance could blossom, so ensure you plan a treat. *Moon in Aries.*

13 SEPTEMBER

A practical approach to work and money management will pay off. Avoid impulsive decisions and be realistic for the best results. *Moon enters Taurus.*

14 SEPTEMBER

You'll appreciate the sense you are making progress with someone special. If finances have been a little tough of late you may discover an innovative way to save or could rethink your budget. *Moon in Taurus.*

15 SEPTEMBER

You can get on well with people and could also make some solid agreements both at home and at work that put you in a more secure place, so take the initiative with your various projects and plans. *Moon enters Gemini.*

16 SEPTEMBER

This is a truly romantic day for you, especially if it's your birthday. Romance, love and all things related to creature comforts will appeal to you. Someone may surprise you with their news, and a delay or misunderstanding is best handled one step at a time to gain clarity. *Moon in Gemini.*

17 SEPTEMBER

You'll enjoy a sense of freedom and the potential to travel, spend time with people you love and feel more vibrant. You may also enjoy working at home on your décor or garden and will find the help you need if there is any heavy lifting. *Moon in Gemini.*

18 SEPTEMBER

Talks and negotiations will be progressive even if you feel you are going over old ground. The good news is you'll get the chance to reconsider some of your agreements and arrangements. You'll enjoy a reunion or a return to an old haunt. It's a good time to discuss your plans with someone close. *Moon enters Cancer.*

19 SEPTEMBER

This is a good time to socialise and network. You'll enjoy the company of like-minded people. If you're looking for a commitment from someone you may attain it. Mid-March Pisces, especially, could make considerable changes to your work and health schedules, so plan ahead! *Moon in Cancer.*

20 SEPTEMBER

Your hard work will pay off, be this in your personal life or at work, so be sure to take the initiative with your plans and activities. You may experience an upbeat change of routine or a spontaneous event that gets you out of your usual schedule. If you're considering a major personal or work investment, ensure you have checked the details. *Moon enters Leo.*

21 SEPTEMBER

The Leo moon brings out your inner lion, and you'll feel more energised and prepared to get ahead at work and with your personal projects. However, you may also appear a little rash, so ensure you don't put anyone's nose out. *Moon in Leo.*

22 SEPTEMBER

You're not known for being impatient yet when the going is too slow for you you can be restless just like anyone else. Take a moment to put your energy into situations you enjoy and you will reap the rewards, and avoid being easily distracted for the best results. *Moon in Leo.*

23 SEPTEMBER

As the sun steps into Libra it marks the equinox, a time when we collectively sense we can achieve more balance and harmony in our lives. Your attention is likely to go increasingly to collaborations and how to find peace and quiet in your life. News or a meeting may be positive, but if you discover a financial anomaly it's better dealt with earlier rather than later. *Moon in Virgo.*

24 SEPTEMBER

This is a super-romantic day for you, so ensure you plan something special. Couples could deepen your understanding of each other, and if you're single this is an excellent time to look for love if you wish for romance and commitment. You'll be inspired by the arts, music and romance. If you're making a key financial or personal commitment, ensure you research your options carefully to avoid mistakes. *Moon in Virgo.*

25 SEPTEMBER

The new moon in Libra signals a fresh project or collaboration. You may be ready to commit to someone or to a project or job, and this is likely to be transformational. If you've been single for a while you may find a partner. If you're a couple but have been going through a tough time you will finally decide which way you will go: whether to commit or go your separate ways.

26 SEPTEMBER

Developments are going to move forward quickly. A romantic situation will be decided on and you could meet someone significant. Key news from someone close will merit careful attention to ensure there are no misunderstandings. It's a good time for romance and socialising. A key meeting could signal considerable change to come. **Moon in Libra.**

27 SEPTEMBER

This is a good time for talks and negotiations, especially in your personal life. A relationship may undergo considerable change as a result of news or discussions. You may enjoy a reunion. If you are a little forgetful, avoid misplacing valuables such as house keys. **Moon in Libra.**

28 SEPTEMBER

You can make a great deal of progress at work, so take the initiative with talks and projects. A trip could be constructive. A meeting is likely to go well. You can accomplish a great deal, so be optimistic and proactive. **Moon in Scorpio.**

29 SEPTEMBER

Your emotions are catching up with you and you may have strong feelings or will gain a deeper understanding of someone close. If you're at work you may need to keep a lid on strong feelings to maintain a professional stance. **Moon in Scorpio.**

30 SEPTEMBER

It's Friday, and you'll appreciate the chance to let off some steam. You'll enjoy doing activities with like-minded people. You may be drawn to a healthy activity or to spiritual development, for example. **Moon in Sagittarius.**

October

career   love   home   health   finance

1 OCTOBER

Key talks to do with shared duties, responsibilities and money will merit careful focus. You may enjoy a reunion. Romance could blossom. You may be inclined to overspend or overindulge, so maintain perspective. ***Moon in Sagittarius.***

2 OCTOBER

A partner or a work colleague may have important news for you. You may enjoy socialising with like-minded people and doing something different. Communications are likely to gradually improve over the coming weeks. ***Moon in Capricorn.***

3 OCTOBER

This is a good day for conversations and meetings with a group, friend or organisation, as you may enjoy get-togethers and collaborations. It's a good day to organise your week. ***Moon in Capricorn.***

4 OCTOBER

You'll appreciate the sense that some relationships are coming out of the woods and that you are able to reach a more light-hearted accord. Be prepared to think outside the box if you need to come up with clever ways to move a joint project forward. ***Moon enters Aquarius.***

5 OCTOBER

You could make some long-term decisions and come to fair and equal agreements, so if you need to find a better way to collaborate and co-operate with someone this is your day to set the wheels in motion! *Moon in Aquarius.*

6 OCTOBER

Once the moon is in your sign you'll feel more emotionally in tune with developments at work and in your personal life. Meanwhile, be prepared to think analytically and logistically about your work and collaborations. *Moon enters Pisces.*

7 OCTOBER

This is an excellent day to focus on health and well-being, not only of your own but also potentially of someone close. A financial matter may deserve close attention as a work or personal project could move forward. Ensure you are on the right track with your big-picture goals if you need to review a circumstance. If not, take action to get back on track. *Moon in Pisces.*

8 OCTOBER

Trust your instinct and be inspired by developments but avoid being too idealistic as this could turn out to be your Achilles heel, especially in a personal and work situation. *Moon enters Aries.*

9 OCTOBER

The Aries full moon will spotlight a fresh cycle in a personal or financial matter. If you feel your vulnerabilities or those of someone close surface, find the time to gain perspective and be practical. And if you feel you or they need expert advice, ensure you seek it as it will be available.

10 OCTOBER

You may find that developments have a therapeutic effect, especially in a shared circumstance. However, if you feel vulnerable ensure you seek guidance, expert help or advice, especially regarding a personal or financial matter. *Moon enters Taurus.*

11 OCTOBER

This is a good day to look for more fair play and balance in key agreements such as legal or personal matters, as you are likely to find it. Be prepared to negotiate and keep emotions out of transactions if possible. *Moon in Taurus.*

12 OCTOBER

You could make progress with your talks and negotiations, especially in connection with someone close. However, if some aspects of your agreements are unclear or if you're unsure of your decisions, avoid making assumptions so you don't make mistakes. *Moon in Taurus.*

13 OCTOBER

You may be surprised by news or developments, especially regarding finances or someone close. If disagreements arise it may stem from a difference in values. If you work hard at finding solutions to problems you'll succeed, so don't give up if some interactions are difficult. *Moon in Gemini.*

14 OCTOBER

This is an excellent day for negotiations, especially regarding work, health and legal matters. If you'd like to make a commitment to someone or to a new project or health routine, this is a good day to do so. *Moon in Gemini.*

15 OCTOBER

You're communicating well and thinking analytically, which is ideal for making a key decision and for work matters. You may wish to make changes at home and your endeavours will go well. If in doubt, trust your instincts. *Moon enters Cancer.*

16 OCTOBER

This is a romantic day and you'll relish putting your feet up and enjoying the company of someone you love. However, if you discover obstacles and delays to your plans avoid feeling too disappointed. You may feel a little forgetful, so avoid misplacing valuables such as house keys. If you find someone's behaviour is mysterious, you'll gain a deeper understanding of them if you look more closely at their values and ideas. *Moon in Cancer.*

17 OCTOBER

This is a good time to get on top of work and domestic chores, as you have the energy to pump into your ideas so your actions will have good results. Collaborations are likely to go well; just ensure you're on the same page and avoid making snap decisions. *Moon in Cancer.*

18 OCTOBER

Another busy day will keep you on your toes. Just avoid over-tiring yourself and biting off more than you can chew at work or with the projects you choose to undertake. *Moon in Leo.*

19 OCTOBER

While you're generally able to get on well with other people this doesn't mean you'll get on with everyone! Someone in a position of power may oppose some of your ideas or you may be caught in someone else's drama, so take things one step at time as this could be an intense day. *Moon in Leo.*

20 OCTOBER

This may be another tense day during which collaborations and relationships are subject to conflict. A power struggle or intense talks will be best approached with a calm attitude and willingness to find common ground or resolve a dispute or difference of opinion. *Moon enters Virgo.*

21 OCTOBER

You have an eye for detail, an ability that will be useful at work. You may be drawn to investing more time in your health and well-being. Find ways to channel strong energy into something productive. *Moon in Virgo.*

22 OCTOBER

There is a lovely romantic tone to the day. The arts, music and a favourite activity will all inspire you. If you're single this is a good day to meet someone new. Couples will enjoy deepening your ties. Some developments may be surprising, so be adaptable if some plans need to be changed at short notice. An investment could pay off, but avoid taking uncalculated risks. *Moon in Virgo.*

23 OCTOBER

Now that the sun will be in Scorpio for the next four weeks you'll feel more passionate about your ventures and more in tune with your intuition, and both these circumstances will put you in a stronger position. This is a good time for constructive talks about how to find more stability in your life and at work. Some aspects of the day may seem like hard work, but if you see your projects through you'll enjoy the results. It's a good day to devise a fresh financial budget and to avoid overspending if you're already in debt. *Moon in Libra.*

24 OCTOBER

A meeting with someone from your past may be a little tense but could be therapeutic, especially if you make time for it by being diligent with your research and workload. *Moon in Libra.*

25 OCTOBER

The partial solar eclipse in Scorpio signals the start of a new chapter that will affect your collaborations, relationships and general activities in life. You may be ready to commit to someone or something new. If you feel tense about a circumstance, ensure you research it more deeply before making a commitment you can't escape. Avoid misunderstandings.

26 OCTOBER

You are generally on an upwards trajectory, even if you feel strong emotions are emerging. Be prepared to manage emotions and avoid making snap judgments, especially about legal, financial and personal matters. Be practical and logical about your decisions. *Moon in Scorpio.*

27 OCTOBER

You may hear good news to do with someone close, your home or a property. If things are moving too quickly, find ways to slow them down if possible. You may not agree with a friend or organisation, so find expert advice if you're unsure of your next step. ***Moon enters Sagittarius.***

28 OCTOBER

As Jupiter steps back into your sign you may find that your emotions and expectations are a little overwhelming or even exaggerated. A past situation may need to be reviewed. If all is well in your life you'll enjoy the current circumstances, but if not you may find expert help will be useful for moving forward financially and in your personal life. ***Moon in Sagittarius.***

29 OCTOBER

Important news and developments will give you the heads-up about an important financial or personal situation. A trip or get-together will be constructive and may take you somewhere different. You'll enjoy feathering your nest with a bright colour scheme or more luxurious textiles. ***Moon enters Capricorn.***

30 OCTOBER

You're better known for being creative, mystical and spiritual yet you have a practical streak that enables you to see the bright side of just about anything and to take reasonable steps to improve just about any circumstance. You'll enjoy socialising with someone who has the same values as you. ***Moon in Capricorn.***

31 OCTOBER

Happy Hallowe'en! You'll enjoy a sociable atmosphere. However, some talks may be a little stressful so ensure you avoid any tricks! ***Moon enters Aquarius.***

November

| career | love | home | health | finance |

1 NOVEMBER

You're not known for being obstinate, yet you can be just as stubborn as anyone! If disagreements arise just double-check you're not walking down a path on which no one will be able to agree. You may need to agree to disagree at some point. Look for clever ways to enjoy me time. ***Moon in Aquarius.***

2 NOVEMBER

You may be inclined to take other people's opinions and situations personally, so ensure you maintain perspective. Someone may feel vulnerable or sensitive and will require delicate handling. ***Moon enters Pisces.***

3 NOVEMBER

You'll enjoy a reunion even if this could involve the need to sort out a financial or personal issue. Be inspired and use your intuition, as this will help you to find good solutions to any problems. ***Moon in Pisces.***

4 NOVEMBER

The moon in your own sign will encourage you to see a difficult circumstance in a good light, but you may tend to be a little idealistic so ensure you are being realistic. A group, friend or organisation may be particularly helpful. ***Moon enters Aries.***

5 NOVEMBER

You may receive unexpected news or bump into someone from out of the blue. If you feel a little vulnerable the best way ahead would be to ensure you have the backing of someone important to you. Ask for support or expert advice if needed. Be prepared to embrace change. *Moon in Aries.*

6 NOVEMBER

You'll be clear about where in your life you need to make changes, as an old pattern is ready for change. The Aries moon may bring your feistiness out, and while this will help you to get things done you may also tend to burn bridges, which is to be avoided. Someone may need your help or vice versa; rest assured it will be available. *Moon in Aries.*

7 NOVEMBER

Keep communication channels open or you could end up with a difficult situation where no one can benefit such as a Mexican stand-off. A financial matter is best approached from a practical perspective. Avoid being idealistic as there is a bottom line to realities at the moment that must be adhered to. *Moon in Taurus.*

8 NOVEMBER

The total lunar eclipse in Taurus will spotlight a key agreement. You may receive news that could alter your direction in your personal life or a collaboration. A legal matter may be decided on or you may be ready to sign a contract that means considerable change to come.

9 NOVEMBER

You may be surprised by news or an unexpected development. You may need to reconsider your stance. Avoid making snap decisions as these could backfire, and be practical with financial matters and prepared to embrace something new. *Moon enters Gemini.*

10 NOVEMBER

This is a truly romantic day, and you may be inspired to adopt a fresh approach to a venture or someone special. You may even adopt an escapist attitude. You may also tend to be easily influenced, so if a contract needs to be signed or an agreement made ensure you double-check the facts. You won't agree with everyone, and a financial matter is best approached carefully. *Moon in Gemini.*

11 NOVEMBER

This is another day to take things carefully with a group, at work or in your personal life, as you may fundamentally disagree about basic matters that unless agreed upon could signal key change. Avoid arguments with someone in a position of authority or in your personal life as these could arise seemingly out of nowhere. *Moon in Gemini.*

12 NOVEMBER

You'll appreciate the chance to relax, unwind and take time out. You may be drawn to altering your appearance or improving your wardrobe. It's a good day for romance, so make a date with someone special. *Moon in Cancer.*

13 NOVEMBER

This is another romantic day and you'll enjoy spending time with someone inspiring. Spiritually inclined Pisces will find you deepen your beliefs and faith. Meditation and psychic work could flourish under these stars. You may need, though, to clear the space to indulge a little in your own activities and interests. *Moon in Cancer.*

14 NOVEMBER

Trust your intuition and avoid being easily influenced by a charming or influential character – unless you want to be, of course! You'll be drawn towards art, expressing yourself more fully with someone close and creating a sense of happiness in your life. Take action to make some projects work well for you. *Moon enters Leo.*

15 NOVEMBER

This is an inspiring time when you can make progress with your various projects, especially in your personal life and creatively. Take the time to ask yourself what your priorities are and where you wish your life to go over the coming weeks and months and then find ways to make your dreams come true. *Moon in Leo.*

16 NOVEMBER

As Venus enters Sagittarius you'll enjoy feeling more upbeat and outgoing and may contemplate a long-distance trip and other ways to broaden your horizons such as joining a study group. You may feel more optimistic and willing to try news ideas and to meet new people. *Moon in Leo.*

17 NOVEMBER

As Mercury joins Venus in Sagittarius, travel and new experiences will increasingly appeal to you over the coming weeks. You may feel readier to step into new territory at work and also in your personal life. If you have a legal matter or a contract to sign you may find you experience a more optimistic phase. *Moon in Virgo.*

18 NOVEMBER

A collaboration with a friend, group or organisation could be transformative and beneficial. You'll enjoy a social or networking event and doing something fun with like-minded people such as sports. *Moon in Virgo.*

19 NOVEMBER

You may discover that your expectations have been unrealistic and may need to reconsider your stance. Perhaps you've been hasty with a decision. A trip or meeting may need to be delayed or postponed; avoid taking it personally as you'll enjoy doing something else instead. ***Moon enters Libra.***

20 NOVEMBER

This is a good time to find more balance in your life and especially in your relationships, so be sure to reach out to someone especially if some talks have been fraught of late. Romance could blossom, so take the initiative. ***Moon in Libra.***

21 NOVEMBER

This is an excellent day for getting together over a mutually enjoyable activity such as a spiritual pastime or an artistic project. You will enjoy being more self-expressive and a sporting event will appeal along with being more physically active. ***Moon enters Scorpio.***

22 NOVEMBER

The sun in Sagittarius for the next four weeks will bring out your inner adventurer and you'll enjoy being more outgoing, physically active and optimistic. If study, legal matters or travel have been on the drawing board you are likely to see more positive action in these areas over the coming weeks. ***Moon in Scorpio.***

23 NOVEMBER

The Sagittarian new moon will kick-start a fresh project or venture. Find the time to research what you truly love to do and put more energy into that. A spiritual, sports, legal or travel initiative could take you places. Make a wish, but as always be careful as it will come true. You may enjoy a more outgoing and sociable phase over the coming weeks.

24 NOVEMBER

Be positive and optimistic, as you'll enjoy feeling a breath of fresh air as a result. Find ways to be healthier and more outgoing; you'll be glad you did! It's a good time to improve your well-being. ***Moon in Sagittarius.***

25 NOVEMBER

There is a therapeutic and healing aspect to the day and you could experience an upbeat development. For some this will be due to an improvement in your health and well-being and for others the chance to be more involved in your pastimes and find time for people you love being with. ***Moon enters Capricorn.***

26 NOVEMBER

This is a good day to meet an expert or find guidance if you are looking for help with a long-term or new project. If you're looking to enter fresh territory you'll find guidance particularly useful. You may wish to improve your health, and this is an excellent time to do so. A sports, health or spiritual activity will be uplifting. *Moon in Capricorn.*

27 NOVEMBER

An unexpected change in a personal circumstance is best approached head-on. Travel, unusual developments and communications may require you to be patient. *Moon enters Aquarius.*

28 NOVEMBER

This is a good day for meetings and negotiations at work. If you'd like to advance your career or to make an impression you may do so. However, it's important to avoid rushing and take things one step at a time. *Moon in Aquarius.*

29 NOVEMBER

You'll enjoy getting out and about although some talks and meetings may seem rushed. Avoid making snap decisions, even if you must be spontaneous and think on your feet. Ask for time to consider propositions if you're put under pressure. *Moon in Aquarius.*

30 NOVEMBER

This is another good day for meetings and to make agreements, especially at work and regarding health and your favourite activities. Be practical and look for exciting ways to add more variety and spice into your spare time. *Moon in Pisces.*

December

career   love   home   health   finance

1 DECEMBER

This is a good day to get things done, and get-togethers are likely to be animated. You may enjoy a trip and will meet like-minded people. There may be an aspect of tension in the air that you may find enjoyable and exciting, but if you feel under pressure take things one step at a time. *Moon in Pisces.*

2 DECEMBER

While this is a proactive time when you can make a great deal of progress, especially at work and with your projects and interests. You may be prone to making mistakes largely due to oversights so ensure you focus, especially at work. A trip or meeting may be delayed. *Moon in Aries.*

3 DECEMBER

This is a therapeutic aspect to the day. A trip, meeting, activity or interest will bring a healing aspect. It's a good time to deepen your spirituality, and if you need expert guidance it will be available. You may be drawn to updating your appearance or wardrobe. *Moon in Aries.*

4 DECEMBER

If you're working you are likely to be productive, but you must keep an eye on details to avoid mistakes and forgetfulness. You may also be easily influenced and overindulge, so if you tend to be a little escapist avoid resuming bad habits. *Moon enters Taurus.*

5 DECEMBER

Your practical and realistic qualities will emerge, and while you'll manage to get things done you may also tend to be fairly hard on yourself, so avoid being too self-critical. A favourite activity may be delayed or postponed due to factors outside your control. **Moon in Taurus.**

6 DECEMBER

You prefer certainty to uncertainty so you may need to dig deep, as delays and ambiguity may arise and especially at work. There could potentially also be misunderstandings. Back up computers to avoid losing information. **Moon enters Gemini.**

7 DECEMBER

An unexpected development or even a spanner in the works needn't dampen your spirits. A lovely activity or a favourite interest will prove to be productive. **Moon in Gemini.**

8 DECEMBER

The Gemini full moon spotlights a fresh chapter in a domestic circumstance and, for some, due to a relationship, trip or study. If you have legal matters to decide you may find that choices come to a head. A new phase at work or in your general direction may affect your personal life. Avoid making impulsive decisions.

9 DECEMBER

You may be surprised by news or a trip or visit. This is likely to be upbeat and it'll provide a sense of potential and positivity. You may bump into an old friend or receive unexpectedly good financial news. **Moon in Cancer.**

10 DECEMBER

You may be conscious that you are turning a corner in the big picture, such as in your status, general direction or career. Consider talks and financial transactions carefully, as you may otherwise regret snap decisions. You won't agree with everyone, so be prepared to communicate clearly to avoid misunderstandings. **Moon in Cancer.**

11 DECEMBER

As Venus joins Mercury in Capricorn you'll feel drawn towards creating more stability and security in your life, and especially via your work and status and in your general direction. Just avoid getting stuck in one groove and remember to be adventurous about your options. **Moon enters Leo.**

12 DECEMBER

This is an excellent day to be more adventurous and outgoing both at work and in your personal activities. If you're looking to make a fresh commitment or find a new way ahead in a relationship or at work, this is a good day to make agreements. ***Moon in Leo.***

13 DECEMBER

This is a good day to focus on boosting your work position and health. Just remember, though, that not everyone may feel as outgoing and proactive as you and you may need to take things one step at a time where your hope for rapid advancement is concerned. ***Moon in Leo.***

14 DECEMBER

While you are optimistic about your ventures, if you discover that you have overlooked an important factor it's a good time to improve your situation. Be clear and concise with communications to avoid misunderstandings. Be prepared to unravel a mystery and be patient with delays. ***Moon enters Virgo.***

15 DECEMBER

You can make progress, especially at work and financially. However, you may be prone to misunderstandings, so ensure you are super clear with arrangements. A travel delay may occur. Back up computers to avoid losing information. ***Moon in Virgo.***

16 DECEMBER

This is another day where being clear with your communications and arrangements will turn out well for you, as mistakes, delays and miscommunications could arise. ***Moon enters Libra.***

17 DECEMBER

A surprise or different event will be enjoyable, and you may gain a sense of validation that you're on the right track both at work and in your personal life. You may experience a financial or ego boost. ***Moon in Libra.***

18 DECEMBER

A project, venture or interest could blossom, so take the initiative. A social, office or seasonal event will raise morale, so be prepared to socialise and network as you're likely to enjoy it! ***Moon in Libra.***

19 DECEMBER

You'll enjoy getting together with like-minded people and enjoying some Christmas cheer. However, some meetings or a trip may be more complex than you'd expected or will need to be postponed or delayed. Take a moment to avoid being impatient with logistics. ***Moon in Scorpio.***

20 DECEMBER

The Scorpio moon will bring out your passionate side and you may surprise yourself with the strength of some of your feelings. You may learn something about yourself or someone close. *Moon in Scorpio.*

21 DECEMBER

The solstice is when the sun enters the zodiac sign of Capricorn. It is a time of reflection when you can gather your wits as you assimilate your progress this year. Over the next four weeks you will increasingly focus on creating more stability and security, especially at work and in your general status. It's a good time to seek the company of people you look up to for inspiration. Some logistics such as travel or work schedules may be complex, so be patient. *Moon in Sagittarius.*

22 DECEMBER

You'll enjoy a sense of hope and optimism, especially in your general direction in life and in your finances and status. You may receive an unexpected compliment or financial boost. *Moon in Sagittarius.*

23 DECEMBER

The new moon and supermoon in Capricorn signals a fresh chapter regarding your status, interests and, for some, in your career. Get set to turn a corner in the most practical way possible. You'll enjoy a reunion or a return to an old haunt.

24 DECEMBER

A trip or reunion will be enjoyable. Romance could flourish, and you'll appreciate the tradition and spirituality of this time of year. Avoid overindulgence, as you'll regret it tomorrow! Avoid being absent-minded as you could misplace something valuable such as the car keys. *Moon in Capricorn.*

25 DECEMBER

Merry Christmas! There is likely to be something a little different about your Christmas Day this year. You'll value the company you have and will enjoy a trip down memory lane. *Moon in Aquarius.*

26 DECEMBER

There is a truly nostalgic feeling to the day and you'll enjoy socialising and, at the least, touching base with someone you admire. Avoid allowing someone annoying to alter your good mood. You'll enjoy music, delicious food and delightful company. *Moon in Aquarius.*

27 DECEMBER

A return to an old haunt will be enjoyable. You'll appreciate a reunion and the opportunity to reminisce. If you're back at work you'll enjoy the change of pace. *Moon in Pisces.*

28 DECEMBER

This is a lovely day for romance and for spending with like-minded people. You may be drawn to indulging more in the arts, good food and music but may also be prone to over-indulging. Try to get important paperwork done before Mercury turns retrograde tomorrow to avoid having to review your work further down the track. *Moon in Pisces.*

29 DECEMBER

A key meeting will be enjoyable. You'll appreciate the chance to socialise and network. Romance could blossom, and singles may meet a like-minded character. You may be drawn to returning to a familiar place. *Moon in Aries.*

30 DECEMBER

A trip or conversation may be more complex than you'd hoped, but if you are diligent with your plans you will succeed. Avoid making snap decisions as these could backfire, and choose your words carefully to avoid inadvertently hurting someone's feelings. *Moon in Aries.*

31 DECEMBER

Happy New Year! You may be under pressure to spend time with a certain group of people or to go to a particular place, but you may prefer to do your own thing. In either case you'll enjoy a beautiful way to see in the new year. *Moon enters Taurus.*

FURTHER INFORMATION

Find out your moon sign and ascendant sign at www.astrocast.com.au. For an in-depth personal astrology chart reading contact Patsy Bennett at patsybennettastrology@gmail.com.
   Further astronomical data can be obtained from the following:

* Michelsen, Neil F. and Pottenger, Rique, *The American Ephemeris for the 21st Century 2000–2050 at Midnight*, ACS Publications, 1997.
* The computer program Solar Fire from Esoteric Technologies Pty Ltd.